ABOUT THE AUTHORS

Mark Austin, Associate Professor at the University of Maryland, College Park, has joint appointments in the Department of Civil Engineering and Institute for Systems Research, and a faculty appointment with the Interdisciplinary Applied Mathematics Program. Mark has a B.E. in Civil Engineering (1st Class Honors) from the University of Canterbury in New Zealand. His M.S. and Ph.D. degrees in Structural Engineering are from the University of California, Berkeley. Mark can be reached at `austin@isr.umd.edu`.

David Chancogne is Manager of the Neural Systems Laboratory and Assistant Research Scientist at the Institute for Systems Research, University of Maryland, College Park. David has an undergraduate degree in computer engineering from Institute National des Sciences Appliquiées, Toulouse, France. You can reach him at `doc@isr.umd.edu`.

CONTRIBUTING AUTHOR

David Mazzoni has a Ph.D. in Electrical Engineering from the University of Maryland, College Park. After working as an Assistant Research Scientist and teaching C, C++, and electrical engineering courses at the University of Maryland, he is now working for the National Security Agency.

INTRODUCTION TO ENGINEERING PROGRAMMING: IN C, MATLAB AND JAVA

Mark Austin
Department of Civil Engineering
University of Maryland
College Park, Maryland

David Chancogne
Institute for Systems Research
University of Maryland
College Park, Maryland

John Wiley & Sons, Inc.
New York Chichester Weinheim Brisbane Singapore Toronto

ACQUISITIONS EDITOR JOE HAYTON
MARKETING MANAGER KATHERINE HEPBURN
PRODUCTION EDITOR PATRICIA McFADDEN
DESIGNER KEVIN MURPHY/NANCY FIELD
COVER DESIGN MICHAEL JUNG
ILLUSTRATION COORDINATOR GENE AIELLO

This book was set in Times Ten by Publication Services and printed and bound by Malloy Lithographing, Inc.
The cover was printed by Phoenix Color.

This book is printed on acid-free paper. ♾

The paper in this book was manufactured by a mill whose forest management programs include sustained yield harvesting of its timberlands. Sustained yield harvesting principles ensure that the numbers of trees cut each year does not exceed the amount of new growth.

Library of Congress Cataloging in Publication Data:

Austin, Mark.
Engineering programming : C. Matlab, and Java / Mark Austin, David Chancogne.
p. cm.
Includes index.
ISBN 0-471-00116-3 (alk. paper)
1. C (Computer program language) 2. MATLAB. 3. Java (Computer program language) 4. Engineering mathematics—Data processing.
I. Chancogne, David. II. Title.
QA76.73.C15A98 1999
620'.00285'5133—dc21 98-8481
CIP

PREFACE

OBJECTIVES AND BACKGROUND

This introductory text teaches concepts in modern engineering computations and the C, MATLAB, and Java programming languages to university students who are studying engineering at the freshman, sophomore, and junior levels. We assume that our readers have finished high school with upper-level courses in mathematics and physics, and are perhaps at the point of taking their first or second year of classes in a specific engineering discipline. This text evolved from class notes and web-based tutorials developed at the University of Maryland, College Park, since the early 1990s.

By the late 1980s, engineering workstations were well established in the marketplace, and the development of software that included graphical user interfaces seemed to be something from which engineers could benefit. When we first encouraged our graduate students to use C, most of them purchased a copy of Kernighan and Ritchie [14] and read the first three to four chapters by themselves. We observed that only the very best students could easily grasp the concepts of pointers and data structures, and use them to design and write high-quality engineering software. This obstacle to development was viewed with considerable consternation—the use of flexible data structures and dynamic memory allocation, coupled with good program design were, after all, the key reasons we recommended C in the first place. The early versions of the class notes were written to help students overcome this obstacle.

Since the early 1990s, our expectations of computers in day-to-day engineering activities has been advanced by remarkable leaps in computer technology. To most engineers in the 1970s and early 1980s, "engineering programming" meant "programming in FORTRAN," even if the task at hand was ill suited to the class of problems for which FORTRAN was originally designed. Currently, "engineering programming" is much more broad based; that is, engineers are writing software programs for a range of applications in FORTRAN, C, C++, and MATLAB. Now that the Internet and World Wide Web (WWW) are well on their way to becoming an integral part of the way engineering companies do business and solve problems, web programming and the Java programming language are likely to join the family of languages in which engineering software will be written.

Our engineering students are acutely aware of these trends, of course. They only need to browse the employment section of *The Washington Post* to see where the jobs are. In addition to having a good understanding of what computing is about, today's graduating engineers need to be adept at selecting the right programming language for a specific job. Some of them will also need the background and skills to design and implement engineering software in a number of programming languages. In recent years, our courses at the University of Maryland have been attended by approximately equal numbers of Civil, Mechanical, and Electrical Engineering students, and many of our undergraduate students are now learning combinations of C, MATLAB, and Java as their first programming languages. Our course notes and this book have been updated to reflect this demand.

SCOPE

The text is partitioned into five parts.

Part 1—Concepts in Modern Engineering Computations

This book begins with an overview of concepts in modern engineering computations. Our goals are to provide students with basic understanding of the types of engineering computations that occur in professional practice, how engineering computations work in a simple computer, and how the advent of computer networks is changing the face of what is possible with engineering computations. In Chapter 1, we briefly describe the ways in which engineers use computers today. We describe the basic hardware components in a simple computer, concepts in a simple operating system, and the role of computer networks in engineering computations. A brief introduction to the Internet and WWW is provided. Chapter 2 contains a high-level introduction to development of engineering software applications. We describe a variety of software development strategies, high- and low-level programming languages, and compilers.

Part 2—C Tutorial

C is a great programming language for writing applications programs that have to manipulate character strings and/or blocks of memory, link with external libraries, interact with a computer's operating system, or possibly solve problems that require sophisticated definition and manipulation of complex application-dependent data types.

The C tutorial is divided into 10 chapters. Chapter 3 is a self-contained tutorial that introduces the basic concepts of C via two case study problems. The basic data types and variables, Hungarian notation for naming variables, operators and expressions, and control of program flow are described in Chapters 4 to 6. Chapter 7, Functions I, is an introduction to the differences between small and large C programs, top-down and bottom-up strategies of program design, and the use of functions in C. Chapters 8 and 9 are particularly important because pointers and arrays, and advanced features of functions, are where C departs from other high-level languages. If students can master these two chapters, then they will be off and running with C. Chapter 10 describes dynamic memory allocation, and its application to the run-time allocation of character strings and small two-dimensional matrices. Finally, the C preprocessor, and input and output (I/O), are covered in Chapters 11 and 12.

Part 3—MATLAB Tutorial

MATLAB is a great programming language for solving simple matrix problems with simple graphics. The program code will be much shorter and simpler than an equivalent implementation in C, FORTRAN, or Java. Chapter 13 is an introduction to programming in MATLAB. Topics include variables and variable arithmetic, matrices and matrix arithmetic, control structures, built-in matrix functions, M-files, and so forth. A brief introduction to MATLAB graphics is contained in Chapter 14. Many other texts weave MATLAB graphics into the introductory sections of MATLAB programming; however, in an effort to keep the tutorial length short, we have separated graphics from programming. Chapter 15 covers the solution of linear matrix equations in MATLAB. We demonstrate the power of MATLAB by working step by step through the formulation and solution of a variety of engineering applications involving families of matrix equations and, where applicable, MATLAB graphics.

Part 4—Java Tutorial

Java is a great programming language for writing engineering applications software that must have platform-independent graphical user interfaces and/or operate across the Internet. Chapter 16 systematically describes the features of Java that make the language unique. Chapter 17 is devoted to the fundamental concepts of object-oriented analysis, design, and program development. Chapter 18 contains an introduction to the Java programming language. Finally, Chapter 19 covers Java graphics. We see how to write Java programs that can move across the Internet and be displayed in a web browser.

Appendices

Appendix 1 is a basic introduction to the UNIX operating system. Appendix 2 describes functions in the standard library.

Reading the Text

We assume that our readers will work through Part 1 of this text first and then move on to either the C or the MATLAB tutorial. The Java tutorial assumes that programmers are already familiar with C.

CASE STUDY PROBLEMS AND PROGRAMMING EXERCISES

In demonstrating how the C, MATLAB, and Java programming languages work, and how they should be designed, written, and compiled, we have tried to select case study problems and programming exercises that will be of interest to students from multiple engineering disciplines. When a student is getting started with a new language, he or she will be concerned with the syntax of the language, how the components of a small program fit together, and the procedure for writing, compiling, and running a program. To ensure that students can focus on these issues (this is a programming text after all), we selected application problems with which most engineering students will already be familiar—solving for the roots of a quadratic equation and evaluating simple mathematical formulae are among the examples repeated in the tutorials.

To help readers to assess the strengths and weaknesses of C, MATLAB, and Java, we solve and compare a small set of problems using each of these languages. We see, for example, that although the interactive solution of a quadratic equation can be easily implemented in either C or MATLAB, implementing the same problem in Java is rather difficult. However, computer programs can be written in Java that have functionality that is almost impossible to replicate in either C or MATLAB.

WORLD WIDE WEB SITE

We have created a WWW site for pointers to further information, electronic distribution of the source code to the computer programs in this book, and communication with our readers. You can access the book's home page at the University of Maryland directly with the Internet address

```
http://www.isr.umd.edu/~austin/book.html
```

A link to this book's home page may also be found at

```
http://www.wiley.com/college/austin
```

the home page for John Wiley and Sons, the publisher of the book.

Despite our best efforts to test and debug the code and programming exercises, a book of this type will inevitably contain errors and omissions. Please check the web site for a list of frequently asked questions, source code patches, and links to web sites that may have moved. If you have constructive suggestions for programming exercises or have identified an error in the text, please send us E-mail from the book home page or directly at austin@isr.umd.edu. Alternatively, you can contact us at engineer@jwiley.com. We want to hear from you and will do our best to respond!

ACKNOWLEDGMENTS

Our "little book project" has benefited from the constructive suggestions, assistance, careful reviews, and encouragement of many friends and colleagues. From the University of Maryland, we want to thank Steve Creighton, Bernie Frankpitt, Asok Ghosh, Wane-Jang Lin, Jim Preston, Roland Schramme, B. K. Voon, and Jianmin You for taking time from their studies to review the chapter drafts. Rachel Albrecht, Nathan Blattau, Amanda Cody, Gregory Douglas, Asok Ghosh, Jim Hozdic, Amy Lau, Joseph Neubauer, and Clara Popescu provided solutions to many of the problems. Without their help, this project would never have made it to completion.

We also received helpful comments and suggestions from Bernard Chancogne (France), Andrew Heunis (University of Waterloo), David Lovell (University of Maryland), Mark and Michelle Townsley (IBM and Cisco), Loc Vu Quoc (University of Florida, Gainesville), David Stewart (University of Maryland), Chris Thewalt (University of California, Berkeley), and Greg Walsh (University of Maryland). We sincerely thank the book reviewers for their many comments and suggestions. They are: James Cohoon (University of Virginia, Charlottesville), Gregory Fenves (University of California, Berkeley), Peter Furth (Northeastern University, Boston), Leon Levine (University of California, Los Angeles), David Rocheleau (University of South Carolina), David Spooner (Rensselaer Polytechnic University), Ruth Ungar (University of Connecticut), Joel Wein (Polytechnic University, Brooklyn), and Richard Whitehouse (Arizona State University).

Finally, we want to thank Jan Poston-Day for her excellent editing, and the nice people at John Wiley and Spectrum Publisher Services for having faith in this project and pushing the production along in a timely manner.

CONTENTS

PART 1

CONCEPTS IN MODERN ENGINEERING COMPUTATIONS

This text begins with a tutorial describing the concepts on which modern engineering computations are built. In our experience, students are much better prepared to learn a new programming language if they are already familiar with these basic concepts.

After briefly explaining the range of application programs that are found in engineering organizations, Chapter 1 quickly reviews the major contributions of computer technology over the past 30 years. This historical review helps us to see where and how technology has evolved, and provides perspective for where computing and computer technologies are likely to head in the next 5 to 10 years. We then examine the hardware components in a simple computer, the components and purposes of a simple operating system, and the role computer networks are playing in modern-day applications of engineering computing. The latter includes introductions to client/server computing, the Internet, and the World Wide Web (WWW).

Chapter 2 introduces the principles on which modern engineering software systems are built. Topics include the hardware-software lifecycle, the economics of software development, top-down and bottom-up development strategies, software modularity, and information hiding. This chapter concludes with an introduction to programming language concepts, including high- and low-level programming languages, compiled versus interpreted languages, scripting and markup languages, and so forth.

1

INTRODUCTION TO ENGINEERING COMPUTATIONS

1.1 APPLICATIONS OF COMPUTERS IN ENGINEERING

Since the 1970s, remarkable advances have occurred in the processing speed of computers, the capacity of computers to store, manipulate, and present large quantities of data and information, and the ability of computers to communicate with other computers over networks. Evidence of these advances can be found in present-day engineering offices where computers are used in at least four broad capacities:

1. For *storage and manipulation of data and information.* Modern databases can store and manipulate a variety of data and information, including commercial off-the-shelf products, materials, and services; experimental data; the results of numerical computations; models of designs; design documents and drawings; Geographic Information Systems (GIS) imagery; and so forth.
2. For *communication over computer networks.* Networking tools and technologies allow for the exchange of data and information over networks, and for computers to jointly contribute to the solution of large engineering analyses. Perhaps the greatest use of computer networks is for communication via E-mail.
3. For *desktop publishing.* Word processing packages such as LaTeX and Microsoft Word, and picture editors such as Corel Draw and Photoshop enhance an engineer's ability to write and edit publications.
4. For *numerical and symbolic computations.* Engineering analysis programs (e.g., programs for control systems and finite element analysis; MATLAB and Mathematica) are needed for the solution of engineering problems. The majority of

engineers use commercial software for numerical and symbolic calculations, requiring preparation/programming of input files, while some engineers write their own software.

From a business point of view, the most useful application programs will directly improve the performance and reliability, productivity, and economic competitiveness of engineering systems development. The participating application programs should be fast and accurate, flexible, reliable, and, of course, easy to use. And they should work together. A good example of the last requirement can be found in modern-day computer-aided design (CAD) systems where engineering analysis programs are integrated with project management tools, databases of project requirements, organizational resources, and commercial off-the-shelf products, materials, and services.

An unfortunate problem caused by these advances is the gap many engineers are finding between their knowledge of these technologies and the opportunities they afford. Solutions to this problem are complicated by the large number of activities in which engineers participate and the inability of many present-day engineering application programs to operate across a variety of hardware platforms and operating systems. Keeping up to date with computational technologies is really a lifelong endeavor because some of the application tools and computer programming languages we will be using in 5 to 10 years are only just being invented.

1.2 RECENT ADVANCES IN COMPUTING

A good way of beginning to understand where computers and programming languages might be headed in the near future is to take a look at where they have come from in the recent past. We therefore begin this section with a little history.

1.2.1 Highlights of Computing Since 1970

For more than a decade now, computers have been providing approximately 25% more power per dollar per year. Together with the aforementioned advances in technology and market-driven forces, these changes have stimulated the exploration of many new ideas and paradigms. Figure 1.1 summarizes, for example, the major "modes of operation" and "key technologies for computing" versus decade for the past 30 to 35 years (this diagram has been adapted from an article in *Scientific American* [44]). The highlights are

1970s: In the early to mid-1970s, *mainframe computers* were commonplace. They had a computational speed of 1 to 2 MIPS (millions of instructions per second) and were largely viewed as machines for research engineers and scientists. Compared to today's standards, *computer memory* was very expensive, and human–computer interaction was primitive. In fact, scientists and engineers interacted with a computer by sitting at a terminal and typing

Decade	BATCH 1960s	TIME SHARING 1970s	DESKTOP 1980s	NETWORKS 1990s
Technology	Medium-Scale Integration	Large-Scale Integration	Very Large-Scale Integration	Ultra-Scale Integration
Users	Experts	Specialists	Individuals	Groups
Objective	Calculate	Access	Present	Communicate
Location	Computer Room	Terminal Room	Desktop	Mobile
Connectivity	Peripherals	Terminals	Desktops	Laptops Palmtops
User Activity	Punch and Try (computer cards)	Remember and Type (interact)	See and Point (drive)	Ask and Tell (delegate)
Data	Alphanumeric	Text Vector	Fonts Graphs	Sound Video
Languages	Cobol, FORTRAN	PL/1, Basic	Pascal, C SQL	C++, Java Perl, Tcl/Tk HTML, VRML

FIGURE 1.1 Paradigms of computing versus decade.

commands on a keyboard. The computer would respond by sending text to the terminal screen.

Most software developers wrote computer programs dedicated to a specific task (e.g., finite element analysis, control systems package, an accounting or stock control system). Many of these packages were written in FORTRAN and run in "batch mode." The ease with which FORTRAN could be used to evaluate mathematical formulae—hence the name *For*mula *Tran*slation—was adequate for most engineering applications, and it can reasonably be argued that the choice of language was suitable for its time (unfortunately, some engineers and educators still think it is adequate).

1980s: In the 1980s, *desktop publishing* systems were developed for individuals at work and at home. Computers such as the Macintosh presented users with a screen containing a window, scroll bar, and button/icon interface components that could be defined and manipulated with a mouse device by simply pointing and clicking icons on the graphical interface.

1990s: The use of computers in engineering is now at a point where mainframe computers are being replaced by high-speed engineering workstations and modern personal computers (PCs) having bit-mapped graphics (a bit is short for binary digit, either a 1 or a 0), global network connectivity (e.g., cellular communications, fiber optic, the World Wide Web), and multimedia (i.e., two or more of the following: graphics, voice, digital sound, video) [33]. *Laptop computers* now provide mobility, without compromising too many of the computational features available on PCs.

It is important to note that computers, once viewed as a tool for computation alone, are now seen as an indispensable tool for computations and mobile communications. Access to this information has expanded from "experts" in the 1970s to "groups of individuals" today. A whole host of new programming languages, operating systems, and application programs have been written to support the new modes of functionality and day-to-day operation enabled by these technology advances. Consider, for example, an engineer who has access to a high-speed PC with multimedia interfaces and global network connectivity, and who happens to be part of a geographically dispersed development team. The team members can use the Internet/E-mail for day-to-day communications, to share project information among team members, to conduct engineering analyses at remote sites, and to access information from databases on project components, materials, and services. Online assembly of joint ventures, online bidding of projects, and online verification of project performance against design standards may become commonplace in the near future.

1.3 COMPUTER HARDWARE CONCEPTS

The three main components in a computer are the *hardware* (including the computer networks connecting individual computers), the *operating system,* and the *application programs* that operate on individual computers and across computer networks. In our opinion, programmers should have a basic understanding of the hardware and operating system components in a simple computer because many computer programs are written to interact with a computer's input/output (I/O) devices and its operating system.

1.3.1 Hardware Components in a Simple Computer

Figure 1.2 is a schematic of the main hardware components in a typical (simplified) PC. Viewed from a high level of abstraction, a computer is an assembly of processor,

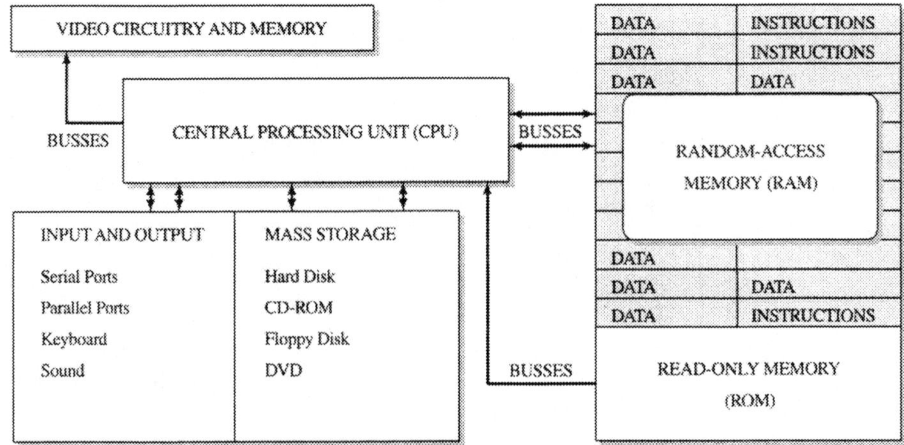

FIGURE 1.2 Hardware model of a personal computer.

memory, and I/O modules. A particular computer may have one or more modules of each type, with these modules being connected in some way to produce the main function of the computer.

In Chapter 2, we see that a computer program is nothing other than a list of instructions that can be followed mechanically by the computer. Machine instructions are expressed as binary numbers—that is, information represented as a sequence of zeros and ones. A computer can execute a program only if it is expressed in a machine language that can drive the mechanical operations of the computer.

The *central processing unit* (CPU) is the engine that controls the operations of the computer by executing instructions. In a conventional CPU, instructions are fetched from main memory, decoded, and executed one at a time. This process is entirely mechanical, and so if a computer program is to execute without error, the machine code instructions must be complete and unambiguous in their intent. Computers are designed so that they can be easily connected to external devices such as printers and keyboards. A second purpose of the CPU is to handle interrupts. When a device sends an interrupt signal to the CPU, it will halt what it is doing, take care of the device request, and then resume the original computation. The ability of a CPU to work on the solution of multiple tasks is called *multitasking*.

Within the CPU the *control unit* controls the fetch, decode, and execute cycles for instructions stored in memory. The *arithmetic control unit* carries out arithmetic and logical operations on words of data. A word of data is as long as the length of the hardware register in bits. The word length of a computer refers to the size of the unit of data in bits that a CPU can process at a time. Computers with a large word length process data faster than computers with a small word length. The first processor had 4-bit word lengths. Currently, 32-bit PCs and engineering workstations are commonplace. In a few years, 64-bit computers will dominate the marketplace. The *internal storage unit* (not to be confused with the computer's primary memory) is fast internal memory that temporarily stores and manipulates data. It also contains busses (i.e., wires) for communication of the CPU with I/O devices, and mass storage known as random-access memory (RAM) and read-only memory (ROM).

The speed of a CPU is closely linked to the size of computer chips from which it is constructed. Broadly speaking, the more transistors a chip has, the more information it can process. State of the art manufacturing processes in 1997 allowed for chips having a miniaturization of 1/290th of a human hair width. The result, Pentium processor technology, has a maximum speed of 200 to 230 millions of cycles per second (i.e., 200–230 MHz). The next generation of Pentium Pro chips (manufactured at miniaturization of 1/400th of a human hair width) will be able to run at speeds of up to 500 MHz. Predictions are that by the year 2001, the next generation of Intel chips will contain 64-bit processing and operate at 1000 MHz.

The primary memory in a computer, called RAM (an acronym for *random-access memory*), stores data and low-level program instructions as sequences of binary digits. Present-day PCs and engineering workstations have 32 to 256 Megabytes (MB) of RAM (see Table 1.1 for a definition of terms), plus some *read-only memory* (ROM). *Mass storage* is where programs, data, images, and so forth are

TABLE 1.1 Terms Used to Quantify Storage

Term	*Abbreviation*	*Number of Bytes/Bits*
Byte	B	1 byte = 8 bits
Kilobyte	KB	1024 = 2^10 bytes
Megabyte	MB	1,048,576 = 2^20 bytes
Gigabyte	GB	1,073,741,824 = 2^30 bytes
Terabyte	TB	2^40 bytes

permanently stored. For example, standard CD-ROMs store up to 650 MB, which is enough memory for approximately 70 minutes of audio/music. The new digital video disc (DVD) format, also sometimes called digital versatile disc, will be able to store up to 12 times as much data [8.5 Gigabytes (GB) using both sides of the disk]. This is enough capacity to hold a full-length feature film with Dolby multichannel digital audio.

A *bus* is an electronic pathway in a digital computer that provides a communication path for data to flow between the CPU and its memory, and between the CPU and peripheral devices connected to the computer (e.g., monitor, printer, keyboard and mouse, network interface). Computer systems are designed so that they can be easily expanded by adding new devices. When a new device is added to a computer, a software package known as a *device driver* must be installed so that the CPU can communicate with the new device. In Figure 1.2, busses provide multiline paths for rapid data transfer between different sections of the main computer board.

1.4 OPERATING SYSTEM CONCEPTS

An *operating system* is the set of programs that provides an interface between the computer hardware and the computer users. The operating system manages the sharing of a computer's resources and its memory contents, the low-level details of loading and executing programs, file storage and retrieval, assignment of processes to the screen and keyboard I/O devices, and communication with other computers. The term *operating system kernel* describes the set of programs in an operating system that implements the most primitive of that system's functions, including those for process management, memory management, basic I/O control, and security. Together these operating system features give the computer much of its functionality, including an environment for writing and running programs. The operating system and its components are also the first programs to run when the computer is turned on.

Two of the most popular operating systems are UNIX and WINDOWS 95™, and, fortunately, there are many similarities in their basic design and functionality. When you are just starting to learn how a new operating system works, understanding how the file system works is the most important (and potentially confusing) first step. In UNIX and WINDOWS 95, for example, you need to know how hierarchies of files are handled by the operating system and the operations that can be used to assemble, manipulate, and navigate a file system hierarchy. You may also need to learn how to "remote login" to another computer over a computer network. Interested readers should refer to Appendix 1 for a detailed discussion of these concepts for UNIX.

1.5 COMPUTER NETWORKING CONCEPTS

A *computer network* is simply two or more computers connected together. Computer networks enable humans and computers to communicate by sending messages, and to share data and information resources by exchanging files. Two types of computer network are as follows:

1. *Local Area Network (LAN).* A LAN is a network where computers are connected together directly. Usually the connection will be some type of cable.
2. *Wide Area Network (WAN).* A WAN is simply a network of LANs connected together. The connections in present-day WANs are becoming a mixture of cable, fiber optic, and satellite communications.

Communication among LANs is handled by special-purpose computers called *routers.* Routers connect LANs to form a WAN. WANs can then be connected to form even larger WANs.

1.5.1 Client/Server Network Architectures

The sharing of information across computer networks is often implemented as two (or more) programs running on separate computers. One program, called the server, provides a particular resource. A second program, called the client, makes use of that resource. The server and client programs may be running on different machines located in separate rooms or even separate countries. Computer networks, where one server provides information to many clients, are said to have *client/server architectures.*

Figure 1.3 shows a simplified network where one server machine is connected to three client machines. Any one of the client machines can send a message to the server machine requesting data, information, or access to certain operating system or application package processes. The server machine will respond by sending the requested information/service to the client.

Client/server network architectures are increasing in popularity because of the advantages they afford. By localizing data, information, and operating system/application package processes on a single server machine, and providing access to client machines on an as-needed basis, maintenance of operating system software and application program software is simplified considerably. Moreover, by moving much of the processing power from stand-alone client machines to powerful server machines, an opportunity exists to design client machines having "minimal" operating system functionality. These so-called "network computers" are expected to retail for considerably less than current PCs.

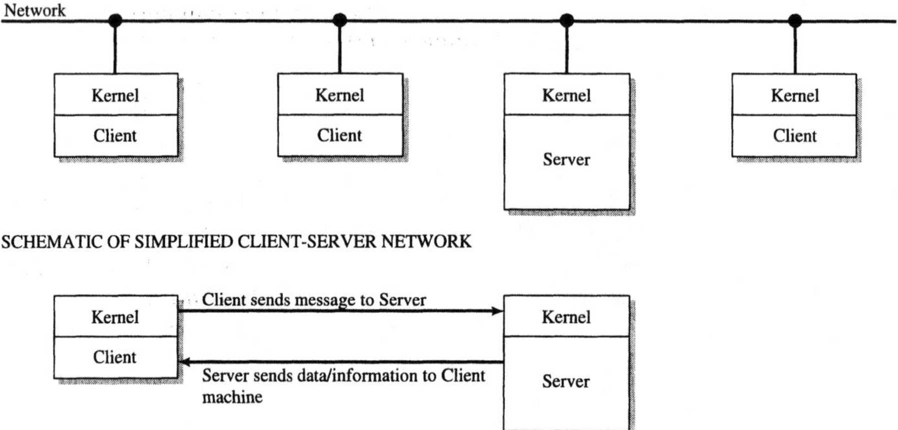

FIGURE 1.3 Model of communication in client/server systems.

1.5.2 The Internet

Millions of computers are now connected together in a massive worldwide network of computers called the Internet. The word *Internet* literally means "network of networks," and on any given day it connects roughly 20 million users in more than 50 countries—see, for example, the countries shaded in black in Figure 1.4. The Internet is rather unique in the sense that nobody owns, is in charge of, or pays for the entire cost of running the Internet.

Development of the Internet dates back to 1969 when the Defense Advanced Research Projects Agency arm of the Department of the Defense commissioned

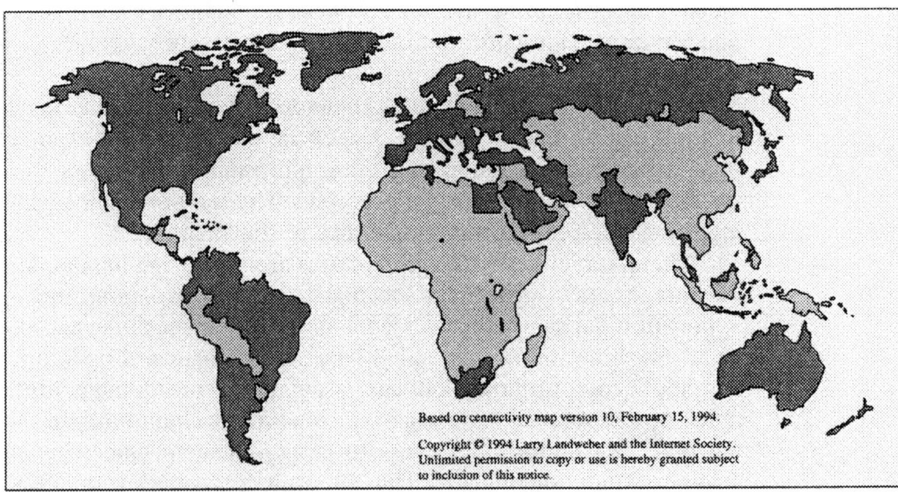

FIGURE 1.4 Countries having access to the Internet.

the construction of an experimental computer network. Work on the Advanced Research Projects Agency Network (ARPANET) centered around a perceived problem in the Department of Defense—how to keep U.S. military sites in communication in the event of a nuclear war. If just a few metropolitan areas were wiped out, communications could be severely disrupted. Two years later the network was connecting 15 nodes, all of them research centers. The Internet has since passed through the watchful eyes of many universities and research organizations, and grown in size to include millions of computer hosts.

Table 1.2 shows the number of hosts on the Internet versus time for August 1981 through July 1996. The estimate for the year 2000 is that 40 million people will be connected to the Internet.

1.5.3 Internet Access

The majority of present-day home users access the Internet using a modem and phone lines—the upper speed, or *bandwidth,* at which information can be transmitted is 33.6 kilobits per second. A modest increase in bandwidth to 64 or 128 kilobits per second is possible with Integrated Services Digital Network (ISDN) technology. With 64 kilobits/sec bandwidth connection to the Internet, users can reserve part of the bandwidth channel for voice or fax calls. Most large research organizations and universities are connected to the Internet with one or more T1 lines having bandwidth 1.46 megabits per second. In the near future, significant increases in bandwidth (i.e., 10 megabits/sec) may be possible with cable modems.

1.5.4 Protocols for Internet Communication

Before two computers can exchange data and information over a network, they must agree on a specification, or protocol, for communication. Protocols cover issues such as how data will be formatted, conventions for control and coordination of information exchange, and handling of errors.

TABLE 1.2 Number of Hosts on the Internet 8/81 to 7/96

Date	*No. of Host Computers*	*Date*	*No. of Host Computers*
Aug. 81	213	Jan. 89	80,000
May 82	235	Oct. 90	313,000
Aug. 83	562	Oct. 91	617,000
Oct. 84	1,024	Oct. 92	1,136,000
Oct. 85	1,961	Oct. 93	2,056,000
Nov. 86	5,089	Oct. 94	3,864,000
Dec. 87	28,174	Jul. 95	6,642,000
Jul. 88	33,000	Jul. 96	12,881,000

At the network level, the Internet Protocol (IP) specifies how data are to be physically transmitted from one computer to another, and the Transmission Control Protocol (TCP) ensures that all the data sent using IP are received without error. Together these protocols are known as TCP/IP, and they form the foundation of many other high-level application-oriented protocols for sending packets of information (e.g., files, E-mail, web pages) across networks.

1.5.5 Internet Domain Names and Addresses

The Internet sends packets of information across a network using a model that is simply an electronic counterpart to the way letters are posted inside an envelope containing a delivery address and a return address. Perhaps the delivery address is the location of your Internet provider and the return address is the location of your home.

Every computer on the Internet has its own unique Internet address. You cannot send an E-mail message to someone, transfer a file via FTP, or access web pages located on a specific computer, unless you know his or her Internet address. In our "letter-and-envelope" analogy, there is the numerical form of an Internet address (it looks like `xxx.xxx.xxx.xxx`), and its vernacular counterpart. Although the numerical form is somewhat akin to a postal zip code and an important part of the address delivery, people naturally prefer to work with addresses written in textual terms. Computer domain names follow a three-part format:

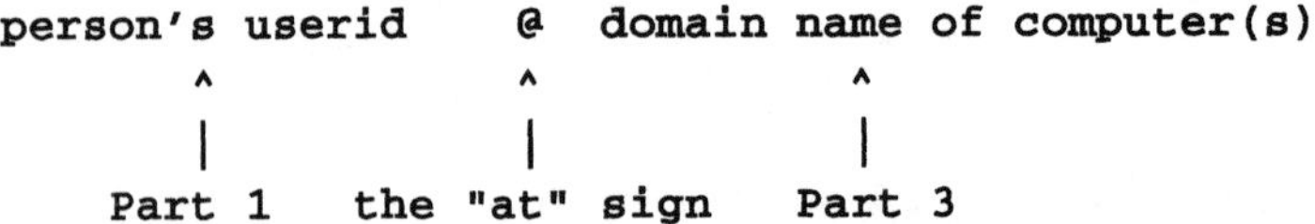

For example, the internet address `austin@isr.umd.edu` has the person id `austin` and the domain name `isr.umd.edu`. The numerical counterpart of `isr.umd.edu` is `128.8.111.4`. As these examples show, there is never blank space between components of the Internet address.

One important point to note is that user ids need not be unique. For instance, two people with the family name Austin can have the login name `austin` as long as they operate on separate domains.

```
austin@isr.umd.edu
austin@kiwi.berkeley.edu
```

The domain name of the computer(s) must be unique, however.

Computer domain names are composed of subdomain names that follow the nomenclature outlined in Tables 1.3 and 1.4. For example, in the computer address `isr.umd.edu`, the subdomain name `edu` tells us that the computer is located at an educational institution. The subdomain name `umd` stands for the University of Maryland. Finally, the subdomain name `isr` represents the collection of computers at the Institute for Systems Research at the University of Maryland.

TABLE 1.3 Organizational Domain Names

Domain	*Meaning*	*Domain*	*Meaning*
com	Commercial	mil	Military
edu	Educational	net	Networking
gov	U.S. government	org	Nonprofit

1.5.6 Internet Services

Using the Internet means sitting at a computer and having access to a number of basic services, including

1. *E-mail.* You can send or receive electronic messages from anyone on the Internet. Anything that can be stored in text file can be mailed. Facilities also exist for converting binary files (e.g., an executable computer program) into a format suitable for transmission via E-mail.
2. *Telnet.* The Telecommunications Network (Telnet) program allows users to remotely login to computers over a network. The computer may be in the next room, or perhaps, on another continent.
3. *Gopher.* Gopher allows a user to request information from an extensive list of gopher servers on the Internet.
4. *File Transfer.* The File Transfer Protocol (FTP) enables the copying of files from one computer to another. Anonymous FTP is a system where an organization makes certain files available for public distribution—you can access such a computer by logging in with the user id "anonymous." Although no special password is required, it is customary to enter your E-mail address.
5. *Usenet.* An abbreviation for "user's network," Usenet is a collection of more than 5,000 discussion groups centered around particular topics. Newsgroups exist for every topic imaginable, including of course, those dedicated to the Internet and its development.

More recently, these basic services have been supplemented by the World Wide Web (WWW), allowing easy access to a wide array of media.

TABLE 1.4 Some Geographic Top-Level Domains

Domain	*Meaning*	*Domain*	*Meaning*
at	Austria	dk	Denmark
au	Australia	fr	France
br	Brazil	jp	Japan
ca	Canada	nz	New Zealand
de	Germany (Deutschland)	uk	United Kingdom

1.5.7 The World Wide Web

By providing millions of users in homes, schools, and industry with access to a wide array of media via an easy-to-use graphical user interface, the Web has captured the honorable distinction of being the most exciting part of the Internet.

Development of the Web began in March 1989, when Tim Berners-Lee of the European Particle Physics Laboratory (part of a larger organization known as CERN) proposed the project as a means of transporting research and ideas effectively throughout the CERN organization. The initial project proposal outlined a simple system of using networked hypertext (see the next section) to transmit documents and communicate among members in the high-energy physics community. The first graphical user interface to the Web was written by the Software Design Group at the National Center for Supercomputing Applications (NCSA). They named their graphical interface Mosaic. Mosaic, and the now famous Microsoft Internet Explorer and Netscape browsers, provide mouse-driven graphical user interfaces for displaying hypertext and hypermedia documents containing forms, paragraphs, lists, and tables in a variety of fonts and font styles. Graphics images can be linked to text and vice versa. Sound and video files can be pointed to by documents and downloaded over the Internet by simply clicking on the appropriate link.

Today's browsers are simply the beginning of where web development is headed. To help ensure that web browsers will be accepted as common business tools, software developers are busy integrating browser technology with office productivity suites (e.g., E-mail, word processors, graphics, spreadsheets, databases) and, in the case of engineering firms, design and analysis software. Work is also currently underway to incorporate *encryption technology* and client authentication abilities into web servers, thereby allowing users to send and receive secure data. These features will ensure that sensitive data is kept private, a prerequisite for commercial transactions over the Internet.

1.5.8 Hypertext and Hypermedia

Hypertext is basically the same as regular text with one important exception—hypertext contains connections within the text to other documents (see Figure 1.5). Suppose, for instance, that you were able to somehow select (with a mouse or with your finger) the phrase "encryption technology" in the previous paragraph. In a hypertext system, you would then have one or more documents related to encryption technology appear before you—a textual description of the applications of encryption technology, or perhaps Webster's definition of encryption. These new texts would themselves have links and connections to other documents. Continually selecting text would take you on a free-associative tour of information. In this way, hypertext links, called *hyperlinks,* can create a complex virtual web of connections.

Hypermedia is hypertext with a difference—hypermedia documents contain links not only to other pieces of text, but also to other forms of media such as sounds, images, and movies. Images themselves can be selected to link to sounds or documents. Hypermedia simply combines hypertext and multimedia.

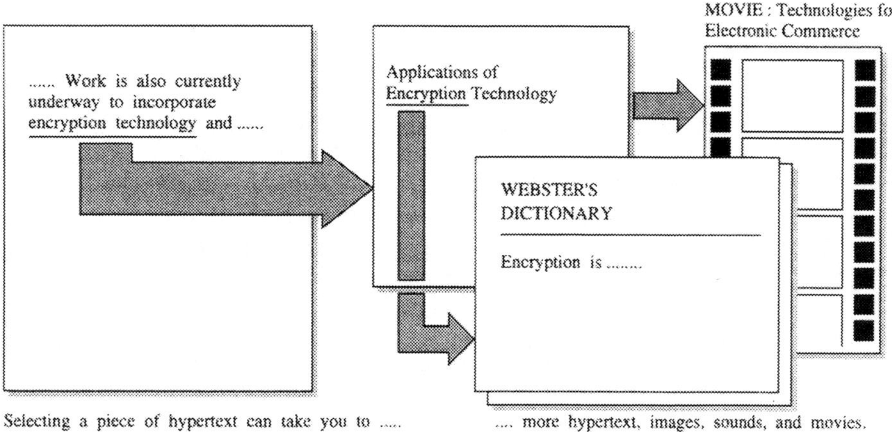

FIGURE 1.5 How hypertext works.

Suppose that you are a project manager in a large multinational engineering organization. Here are some examples of how web-based hypermedia might be used:

1. By clicking a mouse button on a part in an engineering drawing, you are able to see the pathway of project requirements leading to that part being incorporated in the design.
2. A web-based system might provide up-to-the-minute information on the status of a particular project. Clicking on the textual description of a project requirement could start an audio track describing an engineer's rationale for the requirement.
3. By looking at an organization's floor plan, you are able to retrieve information about an office by simply touching a room. An inventory of office equipment, detailed office drawings, and information on the office occupant and their current projects might appear by clicking on the right, center, and left mouse buttons.
4. You are reading a research paper to understand why a new technology is needed by your organization. By selecting text in a research paper, you are able to view a movie of the technology being tested in a laboratory setting. Then by clicking on a mouse button you are able to download and execute an engineering analysis package demonstrating how the technology works for simple case-study problems.

In the implementation of these applications, we expect that the use of hypermedia will elevate a reader's ability to "understand" and "navigate" the concepts presented beyond what is likely to occur with a serial presentation (e.g., a regular book). Realizing this goal requires at the very least, good judgment, attention to detail in document design, and user testing.

1.5.9 How Does the Web Work?

Web software is designed around a distributed client/server architecture (see Figure 1.3). A *web client,* called a web browser if it is intended for interactive use, is a program that can send requests for documents to any web server. A *web server* is a program that, upon receipt of a request, sends the document requested (or an error message if appropriate) back to the requesting client. Because the task of document storage is left to the server and the task of document presentation is left to the client, each program can concentrate on those duties and progress independently of each other.

Figure 1.6 shows the sequence of transactions that would take place when the "Company Floor Plan" is downloaded from a web server and displayed on a web browser. The sequence of events is as follows:

1. A user working at the web client selects a hyperlink in a piece of hypertext connecting to another document, such as "Company Floor Plan."
2. The web client uses the address associated with that hyperlink to connect to the web server at a specified network address and asks for the document associated with "Company Floor Plan." (See the upper half of Figure 1.6.)
3. The web server responds by sending the text and any other media within that text (pictures, sounds, or movies) to the client. The web client renders the information for presentation on the user's web browser window. (This step is shown along the lower half of Figure 1.6.)

The language that web clients and servers use to communicate with each other is called the Hypertext Transfer Protocol (HTTP). All web clients and servers must be able to speak HTTP to send and receive hypermedia documents. For this reason, web servers are often called HTTP servers, and "World Wide Web" is often used to refer to the collective network of servers speaking HTTP as well as the global body of information available using the protocol.

1.5.10 Uniform Resource Locators

The Web employs what are called *Uniform Resource Locators* (URLs) to represent hypermedia links and links to network services within Hypertext Markup Language

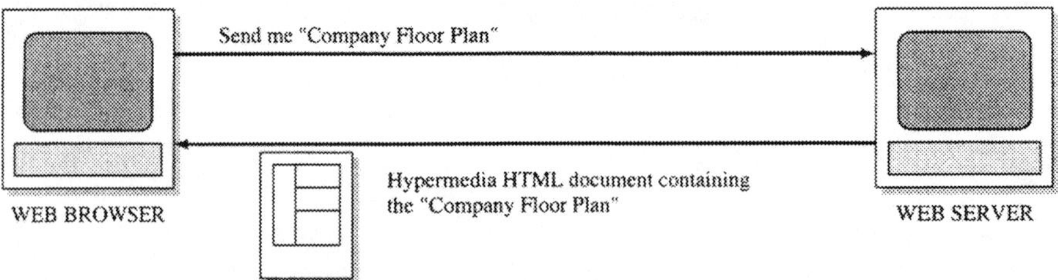

FIGURE 1.6 Web server and web client transactions.

TABLE 1.5 Some Examples of URLs

Uniform Resource Locator	*Description*
`http://www.ence.umd.edu/Welcome.html`	Connects to an HTTP server and retrieves an HTML file
`ftp://rtfm.mit.edu/pub/usenet/`	Opens an FTP connection to the usenet frequently asked questions stored at rtfm.mit.edu
`gopher://gopher.tc.umn.edu/`	Connects to a gopher menu at the University of Minnesota home site, inventor of the Gopher.

(HTML) documents. Almost any file or service on the Internet, including *FTP, Gopher,* and *Telnet,* can be represented with a URL. Table 1.5 contains some examples.

A URL is always a single unbroken line of letters and numbers with no spaces. The first part of a URL (before the two slashes) specifies the method of access; `http` is perhaps the most common. Typically, the second part of the URL is the address of the computer where the data or service is located. Further parts may specify the names of files, the port to connect to, or the text to search for in a database.

Sites that run web servers are often named with a www at the beginning of the network address. For example, the Department of Civil Engineering web server at the University of Maryland has the URL:

`http://www.ence.umd.edu/Welcome.html`

`Welcome.html` is the name of the HTML file for our department home page. You can ask your web browser to connect to this web server by simply specifying the URL in the location window.

1.5.11 Web Search Engines and Robots

A web *search engine* is simply a computer program that allows users to make queries for information residing in a database. The URLs for some of the good search engines on the WWW are as follows:

Search Engine	*Uniform Resource Locator*
AltaVista	`http://www.altavista.digital.com`
Hotbot	`http://www.hotbot.com`
Lycos	`http://www.lycos.com`
Yahoo	`http://www.yahoo.com`

Search engines help you to locate documents containing specific titles, words or phrases, links to specific URLs and host names, images having a specific name,

Java applets, and so forth. Each of these "document types" is located by constructing an appropriate query, and we refer you to online documentation at each search engine for the appropriate details.

Search engines such as AltaVista and Hotbot have indexed the complete contents of tens of millions of web pages. How can they do this? Clearly, humans cannot hope to manually index these quantities of information; the process has to be automated. The short answer to these questions is web robots. A *web robot* is a program that traverses the web's hypertext structure by retrieving a document and recursively retrieving all documents that are referenced.

Web robots can also be used for statistical analysis (e.g., to count the number of web servers), for maintenance (e.g., to detect out-of-date "dead" links), and for resource discovery (e.g., summarize large segments of the web). Resource discovery is perhaps the most exciting application of web robots; it means that rather than relying solely on browsing, a web user can combine browsing and searching to locate information even if the database does not contain the exact item you want to retrieve. It is likely to contain references to related pages, which in turn may reference the target item. These programs are also sometimes called spiders, web wanderers, or web worms.

Further Information

1. Good discussions on current and emerging trends in computing and computer technology periodically appear in *Scientific American.* See, for example, the articles on networked computing in the 1990s by Tesler [44], and the *21st Century Special Issue* from August 1995. Another good source on trends in computing may be found in a series of essays within the text *Technology 2001: The Future of Computing and Communications* [18, 19].
2. Browser plug-ins are software programs that extend the capabilities of a browser, such as Netscape Navigator, in a specific way. Current plug-ins allow for the ability to play audio samples or view video movies from within the browser, and to build and display three-dimensional worlds.

Links to some of these pages can be found at the book home page:

```
http://www.isr.umd.edu/~austin/book.html.
http://www.wiley.com/college/austin/
```

Review Questions

1. Have you been able to acquire an account and logon to a computer system at your school or company? Otherwise, do you have access to a PC that you can use to compile and run C, MATLAB, and Java programs while reading this book?

2. Do you understand the basic purpose of the computer components, such as the floppy disk, hard disk, memory (RAM and ROM), CPU, video display, keyboard, mouse, and so forth?

3. What are the main purposes of an operating system?
4. What is a computer network?
5. Briefly describe how a client/server system works. Can a computer act as both a client and a server at the same time?
6. Why were the Internet and the World Wide Web originally developed?
7. What technology has enabled web search engines, such as Yahoo and AltaVista, to index tens of millions of web pages in just a few years' time?
8. What is hypermedia?

1.6 REVIEW EXERCISES

Problem 1.1: Acquire an account on a UNIX machine and login to your account. When you have logged in successfully, try to "navigate" the file system. For example, start by typing the `pwd` command. This command prints the working directory, or your current location in the file system. Now try `cd ..`, which moves your current directory up to the parent directory. Now try `ls` to list the files in your directory. Now that you are in your parent directory, you can get back to your personal directory by typing `cd` (for change directory). By using `cd ..` and `cd` followed by a directory name, try to navigate and show the directory structure around your "home directory" on the UNIX system. Make a tree-type drawing of the structure.

Problem 1.2: Login to a UNIX machine and try the commands `rm`, `ls`, `cd`, `mkdir`, `rmdir`, and `cat`. Experiment with the online UNIX manual; that is, type `man` (for manual) command, as in `man mkdir`.

Problem 1.3: Try specifying options to the commands on your computer system (e.g., `ls -l` in UNIX). Almost all operating system commands have options so that you can specialize the operation of the command. You will eventually learn how to do this with your C programs (it is convenient when you include command-line options because it lets the user specify particular features of the program without having to ask every time the program is run). You can find the available options for an operating system command via `man` program on UNIX systems.

Problem 1.4: Use the operating system commands explained in Appendix 1 to build a simple directory structure under your UNIX home directory or under the root (C:) on your WINDOWS/NT system. Do not hesitate to create *many* directories; they are, after all, free!

Problem 1.5: Can you get some experience with a text editor such as "vi" or "emacs" on a computer? You will need to have experience with this because you will use an editor to enter your programs before they can be compiled and run. Most PCs come with a basic text editor, and there are many public domain editors you can get free of charge.

2

PRINCIPLES OF ENGINEERING SOFTWARE DEVELOPMENT

2.1 HARDWARE-SOFTWARE LIFE CYCLE

In engineering circles, advances in computer hardware and applications programs are driven by market competition and the need to design, analyze, manufacture, and control complex engineering systems. The complexity of an engineering system can be due to a number of factors including its size (i.e., a large number of interacting parts), nonlinear relationships between the input/output (I/O) parameters, incomplete information, enhanced performance specifications, and so forth. In any case, without the assistance of modern-day computer hardware and engineering applications programs, development of these systems would simply be intractable, if not impossible.

Figure 2.1 is a high-level view of components in the hardware-software life cycle. Typically, it begins with a group of engineers/customers, developers, and stakeholders (e.g., owners of a company) reaching consensus on the need for a new product and its pathway of development. Sometimes the results can be really impressive. Since the mid-1980s, for example, manufacturers of computer hardware have doubled the computational speed of their products every 12 to 18 months.

The economic challenges and difficulty in following up on hardware advances with appropriate software developments are reflected in Figure 2.2. In the early 1970s, software consumed approximately 25% of total costs, and hardware 75% of total costs for development of data-intensive systems. For the most part, computer systems were stand alone, and software developers wrote computer programs dedicated to a specific task (e.g., finite element analysis, control systems package).

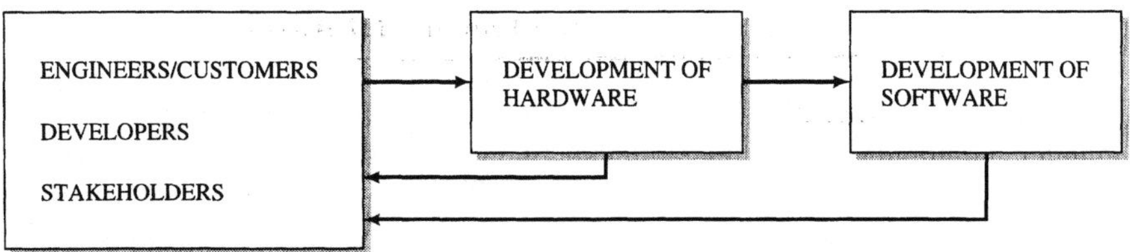

FIGURE 2.1 Hardware-software life cycle.

Currently, the development and maintenance of software typically consumes more than 80% of total project costs. This change in economics is the combined result of falling hardware costs, increased software development budgets, and a need to solve more difficult problems than in the past. Whereas one or two programmers might have written a complete program 20 years ago, teams of programmers are now needed to write today's large software programs. Moreover, for organizations that have made large investments in software, there is great reluctance to discard software just because a new technology has come along. What management

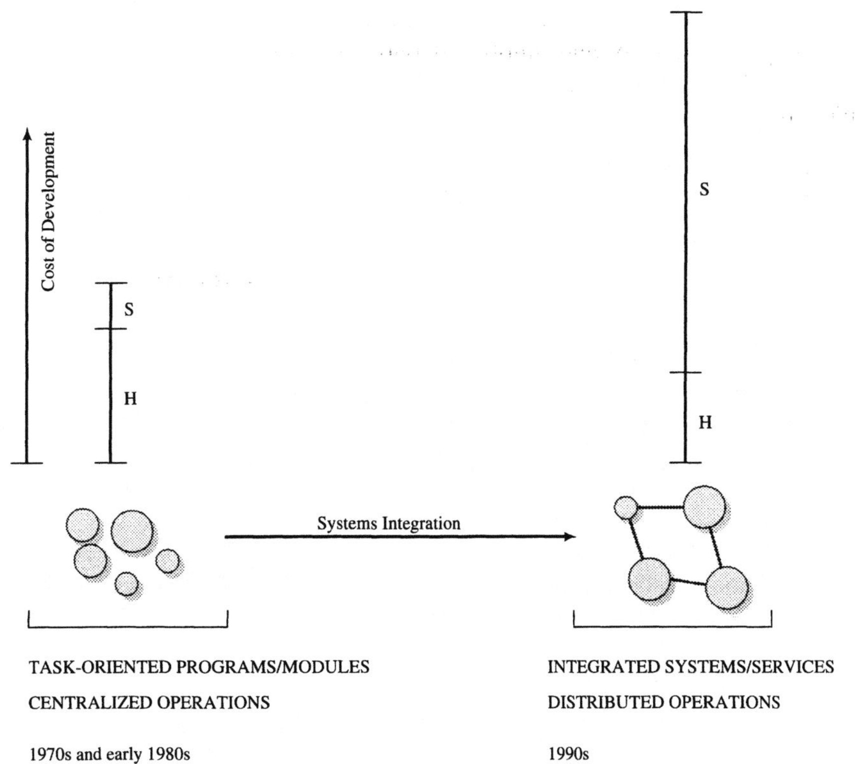

FIGURE 2.2 Economics of software development and integration. H, hardware; S, software.

would like to see instead are the benefits of improved communications without having to reinvest in the basic application-specific software. The objectives of *systems integration* are to try to bring this situation under control, to ensure that the pathway forward maximizes return for the organization, and protects a company's past investments in software and hardware [9]. Systems integration is not a technical discipline in itself, but rather an approach to the management of organizations that recognizes the different ways its parts interact. Understanding an organization's structure and management practices is critically important because it is a prerequisite to computer automation.

If software developments for engineering/business applications are to have any chance of keeping up with advances in computer hardware and networking, future developments will need to pay close attention to software design and reuse of functions, libraries, modules, program architectures, and programming experience. A key component of the solution lies in the judicious choice of programming language(s). In addition to having the ability to compute and evaluate formulae, programming languages now need to handle and manipulate large quantities of data and information, and lend themselves to rapid development of interactive graphics applications in parallel and networked computing environments. Recently developed languages such as Perl, Tcl/Tk, and Java are expected to play a central role in making this happen [2, 27, 46].

2.2 PRINCIPLES OF ENGINEERING SOFTWARE DESIGN

The discipline of software engineering is concerned with the design and implementation of computer programs that work, are correct, and are well written. Software engineering principles can be applied to small and large computer programs alike.

2.2.1 Small and Large Computer Programs

Small Computer Programs

Small computer programs are characterized by the data structures and algorithms they employ, design of the program architecture, and the computational efficiency of the program implementation.

Novice computer programmers tend to write programs that are small, composed of perhaps only a few hundred lines of source code. When you are learning to program in a new language, becoming familiar with its syntax, data types, and control structures are the most important things because without them you cannot transform a small-scale task into step-by-step programming instructions.

Large Computer Programs

In real-world engineering environments it is now commonplace for computer programs to be hundreds of thousands (even millions) of lines long. Many of them are so complex that even the best human minds cannot simultaneously comprehend all the details. It is therefore vitally important that the design and implementation of large computer programs be based on established procedures for software development, including attention to program specification and design, organization, coding, testing, and maintenance of software [4, 26]. Careful planning of these activities is needed because

1. Large programs are most often written by programming teams. Team members must be able to understand one another's work. When the planning, design, and coding of a project takes several years, communication of work among employees is of utmost importance.
2. Large programs are often developed within the constraints of short time-to-delivery contract schedules. Programming teams may not have the luxury of starting again, even after a key design flaw is identified.
3. Well-organized programs are easier to debug. A little extra time spent planning the layout of a program may be saved many times over when it comes time to debug and upgrade the software. Indeed, some estimates place maintenance at 60% to 80% of the overall cost of a software project.
4. Large programs often evolve through a series of versions, or updates. The programmer making updates is likely to be a person other than the original developer.

2.2.2 Models of Software Systems Development

Models of software systems development are an important component of large computer program development because they provide the project participants with a framework for knowing what is expected, and when. In some cases, the model may also form the basis of legal agreements, with contract payments being tied to successful completion of a task identified in the model.

Figure 2.3 is a schematic of two models of software system development that are currently in use. The *waterfall model* [36] views the software development process as a sequence of stages that includes requirements specifications, design and testing, integration, and maintenance (we get to the details of each step in a moment). Each phase of sequential development is completed, via formal review, before the next phase begins. The waterfall model of development is appropriate when the problem and solution method are well understood.

The *spiral model* of development, shown in Figure 2.3b, is simply a sequence of waterfall models with risk analysis and control incorporated at regular stages in the project [3]. This risk-oriented approach to iterative enhancement recognizes that implementation options are not always clear at the beginning of a project. For example, a software project that is scheduled for development over a number of years may need technology that has not yet come to market. Maybe the technology will evolve as expected, and maybe it will not. The radial direction of Figure 2.3b corresponds to the cumulative cost incurred in the project, and the angular direction corresponds to progress made in completing each cycle of the spiral. Each cycle of development has the following phases:

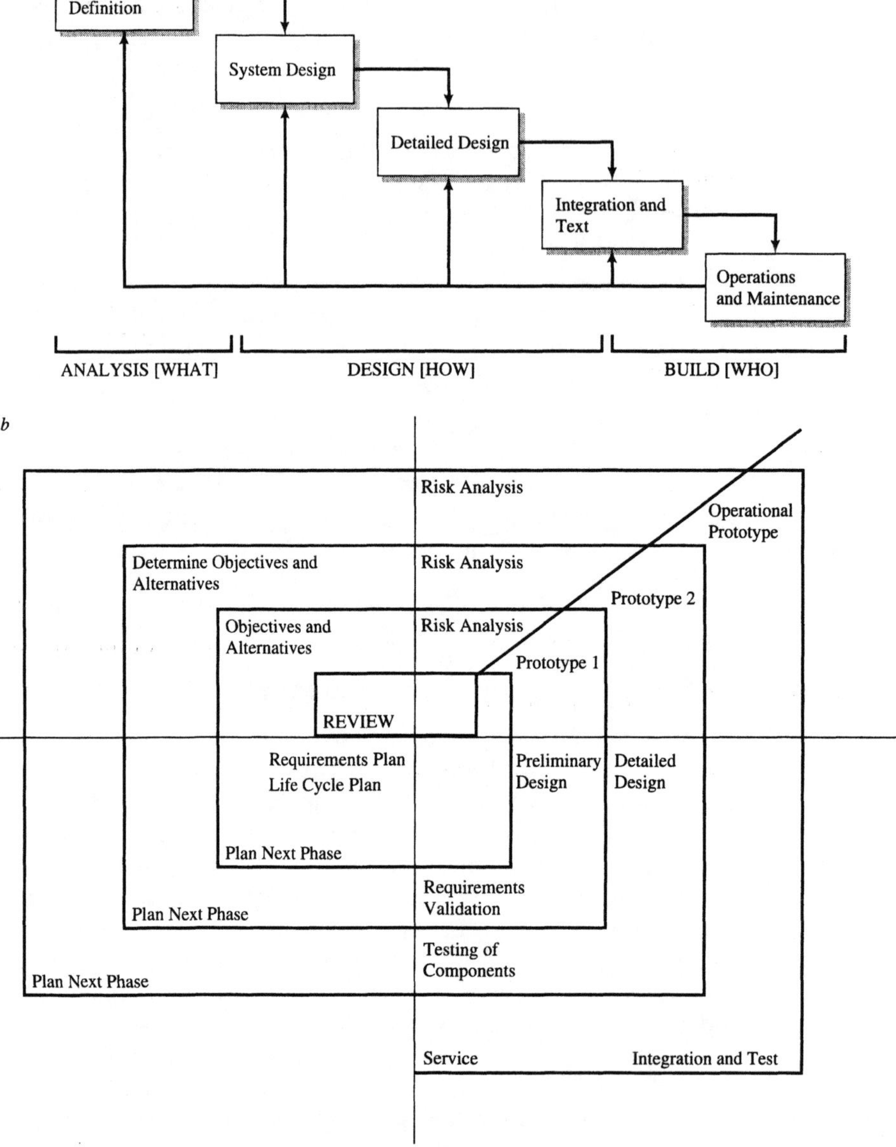

FIGURE 2.3 Models of development for software systems: (a) waterfall and (b) spiral models of systems development.

1. Identify the design and development objectives for the cycle as well as the alternatives that are possible to achieve the goals.
2. Evaluate different alternatives based on objectives and constraints. Where appropriate, identify uncertainties and risks. Risk means "something that can go wrong" as the consequence of incomplete information or perhaps as the result of human errors.

3. Develop strategies such as simulation, prototyping, and benchmarking for resolving uncertainties and risks.
4. Plan the next stage, allowing for any of the possible life cycle models to be used.

Of course many variations on the waterfall and spiral models are possible. For example, some companies develop software incrementally, using a model that is essentially a chain of waterfall models with each link in the chain corresponding to development of a software release. Subsequent releases add capability to previous releases and fix bugs found in previous versions. The second observation tends to be a sore point with many involved in the software industry and leads them to make comments such as "never buy software that is younger than Version 3.0." Clearly they think that it takes at least two software versions just to find and eliminate insidious startup bugs.

2.2.3 Components of Software Systems Development

The key steps in the development of a large software project are as follows.

Requirements Specification

The objective of the requirements specification is to state the goals of the program as carefully as possible. The goals could include, for example, expected input (keyboard/files/IO board) and output. The requirements should also identify any known limitations, possible errors, and accuracy issues.

The importance of the requirements specification is partly due to the economics of project development at the beginning of the software life cycle. As indicated in Figure 2.4, decisions made at the beginning of the software life cycle are inexpensive to make, yet have the greatest commitment of funds. Without a clearly de-

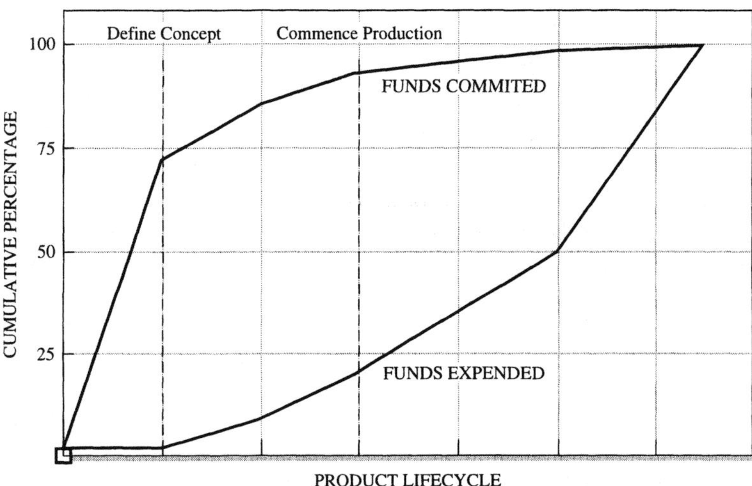

FIGURE 2.4 Funding commitments in product life cycle.

TABLE 2.1 Cost of Correcting Design Errors

Project Phase	*Bug Description*	*Relative Cost Ratio*
Design	Design team	1
Implementation	Programmers	10–20
Quality assurance	QA personnel	70–100
Shipment to customer	Customer	Very expensive

fined requirements specification, there is a greatly increased chance of project failure.

Table 2.1 shows the results of a study by Hewlett-Packard to quantify the relative costs, in terms of money and/or time, of correcting design errors. From an economic point of view, the last thing a manufacturer wants is discovery of a fatal error in the engineering system by a customer.

Analysis

Carefully analyzing a problem and its possible solutions is of utmost importance. Either you have to develop an algorithm yourself, or find one that is already available. Do not hesitate to look for established techniques; for example, an engineering problem might involve solving a set of linear equations using a standard numerical algorithm such as Gaussian Elimination. To develop algorithms from scratch when an already well-thought-out and documented technique is available is a waste of time.

Design

The next most important phase of program development is to develop a viable design that you believe will work. Studies indicate that up to 50% of all errors in the software life cycle are made during the design phase of the software; the remaining errors tend to be programming and syntax errors (as described previously). Unfortunately, design errors are also the most expensive to repair since many appear only at run-time, and often after the software has been delivered to the customer.

Implementation

The implementation phase focuses on the specification, writing, and documentation of modules of code. When the details of specification are particularly complicated, pseudocode is often inserted as an intermediate step. *Pseudocode* is simply a high-level description of the code (or algorithm) to be implemented, where the semantics are less strict than the programming language itself.

Always document program source code so that it can be understood by you and others at a later date. Documentation includes recording details of your specific solution—how the analysis phase will transfer to the program, what language-specific constructs were used, what method of problem decomposition was used, and any important restrictions in your software design. An executable program is the result of the implementation phase.

Test and Verification

In many engineering industries, such as airplane flight control, airport traffic control, nuclear power plant control, medical instruments, and communications network control, reliability of software is the most sought after attribute. The software must execute as expected and without errors. Obtaining software that performs with a high degree of confidence requires a solid program design, a careful implementation, and a carefully designed suite of test problems that may illuminate software bugs and weaknesses. The identification of bugs and weaknesses is highly desirable, because this is the point at which fixing them is easy.

Maintenance

It is frequently stated that programmers spend up to three quarters of their time maintaining existing software. Maintenance activities include (1) repair of coding (and design) errors, (2) adapting the software to changes in the computing environment (e.g., an update in the operating system), and (3) adapting the software to changes in the customers' requirements. Ask yourself how much code you have written in the past that is still in use (by you or others)? Can you easily understand programs that you wrote years ago? Would it be easy to change or modify your programs for a new purpose?

Table 2.2 shows how important it is to write code that can be reused and easily modified for a new purpose. If you are busy reinventing the wheel while other developers are reusing their software, eventually you will not be able to compete. These issues have to be taken into account before and during development of new programs. Once you have written a program without considering these issues, it is difficult and erroneous to shoehorn or force the code into a new application. We must learn to take into account the need for future changes in programs and design programs accordingly.

2.2.4 Modular Program Development

The goal of modular programming is to break a complex task or program into an ensemble of weakly coupled (independent) modules. Each *module* should be viewed as an independently managed resource, with access highly restrained. Programs consisting of well-designed modules are much simpler to design, write, and debug

TABLE 2.2 Reuse of Code in the United States and Japan

	Reuse Rate (%)	*Average Lines per Year*	*Average Errors per 1,000 Lines*
Japan	80	12,447	1.96
United States	30	7,290	4.44

than equivalent programs that are poorly designed [6, 28]. Guidelines for the design of program modules are

1. Psychological studies indicate that the average human can only simultaneously comprehend seven (plus or minus two) pieces of information. Hence, one module should have no more than seven subordinate modules.
2. There should be separation between the controller and worker modules.
3. Every module must perform a task appropriate to its place in the hierarchy.
4. Every module should only receive as much information as it needs to perform its function and, ideally, they should exchange as little information as possible.

Modules should enforce the principle of *information hiding,* namely, that all information about a module should be private to the module unless it is explicitly declared public [28]. Public data should be avoided because it exposes implementation details that make reuse unlikely and maintenance difficult. A key benefit of information hiding is the opportunity it affords for updating the internal details of a module (here we assume that the details of the public interface do not change) without affecting other modules in the system.

Coupling

Coupling measures the extent to which different modules in a system are interconnected with one another (see Figure 2.5). In design we should keep the interfaces as minimal and as simple as possible. Designing for minimal coupling among modules helps to ensure that errors occurring in one module will not propagate across the whole system.

Cohesion

Cohesion is a concept that describes how strongly the attributes and functions of a module are connected. Ideally, a module should just perform one task. In design we should keep related functions together and unrelated functions apart.

The attributes of system coupling and cohesion work together. Generally speaking, modules with components that are well related will have the capability of

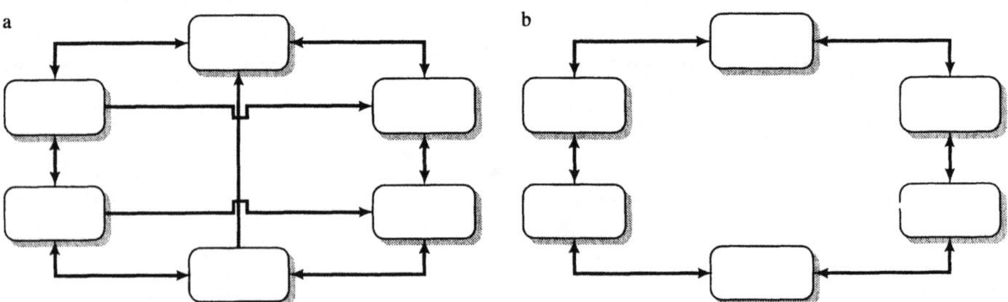

FIGURE 2.5 (a) Highly coupled and (b) loosely coupled systems.

plugging into loosely coupled systems. Modules should be designed within the framework of a well-defined language or grammar. If this principle is followed, then large programs may be divided into smaller modules (which may be compiled separately), and independent modules may be assembled together (i.e., bottom-up design). Modules designed within the framework of a language are easier to maintain and extend.

2.2.5 Abstraction

Programmers often apply techniques of abstraction to the development process, meaning that they concentrate on the essential features of one part (module) of the computer program and abstract from details of the computer program that are not immediately relevant to the current module. In the development of computer software, two types of abstraction are common:

1. *Procedural.* Software development is based on a stepwise refinement of the system's abstract function. This type of abstraction is most common in programming languages such as C, MATLAB, and FORTRAN.
2. *Data.* Software development is based on the system data and the operations that can be applied to the data. Implementations of data abstraction correspond to objects and the operations that can be applied to the objects. This type of abstraction is common in object-oriented programming languages such as C++ and Java.

2.2.6 Top-Down and Bottom-Up Software Design

Techniques of abstraction are often used in conjunction with a combination of top-down and bottom-up development strategies, as shown in Figure 2.6. Top-down software development begins at the conceptual level and passes through three stages:

1. The *high-level design* establishes the important subsystems of the design, the purpose and intended behavior of each subsystem, and the relationship among subsystems. As already mentioned, a good design corresponds to subsystems that are as uncoupled as possible.
2. The *intermediate-level design* breaks subsystems into modules. Each module should have one well-defined purpose, hide its data from other modules, and have a minimal number of connections to other modules in the program [24].
3. The *low-level design* involves detailed specification of algorithms and data structures.

You should notice that top-down design delays detailed decisions about the program flow and data structures until they absolutely have to be made.

The strategy of bottom-up design starts with low-level procedures, modules, and subprogram library routines, and tries to combine them into higher-level entities. A key benefit of bottom-up design is its use of already implemented code. For example,

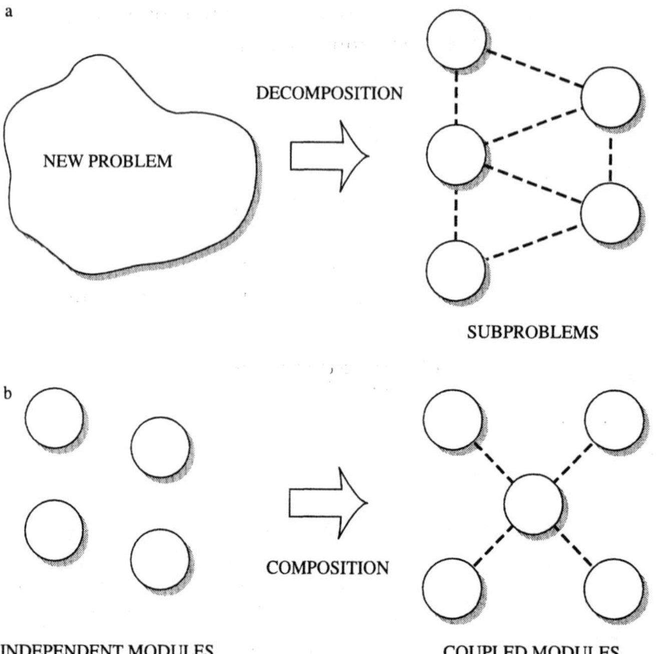

FIGURE 2.6 Schematics of (a) top-down and (b) bottom-up design.

numerical linear algebra packages are one area where libraries are routinely linked to C programs for finite element and numerical analysis, solution of differential equations, and solution of engineering control problems.

Top-down and bottom-up designs are extreme strategies for generating a hierarchical program structure and are often at odds with each other. Often the result of a top-down design is software modules that are of a one-time-only form. They are not amenable to reuse because they were designed as components without a preconceived vision of their future use. Similarly, generic modules suitable for bottom-up design may contain many features not needed to solve a specific task.

Software designers never embark on the construction of a new system without first considering available libraries/modules. Conversely, they never build software modules without a preconceived vision of their future use. A balance of the above-mentioned criteria is usually needed and desirable.

2.3 COMPUTER PROGRAMMING LANGUAGE CONCEPTS

Computer programs are composed of data and software instructions. The software instructions in a computer program tell the computer hardware how to execute a particular task by manipulating various types of data in a precise manner. Programming languages facilitate the development of these software instructions by providing constructs for organizing computations. The best programming languages enable the writing of good computer programs by being easy to read, understand, and modify.

2.3.1 High- and Low-Level Computer Languages

In the earliest days of computing, computers were programmed by entering instructions and data into the computer in binary form. These so-called *machine languages* correspond to the instruction set of a particular computer hardware. They are entirely machine dependent (i.e., very low level) and can be very tedious and error prone to program.

Programming in machine languages was quickly replaced by programming in symbolic *assembly languages,* which make the instructions easy to write and understand by using mnemonics for the machine instructions. For example, the sequence of symbols STO M R1 would store the contents of register 1 in memory location M. Symbolic assembly languages are still low level and tend to be machine dependent. An "assembler" converts the assembly language into corresponding binary code and generates a binary program for execution.

Easy-to-read *high-level languages* have been around since the early 1950s. The term "high level" means that many details in a program's development are handled automatically, thereby providing a pathway for programmers to write less code to get the same job done. For example, a number of high-level programming languages have been designed with the keywords `if` and `for` for the construction of simple branching and looping control structures. Once the program source code has been written, a compiler (see details below) will automatically generate the low-level machine instructions to implement the control structures. Whereas one line of assembly language code must be manually written for each low-level program instruction, high-level programming languages generate (on average) about five machine instructions for each line of code written. And because programmers write approximately the same number of lines of source code per day, irrespective of the development language, application programs can be implemented in a high-level language much faster (and more cheaply) than in an assembly language [5]. Examples of high-level programming languages are FORTRAN, C, C++, and Java. These languages are good for building software components from data structures and algorithms from scratch.

2.3.2 Compiled and Interpreted Programming Languages

Because computer hardware can only follow very low-level machine code instructions, which are difficult for humans to understand and manipulate, engineers usually write computer programs in a high-level programming language.

$$\text{[HIGH-LEVEL LANGUAGE]} \xrightarrow{\text{COMPILER}} \text{[LOW-LEVEL MACHINE LANGUAGE]}$$

A *compiler* translates the computer program source code into machine code instructions. The compiler can be thought of as a type of machine; it only understands a limited range of commands. If the compiler does not receive proper input, it can only try to interpret the error, report what is wrong (i.e., error messages), and exit. C, C++, and FORTRAN are among the programming languages that are compiled. Good programmers have some idea into what the code they write compiles (assembly language, bytecode, or machine code), because it is the efficiency of compiled code that matters, not the original number of source code lines.

In an *interpreted* computer program, high-level statements are read one by one, and translated and executed on the fly (i.e., as the program is running). Scripting languages such as Tcl/Tk and Perl are interpreted, as are application programs written in the MATLAB programming language.

The Java programming language is both compiled and interpreted. High-level Java source code is compiled into a low-level bytecode, and then interpreted by a Java Virtual Machine. Do not worry if some of the details seem a little murky at this point—we fill in the details of how this happens in the Java tutorial.

2.3.3 Procedural and Object-Oriented Programming Languages

Programming languages such as FORTRAN, C, and MATLAB are *procedural* because they enable a complex problem to be decomposed into a hierarchy of functions. Each function has a well-defined set of input parameters and will return a well-defined set of output values.

Programming languages such as C++ and Java, are *object oriented* because they view complex problems as an assembly of data items together with sets of methods (i.e., functions) that can manipulate the data.

2.3.4 Database and Scripting Languages

The rapidly growing complexity of engineering and business software since the 1980s has led to the development of a number of new programming languages for standardized interaction with databases and the rapid deployment of integrated software systems. As a case in point, the Structured Query Language (SQL) specifies the semantics of a database management system, including definitions of the structures and operations of the data model that can be implemented. Database language standards such as SQL facilitate the sharing of database applications with other applications, especially when the life of the application is longer than the life of current equipment, or where the application is to be understood and maintained by programmers other than the original program authors. Of course, programs written in C and C++ can interact with databases via function calls implementing SQL.

High-level *scripting languages,* such as Perl and Tcl (the Tool command language), assume that a collection of software components already exist and are designed for the gluing (or integration) of software components together. Scripting languages are coming into vogue because of the central role they can play in the rapid deployment of graphically based applications programs that operate across the Internet.

2.3.5 Hypertext and Virtual Reality Markup Languages

The Hypertext Markup Language (HTML) is the standard language employed by the Web for creating and recognizing hypermedia documents. HTML documents are usually written in files named with the suffix `.html`. They are nothing more than standard ASCII text files with formatting codes that contain information about layout (text styles, document titles, paragraphs, lists) and hyperlinks. The recent versions of HTML support a host of new features, including interactive forms, defined "hot spots" in images, and more sophisticated mechanisms for formatted page layout.

The Virtual Reality Markup Language (VRML) is a graphic standard that enables construction of interactive three-dimensional scenes within the Web. Figures 2.7 and 2.8 show, for example, three-dimensional wire frame and solid scenes of a house containing rooms, furniture, and so forth [35]. VRML provides the mechanisms for a user to manipulate his or her view of the scene and interact with components in the scene. For instance, an engineer might click on an item of furniture in the solid scene and be presented with detailed top, side, and front elevation drawings of the item.

What is really neat is that by using the Java programming language to glue components of VRML scenes and their behavior together, such an environment could be distributed across a network.

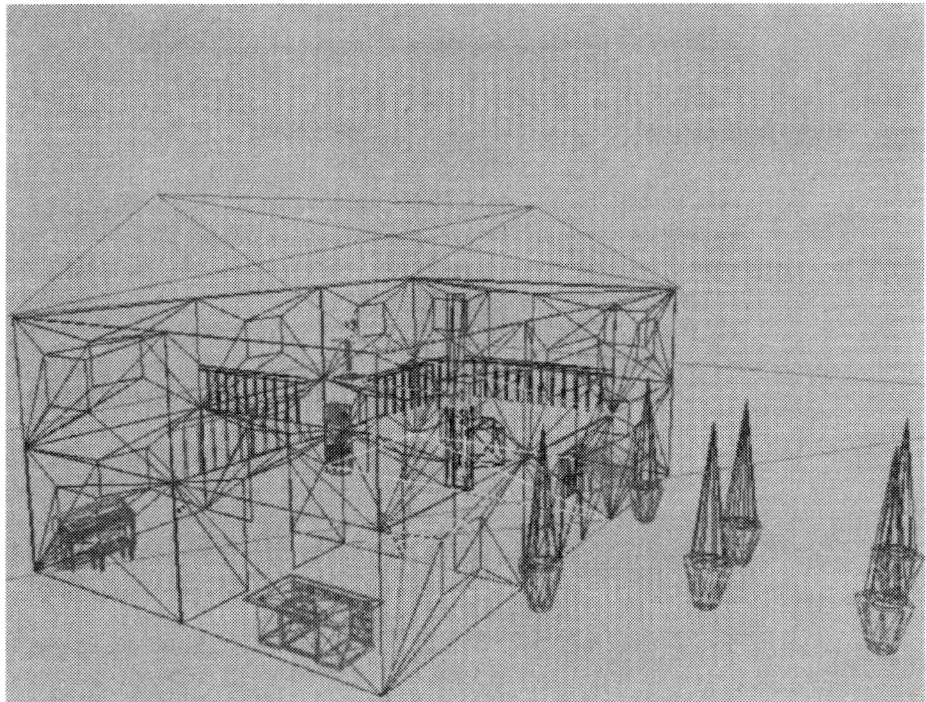

FIGURE 2.7 Wire frame schematic of a house.

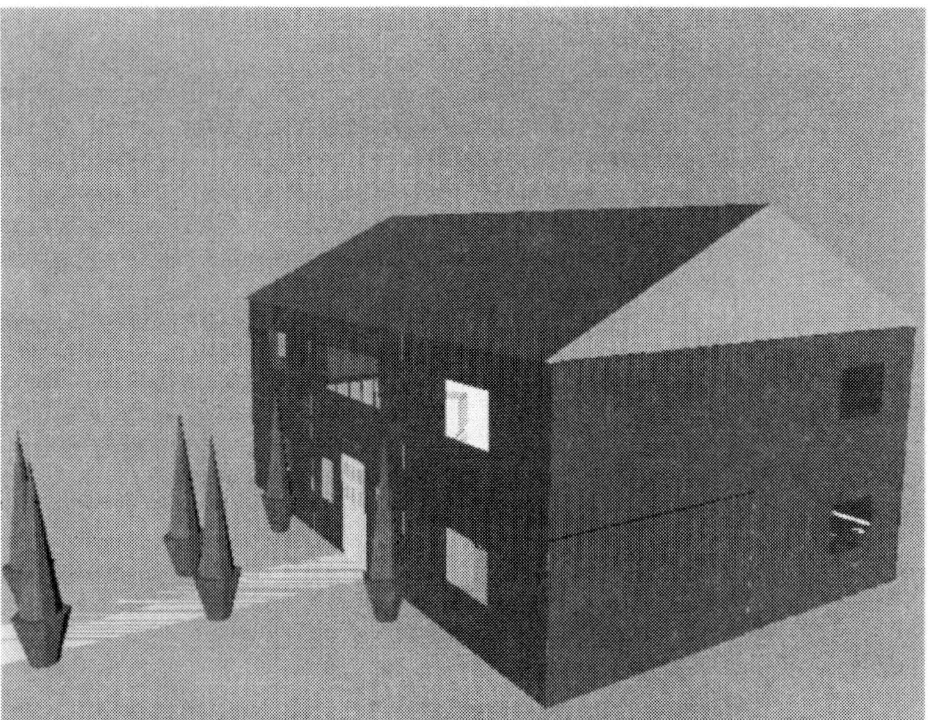

FIGURE 2.8 Three-dimensional representation of a house.

2.4 PROGRAMMING LANGUAGE SELECTION

As indicated in Figure 1.1, the number of programming languages engineers are using is steadily increasing. This trend is due in part to the expanding range of tasks for which engineers are now using computers, and in part by the limited range of tasks current programming languages can handle well. Since computer languages are usually designed with the solution of a certain range of problems in mind, the selection of the right language for the job at hand is of utmost importance.

Here are some rules of thumb for selecting a programming language:

1. Use MATLAB if you need to solve a problem that can be conveniently represented by matrices, solved using operations from linear matrix algebra, and presented using relatively simple two- and three-dimensional graphics. Computing the solution to a family of linear equations, and representing, manipulating, and displaying engineering data are perhaps the two best examples of problems for which MATLAB is ideally suited.

   Not only is the MATLAB programming language exceptionally straightforward to use (every data object is assumed to be an array), but the MATLAB program code will be much shorter and simpler than an equivalent implementation in C or FORTRAN or Java. MATLAB is therefore an ideal language for creating prototypes of software solutions to engineering problems, and using them to validate ideas and refine project specifications. Once these issues have been worked out, the MATLAB implementation can be replaced by a C or Java implementation that enhances performance and allows for extra functionality—for example, a fully functional graphical user interface that perhaps communicates with other software package over the Internet.

Since the early 1990s, the functionality of MATLAB has been expanded with the development of toolboxes containing functions dedicated to a specific area of mathematics or engineering. Toolboxes are now provided for statistics, signal processing, image processing, neural nets, various aspects of nonlinear and model predictive control, optimization, system identification, and partial differential equation computations. MATLAB 5.0 also comes with an application program interface (API) that allows MATLAB programs to communicate with C and FORTRAN programs, and vice versa, and to establish client/server relationships between MATLAB and other software programs.

2. Use C if your program has to manipulate character strings and/or blocks of memory, communicate with the operating system, link easily to external software libraries, and/or communicate with other software packages over a network.

   A wide range of engineering applications are now being written in C. For example, finite element programs that can solve matrix equations involving thousands of unknowns have been written in C. C is the language of choice for systems programming involving graphics packages such as X, Windows NT, and compiler construction tools such as Yet Another Compiler Compiler (YACC) and Lexical Analysis (LEX). Embedded systems, whose purpose is to maintain or control some property or relationship among components of a larger system are also programmed in C. Embedded systems include controllers to run machinery, thermostats, refrigerators, VCRs, and TVs, to name just a few.

3. Use Java for problem solving that involves graphical user interfaces that will work on a variety of computer platforms and/or if your program has to communicate with other software programs and databases across the Internet.

   Because the Java language is relatively new, there simply has not been enough time for sophisticated application programs to be written. However, this situation is rapidly changing. The seeds of development can be found in Java applet programs that solve simple undergraduate engineering problems. See, for example, the collection of engineering applets at the Gamelan web site, and the problems at the end of Chapter 19.

Some of these rules of thumb correspond to advanced language features that are beyond the scope of the introductory tutorials in this book. We therefore suggest that you follow up on points of interest by browsing the computer sections of your local bookstore.

An important point to keep in mind is that these languages are not completely independent, and it makes good sense to implement an application program using more than one programming language when their combination allows for superior functionality and/or lower life cycle development costs. For example, a current limitation of computational applications written in C and C++ is that their graphical interfaces tend to work only on one type of computer system (i.e., UNIX box, PC, or Mac). Commercial applications overcome this limitation by simply creating and maintaining UNIX, PC, and Macintosh versions of an application program, a development process that can be very expensive. In the near future, however, engineering applications having a graphical front end written in Java and a numerical engine written in C or C++ are likely to become quite common. The result will be single versions of an interactive application program that can operate across multiple platforms. Software development costs are expected to drop because the need to create and maintain multiple versions of a program will have been mitigated.

Further Information

1. An ensemble of WWW links to HTML and VRML development resources can be found at the book home page:

   ```
   http://www.isr.umd.edu/~austin/book.html.
   http://www.wiley.com/college/austin/
   ```

2. A good introduction to Tcl and the Tk Toolkit can be found in Osterhout [27].
3. For a good introduction to the use of Java for 3D and VRML Worlds, see Lea *et al.* [17].

Review Questions

1. What are the basic steps involved in the development of software? Why is the process broken down into several steps? Why would you use one language rather than another? Are they all the same?

2. Briefly explain the terms *abstraction, modularity, coupling, cohesion,* and *information hiding.*

3. What are the goals of top-down and bottom-up design?

4. What is the difference between procedural abstraction and data abstraction?

5. What are present-day applications programs written in high-level programming languages?

6. Why does it typically take much longer to write an application program in assembly language than in a high-level programming language?

7. What do the acronyms HTML and VRML stand for? What is the relationship between Java and VRML?

8. For what types of problems is the MATLAB programming language suited? How has the functionality of MATLAB been expanded?

9. For what types of problems is the C programming language suited?

10. For what types of problems is the Java programming language suited?

11. Why does it sometimes make sense to develop a software package using more than one programming language?

PART 2

C PROGRAMMING TUTORIAL

Now that we are familiar with the basic concepts of modern engineering computations, it is time to begin learning the C programming language.

The C programming language tutorial is divided into 10 chapters. Chapter 3 introduces the C language, its history, and the steps needed to write, compile, and run a small C program. These steps are illustrated by working step by step through the development of two programs. The basic data types and variables; Hungarian notation for naming variables, operators, and expressions; and control of program flow are described in Chapters 4 through 6. Chapter 7 is an introduction to the use of functions in C. Chapters 8 and 9 are particularly important because pointers and arrays, and advanced features of functions, are described. These are areas where C departs from other high-level languages. Students who can master these two chapters will be off and running with C. Chapter 10 describes dynamic memory allocation, and its application to the run-time allocation of character strings and small two-dimensional matrices. Finally, the C preprocessor, and input and output, are covered in Chapters 11 and 12.

Appendix 1 is a basic introduction to the UNIX operating system. Appendix 2 contains a detailed summary of functions in the standard C library.

3

GETTING STARTED

3.1 KEY FEATURES OF C

Most newcomers to a language want to know immediately what distinguishes the new language from what they already know. Why is the new language better? What is all the excitement about? How can C possibly be better than FORTRAN? We believe that it is better for many reasons, but most of them will require more in-depth study of the language and its uses. Here are a few differences that are easy to delineate:

1. The language maintains a model that is close to the underlying hardware, and consequently many of the language specifications remain permissive (to allow the expressive power needed to control low-level activities).
2. The language specification is sparse, meaning there are only 32 keywords and few operators. C does not have, for example, an exponentiation operator; there is no built-in input/output (I/O), string manipulation, or math functions (sin, cos, etc). We soon see that these features are supported in libraries.
3. Much of the functionality of a C programming environment comes from external libraries. Some of these libraries are standard and contain groups of functions that are so commonly used that they are provided with the compiler (e.g., functions for I/O, manipulation of character strings, math functions).
4. Because the standard library has been developed over many years, and now has an official standard specification, this approach to program development enhances portability of software across computer platforms.

C has been reluctantly received in many engineering circles. One problem is that it contains features of both high- and low-level languages. C is a high-level language because it uses an English-like syntax for control statements and supports user-defined data types. At the same time, C is a low-level language because it allows variables to be declared and stored in registers, supports operations on bits, and in general gives the programmer access to low-level features of the computer. The C programming language was originally developed with support for these operations in mind.

Experience indicates that programmers who know C have little difficulty learning FORTRAN; however, the opposite is not true. To its detriment, C places few restrictions on the programmer and, as such, assumes that you know what you are doing. Errors are sometimes difficult to find because two C programs may look and read completely differently, and yet be functionally identical. Also, more complex data structures are supported in C, and when these are not documented or understood completely, programs can become difficult to understand. To alleviate this problem area, the novice programmer should try to develop a consistent style of programming (comments, naming conventions, spacing and indentation), with source code that is easy to read and modify when the need arises.

3.2 A LITTLE HISTORY

The C programming language was developed in the early 1970s by researchers at AT&T Bell Laboratories in New Jersey. Although C was originally developed with systems programming in mind (the UNIX operating system is written in C), it now finds application to development of numerical and engineering software as well. In 1978, Kerninghan and Ritchie wrote the book *The C Programming Language* [14]. They were intimately involved in the language's development, and they saw the need for a book to explain its application and capabilities. Indeed, when C compilers were written by vendors other than AT&T, the only specification available for the language was the Kerninghan and Ritchie book. Consequently, the compilers that used the book as a reference are now referred to as "K&R" compilers. Since the late 1970s, several features have been added to the language (and some dropped). In 1984, many of the revisions to K&R C were reported by Harbison and Steele (H&S C) [12]. At about the same time (in 1983), the American National Standards Institute (ANSI) formed a committee (named X3J11) to standardize the C programming language and its run-time libraries, thereby increasing portability of C programs among hardware platforms (i.e., HPs, SUNs, DECs, PCs). These libraries are now called ANSI (standard) C. A draft of this standard was ratified in 1989 [1]. It covers topics such as preprocessor directives, function definitions and bodies, and formal use of standard run-time libraries.

3.3 WRITING AND COMPILING A SIMPLE C PROGRAM

This chapter contains a step-by-step introduction to the process of writing, compiling, and running small C programs. We present two case study programs as an introduction to what C programs look like and how the C language can be employed for the solution of simple problems. Particular attention will be paid to the standard library functions `scanf()` and `printf()` because they handle formatted I/O, respectively. Novice C programmers need to know how to use the function `printf()` because it can be used to print error messages (something you will most likely need to do). Section 3.6 covers the details of compiling and running small C programs in a variety of operating system environments.

3.3.1 User-Defined Code and Software Libraries

Computer programs written in C are a combination of *user-defined code*—that is, the computer program code we write ourselves—and collections of external functions located in *software libraries.* Software library functions are written by computer vendors and are automatically bundled with the compiler. *Software libraries* play a central role in the development of C programs because the small number of keywords and operators in C is not enough to solve real engineering and scientific problems in a practical way. What really makes C useful is its ability to communicate with collections of functions that are external to the user-written source code. This is where much of the real work in C programs takes place.

The ANSI C standard requires that certain libraries are provided with all implementations of ANSI C. For example, the standard library contains functions for I/O, manipulation of character strings, handling of run-time errors, dynamic allocation and deallocation of memory, and functions for C program interaction with the computer's operating system. Mathematical formulae are evaluated by linking a C program to the math library. Engineering application programs may also communicate with graphical user interface, numerical analysis, and/or network communications libraries.

Generally speaking, if there is a library function that meets your needs, by all means use it. The judicious use of library functions will simplify the writing of your C programs, shorten the required development time, and enhance C program portability. Software is said to be portable if it can, with reasonable effort, be made to execute on computers other than on the one on which it was originally written.

3.3.2 Program Development Cycle

When you are a novice C programmer, the two most important issues you are likely to be concerned about are learning the syntax of the C language and becoming familiar with the step-by-step details of planning, writing, compiling, running, testing, and documenting small C programs. The pathway of C program development is summarized in Figure 3.1. They key steps are as follows:

1. *Develop Pseudocode.* Pseudocode is a nickname for an English description of ideas that will eventually be translated into a programming language. Like most engineering design processes, development of pseudocode descriptions is inherently iterative. Pseudocode descriptions begin with general high-level statements of the required problem-solving procedures and are successively

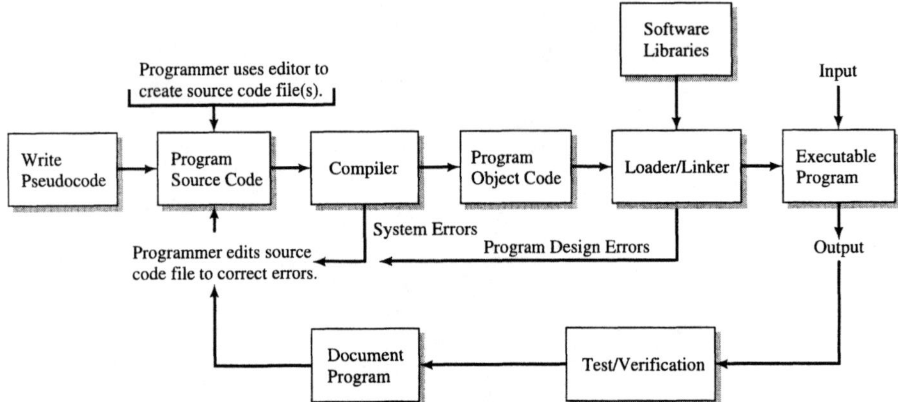

FIGURE 3.1 Program development cycle.

refined until they look "more or less" like a program. For us, pseudocode is a description of the program steps that can eventually be written in C.

Beginning the program development cycle with a pseudocode problem description is important because it forces us to deal with design issues at an early stage, when corrections and changes are easy to make. For example, with a pseudocode description of a problem-solving procedure in hand, the correctness of an algorithm can be tested by stepping through it in your head or on scratch paper. Most experienced programmers will attest to the fact that errors in logic are the most difficult to find, especially in the latter stages of program development. Getting programs to compile (syntax, structure, etc.) is the easy part.

2. *Edit Program.* The pseudocode is translated into a C program by using a text editor for the creation of source code files containing a description of the problem to be solved. Most computer systems support a variety of text editors. Because some of them will be much easier to learn and use than others, it is a good idea to ask your instructor for advice on the best place to start and for information on basic editor commands to insert and modify text.

   All file names in our C programs will consist of a base name with an optional period and suffix. The first character of the file name must be a letter, possibly followed by more letters and numbers. C source code files are where the C language description of our engineering problem descriptions will go and, by convention, they will be stored in files having names with a `.c` suffix. Header files contain function declarations and symbolic constants, and act as an interface between user-defined C code and one or more external software libraries. By convention, header file names will have a `.h` suffix. We soon see that object files are generated by the compiler and have a `.o` suffix. The suffix convention is used by compilers to identify the type of information stored in a file.

3. *Compile Program.* A C compiler is a computer program that translates high-

level problem descriptions, written in the C language, into equivalent low-level language descriptions that can be understood by a particular type of computer (i.e., the computer hardware). You should think of the C compiler as a type of machine that only understands the grammatical rules of the C programming language. If the compiler does not receive proper input, it can only try to interpret the error, report what is wrong by printing error messages, and exit. If the rules of the language are satisfied, however, the compiler will generate one or more object files containing low-level machine language instructions. The linker is a software program that resolves all cross-references among object files, connects the user-written code to relevant software library modules and, finally, generates a single executable program file. The chain of "compilation activities" is summarized by the center row of blocks in Figure 3.1.

4. *Performance Analysis.* Performance analysis consists of an evaluation of the program performance with respect to the design specifications. As indicated on the right-hand side of Figure 3.1, most computer programs will receive some form of input from the keyboard, or perhaps from a file, and generate output to the computer screen, or perhaps to a file. The critical question to ask at this point is "does the computer program do what it was designed to do?"
5. *Debug and Test Program.* The first few drafts of a C program nearly always contain errors (or bugs). You will need to correct (or debug) your program if there are syntax, executional, or logic errors, as determined in the performance analysis or compilation. Syntax errors are those encountered when the program is compiled into machine code; if you have typing errors, then the compiler will not be able to understand what you are doing. Execution errors are found when the program is run, for example, if the bounds of an array are exceeded or, perhaps, if division by zero occurs. Logic errors are usually discovered after the program has finished executing or during execution. If execution does not proceed as expected, then perhaps there is a flaw in the logic of the program. In each case, symbolic debuggers such as `dbx` [21] may be used to interactively run the program and detect errors (see following comment). It may be faster and easier to go back and reconsider the design of the program. Have you effectively transferred the design to C, or is there a flaw in the design? Answering these questions first may lead to a solution faster than learning a whole new bag of tricks with a debugger.
6. *Document Code.* You should document your source code so that other programmers know what the source code does and how it may be used. The process of documenting your program should be integrated into the program development cycle. Some (experienced) programmers will tell you that they first develop the code and then document it. It is our experience, however, that with the pressures of life being what they are (everyone is pressed for time), this strategy of development results in code that works but is poorly or never documented.

In this solution of practical engineering problems, several iterations of Steps 1 through 6 may be required before a fully developed, correct, working program is obtained. Indeed, the purpose of the looping constructs in Figure 3.1 is to show that when an error occurs in the language syntax, program design, and/or program performance, the programmer must return to Steps 1 and 2, make the necessary adjustments to the program design/source code, and recompile and test the program.

3.4 PROGRAM 3.1: PRINT APPROXIMATE VALUE OF π

3.4.1 Problem Statement and Source Code

Our first C program simply prints an approximate value of π to the computer screen. The problem-solving procedure can be represented by two lines of pseudocode, namely

```
Set constant for approximate value of pi.
Print approximate value of pi.
```

The entire contents of Program 3.1 are written in one file (we call it `first.c`).

PROGRAM 3.1: PRINT APPROXIMATE VALUE OF π

```
/*
 * ===================================================================
 * Print value of "pi" to computer screen
 *
 * Written by: Mark Austin                             January, 1994
 * ===================================================================
 */

#include <stdio.h>  /* Standard Input/Output function declarations */

#define PI 3.1415926

int main( void ) {

    printf("Approximate value of PI = %f \n", PI );
    return (0);
}
```

All that Program 3.1 does is output

```
Approximate value of PI =   3.141593
```

to the computer screen. Even though it is only 20 lines long, Program 3.1 contains many of the features of C (e.g., comments, preprocessor directives, header files, a `main ()` function, standard library functions) that you will need to write programs.

3.4.2 Comment Statements

Comment statements begin with the two-character sequence /* and end with first occurrence of the character pair */ (they are used symmetrically). Comment statements may contain any number of characters and are always treated as white space; in other words, the C compiler ignores all text following /* up to and including the matching */. Avoid nested comment statements (comments inside of comments).

Comment statements, if well conceived and well placed, can significantly enhance the readability of code. You will find that if you or others have not looked at a particular program for a while, then well-conceived and well-placed comments can make a big difference in whether the purpose and operation of the code can be quickly recalled.

3.4.3 Layout of the Program Source Code

C is a free-form language, meaning that programs do not have to be arranged on a page in a strict format. You may put several statements on a single line or spread a single statement over several lines. Comment statements may be arbitrarily positioned. The C programming language regards the space between characters as white space that will be disregarded by compilers. *White space* is officially defined as

- Blanks (or spaces—literally, the space character)
- New lines (carriage returns—what you type at the end of each line)
- Horizontal and vertical tabs (used in aligning text)
- Comment (/* this is a comment! */)
- Formfeeds (used to separate pages when listing source code)

In Program 3.1, we use white space and blank lines to separate significant sections of code (blank lines are like punctuation in a sentence) and to make the program source code as readable and easy to understand as possible. Readability of a computer program can also be enhanced with the use of (1) descriptive names for variables/identifiers, (2) attention to indentation of blocks of code, (3) consistent placement of braces and use of parentheses, and (4) informative comments that enhance the meaning of code. A second technique for helping readers to find their way around source code is to lay out every C source file in the same way. In Program 3.1, we adopt the following layout:

```
Block of comments explaining purpose of source code in file.
Header files for declarations.

int main() {
Declare variables and constants for main() function block.

   List of statements to be computed;

}

Other user-defined functions (if necessary).
```

Once you establish a style of programming and code layout that works and is easy to read, it is a good idea to stick to it. This strategy of programming makes the inevitable task of finding and correcting programming errors easier.

3.4.4 The `main()` Function

Functions play a central role in the development of C programs because they allow for the partitioning of large problems into smaller (manageable) subproblems, and they enable the development of hierarchical problem-solving strategies. Every C program must have one user-defined function called `main()`, because this is where C programs begin their execution. The script of code

```
int main ( void ) {     <===== header and opening brace for main() function.

}                       <===== closing brace for body of function main().
```

shows the general structure of function `main()` in Program 3.1. Functions contain a header and a body enclosed within opening and closing curly braces {· · ·}. A function header takes the form

```
returnType functionName ( list of arguments )
```

and it is composed of a function name, a list of zero or more arguments, and a return type. In Program 3.1, the keyword `int` tells the compiler that function `main()` will return an integer value. The keyword `void` between brackets indicates that main will not have any arguments.

Because C is a free-form language, an alternative and equally good declaration for `main()` is

```
int main ( void )           <===== header for function main().
{                           <===== opening brace for body of function main().
}                           <===== closing brace for body of function main().
```

where the curly braces have been aligned on the first column. In most of the listings in this text, we employ the former style of formatting because it conserves "vertical white space"; that is, it reduces the number of lines that you will read in a listing. A typical function body will contain a series of declarations and statements

```
{
    C_statement_1;
    C_statement_2;

    C_statement_m;
}
```

which will be executed in the order in which they appear. Declarations define the memory locations that will be employed by the program during its execution.

Statements specify the operations that will be computed during the program's execution. For example, the body of Program 3.1 contains two statements:

```
printf("Approximate value of PI = %f \n", PI );
return (0);
```

printf() is a general-purpose standard library function for generating formatted output and return is a statement for returning a value from the function execution. Like all functions in C, printf() is called by giving the function name followed by a list of arguments enclosed within parentheses—we expand on its capabilities in this chapter and in Chapter 12. Statements in C are terminated by a semicolon (;).

The program execution for Program 3.1 begins at the top of function main(), switches to function printf(), and back to main().

3.4.5 Header Files and the C Preprocessor

All ANSI C compilers require declarations for library functions before they are used in a program. The function declarations will tell the C compiler how the functions in the library will be called and what contents (if any) will be returned by the function. You do not really have to know how the library functions work; the library writers deal with the details so that you can concentrate on your specific program.

Whenever you use a C compiler, a program called the "C preprocessor" will scan the source code files and respond to any lines beginning with a pound symbol # followed by certain keywords. For example, the command #include tells the C preprocessor to replace a single line in the program source file by the contents of the file name listed between the <brackets>. In Program 3.1, the directive

```
#include <stdio.h>    /* include declarations for I/O functions */
```

tells the C preprocessor to find and insert the contents of the header file (so called because these files are usually included at the top or head of a program) stdio.h just as if it had been manually inserted by the programmer. Header files act as interfaces between the user-defined source code and object modules located in software libraries such as the standard library(ies), and contain the details on how library functions should be used. As a case in point, the stdio.h header file contains function declarations and variable constants used by the standard library for I/O. A C compiler uses this information to ensure that the user-defined code calls functions in the standard library in the correct way.

Figure 3.2 is a schematic of the header files, user-defined functions, and library functions that play a role in the development of Program 3.1. The one-way arrow from header file stdio.h to the box containing main() signifies that first.c will read (or include) the contents of stdio.h. The use of two-way arrows between the boxes containing main() and printf() signifies that when the program is executed, the program control will switch from main() to printf(), and then back to main().

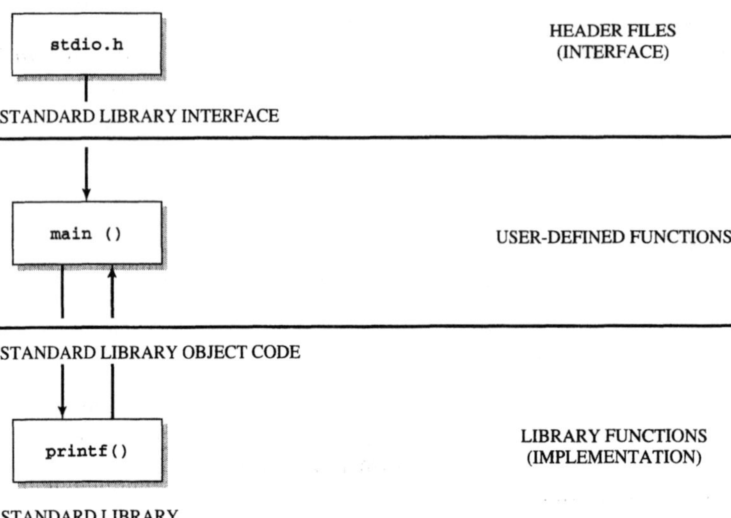

FIGURE 3.2 Architecture of Program 3.1.

3.4.6 Symbolic Constants

The `#define` preprocessor directive may be used to define a symbolic constant that assigns an identifier (i.e., a name) with a constant. The names of symbolic constants should be selected so that they are easy to remember. In Program 3.1, the directive

```
#define PI 3.1415926
```

makes the name `PI` synonymous with the constant 3.1415926. During the initial phases of program compilation, the C preprocessor searches through the source code for references to `PI` and replaces each occurrence with 3.1415926. Now suppose at a later date precision is added to our approximation of `PI` by updating the directive

```
#define PI 3.14159265358979332846
```

All instances of `PI` can be updated by simply recompiling the computer program.

3.4.7 Standard Output with `printf()`

`printf()` is a versatile standard library function for accessing the terminal screen and producing formatted output. Its capabilities include

- Automatic formatting of numerical output when no other specification is given
- The ability to accept a variable number of arguments
- The ability to determine output formats at run-time (e.g., `%*.*f`)
- The ability to return the number of bytes output

The beauty of putting `printf()` in the standard library and providing programmers with the mechanisms to call function in external libraries is that it leaves the programmer free to concentrate on development of code for problem solving.

The C statement

```
printf("Approximate value of PI = %f \n", PI);
```

calls `printf()` with two arguments, a string constant

```
"Approximate value of PI = %f \n"
```

and the constant `PI`. The contents of the function argument between quotes ". . . ." is called a character string. The sequence of characters `%f` is an example of a conversion specification. Conversion specifications begin with a percent sign (`%`) and are followed by one or more formatting options for output, left/right justification, numeric signs, size specification, precision specification, decimal points, and padded zeros. In this particular case, the `%f` simply tells `printf()` to output the contents of `PI` as a floating point number. By default, the floating point number will be printed with six decimal places of precision.

We use the `'\n'` escape character to print a carriage return and advance the screen output (or cursor) to the beginning of a new line. Omitting a new line character in `printf` statements will result in long stream of output on the same line—the output will either run off the right-hand side of the computer screen, or possibly jump to the next line automatically (actual behavior will depend on the computer system). For a detailed description of escape characters, see Table 12.3.

One of the neat features of `printf()` is its ability to accept a variable number of arguments. In practical terms, one argument value must be added to the argument list of `printf()` for every field with a `%` specifier in the string constant. For example, the script of code

```
Modified printf() statement                               Output
===========================================================================
printf("PI = %5.3f  2*PI = %5.3f\n", PI, 2*PI);          PI = 3.141 2*PI = 6.283
```

shows how a single call to `printf()` can print two floating point numbers. Now a brief word of warning. When the number to be formatted will not fit within the specified field (e.g., if π happened to be greater than 10^7), `printf()` outputs the whole value. This is the only logical thing to do that will not result in a loss of information.

Alternative Conversion Specifications

Our approximation of PI could have been printed using a number of user-defined formatting options; for example, the left- and right-hand columns of the following table

Modified `printf()` *statement*	*Output*
`printf(" PI = %f \n", PI );`	`PI = 3.141593`
`printf(" PI = %14.7f \n", PI );`	`PI =      3.1415926`
`printf(" PI = %14.7e \n", PI );`	`PI =  3.1415926e+00`
`printf(" PI = %14.7E \n", PI );`	`PI =  3.1415926E+00`
`printf(" PI = %14.7g \n", PI );`	`PI =       3.141593`
`printf(" PI = %14.7G \n", PI );`	`PI =       3.141593`
`printf(" PI = %-14.7f \n", PI );`	`PI = 3.1415926`
`printf(" PI = %-14.7e \n", PI );`	`PI = 3.1415926e+00`

show modifications to the print statement in Program 3.1 and the output that results. The format specification `%14.7f` tells `printf()` to output the contents of `PI` as a floating point number in a field 14 digits wide (including the decimal point), with 7 digits of precision to the right-hand side of the decimal point. To ensure that the specification has enough width for the decimal point and the minus sign (if needed), the total number of digits in the output field should be at least three larger than the number of digits appearing after the decimal point.

The floating point specifications `e` and `E` tell `printf` to output the floating point number in exponential format. Unless the floating point number to be printed equals zero, the number before the letter `e` will represent a value between 1.0 . . and 9.99 . . . The two-digit part after the `e` represents an exponent value expressed as a signed decimal integer. The floating point number will be approximately equal to the first component multiplied by 10 raised to the value of the exponent. The total number of digits in the output field should be at least seven larger than the number of digits appearing after the decimal point. The floating point specifications `g` and `G` tell `printf` to select the better of the `f` or `e` formats. Although the rules for selecting the format are implementation dependent, as a general guideline, if the number to be printed falls within the range-of-conversion specification, use of the `f` format is likely. Otherwise, the floating point number will be printed in exponential format. In the seventh and eighth print statements, the output is left justified by inserting a minus (-) at the front of the conversion specification.

3.5 PROGRAM 3.2: COMPUTE AND PRINT AREA OF CIRCLE

3.5.1 Problem Statement and Source Code

In our second C program, we prompt a user for a circle radius, read the circle radius supplied as keyboard input, check that the radius is greater than zero, and finally compute and print the circle radius and area. The pseudocode for this simple problem is

```
prompt and wait for user to supply radius of circle
read the circle radius supplied as keyboard input

check that radius is greater than zero.
```

```
if radius less than or equal to zero.
   print error message and terminate program execution.

use math library functions to compute an approximate value of pi.
compute and print area of circle.
```

Notice how we have indented the fourth line of pseudocode to highlight the relationship between the outcome of the radius test, and the need to print an error message and terminate the program execution.

Compared to Program 3.1, the source code for Program 3.2 is a lot more representative of simple C programs that you are likely to write. Program 3.2 employs functions in the standard library for program I/O and a function in the math library to compute an approximate value of π. It is also our first program containing floating point variables, arithmetic expressions, assignment statements, and branching constructs for flow of program control.

PROGRAM 3.2: COMPUTE AND PRINT AREA OF CIRCLE

```
/*
 * ===================================================================
 * Compute Area of a Circle : Coefficients are defined in main program.
 *                          : Radius and area of circle are printed to
 *                            screen.
 *
 * Written by: Mark Austin                                January, 1994
 * ===================================================================
 */

#include <stdio.h>  /* Standard Input/Output function declarations      */
#include <math.h>   /* Math functions, such as sqrt(x), and constant M_PI */

int main( void ) {
float fRadius; /* Radius of circle  */
float   fArea; /* Area of circle    */
float     fPi; /* Variable for "pi" */

  /* [a] : Prompt User for "radius of circle" */

  printf("==========================================\n");
  printf("Please input the circle radius (Radius > 0):");
  scanf("%f", &fRadius);

  /* [b] : Check that the radius is greater than zero */
```

```
    if( fRadius <= 0 ) {
        printf("ERROR >> Circle radius must be greater than zero\n");
        exit (1);
    }

    /* [c] : Compute Area of Circle */

    fPi   = 4.0*atan( 1.0 );
    fArea = fPi*fRadius*fRadius;

    /* [d] : Print Radius and Area */

    printf("Radius of Circle = %8.3f \n", fRadius );
    printf("Area of Circle   = %8.3f \n", fArea );
    return (0);
}
```

Assume that Program 3.2 has been compiled into an executable file called `AREA`. The script of code

```
prompt >>
prompt >> AREA
=============================================
Please input the circle radius (Radius > 0): 2.5
Radius of Circle =    2.500
Area of Circle   =   19.635
prompt >> AREA
=============================================
Please input the circle radius (Radius > 0): -10
ERROR >> Circle radius must be greater than zero
prompt >>
```

shows how Program 3.2 prompts and waits for the user to supply a circle radius at the keyboard, and then computes and prints the area of a circle. With a user-defined radius of 2.5, the circle area for test case 1 evaluates to $\pi r^2 = \pi \cdot 2.5^2 = 19.635$. Test case 2 shows the error messages that are generated when a negative circle radius is supplied at the keyboard.

3.5.2 Header Files and the C Preprocessor

Program 3.2 has one user-defined function called `main()`. Function `main()` calls the standard library functions `printf()` and `scanf()` for formatted output to the computer screen and formatted input from the keyboard, and `exit()` for the controlled termination of the program's execution. Rather than use a symbolic constant for an approximate value of π, Program 3.2 computes an approximate value of π via the math library function `atan()`.

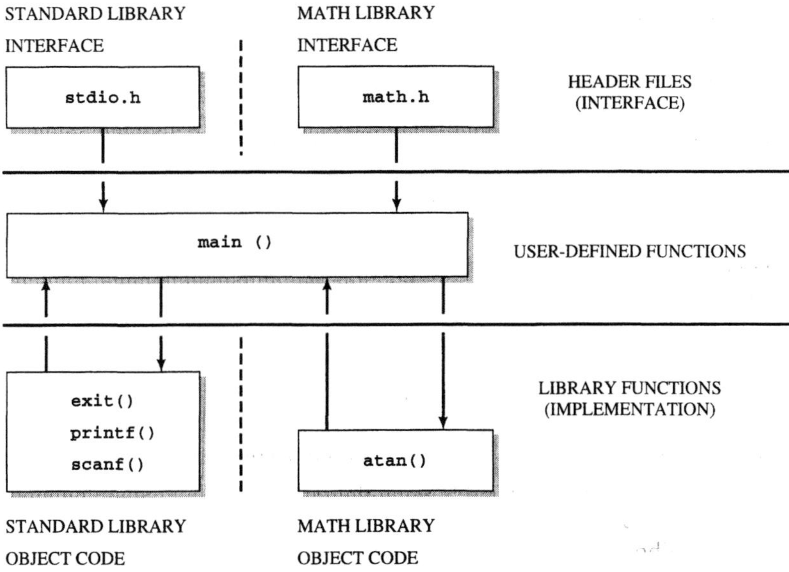

FIGURE 3.3 *Architecture of Program 3.2.*

The arrangement of header files, user-defined functions, and library functions for the development of Program 3.2 is summarized in Figure 3.3. We begin our development of Program 3.2 with the C preprocessor statements

```
#include <stdio.h>
#include <math.h>
```

because the compiled program will call functions in both the standard and the math libraries. The C preprocessor will replace the line `#include <stdio.h>` with the contents of the standard library header file and the line `#include <math.h>` with the contents of the math library header file. (This process is depicted by the one-way arrows at the top of Figure 3.3.)

The math library header file contains declarations for a wide range of mathematical constants and mathematical functions. One such constant is `M_PI`, an approximate value of π given by

```
#define M_PI   3.14159265358979323846
```

Of course we could have used this approximation in Program 3.1. The math library header file contains function declarations for `sqrt` (a function to compute the square root of x, where $x \geq 0$), `pow` [a function to compute x^y with the function call $pow(x, y)$], `sin` and `cos` (for computation of sine x and cosine x, where x is

TABLE 3.1 Some Important Functions in the Math Library

Function	*Purpose*	*Argument(s)*	*Result*
`abs(x)`	Return absolute value of integer argument.	integer	double
`acos(x)`	Return arc cosine of double argument x.	double	double
`asin(x)`	Return arc sine of double argument x.	double	double
`atan(x)`	Return arc tangent of double argument x.	double	double
`cos(x)`	Return cosine of angle x (radians).	double	double
`exp(x)`	Return exponent of argument x.	double	double
`fabs(x)`	Return absolute value of double argument.	double	double
`log(x)`	Return natural logarithm of argument x.	double	double
`log10(x)`	Return base 10 logarithm of argument x.	double	double
`pow(x,y)`	Return x^y with function call $pow(x, y)$.	double	double
`sin(x)`	Return sin of angle x (radians).	double	double
`sqrt(x)`	Return square root of positive argument x.	double	double
`tan(x)`	Return tangent of angle x (radians).	double	double

in radians), and so forth. Table 3.1 contains a summary of commonly used mathematical functions, together with a description of their purpose, arguments, and results. Once the appropriate function declarations are in place, a programmer may call the functions as needed.

3.5.3 Keywords in C

The C language has 32 keywords (or reserved words) that are part of the language itself. Among other things, the C keywords participate in the declaration of data types and the specification of control and looping constructs, and as such, must not be used for user-defined variable names, function names, or names of constants. Programs 3.1 and 3.2 employ the keywords

```
float        if        int        return        void
```

A complete list of keywords is located in Chapter 4.

3.5.4 Basic Data Types

A fundamental purpose of computer programs is manipulation of constants and variables. In the C programming language, constants and variables are assembled from four basic data types. The data type `char` stores characters; the data type `int`, integers; the data type `float`, floating point numbers; and the data type `double`, floating point numbers with double precision. All the data types that we see later in this text, including arrays and pointers, are assembled from these four basic data types.

On modern engineering workstations and PCs having a 32-bit word size, individ-

TABLE 3.2 Range and Precision of Basic Data Types

Data Type	*No. of Bytes*	*Range and Precision*
`char`	1	0–255
`int`	4	Maximum = 2,147,483,647 Minimum = −2,147,483,648
`float`	4	Maximum value = 3.402 × 10^38 Minimum value = 3.402 × 10^−38 Floating point numbers are represented to approximately 6–7 decimal places of accuracy.
`double`	8	Maximum value = 1.797 × 10^308 Minimum value = 1.797 × 10^−308 Double precision numbers are represented to approximately 15–16 decimal places of accuracy.

ual characters are stored in 1 byte of memory (i.e., 8 bits of memory), integers and floats in 4 bytes of memory (i.e., 32 bits of memory), and double precision floating point numbers in 8 bytes of memory (i.e., 64 bits of memory). The precision and range of numbers and characters that can be stored by each of the basic data types is summarized in Table 3.2.

3.5.5 Declaring Variables

The names and data types of all variables must be defined before they are used in an executable block of statements. The declarations

```
int main ( void ) {
float fRadius; /* Radius of circle   */
float   fArea; /* Area of circle     */
float     fPi; /* Variable for "pi" */

          ...... details omitted .....
}
```

tell the compiler to allocate memory for three variables, `fRadius`, `fArea`, and `fPi`. Each variable will be of data type `float`, and we indicate the data type by providing the prefix `f..` to the variable name. Similarly, character variables will have the prefix `c..`; integers, the prefix `i...`; and double precision floating point numbers, the prefix `d...`. This variable naming scheme is called Hungarian notation, and we fully describe its capabilities in Chapter 4.

In keeping with the layout of programs described in the previous section, all the variables for Program 3.2 are declared at the top of the body of function `main()`. This practice makes the variable declarations in a program easy to find and helps to avoid the irritating problems of variables having multiple declarations, almost the same name, and so forth.

3.5.6 Standard Input with scanf()

The abbreviated block of statements

```
float fRadius; /* Radius of circle */

printf("Please input the circle radius (Radius > 0):");
scanf("%f", &fRadius);
```

shows the essential details of declaring a floating point variable `fRadius`, prompting the user for a circle radius, and calling the standard library function `scanf()` to read formatted input from the keyboard in a prespecified location.

Like `printf()`, the first argument to `scanf()` is a format string containing the specifications for one or more fields of expected input. The first part of the specification, `%f`, tells `scanf()` to expect input in the form of a floating point number, the contents of which will be stored at memory location `&fRadius`. The `&` preceding the variable name evaluates to the address of `fRadius`, rather than the value of `fRadius` itself. It is important to note at this point that the format specifiers for `scanf()` are similar to those for `printf()` but are not identical. When in doubt, refer to Table 12.4.

3.5.7 Arithmetic Expressions

Like many other programming languages, an expression in C is a sequence of symbols, also called tokens, that can be evaluated to a numerical quantity. An expression may be as simple as a single token and as complicated as a long sequence of tokens.

The C language supports five arithmetic operators that operate on two numbers. The operators are `*` and `/` for multiplication and division, `+` and `-` for addition and subtraction of two numbers, and the modulus operator `%`. The modulus operator computes the integer remainder in a division between two integers. For example `5%3` equals `2` because `5 = 3*1` + remainder `2`. The C language also supports the unary operators `+` and `-` for the definition of positive and negative numbers (e.g., `+fArea` and `-fArea`).

Table 3.3 contains a summary of the hierarchy and order of evaluation for these operators. The sequence of evaluation for arithmetic expressions is determined by the hierarchy (or precedence) of operators in the expression and by whether operator association is left to right or right to left. Operators having precedence 1 are evaluated before those of level 2, and those of level 2 are evaluated before operators of level 3. A complete summary of all the operators in the C language, and their precedence levels, is located in Table 5.1.

When an expression contains operators of equal precedence, evaluation is

TABLE 3.3 Precedence and Association of Basic Arithmetic Operators

Operator	*Purpose*	*Precedence*	*Association*
-	Unary minus	2	Right to left
+	Unary plus	2	Right to left
*	Multiplication	3	Left to right
/	Division	3	Left to right
%	Modulus	3	Left to right
+	Addition	4	Left to right
-	Subtraction	4	Left to right
=	Assignment	14	Right to left

left to right (for `*`, `/`, `+`, and `-`) and right to left for the unary minus (`-`). The arithmetic expression

```
fPi*fRadius*fRadius;
```

contains only the multiply operator `*` and is evaluated left to right. First, `fPi` is multiplied by `fRadius`; then, `fPi*fRadius` is multiplied by `fRadius`.

Instead of using a symbolic constant for an approximate value of π, Program 3.2 computes π via functions in the math library. More precisely, we know from basic trigonometry that tan (45°) = 1 and that 45 degrees corresponds to $\pi/4$ radians. It follows that $\pi = 4*\tan^{-1}(1)$ radians. The function declaration for `atan`

```
double atan ( double );
```

is located in `math.h`, and indicates that `atan` will accept one argument of type `double` and return a result of type `double`. Once a function declaration is in place, the compiler can insert the appropriate code needed to link in the complete details of the compiled function later. A compiler does not need to know what a function does (or how it does it), it only needs the function interface. The arithmetic expression

```
4.0*atan( 1.0 );
```

directs the program control to the function `atan(1.0);` to compute the arc tangent of 1.0 (i.e., $\pi/4$) and multiplies the result by `4.0`. The `atan` function is used (or called) by giving its function name followed by a list of arguments enclosed in parentheses. More important, a function can be used anywhere that a value is required in an expression since the value of a function is its return type. If a function returns a type `type` (e.g., int, float, or double), then wherever a `type` is expected, the function call may be substituted. Engineers always use this abstraction in mathematical expressions. We assign expressions to functions such as `f(x)` so that they can be manipulated more easily and proceed to use `f(x)` in other expressions as if we had substituted the original expression there. This makes mathematics and programs easier to read because we can use abstractions to simplify explicit formulas and solve difficult problems.

3.5.8 Assignment Statements

We use the equals character (=) to create assignment statements

```
identifier = expression;
```

that assign a value to an identifier. For example, in Program 3.2, the statements

```
fRadius = 2.0;
fPi     = 4.0*atan( 1.0 );
fArea   = fPi*fRadius*fRadius;
```

assign the value `2.0` to variable `fRadius`, an approximate value of π to `fPi`, and the results of the arithmetic expression `fPi*fRadius*fRadius` to `fArea`. Notice that each of these statements is terminated with a semicolon.

The C language permits multiple assignments within a single statement. For example, it is conceivable that in a modified version of Program 3.2 we could declare the variables

```
float fArea1;
float fArea2;
```

and initialize their values in just one statement:

```
fArea2 = fArea1 = fPi*fRadius*fRadius;
```

Because assignment operators evaluate right to left, evaluation of this statement will begin with `fPi*fRadius*fRadius` and its assignment to `fArea1`. Finally, the value of `fArea1` will be assigned to `fArea2`.

The purpose of Figure 3.4 is to show the values of variables in memory before

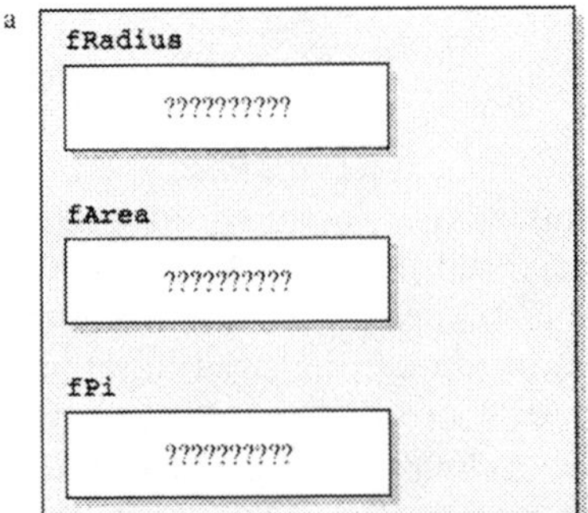

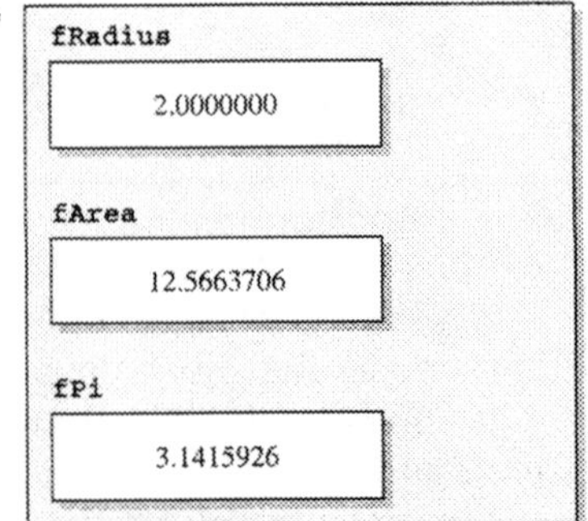

FIGURE 3.4 Value of variables in memory (a) before and (b) after execution.

program execution and at the end of program execution. As a general rule of thumb, variables should be assumed to hold meaningless value unless they are explicitly assigned a value at compile time or until they are assigned a value during the program execution.

All expressions may be classified as being either an `rvalue` or an `lvalue`. An `rvalue` is an expression that can be evaluated but cannot be changed. In contrast, `lvalues` correspond to expressions that have a location in memory, and as such, can be modified during the program execution. Program 3.2 has three variable expressions and three arithmetic expressions.

Expression	`lvalue`	`rvalue`
`fRadius`	Yes	Yes
`fArea`	Yes	Yes
`fPi`	Yes	Yes
`2.0`	No	Yes
`4.0*atan( 1.0 )`	No	Yes
`fPi*fRadius*fRadius`	No	Yes

Usually, an `lvalue` appears on the left-hand side of an = assignment, and `rvalues` are on the right-hand side of the = assignment. The variables `fRadius`, `fArea`, and `fPi` are both `lvalue` and `rvalue` because they have memory location and can be evaluated during the program execution.

3.5.9 Program Flow and Control

Statements in a C program are executed sequentially. For the solution of practical problems, however, mechanisms are needed for the branching of a program's control of flow and for the efficient computation of repetitive operations inside a loop. Block `/* [b] */` contains our first example of the `if` branching control structure.

```
if( fRadius <= 0 ) {

    .... Statements of C code deleted .....

}
```

The construct `fRadius <= 0` is a relational expression that will evaluate to either true or false. The block of C statements within the braces $\{\cdots\}$ will be executed only when the relational expression evaluates to true. In this case, the relational expression evaluates to true when `fRadius` is less than or equal to zero; in other words, we want to ensure the circle radius is greater than zero before computing an area. We return to the topic of relational expressions, and branching and looping constructs, in Chapter 6.

The block of C statements within the braces

```
printf("ERROR >> Circle radius must be greater than zero\n");
exit (1);
```

will be executed when the expression `fRadius <= 0` evaluates to true. After the error message

```
ERROR >> Circle radius must be greater than zero
```

is printed, the function called `exit(n)` will terminate the program's execution with cleanup activities. A nonzero value of `n` indicates an unsuccessful program termination.

3.6 COMPILING AND RUNNING SMALL C PROGRAMS

Now that we have seen what the syntax of a simple C program looks like, we move on to the problem of compiling and running C programs in a variety of operating system environments.

Today's marketplace is dominated by two kinds of C compilers. The so-called "older compilers" still in use on many UNIX and PC machines, adhere to the original K&R style of C programming developed in the 1970s. Since the early 1990s, K&R C has been superseded by the ANSI standard C, the style and language rules we use throughout this text. All the compilers released in the last few years comply with the ANSI standard.

For the purposes of illustrating the process of compiling and running a small C program, we assume that all the user-defined code is located within (at most) two files named `file1.c` and `file2.c`. The simplest way of compiling a one-file C program is with the command syntax

```
prompt >> name_of_compiler file_name.c
```

Here prompt >> is the prompt of the (UNIX) shell. The system prompt on your computer will probably be different; for instance, many UNIX computer systems help users to keep track of their location in the file system by including this information in the UNIX prompt. `name_of_compiler` is the name of the C compiler on your computer, and `file_name.c` is the file of source code to be compiled.

There is an ANSI compiler available on the UNIX machines written and distributed by the Free Software Foundation called `gcc` (Gnu C compiler). Using the Gnu C compiler, a one-file C program can be compiled by simply giving the command:

```
prompt >>
prompt >> gcc file1.c
prompt >>
```

TABLE 3.4 Types of Compilers

Compiler	*Description*	*Example*
`bcc`	Borland compiler	`bcc file1.c`
`cc`	Kernighan and Ritchie compiler	`cc file1.c`
`gcc`	Gnu C compiler	`gcc file1.c`
`tcc`	Turbo C compiler	`tcc file1.c`

If there are no syntax errors in the source file, the ANSI compiler `gcc` will generate an executable program file called `a.out`. This is the file you have been waiting for. You can execute the computer program by simply typing `a.out` at the operating system prompt. For example,

```
prompt >> a.out
```

The operating system will load the executable program file `a.out` into memory and execute it.

We realize that you may not have `gcc`; therefore, Table 3.4 provides a summary of compilers that may be operated with keyboard commands. In PC operating system environments, there is a general trend toward high-level language compilers being sold as part of a development environment, where word processors, compilers, linkers, and loaders are combined into one integrated software package.

3.6.1 Optional Compiler Arguments

Most C compilers accept a range of optional arguments, which are flagged with a minus sign. In this section, we look at three of the most useful command options. These options are (1) rename the program executable file, (2) reduce the time needed to compile a program within each iteration of the edit–compile–test cycle, and (3) help you to identify run-time errors in your programs.

We look at item (1) first. A shortcoming of our compilation command is that the C compiler always generates an executable file with the file name (`a.out`). Multiple executable programs cannot coexist in the same UNIX directory because the compiler will, by default, destroy one executable program when it tries to create another. This problem can be easily fixed by providing meaningful program names via the compiler command option `-o` (for output). To do this, append a suitable output executable file name with `-o` (for output) like this

```
prompt >> gcc file1.c -o PROGRAM1
```

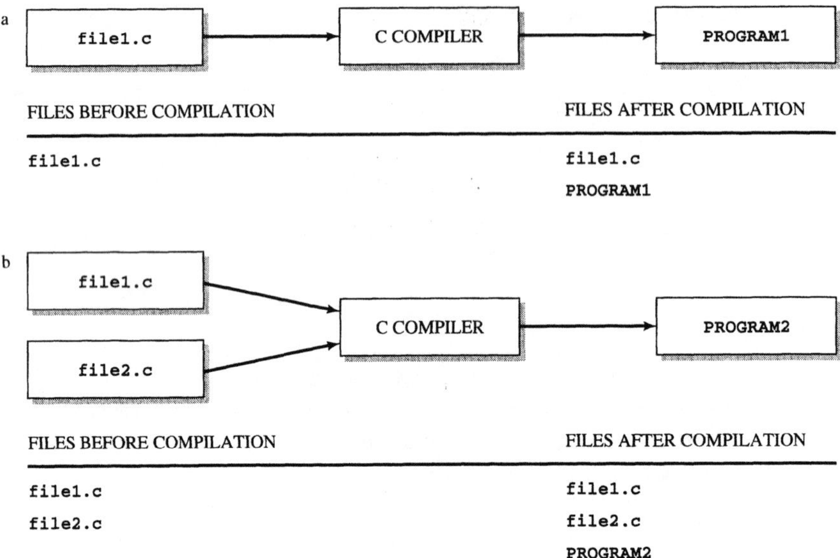

FIGURE 3.5 Compilation of (a) one- and (b) two-file C programs.

and the compiler will put the executable program into the file named `PROGRAM1`. A schematic of files before and after compilation is shown in Figure 3.5a.

The next level of difficulty occurs when the source code for a C program is partitioned into two (or more) source files. Assume, for purposes of discussion, that you are working on the development of a two-file C program having source file names `file1.c` and `file2.c`. A suitable command for compiling this program is

```
prompt >> gcc file1.c file2.c -o PROGRAM2
```

A schematic of files, before and after compilation, is shown in Figure 3.5b. At an intermediate point of program development, you may have just finished editing `file2.c`, and want to recompile and run the `PROGRAM2`. The command

```
prompt >> gcc file1.c file2.c -o PROGRAM2
```

recompiles the contents of both `file1.c` and `file2.c`, even though the former has not been changed. Although this point may seem like a minor inconvenience, many computer programs in real-world engineering applications often have hundreds of source files. A lot of time may be needed to compile an entire program on one of today's engineering workstations. This inefficiency can be easily avoided by setting the flag `-c`. It tells the compiler to produce an object file (`.o`) for each source file. Compilers use the existence and age of object files to determine which source files need recompiling. The rules for compilation are as follows:

1. A source file will be compiled if its matching object file does not exist.
2. A source file will be recompiled when the age of the matching object file is older than the source file.

The flag `-g` tells the compiler to produce symbol table information so that debugger tools such as `dbx` may be used to identify run-time errors in a program. So, for example, if the command to compile our two-file program is modified to

```
prompt >> gcc file1.c file2.c -c -g -o PROGRAM2
```

then the executable file `PROGRAM2` will contain the symbol table needed by `dbx` for the run-time identification of program errors. The list of program files before and after compilation is as follows:

Files before Compilation	*Files after Compilation*	
file1.c	file1.c	file1.o
file2.c	file2.c	file2.o
	PROGRAM2	

3.6.2 Linking Software Libraries to Program Object Code

During the latter stages of the program compilation, the program object code will be linked to one or more external software libraries. This process is illustrated on the right-hand side of Figure 3.1. All C programs link their program object to the standard library by default. Functions in the math library can be linked to a program's object code by adding the option `-lm` to the compilation command.

3.6.3 Redirection of Standard I/O

Instead of directing output directly to the terminal, UNIX systems allow output from a computer program to be redirected to a file with a command of the form

```
prompt >> myProg > outputFile
```

Input that would normally come from the keyboard can be read from a file instead with commands of the type

```
prompt >>  myProg < dataFile
```

The simultaneous redirection of input from a file, and the echoing of the output to another file, is easily accomplished by extending the command to

```
prompt >>  myProg < dataFile > outputFile
```

This approach to program execution is a sort of "poor person's I/O" because only one stream of input and one stream of output can exist to/from at program. In Chapter 12 we see how to write C programs in which multiple streams of I/O control are handled by a rich set of library functions.

3.7 PROGRAMMING GUIDELINES

Here are some simple programming guidelines.

3.7.1 Vertical Layout

Try to keep code that is important to the problem and structure of the solution on a single page, formatted the way we read text, left to right, top to bottom. This is not always obvious since any meaningful program will occupy more than one page. That is where functions help, you can split the code into several function calls, each of which can be understood on their own. If the function code is effectively encapsulated, it can then be considered an abstraction in the calling routine and the details of its operation are not important at that point. An examiner of the code can read the details of the function separately if he or she is really interested. If the reader must keep flipping between screens and/or pages, then it becomes harder to concentrate on the important details of the program. When function design is covered in Chapter 7, we see how easily this is achieved.

3.7.2 Braces

Place opening curly braces on a line with the structure that requires them. Place the closing curly brace directly under the structure that requires it. The systematic positioning of the opening and closing braces in this manner facilitates the identification of blocks of source code.

3.7.3 Indents

Highlight the structure of your source code by indenting and aligning code blocks three or four spaces from the previous indentation. Do not use tabs unless your editor replaces them with a few spaces. Tabs on most systems default to eight spaces, and this is too much space. This not only pushes code off the right side of the page, but it also makes code listings appear to be chopped up.

Other factors related to style are covered as we proceed to more advanced sections of the tutorial. At this point, the primary goal is to lay out your code on the printed page (or screen) in a consistent and readable format. Readable code implies the following: short listings, proper use of indentation and braces, and a clear concise structure. Although these characteristics take on more meaning with experience, it certainly does not hurt to start with some simple ground rules based on the knowledge of experienced programmers.

REVIEW QUESTIONS

1. Have you found an editor and a compiler on your computer system? Have you tried an edit–compile–run test?
2. Can you see the merits of a careful design for programs (rather than just "hacking" code)? Can you imagine writing several thousand lines of code without doing a design first? Do you think the program would run correctly? How much confidence would you have in the result? (A good "confidence test" is to ask yourself if you would "bet a paycheck" that there are no bugs in the program!)
3. Why should your source code be formatted so that it is easy to read?
4. What is the purpose of the C preprocessor?
5. What characters always surround a code "block"? Where do you place variable definitions in a program block?
6. When are comments useful? Give an example of cases where they are useful and one where they are not.
7. What does a function declaration tell the compiler? What are the critical parts? Why does it need to know this information?
8. What is a library function? Why are libraries used?
9. What is a function argument?
10. What is a compiler option? How is the math library linked to a program?
11. Why do we link library code into our programs?

3.8 PROGRAMMING EXERCISES

Problem 3.1 (Beginner): Rewrite Program 3.1 so that it prints the value of π as defined by the constant `M_PI` located in the math library header file `math.h`.

Problem 3.2 (Beginner): It is well known that the formula for converting a temperature in Celsius to Fahrenheit is

$$°F = \frac{9}{5} \cdot °C + 32 \tag{3.1}$$

Write a C program that will prompt the user for the temperature in degrees Celsius, and compute and print the equivalent temperature in Fahrenheit.

Problem 3.3 (Beginner): The volume of a sphere of radius r is

$$\text{Volume} = \frac{4}{3}\pi r^3 \tag{3.2}$$

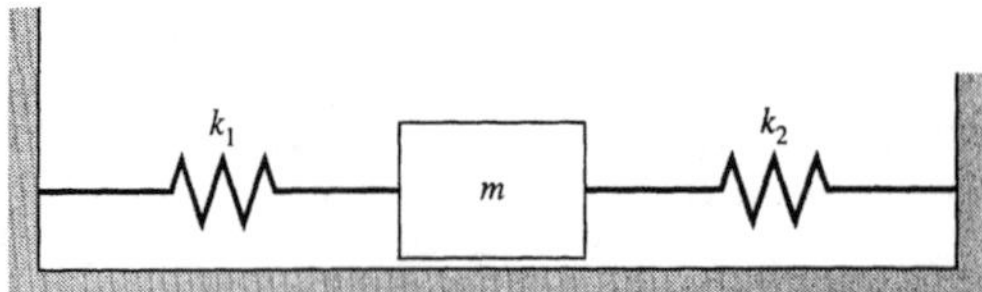

FIGURE 3.6 Mass-spring system.

Write a C program that will prompt the user for a sphere radius, and then compute and print the volume of the sphere. You should use the `pow()` function in the math library to compute r^3.

Problem 3.4 (Beginner): Figure 3.6 shows a mass m resting on a frictionless surface. The mass is connected to two walls by springs having stiffnesses k_1 and k_2. The natural period of the mass-spring system is

$$T = 2\pi \sqrt{\frac{m}{k_1 + k_2}} \tag{3.3}$$

Write a C program that will prompt a user for m, k_1, and k_2, check that the supplied values are all greater than zero, and then compute and print the natural period of the mass-spring system.

Problem 3.5 (Beginner): The area of a triangle having side lengths a, b, and c is

$$\text{Area} = \sqrt{s(s-a)(s-b)(s-c)} \tag{3.4}$$

where $s = (a + b + c)/2$. Write a program that will prompt the user for the three side lengths of the triangle, and then compute and print the area of the triangle via Equation 3.4.

Note. To ensure that the triangle is well defined, your program should check that all side lengths are greater than zero and that the sum of the shorter two side lengths exceeds the length of the longest side.

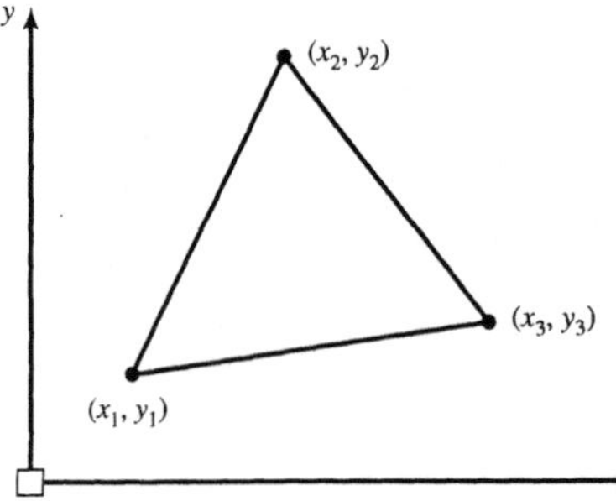

FIGURE 3.7 Vertex coordinates for triangle.

Problem 3.6 (Beginner): Figure 3.7 shows a triangle defined by the vertex coordinates (x_1, y_1), (x_2, y_2), and (x_3, y_3). Write a C program that will

1. Interactively prompt a user for the x and y coordinates at each triangle vertex.
2. Print the triangle vertices in a tidy table.
3. Compute and print the area of the triangle (make sure that it is positive) and its perimeter.

4 BASIC DATA TYPES AND VARIABLES

This chapter describes the basic data types provided by the C language. Basic data types are important because their capabilities and limitations affect nearly all the engineering and scientific programs we develop.

4.1 BASIC DATA TYPES IN C

The word `data` is used to describe any type of information that may be manipulated by a computer. A binary digit, or `bit`, is the smallest item of data that a computer can manipulate. Each bit can have two possible values: `1` or `0`.

Groups of bits are used to represent various types of information. For example, a group of four bits, commonly called a "nibble," is capable of representing the integers zero through fifteen.

`0000`	zero	`0100`	four	`1000`	eight	`1100`	twelve
`0001`	one	`0101`	five	`1001`	nine	`1101`	thirteen
`0010`	two	`0110`	six	`1010`	ten	`1110`	fourteen
`0011`	three	`0111`	seven	`1011`	eleven	`1111`	fifteen

Although some of the first microprocessors manipulated groups of 4 bits at once, these processors were very limited. As higher-density integrated circuits became possible, 8-bit microprocessors quickly took hold.

A group of 8 bits is commonly called a `byte` and, in the C programming language, a byte is the basic unit of measure for memory needed to store a particular

TABLE 4.1 Introduction to Basic Data Types in C

Type	*Size*	*Description*
`char`	1 byte	Characters or small integer variables
`int`	2 or 4 bytes	Integer values
`float`	4 bytes	Floating point numbers
`double`	8 bytes	Floating point numbers

data type. Since a byte is composed of 8 bits, it can represent $2^8 = 256$ different values, where the actual values range from 0 to 255. The 256 combinations can also be used to represent negative values. It is all a matter of interpretation, and we discuss the issue of signed values in Section 4.2. If more than 256 distinct values are needed in a number, then groups of bytes may be used to expand the range.

The C language contains four basic data types: characters, integers, and two floating point types. A brief summary of the size and use of each data type is given in Table 4.1. In the following subsections, we also see that each data type can be supplemented with qualifiers.

4.2 CHARACTERS

Because the use of text is central to computing and its applications, it should be no surprise that the `char` is one of the most important C data types. Many programs exist solely for the manipulation of characters. A `char` occupies 1 byte of storage.

A standard representation for all the common characters used in modern computers is the American Standard Code for Information Interchange, or ASCII code. This code simply assigns a unique value to each of the printing characters, numbers, punctuation marks, and other nonprinting characters used for controlling computers. For example, all the characters in this text have a unique ASCII code or value. In addition, there are ASCII codes for nonprinting characters, whose purpose may be to format the text on a page.

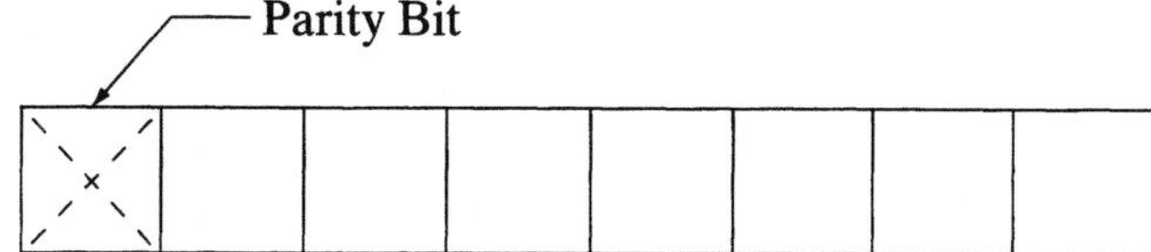

The ASCII format employs an 8-bit code with 1 parity bit. At one time, the primary use of the parity bit was to detect errors in the transmission of bytes; it was set so that the total number of `1s` in each byte would be either `odd` or `even` [39]. This left 7 bits to encode a maximum of 128 (i.e., $128 = 2^7$) distinct characters, including lower- and uppercase letters, numbers, punctuation, and special characters such as + and #. Currently, this use of the parity bit has become less common, with many PCs now using the eighth bit to represent an extended range of characters (e.g., graphical symbols or other unusual characters).

TABLE 4.2 ASCII Character Format

0 nul	32	64 @	96 '
1 soh ^A	33 !	65 A	97 a
2 stx ^B	34 "	66 B	98 b
3 etx ^C	35 #	67 C	99 c
4 eot ^D	36 $	68 D	100 d
5 enq ^E	37 %	69 E	101 e
6 ack ^F	38 &	70 F	102 f
7 bel ^G	39 '	71 G	103 g
8 bs ^H	40 (	72 H	104 h
9 tab ^I	41)	73 I	105 i
10 lf ^J	42 *	74 J	106 j
11 vt ^K	43 +	75 K	107 k
12 np ^L	44 ,	76 L	108 l
13 cr ^M	45 -	77 M	109 m
14 so ^N	46 .	78 N	110 n
15 si ^O	47 /	79 O	111 o
16 dle ^P	48 0	80 P	112 p
17 dc1 ^Q	49 1	81 Q	113 q
18 dc2 ^R	50 2	82 R	114 r
19 dc3 ^S	51 3	83 S	115 s
20 dc4 ^T	52 4	84 T	116 t
21 nak ^U	53 5	85 U	117 u
22 syn ^V	54 6	86 V	118 v
23 etb ^W	55 7	87 W	119 w
24 can ^X	56 8	88 X	120 x
25 em ^Y	57 9	89 Y	121 y
26 eof ^Z	58 :	90 Z	122 z
27 esc ^[	59 ;	91 [	123 {
28 fs ^\	60 <	92 \	124 |
29 gs ^]	61 =	93]	125 }
30 rs ^^	62 >	94 ^	126 ~
31 us ^_	63 ?	95_	127 del

Table 4.2 shows the character encodings for the ASCII format. The ASCII format begins with what is called a NULL character (where all of the bits are set to 0) and proceeds through several codes used in the transmission and formatting of text. The first printing character (i.e., the underscore) is not reached until the 32nd code. The space character, code 33, separates all the words on this page. Codes 34 through 64 cover the punctuation symbols, arithmetic operators, and digits. The first alphabet character, A, is reached at code number 65. After all

the uppercase letters, there are a few more punctuation characters followed by all the lowercase letters (starting at code 97) and finally the remaining punctuation codes (codes 123 to 126). We have arranged the ASCII character encodings into four columns so that you can see how the lower- and uppercase letters line up.

Although the nonprinting codes cannot be seen directly, they are an important part of the ASCII set. For example, the carriage return and line feed at the end of each text line provides vertical formatting of text. The idea for using a character to represent a carriage return originated with the typewriter, which had a type of wand attached to the "carriage" (or roller) that held the paper. When the wand was pushed from right to left, it would advance (roll) the page and at the same time return the carriage to the right so that the typed text would start on the left of the next line. With the advent of computers, the same idea was needed for arranging text vertically and the terminology was carried over. The computer (ASCII) code for carriage return now just positions the cursor (or print head, or laser) on the left to start a new line. Because a new line normally starts below the previous, a "newline" character is usually combined with the carriage return. The two terms, carriage return and line feed, are often used synonymously. They were sometimes separated to allow overwriting certain characters. For example, characters could be underlined by typing them, then executing a carriage return (without a newline) followed by typing underscore '_' characters under the characters to be underlined. This is also a carry over from now obsolete technology and is seldom used.

Remark 4.1

The ASCII character format is designed to handle the range of characters in the English language, numerals, and various symbols for punctuation. Tens of thousands of characters are needed to store some Chinese dialects. Extensions of the C language to handle large multiple-byte character sets have been proposed [30, 32].

4.2.1 Defining Character Variables in C

Character types in C are defined with the `char` keyword. Program 4.1 demonstrates how a character variable is defined and initialized.

PROGRAM 4.1: C PROGRAM CONTAINING VARIABLES

```
int main( void ) {   /* Beginning of the (main) block.                 */
char cAChar;         /* We put variable definitions here.             */

     cAChar = 65;    /* Executable statement : assign the code for 'A' */
                     /* to "cAChar"                                    */

}                    /* End of (main) block                            */
```

Program 4.1 does not generate any output. We simply note that a `char` can hold any of the values in the ASCII set, so we could assign the code for the character `A` to `cAChar` with the following statement:

```
cAChar = 65;     /* Executable statement : assign the code */
                 /* for 'A' to "cAChar"                    */
```

The layout of bits in `cAChar` is

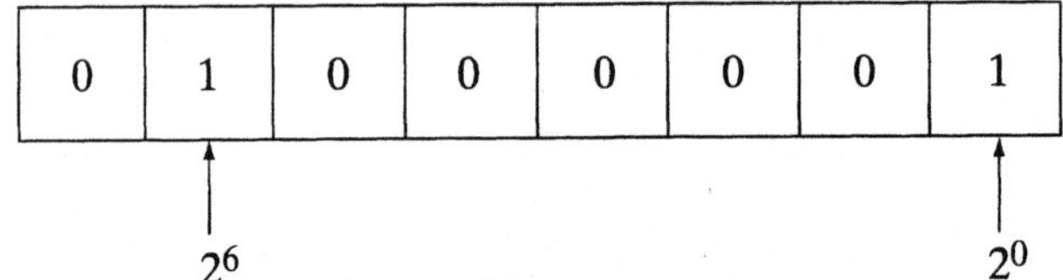

The individual bits within a byte are numbered right to left, starting from 0. Each bit represents a power of 2. The rightmost bit represents 2^0, bit 1 represents 2^1, bit 2 represents 2^2, and so forth. The bit setting signifies the power of 2s weight in a numbers representation. So, for example,

$$65 = 1 \cdot 2^6 + 0 \cdot 2^5 + \cdots + 1 \cdot 2^0 \quad (4.1)$$

You should also notice that we had to look up the code for character `A` in Table 4.2, a practice that is both tedious and error prone. Fortunately, there is a better way to initialize characters using character constants.

4.2.2 Character Constants

Character constants in C are a single character surrounded by single quotes ’ ’. They evaluate to the equivalent ASCII code given in the Table 4.2. For example, the character constant ’a’ evaluates to (is equivalent to) the decimal number 97. A common source of confusion with new C programmers is the distinction between zero and the ’0’ character. Zero evaluates to 0 (the integer: $0 = 0_{10} = 00000000_2$) and the character ’0’ evaluates to decimal 48 (the character: ’0’ $= 48_{10} = 0011000_2$).

We can use a single-quoted character constant to rewrite the previous code that assigns `cAChar` the character `A`

```
cAChar = 'A';  /* assign 'A' to character variable "cAChar" */
```

Because the character constant ’A’ evaluates to the equivalent ASCII code (decimal 65), it is effectively the same statement as in the previous version. The purpose of the second version is, however, much clearer than the first. In addition, the compiler can look up the code for ’A’ more reliably than we can.

4.2.3 Escape Characters

The C language uses escape characters to represent nonprinting control characters that are difficult to enter into the source program directly. In Table 4.2, for example,

TABLE 4.3 Character Escape Codes

	Character Escape Codes
n	Newline forces output to start on a new line.
t	Horizontal tab moves cursor to next tab stop.
v	Vertical tab moves cursor to next vertical tab stop.
r	Carriage return forces output to go back to the beginning of the same line.
b	Backspace moves cursor back one position.
f	Formfeed forces output to skip to the beginning of the next page.
\\	Used to represent backslash character.
\'	Needed to represent single-quote character inside character constants.
\"	Represents a double-quote character inside strings.
nnn	Consists of a backslash followed by one, two, or three octal digits. In particular, the \0, or NULL character, is used to mark the end of a string.

`nul` is an abbreviation for NULL (or 0), `tab` for horizontal tab, `vt` for vertical tab, `cr` for carriage return, `bel` for bell, `bs` for backspace, `esc` for escape, and `nl` for newline.

The most common way to write escape characters is as a double-character sequence, where a backslash is followed by a printing lowercase letter (see Table 4.3). For example, escape sequences are used frequently in print statements to format the output so that it is more readable. The most common escape sequence in C is the *n*, which is used as the line terminator.

Escape characters may also be directly referenced via their octal number. An octal constant is specified as '*XXX*', where *XXX* represent the octal digits of the number. For example, horizontal tab (also known as control I) is the ninth ASCII character and is written '\011'.

Remark 4.2

A character such as `cAChar` can assume 256 distinct values because 1 byte of memory is allocated to store its contents. Most often the values are assumed to range from 0 to 255.

Interpreted Range of Values : unsigned char	signed char
0	-128
1	-127
....	.....
254	126
255	127

It is important to keep in mind, however, that because characters are signed by default, they can also be used to represent a count that includes negative numbers (e.g., −128 to 127). Programmers should exercise good judgment in the use of chars to represent values other than the traditional 0 to 255 range. Suppose, for example, that we need a variable to count through a maximum of 31 days in a month. Although it is technically possible to store these values in a `char`, many readers would quickly become confused by this usage because characters are nearly always used to represent printable text. A much better approach would be to use the `int` variable, as described in Section 4.3.

4.3 INTEGERS

The integer data type is another of the fundamental data types in C. The keyword for the integer type is `int`, and it plays a central role in the declaration of integer data types. Consider, for example, the declarations

```
int iPennies;
int iCounter;
```

for the integers `iPennies` and `iCounter`. Initial values can also be supplied in definitions, as with

```
int iCounter = 0;
int iNickels = 5;
```

If initial values are not supplied for a variable before its use, then the initial value will be indeterminate (i.e., garbage!). The task of assigning initial values to variables is left to the programmer, either when the variables are defined or as explicitly assigned before their actual use.

Computers will allocate either 2 or 4 bytes for an `int`. While the following is not a hard-and-fast rule, generally an `int` will be the same size as the computer architecture's registers. The strategy of making the natural word size for a particular architecture match that of an integer leads to enhanced performance for manipulation of integer types by the CPU.

The range of values that an `int` can store depends on how large it is (how many bytes of storage it occupies). If the size of an integer is 2 bytes, then it can take on 2^{16} (or 65,536) different values. A 32-bit integer can have 4,294,967,296 different values. Knowing the range of integers is important because your program will not operate as expected if that range is exceeded (more on that later). In general, integers are signed, meaning that they can have negative as well as positive values. If half of the states are used to represent the negative integers, then the maximum and minimum possible machine representations are $2^{31} - 1$ (about 2 billion).

TABLE 4.4 Summary of Integer Data Types on PCs

Type	*Size*	*Range*
`unsigned char`	8 bits	0–255
`char`	8 bits	−128–127
`enum`	16 bits	−32,768–32,767
`unsigned int`	16 bits	0–65,535
`short`	16 bits	−32,768–32,767
`int`	16 bits	−32,768–32,767
`unsigned long`	32 bits	0–4,294,967,295
`long`	32 bits	−2,147,483,648–2,147,483,647

4.3.1 Short and Long Integers

To accommodate machines with different integer sizes, C provides for the data types `short int` and `long int` in addition to `int`. Most often these data types are simply written as `short` and `long`. As summarized in Table 4.4, short and long ints will be at least 16 and 32 bits, respectively. It is important to note that although the actual number of bytes in each data type will be implementation dependent, the ANSI standard guarantees that the number of bytes in

```
short   <=  int   <=  long
```

Because `long` integers will often use more memory than a `short` or `int`, it follows that `long` integers will have the ability to store a range of integer values that is much greater than is possible with an `int`.

4.3.2 Unsigned Integers

Unsigned integers are used to represent only positive integer values. They give twice the range of signed integers because they do not need one of the bits to represent the sign; details can be found in Table 4.4 and Figure 4.1. The `unsigned` keyword is used to represent unsigned integer values:

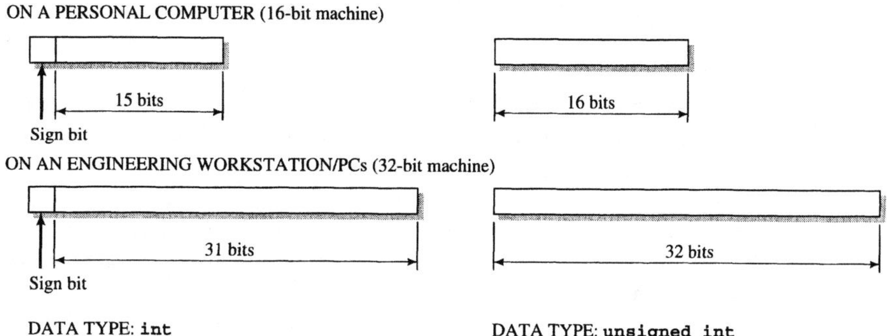

FIGURE 4.1 Bits in `int` and `unsigned int`.

```
unsigned int uiPennies;
unsigned uUpCounter;   /* Note : the int specifier is not required        */
                       /*        because it is the default.               */
```

When you are designing a program, choose variable types and names carefully. For those cases where an integer variable does not need to be negative, declaring it as unsigned provides a larger range (double the signed range), and also makes it clear to anyone reading the code that the variable is never intended to be negative. The latter is more important than the range.

4.3.3 Integer Constants

Integer constants are as expected (0, 1, −56, 255, −15,001) and are represented internally within the computer hardware in what is called *"2s complement* form." No commas, decimal points, or other characters are allowed in integer constants. If an integer constant falls outside the range of an `int`, then it will be stored as a `long` constant. A long constant can also be ensured by using the suffix `l`, or `L` as in `-200000L`. To ensure that an unsigned value is stored, use the suffix `u`, or `U` as in `50000U`. The combination of these yields an `unsigned long` type: `5000000UL`. It is a good idea to use these terminal specifiers since it makes the desired type explicit to increase readability and preclude potential maintenance errors.

4.4 SINGLE AND DOUBLE PRECISION FLOATING POINT NUMBERS

Floating point numbers and floating point arithmetic play a central role in scientific and engineering computations, and there are several issues we should be aware of when using and combining floating point numbers.

First, computers use a finite number of bits (e.g., 32 or 64 bits) to store real numbers in binary format; therefore, not all numbers can be represented exactly. For example, although the fraction 1/10 can be written 0.10 in base 10, its decimal representation in base 2 has infinite length. Hence, a computer cannot store the exact value of 1/10. We also need to deal with the problem of finite precision arithmetic. Unlike arithmetic in pure mathematics, basic arithmetic operations on a computer often leads to errors (e.g., round-off, truncation, loss of significant digits, out of range, divide by zero, infinity). Most computers mitigate this problem by supporting two levels of precision for floating point computations. Single precision arithmetic corresponds to approximately 6 decimal digits of accuracy. Double precision arithmetic increases the number of digits of accuracy to approximately 16 or 17.

A second issue is "reliability of computations across computing platforms." When the same computer program is executed on two different computers that have the same level of precision for single and double precision floating point numbers, the numerical results should be identical. In practice, however, this has not been the case; computers have handled truncation and round-off errors in their own particular ways. This unsatisfactory situation is addressed by the IEEE floating

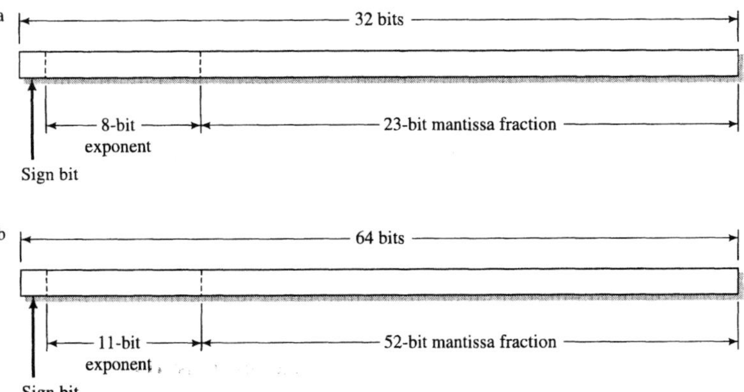

FIGURE 4.2 IEEE floating point arithmetic standard for (a) 32-bit words and for (b) double precision floats.

point standard, which provides computer hardware manufacturers with standards for storing floating point numbers and handling errors in floating point arithmetic. Improved portability of software is the main reason for completely specifying the results of arithmetic operations. When a program is moved from one machine to another and both support IEEE arithmetic, any intermediate results that differ must be because of errors in the software, not differences in arithmetic [11, 16, 42].

4.4.1 Floating Point Variables

Floating point variables and constants are used by engineers and scientists to represent values outside of the integer range. In their simplest form, they represent numbers such as `3.4`, `-45.33`, and `2.714`. Exponential notation can be used to represent numbers that are either very large or very small in magnitude. Some examples are

```
3.0e-25     4.5e+05     2.34567890098e+19
```

Figure 4.2 shows how the IEEE standard specifies storage of single and double precision floating point numbers in exponential format. The notation for exponential format contains three parts, a `sign` σ, a `mantissa` m, and an `exponent` E. A floating point number X will take the form

$$X = \sigma \cdot m \cdot 2^E$$

The signed mantissa is interpreted as a fraction $0 < m < 1$ and is assumed to follow a 1 (this part is not stored). If Δx is the interval of length between two numbers that can be represented, then we observe that Δx increases in proportion to the magnitude of the number being represented and decreases in proportion to the number of digits stored in the mantissa.

In the C programming language, single and double precision floating point

TABLE 4.5 Type, Length, and Range of Floating Point Numbers on a 32-bit Computer

Type	*Length*	*Range*
`float`	32 bits	3.4×10^{-38} to 3.4×10^{38}
`double`	64 bits	1.7×10^{-308} to 1.7×10^{308}
`long double`	80 bits	1.1×10^{-4932} to 1.1×10^{4932}

numbers are declared with the keywords `float` and `double`, respectively. There are in fact three data types for floating point numbers, `float`, `double`, and `long double`, and available accuracy and range increases with storage requirements. For single precision storage, the mantissa is bounded by 23 bits and the signed exponent by 8 bits. Together the mantissa and exponent are capable of representing numbers to about six significant digits accuracy, with exponents covering the range 10^{-38} to 10^{38}. For double precision storage, the mantissa is 52 bits long, and the range of storage is increased to 10^{-308} to 10^{308}. Table 4.5 shows the length and range of numbers that can be stored with data type `long double`.

Example Program

Program 4.2 computes and prints the storage requirements for each basic data type in C.

PROGRAM 4.2: PRINT SIZE OF SOME BASIC DATA TYPES

```
/*
 * ====================================
 * Print size of basic data types in C.
 * ====================================
 */

#include <stdio.h>

int main( void ) {
char      cName;
float    fMiles;
int      iCount;
double    dDist;

   /* [a] : Announce program */

   printf( "storage1.c : print size of basic data types \n" );
   printf( "-------------------------------------------- \n" );
```

```
  /* [b] : Now list variables and their storage requirements */

  printf( "\"cName\"  occupies %2i bytes of storage\n", sizeof( char ));
  printf( "\"fMiles\" occupies %2i bytes of storage\n", sizeof( float ));
  printf( "\"iCount\" occupies %2i bytes of storage\n", sizeof( int ));
  printf( "\"dDist\"  occupies %2i bytes of storage\n", sizeof( double ));

}
```

When Program 4.2 is compiled on a SUN SPARCstation, the generated output is as follows:

```
storage1.c : print size of basic data types
-------------------------------------------
"cName"  occupies  1 bytes of storage
"fMiles" occupies  4 bytes of storage
"iCount" occupies  4 bytes of storage
"dDist"  occupies  8 bytes of storage
```

This program shows that the storage size of any C language type can be determined using the `sizeof` operator. `sizeof` returns the size, in bytes, of its argument's type. For example, the `sizeof( char )` is 1 (byte) and the `sizeof( int )` is 4 bytes on most UNIX and modern PC systems but only 2 bytes on DOS systems. It is not important to memorize the size of any variable type because it can always be easily determined using the `sizeof` keyword. Programs that use `sizeof` intelligently are, in general, more portable. The program can then make decisions based on the sizes of variables on the current machine. We review other uses of `sizeof` later in this text that make memory allocation much easier and, as usual, more portable.

Remark 4.3

Several extensions to Standard C are being considered with the goal of making C numerically competitive with FORTRAN. These extensions include IEEE floating point support (to handle error conditions in numerical computations), mechanisms for complex arithmetic, and extended integers that contain more than 32 bits. For details, see Jervis [13].

4.5 ENUMERATION DATA TYPES

The readability and reliability of C programs can be improved with the use of meaningful names instead of integral constants. Suppose, for example, that a program needs to deal with the days of the week, or months in a year. Our own choice of integers to represent months can be intuitive, as in Jan = 1, Feb = 2, and so forth. Similarly, we could assign daily values using Sun = 1, Mon = 2, or Mon = 1, Tue = 2, etc. Because an established standard for numbering days of the week does not exist, one programmer might choose to begin numbering days of the week with 1, and another programmer might begin numbering from 0. Unfortunately, use of constants like 1, 2, 3 . . . leads to subtle program bugs that can be difficult to find.

The C programming language mitigates this problem by allowing small integer values to be represented with enumerative type names. For example, the declarations

```
enum weekday   { Mon, Tue, Wed, Thu, Fri, Sat, Sun };          or
enum dayofweek { Mon = 1, Tue, Wed, Thu, Fri, Sat, Sun };
```

establish enumerated data types for the days of the week. If the first value is not specified, it starts with 0. If a value is specified, the next unspecified value is one more than the previous. In the second example, the value of `Tue` will be 2 and the rest will follow consecutively.

A key advantage to using `enum` types in C is that the compiler will check values you assign to `enum` variables. So, if we define

```
enum weekday wToday;
```

and assign `Sun` to the variable `wToday`, the compiler should not complain. But if we try to assign 8 to `wToday`, the compiler will complain since it was not one of the "enumerated" values that `wToday` can use. This strategy of programming prevents bugs from occurring, while also making C programs more readable and maintainable (both admirable goals). Weekdays are much more intuitive labels for days of the week than some contrived numbering system.

Example Program. With the discussion on enumeration data types in place, Program 4.3 uses enumerated data types to print days of the week and days of the weekend.

PROGRAM 4.3: PRINT DAYS OF THE WORK WEEK AND WEEKEND

```
/*
 * ========================================
 * Print days of the work week and weekend
 * ========================================
 */
```

```
#include <stdio.h>

int main( void ) {
enum day { Sun = 1, Mon, Tue, Wed, Thur, Fri, Sat };
enum day eDay;

     eDay = Sun;
     printf("Day %4d is on the weekend\n", eDay);
     eDay = Mon;
     printf("Day %4d is a work day \n", eDay);
     eDay = Tue;
     printf("Day %4d is a work day \n", eDay);
     eDay = Wed;
     printf("Day %4d is a work day \n", eDay);
     eDay = Thur;
     printf("Day %4d is a work day \n", eDay);
     eDay = Fri;
     printf("Day %4d is a work day \n", eDay);
     eDay = Sat;
     printf("Day %4d is on the weekend\n", eDay);
}
```

Program 4.3 generates the output

```
Day    1 is on the weekend
Day    2 is a work day
Day    3 is a work day
Day    4 is a work day
Day    5 is a work day
Day    6 is a work day
Day    7 is on the weekend
```

You should note that because items of the enumerated data type are actually stored as integers, they can also be printed as integers.

4.5.1 Use of Magic Numbers

A magic number is simply a user-defined constant/number in a computer program's source code, which plays a special role in the solution procedure for a specific problem. The magic number could serve any number of roles, including the initial or final value in a looping construct, an array limit, or, perhaps, a sentinel value.

For example, the script of code

```
/* Version 1 : Magic Number Example */

int main ( void ) {
char caaNames [3][3];
int iNoRows      = 3;
int iNoColumns   = 3;

        .... details of code ....

}
```

uses the magic number `3` to define the size of a two-dimensional array of characters, and as the initial value of the integers `iNoRows` and `iNoColumns`. We discourage the use of magic numbers because their values are often arbitrary. Moreover, if at a later date the problem size changes, then the programmer must manually edit all the source files and update the relevant instances of `3` to the new problem size. This procedure is, at best, error prone.

Prior to the ANSI C standard, most constants were defined using the preprocessor in statements such as

```
#define SIZE 3
```

An improved version of our magic number example would be

```
/* Version 2 : Magic Number Example */

#define SIZE 3

int main ( void ) {
char  caaNames [ SIZE ][ SIZE ];
int iNoRows      = SIZE;
int iNoColumns   = SIZE;

        .... details of code ....

}
```

The style of programming in Version 2 is a considerable improvement over Version 1 because only one number needs to be updated when the problem size changes. The C preprocessor will substitute all instances of the definition `SIZE` with the number 3 when this second version of the program is recompiled.

With ANSI C, the enum keyword was added with the ability to define integral constants, rather than use the preprocessor, as in

```
/* Version 3 : Magic Numbers Eliminated */

enum { ProblemSize = 3 };

int main ( void ) {
char  caaNames [ ProblemSize ][ ProblemSize ];
int iNoRows      = ProblemSize;
int iNoColumns   = ProblemSize;

        .... details of code ....

}
```

Although the second and third versions appear to be functionally equivalent, the *enum* version is superior to the *define* version because the former is handled by the compiler. The compiler can find errors more easily than the preprocessor.

Suppose, for example, that we use *defines* in a program that handles dates and days of the week. During an intermediate step of the program development, the source code for a computer program might look like

```
#define MONDAY    1
#define TUESDAY   2
#define WEDNESDAY 2
#define THURSDAY  4
#define FRIDAY    5
```

Notice that there is a mistake in the code. `WEDNESDAY` has the wrong value (they are arbitrary to some degree, but they should at least be sequential!). This type of error can occur easily, and there is no help from the compiler in detecting it. Also, these problems are so common that some languages include support for this type of list. The ANSI C committee was also aware of the benefits of a list, and so they added the ability to "enum"erate a list of values to C. If we define, for example, two new types *weekday* and *typeofday*

```
enum weekday {    Monday = 1, Tuesday, Wednesday, Thursday, Friday };
enum typeofday { Workday = 1, Weekend };
```

then the values of each list can only take on values defined within the list. New variables may be defined, as in

```
enum weekday   wToday = Monday;
enum typeofday wType;
```

and in another point in the computer program we might use code such as this

```
wToday = Monday;
 wType = WorkDay;

.......

wToday = Saturday;
 wType = Weekend;
```

to classify days of the week as being either work days or weekend days.

4.6 VARIABLE ATTRIBUTES: TYPE, ADDRESS, NAME, AND VALUE

A variable (also called an identifier) is an object that has four important attributes, a type, a storage address (or location) in computer memory, a name, and a value. All four parts must be known before a variable may be used in a program. These declarations will take the form

```
type variableName;                    or
type var1, var2, var3;
```

where `var1`, `var2`, and `var3` all have the same type. For example, the declaration

```
int iVal = 10;
```

defines an integer called `iVal` and initializes its contents to `10`.

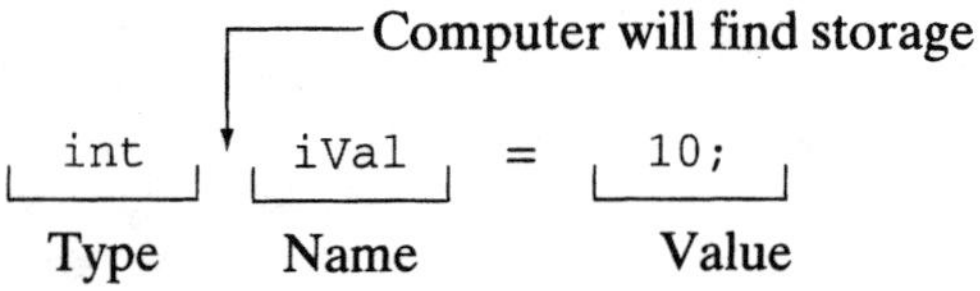

```
              ┌──────Computer will find storage
              ↓
   int      iVal    =    10;
  └───┘    └────┘       └───┘
  Type      Name        Value
```

The variable type (`int` in this case) determines (1) the amount of memory that will be used to store the variable, (2) the values that the variable can take, and (3) the operations that may be applied to the variable. When a compiler encounters a variable declaration, it will enter the variable name and type into a symbol table (so it knows how to use the variable throughout the program) and generate the necessary code for the storage of the variable at run-time. The purpose of the label "computer will find storage" inserted immediately after the `type` definition is to highlight the compiler's responsibility in determining where a variable will be stored. The physical location of a variable's storage is something the programmer has no control over. In contrast, the programmer is fully responsible for indicating the `type`, `name`, and `value` of the variable.

The value of a variable is directly available by using the variable name. In

TABLE 4.6 Characteristics of Variables

Declaration	*Type/Size (in Bytes)*	*Location*	*Value*
`float fAngle = M_PI;`	float/4	`0xffe0`	M_PI
`int iStartVal = 1;`	integer/2	`0xffe4`	1
`char cInChar = 'A';`	character/1	`0xffee`	65
`int iaPrimes[ 4 ];`	integer/4*`sizeof( int )`	`0xffe6`	???
`char caInBuf[ 80 ];`	array of char/80	`0xffef`	???

other words, the value of `iVal` is simply `iVal`, and if `iVal` is used in an expression, the code generated by the compiler will automatically fetch the current value. The address of a variable in computer memory at run-time can be found by applying the special operator `&` to the front of the variable name. For example, the address `iVal` is given by `&iVal`.

Table 4.6 shows an ensemble of variable declarations, along with their type and size, location in memory, and value. For each case, the compiler automatically takes care of assigning variables to valid locations; they are shown in the third column of Table 4.6, and for our particular implementation, just happen to begin at location `0xffe0`. Because the compiler knows the size of each variable type, memory for variables can be allocated and the distance between addresses of adjacent variables can be computed.

The fourth entry of Table 4.6 is an array of four integers that has the name `iaPrimes`. The fifth entry in Table 4.6 is an array of 80 characters and has the name `caInBuf`. We discuss arrays in depth in Chapter 8.

Example Program. Program 4.4 demonstrates variable storage for each basic data type in C.

PROGRAM 4.4: PRINT STORAGE OF BASIC DATA TYPES

```
/*
 *  ==========================================
 *  Illustrate how variables are stored in C.
 *  ==========================================
 */

#include <stdio.h>

int main( void ) {
float       fMiles;
int    iCount, iNum;
double dDist, dTemp;

   /* [a] : Announce program */
```

```
  printf( "STORAGE.C will illustrate how variables are stored in memory \n" );
  printf( "------------------------------------------------------------ \n" );

  /* [b] : Now list variables and their addresses. */

  printf( "\"fMiles\" occupies %i bytes of storage that begins at location
    %x\n", sizeof( float ), &fMiles );
  printf( "\"iCount\" occupies %i bytes of storage that begins at location
    %x\n", sizeof( int ), &iCount );
  printf( "\"iNum\"   occupies %i bytes of storage that begins at location
    %x\n", sizeof( int ), &iNum );
  printf( "\"dDist\"  occupies %i bytes of storage that begins at location
    %x\n", sizeof( double ), &dDist );
  printf( "\"dTemp\"  occupies %i bytes of storage that begins at location
    %x\n", sizeof( double ), &dTemp );
}
```

The output generated by Program 4.4 is

```
STORAGE.C will illustrate how variables are stored in memory
-------------------------------------------------------------
"fMiles" occupies 4 bytes of storage that begins at location f7fff7dc
"iCount" occupies 4 bytes of storage that begins at location f7fff7d8
"iNum"   occupies 4 bytes of storage that begins at location f7fff7d4
"dDist"  occupies 8 bytes of storage that begins at location f7fff7c8
"dTemp"  occupies 8 bytes of storage that begins at location f7fff7c0
```

Program 4.4 employs the `sizeof` operator to compute the required storage, in bytes, for each basic data type. You should notice how the amount of storage needed for each variable can be related to the storage addresses that are printed. You should not attempt to memorize the size of a variable type because it can always be easily determined using the `sizeof` keyword. Programs that use `sizeof` intelligently are, in general, more portable because they can make decisions based on the sizes of variables on the current machine.

4.7 VARIABLE NAMING CONVENTIONS

Variable names consist of a sequence of letters, digits, and underscores, with uppercase letters being distinguished from lowercase letters. A variable name cannot

TABLE 4.7 List of Keywords in ANSI C

auto	default	float	register	struct	volatile
break	do	for	return	switch	while
case	double	goto	short	typedef	
char	else	if	signed	union	
const	enum	int	sizeof	unsigned	
continue	extern	long	static	void	

start with a digit, and it cannot have the same name as a reserved word, as shown in Table 4.7.

In this text, we use a modified form of "Hungarian notation" to name the variables in our C programs. Hungarian notation was started by the legendary Microsoft programmer Charles Simonyi [29], and it prefixes a variable by a letter or letters to tell the programmer what type of data the variable represents. Consider, for example, use of Hungarian notation for an integer variable that will represent a count. A good definition is

```
int iCount;
```

Notice the leading `i` before the name (the true name begins with a capital letter) `Count`. For those applications where the value of `Count` will never be negative, the unsigned variable type should be used. An appropriate name for our count variable is

```
unsigned int uiCount;
```

or, more tersely,

```
unsigned uCount;
```

Note the leading `ui`, which just picks up the first character of the defining types `unsigned` and `int` before starting off the primary name `Count` with a capital `C`. This is always the case with the leading capital letter in a variable name. As soon as the type information ends, we start the actual—hopefully, intuitive—part of the name with a capital letter. If it is necessary to use longer names with concatenated words, then capitalize each word, as in `DayOfWeek`. The underscore character '_' can also be used in variable names, but it is more difficult to type and adds little to the readability. We think that the style of using capital letters is clearer (and easier to type) than using `under_scores_all_over_the_place`.

TABLE 4.8 Prefix Characters for Hungarian Notation

C Type	*Prefix Characters*	*Example Definition*
`char`	`c`	`char cInputVal;`
`unsigned char`	`uc`	`unsigned char ucLowByte;`
`int`	`i`	`int iPosition;`
`unsigned int`	`ui`	`unsigned int uiCount;`
`long`	`l`	`long lExtent;`
`unsigned long`	`ul`	`unsigned long ulDiskSize;`
`char [] (array)`	`ca`	`char caBuffer[eMaxChar];`
`char * (pointer)`	`cp`	`char * cpNextChar;`
`float`	`f`	`float fX, fY, fZ;`
`double`	`d`	`double dBeamWidth;`
`FILE * (pointer)`	`Fp`	`FILE * FpInFile;`
`enum`	`e`	`enum {`*`Mon, Tue,`*` ...} eToday;`
`struct`	`s`	`struct sWeather;`

Table 4.8 contains a suggested list of prefix characters for many of the common data types. Remember that C does not gain additional information from these characters, they are merely a notational convenience that will enhance software readability. There is no need to memorize the prefixes in the center column of Table 4.8. The appropriate prefix is just the first character from the type definition on the left. The choice of prefix characters is not cast in stone or entirely self-consistent either (e.g., `Fp` for `FILE *` distinguishes it from `fp` for `float *`). The important point is that we use the prefixes to enhance the program's readability, while reducing the chance for type conversion problems.

Because Hungarian notation constantly reminds us of the data type for each variable, use of this naming convention can help avoid errors in code before they turn into bugs. Consider, for example, situations where C will perform automatic type conversion. If we assign a long integer type to a possibly smaller storage type (int or short), then the value may be truncated and precision lost. This could cause problems if the precision was necessary for proper operation of the program. Another case is when a floating point value is assigned to an integral variable. The float will be truncated, and if we notice the type information on the variable names, we may avoid a costly and silent error. These two examples may not seem convincing at first. The true beauty of Hungarian notation will come into play when we get to the difficult parts of C: arrays and pointers.

Avoid using variable names such as `i`, `j`, `k`, and `n`, because they carry little meaning. Although it is true that they are often used in mathematical functions as indices and counters, it is better to avoid making assumptions about the reader's background or familiarity with common mathematical usage. The tendency to name variables with single characters that frequently are unrelated to their actual use may also stem from the fact that many of the first compilers had limited parsing ability (and many of the first programmers could not type!). If variable names were longer than some arbitrarily small value, then the compilers could not distinguish them. However, all new ANSI compilers consider 31 characters of any name to be significant, so we should not avoid using long names for variables if they are more meaningful.

Programming Tip. It is considered bad programming practice to use identifier names that differ only in the case of their capital letters, as in `Example` and `example`, or to use groups of compound words separated by combinations of hyphens and underscores (e.g., `max-string-length`, `max_string_length`).

Review Questions

1. Why are escape codes necessary for certain characters?
2. Can you find the limits of integers on your computer? Why might they be different than another computer?
3. Why is the use of "magic numbers" discouraged?
4. How can you find a variable's address? Why might you want to know it? Did you ever concern yourself with this concept in other languages?
5. Why is the use of Hungarian notation for variable naming important? (If you are not convinced, you may change your mind after using pointers for a while.)

4.8 PROGRAMMING EXERCISES

Problem 4.1 (Beginner): Write a short C program that will print

```
The quick brown fox     "jumps"
                        over
                        the lazy dog
```

to the computer screen. The first line of output should include the quotation marks, and the second and third lines should be aligned by three tab stops.

Problem 4.2 (Beginner): Write a C program that will print the letters and corresponding ASCII character formats as shown in the third and fourth columns of Table 4.2. The output from your program should look similar to the following:

```
A 65          a  97
B 66          b  98
C 67          c  99

.... lines of output removed ....

Y 89          y  121
Z 90          z  122
```

Problem 4.3 (Beginner): Write a C program that will compute and print n and 2^n for values $n = 1$ through 35. The output from your program should look similar to the following:

```
 ii          2^ii
================
  1             2
  2             4
  3             8

... lines of output removed ...

 30    1073741824
 31   -2147483648
 32             0
 33             0
 34             0
 35             0
```

You should find that when n reaches 31, an error in the evaluation will occur because the integer exceeds the maximum value that can be stored by the `int` data type. Although the exact details of how subsequent values of n are handled will be system dependent, most systems will simply start over again beginning with zero.

Problem 4.4 (Beginner): The ANSI header file `limits.h` contains detailed information on the maximum and minimum values that can be represented by various integer data types. For example, on a SUN workstation, the `limits.h` contains the lines

```
#define INT_MIN (-2147483647-1) /* min value of an "int" */
#define INT_MAX   2147483647    /* max value of an "int" */
```

With this information in hand, extend your solution to Problem 4.3 so that integer overflows are handled with the error message

```
Error : Integer Overflow
```

After a variable has suffered an integer overflow, all subsequent calculations involving that variable should be labeled with the same message. This means that the last six lines of program output should look similar to the following:

```
30    1073741824
31   Error : Integer Overflow
32   Error : Integer Overflow
33   Error : Integer Overflow
34   Error : Integer Overflow
35   Error : Integer Overflow
```

Note. You can easily find the location of `limits.h` on a UNIX system by typing

```
prompt >> whereis limits.h
```

Problem 4.5 (Beginner): Convert the program

```
#include <stdio.h>

main ( void ) {
char    a =  'A';
int     i =    0;
long    j          = -100000;
unsigned long k = 100000;
float   y =   2.4;
double x =   3.4;

  printf(" char a            = %c\n", a );
  printf(" int  i            = %d\n", i );
  printf(" long j            = %d\n", j );
  printf(" unsigned long k = %d\n", k );
  printf(" float  y          = %f\n", y );
  printf(" double x          = %f\n", x );
}
```

to Hungarian notation.

Problem 4.6 (Beginner): Write a C program that will display the storage required (in bits and bytes) by all the intrinsic types permitted in C. Display this information in a table similar to the following:

```
=================================================================
TYPE                        BYTES    BITS       Minimum      Maximum
=================================================================
char (signed)                  1       8          -128          127
char (unsigned)                1       8             0          255
int (signed)                   4      32   -2147483648   2147483647
...
float                          4      32   1.17549e-38  3.40282e+38
...
double (long)                  8      64 2.22507e-308 1.79769e+308
```

The size in bytes for any standard type can be determined by using the operator `sizeof`. The minimum and maximum values can be determined (for any ANSI standard implementation) by `#include`ing the files `limits.h` and `float.h`. These files contain important constants that you can access. For example, to print the minimum value that an `int` and a `float` can hold on your computer, you could compile and execute the code fragment

```
#include <float.h>  /* floating point type info */
#include <limits.h> /* integer type info */
#include <stdio.h>

int main( void ) {
    ...
    printf( "\nThe minimum float value is %g", FLT_MIN );
    printf( "\nThe maximum int value is %i",   MAX_INT );
    ....
}
```

Note. The command

```
prompt >> whereis float.h
```

will give you the location of `float.h` on your UNIX system.

5

OPERATORS AND EXPRESSIONS

5.1 ARITHMETIC OPERATORS AND EXPRESSIONS

The arithmetic operators that may be used on integers and floating point numbers are

```
+ - * /
```

where the symbols take their usual meaning of addition, subtraction, multiplication, and division. These operators are called `binary operators`, not because all numbers are ultimately stored as binary numbers, but because the operator has two arguments—one on the left and one on the right. The modulo operator

```
%
```

applies only to integers and returns the remainder after integer division. More precisely, if `iA` and `iB` are integers, then

```
iA % iB = k*iB + iR
```

where `k` is the number of times `iB` divides into `iA`, and `iR` is a remainder that falls into the range `0` through `iB-1`. For example, 0%4 = 0, 1%4 = 1, 2%4 = 2, 3%4 = 3, 4%4 = 0, and so forth.

5.2 ASSIGNMENT OPERATIONS

Assignment expressions normally take the form

```
A = B;
```

where B is the result of an arithmetic operation. For example, the expression

```
iCount = 1;
```

assigns the value of 1 to the integer iCount. The assignment operator is the familiar = sign. The expression

```
iCount = iCount + 1;
```

adds 1 to the old value of iCount and assigns the result to iCount. The new value of iCount is 2. From an algebraic point of view, statements of the type

```
iCount = iCount + 1;
```

are meaningless because iCount can never equal iCount + 1. In computer languages, these statements take a different interpretation, and perhaps the actual intent would be clearer if we could write assignment expressions as

```
iCount ← iCount + 1
```

to indicate that iCount is assigned the previous value of iCount plus 1.

The right-hand side of the assignment expression is called the rvalue, and it can be any value, variable, or otherwise. The left-hand side of an assignment is called an lvalue. All lvalues must have storage associated with them so that the results of the right-hand side expression can be saved. In our introductory example, the rvalue is iCount + 1, and the lvalue is iCount. Now, consider a counterexample. Statements of the type

```
1 = iCount;
```

make little sense because there is nowhere to store the results of the right-hand side expression (i.e., 1 is not an lvalue). To minimize typing and to better reflect what is being done, statements of the form

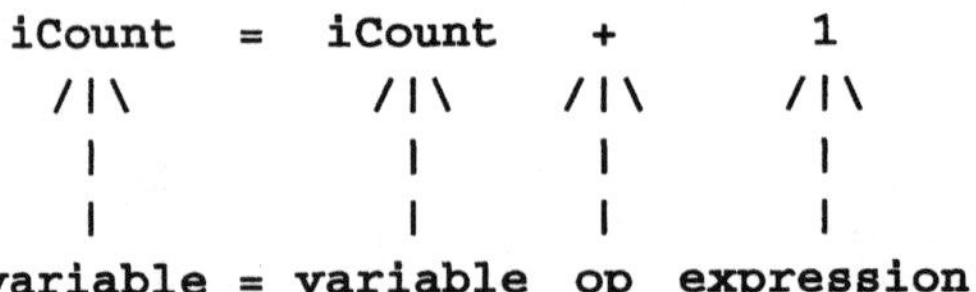

can also be written (in shorthand form)

```
variable op= expression
```

where op can be any of the arithmetic operators +, -, *, /, or %, and some others to be covered later in this text. For example, the statement

```
iCount = iCount + 1;
```

can be shortened to

```
iCount += 1;
```

and decrement operations of the type iValue = iValue - 1 can be rewritten as iValue -= 1. Similarly, division operations of the type

```
fValue = fValue / 2.0;
```

can be shortened to

```
fValue /= 2.0;
```

Use of the shorthand notation for assignments will sometimes result in faster execution because the compiler can directly translate this into an assembly-level operation. In contrast, the expression iCount = iCount - 1 means load iCount into the central processing unit (CPU) register, decrement its value by the constant 1, and then restore the value in memory. There are low-level assembly operations that will do this all directly (in place, without loading and restoring the value). A good optimizing compiler will be able to notice and use these faster forms.

5.3 INCREMENT/DECREMENT OPERATORS

C provides two special operators, ++ and --, to increment and decrement variables in shorthand form. Instead of writing iValue = iValue + 1 or iValue += 1 to increment a variable, you can simply write iValue++ or ++iValue.

What is the difference between iValue++ and ++iValue? There is not much difference in the case of an isolated (single-line) statement. There is, however, a major difference when the operator precedes or comes after a variable in more complicated expressions. If ++ comes after an object's name, then it is called the postincrement operator. If the ++ comes before an object's name, then it is called a preincrement operation. When ++iValue is employed in an expression, the value of iValue is incremented *before* the expression is evaluated. The opposite is true when postfix notation is used.

To illustrate this point, say that iCount = 10. The pair of statements

```
iCount += 1;
iNewCount = iCount;
```

can be replaced with the single statement

```
iNewCount = ++iCount;
```

The value of iCount is first incremented by one to 11 and then the result is assigned to iNewCount. At the conclusion of this statement's execution, iCount and iNewCount will both equal 11. The same statement with a postincrement operator

```
iNewCount = iCount++;
```

will set iNewCount equal to 10, and then increment iCount by one to 11. Pre- and postincrement operators can only be applied to variables. They cannot be used on constants or expressions (e.g., the statement 3++ is both illegal and nonintuitive.

Computer Program: Pre- and Postincrement Operators

The following computer program demonstrates use of pre- and postincrement operators.

PROGRAM 5.1: PRE- AND POSTINCREMENT OPERATORS

```
/*
 * ========================================
 * Test Pre- and Postincrement Operations
 * ========================================
 */

int main( void ) {
int iCount1, iCount2;

   /* [a] : Test Postincrement Operators */

   iCount1 = 5;
   printf( "The value of   iCount1 is : %4d\n", iCount1 );
   printf( "The value of iCount1++ is : %4d\n", iCount1++ );
   printf( "The value of iCount1-- is : %4d\n\n", iCount1-- );
```

```
   /* [b] : Test Preincrement Operators */

   iCount1 = 5;
   printf( "The value of   iCount1 is : %4d\n", iCount1 );
   printf( "The value of ++iCount1 is : %4d\n", ++iCount1 );
   printf( "The value of --iCount1 is : %4d\n\n", --iCount1 );

   /* [c] : Test Pre- and Postincrement Operators */

   iCount2 = iCount1++;
   printf( "The value of \"iCount2 = iCount1++\" is : %4d\n", iCount2 );
   iCount2 = ++iCount1;
   printf( "The value of \"iCount2 = ++iCount1\" is : %4d\n", iCount2 );
}
```

The output from Program 5.1 is conveniently divided into three blocks:

```
The value of   iCount1 is :   5
The value of iCount1++ is :   5
The value of iCount1-- is :   6

The value of   iCount1 is :   5
The value of ++iCount1 is :   6
The value of --iCount1 is :   5

The value of "iCount2 = iCount1++" is :   5
The value of "iCount2 = ++iCount1" is :   7
```

The initial value of `iCount1` is 5 at the beginning of each block. The first block of output demonstrates the behavior of postincrement operations. In the second `printf` statement (containing `iCount1++`), the value of `iCount1` is incremented to 6 after the `printf` function is called. Similarly, in the third `printf` statement (containing `iCount1--`), `iCount1` is decremented to 5 after the `printf` function is called.

The second block of output demonstrates the behavior of preincrement operations. In the `printf` statement containing the expression `++iCount1`, the value of `iCount1` is incremented to 6 before its value is printed. The statement containing the expression `--iCount1`, decrements its value by one before `printf` is called.

The third block of source code examines the results of pre- and postincrement operations combined with assignment operations. The statement

```
iCount2 = iCount1++;
```

assigns the current value of `iCount1` to `iCount2` and then increments `iCount1` by one. At this point, `iCount1` equals 6 and `iCount2` equals 5. Finally, the statement

```
iCount2 = ++iCount1;
```

increments `iCount1` by one and assigns 7 to `iCount2`.

5.4 ARITHMETIC EXPRESSIONS AND PRECEDENCE

Table 5.1 contains a 15-level precedence hierarchy of operators together with their order of evaluation. In this section, we focus on the arithmetic operands located at levels 2, 3, and 4, and the unary plus and unary minus operators at level 2 of Table 5.1. For a brief preview of the operators appearing later in this tutorial, see Remark 5.1.

The rules for evaluation of operators are as follows:

1. Operators having a high precedence level (i.e., low numerical value) will be evaluated before those having a low precedence level (i.e., high numerical value).
2. If an expression contains more than one operator at the same level of precedence, then the right-to-left and left-to-right rules of evaluation apply. The operators in categories 2, 13, and 14 are evaluated from right to left. The operators at all other levels are evaluated from left to right.

TABLE 5.1 Hierarchy of Operator Evaluation

Operator	*Precedence*	*Order of Evaluation*
`() [] -> .`	1	Left to right
`! ++ -- + - * & sizeof (type)`	2	Right to left
`* / %`	3	Left to right
`+ -`	4	Left to right
`<< >>`	5	Left to right
`< ≤ > ≥`	6	Left to right
`== !=`	7	Left to right
`&`	8	Left to right
`^`	9	Left to right
`|`	10	Left to right
`&&`	11	Left to right
`||`	12	Left to right
`?:`	13	Right to left
`= += *= /= &=`	14	Right to left
`^= |= <<= >>=`		
`,`	15	Left to right

Remark 5.1: Preview of Operators in Table 5.1

The level 1 operators have the highest precedence and associate left to right. The parentheses ( ) operator can be used to override any of the lower precedences as desired and is used for function calls. The [ ], – >, and . operators are used in the dereferencing of arrays, data structures, and unions. Their usage for arrays is discussed in Chapter 8.

At level 2 are the unary plus and unary minus operators, which act on a single term (e.g., iStart = –10, iVal = +4;), the pre- and postincrement (++) and decrement (– –) operators; and the bitwise not (~), the pointer dereference (*), the "address of" (&), and the cast and sizeof operators [e.g., (int *)]. Together with the operators at levels 13 and 14, these unary operators associate right to left.

Level 3 contains the multiplicative arithmetic operators, * and /, and the integer modula (or remainder) operator (%). Levels 4 through 6 contain the arithmetic operators (+) and (–), followed by the bitwise shift operators (<< and >>), the logical comparison operators (<, <=, >, and >=), and the logical equality operators (== and !=). Details are found in Chapter 6. Levels 8 to 12 contain the bitwise-AND operator (useful for bitwise masking), the bitwise exclusive-OR operator (^), the bitwise-OR operator (|), the logical-AND operator (&&), and the logical-OR operator (||). Levels 13 through 15 contain the tertiary operator (useful for inlining if-else type expressions), followed by the assignment operators, and finally the comma (,) operator.

Some points to keep in mind are

1. Do not confuse logical and bitwise operators; they will frequently compile without error when transposed in expressions.
2. Remember that all the operators at precedence levels 2, 13, and 14 evaluate right to left. The need for right to left evaluation is most obvious for the assignment operator, where we want

   ```
   iVal = iCount = 0;
   ```

   to associate right to left, not from left to right.
3. The associativity rules are only important when you have more than one operator in the same level in the same expression. If the operators are from different levels, then the higher precedence operator is always evaluated first.

Now look at three specific examples and see how these rules apply.

Example 1. Let `fValue` be a floating point number equal to 4.0. The expression

```
fValue / 2.0 + 3.0; ===> 4.0 / 2.0 + 3.0 <=== Starting expression
                    ===> 2.0 + 3.0       <=== Step 1 of evaluation
                    ===> 5.0             <=== Step 2 of evaluation
```

contains two operators. The division operator (/) has precedence level 3, and the addition operator (+) has precedence level 4. Because both operators evaluate left to right, and because division has the higher precedence (i.e., lower precedence number), the subexpression `fValue / 2.0` is evaluated and `3.0` is added to the intermediate result. The final result is `5.0`. Moreover, if the expression is rewritten as

```
 3.0 + fValue / 2.0 ===> 3.0 + 4.0 / 2.0 <=== Starting expression
                    ===> 3.0 + 2.0       <=== Step 1 of evaluation
                    ===> 5.0             <=== Step 2 of evaluation
```

then these rules will ensure that the expression evaluates to the same numerical result.

We often use the phrase "evaluates to" in conjunction with expressions that may have intermediate results. The terminology implies that the compiler (and/or the run-time code) will process the expression, possibly changing and simplifying its form. But in the end, the result of any processing is what the expression `evaluates to`.

Example 2. The importance of the parentheses operator (i.e., `()`) stems from its level 1 precedence (the highest level possible) and the ease with which programmers can use parentheses to affect the order of evaluation in expressions. Suppose, for example, that you were unsure of (or forgot) the precedence of the addition and division operators in Table 5.1. You could enforce the desired order of evaluation in this example by placing parentheses around the intermediate and final results:

```
(3.0 + (fValue/2.0)) ===> (3.0 + (4.0/2.0)) <=== Starting expression
                     ===> (3.0 + 2.0)       <=== Step 1 of evaluation
                     ===> 5.0               <=== Step 2 of evaluation
```

Because division and multiplication have the same highest level of precedence (level 3) in the expression, the intermediate results `10.0/2.0`, `18.0/4.0`, and `4.5` are computed in that order. Addition comes next. Finally, the result of the arithmetic expression is assigned to `fValue`. The assignment operator at level 14 makes sense; its low precedence means that it will be done last.

Expressions for the intermediate results can be enclosed within brackets without changing the numerical result:

```
fValue = ( 10.0 / 2.0 ) + ( 3.0 * 6.0 / 4.0 );
```

Example 3. Because assignment operator evaluates right to left, statements of the form

```
fX = fY = 0;
```

assign `0` to `fY`. The value of `fY` is then assigned to `fX`. Operators within a single category have the same precedence.

Integer Arithmetic

Integer division truncates what we think of as the fractional components of all intermediate and final arithmetic expressions. In the integer expression 1/2, we think the result is one half or .5, but there is obviously no way to store .5 in an integer, so the result is 0. Although this may seem obvious, many subtle bugs in numerical calculations can be traced to truncation in arithmetic expressions. For example, the expression 18/4 will evaluate to 4 (and not 4.5), and the result of

```
iValue = 5 + 18/4;   ===> 5 + 4 <=== Step 1 of evaluation
                     ===> 9     <=== Step 2 of evaluation
```

will be `9`. Suppose what we really wanted was

$$iVal = \frac{10}{\left[2 + \frac{3*6}{4}\right]}$$

Without parentheses, the expression

```
iValue = 10/2 + 3*6/4 ===> 5 + 18/4 <=== Step 1 of evaluation
                      ===> 5 + 4    <=== Step 2 of evaluation
                      ===> 9        <=== Step 3 of evaluation
```

will evaluate to `9`. The order of evaluation can be adjusted by inserting parentheses around those parts of the expression that should be evaluated first. Now we have

```
iValue = 10/(2 + 3*6/4) ===> 10/(2 + 18/4) <=== Step 1 of evaluation
                        ===> 10/(2 + 4)    <=== Step 2 of evaluation
```

```
===> 10/6              <=== Step 3 of evaluation
===> 1                 <=== Step 4 of evaluation
```

Unary Plus and Unary Minus

The unary minus has precedence level 2. For example, in Chapter 3, we computed the area of a circle with the code

```
fArea = fPi*fRadius*fRadius;
```

The same numerical result would be obtained with

```
fArea = --fPi*-fRadius*-fRadius;
```

Here we have applied the unary minus twice to `fPi` and once to each occurrence of `fRadius`. The arithmetic sequence `--fPi` is evaluated as if it were written `-(-fPi)`, with the contents inside the brackets `(...)` being evaluated first.

Computer Program: Resistors in Parallel. The following computer program computes the combined resistance of three resistors in parallel.

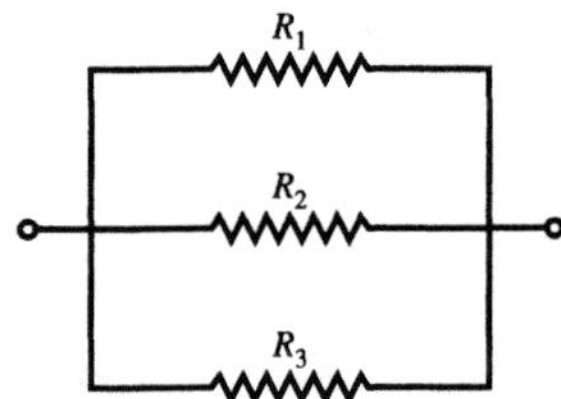

$$\text{Combined resistance} = \left[\frac{1}{\frac{1}{R_1} + \frac{1}{R_2} + \frac{1}{R_3}}\right] \tag{5.1}$$

when R_1 = 1.5 ohms, R_2 = 2.5 ohms, and R_3 = 3.5 ohms.

PROGRAM 5.2: RESISTORS IN PARALLEL

```
/*
 * ====================================================
 * Combined Resistance of Three Resistors in Parallel
 * ====================================================
 */
```

```
#include <stdio.h>

int main( void ) {
  float fR1 = 1.5F;
  float fR2 = 2.5F;
  float fR3 = 3.5F;
  float fCombinedResistance;

  /* [a] : Print properties of individual resistors */

     printf( "Resistor 1 is %8.3f ohms\n", fR1 );
     printf( "Resistor 2 is %8.3f ohms\n", fR2 );
     printf( "Resistor 3 is %8.3f ohms\n", fR3 );

  /* [b] : Compute and print combined resistance */

     fCombinedResistance = 1.0 / ( 1.0/fR1 + 1.0/fR2 + 1.0/fR3 );
     printf( "Combined Resistance is %8.3f ohms\n", fCombinedResistance);
}
```

The output from Program 5.2 is

```
Resistor 1 is    1.500 ohms
Resistor 2 is    2.500 ohms
Resistor 3 is    3.500 ohms
Combined Resistance is    0.739 ohms
```

Notice that we have initialized the individual resistors with statements of the form `float fR1 = 1.5F`, and not `float fR1 = 1.5`. By default, constants of the form `1.5` will be of type `double`. When we write

```
float fR1 = 1.5;
```

the compiler will automatically convert the constant from type `double` to type `float` when the assignment is made. The declaration

```
float fR1 = 1.5F;
```

tells the compiler to store `1.5` as a float, thereby avoiding the need for a data conversion during the initialization of `fR1`. In the evaluation of the determinant of Equation 5.1

```
( 1.0/fR1 + 1.0/fR2 + 1.0/fR3 )
```

the entire contents are enclosed within brackets, but individual terms are not. We obtain the correct numerical result because divisions have precedent level 3 and addition has precedent level 4. This means that `1.0/fR1` and `1.0/fR2` will be computed before their sum is evaluated.

Computer Program: Horner's Rule. Let $f(x)$ denote a polynomial of degree n in a single variable x, which takes the form

$$f(x) = a_o + a_1 \cdot x + a_2 \cdot x^2 + a_3 \cdot x^3 + \cdot \cdot \cdot + a_n \cdot x^n \tag{5.2}$$

where all the coefficients $a_o, a_1, \cdot \cdot \cdot, a_n$ are nonzero. We are interested in evaluating the polynomial at a specific value, $f(r)$. One approach is to compute each of the product terms in Equation 5.2 and then sum their values. (This calculation requires $\frac{n(n+1)}{2}$ multiplications, assuming that n multiplications would be required to calculate x^n.) An alternative method, which is known as Horner's rule, consists of rewriting Equation 5.2 in nested form

$$f(x) = a_o + x \cdot \{a_1 + x \cdot [a_2 + x \cdot (a_3 \cdot \cdot \cdot + x \cdot a_n)]\} \tag{5.3}$$

Program 5.3 demonstrates evaluation of the polynomial

$$f(x) = 2 + 3 \cdot x + 4 \cdot x^2 + 5 \cdot x^3 + 6 \cdot x^4 \tag{5.4}$$

when it is written in the formats of Equations 5.2 and 5.3.

PROGRAM 5.3: USING HORNER'S RULE TO EVALUATE A POLYNOMIAL

```
/*
 * ==============================================================
 * Evaluation of        f(x)  = 2 + 3.x + 4.x^2 + 5.x^3 + 6.x^4
 * using Horner's Rule        = 2 + x.(3. + x.(4 + x.(5. + 6.x)))
 * ==============================================================
 */

#include <stdio.h>
#include <math.h>

int main( void ) {
  float fA = 2.0;
  float fB = 3.0;
  float fC = 4.0;
  float fD = 5.0;
  float fE = 6.0;
  float fX1;

/* [a] : Prompt user for value of function variable */

   printf("Please enter coefficient fX : ");
   fflush(stdout)
   scanf("%f%*c", &fX);
```

```
/* [b] : Evaluate polynomial as sum of product terms */

   fX1 = fA + fB*fX + fC*fX*fX + fD*fX*fX*fX + fE*fX*fX*fX*fX;
   printf("Sum of Product terms        : F(%4.2f) = %4.2f\n", fX ,fX1 );

/* [c] : Evaluate polynomial using Horner's Rule */

   fX1 = fA + fX*(fB + fX*(fC + fX*(fD + fX*fE)));
   printf("Using Horner's Rule         : F(%4.2f) = %4.2f\n", fX ,fX1 );
}
```

The input and output from a typical session of Program 5.3 is

```
Please enter coefficient fX : 2.0
Sum of Product terms        : F(2.00) = 160.00
Using Horner's Rule         : F(2.00) = 160.00
```

Both function evaluations require four addition operations. The computational benefit of Horner's rule crops up in the number of required multiplication operations. While the former polynomial evaluation uses 10 multiples, use of Horner's rule gives the same result with only four multiplication operations.

5.5 MIXED EXPRESSIONS AND DATA TYPE CONVERSIONS

When an arithmetic expression is evaluated, it is important to ensure that all its components are of a compatible type. The consequences of not paying attention to these details can lead to erroneous numerical results; for example, in Section 5.4, we saw how the fractional result of integer expressions will be automatically truncated to 0. Now consider the situation where there is more than one data type in a single expression, namely

```
fVal = M_PI / 4;
```

Would it make sense to convert `M_PI` to an integer before dividing by 4? No. It makes more sense to convert both to the larger (more information) type so no information is lost. This is the approach taken by C when a mixed expression is encountered. More precisely, the rules for data conversion are

1. If either operand is long double, convert other to long double, otherwise
2. If either operand is double, convert the other to double, otherwise
3. If either operand is float, convert the other to float, otherwise
4. Convert char and short to int
5. If either operand is long, convert the other to long

When this set of rules is used in assignment statements, the value of the statement to the right-hand side of the assignment operator (i.e., =) is converted to the type of the left-hand side. For example,

```
fValue = iValue; /* Converts the integer to a float before assigning it. */
iValue = fValue; /* Converts (truncates) the floating point value before */
                 /* the assignment is made                               */

int iValue;      /* see example below */
char   cIn;

iValue =    cIn; /* convert char to int : no information lost */
cIn    = iValue; /* convert int to char : truncation occurs   */
```

Because the number of bytes in an `int` is always greater than the number of bytes in a `char`, the transformation from integer to char does not lose any information. In the conversion back to `char`, the `int` will be truncated to the char's original contents.

Implicit conversions also occur in assignment operations. For example, suppose the `rValue` of an assignment is a float and the `lvalue` is an integer as in

```
int iCount;
int iValue = 2;

iCount = 3.14 * iValue;
```

Let us examine the implicit conversions going on in evaluation of this expression. The rvalue `3.14 * iValue` has the binary `*` operator in it; therefore, `iValue` must be promoted to type `float`, and the multiplication performed. Now, the lower precedence assignment must be done. In this case, the `lvalue` is of type `int`; thus, the `rvalue` is converted to type `int`. A simple rule that works in almost all type conversions is that the smaller of the two types will be promoted to the larger (widening), if necessary. Although a widening of types tends to be well behaved, contractions of types (i.e., `double` to `int`) will result in the loss of the fractional component or loss of precision. It is important to keep these issues in mind when writing arithmetic expressions with different types.

Remark 5.2

In Program 5.2, the statement

```
fCombinedResistance = 1.0 / ( 1.0/fR1 + 1.0/fR2 + 1.0/fR3 );
```

may also be written

```
fCombinedResistance = 1 / ( 1/fR1 + 1/fR2 + 1/fR3 );
```

with the floating point constants being replaced by integer constants. Because the variables `fR1`, `fR2`, and `fR3` are floats, expressions of the type `1/fR1` will be converted to `1.0/fR1` before evaluation takes place (see Rule 3).

Remark 5.3

If dX and dY are variables of type double, then the (math library) function call `pow( dX, dY )` will return dX raised to the power dY. Hence, a third way of evaluating Equation 5.4 is with the script of code

```
fX1 = fA + fB*fX + fC*pow( fX, 2.0 ) + fD*pow( fX, 3.0 ) + fE*pow( fX, 4.0 );
printf("Using Power Math Functions : F(%4.2f) = %4.2f\n", fX ,fX1 );
```

You should note that we have called `pow(...)` with the first argument being a float. By Rule 2, the float will be converted to a double before the argument is passed to `pow(...)`.

Explicit Conversion

Explicit conversions of type are called `casts`. The syntax of an explicit type conversion, or cast, is

```
(type-name) expression
```

The cast explicitly forces conversion of `expression` to type `type-name`. For example,

```
fVal = (float) 1 / 2;
```

assigns 0.5 to `fVal`. Here are the steps taken by the compiler:

1. Casts have highest precedence, so the integer `1` is converted to a float.
2. The `/` operator has next highest precedence, so type conversion is done on the expression's arguments. The integer `2` is converted to `2.0`.
3. The division is computed, yielding a float 0.5.
4. 0.5 is assigned to `fVal`. No type conversion is necessary since it is already a float.

Question: What would the value of `fVal` be after the following?

```
fVal = (double) (1/2);
```

Here is what happens:

1. The integer expression `1/2` is evaluated first, since the ( ) have the highest precedence.
2. The result of (`1/2`) is an integer 0. It is converted to double.
3. The double `rvalue` is converted to a float `lvalue`.
4. `fVal` is assigned the value 0.0.

Casts should be used with care because, in effect, we are telling the compiler "just do this, even though precision may be lost." For example, in the script

```
int     iValue = 3;
char    cAChar;

cAChar = (char) iVal;
```

truncation of the integer will occur because a `char` is smaller than an `int`.

5.6 BITWISE OPERATIONS AND APPLICATIONS

The ability to manipulate individual bits in a character or integer is an essential part of low-level systems programming for device drivers and communications protocols. If you are not concerned with these applications, then skip this section and return to it later if needed.

The C programming language supports four logical bitwise operators and two bitwise shift operators. Table 5.2 contains a brief description of each operator and its hierarchy of evaluation.

5.6.1 Logical Operations

The logical bitwise operators are similar to the boolean operators that we encounter in Chapter 6 for program control. The bitwise-OR operator, | (or), compares its

TABLE 5.2 Summary of Logical and Shift Bit Operations

Operator	*Description*	*Symbol(s)*	*Hierarchy*
Logical	Bitwise-AND	&	8
	Bitwise EXCLUSIVE-OR	^	9
	Bitwise-OR	|	10
	Bitwise complement (bitwise-NOT)	~	2
Shift	Shift left	<<	5
	Shift right	>>	5

two operands one bit at a time and sets a bit in the result if either of the corresponding operand bits is set (i.e., has value of 1). For example, if

```
unsigned char ucValue1 = 'A'; /* bit pattern is 01000001 */
unsigned char ucValue2 =   9; /* bit pattern is 00001001 */
```

then

```
    01000001
  | 00001001
------------
  = 01001001
```

The bitwise-AND operator, & (and), sets only those bits whose corresponding operand bits are both set. For example,

```
    01000001
  & 00001001
------------
  = 00000001
```

The bitwise EXCLUSIVE-OR operator, ^ (exclusive-or), sets those bits when one or other (but not both) bits of the original operand are set. For example,

```
    01000001
  ^ 00001001
------------
  = 01001000
```

The bitwise complement (or bitwise-NOT) operator, ~, flips each bit by making each 1 a 0, and vice versa. For example,

```
  ~ 01000001          ~ 00001001
------------        ------------
  = 10111110          = 11110110
```

5.6.2 Shift Operations

The shift operator moves the bit pattern one or more positions to the left or right, as specified by the right operand. For example,

```
The bit pattern of (ucValue2 << 1) is 00010010
The bit pattern of (ucValue2 << 2) is 00100100
The bit pattern of (ucValue2 << 3) is 01001000
The bit pattern of (ucValue2 << 4) is 10010000
The bit pattern of (ucValue2 << 5) is 00100000
```

Bits that fall off the end of the byte boundary are lost. The shift operation `(ucValue2 << 1)` does not affect `ucValue2` itself, unless of course, the shift operation is used in conjunction with an assignment. For example,

```
ucValue2 = ucValue2 << 1;
```

Now `ucValue2` equals $1 \cdot 2^4 + 1 \cdot 2^1 = 18$.

5.6.3 Mask Operations

The bitwise-AND operator can be used to mask out bits. A mask is a bit pattern that when `&'ed` with a variable, zeros out any bits that are not ones in the mask but leaves the remaining bits of the variable with their original value. For example, if `MASK = 7` (bit pattern is `0000 0111`), then

```
00001001 & MASK ==> 0000 0001
```

The mask has set the five uppermost bits to zero. Similarly, a mask used with the bitwise-OR operator turns all the bits on where the mask has ones, and leaves all remaining bits unchanged.

Mask operations play a central role in the development of code to print the individual bits in a character or integer. For example, if

```
unsigned char ucTestChar = 'A';
```

then the operation `(ucTestChar & (1 << iBit))` will evaluate to a nonzero number if the `ith` bit from the left-hand side of the byte is nonzero.

Numerical Example

Program 5.4 prints the bits in the character `'A'`.

PROGRAM 5.4: PRINT BITS IN CHARACTER

```
/*
 * ===================================================================
 * Use shift operators and mask to print individual bits in a character
 * ===================================================================
 */

#include <stdio.h>

int main( void ) {
unsigned char ucTestChar = 'A';
int iBit;
```

```
  printf( "The binary value of %d is : ", ucTestChar );

  for(iBit = 7; iBit >= 0; iBit = iBit - 1 ) {
      if((ucTestChar & (1 << iBit )) != 0 )
         printf( "1" );
      else
         printf( "0" );
  }
  printf("\n");
}
```

The output from Program 5.4 is

```
The binary value of 65 is : 01000001
```

The binary value of a character is printed by systematically varying `iBit` from 7 to 0. A `1` (one) is printed when the mask operation evaluates to nonzero. Otherwise, `0` is printed.

5.7 SUBTRACTIVE CANCELLATION

Subtractive cancellation is the loss of information that occurs when two floating point numbers of almost equal size are subtracted using finite precision arithmetic.

To see how this loss of information occurs, assume that X and $X + \Delta X$ are 32-bit floating point numbers and that ΔX is extremely small compared to X. If the numbers are stored according to the IEEE floating point standard (for details, see Figure 4.2), then the bit patterns in X and $X + \Delta X$ will be identical except for a small number of the rightmost bits.

When the difference $X + \Delta X - X$ is computed, all the bits in the mantissa will cancel, except for the few rightmost bits (see Figure 5.1). Instead of having 23

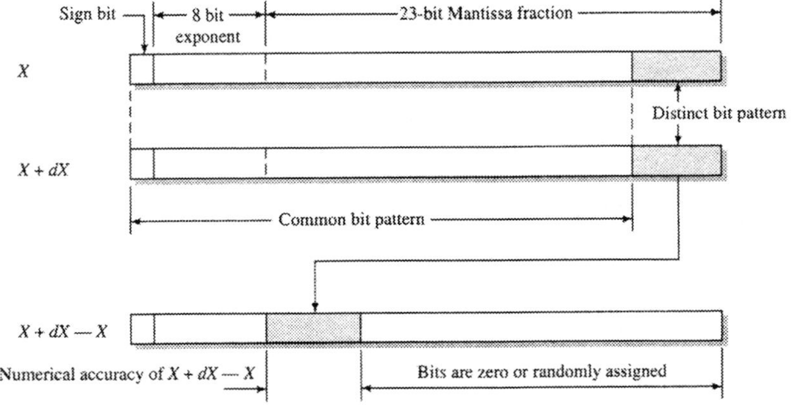

FIGURE 5.1 Subtractive cancellation of $X + \Delta X - X$.

bits of numerical precision, the result of the difference calculation will be accurate to only a few bits. The remaining bits in the mantissa may be zero or randomly assigned. Hence, any further calculations involving the result of $X + \Delta X - X$ will have only a few digits of accuracy, since a chain of computations cannot be stronger than its weakest link.

The standard technique for avoiding a loss of information due to subtractive cancellation is to rewrite appropriate formulae so that cancellation is avoided. The results can be very dramatic, as demonstrated in the following simple numerical example.

Numerical Example

Consider numerical evaluation of the formula

$$f(x) = \left[\frac{1 - \cos(x)}{x^2}\right] \tag{5.5}$$

very near to $x = 0$. Using a Taylor series approximation for $\cos(x)$, it is easy to show that $f(0) = 0.5$. When we attempt to evaluate Equation 5.5 for values of x very close to zero, subtractive cancellation is likely to occur because $\cos(x) \approx 1.0$. A mathematically equivalent form of Equation 5.5 is

$$f(x) = \left[\frac{1 - \cos(x)}{x^2}\right] \cdot \left[\frac{1 + \cos(x)}{1 + \cos(x)}\right] = \left[\frac{\sin^2(x)}{x^2 \cdot [1 + \cos(x)]}\right] \tag{5.6}$$

With the rightmost term of Equation 5.6 in hand, Program 5.5 computes Equations 5.5 and 5.6 for a sequence of x-values that systematically approach zero.

PROGRAM 5.5: SIMULATIVE SUBTRACTIVE CANCELLATION

```
/*
 * ===============================================================
 * Demonstrate Numerical Errors due to Subtractive Cancellation
 * ===============================================================
 */

#include <stdio.h>
#include <math.h>

float Function1 ( float fX ) {
      return (1.0-cos(fX))/fX/fX;
}

float Function2 ( float fX ) {
      return sin(fX)*sin(fX)/fX/fX/(1.0 + cos(fX));
}
```

```
int main( void ) {
float fX = 1.0;
int iCount;

   for (iCount = 1; iCount <= 8; iCount ++ ) {
        fX = fX/10.0;
        printf( "fX = %10.3e : Function1 = %10.8f : Function2 = %10.8f \n",
                fX, Function1( fX ), Function2( fX ));
   }
}
```

In Program 5.5, `Function1()` returns the result of Equation 5.5, and `Function2()`, the rightmost term in Equation 5.6. The program's output is as follows:

```
fX = 1.000e-01 : Function1 = 0.49958348 : Function2 = 0.49958348
fX = 1.000e-02 : Function1 = 0.49999583 : Function2 = 0.49999583
fX = 1.000e-03 : Function1 = 0.49999997 : Function2 = 0.49999997
fX = 1.000e-04 : Function1 = 0.50000000 : Function2 = 0.50000000
fX = 1.000e-05 : Function1 = 0.50000018 : Function2 = 0.50000000
fX = 1.000e-06 : Function1 = 0.50004458 : Function2 = 0.50000000
fX = 1.000e-07 : Function1 = 0.49960050 : Function2 = 0.50000000
fX = 1.000e-08 : Function1 = 0.00000000 : Function2 = 0.50000000
```

You should notice that even though `fX` and the results of the function evaluations are single precision, all the intermediate computations are in double precision. Still, the output clearly shows how subtractive cancellation of terms in Equation 5.5 leads to errors in the evaluation at $f(x)$ and how Equation 5.6 avoids subtractive cancellation completely.

Problems of subtractive cancellation crop up in a number of engineering applications. Problem 7.8 describes how subtractive cancellation can lead to poor numerical results in the computation of roots for quadratic equations and how the solution procedure can be rewritten to mitigate the problem.

Review Questions

1. Why is it arbitrary whether you use preincrement or postincrement in an expression with a single statement? For example,

```
++iCount;   /* or */
iCount++;
```

2. Why is 1/2 equal to 0 in C?

3. How can you override operator precedence in an expression to ensure that addition is done before multiplication?

4. Why might bitwise operations be important when C is used in operating system software (or control systems)?
5. How could you use shift operations to speed up some calculations? Why does this work?
6. Why do you have to `#include <math.h>` before you can use the trigonometric functions?
7. Why might subtractive cancellation be a problem in some programs?

5.8 PROGRAMMING EXERCISES

Problem 5.1 (Beginner): Write a program that defines, initializes, evaluates, and prints the results of the following expressions:

```
iCount = iCount + 1;
iVal = iCount / 2;
```

Verify that the expression `iVal = ++iCount / 2;` will produce the same results.

Problem 5.2 (Beginner): Write a program that defines, initializes, evaluates, and prints the results of the following expressions:

```
iVal = iCount / 2;
iCount = iCount - 1;
```

Verify that the expression `iVal = iCount-- / 2;` will produce the same results.

Problem 5.3 (Beginner): Write a program that reads in floating point values (use float for storage). Prompt for, read, and store various floating point values. After reading in the values, print them back to standard output. Try to find values where the output value is NOT the same as your input. *Hints:*

```
printf( "\nEnter a floating point value -->" );
scanf( "%f", &fValue );
printf( "\nYou entered -->%g", fValue );
```

Problem 5.4 (Beginner): The reactance of a capacitor X_c is given by the expression

$$X_c = \frac{1}{\omega C} \tag{5.7}$$

where $\omega = 2\pi f$. The frequency and capacitance of the capacitor are given by f and C, respectively. Write a computer program that will prompt the user for the frequency f and capacitance C of a capacitor. The program should print the value of ω and the reactance of the capacitor for frequencies $0.1 \cdot f$, f, and $10 \cdot f$.

Problem 5.5 (Beginner): The inductive reactance of a circuit consisting of an inductor with inductance L in henries at a frequency f in Hz is given by the formula

$$X_L = 2\pi fL = \omega L \tag{5.8}$$

where $\omega = 2\pi f$. Write a program to prompt the user for a value of L and a frequency f. Print the values of inductive reactance for $0.1 \cdot f$, f, and $10 \cdot f$.

Problem 5.6 (Beginner): The frequency at which a series LC circuit is resonant is given by the formula

$$f = \frac{1}{2\pi\sqrt{LC}} \tag{5.9}$$

This occurs when $X_L = X_C$ (see Problems 5.4 and 5.5). Write a program that prints the series resonant frequency, given values for L and C.

Problem 5.7 (Beginner): The output amplitude of a low-pass Butterworth filter with k elements is given (in dB) by

$$A = \frac{1}{\sqrt{\left[1 + \left(\frac{f}{f_c}\right)^{2k}\right]}} \tag{5.10}$$

where f_c is the frequency for an insertion loss of 3 dB. For a 3-dB frequency of 1,000 Hz, write a program to find the output amplitude of a 3-element filter for $f = 0.01 \cdot f_c$, $0.1 \cdot f_c$, f_c, $10 \cdot f_c$, and $100 \cdot f_c$.

Problem 5.8 (Beginner): Figure 5.2 shows the trajectory of a projectile launched with velocity V_o at angle θ to a horizontal plane. Assuming that all effects of air resistance may be neglected, the horizontal distance traveled as a function of time, $H(t)$, is

$$H(t) = V_o \cdot \cos(\theta) \cdot t \tag{5.11}$$

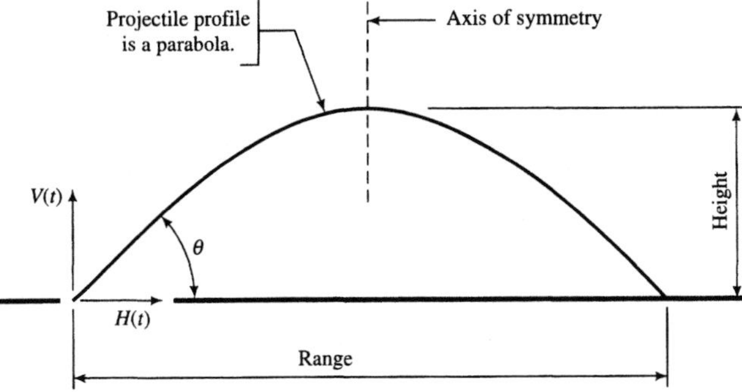

FIGURE 5.2 Trajectory of projectile.

The vertical distance of the projectile from the horizontal ground, $V(t)$, is given by

$$V(t) = V_o \cdot \sin(\theta) \cdot t - \frac{1}{2} g t^2 \tag{5.12}$$

where g is acceleration due to gravity. By noting that the maximum height of the projectile corresponds to the mathematical condition $dV/dt = 0$, and that the projectile profile will be parabolic and symmetric about its highest point, it is relatively easy to show that the total time of flight will be

$$\text{Total flight time} = \left[\frac{2 \cdot V_o \cdot \sin(\theta)}{g} \right] \tag{5.13}$$

and the range of flight will be

$$\text{Range of flight} = \left[\frac{V_o^2 \cdot \sin(2\theta)}{g} \right] \tag{5.14}$$

With this background in place, write a computer program that will compute and print the flight times and projectile range for launch angles, beginning at 0 degrees and increasing in increments of 5 degrees up to 90 degrees. You should observe that the maximum range occurs when $\sin(2\theta) = 1$ (i.e., $\theta = 45$ degrees) and that the maximum flight time occurs for $\sin(\theta) = 1$ (i.e., $\theta = 90$ degrees).

Problem 5.9 (Beginner): Write a C program that will prompt a user for a positive floating point number, `A`, and then use the divide-and-average formula:

$$x_{n+1} = 1/2 \left[x_n + \frac{A}{x_n} \right] \tag{5.15}$$

to compute its square root. Your program should use the criterion

$$\left| \frac{x_{n+1} - x_n}{x_n} \right| \leq \varepsilon \tag{5.16}$$

for a test on convergence, where ε is a very small number. Print the number `A`, its square root, and the number of iterations needed to compute the result. You should find that Equation 5.15 will converge rapidly when a good starting value for the iteration is selected. Try $x_o = A/2$.

Problem 5.10 (Intermediate): Modify Program 5.4 so that the bits in a character are printed within a single function. Details of the `PrintBitsInByte ()` are as follows:

```
#include <stdio.h>
#include <limits.h>

/* Print bit pattern within a byte */
```

```
void PrintBitsInByte (unsigned char ucByte) {
int iBitCount;

for( iBitCount = CHAR_BIT - 1; iBitCount >= 0; iBitCount-- ) {
        printf( "%c", (ucByte & (1 << iBitCount) '1' : '0'));
  }
}
```

Use `PrintBitsInByte()` to print the result of bitwise logical and bitwise shift operations.

Problem 5.11 (Beginner): Write a computer program that uses the math library function "exp" to find the value of e^1 (i.e., `#include <math.h>`). The accuracy of this value will be double precision. Then write the necessary C code to evaluate the exponential function using a series approximation with `enum{NoTerms = 7}` terms. Recall that the Taylor series expansion

$$f(n)\,|_{x=0} = \sum_{n=0}^{\infty} \frac{f^n(0)x^n}{n!}$$

gives us an expression for approximating e^x around 0. Hence, for `NoTerms` equal to 7, the series approximation gives

$$e^x \approx 1 + x + \frac{x^2}{2!} + \frac{x^3}{3!} + \cdot\cdot\cdot + \frac{x^7}{7!} \tag{5.17}$$

Compute and sum the appropriate values for individual terms in the series. Compare the series approximation with the numerical results returned from the math library function.

Problem 5.12 (Intermediate): Use Horner's rule to rewrite Equation 5.17. Now let S_x be the numerical result of the Taylor series expansion and M_x be the numerical result from the math library. You should assume that for a wide range of xs, M_x will be highly accurate. Hence, the absolute error in the approximations is

$$\text{Absolute error} \approx |S_x - M_x| \tag{5.18}$$

and the relative error in the approximations is

$$\text{Relative error} \approx \left|\frac{S_x - M_x}{M_x}\right| \tag{5.19}$$

Write a computer program that will print the results of both the series approximation and the value obtained by using the math library function exp(x).

Devise a numerical experiment that shows how the accuracy of the numerical results varies with the value of x. Try both positive and negative values (e.g., $x = +10$ and $x = -10$). For each value of x, compute and print the absolute and relative errors.

Problem 5.13 (Beginner): Let x be a positive floating point number and dx be a floating point number whose magnitude is very small compared to x. Write a C program that will systematically evaluate the expression

$$\sqrt{x + dx} - \sqrt{x} \tag{5.20}$$

for $|dx| \to 0$. Show that errors due to subtractive cancellation can be avoided by rewriting Equation 5.20 as

$$\frac{dx}{\sqrt{x + dx} + \sqrt{x}} \tag{5.21}$$

We recommend that you use variables of type `double` for all floating point variables and the math function `sqrt()` for the square root evaluations.

6

CONTROL OF FLOW

6.1 INTRODUCTION

This chapter examines C's relational and logical operands and control structures, which allow a computer program to take a course of action that depends on the data, logic, and calculations currently being considered.

6.2 RELATIONAL AND LOGICAL OPERANDS

Relational and logical operators are used to test the relationship between two (or more) values. By definition, the C programming language considers an expression to be `true` if its numerical value is nonzero. Otherwise, the evaluated expression will be numerically equal to zero and interpreted as `false`.

Table 6.1 contains a summary of relational and logical operators, and their hierarchy of precedence for evaluation, as defined in Table 5.1. Operators of equal precedence are listed on the same line. The first point to note is that relational operators at levels 6 and 7 have lower precedence than arithmetic operators (levels 3 and 4), but higher precedence than assignment operators (level 14).

6.2.1 Relational Operators

Relational operators are used to determine the relationship between two values. For the purposes of illustration, let `fA = 1.0`, `fB = 2.0`, and `fC = 3.0`. Valid

TABLE 6.1 Relational and Logical Operators

Operator	*Description*	*Symbol(s)*	*Hierarchy*
Relational	Is less than	`<`	6
	Is greater than	`>`	6
	Is less than or equal to	`<=`	6
	Is greater than or equal to	`>=`	6
	Is equal to	`==`	7
	Is not equal to	`!=`	7
Logical	(Unary) negation	`!`	2
	Logical and	`&&`	11
	Logical or	`||`	12

examples of relational expressions, with their numerical and true–false interpretations, are as follows:

Expression	*Numerical Value*	*Interpretation*
`fA < 3.4`	1	True
`fA + fB < 3.4`	1	True
`fA + fB == 3.4`	0	False
`fA + fB != 3.4`	1	True
`fC == 'w'`	0	False

In each case, the variable(s) on the left-hand side of the statement are evaluated and tested against evaluated variable(s) on the right-hand side of the statement. The first example evaluates to a nonzero value because `fA` is less than `3.4`. The "`==`" operator tests for the equivalence of two operands

```
expr1 == expr2
```

and returns nonzero value (usually 1) when `expr1` is equivalent to `expr2`. Conversely, the not equals operator, `!=`, tests for the inequality of two operands

```
expr1 != expr2
```

and will return a nonzero value (i.e., true) when `expr1` is not equal to `expr2`.

Note. A common programming error is to confuse the equivalence operator (`==`) with the assignment operator (`=`).

6.2.2 Logical Operators

The C language provides three logical operators, which allow two or more test conditions to be combined and used within a single control structure (see Table 6.1). Their syntax is

```
Not operator :      !expression1
And operator :      expression1 && expression2
Or  operator :      expression1 || expression2
```

where `expression1` and `expression2` are C expressions. The first operator is unary (only operates on one argument), and the second and third operators are binary.

For the purposes of illustration, let `iValue1 = 1`, `iValue2 = 2`, and `iValue3 = 3`. Examples of valid logical operations are as follows:

Expression	*Numerical Value*	*Interpretation*
`2 || 3`	1	True
`iValue1 - 1 || iValue2 - 2`	0	False
`iValue1 == 1 && iValue2 == 2`	1	True
`iValue1 == 2 && iValue2 == 1`	0	False
`iValue1 != 1 && iValue2 == 1`	0	False
`!iValue1`	0	False
`!iValue1 && iValue2`	0	False

The logical not operator "`!`" has a very high precedence (level 2), and so it evaluates early in expressions with lower-level operators. For example, `!iValue1 && iValue2` will evaluate as `(!iValue1) && iValue2` and not as `!(iValue1 && iValue2)`.

Compared to the logical not operator, the `or` (||) and `and` (&&) operators have very low precedence (levels 11 and 12). The evaluation of conditional expressions that have the form

```
iValue1 < iValue2 && iValue3 > iValue2
```

will begin at the left-hand side of the compound expression, and move left to right, evaluating terms until the truth value is determined. The comparisons `iValue1 < iValue2` and `iValue3 > iValue2` have level 6 hierarchy and are evaluated first. Then the logical `and` operator (at level 11 hierarchy) is evaluated. There is no need to provide two levels of parentheses, as in

```
(iValue1 < iValue2) && (iValue3 > iValue2)
```

because the relational and logical operators have different levels of hierarchy.

The evaluation of a logical expression will cease as soon as the compiler knows the result; for example, the evaluation of `expr1 && expr2` will stop when `expr1` is false, and the evaluation of `expr1 || expr2` will stop when `expr1` is true. For our test suite of variables, evaluation of the logical expression

```
iValue1 < 0 && ....
```

ceases as soon as it is determined that `iValue1 < 0` is false.

Expressions involving relational and logical operators are not restricted to constant and variable comparisons. When function calls are embedded within conditional statements, the return value from the function will be used in the comparison. Function calls have high precedence. So, for example, the script of code

```
LoopControl == 0 && (SafeCond == CheckSystemSafety())
```

will evaluate to true if `LoopControl` equals zero and the return value from `CheckSystemSafety()` is equivalent to `SafeCond`.

Remark 6.1

Because there is no guarantee that a floating point value will have an accurate internal representation, floating point numbers should not be used in situations where the results of a numerical computation critically depend on exact comparisons of numbers. For example, because 1.1 in binary format has infinite length and cannot be represented exactly by IEEE format, on some computers the simple `for` loop

```
float fVal;
for (fVal = 0.0; fVal != 1.1; fVal = fVal + 0.01)
     printf ("fVal = %f", fVal);
```

will continue indefinitely because the simple test `fVal != 1.1` may never evaluate to true.

6.3 SELECTION CONSTRUCTS

Selection constructs in C allow us to control the path of execution through the statements of a program based on the results of conditional statements. Most real-world programs make comparisons at run-time and proceed differently depending on the results of the comparisons. We need language constructs that support changes in control flow, and in C there are several.

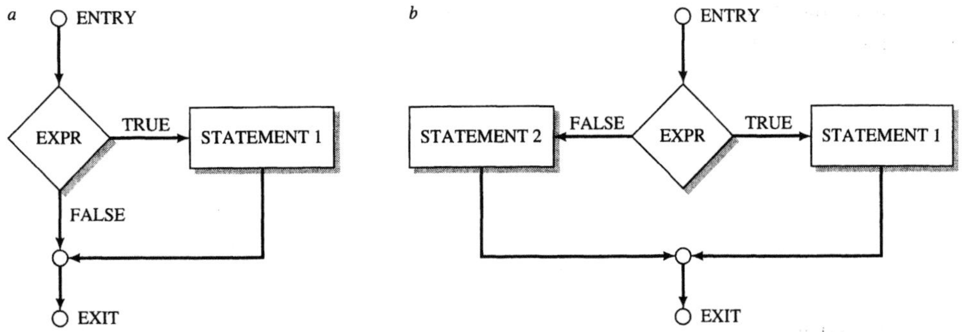

FIGURE 6.1 *The* `if` *and* `if-else` *selection structures.*

6.3.1 If and If-Else Statements

Two of the simplest and most widely used constructs for control of program flow are the `if()` and `if()-else` statements. Their structure is illustrated in Figure 6.1. The `if()` statement syntax is

```
if( conditional_expression )
    statement1;
```

The `if()` construct will execute `statement1;` when the conditional expression evaluates to a nonzero value (i.e., true). When the conditional expression evaluates to zero (i.e., false), the program execution will proceed directly to the first statement after `statement1`.

Conditional expressions may be anything that evaluates to zero or nonzero. It is possible, for example, to insert arithmetic expressions within the condition field

```
if( fAngle <= M_PI/2.0 )
    fAngle = ProcessAngle( fAngle );
```

The statement `fAngle = ProcessAngle(fAngle);` will be executed if `fAngle <= M_PI/2.0` evaluates to a nonzero number. Similarly, the script of code

```
if( sin( fAngle ) != 0.0 )
    fAngle = ProcessAngle( fAngle );
```

will call `ProcessAngle( fAngle )` if the math function `sin( fAngle )` returns a value that is not equal to zero. Another common situation is statements of the type

```
enum { Max = 3 };

if( Max == iVal )
    DoIfTrue();
```

We believe that it is good programming practice to put `Max` on the left instead of the right, because programmers often mistakenly write the assignment operator instead of the equivalence operator, as in

```
if( iVal = Max )        /* Poor programming style : Also */
                        /* note error in code */
    DoIfTrue();
```

Here `Max` is unintentionally assigned to `iVal`. The value of the result `(Max)` determines the condition in the `if` statement. If `Max` happens to be nonzero (i.e., true), then function `DoIfTrue()` will always be called. Alternatively, if `Max` equals zero, then `DoIfTrue()` will never be called. In either case, a compiler will happily compile the code without notification of an error. If, however, an assignment is accidentally made, as in

```
if( Max = iVal )
    DoIfTrue();
```

then the compiler will detect an assignment to an enumerated type and, at the very least, generate a warning message. With this style of programming in mind, a construct that you will often see is

```
if( EOF == (iInputChar = getchar()) )
    printf( "\nAt end of File. " );
```

Here the return value from `getchar()` is assigned to the integer `iInputChar` before the comparison is made. The program will print

```
At end of File.
```

when the returned character matches the end-of-file character (EOF). Notice that the EOF is positioned on the left side of the relational expression. This script of code could have been written more explicitly as

```
iInputChar = getchar();
if( EOF == iInputChar )
    printf( "\nAt end of file. " );
```

Many programmers would argue that the second script of code is easier to read than the first and, therefore, better. There are, however, cases where the former represents the desired behavior (despite the poor program readability). A case in point is error checks for the input on a call to `scanf()`

```
if( scanf( "(%f, %f)", &fValRe, &fValIm) ) < 2 )
    printf( "\nError: re-enter data..." );
```

scanf() returns the number of fields that were scanned and stored. If the input is not correct, the number of fields scanned will be less than expected and an error message will be printed.

6.3.2 Block Statements

Block statements are needed for situations where more than one statement must be executed when a condition is true. In a continuation of the examples given previously, suppose that we wanted to execute the statement pair

```
fAngle = ProcessAngle( fAngle );
iNext  = iValue + 1;
```

when sin(fAngle) evaluates to a nonzero number. This can be accomplished by using left and right braces – { and } – to bundle multiple statements into a single *block*. The aforementioned example would be written

```
if( sin( fAngle ) != 0.0 ) {
    fAngle = ProcessAngle( fAngle );
    iNext  = iValue + 1;
}
```

The use of curly braces is optional when only one statement follows the if conditional. In other words,

```
if( conditional_expression )
  statement1;
```

is functionally equivalent to

```
if( conditional_expression ) {
  statement1;
}
```

Remark 6.2

C is a free-form language, meaning that white space and end-of-line characters are ignored by the compiler, as are the placement of the braces. Still, the layout of a program's source code can become a religious issue for many programmers. For example, an equivalent block statement is

```
if( sin( fAngle ) != 0.0 )
    {
    fAngle = ProcessAngle( fAngle );
    iNext  = iValue + 1;
    }
```

Although the second compound statement is probably the most *structured* and obvious grouping, the first form also has its merits. For one, program listings are shorter because the block statement uses fewer lines—this is a good reason why you will see books written using this style. The first form also shows clearly where the "end" of the `if` statement is since the closing brace } aligns with the `if` statement. We adopt the first style in this book. The important point with regard to indenting, use of white space, and block alignment is to adopt a style and stick to it. Use of a consistent style will make your code easier to read.

6.3.3 If-Else Statements

An important limitation of the `if()` programming construct is that it leads to multiple blocks of code that look similar to the following:

```
if( iCount < MaxCount ) {
   iVal  = ProcessAngle( fAngle );
   iNext = iVal + 1;
}

if( iCount >= MaxCount ) {
   iNext = iVal - 1;
   iCount--;
}
```

Having to write the condition one way and then rewrite it to encompass the opposite case seems redundant. This situation is equivalent to an if-else condition and, fortunately, such a construct is supported in C. The if-else programming construct

```
if( conditional_expression )
   statement1;
 else
   statement2;
```

allows a computer program to choose between two paths before continuing its execution. As expected, `statement1` will be executed when `condition_expression` evaluates to true. Otherwise, `statement2` will be executed. Either of these statements can be a block statement as in

```
if( condition ) {
  statement3;
  statement4;
} else {
  statement5;
  statement6;
}
```

Here the style of indenting starts to show its strengths since the flow of execution is implied by the layout of code.

6.3.4 Chained (and Nested) If-Else Clauses

If statements can be chained with the else clause to form a sequence of "else if" constructs and a programming construct that allows for the selection among multiple paths in program flow. The general layout is

```
if( conditional_expression1 )
    statement1;
else if( conditional_expression2 )
    statement2;
else  if( conditional_expression3 )
    statement3;
else
    defaultStatement;
```

`Statement1` will be executed if `conditional_expression1` is true; `statement2` will be executed if `conditional_expression2` is true, and so forth. If none of the conditional statements evaluate to true, then `defaultStatement` will be executed by default. After the corresponding statement has been executed, the program execution will jump to the end of the chained if-else clause. In the script of code

```
if( Monday == eDay )
    doStartWeek();
else if( Tuesday == eDay )
    doGettingRolling();
else if( Wednesday == eDay )
    doHumpDay();
else if( Thursday == eDay )
    doAlmostDone();
else if( Friday == eDay )
    doTGIF();
else
    doHomework();
```

function `doStartWeek()` will be called if `eDay` equals Monday; function `doGet Rolling()` will be called when `eDay` equals Tuesday, and so forth. Code of this type can get out of hand when we have many different conditions for which to test. However, it does make explicit exactly what is going on—there should be no ambiguity. Maintenance of code such as this is not difficult and usually does not introduce errors since the control flow is explicit.

You should note that the `else if` is not one word, and any of the above statements could be a block statement. Moreover, the else statement always goes with the last `elseless` if statement (this rule is a common source for programming errors!). So, for example, the left- and right-hand scripts of code

```
enum { Max = 25, BaseTen = 10 };

   if( iVal < Max )                               if( iVal < Max ) {
      if( iVal < BaseTen)                            if( iVal < BaseTen)
         iVal = iCount;       <== the same as ==>       iVal = iCount;
   else                                              else
      iVal = iCount + BaseTen;                    iVal = iCount + BaseTen;
                                                  }
```

have the same functionality. Assume for the purposes of discussion that the value of `iVal` is less than `Max` but greater than `BaseTen` (say, the value 11) when this block of code is reached. The first if condition will evaluate to true. The second if statement will be executed and will evaluate to false. It follows that

```
iVal = iCount;
```

will not execute. What happens next? From the way the left-hand block of code is indented, it would seem that the `else` clause will be executed if the first if is not true. This is an incorrect assumption. The `else` condition is actually connected to the condition of the second if statement. In other words, the left-hand script has code indentation that is totally misleading. To force the else condition to act on the first if statement, we must rewrite this fragment as

```
enum { Max = 25, BaseTen = 10 };

if( iVal < Max ) {
   if( iVal < BaseTen)
       iVal = iCount;
} else
   iVal = iCount + BaseTen;
```

The use of parentheses explicitly tells the compiler which `if` to associate the `else` with and removes the ambiguity in reading the program code.

6.3.5 Tertiary Condition Operator

We have just seen that the condition operator serves as a concise form of the `if-else` construct. For example, the script of code

```
if( iA > iB)
  iZ = iA;
else
  iZ = iB;
```

assigns to iZ the maximum of iA and iB. The tertiary operator allows this assignment to be accomplished in a single expression. The syntax is

```
conditional_expression ? value1 : value2
```

If the conditional expression, conditional_expression, evaluates to true (i.e., nonzero), then the condition operator is assigned value1. Otherwise, the condition operator is assigned value2. With these rules in place, the aforementioned script of code may be rewritten:

```
iZ = ( iA > iB ) ? iA : iB;
```

Strictly speaking, the brackets () are not necessary because the comparison operator has precedence level 6, and tertiary operator is at level 13. We use the brackets () because it makes an otherwise confusing operator easier to understand.

6.3.6 Switch Statement

The switch statement is a multiway conditional test that is C's counterpart to FORTRAN's computed goto statement (see Figure 6.2). The general syntax is as follows:

```
switch( expression ) {
  case constant1Expr:
       statement 11;
       statement 12;
       break;
  case constant2Expr:
       statement 21;
       statement 22;
       ... etc ...
       break;
  default:
       stmtDefault;
  }
```

The expression at the top of the switch statement must be an integer type, as must each individual case constant1Expr, constant2Expr, and so forth. The expression at the top of the switch is evaluated, and the result is compared against each case expression. The corresponding block of statements is executed when a match is found. The default statements will be executed when the expression

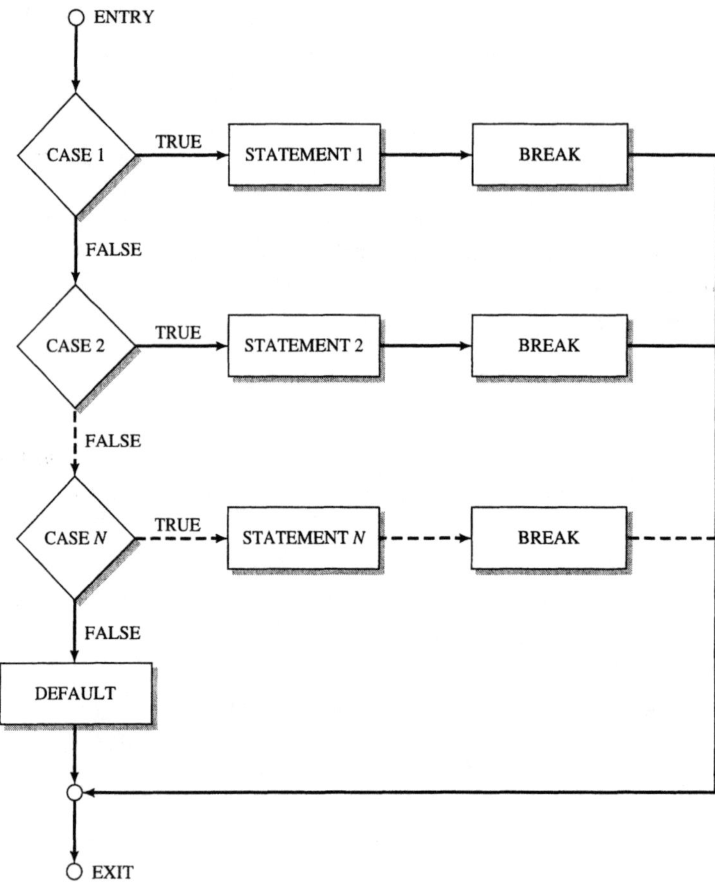

FIGURE 6.2 The `switch` selection structure.

does not match any of the `case` statements (notice that the `default` statement is like an `else` for the whole structure). For example,

```
switch( eDay ) {
   case Monday:
         doStartWeek();
         break;
   case Tuesday:
         doGettingRolling();
         break;
   case Wednesday:
         doHumpDay();
         break;
   case Thursday:
         doAlmostDone();
         break;
```

```
    case Friday:
         doTGIF();
         break;
    default:
         doHomework();
}
```

The use of break statements at the end of each case causes an immediate exit from the `switch()` (and other) statements. Without the break statements in place, the program execution would fall into the next, and all remaining, statements. Case statements may be nested—for example,

```
switch( eDay ) {
    case Monday:
    case Tuesday:
    case Wednesday:
    case Thursday:
    case Friday:
         doWeekDayExec();
         break;
    case Saturday:
    case Sunday:
         doTheWeekEnd();
         break;
    default:
         notADay();
         break;
}
```

Function `doWeekDayExec()` will be called when `eDay` is `Monday` through to `Friday`; `doTheWeekEnd()` will be called for `Saturday` and `Sunday`, and `notADay()` when `eDay` does not match a valid day of the week.

6.4 ITERATION CONSTRUCTS

Most of our computer programs will need the ability to loop (or iterate) over one or more statements while some condition is met. The process of iteration generally involves three components—initialization, testing, and incrementing. During the initialization phase, initial values are assigned to any variables that will be used within the loop. Whether the loop is entered or not initially, and whether looping continues, is determined by some expression that can be checked. Most iterating loops will increment a "loop control variable" during each cycle of the iteration.

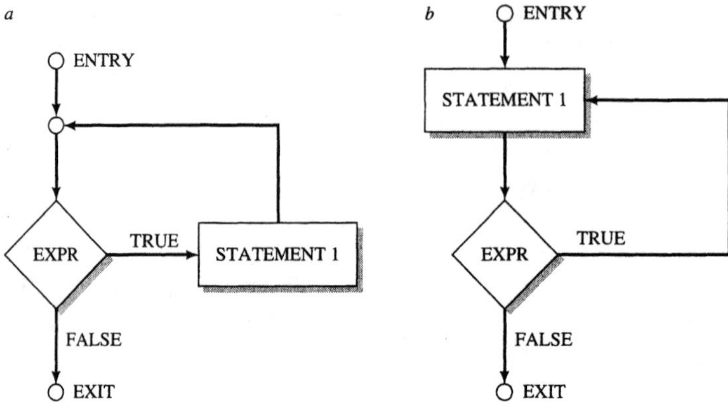

FIGURE 6.3 The (a) `while` and (b) `do-while` iteration structures.

Figure 6.3 illustrates two conceptual structures for implementing the `while` and `do-while` iteration constructs. The conditional checkbox in the left-hand schematic is located at the beginning of the iteration loop. Execution of the while loop will continue until the expression evaluates to false. The control structure of the right-hand schematic, in contrast, shows checking of an expression after the loop statement (or block of loop statements) is executed. This means that the "do-while loop" will always be entered, and the statement (or block of statements) executed at least once.

6.4.1 While Statements

The `while()` looping construct has the syntax

```
while( conditional_expression )
   statement;
```

or equivalently, with a block statement

```
while( conditional_expression ) {
   statement1;
   statement2;
   ...
   statementN;
}
```

The `while` statement is a useful mechanism for controlling the repetition of actions while `conditional_expression` is true. Consider, for example, the short script of code to compute factorials:

```
/* Compute iN Factorial (i.e., iN! ) */

int iN                    = 5;
int iCount                = 1;
unsigned int uiFactorial = 1;

while( iCount < iN )
   uiFactorial *= ++iCount;
```

The `while` conditional statement is entered with the loop control variable `iCount = 1`, the summing variable `uiFactorial = 1` and `iN = 5`. The value of the iteration variables, conditional expression, and `uiFactorial` at the end of the loop in each of the four iterations is as follows:

Iteration	`iCount`	`iN`	`iCount < iN`	`uiFactorial *= ++iCount;`
1	2	5	True	`2 <== 2*1`
2	3	5	True	`6 <== 3*2`
3	4	5	True	`24 <== 4*6`
4	5	5	False	`120 <== 5*24`

The conditional expression `iCount < iN` will evaluate to zero at the top of the fifth iterate, at which point the result of our 5! calculation is 120. The same factorial could have been computed with the code

```
int iCount = 1;
unsigned int uiFactorial = 1;

while( iCount < 5 ) {
   uiFactorial *= ++iCount;
}
```

The second version is less desirable than the first version because it employs the magic number 5. For a detailed discussion of the reasons why magic numbers correspond to poor programming practice, see Chapter 4.

6.4.2 Do-While Statement

The `do-while()` looping construct is appropriate when at least one iteration of a loop is required. The construct will execute a statement (or possibly a block of statements) and then evaluate a conditional expression to see if a further loop of computations is needed. The syntax for the simple and the blocked *do-while* statements is

```
do statement1;
   while( conditional_expression );
```

```
do {
   statement1;
   statement2;

   ... etc ...

   statementN;
} while( conditional_expression );
```

You should notice that in both constructs a semicolon (`;`) appears after the while closing parentheses. When the `conditional_expression` evaluates to a nonzero value, a new loop of the statements will be executed.

Consider, for example, a script of code that prompts a user to input two coordinate pairs entered as (x, y) values from the keyboard:

```
float fX, fY;
enum { TwoDim = 2 };

do {
   printf( "\nEnter the starting coordinate as (fX, fY) -->" );
   fflush( stdin );
   iArgs = scanf( "(%f,%f)", &fX, &fY );
} while( iArgs != TwoDim );
```

The number of items read by `scanf()` is assigned to `iArgs`. The conditional part of the do-while statement checks that two values have been read. If an input error has occurred, and scanf has read something other than two value, the user will be prompted another time for input. Within the body of the loop, `fflush(stdin)` flushes the contents of the standard input buffer and prevents the input from getting out of sync with the expected input. The use of `fflush()` also eliminates the need for synchronization of carriage returns at the beginning (or end, in a sequence) of scanfs (for a detailed discussion on buffered I/O, see Chapter 12).

6.4.3 For Statement

One problem with the `while()` and `do-while()` looping constructs that crops up in many real-world application programs is lengthy loop bodies that may span multiple pages. In fact, on a printout of the source code, each of the three looping components—initialize, condition, and increment—may be on a separate page. This separation of information diminishes readability of the program source code and can make debugging of programs more difficult than necessary.

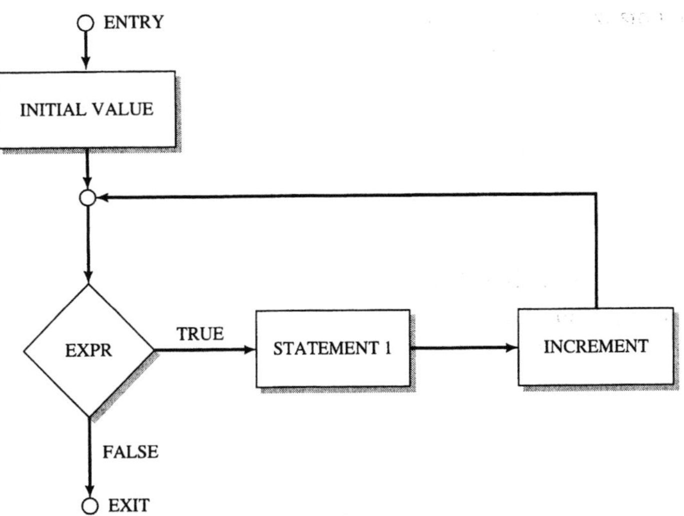

FIGURE 6.4 The `for` iteration structure.

C's `for()` looping construct solves this problem by putting the initialize, continuation, and increment operations in one location (see Figure 6.4). Here is the syntax

```
/* Syntax of for loop containing a single statement */

   for( initialization ; continuation ; increment )
      statement1;

/* Syntax of for loop containing a block of statements */

   for( initialization ; continuation ; increment ) {
      statement1;
      statement2;

      ... etc ...

      statementN;
   }
```

for loops containing a single statement and loops containing a block of statements. In both cases, `continuation` is a relational/logical expression that will evaluate to either true or false. Just like the previously discussed loop/selection constructs, for loops will continue while the `continuation` evaluates to true. The `initialization` can be zero or more statements that initialize variables employed in the for loop. Similarly, `increment` can be zero or more statements that are executed at the conclusion of each loop. The use of parentheses is optional when only one statement follows the `for` loop construct.

For example, the simple `for` loop

```
int iCount,
enum { MaxValue = 3};

for( iCount = 0; iCount <= MaxValue; iCount = iCount + 1 )
     printf("*** iCount = %3d\n", iCount );
```

generates four lines of output

Loop	`iCount`	`iCount <= MaxValue`	*Output*
1	0	True	`*** iCount = 0`
2	1	True	`*** iCount = 1`
3	2	True	`*** iCount = 2`
4	3	True	`*** iCount = 3`
5	4	False	

The initialization condition is `iCount = 0`. All that the body of the for loop does is call `printf()`. At the conclusion of each loop, `iCount` is incremented by one, and the `continuation` is evaluated to see whether another iteration is required. In this example, looping continues until the beginning of the fifth loop, at which point `iCount <= MaxValue` evaluates to false.

If `iCount` was expected to iterate over a range of integers other than zero to `MaxValue` then a suitable extension of this code would be

```
int iCount,
enum { MinValue = 3, MaxValue = 8 };

for( iCount = MinValue; iCount <= MaxValue; iCount = iCount + 1 )
     printf("*** iCount = %3d\n", iCount );
```

Now the starting and finishing values of the for loop are controlled by `MinValue` and `MaxValue`, respectively, and for the settings shown, `iCount` would be printed from 3 to 8.

It is important to know that any one of the expressions in the `for` loop can be left out but that the semicolons (`;`) must always be there. For example, the script of code

```
int iCount,
enum { MinValue = 3, MaxValue = 8 };

iCount = MinValue;
for( ; iCount <= MaxValue ; ) {
     printf("*** iCount = %3d\n", iCount );
     iCount = iCount + 1;
}
```

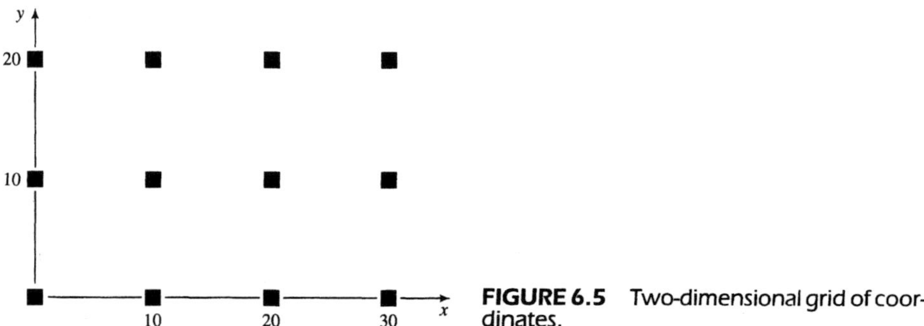

FIGURE 6.5 Two-dimensional grid of coordinates.

is functionally equivalent to the previous script. We do not like this style of programming because it separates the initialization, continuation, and increment components, the key reason for having the `for` loop in the first place.

For looping constructs can be nested and can include more than one statement in their `initialization` and `increment` components. Suppose, for example, that we want to generate and print the coordinates in a two-dimensional rectangular grid as shown in Figure 6.5. An easy way of generating the node numbers and coordinates is to use two levels of for loops, as in

```
float MinXcoord = 0.0, MaxXcoord = 30.0;
float MinYcoord = 0.0, MaxYcoord = 20.0;
float fXcoord, fYcoord;
int   iNodeNo = 1;

for( fXcoord = MinXcoord; fXcoord <= MaxXcoord; fXcoord = fXcoord + 10.0 ) {
     for( fYcoord = MinYcoord; fYcoord <= MaxYcoord;
          fYcoord = fYcoord + 10.0, iNodeNo = iNodeNo + 1 ) {
          printf("*** Node %2d : (x,y) = %8.3f %8.3f\n",
                 iNodeNo, fXcoord, fYcoord );
     }
}
```

The output is

```
*** Node  1 : (x,y) =   0.000  0.000
*** Node  2 : (x,y) =   0.000 10.000
*** Node  3 : (x,y) =   0.000 20.000
*** Node  4 : (x,y) =  10.000  0.000
*** Node  5 : (x,y) =  10.000 10.000
*** Node  6 : (x,y) =  10.000 20.000
*** Node  7 : (x,y) =  20.000  0.000
*** Node  8 : (x,y) =  20.000 10.000
*** Node  9 : (x,y) =  20.000 20.000
```

```
*** Node 10 : (x,y) = 30.000  0.000
*** Node 11 : (x,y) = 30.000 10.000
*** Node 12 : (x,y) = 30.000 20.000
```

Points to note are as follows:

1. We have introduced `MinXcoord`, `MinYcoord`, `MaxXcoord`, and `MaxYcoord` to represent the beginning and end coordinate values used in the two for loops. The use of variables in this context makes sense because the code can be easily updated to reflect changes in the number of nodes and size of the rectangular grid.
2. When space permits, it is good programming practice to put all of the `for` loop control information—initialization, continuation, and increment—on a single line. Because the inner loop of our grid example contains several lengthy statements, the source code will be easier to read if the loop specification is spread over several lines:

```
...... details of outer loop removed ....

    for( fYcoord = MinYcoord; fYcoord <= MaxYcoord;
         fYcoord = fYcoord + 10.0, iNodeNo = iNodeNo + 1 ) {

              ...... details of inner loop removed ....
    }
```

In either case, this style of programming is a form of control flow *encapsulation* because it keeps the important information related to the loop in a single location. Adhering to this style of programming will, in our opinion, make your code more readable and maintainable, especially when loops are nested.

3. You should note that the continuation part of the inner loop contains two executable statements—`fYcoord = fYcoord + 10.0` and `iNodeNo = iNodeNo + 1`—separated by a comma.

6.4.4 Break and Continue Statements

We have already seen that the break statement will force an immediate exit from the cases of a `switch()` statement. Break statements can also be used to force an immediate exit from `while()`, `for()`, and `do-while()` loops. It may be convenient, for example, to use a `break` for an early exit from a looping structure.

```
int ii;

for( ii = 1; ii <= 5; ii = ii + 1 ) {
   printf("*** Inside loop : ii = %2d\n", ii );
   if( ii >= 3 )
        break;
}
printf("*** Broken from loop !!\n");
```

The details of variables in the loop and the early exit are as follows:

Loop	ii	ii <= 5	*Output*
1	1	True	*** Inside loop : ii = 1
2	2	True	*** Inside loop : ii = 2
3	3	True	*** Inside loop : ii = 3
			*** Broken from loop !!

In our opinion, the use of break statements should be avoided because it leads to code having multiple exit points. A fundamental tenet of structured programming is that there should be only one entry and exit location from loop structures.

The `continue` statement causes the next iteration of an enclosing `for()`, `do-while()`, or `while()` loop to begin. It is a form of *local goto* that jumps over the remaining instructions in the loop. For example, the script of code

```
int ii;

for ( ii = 1; ii <= 5; ii = ii + 1 ) {
    if ( ii >= 3 )
         continue;

    printf("*** Inside loop : ii = %2d\n", ii );
}
printf("*** Broken from loop : ii = %2d !!\n", ii );
```

generates the output

Loop	ii	ii <= 5	*Output*
1	1	True	*** Inside loop : ii = 1
2	2	True	*** Inside loop : ii = 2
3	3	True	
4	4	True	
5	5	True	
6	6	False	
			*** Broken from loop : ii = 6 !!

Just like the `break` statement, we discourage the use of `continue` because it makes control flow difficult to follow and hard to maintain. Rather than use break and continue statements, rethink the logic of the problem to ensure that a more structured solution is not possible. In other words, use break and continue sparingly.

6.5 COMPARISON OF LOOPING CONSTRUCTS

Groups of statements may be initialized within the `for()` construct. For example, the block of statements

```
for( initialization ; continuation ; increment ) {
    statement1;
}
next_statement;
```

are semantically equivalent to

```
initialization;
while( continuation ) {
        statement1;
        increment;
}
next_statement;
```

Remark 6.3: Indentation of Code and Blank Lines

Indentation of code often improves the readability of a C program. Consider the following two segments of code and the difference that the indentation makes. In the first code segment, the code lines are not indented at all:

```
for(i = 1; i <= 20; i++)
for(j = 1; j <= 20; j++) {
matrixitem = a[i][j];
printf("MatrixItem[%2d][%2d] = %8.4f\n,i,j,matrixitem);
}
```

The second code segment is functionally identical to the first but uses indentation to make the structure of the nested `for` loop easier to recognize:

```
for(i = 1; i <= 20; i++)
   for(j = 1; j <= 20; j++) {
      matrixitem = a[i][j];
      printf("MatrixItem[%2d][%2d] = %8.4f\n,i,j,matrixitem);
   }
```

Most programmers will use two, three, or four spaces for each level of nesting. A full tab (i.e., eight spaces) of indentation is always too much. For each level of nesting, all C statements are indented by the same amount.

Blank lines can also be used judiciously to enhance the readability of source code. This "vertical white space" is usually inserted between sections of code that are logically distinct. So, if we have a section of code at the beginning of a program that initializes variables, follow it with a blank line before proceeding to the next section of code. A blank line after the variable definitions at the beginning of a new block is also nice for distinguishing definitions from the executable statements that follow.

REVIEW QUESTIONS

1. How do you override the order of evaluation of logical operations?
2. How can you avoid many bugs by putting constants on the left side of equality comparisons?
3. Does the compiler consider the way you indent your program text to be important?
4. Which statement is the else statement associated with in all cases?
5. What are common purposes for while, do-while, and for loops used? Does each have a common attribute? Can the for loop be used to replace the others? Should you replace the others?
6. Why are `continue` statements undesirable? Write a block of code that has the same functionality as

```
int ii;

for ( ii = 1; ii <= 5; ii = ii + 1 ) {
    if ( ii >= 3 )
        continue;

    printf("*** Inside loop : ii = %2d\n", ii );
}
printf("*** Broken from loop : ii = %2d !!\n", ii );
```

but does not contain a `continue` statement.

6.6 PROGRAMMING EXERCISES

Problem 6.1 (Beginner): Write a complete program to calculate the amount of money A accumulated after n periods if the principal P is deposited in an account that draws an annual interest I (in percent). Use the formula

$$A = P \cdot [1 + I]^n \tag{6.1}$$

Problem 6.2 (Beginner): The current–voltage relationship for a p-n diode is given by

$$I = I_s \cdot e^{\left(\frac{qV}{kT}-1\right)} \tag{6.2}$$

where I is the current; I_s, the saturation current; V, the voltage across the junction; q, the electronic charge ($1.6 \cdot 10^{-19}$ Coulomb); k, the Boltzmann constant ($1.38 \cdot 10^{-23}$ J/°K); and T, the junction temperature.

Write a program to calculate I as V varies from -0.25 V to 1 V in increments of 0.125 V. For each current–voltage, assume a junction temperature of 300°K, and a saturation current I_s of 1 μ A. Plot your results using MATLAB (for details, see the MATLAB tutorial).

Problem 6.3 (Beginner): Figure 6.6 shows a sphere of radius r and density ρ floating in water. The weight of the sphere will be $4/3\rho\pi r^3$. The volume of the spherical segment displacing water is $1/3\pi(3rd^2 - d^3)$.

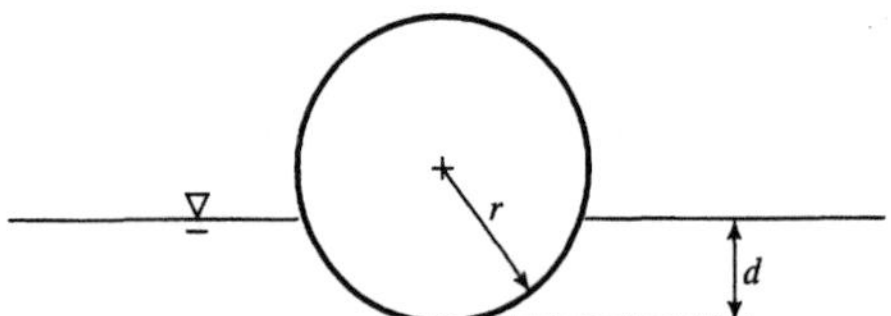

FIGURE 6.6 Sphere floating in water.

Write a C program that will compute and print the depth to which a sphere will sink as a function of its radius for $\rho = 0$ to $\rho = 1$ in increments of 0.1. Use MATLAB or some other graphical package to plot the results.

Problem 6.4 (Intermediate): Write a program to calculate the series approximation

$$\sin(x) = \sum_{n=0}^{\infty} \frac{f^n(0)x^n}{n!} = x - \frac{x^3}{3!} + \frac{x^5}{5!} - \frac{x^7}{7!} + \cdots$$

about $x = 0$ for an arbitrary number of series terms n. Try to formulate your solution to this problem in terms of Horner's rule (for details, see Chapter 4).

Then devise a numerical experiment to show how, for a given level of accuracy ε, more terms are needed as the argument x moves away from 0. Extend the functionality of your program so that new terms will be added to the series approximation until the error is smaller than ε.

Problem 6.5 (Intermediate): Write a program that will prompt a user for a base 10 integer in the range 0 . . . 255, and then convert and print the equivalent binary number (base 2).

Hints. Each digit of a base 10 number is a power of 10 (10^0, 10^1, 10^2 . . .), whereas each digit of a binary number is a power of 2 (2^0, 2^1, 2^2, 2^3,. . .). To convert a decimal (base 10) value to binary (base 2) form, write a loop that divides the entered decimal value by a power of 2^n, where n represents the binary digit power.

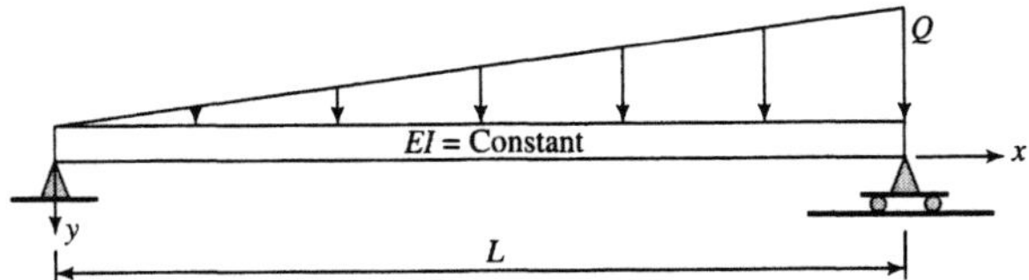

FIGURE 6.7 Linear elastic beam with linear loading.

Take the remainder of this division (i.e., the modulo operator `%`) and continue the division process with the remainder on each pass. If the division yields 1, then that binary digit will be 1.

Problem 6.6 (Intermediate): Develop an algorithm and write a computer program that will convert a binary number to its decimal equivalent.

Problem 6.7 (Intermediate): Figure 6.7 shows a linear elastic beam carrying a triangular loading. The deflection of a beam with constant cross-section inertia (I) and modulus of elasticity (E) is given by the Fourier series

$$y(x) = \left[\frac{2QL^4}{\pi^5 EI}\right] \sum_{n=1}^{\infty} \left[\frac{(-1)^{n+1}}{n^5}\right] \cdot \sin\left(\frac{n\pi x}{L}\right) \tag{6.3}$$

where Q is the distributed loading (i.e., with units force/length) applied to the right-hand side of the beam.

The bending moment is given by

$$M(x) = EI \cdot \frac{d^2 y(x)}{dx^2} \tag{6.4}$$

Write a C program to evaluate the deflection and bending moment along the beam at spacing intervals of $L/10$. Include a test for terminating the series summation when a given level of accuracy is obtained.

7

FUNCTIONS I

7.1 INTRODUCTION

This chapter examines the central role played by functions in the design and implementation of C programs.

We begin with a little background. Three or four decades ago when high-level programming languages were being developed for this first time, researchers recognized the need for a facility that would enable the creation of building block hierarchies in the structure of computer programs, and for the efficient development and computation of repetitive tasks, possibly at several different locations in a computer program. Program language developers envisioned that a programmer would write a block of code for the solution to a specific task just once and then allow the program to call the block of code whenever it was needed [7]. In the C programming language, this facility is the function construct [1]. (In the FORTRAN and Pascal programming languages, this facility is called subroutines and procedures, respectively.)

So what exactly is a function? In mathematics, a function is a well-defined concept. If the set of all real numbers is denoted $\mathbb{R}^1$, then $g(x)$ is a function from $\mathbb{R}^1$ into $\mathbb{R}^1$ if all two ordered pairs (x, y) are unique. The left-hand schematic in

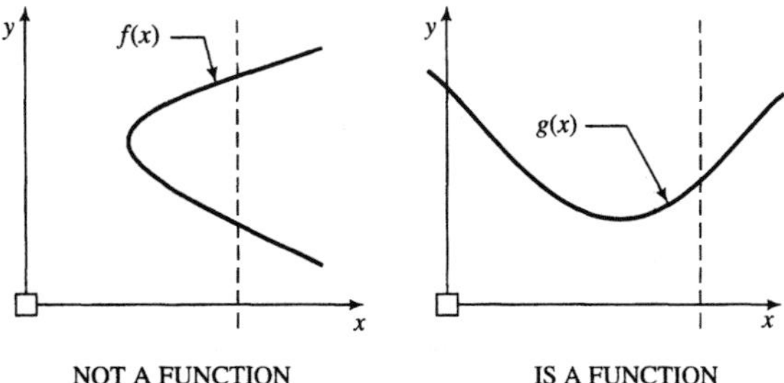

FIGURE 7.1 What is a function?

Figure 7.1 shows that $f(x)$ is not a function because there exists values of x with ordered pairs $[x, f(x)]$ that are multivalued. However, the mapping $y = g(x)$ is a function because it returns a unique of y for each argument x. We often define functions in engineering applications to simplify notation, and we can use this ability in C in a similar way. For example, it is clearer to define a function as

$$f(x) = x^2 + 2x \tag{7.1}$$

and refer to it as $y = f(x)$ than to always write $y = x^2 + 2x$.

Functions in the C programming language share many of the same attributes as functions in mathematics, namely:

1. *Name:* All C functions will have a name.
2. *Argument List:* Most functions in C will pass information from the calling function via an argument list. Occasionally, we encounter functions that have empty (void) argument lists.
3. *Return Value:* Most C functions return information to the calling function via the return value. A few functions do not return a data type at all (void return type).

The three operations that can be applied to the name of a function are as follows:

1. Call the function by appending to its name brackets, enclosing a list of argument expressions separated by commas.
2. Use the function name as a parameter argument to another function—in this case, a pointer to a function is passed.
3. Assign the function to a variable of the appropriate pointer type.

Operational items 2 and 3 involve advanced features of C and are not covered in this tutorial.

7.1.1 Library and User-Defined Functions

Functions in C are either library or user-defined functions. Library functions are simply groups of related C functions collected into a single file archive; they fill out the language and give it most of its functionality. These archives are (most often) written by computer vendors and are automatically bundled with the compiler before it is shipped. For example, in this text we make extensive use of the standard library and the math library.

User-defined functions are the ones we write ourselves, and we get to the details of doing this in a moment. Most user-defined functions are the result of the design phase of software development and are written to fulfill a specific purpose in a programming project. Although most user-defined functions do not (initially) constitute a library, they can be grouped into a library if desired. Indeed, it does not hurt to keep in mind that functions we define might eventually be used in a library (this is certainly a noble goal when writing functions).

7.2 FUNCTIONS REQUIRED IN A C PROGRAM

In the development of C programs for engineering applications, the "design phase" is perhaps the most important component of the software development process. The program design includes the identification of key operations in the problem-solving process and the mapping of these operations to specific C functions. The C functions should be organized into a hierarchy that solves the problem at hand (the top priority) and makes the solution procedure seem as simple as possible.

All C programs must have the function called `main()` because this is where the program's execution will begin. The function `main()` may call other user-defined and library functions, which may in turn call functions themselves. Library functions should be used when it is clear that they will reduce the complexity and time of program development. The trade-off in using library versus user-defined functions lies in a C program's functionality. Many C programs will not have the required problem-solving capacity without a significant amount of user-defined code. A couple of iterations of development may be needed to find the right balance between library and user-defined code. You should view the extra time needed to organize the code as a good long-term investment. The benefits will be simplified maintenance of the program throughout its lifetime and enhanced reuse of the software at a later date.

7.3 WRITING USER-DEFINED FUNCTIONS

7.3.1 Function Declarations

The C programming languge requires that C functions be declared before they are called. Function declarations (or prototypes) take the form

```
returnType FunctionName ( zero or more argument declarations );
```

and tell the compiler the number and type of arguments that will be passed to a function, and the type of value returned from the function. The script of code

```
void  createStack( int iSize );
float complexMagnitude( float fRe, float fIm );
void  matrixPrint( char *, double **, int , int );
```

shows an ensemble of function declarations for an ANSI compliant compiler. Look at these declarations in detail. The name of the first function is `menuPrint`. The term `void` before the function name indicates that `menuPrint` will not return a value (by default, functions are assumed to return an integer). Use of the term `void` between brackets following the function name (i.e., `( void )`) tells the ANSI compiler that `menuPrint` will have an empty argument list. The function `createStack` has one integer argument and returns nothing. The function `complexMagnitude` has two arguments of type float and returns an object of type float. The declaration for `matrixPrint` uses concepts we cover in Chapters 8 and 9. The function has four arguments: a character pointer, a pointer to a pointer of type double, and two integers. `matrixPrint` does not return a data object.

Although the use of identifiers, such as `iSize`, `fRe`, and `fIm`, in function declarations enhances readability of the program source code, this information is not used by a compiler. We could have simply written

```
void  createStack( int );
float complexMagnitude( float , float );
```

The compiler only needs to know the data type being passed as a function argument.

C compilers will assume that all functions return an integer, unless explicitly stated otherwise. However, for clarity of programming, we always explicitly state the return type from functions. Once a function declaration is in place, the compiler can insert the appropriate code needed to link in the complete details of the compiled function later (see Figure 11.1). A compiler does not need to know what a function does (or how it does it), it only needs the function interface.

The compiler handles the details of a function call using information that has been provided. Suppose, for example, the aforementioned function declarations are located in a header file or at the beginning of a function block. The compiler will know the name of each function, the number and type of its arguments, and the return type. When a function call is actually made later in the program, the compiler checks that you have provided the correct number and type of arguments, and that the return type is used in a manner consistent with its declaration. Implicit type conversions are performed (as required) so that programmers are not overburdened with unnecessary details (if you specify a `float` argument but actually call the function with an `integer`, it only makes sense to convert the `int` to `float`). At this point, the compiler is ready to generate code for the function call.

It is also important to realize that the operational details of the functions (i.e., the implementation) need not be known to call them. In fact, we soon see that function definitions and function declarations are often located in different files that are compiled separately. If the functions are part of a library (e.g., the math or standard library), then we may not know the definitions of the functions. All that is required is a declaration and sufficient knowledge of the function's operation (included in some type of documentation). Compiler vendors provide a header file with declarations, constants, and so on, and a compiled object file for the library that we can link into our programs.

Remark 7.1

We conform to ANSI C guidelines and declare all functions before their use, and specify the type of all arguments and the function return type. Previous versions (old style) of C had more leeway in argument and return type definition. For example, the aforementioned function declarations in the classic K&R style of C would be

```
void  menuPrint( );
void  createStack( );
float complexMagnitude( );
void  matrixPrint( );
```

Old style function declarations contain a function name and return type. However, information on the function arguments is not provided. This style of programming was specifically changed in ANSI C since it was a common source of errors.

7.3.2 Filling in User-Defined Functions

When we write our programs, we fill in the implementation details of our functions in a formal definition. The structure of a function is

```
returnType
functionName ( list of argument declarations ) <== function header
{
                                      <== beginning of function body

   body of function;

}                                     <== end of function body
```

Every function has a `header` and a `body`. Function headers consist of the data type returned by the function (the default is `int`), a unique function name that (hopefully) represents what the function does, and a list of zero or more function arguments. The details of the function header should be in direct correspondence with the function *declaration.* Normally terms will match exactly, although the parameter names can be different. In fact, many programmers copy it over directly to avoid typographic errors. The body of a function contains an opening brace, declarations (if any), C statements (possibly other function calls), and a closing brace signifying the end of the function.

Example. The complete source code for the `complexMagnitude()` function declared previously is

```
/*
 * ======================================================================
 * complexMagnitude() : return magnitude of complex number represented by
 * the components in the argument list (i.e., (fRe,fIm))
 *
 * Input  : float fRe  -- Real component of complex number.
 *          float fIm  -- Imaginary component of complex number.
 * Output : float fMag -- Magnitude of complex number.
 *
 * Note : use of sqrt() implies that #include <math.h> precede this code.
 * ======================================================================
 */

float
complexMagnitude( float fRe, float fIm )

float fMag;

      fMag = sqrt( fRe*fRe + fIm*fIm );

      return (fMag);

}
```

As suggested by the function name, `complexMagnitude()` computes the magnitude of the complex number represented by the real and imaginary components passed to it as arguments. You should observe the one-to-one match in the details of the function declaration and function header. `fMag` is a local variable known only to the block of code in which it is defined. When the function returns to the calling routine, the value of `fMag` is lost.

7.4 CASE STUDY PROGRAM: QUADRATIC EQUATION SOLVER

In this section, we demonstrate the process of writing user-defined functions by working step by step through the development of a computer program that will interactively prompt a user for a quadratic equation, and then compute and print its roots.

Problem Statement

It is well known that the roots of a quadratic equation are given by solutions to

$$p(x) = ax^2 + bx + c = 0 \tag{7.2}$$

A number of solution cases exist. For example, when both $a = 0$ and $b = 0$, we consider the equation to be `extremely degenerate` and leave it at that. When $a = 0$ and $b \neq 0$, we consider the case `degenerate`; in this situation, the equations reduce to $p(x) = bx + c = 0$, which has one root. Otherwise, we have

$$\text{Roots} = \left[\frac{-b \pm \sqrt{b^2 - 4ac}}{2a}\right] \tag{7.3}$$

The term $b^2 - 4ac$ is known as the discriminant of the quadratic equation.

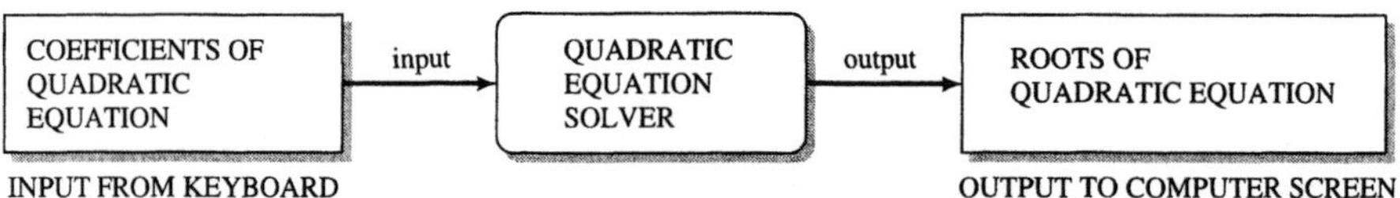

FIGURE 7.2 Quadratic equation solution procedure.

Figure 7.2 is a high-level schematic of the problem-solving procedure that will be followed. The program will begin its execution by prompting a user for the equation coefficients a, b, and c. After the coefficients have been specified at the keyboard and read by the computer program, the roots of the quadratic equation will be computed and printed to the computer screen along with an appropriate message for the type of solution. Appropriate messages are `Extremely degenerate`, `Degenerate`, `Two real roots`, and `Two complex roots`. For example, if 1, 2, and 3 are real for a, b, and c, the computer program will print

$$\text{Two complex roots} \quad : \quad \text{Root 1} = -1.0000 + 1.414214\,i \tag{7.4}$$

$$: \quad \text{Root 2} = -1.0000 - 1.414214\,i \tag{7.5}$$

Pseudocode for Quadratic Equation Solver

Because this problem contains numerous details and types of solution, we refine our pseudocode over several iterations of development.

Iteration 1: A first-cut pseudocode version for this task might look similar to the following:

```
announce the quadratic equation solving program
request a, b, and c from the user

calculate the discriminant
if the discriminant is >= 0 then the roots are real:
   compute and print real roots x1 and x2
```

```
else the roots are complex
   the real part is -b/2a
   the imaginary part is the square root of (the negative of the
                                                 discriminant) / 2a

print the results
```

Here we indent certain statements to show the structure of the eventual program. Once preliminary ideas are written this way, the steps can be refined until the pseudocode is close to the target language. A second structured technique is to take each statement and generate a whole block of pseudocode statements for each.

Iteration 2: Using successive refinement, we can develop this pseudocode further into

```
print "quadratic equation solving program"
print "Enter the coefficients a, b, and c"
read the coefficients

discriminant = b^2 - 4ac
if the discriminant is > 0 then equation has real roots x1, x2.
   x1 = -b/2a - sqrt( discriminant) / 2a
   x2 = -b/2a + sqrt( discriminant) / 2a
else, the discriminant is < 0, and roots are complex numbers
   (re, im) with
   re = -b/2a
   im = sqrt( - discriminant) / 2a
   print complex roots
```

Iteration 3: Iteration 2 still does not look like C code, so at least one more stage of development is desirable

```
define variables for a, b, c, discriminant
print "quadratic equation solving program"
print "Enter the coefficients a, b, and c"

scanf for a,b,c
if( a equal to zero )
    compute roots to determinate equations
    exit

discriminant = b^2 - 4ac
if (discriminant > 0.0)  /* the roots are real */
   root1 = -b/2a - sqrt( discriminant )/2a
   root2 = -b/2a + sqrt( discriminant )/2a
   print "The first root is " root1
   print "The second root is " root2
```

```
else  /* the roots are complex */
   re = -b/2a
   im = sqrt( -discriminant )/2a
   print "The first  complex root is", re, im
   print "The second complex root is", re, -im
```

This version of pseudocode is close to C, and we are ready to begin designing and writing the C code for our quadratic equation solver.

Program Modules for Quadratic Equation Solver

A key issue in the design of almost every C program is the problem of finding a good balance in the use of user-defined functions and library functions. The advantage of user-defined functions is that they enable the development of customized problem-solving procedures. However, writing and testing user-defined code can be a very time-consuming process. The benefit of library functions is that they enable reuse of code that has already been written and thoroughly tested. Judicious use of library functions can result in significant reductions in the time and effort needed to write and test C programs. Obtaining a good balance in the use of user-defined code and library functions requires experience and, to some extent, is an art. This means that novice C programmers must place a priority on becoming familiar with the availability and purposes of library functions.

With these points in mind, Table 7.1 shows the mapping "tasks to C functions" that are implemented in Program 7.1. The heart of our quadratic equation solution procedure is contained in three user-defined functions: `main()`, `quadratic()`, and `discriminant()`. The standard library functions `printf()` and `scanf()` handle formatted output and input, respectively (there is no point in reinventing the wheel here). Evaluation of Equation 7.3 requires a square root calculation, and this is handled by the function `sqrt()` located in the math library.

TABLE 7.1 Function Modules for Quadratic Equation Solver

Task	* *User-Defined Functions*	*Standard Library*	*Math Library*
Read coefficients	* `main()`		
Solve quadratic equation	* `quadratic()`		
Compute discriminant	* `discriminant()`		
	*		
Standard output to screen	*	`printf()`	
Standard input from keyboard	*	`scanf()`	
Square root computation	*		`sqrt()`

PROGRAM 7.1: COMPUTE ROOTS OF QUADRATIC EQUATION

```
/*
 * ===========================================================================
 * Solve Quadratic Equations : Coefficients are read in from keyboard
 *                           : Roots of Quadratic are printed to screen.
 *
 * Note : Naive implementation of quadratic equation solver. This algorithm
 *        does not take into account possible loss of accuracy when two
 *        floating point numbers of almost equal size are subtracted.
 * ===========================================================================
 */

#include <stdio.h>   /* Standard Input/Output function declarations */
#include <math.h>    /* Math functions, such as sqrt(x).            */

/* Function Declarations */

float discriminant( float , float , float );
void quadratic ( float , float , float );

/* Main Program for Quadratic Equation Solver */

int main( void ) {
float   fA, fB, fC;          /* Coefficients for Quadratic Equation   */

   /* [a] : Print Welcome Message */

   printf("Welcome to the Quadratic Equation Solver (Version 1)\n");
   printf("===================================================\n");

   /* [b] : Prompt User for Coefficients of Quadratic Equation */

   printf("Please enter coefficients for equation a.x^2 + b.x + c\n");
   printf("Enter coefficient a : ");
   scanf("%f%*c", &fA);
   printf("Enter coefficient b : ");
   scanf("%f%*c", &fB);
   printf("Enter coefficient c : ");
   scanf("%f%*c", &fC);

   /* [c] : Print Quadratic Equation to Screen */

   printf("Equation you have entered is : %g.x^2 + %g.x + %g\n", fA, fB, fC);
```

```
   /* [d] : Compute Roots of Quadratic Equation */

   quadratic ( fA, fB, fC );
   return (0);
}

/*
 * ==============================================================
 * quadratic() : Compute roots to Quadratic Equations
 *
 * Input  : float fA -- Coefficient "fA" in quadratic equation
 *          float fB -- Coefficient "fB" in quadratic equation
 *          float fC -- Coefficient "fC" in quadratic equation
 * Output : void
 * ==============================================================
 */

void quadratic ( float fA, float fB, float fC ) {
float fRoot1, fRoot2;       /* Real roots 1 and 2 of quadratic equation */
float  fDiscriminant;       /* Discriminant of quadratic                */

   /* [a] : Compute Roots of simplified equations : fA equals zero */

   if(fA == 0 && fB == 0) {
      printf("Cannot solve Extremely degenerate equation " );
      printf("%14.8g = 0.0\n", fC );
      exit (1);
   }

   if(fA == 0 && fB != 0) {
      fRoot1 = - fC/fB;
      printf("Degenerate Root : Root = %14.8g\n", fRoot1 );
      exit (1);
   }

   /* [b] : Compute Roots of Quadratic Equation : fA not equal to zero */

   fDiscriminant = discriminant( fA, fB, fC );
   if(fDiscriminant >= 0) { /* Case for Two Real Roots */

      fRoot1 = -fB/2.0/fA - sqrt( fDiscriminant )/2.0/fA;
      fRoot2 = -fB/2.0/fA + sqrt( fDiscriminant )/2.0/fA;

      printf("Two real Roots : Root1 = %14.8g\n", fRoot1 );
      printf("               : Root2 = %14.8g\n", fRoot2 );
   } else {                   /* Case for Complex Roots */
```

```
      printf("Two complex roots : Root1 = %14.8g + %14.8g i\n", -fB/2.0/fA,
              sqrt( -fDiscriminant )/2.0/fA);
      printf("                  : Root2 = %14.8g + %14.8g i\n", -fB/2.0/fA,
             -sqrt( -fDiscriminant )/2.0/fA);
   }
}

/*
 * ===========================================================
 * discriminant() : Compute discriminant of quadratic equation
 *
 * Input  : float fA -- Coefficient "fA" in quadratic equation
 *          float fB -- Coefficient "fB" in quadratic equation
 *          float fC -- Coefficient "fC" in quadratic equation
 * Output : float    -- Numerical value of discriminant.
 * ===========================================================
 */

float discriminant( float fA, float fB, float fC ) {
float fDiscriminant;

     fDiscriminant = fB*fB - 4.0*fA*fC;
     return(fDiscriminant);
}
```

Compiling and Running the Program

Program 7.1 is compiled into an executable program called `QUADRATIC` with the command

```
gcc quadratic.c -o QUADRATIC -lm
```

The command option `-lm` tells the compiler to link Program 7.1 with the math library. Now that the program is compiled, we can run and test it to make sure it performs as expected. The following scripts show interactive input and generated output for test cases covering distinct real roots and complex roots:

Case 1. Two real roots: `fA = 1`, `fB = 2`, `fC = 1`.

```
prompt >> QUADRATIC
Welcome to the Quadratic Equation Solver (Version 1)
====================================================

Please enter coefficients for equation a.x^2 + b.x + c
Enter coefficient a : 1.0
```

```
Enter coefficient b : 2.0
Enter coefficient c : 1.0
Equation you have entered is : 1.x^2 + 2.x + 1
Two real roots : Root1 =              -1
               : Root2 =              -1
prompt >>
```

Case 2. Two complex roots: `fA = 1`, `fB = 1`, `fC = 1`.

```
prompt >> QUADRATIC
Welcome to the Quadratic Equation Solver (Version 1)
====================================================

Please enter coefficients for equation a.x^2 + b.x + c
Enter coefficient a : 1.0
Enter coefficient b : 1.0
Enter coefficient c : 1.0
Equation you have entered is : 1.x^2 + 1.x + 1
Two complex roots : Root1 =           -0.5 +    0.8660254 i
                  : Root2 =           -0.5 +   -0.8660254 i
prompt >>
```

These results can be verified with an easy hand calculation.

Program Architecture

Figure 7.3 is a schematic of the header files, and user-defined and library functions that make up Program 7.1. Once again the header files `stdio.h` and `math.h` act as interfaces between the user-defined code and compiled functions in the standard library and the math library. The dashed-line boxes and arrows indicate that the user-defined source code is partitioned into three functions, and that the program control will pass from `main()` to `quadratic()`, onto `discriminant()`, and back to `main()`. The solid two-way arrows indicate switching of the program control from the user-defined code to/from the standard library functions `printf()`, `scanf()`, and `exit()`, and the math library function `sqrt()`. The library function `exit()` causes a controlled termination of the program execution.

Function Declarations

All that a compiler needs to check that a function is being called (or used) correctly is its declaration. The statements

```
float discriminant( float , float , float );
void  quadratic ( float , float , float );
```

are function declarations for `discriminant` and `quadratic`. The first declaration tells the compiler that a function named `discriminant` has three floating point

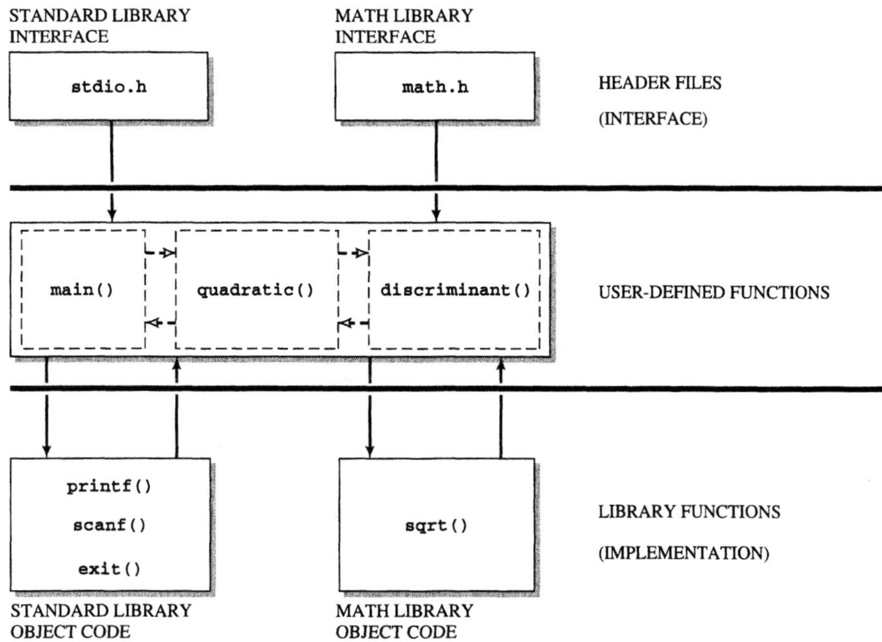

FIGURE 7.3 Architecture of Program 7.1.

number arguments and will return an object of type float. The second declaration tells the compiler about a function called `quadratic` having three arguments of type float. The keyword `void` indicates that `quadratic` does not have a return value.

You should observe that in Program 7.1, functions `quadratic()` and `discriminant()` are both called before the source code details are given.

Function Calls

A function is used (or called) by appending to its name a list of arguments enclosed within parentheses. As a general rule of thumb, a function having a specific return value may be positioned anywhere in source code where that data type will work. With the function declaration for `discriminant()` in place at the top of Program 7.1, for example, we can make the function call

```
fDiscriminant = discriminant( fA, fB, fC );
```

even before the source code details of `discriminant()` appear. A compiler will check that the function call has the correct number and type of function arguments and that the `discriminant()` return value is being used in a manner consistent with the remainder of the statement in which the function call appears. In this particular case, both the left- and right-hand sides of the assignment statement are of type float.

Function calls may be embedded inside mathematical expressions in much the same way mathematical expressions are written on paper. The statement

```
fRoot1 = -fB/2.0/fA - sqrt( fDiscriminant )/2.0/fA;
```

is an arithmetic expression for variable `fRoot1`. At an intermediate stage of the expression's evaluation, the program control will be directed to the math library function `sqrt()` for calculation of the square root of `fDiscriminant`. The double value returned by `sqrt()` is used just as if it were a variable of the same data type. Of course, we could have also written the code as

```
fSqrt  = sqrt( fDiscriminant );
fRoot1 = -fB/2.0/fA - fSqrt/2.0/fA;
```

The two-line block of code is less efficient than its one-line counterpart because the `double` value is first assigned directly to `fSqrt`, and then in the next statement, `fSqrt` is used in the calculation of `fRoot1`.

Type Conversion of Function Arguments

Function declarations in ANSI C enable automatic type conversion of function argument types, meaning that during a function call, all the arguments to that function will be coerced to the declared type. For example, Program 7.1 calls the math library function `sqrt()`. The function declaration for `sqrt()` is

```
double sqrt ( double );
```

Yet when the function is called, as in

```
fRoot1 = -fB/2.0/fA - sqrt( fDiscriminant )/2.0/fA;
```

the argument to `sqrt()` is of type float (i.e., only four bytes). ANSI C compilers take care of the incompatibility by generating low-level code that will automatically convert `fDiscriminant` to type double before making the function call.

It is important to note at this point that automatic type conversion of function argument types is not supported by many of the early (non-ANSI compliant) C compilers. The problem of making sure function argument types match is left entirely to the programmer. The problem with this program development strategy is that errors do not show up until run-time when a program either crashes because it cannot access a variable, or perhaps it generates incorrect results because the value of variables was corrupted during a function call. Tracking down run-time errors of this type can be extremely difficult.

Return Statements

The `return` statement terminates execution of a function and passes control back to the calling environment. For example, the last statement in function `main()` is

```
return (0);
```

indicating a successful completion of the program execution. In some implementations of ANSI C compliant programs, you will see

```
return EXIT_SUCCESS;
```

When a return statement contains an expression the expression will be evaluated first, and then converted to the return type of the function (if necessary) and passed back to the calling environment. For example, function `discriminant` returns a float equal to the result of

```
fDiscriminant = fB*fB - 4.0*fA*fC;
return(fDiscriminant);
```

The same functionality can be achieved by simply writing

```
return(fB*fB - 4.0*fA*fC);
```

Flushing Standard Output

The `printf()` function often stores characters in a buffer and will flush output to the screen only when an end of line is encountered. If you are writing a program that will prompt a user for input on the same line as the prompt, sometimes the prompt will not show on the screen. This problem can be fixed by explicitly flushing the output to the screen with the function call `fflush(stdout)`:

```
printf("Enter coefficient a : ");
fflush(stdout);
```

Reading Standard Input

The function `scanf()` reads line-buffered input from the keyboard and stores it in a prespecified location. Line buffered means that a whole line of input is read in until the new line character is received. Each input line is entered into an input buffer as you type, and when you hit ⟨Enter⟩, `scanf()` actually processes it. The block of statements

```
float fA, fB, fC;

...... details omitted ......

printf("Enter coefficient a : ");
scanf("%f%*c", &fA);
```

in Program 7.1 prompts the user for quadratic equation coefficient `a` (to be stored in variable `fA`) and waits for input to be supplied at the keyboard.

Like `printf()`, the first argument to `scanf()` is a format string containing the specifications for one or more fields of expected input. The first part of the specification, `%f`, tells `scanf()` to expect input in the form of a floating point value, the contents of which will be stored at the memory location `&fA`. The `&` preceding the variable name evaluates to the address of `fA`, rather than the value of `fA`. The second part of the format specification, `%*c`, means one or more characters, and it ensures that the carriage return character will be read and discarded. We present a detailed explanation as to why this feature is needed in Chapter 12.

7.5 CALL-BY-VALUE MECHANISM FOR FUNCTION CALLS

The C programming language passes arguments to functions "by value," meaning that when a constant, variable, or arithmetic expression is explicitly listed as an argument in a function call, its value will be evaluated and passed to the function. Unless special programming procedures are employed (and we describe them in Chapter 9), the function that is called will not have access to blocks of memory employed by the calling function.

Computer Program. We now demonstrate how the "call-by-value" mechanism works in practice by working step by step through an example.

Program 7.2 is an assembly of two functions, `main()` and `tryChange()`, located within a single file. It demonstrates, via a devil's advocate approach, how the call-by-value mechanism works.

PROGRAM 7.2: DEMONSTRATE CALL-BY-VALUE MECHANISM

```
/*
 * ========================================
 * Demonstrate "call-by-value" mechanism.
 * ========================================
 */

#include <stdio.h>

int main( void ) {
int iVal = 4, iReturnVal;
int tryChange(int iVal);          /* function declaration */

   /* [a] : Pass value of iVal to tryChange() */

   printf("In main() : Passing value of iVal to \"tryChange\"\n" );
```

```
   iReturnVal = tryChange( iVal );
   printf("In main() : Now iVal        = %i\n", iVal );
   printf("                 iReturnVal = %i\n", iReturnVal );
}

/*
 * ===========================================================
 * tryChange() : Test program for changing parameters.
 *
 * Input  : int iPassed -- integer passed to tryChange();
 * Output : int iPassed -- modified value of iPassed.
 * ===========================================================
 */

int tryChange(int iPassed ) {
enum{ AddVal = 103 };

   /* [a] : Change a parameter that was passed by value */

   printf("In tryChange() : iPassed = %i\n", iPassed);
   printf("In tryChange() : Adding %i to iPassed...\n", AddVal );
   iPassed += AddVal;
   printf("In tryChange() : Now iPassed = %i\n", iPassed);

   return iPassed;
}
```

The output generated by Program 7.2 is

```
In main() : Passing value of iVal to "tryChange"
In tryChange() : iPassed = 4
In tryChange() : Adding 103 to iPassed...
In tryChange() : Now iPassed = 107
In main() : Now iVal       = 4
                iReturnVal = 107
```

The program execution begins with `main()` calling `tryChange()` with one argument—then we try, from `tryChange()`, to change the value of the argument declared in `main()`. Our experiment fails because the copy of the variable is changed and not the original variable declared in `main()`!

Figures 7.4a through 7.4d are schematics of contents in the computer stack at critical stages of execution for Program 7.2. We have only labeled memory locations for variable declarations in `main()` and `tryChange()`. Although we normally think

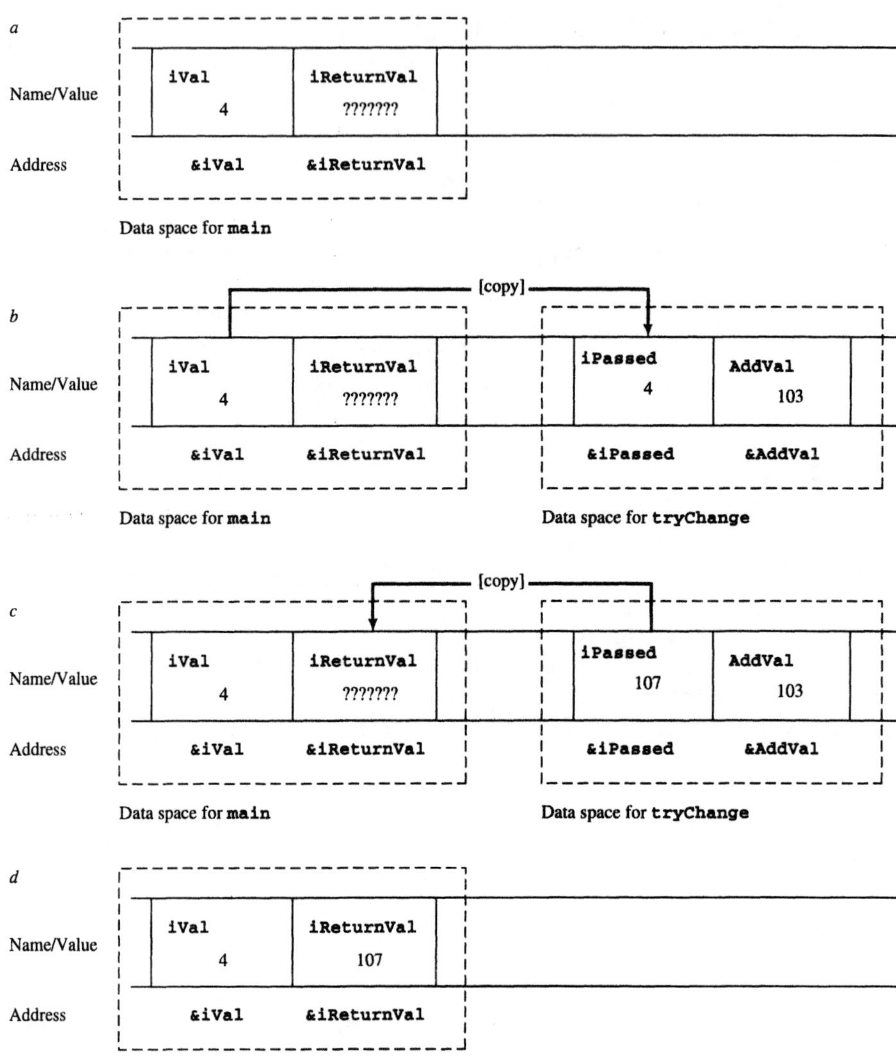

FIGURE 7.4 Schematics of memory layout in Program 7.2: (a) layout of memory before function call; (b) at beginning of function call; (c) at end of function call; and (d) after function call.

of a computer stack as a data structure that grows and contracts in the vertical direction, we have drawn it horizontally, left to right, simply because it is easier to pack four schematics onto one page. We now note:

1. Figure 7.4a shows the layout of memory when Program 7.2 has entered `main()` but before `tryChange()` is called. Variable `iVal` has the value `4`. Memory for `iReturnVal` is allocated, but its value remains uninitialized.

2. Two important uses of the computer stack are storage of function arguments and storage of temporary allocation of memory for local variables that are needed while a function executes. With this in mind, Figure 7.4b shows the layout of memory after Program 7.2 has entered `tryChange()` and memory for the local variable `AddVal` is on the computer stack. We use two dashed boxes to signify that the data space for `main()` on the computer stack is in a separate location than the data space for `tryChange()`. The arrow → signifies that when function `tryChange()` is called with `iVal` as an argument, the value of `iVal` (i.e., `4`) is copied onto the storage location for `iPassed`.
3. When the program execution jumps to `tryChange()`, function arguments and local variables will be accessed from the data space for `tryChange()`. Note that the choice of variable names in `tryChange()` has no bearing on the behavior of the program. For instance, we could have defined `tryChange()`

```
int tryChange( int iVal ) {
enum{ AddVal = 103 };

     .... details of tryChange removed ....

     return iVal;
}
```

   with same variable name as in `main()`, and the program output would be exactly as shown here.
4. Figures 7.4c shows the layout of memory after the arithmetic operation

```
iPassed += AddVal;
```

   and at the point where program control is about to return to `main()`. As reflected in the program output, `iPassed` now takes the value `107`. The left-to-right arrow ← signifies that the return value from `tryChange()` is assigned to `iReturnVal` in `main()`.
5. Figure 7.4d shows the layout of memory after the program execution has returned to `main()`. The key point to note is that the data space for `try-Change()` is no longer available.

7.6 SCOPE AND STORAGE OF VARIABLES AND FUNCTIONS

In this section we look at those features of C that may be used to control the scope and storage of variables and functions.

We begin with a few basic concepts. Declarations for variables and functions introduce the name and type of a variable or function to a program. The scope of a variable or function is the range over which it is defined. The scope of a variable or function is often tied to the file structure of a computer program.

By default, the arguments to a function and variables defined within a function are local to the function. Because no other functions can have access to them, we say that their scope is local (or internal). These variables and arguments are also called automatic because they only exist and are valid from the point of declaration to the end of the enclosing function (see following example). This is the safest and best way to have it. We say that data types and functions are external when they can be accessed by other functions. In the following programs, we see that the scope of an external variable exists from the point of its declaration to the end of the file in which it is defined.

In contrast to variables that are internal to a particular function, memory for external variables is not automatically allocated on the stack; their values persist. It is also important to note that functions cannot be internal (i.e., we cannot define a function inside of a function).

7.6.1 Scope of Variables in a One-File C Program

Program 7.3 is a small C program that contains three functions that are all located within a single file.

PROGRAM 7.3: SCOPE OF VARIABLES IN A ONE-FILE PROGRAM

```
/*
 * ===============================================================
 * scope1.c: Demonstrate scope of variables in a 1 file C program.
 * ===============================================================
 */

#include <stdio.h>

enum {freezing = 32};
float fTemperature = freezing;   /* Global float variable, which
                                    is visible throughout rest
                                    of this file, and also
                                    visible to other files */

int main( void ) {
void testFunction1();
void testFunction2();

   printf("In main() : fTemperature = %f\n", fTemperature);
   testFunction1();
   testFunction2();
   printf("In main() : fTemperature = %f\n", fTemperature);
}
```

```
/*
 * ======================
 * Test functions 1 and 2
 * ======================
 */

int iValue1 = 5;

void testFunction1() {
int iValue2 = 2;

   printf("In testFunction1() : iValue1      = %d\n", iValue1);
   printf("In testFunction1() : iValue2      = %d\n", iValue2);

   /* Increment fTemperature by 32 */

   fTemperature += 32.0;
}

void testFunction2() {
int iValue1 = 2;

   printf("In testFunction2() : iValue1      = %d\n", iValue1);
}
```

The output generated by Program 7.3 is

```
In main() : fTemperature = 32.000000
In testFunction1() : iValue1      = 5
In testFunction1() : iValue2      = 2
In testFunction2() : iValue1      = 2
In main() : fTemperature = 64.000000
```

Points to note are as follows:

1. Variables declared within the body of a function are said to be `local`—they come into existence when the function is entered, and they are lost when the function is exited. Variables of this type are `local` because they can be accessed only from within the defining function. In Program 7.3, for example, the scope of variable `iValue2` is restricted to the braces defining the body of `testFunction1()`.
2. Variables defined outside of a function block are effectively global. Global variables are defined in the current file from the point of declaration/definition to the end of the file and from any other file in the project. In Program 7.3,

the variables `fTemperature` and `iValue1` are global. `fTemperature` is known to all functions in the file. `iValue1` is declared between functions `main()` and `testFunction1()`; it is (semi) global in the sense that it is known only to functions `testFunction1()` and `testFunction2()`.

3. Programming with global variables is a good idea if you need to minimize the number of arguments to functions (as in FORTRAN common blocks). In general, however, the benefits of global variables are more than offset by the negative aspects of their use. More specifically, if many functions have access to a particular variable (or group of variables), then pinpointing the source of programming errors may become very time consuming. In our opinion, it is far better to keep variables local and accessible by a limited amount of code.
4. There are a few ways to override the global nature of variables defined outside of function blocks. In `testFunction2()`, the local `iValue1` overrides the global declaration appearing in the middle of the program: This is reflected by the printing of `iValue1 = 2`, instead of the global variable of the same name, which has the value `5`. A second way of overriding the global nature of variables is with the `static` storage specifier. This technique will be demonstrated in section 7.6.2.
5. The function declarations

```
void testFunction1();
void testFunction2();
```

in `main()` tell the compiler to expect two functions called `testFunction1()` and `testFunction2()`, both of whom will return data type `void`. Omitting these declarations leads to an error. First, the compiler thinks that the functions will return an object of type `int`. Then when the details of the functions are actually compiled—in the lower half of Program 7.3—the function declarations appear with `void`. As a result, compilers will complain that the data types returned by the functions are incompatible.

7.6.2 Scope of Variables in a Two-File C Program

All C programs may be viewed as an assembly of external functions and variables, which may be referenced from locations outside the file in which they are defined. A reference to an identifier not declared in the same file is said to be `external` and `unresolved` at assembly time. This attribute of functions and variables is a key feature promoting the development of modular programs.

Program 7.4 contains the same three functions as Program 7.3 but now the functions are located in two files. Program 7.4 also demonstrates use of the keyword `static` to restrict the scope of variables to a single file and to retain the value of variables between function calls.

PROGRAM 7.4: SCOPE OF VARIABLES IN A TWO-FILE PROGRAM

```
/*
 * ==============================================================
 * File1 : Demonstrate scope of variables and functions in a two
 *         file C program.
 * ==============================================================
 */

#include <stdio.h>

/* Declarations for (external) Functions */

void testFunction1();
void testFunction2();

/* Declarations for Global and File-level Variables */

enum {freezing = 32};
float fTemperature = freezing;  /* Global float variable, which is
                                   visible throughout rest of this
                                   file, and also visible to other
                                   files. */
static int iValue1 = 10;        /* Scope of iValue1 restricted to
                                   this file. */

int main( void ) {
int iCount;

   /* [a] : Increment Variables in External File */

   printf("In main() : iValue1      = %d\n", iValue1 );
   printf("In main() : fTemperature = %f\n", fTemperature);
   testFunction1();
   printf("In main() : fTemperature = %f\n", fTemperature);

   /* [b] : Call testFunction2() three times */
   for(iCount = 1; iCount <= 3; iCount++ )
       testFunction2();

   printf("In main() : Finished calling testFunction2() three times\n");
   printf("In main() : fTemperature = %f\n", fTemperature);
}
```

```
void testFunction1() {

   printf("In testFunction1() located in file 1 : Value1 = %d\n", iValue1);
}
```

```
/*
 * ===================================================================
 * File2 : Demonstrate Scope of Variables and Functions in a two file
 *         C program. This file contains test function 2 and "static"
 *         test function 1.
 * ===================================================================
 */

#include <stdio.h>

float fTemperature;
static int iValue1 = 5;

static void testFunction1() {

   printf("In testFunction1() located in file 2 : Value1 = %d\n", iValue1);
   fTemperature += 32.0;

}

void testFunction2() {
static enum { First, NotFirst } eCall = First;
static int iNoCalls = 1;

   if( First == eCall ) {
        printf("In testFunction2() : First Call !!\n" );
        testFunction1();
        eCall = NotFirst;
   } else {
        iNoCalls += 1;
        printf("In testFunction2() : No Calls = %d\n", iNoCalls );
   }
}
```

The output generated by Program 7.4 is

```
In main() : iValue1      = 10
In main() : fTemperature = 32.000000
In testFunction1() located in file 1 : Value1 = 10
In main() : fTemperature = 32.000000
In testFunction2() : First Call !!
In testFunction1() located in file 2 : Value1 = 5
In testFunction2() : No Calls = 2
In testFunction2() : No Calls = 3
In main() : Finished calling testFunction2() three times
In main() : fTemperature = 64.000000
```

Points to note are as follows:

1. The statement pair

```
enum {freezing = 32};
float fTemperature = freezing;
```

at the top of File 1 makes `fTemperature` global to all functions in File 1. The scope of `fTemperature` is extended to File 2 with the statement

```
float fTemperature;
```

at the top of File 2. A declaration is required at this point so that the compiler will be able to distinguish between local and externally defined variables.

2. In the development of modules of code, situations often arise where a variable (or function) needs to be accessed by many functions within a single module but should be hidden from other modules. The visibility of external variables and functions may be restricted by adding the storage class `static` to their declarations. Two key points that you should remember are

- Static functions will be known only to other functions in the same file. Functions cannot access static data or call static functions defined in another file. This is a form of encapsulation.
- Static variables are only visible within the current file from the point of definition to the end of the file.

We expand on the idea of encapsulation when we get to object-oriented programming with Java. For now we note that in File 2 of Program 7.4 the function `testFunction1()` is declared with the modifier `static`, is known only to other functions in File 2, and in particular is hidden from `main()` in File 1. Another function called `testFunction1()` is located in File 1. When Program 7.4 is run, two calls to `testFunction1()` occur—one from `main()`

and another from `testFunction2()`. Even though the function names are identical, the program is directed to different parts of the program, as controlled by the scope of functions.

3. By default, all variables defined inside a function have local scope with automatic storage. This means that their values are lost after the function call is complete. Suppose, however, that we want to have an internal variable retain its value between function calls. This could be useful, for instance, if we want to keep track of the number of times a function was called during the program execution.

   Fortunately, C provides a mechanism to change internal variables so that their value is maintained between function calls. If a variable declaration is preceded by the keyword `static`, then the variable is not allocated on the stack. Instead, it is stored with other persistent values throughout the program (like, external variables).

4. One useful application of static locals is in cases where we want to do something the first time a function is called and then respond differently on subsequent calls. In `testFunction2()`, variables `eCall` and `iNoCalls` are declared to be static. When `testFunction2()` is called for the first time, `eCall` equals `First`. After `testFunction1()` is called, `eCall` is set to `NotFirst`. All subsequent calls to `testFunction2()` simply increment `iNoCalls` by 1 and print a message.

5. Our current version of `testFunction2()` prints a message every time the function is called. How would you modify Program 7.4 so that only the total number of function calls is printed? One difficulty is that our current implementation keeps track of `iNoCalls` from inside `testFunction2()`. Since the scope of `iNoCalls` is local to `testFunction2()`, it cannot be accessed from outside the function. To solve this problem we need to keep the count code separate from the normal operation of `testFunction2()` and to put the print statement in another function, which may access `iNoCalls`. Here is a solution:

```
static int iNoCalls = 1;

void testFunction2() {
static enum { First, NotFirst } eCall = First;

   if( First == eCall ) {
       printf("In testFunction2() : First Call !!\n" );
       testFunction1();
       eCall = NotFirst;
   } else {
       iNoCalls += 1;
       printf("In testFunction2() : No Calls = %d\n",
              iNoCalls );
   }
}
```

```
void printTotal( void ) {
    printf("testFunction2() was called %i times.", iNoCalls);
}
```

By moving the definition for iNoCalls outside and above testFunction2(), and making it static, the scope of iNoCalls is still restricted to testFunction2() and printTotal(). This strategy of programming is useful for encapsulating functions that should be private and not visible to the rest of the program. Object-oriented techniques need this type of modifier so that certain functions will not be called outside of the designated file.

7.7 PACKAGING OF PROGRAM MODULES

In Program 7.4, communication of function and variable information between files is achieved with the use of declarations at the top of file1.c and file2.c. A much better (and simpler) approach to program development is to declare global variables and external functions in a single header file, and then ask the C preprocessor to include the declarations from the header file. This approach to program development is better because

1. It minimizes the possibility of programming inconsistencies. When global variables and function declarations are positioned at the top of files in large multifile programs, maintaining consistency across files requires a lot of attention to detail.
2. It promotes development of modular multifile programs where groups of related functions are placed within the same file, and compiled and tested separately. Indeed, it is often useful to think of header files acting as "public interfaces" to external code with the internal details of the corresponding source code remaining "private." A good example of this concept is the header file stdio.h and its role as an external interface to the standard C library. Most C programmers have little idea how I/O tasks are actually accomplished. All that programmers really need to know is how the library functions should be called and linked together to generate a working program.

Program 7.4 can be easily modified to incorporate the "header file concept." If we define the header file function.h

```
/*
 * ===========================================================
 * function.h : Declarations for global variables/functions
 *              in file1.c and file2.c.
 * ===========================================================
 */
```

```
void testFunction2();
float   fTemperature;
```

and modify the top of `file1.c` to

```
/*
 * =========================================================
 * file1.c : Demonstrate scope of variables and functions
 *           in a two file C Program.
 * =========================================================
 */

#include <stdio.h>      /* interface to standard library */
#include "function.h"  /* global variables/functions in */
                        /* file1.c and file2.c.          */

enum { freezing = 32 };
fTemperature = 32;

    ..... C code removed ....
}
```

and the top of `file2.c` to

```
/*
 * =========================================================
 * file2.c : Demonstrate scope of variables and functions
 *           in a two file C program.
 * =========================================================
 */

#include <stdio.h>      /* interface to standard library */
#include "function.h"  /* global variables/functions in */
                        /* file1.c and file2.c           */


static int iValue1 = 5;

    ..... C code removed ....
```

then the modified program architecture and pathway of compilation is as shown in Figure 7.5. Compiling Program 7.4 with a command such as

```
gcc file1.c file2.c -c -o TESTSCOPE
```

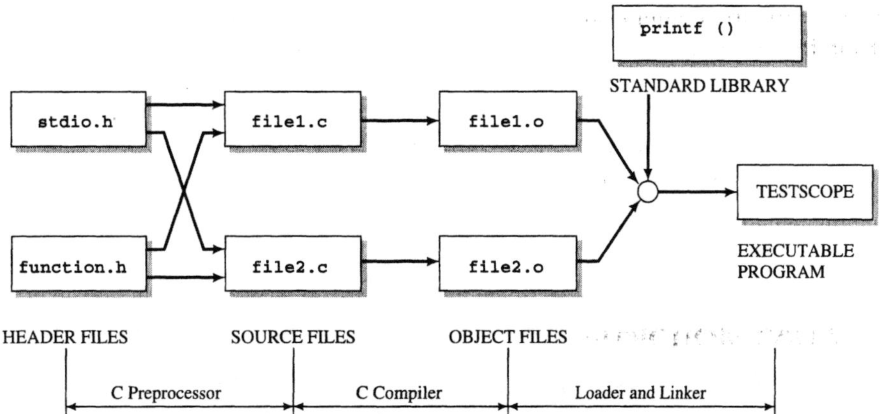

FIGURE 7.5 Pathway of compilation for Program 7.4.

will cause the C preprocessor to replace the lines

```
#include <stdio.h>      /* interface to standard library */
#include "function.h" /* global variables/functions in */
                        /* file1.c and file2.c           */
```

with the contents of `stdio.h` and `function.h`, respectively. The angled brackets (i.e., <>) in the first statement tell the C preprocessor to find `stdio.h` by systematically searching the directories listed in the shell variable `path` of the user's account. (As explained in Chapter 11, this list of directories will be operating system dependent.) The use of quotations (i.e., ". . .") in the second statement tells the C preprocessor to first look in the current working directory for the named file and, if required, search the directories listed in the user's path.

7.8 MATH LIBRARY FUNCTIONS

Table 3.1 contains a summary of the most commonly used math functions, and Appendix 2 contains a detailed description of the function prototypes for the math library. Most of the math library functions have one or two arguments of type `double` or `int` and return a numerical value of type `double`. For example, if `dX` is a variable of type `double`, then

```
cos( dX )
```

returns the cosine of `dX` (`dX` must be in radians) as a double. Automatic type conversion is done on all math library function arguments (i.e., `int` to `double`), if necessary, after the `math.h header` file is included (an ANSI C requirement).

Type conversion will also be done on return values, so if the result of a math function is stored in a `float` or `int`, the value will be truncated with a possible loss of precision.

It is important to keep in mind that many math functions have boundaries (or domains) over which they are defined. For example, the logarithm of a negative number is undefined, and calling

```
dY = log( dX );
```

with a negative `dX` will result in a domain error. Similarly, math functions can sometimes return values whose magnitudes are so large that the result cannot be stored within the bounds of a `double`. This is called a range error, and it can be easily simulated by calling the `exp` function with a very large argument. For example,

```
dY = exp( 5000 );
```

In this case, the returned value will be represented by `NaN`, an acronym for `Not a Number`. Some of the older implementations of C will simply set the function to the maximum `double` value.

Computer Program. Program 7.5 demonstrates the use of several math library functions, and simulates domain and range errors for math functions.

PROGRAM 7.5: EXERCISE FUNCTIONS IN MATH LIBRARY

```
/*
 * ===================================================================
 * math.c: Demonstrate simple math library functions and application
 *         of errno.h for checking range and domain errors.
 *
 * Math Functions used here : fabs(x), sin(x), tan(x), atan2(y,x),
 *                            floor(x), and log(x).
 * User-defined functions   : trunc(x) -- truncate small values of x.
 * ===================================================================
 */

#include <stdio.h>
#include <math.h>
#include <errno.h> /* to allow checking of int errno */

/* Define precision for loops and truncation */

static const float kfEpsilon = 1E-5;

/* A function that truncates small values to 0 */

double trunc( double dValToTruncate ) {
```

```
   if( fabs( dValToTruncate ) < kfEpsilon )
      return 0.0;
   else
      return dValToTruncate;
}

int main( void ) {
double dAngle; /* for angles in this example      */
double dTang;  /* for the tangent of a test angle */
double dLimit; /* limit for angles                */
double dNum;   /* for PI fraction calculation     */
double dY1, dY2, dY3;

/* [a] : Find and print the sin of angles from 0 to PI in PI/6 */
/*       increments.                                            */

   dLimit = M_PI + kfEpsilon;

   for( dAngle = 0.0; dAngle < dLimit; dAngle += M_PI/6 )
      printf( "sin(%4.2g) = %-4.2g\n", dAngle, trunc( sin( dAngle ) ) );

/* [b] : Find the tangent of -3 PI / 4 */

   dTang = tan( -3*M_PI_4 );
   printf( "The tangent of %g (-3PI/4) radians is %g\n", -3*M_PI_4, dTang);

/* [c] : Find the angle with tangent -root2 / -root2 in the third */
/*       quadrant                                                  */

   dAngle = atan2( -M_SQRT2, -M_SQRT2 );
   printf( "The angle with tangent %g/%g is %g\n",
           -M_SQRT2, -M_SQRT2, dAngle );
   printf( "Checking, this value should be %g\n", -3*M_PI_4 );

/* [d] : Find a rational expression in terms of PI. */
/*       We know it's a fraction of 4.              */

   dNum = floor( dAngle*4/M_PI );
   printf( "Expressed as a PI fraction this is %g PI / %g\n", dNum, 4.0 );

/* [e] : test for domain and range errors in math functions */

   /* [e.1] : domain error: for negative argument to log(x) */

   printf( "\nCurrent value of errno: %i", errno );
   dY1 = log( -1 );
   printf( "\nValue of dY1 after log(-1) is %f : errno = %i", dY1, errno );
```

```
    if( EDOM == errno ) { /* EDOM #defined in errno.h above */
        printf( "\nDomain error occurred in log function." );
        errno = 0;          /* reset error status */
    }

    /* [e.2] : range error: for log( 0 ) */

    dY2 = log( 0 );
    printf( "\nValue of dY2 after log(0) is %f : errno = %i", dY2, errno );
    if( ERANGE == errno || EDOM == errno ) {
        printf( "\nRange or domain error occurred in log function." );
        errno = 0;          /* reset error status */
    }
    printf( "\n" );

    /* [e.3] : range/overflow error: for 10^1000 */

    dY3 = pow( 10.0, 1000.0 );
    printf( "\n );
    printf( "Value of dY3 after pow(10, 1000) is %f : errno = %i",
            dY3, errno );
    if( ERANGE == errno ) {
        printf( "\nRange error occurred in pow() function." );
        errno = 0;         /* reset error status */
    }
    printf( "\n" );

/* [f] : Simulate sequence of calculations containing error conditions */

    dY1 = 1.0/0.0;
    dY2 = 2.0*dY1;
    dY3 = dY2/dY1;
    printf( "Value of dY1 = 1.0/0.0 = %f\n", dY1 );
    printf( "         dY2 = 2.0*dY1 = %f\n", dY2 );
    printf( "         dY3 = dY2/dY1 = %f\n", dY3 );
}
```

The output from Program 7.5 is

```
sin(   0) = 0
sin(0.52) = 0.5
sin(   1) = 0.87
sin( 1.6) = 1
sin( 2.1) = 0.87
sin( 2.6) = 0.5
sin( 3.1) = 0
```

```
The tangent of -2.35619 (-3PI/4) radians is 1
The angle with tangent -1.41421/-1.41421 is -2.35619
Checking, this value should be -2.35619
Expressed as a PI fraction this is -3 PI / 4

Current value of errno: 0
Value of dY1 after log(-1) is NaN : errno = 33
Domain error occurred in log function.

Value of dY2 after log(0) is -Inf : errno = 33
Range or domain error occurred in log function.

Value of dY3 after pow(10, 1000) is Inf : errno = 34
Range error occurred in pow() function.
Value of dY1 = 1.0/0.0 = Inf
         dY2 = 2.0*dY1 = Inf
         dY3 = dY2/dY1 = NaN
```

Points to note are as follows:

1. The header file `math.h` has accurate values for many common constants, including e (`M_E`), π (`M_PI`), $\pi/2$ (`M_2_PI`) and the square root of 2 (`M_SQRT2`). For a complete list, find and look at `math.h` on your system.
2. In Part [a], we compute and print the sin of angles from 0 to π in $\pi/6$ increments. Because floating point values are not exact, the loop limit is set just above `M_PI` so that `M_PI` will be included in the loop. The message here is "do not do exact comparisons on floating point values." You may, in fact, get infinite loops if you use expressions such as

   ```
   for( dAngle = 0.0; dAngle != M_PI; dAngle += M_PI/6 ) {
        ... details of code removed ...
   }
   ```

   because `dAngle` may never be exactly equal to `M_PI`.
3. Function `trunc()` is included in the listing so that values close to zero can be truncated before printing. Without `trunc()`, values like `5.7e-16` would be printed for `sin(3.14..)`, where the argument to the sin function is close but not exactly equal to π. Also note that the `fabs()` function is used to find the absolute value of a floating point number. There is also a `abs()` function that takes an integer argument and returns a `double`. Be careful not to use `abs()` to find the absolute value of a floating point argument. The compiler will convert a `float` or `double` to an `int` and then return the absolute value of the truncated value. Use only `fabs` when dealing with floating point values.
4. One of the neat things about C is the facilities it provides for the detection of range and domain errors. Error checking can be instigated by including

the C library header file `errno.h` at the top of the C program. The header file contains declarations for the integer `errno` and a number of constants (details given as follows). When a program begins its execution, `errno = 0`. However, should a mathematical function encounter a range or domain error, then `errno` will take a nonzero value indicating the type of error. More precisely, `errno = EDOM` when a domain error has occurred [e.g., `log(x) : x < 0`], and `errno = ERANGE` when the result of a mathematical function cannot be calculated and stored in a variable of type double. After a math function error has been detected, `errno` must be reset to zero before the next math function is called.

5. Program 7.5 does not crash in Section [f] as one might expect. The program signals, instead, a series of run-time errors in the calculations by printing `NaN`s and `Inf`s (for infinity). `NaN` and `Inf` are part of the Institute for Electrical and Electronics Engineers (IEEE) standard for floating point calculations and are mechanisms for reflecting erroneous conditions that may arise during calculations.

   Once a `NaN` is produced at some point in a calculation, as in divide by zero or an out-of-range result, all subsequent calculations involving a `NaN` will also produce a `NaN`.

Review Questions

1. What are the attributes of all functions? At most, how many values can be returned by a C function?
2. What are the advantages and disadvantages of C program development using library and user-defined functions?
3. Why is `main()` considered a function? Does it have all the attributes of a function? How many copies of `main()` can a C program have?
4. Why should you bother to split a program into several functions if you could put it all in one?
5. What is the purpose of a function declaration? Why can the compiler compile a program with only the declaration and no knowledge (yet) of how the function actually does its work (i.e., without the definition)?
6. What does the function declaration

```
float complexMagnitude( float fRe, float fIm );
```

   tell the compiler?
7. What is the purpose of a `return` statement? Why is the use of multiple `return` statements within a function sometimes considered bad programming practice?
8. Why does the compiler need the function definition to complete the link phase?
9. What is the scope of a variable?

10. Briefly explain two purposes of the keyword `static`.

11. Briefly explain how `range` and `domain` errors occur with mathematical functions.

12. What is wrong with the block of code

```
for( dAngle = 0.0; dAngle != 2*M_PI; dAngle += M_PI/12 ) {
     ... details of code removed ...
}
```

How would you fix the problem?

7.9 PROGRAMMING EXERCISES

Problem 7.1 (Beginner): Write a function that will calculate the value of $f(x)$ given the value of x, where

$$f(x) = x^2 + 2x \tag{7.6}$$

The complete solution should include both an interface file (with the function declaration and a short description of the function in it) and an implementation file, containing the actual function definition. You should assume that the value of x will be considered a float.

Note. Do not represent x in the program as a variable named "x." Instead, choose an appropriate Hungarian notation name.

Problem 7.2 (Beginner): Write a nonrecursive (iterative) factorial function and represent the result as an `unsigned int`. Why is an `unsigned int` appropriate for the result? Your function declaration should be set up to receive an integer argument. Why is an int value appropriate for the argument?

Write a test program to determine the range of factorial values that can be calculated without error.

Problem 7.3 (Beginner): In this chapter we wrote a function that calculates and returns the magnitude of a complex number. Write a test program that will exercise this function. Use one file for the test program source code and a second file for the complex number calculation. Develop a header file that acts as a suitable interface file.

Problem 7.4 (Beginner): Write a program that demonstrates how a static variable can be used to allow a function to "remember" whether it has been called before. The first time the function is called, it should print "initializing" to standard output. The second and subsequent times it is called, it should print "processing" to standard output.

Problem 7.5 (Beginner): Write a program that uses the math library functions to calculate

$$\frac{\sin(x)}{\cos(x)} \tag{7.7}$$

and return the value. Compare this to the math function tan(x) for the same arguments. What are the domains of the function arguments that give valid answers?

Problem 7.6 (Beginner): The voltage across an inductor of inductance L is given by

$$v_L = L \cdot \frac{di}{dt} \tag{7.8}$$

where i is the instantaneous current and t is the time. You can approximate di/dt with $\Delta i/\Delta t$, where Δi is the amount the current changes by in a small time interval Δt. Using these approximations, write a function with three arguments, L, Δi, and Δt. Have your function calculate and return the voltage across an inductor for a fixed change. Call your function several times and print the results for decreasing time intervals Δt.

Problem 7.7 (Intermediate): A key limitation of the quadratic equation solver in Program 7.1 is the absence of checking for loss of numerical accuracy due to subtraction cancellation. We note from Equation 7.3 that this will occur whenever the quadratic equation has two real roots, and either coefficient a or coefficient c (or both) is very small compared to coefficient b.

Rather than naively applying Equation 7.3 directly, numerical accuracy can be improved by computing the quantity

$$Q = -0.5 \cdot [b + \text{sign}(b) \cdot \sqrt{b^2 - 4ac}] \tag{7.9}$$

where sign(b) is a function that gives `1` for positive b and `-1` for negative b. Equation 7.9 follows from multiplying Equation 7.3 by the unity fraction

$$\left[\frac{-b \mp \sqrt{b^2 - 4ac}}{-b \mp \sqrt{b^2 - 4ac}}\right]$$

The roots of the quadratic are `c/Q` and `Q/a`, respectively. Extend Program 7.1 so that it avoids numerical errors due to subtractive cancellation. Develop some test case problems to show that your improved implementation works even when Program 7.1 provides inferior solutions.

Problem 7.8 (Intermediate): An efficient way of computing the cube root of a number `N` is to compute the root of

$$f(x) = x^3 - N = 0 \tag{7.10}$$

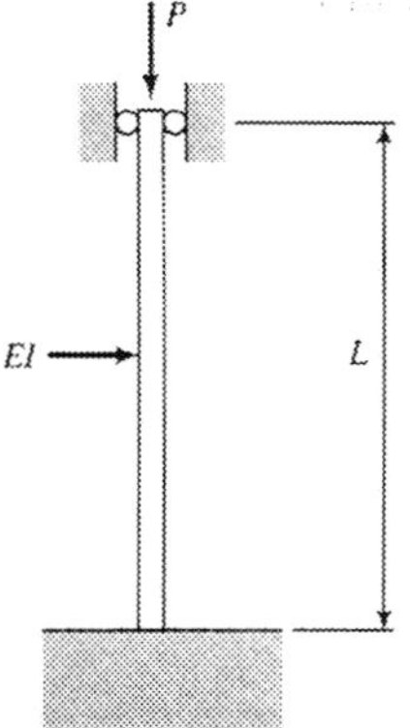

FIGURE 7.6 Column carrying axial load.

with the method of Newton Raphson, namely

$$x_{n+1} = x_n - \left[\frac{f(x_n)}{f'(x_n)}\right] \tag{7.11}$$

Substituting Equation 7.10 into Equation 7.11 and rearranging terms gives the recursive relationship

$$x_{n+1} = \frac{1}{3} \cdot \left[\frac{2x_n^3 + N}{x_n^2}\right] \tag{7.12}$$

Write a C program that will prompt the user for a number `N`, and compute the cube root of `N` via Equation 7.12. Your program should use the criterion

$$\left|\frac{x_{n+1} - x_n}{x_n}\right| \leq \varepsilon \tag{7.13}$$

for a test on convergence, where ε is a very small number. For a range of positive and negative values of `N` and zero, print the number `N`, its cube root, and the number of iterations needed to compute the result.

Problem 7.9 (Intermediate): Figure 7.6 shows an elastic column fixed at its base and pinned at the top. The critical buckling load, P_{cr}, corresponds to the solution of

$$\lambda = \tan[\lambda] \tag{7.14}$$

where $\lambda = L \cdot \sqrt{P_{cr}/EI}$. Write a C program that will use the method of Newton Raphson to find the lowest `positive root` to Equation 7.14, and compute and print the critical Euler buckling load for the column.

8

ARRAYS AND POINTERS

8.1 NEED FOR ARRAYS AND POINTERS

Arrays and pointers in C are where the language departs from the fixed structure of other procedural languages (e.g., FORTRAN, Basic), and it is probably one of the reasons C is so popular. Some programmers will argue that in the case of pointers, "notorious" is a better word. The developers of C needed a language that could be used to write programs for the implementation of operating systems, process control, embedded systems, and so forth. In addition to the evaluation of deterministic formulas, these applications must be able to handle interaction of the application with the operating system, interrupts, and network communications. Occasionally, you will hear the argument that just about *any* language could be used to solve these types of problems. The question you should ask yourself is—but would the solution in Basic or FORTRAN be readable, maintainable, or otherwise elegant? The answer is probably not. New structures and representations are required—pointers, multidimensional arrays, unions, and structures are all features of C that allow engineers to write programs in a way that mimics solutions to real-world problems.

Probably the best way to learn how to use arrays and pointers is through practice and careful study. Arrays are important to engineers because so many problems involve parameters that can be treated as arrays—for example, character strings, sets of linear equation coefficients, vectors, matrices, and coordinates are just a few applications. Pointers may, at first, seem strange and unnecessary. It is important to keep an open mind. The power of pointers will become apparent, especially as we move onto dynamic memory allocation.

Arrays and pointers share many similarities and, in some cases, can be used interchangeably. This chapter explains, for example, how C compilers treat arrays and pointers in a similar way. Although the translation of an array-to-pointer representation is transparent to the programmer, the best programmers are aware of its implications on `compile-time` and `run-time` behavior, and will exploit these translations in their programming.

8.2 INTRODUCTION TO ARRAYS

Arrays are useful whenever a group of tightly related variables is required. Suppose, for example, that you want to store the amount of rainfall measured in inches over the period of a week. Over a month. Over a year. This problem is a candidate for the use of arrays because each element of the array contains similar information. The only difference is the index into the array (day, month, or year).

8.2.1 Definition of Arrays

An array is defined by appending brackets and an array size to the variable name. To generalize, array definitions look as follows:

```
type taVar[ constant size ];   /* note the 'a' prefix */
```

where `type` can be any intrinsic (`char`, `int`, `float`, etc.) or user-defined data type, and the `size` within the brackets must be a constant. The array declaration will result in a fixed size of memory being reserved for the array's use. For example, the array declaration

```
int iaArray [ 4 ];
```

requests a contiguous block of memory for the storage of four variables of type `int`. The elements of array `iaArray` are `iaArray[0]`, `iaArray[1]`, `iaArray[2]`, and `iaArray[3]`.

iaArray [0]	iaArray [1]	iaArray [2]	iaArray [3]

Note that the valid array indices run from `0` to `4 - 1`, and not from `1` to `4` as one might initially expect.

The size of an array can also be #defined with the preprocessor or specified via an enum variable. Equivalent definitions for iaArray are

```
#define ARRAYSIZE 4
int iaArray[ ARRAYSIZE ];
```

and

```
enum { ArraySize = 4};
int iaArray[ ArraySize ];
```

Among the three methods of array definition, use of the enum variable is preferable because it names the size of the array. Frequently the size of the array is used in loops and, therefore, the enumerated size can also be used there. Also, if the array size changes in the future, only one value would have to be changed (ArraySize).

8.2.2 Array Indexing

Array values are accessed by referring to a specific element with an index. In some applications, the index will be a literal constant and in others it will be a variable. If iIndex is a variable of type int, then the elements of iaArray may be accessed with the expression iaArray[iIndex]. The script of code

```
enum { ArraySize = 4 };
int iIndex;
int iaArray[ ArraySize ];

  for( iIndex = 0; iIndex < ArraySize; ++iIndex )
       iaArray[ iIndex ] = 0;
```

shows a typical use of array values being set to zero inside a for loop. Valid array indices run from 0 to ArraySize-1, where ArraySize is the size of the array. When we write iaArray[iIndex], the compiler generates object code to retrieve the contents of memory at a specified offset distance from the starting location of the array.

Suppose that we want to retrieve the value of iaArray[2]. Figure 8.1 shows how the contents of iaArray[2] are accessed at an offset distance 2*sizeof(int) bytes from the base address of iaArray. This mechanism works because the location and dimensions for array storage are known at compile time. At run-time, this information is actually encoded in the binary code generated by the compiler, which means that the programmer must have ensured that the code is correct and memory access does not deviate from the stated bounds (which cannot be changed for standard arrays).

You can use the & operator to get the address of an array element, just as you would for any other variable. So, for example, &iaArray[2] is the address of the

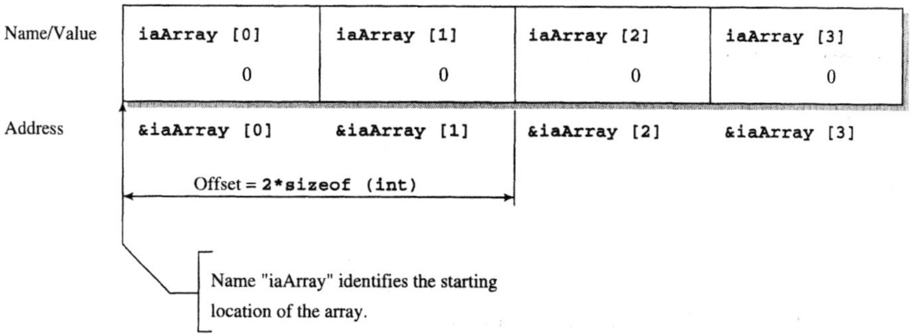

FIGURE 8.1 Components of one-dimensional array of integers.

index 2 element in `iaArray`. The index 2 element and the base address of `iaArray` are related by the expression

```
&iaArray [ 2 ] = &iaArray [ 0 ] + 2 * sizeof ( int );
```

`sizeof` is an operator, not a library function, that returns the number of bytes occupied by its operand. We say that an array is being dereferenced when brackets and an index are used with the array name to access the contents of a specific array element. The brackets remove a level of indirection since the array name without any brackets (e.g., `iaArray`) evaluates to the address of the first element at index 0 (e.g., `iaArray <==> &iaArray[0]`).

Our use of Hungarian notation is consistent in that `iaArray` must evaluate to `ia` or `integer array` exactly as we have defined it. The brackets and index that follow the array name dereference the array name (type `integer array`) and yield a *specific* element of the array (the index 2 element), which is type `int`. In other words, the brackets effectively remove (or cancel) the `a` type prefix leaving only the '`i`', or type `int` in this case. `iaArray` evaluates to an integer array, which is the address of the first integer in the array. We return to the topic of addresses in the sections on character arrays and pointers, and again in the section on passing arrays to functions.

8.2.3 Array Bounds

In C there is no checking of array bounds; the compiler will simply assume that you will only use the memory you have requested. Novice C programmers should make a special effort to keep this point in mind because array index errors (bugs) are particularly common and are among the most insidious to find. If you try to access `iaArray [4]`, then you are actually going beyond the end of the array. This leads to one of two possibilities. Either the operating system detects the fault and core dumps with a segmentation fault, or other variables are corrupted quietly or the operating system is corrupted. If we are lucky, a segmentation fault occurs and the program will terminate. If we are not, something (variables, or the operating system) becomes corrupted and it is only a matter of time before the program and/

or computer crashes. This can happen in subtle and otherwise misleading ways, and you may not suspect the true reason for the fault. If we are unlucky enough to not get a segmentation fault (a situation that would be immediately apparent), a variable allocated after the array may be modified. In this case, the damage is not obvious and may totally mislead the programmer into thinking something else is wrong. The bottom line is—do not access memory outside of the allocated array bounds.

One way of safeguarding against illegal array accesses is to use the `assert` macro to evaluate the validity of an array access before the array access actually takes place. For example, `assert` in the script of code

```
#include <assert.h>

assert( iIndex > = 0 && iIndex < ArraySize );

..... expression involving iaArray [ iIndex ] ....
```

will evaluate to true if `iIndex` is greater than or `equal` to zero and less than `ArraySize`. An error message will be printed and the program's execution will be terminated when the logical expression argument evaluates to false.

8.3 INITIALIZING THE CONTENTS OF AN ARRAY

After an array is specified (or allocated), the array will have random values until its contents are initialized. The contents of an array may be initialized in a number of ways: (1) initialization lists, (2) explicit array initialization, or (3) static allocation (default initialization).

8.3.1 Initialization Lists

When an array is defined, the initial values can be specified in a list, as in

```
int iaVol[10] = {0, 1, 2, 3, 4, 5, 6, 7, 8, 9};
```

The list of initial values are comma separated inside curly braces. It is not necessary to specify the array size if an initialization list is included. In the declaration

```
int  iaVol[] = {2,3,4};
```

the array size is implicitly determined by the number of initializers, in this case three. The compiler will automatically calculate the array size from the list in this case.

Even though the compiler can calculate array sizes if an initialization list is used, it is often good programming practice to define the size of an array as a symbolic constant. This might help prevent array-bound errors in the future if and when the code is changed. In the following code, both the number of elements and the initial values are known when the array is defined:

```
#define MONTHS 12
...
     int iaDaysInMonth[ MONTHS ] = { 31, 28, 31,
                                     30, 31, 30,
                                     31, 31, 30,
                                     31, 30, 31 };
```

Memory is allocated for 12 integers. They are then initialized with the list of the number of days in each month. If we want a constant array (which might be the best choice here since the values probably should not be changed), we need to specify that the array values are going to be considered constants and provide an initialization list. The required syntax is:

```
#define MONTHS 12
...
     const int kiaDaysInMonth[ MONTHS ] = { 31, 28, 31,
                                            30, 31, 30,
                                            31, 31, 30,
                                            31, 30, 31 };
```

Use of the keyword `const` indicates that the array values are to be initialized and never changed thereafter.

Rather than use the preprocessor to define constant array sizes, we could use a type `enum` to accomplish the same thing:

```
enum  { Months = 12 };
const int kiaDaysInMonth[ Months ] = { 31, 28, 31,
                                       30, 31, 30,
                                       31, 31, 30,
                                       31, 30, 31 };
```

This works well since the value for the `enum` type `MonthsInYear` is considered a constant once it is specified in this way, and the number of months in a year probably will not be changing anytime soon.

A compile-time error will occur when the number of elements in the initialization list exceeds the specified array size. This feature of C is a good reason for specifying the array size; generally, it is better to get a compile-time error than to have a design flaw lurking in the code unnoticed. If the number of initializers is less than the size of the array, then the remaining elements will be initialized to 0.

8.3.2 Explicit Array Initialization

Explicit array initialization occurs when the array values are calculated in the program and assigned to the array, following the array definition. Often, the initial values of an array are explicitly assigned inside a loop:

```
enum { WeekDays = 7 };
float faWeeklyRain[ WeekDays ];
int iDay;
  for( iDay = 0; iDay < WeekDays; ++iDay )
      faWeeklyRain[iDay] = 0.0F;
```

Sometimes the initial values of an array may not be known at definition time, or there may be too many to list. An explicit loop is required in either case. In the loop shown above, notice how `iDay` starts at `0` and counts up to `less than WeekDays`.

8.3.3 Static Allocation

Variables and arrays are automatic by default. By automatic we mean that:

1. The scope of variables and arrays is limited to the block of code in which they are defined, and
2. The array is allocated on the stack and is, therefore, temporary. When the executing program is finished with the block of code, all values of the variables and arrays are lost.

Arrays that are defined to be `static` will be provided with so-called "permanent" storage that persists for the program's run-time. By default, all the values in the array will be initialized to `0`.

In the previous definition of `faWeeklyRain`, all the values were unknown (random) after the definition and were subsequently set to `0.0F` by the program. In the listing

```
enum { WeekDays = 7 };
static float faWeeklyRain[  WeekDays ];
```

all the array members are initialized to zero since the array is `static`. Generally speaking, it is bad programming practice to use `static` only to achieve automatic initialization.

8.4 CHARACTER ARRAYS

Although it is common to refer to sequences of characters as character strings, they are really just character arrays. The importance of character strings stems from their wide use in computing. Not only are they the basic medium in which computer programs are written, but also they play a central role in text manipulated by text editors and word processors and are the principal medium of exchange for input and output (I/O).

C does not have a basic data type to represent character strings as some other languages do (C does not need it!). A string is simply stored as a one-dimensional array of type `char`. By convention, a character string is terminated by the null character '\0', otherwise known as the end-of-string sentinel (the null character should not be confused with the printable zero character `'0'`). A 0 character is represented internally by a decimal 48, and is definitely a different animal from a literal 0 (00000000 in binary). See the ASCII table in Chapter 4. Many of the functions that we use to manipulate strings [e.g., `printf()`] will rely on the sentinel convention.

8.4.1 Initializing Character Arrays

There are several mechanisms for initializing the contents of a character string. The simplest, character-by-character initialization, is demonstrated in the script

```
enum { myCharacterArray = 6 };
char caMystring[ myCharacterArray ];

     caMystring[0] =  'o';
     caMyString[1] =  'z';
     caMyString[2] =  'o';
     caMyString[3] =  'n';
     caMyString[4] =  'e';
     caMyString[5] = '\0';
```

Notice that a character array must be long enough to store the printable string characters plus its terminating '\0'. A character string does not need to use the entire contents of a character array. For example, if we had defined `caMyString` with

```
enum { MaxString = 80 };
char caMystring[MaxString];

     caMyString[0] =  'o';
     caMyString[1] =  'z';
     caMyString[2] =  'o';
     caMyString[3] =  'n';
     caMyString[4] =  'e';
     caMyString[5] = '\0';
```

then only six elements are assigned a value, and a large part of the character array `caMyString` remains unused. If a single character array is required to store a number of character strings, then a reasonable programming strategy is to allocate enough space to hold the longest string that is anticipated. Then the actual string can vary in size with the usual `'\0'` at the end.

Character strings may also be stored as a finite sequence of characters enclosed in double quotes. Three examples are

```
"ozone"
"this is a longer string"
"x = y"
```

When the compiler encounters a double-quoted string, it allocates storage for the string and initializes the storage with the characters from the string. The string is automatically terminated with a '\0'. When a string is used to initialize a character array, as in

```
char caMyString[] = "a test string";
```

the compiler determines the size of the string, generates code that will allocate the required memory, and copies the string's contents to the memory at run-time.

8.4.2 Double Quotes vs. Single Quotes

There is an important distinction between double quotes surrounding a string and single quotes surrounding a single character. When double quotes surround a string, it evaluates to the address of the first character in the string. When single quotes surround a character, it evaluates to that character (as in caMyString[0] ='o';). Do not confuse the two cases. Double-quoted strings are constant character arrays. They simplify initialization and storage of strings that are used frequently in programs. The format strings used in printf() statements are a good example:

```
printf( "Enter the next value:");
```

Here the prompt

```
"Enter the next value:"
```

is a constant character string. When printf() is called, the address of the first character in this string is actually what is passed to printf().

Example. Another reason for terminating every string with a '\0' is that very terse and powerful code can be written with this format. For example, we could write a string print function that is used in this format:

```
int printString( char caBuffer[] ) {
int iCharIndex = 0;

    /* loop while still more chars to print */
    while( caBuffer[iCharIndex] != '\0' )
    putchar( caBuffer[iCharIndex++] );
}
```

Printing will stop as soon as the terminating '\0' is reached in the string.

8.5 APPLICATIONS OF ONE-DIMENSIONAL ARRAYS

In this section, we use one-dimensional arrays in the solution of two completely different problems. First, we compute the numerical solution to an ordinary differential equation for the profile of a cable in a simple suspension bridge. In our second problem, we compute and plot a histogram of uniformly distributed random numbers.

8.5.1 Profile of Cable in Simple Suspension Bridge

Problem Statement

Suppose that the cable profile of a small suspension bridge carrying a uniformly distributed load

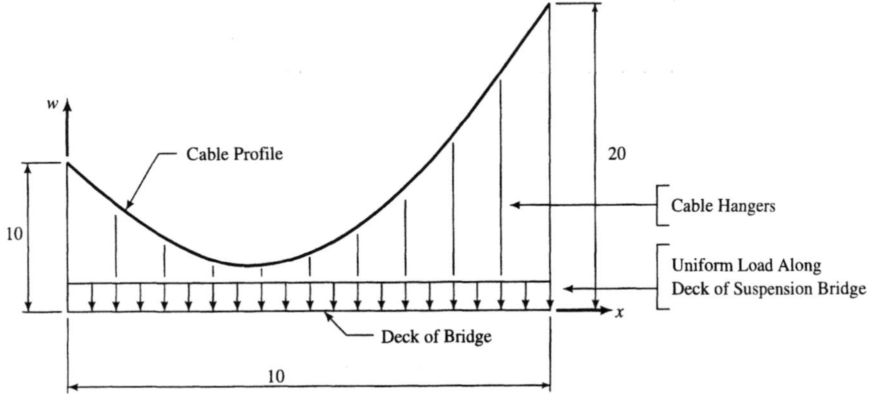

corresponds to the solution of the differential equation

$$\frac{d^2w}{dx^2} = 1.0 \tag{8.1}$$

with the boundary conditions $w(0) = 10$ and $w(10) = 20$. It is easy to show that the analytic solution to the cable profile is

$$w(x) = \frac{1}{2}x^2 - 4x + 10 \tag{8.2}$$

We can compute a numerical solution to the cable profile by dividing the horizontal axis into 10 regions along the x axis, with nine internal nodes, and approximate Equation 8.1 with a suitable finite difference equation.

Method of Finite Differences

In the method of finite differences, the derivative terms in the underlying differential equation are replaced by their finite difference equivalents. To see how the finite

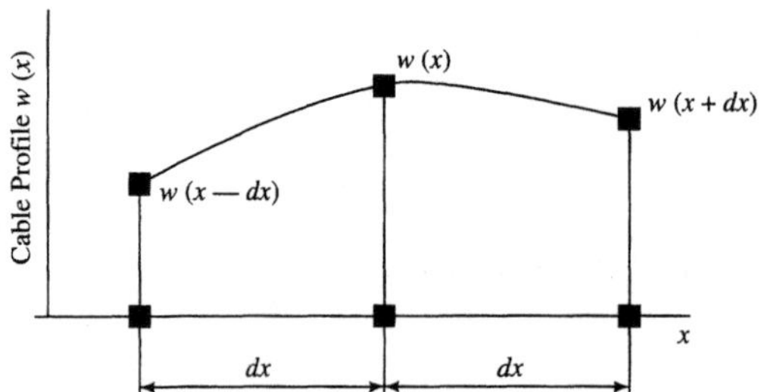

FIGURE 8.2 One-dimensional grid of regularly spaced nodes.

difference approximations apply, suppose that we have a one-dimensional grid of regularly spaced nodes, as shown in Figure 8.2.

There are numerous ways to express the first derivative of $w(x)$ with respect to x. For instance, a forward difference approximation can be obtained by writing the truncated Taylor series approximation for $w(x + dx)$ in terms of $w(x)$:

$$w(x + dx) = w(x) + \frac{dw(x)}{dx} \cdot dx + O(dx^2) \tag{8.3}$$

Rearranging Equation 8.3 gives

$$\frac{dw}{dx}_{forward} = \left[\frac{w(x + dx) - w(x)}{dx}\right] + O(dx) \tag{8.4}$$

Here we use the notation $O(dx)$ to indicate that the finite difference will be first-order accurate. A backward difference approximation to $dw(x)/dx$ can be obtained by writing down the truncated Taylor series approximation for $w(x - dx)$ in terms of $w(x)$, and rearranging terms. The result is

$$\frac{dw}{dx}_{backward} = \left[\frac{w(x) - w(x - dx)}{dx}\right] + O(dx) \tag{8.5}$$

The second derivative of $w(x)$ with respect to x is given by the finite difference of the first derivative approximations, namely

$$\frac{d^2w}{dx^2} = \left[\frac{\frac{dw}{dx}_{forward} - \frac{dw}{dx}_{backward}}{dx}\right] \tag{8.6}$$

$$= \left[\frac{w(x + dx) - 2 \cdot w(x) + w(x - dx)}{dx^2}\right] + O(dx^2) \tag{8.7}$$

The term $O(dx^2)$ indicates that our finite difference approximation of the second derivative will have an error that is proportional to the square of the mesh size dx.

Finite Difference Mesh for Cable Profile

With Equation 8.7 in hand, we can now write the finite difference approximation to Equation 8.1 as

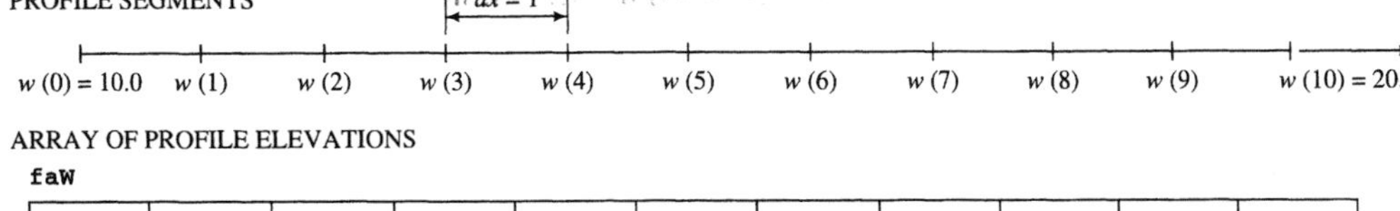

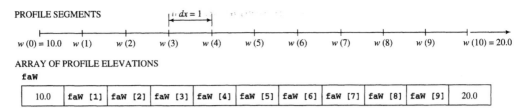

FIGURE 8.3 Array storage of cable elevations.

$$\frac{d^2w}{dx^2} \approx \left[\frac{w(x + dx) - 2 \cdot w(x) + w(x - dx)}{dx^2}\right] = 1.0 \tag{8.8}$$

Equation 8.8 can be rearranged to give

$$w(x) = \frac{1}{2} \cdot [w(x + dx) + w(x - dx) - dx^2] \tag{8.9}$$

Now we are ready to partition the horizontal axis of the bridge deck into 10 segments of equal length (i.e., $dx = 1.0$).

Figure 8.3 suggests that a natural way of storing the cable profile elevation is with a one-dimensional array of floats and with the boundary elevations `w(0) = 10.0` and `w(10) = 20.0` inserted at the array endpoints.

Computer Program

We can compute the elevation of the cable profile at each internal node by systematically walking along the array and evaluating Equation 8.9 at each node. The array will contain the correct elevations when the change in profile shape barely changes from one iteration to the next.

PROGRAM 8.1: PROFILE OF CABLE IN SIMPLE SUSPENSION BRIDGE

```
/*
 *  ====================================================================
 *  Problem : Use finite difference approximation and iterative solution
 *            technique to compute cable profile in a simple suspension
 *            bridge.
 *  ====================================================================
 */

#include <stdio.h>
#include <math.h>

#define max(a, b) ((a) > (b) ? (a) : (b))

enum { LeftHandElevation  = 10 };  /* Elevation of left-hand support   */
enum { RightHandElevation = 20 };  /* Elevation of right-hand support  */
enum { BridgeWidth        = 10 };  /* Span length of Suspension Bridge */
enum { Nodes              = 11 };  /* No of finite difference nodes    */
```

```
int main( void ) {
float faW[ Nodes ];
float fTempW, fMaxChange;
float fdX = BridgeWidth/((float) (Nodes - 1));
int ii;

    /* [a] : Initialize cable profile */

    faW[ 0  ]         = (float) LeftHandElevation;
    faW[ Nodes - 1 ] = (float) RightHandElevation;

    for( ii = 1; ii <= Nodes - 2; ii = ii + 1 ) {
         faW[ ii ] = 0.0;
    }

    /* [b] : Compute profile over interior points */

    fMaxChange = max( LeftHandElevation, RightHandElevation );
    while( fMaxChange > 0.001 ) {
        fMaxChange = 0.0;

        /* [b.1] : Update profile on interior points */

        for( ii = 1; ii <= Nodes - 2; ii = ii + 1 ) {
             fTempW     = 0.5*(faW[ ii-1 ] + faW[ ii+1 ] - fdX*fdX);
             fMaxChange = max( fMaxChange, fabs( faW[ii] - fTempW ) );
             faW[ ii ]  = fTempW;
        }
    }

    /* [c] : Print x-coordinate and cable profile */

    printf("Cable profile                        \n");
    printf("================================ \n");
    printf("      X  Numerical  Analytical \n");
    printf("  Coord  Elevation    Solution \n");
    printf("================================ \n");

    for( ii = 0; ii < Nodes; ii = ii + 1 ) {
         printf("  %5.2f",    ii*fdX );
         printf(" %11.3f",    faW[ii] );
         printf(" %11.3f\n", 0.5*ii*fdX*ii*fdX - 4.0*ii*fdX + 10.0 );
    }
}
```

Program 8.1 generates the output

```
Cable profile
==================================
       X   Numerical  Analytical
   Coord   Elevation    Solution
==================================
    0.00      10.000      10.000
    1.00       6.496       6.500
    2.00       3.994       4.000
    3.00       2.492       2.500
    4.00       1.991       2.000
    5.00       2.491       2.500
    6.00       3.992       4.000
    7.00       6.493       6.500
    8.00       9.995      10.000
    9.00      14.498      14.500
   10.00      20.000      20.000
```

The first column of output contains the x coordinate of nodes in the cable profile; the second column, the cable elevations computed with the finite difference computation; and the rightmost column, the theoretical cable elevations. Notice that the minimum elevation of the cable profile occurs at $x = 4$.

Points to note are as follows:

1. The cable profile is stored in a one-dimensional array `faW` containing `Nodes` elements. Part `[a]` initializes the left- and right-hand cable elevations to `10` and `20`, respectively, and sets the elevations of the internal nodes to zero.

   ARRAY OF PROFILE ELEVATIONS AT THE END OF BLOCK [A]
   `faW`

10.0	0.0	0.0	0.0	0.0	0.0	0.0	0.0	0.0	0.0	20.0

   The initial condition for the cable profile is really quite arbitrary. For example, a second method would be to compute the equation of a line passing through the right- and left-hand endpoints, and set the initial cable elevations to lie along the line.

2. The variable `fMaxChange` keeps track of the maximum change in cable profile elevation at nodes `faW[2]` through `faW[9]`, from one iteration to the next. The line of code

   ```
   fMaxChange = max( LeftHandElevation, RightHandElevation );
   ```

   initializes `fMaxChange` to the larger of `LeftHandElevation` and `RightHandElevation` so that the looping construct will be entered.

3. The heart of Program 8.1 lies in block `[b]`, where a two-level looping construct systematically evaluates Equation 8.9 at nodes `faW[1]` through `faW[9]` until convergence of the cable profile occurs. `fMaxChange` is set to zero at the beginning of each iterate of the outer loop. This particular implementation of the algorithm will update the cable profile until `fMaxChange` is less than `0.001`.
4. The contents of `faW` at the end of the first iteration of profile computations are

   ARRAY OF PROFILE ELEVATIONS AT THE END OF ITERATION 1
   `faW`

10.0	4.50	1.75	0.375	−0.312	−0.656	−0.828	−0.914	−0.957	9.021	20.0

   and `fMaxChange` equals 9.02 (see `faW[9]`). The need for continued computations is handled by the relational expression (`fMaxChange > 0.001`). It evaluates to `true`, thereby indicating the need for a second iteration of computations. At the end of the second iteration, the contents of `faW` are

   ARRAY OF PROFILE ELEVATIONS AT THE END OF ITERATION 2
   `faW`

10.0	5.375	2.375	0.531	−0.562	−1.195	−1.555	−1.756	3.133	11.066	20.0

   and `fMaxChange` equals 4.089 (see `faW[8]`). `fMaxChange` has decreased in value, as expected, but the convergence is rather slow. The looping process continues for 69 iterations, at which point the contents of `faW` are

   ARRAY OF PROFILE ELEVATIONS AT THE END OF ITERATION 67
   `faW`

10.0	6.496	3.994	2.492	1.991	2.491	3.992	6.493	9.995	14.498	10.0

   and `fMaxChange` = 0.000992. The computations are complete because `(fMaxChange > 0.001)` evaluates to `false`.
5. Our numerical experiments indicate that the profile shape is sensitive to magnitude of the convergence criteria. For example, when the limit on convergence is relaxed from `0.001` to `0.1`, the minimum value of the numerically computed cable profile moves down to `1.14`.

Many types of engineering problems can be solved using one- and two-dimensional arrays and the "iterative solution" procedure demonstrated in this problem. Later in this chapter, for example, we use exactly the same strategy to compute the steady-state distribution of temperature in a chimney cross-section. A number of the programming exercises in this tutorial also require iterative solution procedures.

8.5.2 Generate Histogram of Uniformly Distributed Random Numbers

In our second application of one-dimensional arrays, we generate a family of random numbers that are uniformly distributed between zero and one, and construct a histogram of the scaled random numbers. We select this example because "numbers selected at random" are useful for a wide range of engineering and computer applications. Here are two application areas:

1. *Simulation of Natural Phenomena.* Use of random numbers can add realism to computer simulations of natural phenomena (e.g., random fluctuations in an external environment, natural variations in the properties of a system). In these cases, simulation is appropriate when a model calls for imitation of a situation where a pattern of behavior is discernible, but where we can say in only approximate terms what will happen. Although we may not be able to predict with exact certainty how these systems will behave, it is usually possible to look at the behavior of these systems as a whole and make sensible statements about average behavior of the overall system.
2. *Numerical and Optimization Algorithms.* During the past few decades, random numbers have been used in the design of algorithms to solve problems in numerical analysis and simulated annealing methods of optimization.

The term "random number" is difficult to define; it does not make much sense to say, for example, that the number 1 is random. A more rational interpretation of random number stems from the notion of one or more numbers being obtained by chance. Each number in the sequence should have (1) nothing to do with other numbers in the sequence, and (2) a specified probability of falling within a specified range of values. The sum of specified probabilities must be one.

A uniform distribution on a set of random numbers occurs when each of the possible numbers is equally probable; put another way, any one number in the range is just as likely to be selected as any other. Suppose that we want to generate a sequence of `N` random integers covering the interval 1 to 6. An easy way of doing this would be to set up an experiment where a die is thrown N times, with the number on the upturned face being recorded after each throw. If the die is fair (i.e., each of the numbers 1 to 6 is equally likely to appear), then the number of recorded 1s, 2s, . . . 6s will be approximately equal. We say that this experiment generates a uniform distribution of integers from 1 to 6, with each outcome having a 1/6 probability of being realized. A diagram of discrete outcomes and their probabilities is shown in Figure 8.4. A second type of uniform distribution occurs when random numbers are drawn from a continuous interval (e.g., $x = a$ and $x = b$), as shown in Figure 8.5.

Uniformly distributed numbers should be distinguished from random numbers that are generated from different distributions (e.g., the Gaussian or normal distribution). In the following chapters and exercises, we see that the latter distributions are nearly always obtained via a suitable transformation of uniformly distributed

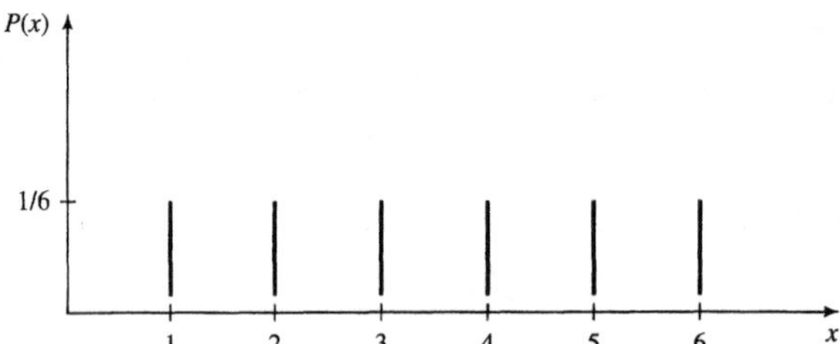

FIGURE 8.4 Discrete random numbers.

random numbers. Therefore, uniformly distributed numbers are the foundation for generation of random numbers generated from a variety of statistical distributions.

Characteristics of Probability Distributions

It is important to note that, in Figure 8.4, the sum of probabilities for discrete outcomes equals one and, for Figure 8.5, the integral of probability from $x = a$ to $x = b$ equals one.

For discrete probability distributions, the average (or mean) value μ of the distribution is given by

$$\mu = \sum_{i=1}^{N} p(x_i) \cdot x_i \tag{8.10}$$

and the variance by

$$\sigma^2 = \sum_{i=1}^{N} p(x_i) \cdot (x_i - \mu)^2 = \sum_{i=1}^{N} [p(x_i) \cdot x_i^2] - \mu^2 \tag{8.11}$$

In Equations 8.10 and 8.11, x_i is the value of the ith random number, which will occur with probability $p(x_i)$. N is the total number of items in the sample size.

The average (or mean) value μ of the continuous uniform distribution is given by

$$\mu = \int_a^b p(x) \cdot x \, dx = \frac{(a + b)}{2} \tag{8.12}$$

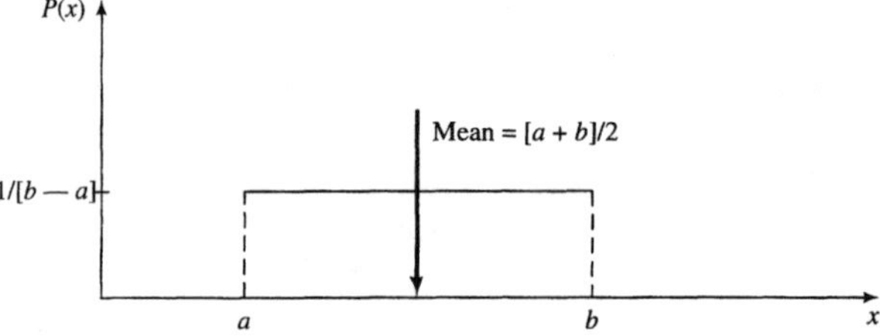

FIGURE 8.5 Uniformly distributed random numbers.

and the variance by

$$\sigma^2 = \int_a^b p(x) \cdot (x - \mu)^2 \, dx = \int_a^b p(x) \cdot x^2 \, dx - \mu^2 = \frac{(b-a)^2}{12} \tag{8.13}$$

The standard deviation of the uniform distribution, $\sigma = (b - a)/\sqrt{12}$, corresponds to the square root of the variance.

Generation of Uniformly Distributed Random Numbers

Before the days of computers, die and urn (i.e., pulling items from a closed bag) experiments were a common means of generating distributions of random numbers. During the past 30 years, a great deal of effort has been devoted to the development of algorithms for the mechanical generation of random numbers on computers and their use within computer programs. Many random number generators in use today are not very good. The sequences of numbers may appear random but may, in fact, not be random at all. A common fault of early schemes was their tendency to degenerate into cycles having short periods of repetition. As pointed out by Knuth [15], devising schemes for the foolproof generation of random numbers is exceedingly difficult.

Most of today's random number generators are special cases of linear congruential sequence schemes, namely

$$X_{n+1} = (aX_n + c) \bmod m, \quad n > 0 \tag{8.14}$$

where m is the modulus of the sequence ($m > 0$), a is the multiplier ($0 \le a < m$), c is the increment ($0 \le c < m$), and X_o is the starting value for the sequence of random numbers ($0 \le X_o < m$). The heart of this method lies in the careful selection of numbers m, a, c, and X_o, followed by testing of the generator on a particular computer to ensure the generated numbers are in fact random. Extensive discussion on these procedures may be found in Chapter 3 of Knuth [15]. In summary, modulus m should be taken as a large number, since the period of the sequence cannot be larger than m elements. A convenient strategy is to set m equal to the computer's word size (i.e., 32-bit word size on engineering workstations), so that $(aX + c)$ mod m is easy to compute. We select the multiplier a so that the period of random numbers is maximized in length. The increment c should be relatively prime with respect to m. The starting value for the random numbers, X_o, may be selected randomly.

A minimal standard for generation of uniformly distributed random numbers can be achieved with the coefficients

$$m = 2^{31} - 1 = 2{,}147{,}483{,}647 \text{ and } a = 7^5 = 16{,}807 \text{ and } c = 0 \tag{8.15}$$

This generator has been tested extensively and is known to produce distributions of random numbers that pass a standard set of statistical tests.

Unfortunately, this algorithm cannot be implemented on standard 32-bit machines without an arithmetic overflow occurring during the calculation of a times $m - 1$. Schrage [37] proposed a novel algorithm that can compute uniformly distributed random numbers with these coefficient settings and avoid the problem of

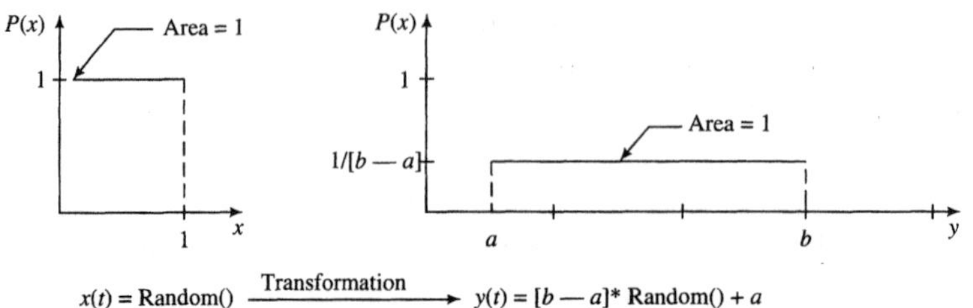

FIGURE 8.6 Transformation to scale random numbers.

overflow in computer arithmetic. The algorithm is suitable for implementation on computers having a 32-bit word size. The appropriate congruential sequence is given by

$$X_{n+1} = a(X_n \bmod q) - r\left[\frac{X_n}{q}\right] + m \cdot \delta(X_n) \tag{8.16}$$

with modulus $m = 2^{31} - 1 = 2{,}147{,}483{,}647$ (a 31-bit prime number) and multiplier $a = 7^5 = 16{,}807$. Coefficient q and r are the quotient and remainder of m/a (i.e., $q = 127{,}773$ and $r =$ the remainder). Coefficient $q = 127{,}773$ is defined by the quotient m/a, and coefficient $r = 2{,}836$ by the remainder in ma. We define $\delta(X_n) = 1$ when $a(X_n \bmod q) - r\left[\frac{X_n}{q}\right] < 0$. Otherwise, $\delta(X_n) = 0$.

Equation 8.16 will return (integer) random numbers uniformly distributed between zero and `m-1`, exclusive of the endpoint values. The range of the computed random numbers may be normalized to `[0,1]` by dividing X_{n+1} by m (i.e., X_{n+1}/m). Further adjustments to the range of a uniform distribution of random numbers are done on a case-by-case basis. For details, see the next section.

Scaling the Range of Uniform Random Numbers

Engineering applications often require a uniform distribution of random numbers that cover the interval `[a,b]`, where a and b take values other than zero and one. Let `Random()` be a function that returns random numbers uniformly distributed between `[0,1]`. As indicated in Figure 8.6, the range of random numbers may be scaled to the interval `[a,b]` with the transformation

$$y(t) = (b - a) \cdot \text{Random}() + a \tag{8.17}$$

Problem Statement and Program Source Code

Program 8.2 uses the user-defined function `Random()` to generate 1,000 random numbers uniformly distributed between zero and one. We apply the linear transformation

$$y(t) = 20 \cdot \text{Random}() + 10 \tag{8.18}$$

to rescale the range of the uniformly distributed random numbers from `[0,1]` to `[10,30]`. Finally, the distribution of scaled random numbers is plotted in a histogram. Theoretical considerations indicate that the average value of the scaled random numbers should be very close to 20 (see Figure 8.5, with a = 10 and b = 30). We also expect that the standard deviation will be approximately equal to $10/\sqrt{3} \approx 5.77$.

PROGRAM 8.2: GENERATE AND PRINT RANDOM NUMBERS

```
/*
 * ===========================================================================
 * The purposes of this computer program are to:
 *
 *     -- Generate a family of 1000 random numbers that are uniformly
 *        distributed within the interval [0,1].
 *     -- Scale the distribution so that the numbers range [10,30].
 *     -- Compute the average and standard deviation of the scaled
 *        distribution.
 *     -- Output histogram of random numbers.
 *
 * Note : We use our own function "Random()" to generate uniformly
 *         distributed random numbers. This function ONLY WORKS on
 *         computers having a 32-bit word architecture.
 * ===========================================================================
 */

#include <stdio.h>
#include <math.h>

void   InitRandom( long int );
double Random();

enum { SampleSize = 1000, HistogramSize = 20 };

int main( void ) {
int iaHistogram [ HistogramSize ];
int iCount, iInterval;
float fRandomNo, fAverage, fVariance;
float fSum        = 0.0;
float fSumSquares = 0.0;

  /* [a] : Zero-out elements of histogram array */

  for(iCount = 0; iCount < HistogramSize; iCount = iCount + 1)
      iaHistogram [ iCount ] = 0;
```

```
  /* [b] : Initialize Seed for Random Numbers */

  InitRandom((long) 12);

  /* [c] : Generate, scale, and catalogue random numbers */

  for(iCount = 1; iCount <= SampleSize; iCount = iCount + 1) {

       fRandomNo = 20*Random() + 10;
       fSum += fRandomNo;
       fSumSquares += fRandomNo*fRandomNo;

       iInterval = (int) floor( fRandomNo ) - 10;
       iaHistogram [ iInterval ] += 1;

  }

  /* [d] : Standard deviation and average of scaled random numbers */

  fAverage  = fSum/SampleSize;
  fVariance = fSumSquares/SampleSize - fAverage*fAverage;

  printf("** Random No. -- Average            = %8.5f\n", fAverage );
  printf("**            -- Variance           = %8.5f\n", fVariance );
  printf("**            -- Standard Deviation = %8.5f\n",
         sqrt(fVariance) );

  /* [e] : Output histogram of random numbers */

  printf("\n");
  for(iCount = 10; iCount < 30; iCount = iCount + 1)
      printf(" %5.1f %5d \n", (iCount + 0.5),
             iaHistogram[ iCount-10 ] );

}

/*
 * ====================================================
 * Random() : Generate Uniformly Distributed Random Numbers
 * ====================================================
 */

static unsigned long int uliSeed = 1;

void InitRandom( long int iMySeed ) {
     uliSeed = iMySeed;
}
```

```
double Random() {
long int liA = 16807;
long int liM = 2147483647;
long int liQ = 127773;
long int liR = 2836;
long int liTempSeed;

    liTempSeed = liA*( uliSeed%liQ ) - liR*( uliSeed/liQ );
    if( liTempSeed >= 0 )
        uliSeed = liTempSeed;
    else
        uliSeed = liTempSeed + liM;

    return( ((double) uliSeed)/liM );
}
```

The abbreviated output from Program 8.2 is

```
** Random No. -- Average              = 19.91072
**            -- Variance             = 34.90170
**            -- Standard Deviation =  5.90777

   10.5       57
   11.5       57
   12.5       35

   ..... details of array output removed ...

   27.5      42
   28.5      56
   29.5      58
```

The first three lines of output indicate that the sample average is close to the theoretical average (19.91 vs 20), and the sample standard deviation is close to the theoretical standard deviation (5.91 vs 5.77). The first column of array output contains the mid-interval values for each entry in the histogram (details follow). Column two of the array contains the number of scaled random numbers falling into each of the intervals `10-11`, `11-12`, and so on, up to `29-30`.

Figure 8.7 is a histogram of the number of generated random numbers. Notice that the total height of the individual columns is 1,000, the number of generated random numbers.

Program 8.2 has three user-defined functions, `main()`, `Random()`, and `Init-Random()`. Points to note are as follows:

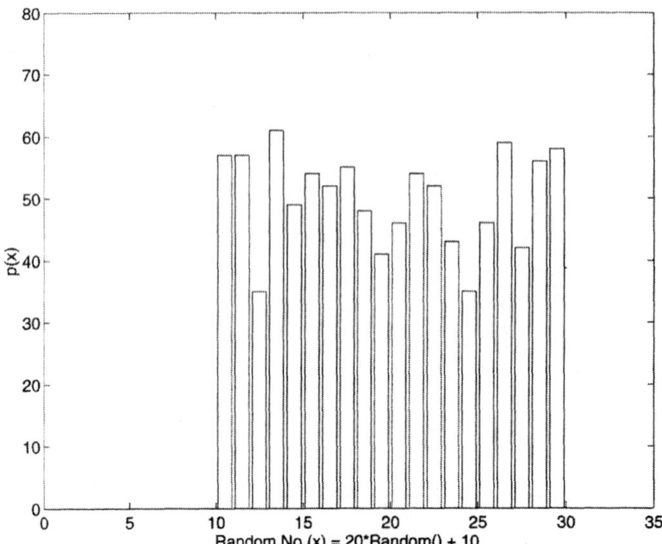

FIGURE 8.7 *Histogram of scaled random numbers.*

1. The statement

```
enum { SampleSize = 1000, HistogramSize = 20 };
```

establishes the constants `SampleSize` and `HistogramSize` for the number of random numbers to be generated and the size of the histogram, respectively. The declaration

```
int iaHistogram [ HistogramSize ];
```

sets up a one-dimensional array of 20 integers that will store the number of scaled random numbers falling within the integer intervals `10-11`, `11-12`, `... 29-30`.

At the conclusion of the analysis, `iaHistogram[0] = 57` stores the number of scaled random numbers that fall into the interval `10-11`, `iaHistogram[1] = 57` the number of random numbers within the interval `11-12`, and so forth. The average height of the columns is `20`.

2. We call `InitRandom()` to initialize the seed for the random number generator. Individual random numbers are generated by the function `Random()`. The declarations

```
void   InitRandom( long int );
double Random();
```

indicate that `InitRandom()` will have one argument, a `long int`, but will not return a type. `Random()` is a function that has zero arguments and returns type double. Chapter 7 contains a discussion on function declarations.

3. The seed for the random number generator, `uliSeed`, is declared and initialized in the two-part block of code:

```
static unsigned long int uliSeed = 1;

void InitRandom( long int iMySeed ) {
     uliSeed = iMySeed;
}
```

Our use of the qualifier `static` in the declaration for `uliSeed` restricts the scope of the variable to the file in which it is declared and ensures that `uliSeed` will retain its value throughout the program's execution. The default value of `uliSeed = 1` can be changed by calling `InitRandom()` with an appropriate positive integer as an argument. Each starting seed value will generate a unique sequence of random numbers, and you should observe that the same sequence of random numbers will always be returned by the same seed. To see this, just execute Program 8.2 several times and compare results.

4. Equation 8.16 is implemented by the block of statements within `Random()`. The generated random number, `uliSeed`, will be an integer value greater than zero and less than `liM` (i.e., $2^{31} - 1 = 2{,}147{,}483{,}647$). The return statement converts (temporarily) `uliSeed` from an integer to a floating point number of type double and then divides the result by `liM`. These two steps scale the range of random numbers from `[ 0, 2,147,483,647 ]` down to `[ 0, 1 ]`, end-points excluded. The scaled random number is returned to the calling program as a floating point number of type double.

5. Because each of the 1,000 random numbers in our numerical experiment are independent and of equal importance, $p(x_i) = 1/1{,}000$, where `1000` is the number of generated random numbers. The mean value of the sample is given by Equation 8.10, namely

$$\mu = \sum_{i=1}^{N} p(x_i) \cdot x_i = \frac{1}{1{,}000} \cdot \sum_{i=1}^{1{,}000} x_i = 19.91 \tag{8.19}$$

and the variance by Equation 8.11, namely

$$\sigma^2 = \sum_{i=1}^{N} [p(x_i) \cdot x_i^2] - \mu^2 = \frac{1}{1{,}000} \cdot \sum_{i=1}^{1{,}000} x_i^2 - 19.91^2 = 34.901 \tag{8.20}$$

The abbreviated block of code

```
for(iCount = 1; iCount <= SampleSize; iCount = iCount + 1) {

     fSum += fRandomNo;
     fSumSquares += fRandomNo*fRandomNo;

}
```

shows how `fSum` keeps track of the sum of the x_i values. Once this calculation is complete, the statements

```
fAverage = fSum/SampleSize;
fVariance = fSumSquares/SampleSize - fAverage*fAverage;
```

evaluate Equations 8.19 and 8.20.

8.6 Multidimensional Arrays

The C programming language does not provide a definition for multidimensional arrays. Instead, C allows for the construction of one-dimensional arrays of generic elements. Since there is no limitation as to what the elements of the array can be, multidimensional arrays correspond to an array where the elements of the array are arrays themselves.

We begin by seeing how multidimensional arrays arise in engineering practice. Consider the two linear equations

$$v_1 = 110 \cdot i_1 - 10 \cdot i_2 \text{ and } v_2 = 10 \cdot i_1 - 15 \cdot i_2 \tag{8.21}$$

where i_1 and i_2 and v_1 and v_2 are currents and voltages in an electric circuit, respectively. In matrix form, these equations may be rewritten:

$$\begin{bmatrix} v_1 \\ v_2 \end{bmatrix} = \begin{bmatrix} 110 & -10 \\ 10 & -15 \end{bmatrix} \cdot \begin{bmatrix} i_1 \\ i_2 \end{bmatrix} \tag{8.22}$$

The C programming language allows for the representation of matrices as a two-dimensional array of floats. Two-dimensional arrays are implemented as an array of arrays, and in the case of Equation 8.22, each element of the array will be a row consisting of two columns (or two `floats`).

The details of C code needed to declare and initialize the array are as follows:

```
enum{ Rows = 2, Cols = 2 };
float faaResVals [ Rows ][ Cols ];

faaResVals [0][0] = 110;
faaResVals [0][1] = -10;
faaResVals [1][0] =  10;
faaResVals [1][1] = -15;
```

You should think of the array contents and array values as having the layout

```
      |          Column 1          Column 2
==========================================
Row 1 | faaResVals [0][0] faaResVals [0][1]
Row 2 | faaResVals [1][0] faaResVals [1][1]
```

```
      |          Column 1         Column 2
==========================================
Row 1 |               110              -10
Row 2 |                10              -15
```

Now we check the Hungarian notation with this array. We have used the prefix `faa . . .` in the array name `faaResVals` to indicate that the matrix is an array of arrays. `faaResVals` has two elements, each being an array of two floats. The array's contents are accessed by dereferencing the array name. By our Hungarian dereferencing convention, each bracketed term effectively cancels an 'a' in the prefix scheme. When we use one set of brackets, as in `faaResVals [m]`, the array name is dereferenced once. The result `fa...` is the one-dimensional array of floats corresponding to the *m*th row of `faaMatrix`. When we use two sets of brackets, as in `faaResVals[m][n]`, the array name is dereferenced twice. The result `f...` is the float located at the *m*th row and *n*th column. Notice that at each level of dereferencing indices start at `0` and go to `NoRows-1` and `NoCols-1`.

Why should we be concerned about the use of array names without the same number of brackets as the dimension? Because it allows us to operate on subarrays, especially in function calls, and to assemble multidimensional arrays using dynamic memory allocation of one-dimensional arrays. We return to the latter topic in Chapter 10.

8.6.1 Patterns of Storage for Multidimensional Arrays

Arrays of any dimension are stored as a linear progression of values in memory, starting at some constant base address. Now suppose that we are working with the two-dimensional array

```
float faaArray[3][4];
```

having three rows of four elements each. All array elements are floats. The layout of array elements is a sequential region of storage starting with row 1 and ending with row 3, as shown in Figure 8.8. The base address for `faaArray` is `&faaArray[0][0]`. When the compiler generates object code to access an arbitrary element, say `faaArray[1][3]`, the starting address of the 2nd row must be calculated first. It is at offset distance four floats times 4 bytes per float = 16 bytes from the base address of `faaArray[0][0]`. Then, within the 2nd row, the 4th element is three floats (i.e., 12 bytes) away. In this procedure, two multiplications and one addition are needed to compute the offset distance for `faaArray[1][3]`, namely

```
&faaArray[1][3] = &faaArray[0][0] + offset_distance;

where  offset_distance = (1*4 + 3)*sizeof(float)  bytes.
```

The offset distance is calculated as `1` times the size of four floats, plus `3` times the

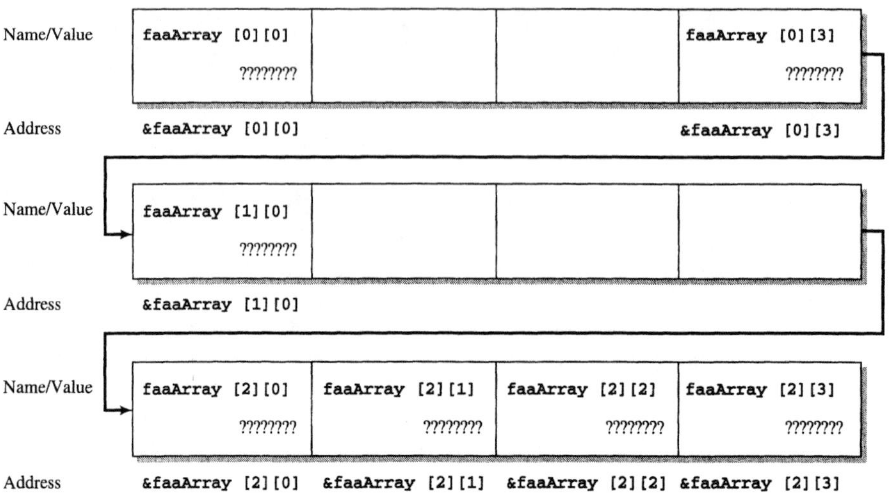

FIGURE 8.8 *Layout of memory in two-dimensional array.*

size of one float. Even more multiplications (i.e., one for each level of indirection) are needed to compute the offset distance for elements in three and higher dimensional arrays. This overhead can seriously affect the efficiency of a large matrix multiplication package. Every access to the elements of the arrays (both reading and writing) requires multiplications to calculate the specific storage location.

8.6.2 Initializing Multidimensional Arrays

Because multidimensional arrays in C are really just assemblies of single dimensional arrays, the concepts for initializing single-dimensional arrays carry over to multidimensional arrays. We have already seen an example of explicit array initialization for array `faaResVals` (e.g., `faaResVals[0][0] = 110`). Multidimensional arrays can also be initialized with lists. Because each element of a multidimensional array is an array itself, the initialization list must also correspond with an array. So, for example, to initialize `faaResVals`, we could use

```
enum{ Rows = 2, Cols = 2 };
float faaResVals[ Rows ][ Cols ] = { {110, -10}, {10, -15} };
```

This procedure is sometimes more convenient than explicit array initialization. When an initialization list is used in a multidimensional array declaration, sizes must be supplied for the 2nd, 3rd, 4th . . . array dimensions. Specification of the first array dimension is optional. For example, if we simply write

```
enum{ Cols = 2 };
float faaResVals[ ][ Cols ] = { {110, -10}, {10, -15} };
```

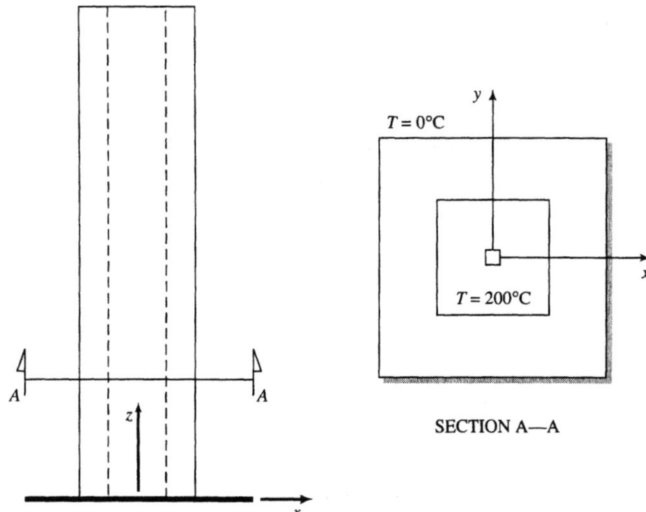

FIGURE 8.9 Front elevation and cross-section of tall chimney.

the compiler will deduce that because there are two columns and the total array size is four floats, the array must be partitioned into two rows.

8.7 APPLICATION OF TWO-DIMENSIONAL ARRAYS

This section uses a finite difference approximation to Laplace's equation and a two-dimensional array of floats to compute and store the steady-state distribution of temperature in the cross-section of a tall chimney.

We select this problem because it is typical of many that naturally occur in the analysis of equilibrium states of physical systems. For example, with suitable simplifying assumptions, Laplace's equation can also describe (1) the irrotational flow of an incompressible fluid, (2) electrostatic and magnetostatic potentials, and (3) the hydraulic head associated with the steady-state flow of ground water in a uniform porous medium.

8.7.1 Heat Conduction Problem

Figure 8.9 shows the front elevation and square-shaped cross-section A-A for the tall chimney. The chimney is constructed from a material that is homogeneous and isotropic (i.e., the material has the same material properties in all directions). At the cross-section, the inside and outside temperatures are 200°C and 0°C, respectively, and there is neither a net flow of heat to or from the chimney (i.e., it is in thermal equilibrium). Finally, we assume that at the chimney cross-section, the distribution of temperature is constant along the z-axis.

Because the chimney is constructed from a material that is homogeneous, thermal conductivity will not vary with position, and because the material is isotropic, thermal conductivity will not vary with direction. The steady-state distribution of temperature $T = T(x, y)$ throughout the chimney cross-section is given by solutions to Laplace's equation

$$\frac{\partial^2 T(x,y)}{\partial x^2} + \frac{\partial^2 T(x,y)}{\partial y^2} = 0 \tag{8.23}$$

with boundary conditions $T = 0°C$ along the exterior of the chimney, and $T = 200°C$ along the chimney interior.

Finite Difference Mesh for Chimney Cross-Section

The chimney cross-section is symmetric about the x- and y-axes, and the two diagonal axes. Our computational model takes advantage of symmetries about the x- and y-axes by modeling only one quarter of the chimney cross-section, as shown in Figure 8.10a. Two new boundary conditions are needed for this model; along the y-axis the temperature gradient $dT/dx = 0$, and along the x-axis $dT/dy = 0$.

If dx and dy are the mesh distance in the x-axis and y-axis directions, then a suitable finite difference approximation to Equation 8.23 is

$$\left[\frac{T(x + dx, y) - 2T(x, y) + T(x - dx, y)}{dx^2}\right] + \left[\frac{T(x, y + dy) - 2T(x, y) + T(x, y - dy)}{dy^2}\right] = 0 \tag{8.24}$$

Equation 8.24 is simply the two-dimensional counterpart of the finite difference approximation derived for the cable profile problem. If $dx = dy$, then Equation 8.24 can be rearranged to give

$$4T(x, y) - T(x - dx, y) - T(x + dx, y) - T(x, y + dy) - T(x, y - dy) = 0 \tag{8.25}$$

The leftmost schematic of Figure 8.10b shows the weighting of discrete temperatures in the finite difference approximation. The nodes along the x-axis (i.e., $y = 0$) satisfy the finite difference equation

$$4 \cdot T(x, 0) - T(x - dx, 0) - T(x + dx, 0) - 2T(x, dy) = 0 \tag{8.26}$$

and along the y-axis (i.e., $x = 0$)

$$4 \cdot T(0, y) - 2T(dx, y) - T(0, y + dy) - T(x, y - dy) = 0 \tag{8.27}$$

The finite difference mesh has 65 nodes, 26 of them being on the interior (i.e., $T = 0°C$) and exterior (i.e., $T = 200°C$) boundaries. This leaves 39 nodes on the chimney interior for evaluation. Instead of evaluating the temperature stencils at all 39 interior nodes, we compute temperature only at the 21 nodes labeled with small filled black boxes and fill in the remaining unknowns by noting the symmetry in temperature along the line $x = y$. The 4-node stencil is used at nodes 1 to 3, and the 5-node stencil is used at nodes 4 to 21.

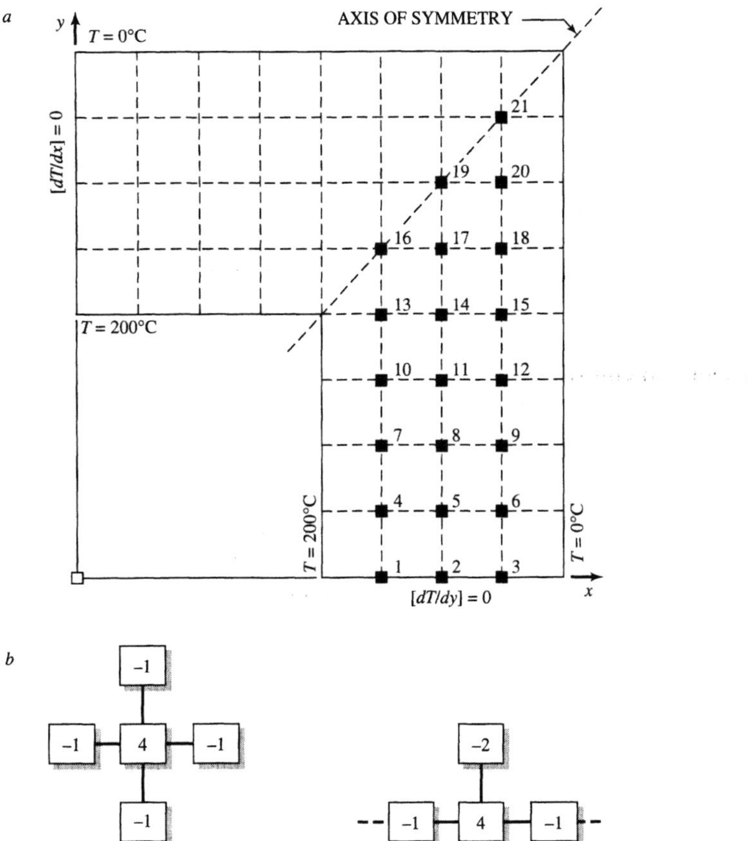

FIGURE 8.10 *(a)* Finite difference mesh and *(b)* finite difference stencils for Equation 8.23.

Computer Program

Program 8.3 uses a simple looping construct and a (9 × 9) matrix called `faaTemp` to compute and store temperatures at the finite difference nodes.

PROGRAM 8.3: DISTRIBUTION OF TEMPERATURE IN CHIMNEY CROSS-SECTION

```
/*
 *  ===================================================================
 *  : Finite difference computation for temperature
 *    distribution in cross-section of chimney.
 *  ===================================================================
 */
```

```
#include <stdio.h>

#define max(a, b) ((a) > (b) ? (a) : (b))

enum { Rows = 9, Cols = 9 };        /*  size of finite difference grid */
enum { InsideTemp = 200 };          /*  temperature inside chimney     */

int main( void ) {
float faaTemp[ Rows ][ Cols ];
float fTempSum, fMaxChange;
int iIndexi, iIndexj;

  /* [a] : Initialize Temperatures */

  for( iIndexi = 0; iIndexi < 5; iIndexi = iIndexi + 1 ) {
      faaTemp[ 4  ][ iIndexi ] = InsideTemp;
      faaTemp[ iIndexi ][  4 ] = InsideTemp;
  }

  for( iIndexi = 5; iIndexi < Rows; iIndexi = iIndexi + 1 ) {
      for( iIndexj = 0; iIndexj < iIndexi; iIndexj = iIndexj + 1 ) {
           faaTemp[ iIndexj ][ iIndexi ] = 0.0;
           faaTemp[ iIndexi ][ iIndexj ] = 0.0;
      }
  }

  /* [b] : Compute temperatures over interior points */

  fMaxChange = InsideTemp;
  while( fMaxChange > 0.5 ) {
      fMaxChange = 0.0;

      for( iIndexi = 5; iIndexi <= 7; iIndexi = iIndexi + 1 ) {

         /* [b.1] : Temperature along edges 3 and 6 */

         fTempSum = faaTemp[ iIndexi+1 ][0] + faaTemp[ iIndexi-1 ][0] +
                    2*faaTemp[ iIndexi ][1];
         fMaxChange = max( fMaxChange,
                           fabs(faaTemp[ iIndexi ][ 0 ] - fTempSum/4.0) );

         faaTemp[ iIndexi ][ 0 ] = faaTemp[0][ iIndexi ] = fTempSum/4.0;

         /* [b.2] : Temperature inside region */

         for( iIndexj = 1; iIndexj <= iIndexi; iIndexj = iIndexj + 1 ) {
            fTempSum = faaTemp[ iIndexi+1 ][ iIndexj ] +
```

```
                    faaTemp[ iIndexi-1 ][ iIndexj ] +
                    faaTemp[ iIndexi ][ iIndexj+1 ] +
                    faaTemp[ iIndexi ][ iIndexj- 1];

            fMaxChange = max( fMaxChange,
                              fabs( faaTemp[iIndexi][iIndexj] -
                                    fTempSum/4.0));

            faaTemp[ iIndexj ][ iIndexi ] = fTempSum/4.0;
            faaTemp[ iIndexi ][ iIndexj ] = fTempSum/4.0;
         }
      }
   }

   /* [c] : Print temperatures : (null) quantities = inside of chimney */

   printf(" temperature = [ \n");
   for( iIndexi = 0; iIndexi < Cols; iIndexi = iIndexi + 1 ) {
      for( iIndexj = 0; iIndexj < Rows; iIndexj = iIndexj + 1 ) {
          if( iIndexi < 4 && iIndexj < 4 )
              printf("   NaN ");
          else
             printf(" %5.1f ", faaTemp[ iIndexi ][ iIndexj ]);
      }
      printf(";\n");
   }
   printf(" ]; \n");
}
```

Points to note are as follows:

1. The looping construct

   ```
   for( iIndexi = 0; iIndexi < 5; iIndexi = iIndexi + 1 ) {
       faaTemp[ 4  ][ iIndexi ] = InsideTemp;
       faaTemp[ iIndexi ][  4 ] = InsideTemp;
   }
   ```

   initializes the nodes along the chimney interior to $T = 200°\text{C}$. The second block of code in part `[a]` initializes the remaining nodal temperatures to $T = 0°\text{C}$.
2. The heart of Program 8.3 is in block `[b]`, where a looping construct iterates over the 21 nodes with unknown temperature until convergence is achieved. Section `[b.1]` evaluates

$$T(x,0) = \left[\frac{T(x-dx,0) + T(x+dx,0) + 2 \cdot T(x,dy)}{4}\right] \tag{8.28}$$

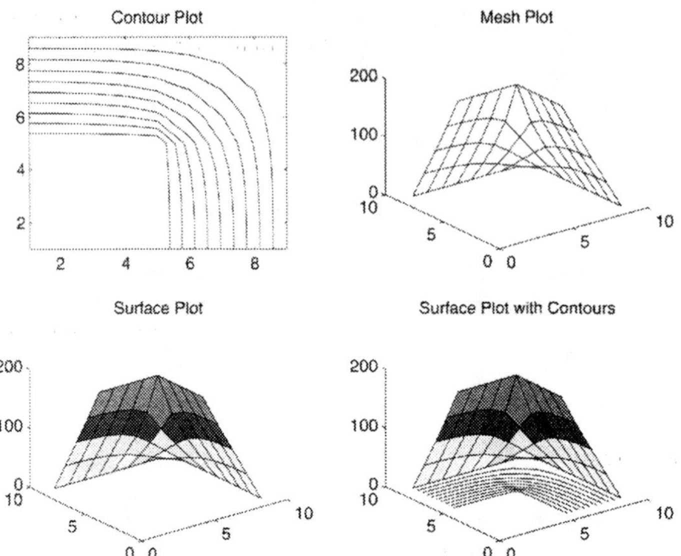

FIGURE 8.11 Temperature profiles in chimney cross-section.

and Section [b.2]

$$T(x, y) = \left[\frac{T(x - dx, y) + T(x + dx, y) + T(x, y + dy) + T(x, y - dy)}{4}\right] \quad (8.29)$$

At the beginning of each iterate, `fMaxChange` is set to zero. The iterations continue until the maximum change in nodal temperature between iterates is less than one half a degree.

3. In part [c] of Program 8.3, a matrix of temperatures is generated in a format suitable for reading by MATLAB [22].

```
temperature = [
  NaN    NaN    NaN    NaN   200.0  147.3  96.5  47.7   0.0 ;
  NaN    NaN    NaN    NaN   200.0  146.9  96.0  47.4   0.0 ;
  NaN    NaN    NaN    NaN   200.0  145.2  93.9  46.1   0.0 ;
  NaN    NaN    NaN    NaN   200.0  140.4  88.9  43.2   0.0 ;
200.0  200.0  200.0  200.0   200.0  128.2  78.8  37.8   0.0 ;
147.3  146.9  145.2  140.4   128.2   94.3  60.6  29.6   0.0 ;
 96.5   96.0   93.9   88.9    78.8   60.6  40.2  19.9   0.0 ;
 47.7   47.4   46.1   43.2    37.8   29.6  19.9  10.0   0.0 ;
  0.0    0.0    0.0    0.0     0.0    0.0   0.0   0.0   0.0 ;
];
```

Figure 8.11 shows a variety of contour and mesh plots of temperature in the chimney cross-section. Please see the MATLAB tutorial for the list of commands used to create this plot. As mentioned in Section 7.8, `NaN`s usually result from arithmetic operations that are ill defined, such as division by zero. In MATLAB, however, NaNs are used to represent matrix elements that are missing.

8.8 POINTERS

A pointer is simply a variable that holds the address of an object in the program. In addition to the four basic attributes that all variables possess, pointers have a fifth attribute called the indirect value. We cannot overemphasize the importance of the indirect value because once it is clearly understood, the full power of the C language will be at your fingertips.

8.8.1 Motivation and Need for Pointers

A key problem with multidimensional matrices is expensive access methods that require one multiplication for each level of indirection. If we could store the address of each row in the array, then no multiplications would be required to find the row address. Elements in a two-dimensional array would be accessed by first getting the row address and adding to it the offset of the column (see Figure 8.12). To store addresses, we need some type of variable that can hold an address. In C, this variable is called a pointer.

8.9 POINTER TYPE, ADDRESS, NAME, VALUE, AND INDIRECT VALUE

All variables have four important attributes: (1) name; (2) type (which determines their size); (3) value; and (4) storage location (or address). For example, the declaration:

```
int iVal = 10;
```

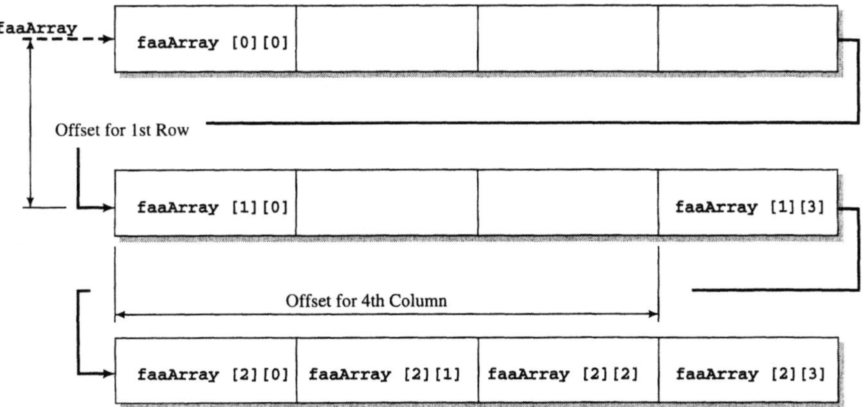

FIGURE 8.12 *Offset access of a two-dimensional array.*

defines an integer called `iVal` and initializes its contents to 10. The address of `iVal` is given by `&iVal`. The variable type—`int` in this example—determines: (1) the amount of memory that will be used to store the variable, (2) the values that the variable can take, and (3) the operations that may be applied to the variable.

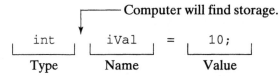

```
                       ┌──── Computer will find storage.
                       ▼
   int            iVal       =     10;
 └──────┘       └──────┘         └──────┘
   Type           Name             Value
```

A pointer is a new type that has five attributes. In addition to the four attributes common to all variables (i.e., name, value, address, type), pointers have a fifth attribute called an indirect value. Pointer declarations are composed of three parts–the data type, an asterisk * (or star) character that precedes the pointer's name, and the pointer name itself. Once defined, a pointer should be explicitly initialized to the address of a valid object of the specified type. For example, the statement

```
int * ipToVal = &iVal;
```

defines

```
                       ┌──── Computer will find storage.
                       ▼
   int*          ipToVal     =    &iVal;
 └──────┘       └──────┘         └──────┘
   Type           Name             Value
```

a pointer of type `int` called `ipToVal`, which takes the address of `iVal` as its initial value. Our use of Hungarian notation helps to clarify what is going on. The type prefix `ip...` follows directly from the definition `(int *)`, thereby making type information explicit in the variable's name.

The indirect value of a pointer is obtained by preceding a pointer's name with the * operator. The result is that the actual value of the object referred to by the pointer. This is why the * operator is often called the indirection or dereferencing operator. For example, when we write

```
* ipToVal
```

we are dereferencing the pointer `ipToVal`. The * operator changes the data type from integer pointer to just integer. For variables having names that are defined with Hungarian notation, dereferencing a pointer effectively cancels out a `p`. So, in our example, the data type `ip...` is effectively changed to an int type prefix `i....`

Computer Program. The basic features of pointers are illustrated in Program 8.4.

PROGRAM 8.4: INITIALIZE AND PRINT A POINTER

```
/*
 *  ======================================================================
 *  Initialize and print a pointer.
 *  ======================================================================
 */

#include <stdio.h>           /* for printf() prototype */

int main( void ) {
int iSomeInt = 10;           /* Define an integer, initialize it to 10 */
int   *ipPtrToInt;           /* Define the pointer, as yet uninitialized */

    ipPtrToInt = &iSomeInt;  /* Initialize pointer to iSomeInt */

    printf("The value    of *ipPtrToInt is %d\n", *ipPtrToInt );
    printf("The location of    iSomeInt is %p\n",  ipPtrToInt );
}
```

Points to note are as follows:

1. After the integer `iSomeInt` is defined and initialized to 10, `ipPtrToInt`, a pointer of type `int`, is assigned the address of `iSomeInt`. We say that `ipPtrToInt` refers to (or points to) the integer `iSomeInt`. Program 8.4 then prints the dereferenced contents of `ipPtrToInt` and the (system-dependent) address of `ipPtrToInt` in memory. A typical script of output is

```
The value    of *ipPtrToInt is  10
The location of    iSomeInt is  f7fff7dc
```

2. Figure 8.13 is a schematic of the memory layout at two stages of the program execution. Like variables, pointers will have undefined (or random) values until they are initialized. We represent this with the use of question marks in the right-hand side of Figure 8.13a. Figure 8.13b summarizes the layout of memory after the assignment statement. We fill in the value of `ipPtrToInt` with `&iSomeInt` and connect `ipPtrToInt` to `iSomeInt` with an arrow to signify their relationship.
3. Now that `ipPtrToInt` knows where `iSomeInt` is stored, `ipPtrToInt` can be used to access the contents of `iSomeInt` and, if required, change the contents of `iSomeInt`. More precisely, the value that `ipPtrToInt` references can be changed by preceding the pointer name with a `*`, and assigning a new value, as in

```
*ipPtrToInt = 20;
```

Now the value of integer `iSomeInt` is `20`.

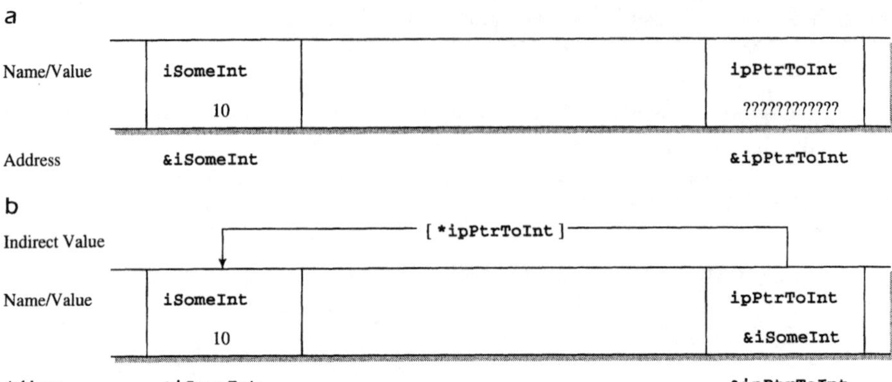

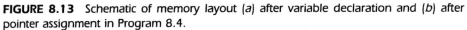

FIGURE 8.13 Schematic of memory layout *(a)* after variable declaration and *(b)* after pointer assignment in Program 8.4.

8.9.1 NULL and Void Pointers

The NULL Pointer

A NULL pointer setting explicitly indicates that a pointer does not point to an object. As a result, NULL does not take the address of an object and, conversely, the address of operator & will never yield a NULL pointer. The script of code

```
#include <stdio.h>

int main( void ) {
int *ipPtrToInt;
    ipPtrToInt = NULL;
}
```

shows the essential details of defining a pointer and initializing its contents to NULL. Readers should note that although a NULL pointer is known not to point to any object, an uninitialized pointer might point anywhere. The NULL macro is defined in the header file stdio.h.

The Void Pointer

A void pointer is a generic type for the comparison of arguments. It is written void *. Unlike regular pointers, a void pointer can point to any type in C. A void pointer can hold any type of pointer, and any pointer can be assigned to a void * without a cast. Here are a few examples of void * usage:

```
int iVal1;
char  cIn;
void * vpHold;
char * cpChar   = &cIn;
int  * ipValue = &iVal1;
int  * ipExtent;
```

```
vpHold    = ipValue;
ipValue   = (int*) vpHold;
ipExtent  = (int *) vpHold;
```

In the final two statements we see that a cast is required when a `void *` is assigned to any other type of pointer. This makes sense since the `void *` carries no type information with it.

8.9.2 Size of Pointers

We already know that characters are stored in 1 byte, integers and floats in 2 or 4 bytes, and doubles in 8 bytes. We also know that a pointer simply holds the address of a variable. If the purpose of the pointer is to store an address in computer memory, then we should expect that all pointers will have the same size, irrespective of their type (this argument is somewhat akin to the use of fixed-size address labels on small and large envelopes). Two questions that this argument leaves unanswered are (1) how many bytes are needed to store a pointer?, and (2) are pointers the same size on all computers?

Computer Program. Program 8.5 answers question 1 by printing the size of pointers (in bytes) for each of the four basic data types in C.

PROGRAM 8.5: PRINT SIZE OF POINTERS

```
/*
 *  ============================================================
 *  Print size of pointers (in bytes) for basic data types.
 *  ============================================================
 */

#include <stdio.h>    /* for printf() prototype */

int main( void ) {
char   *cpChar;   /* pointer of data type character */
int     *ipVar;   /* pointer of data type integer   */
float  *fpVar;    /* pointer of data type float     */
double *dpVar;    /* pointer of data type double    */

  /* [a] : Print size of pointers for basic data types */

     printf( "The sizeof \"cpChar\" is %d bytes\n", sizeof ( cpChar ) );
     printf( "The sizeof \"ipVar\"  is %d bytes\n", sizeof ( ipVar ) );
     printf( "The sizeof \"fpVar\"  is %d bytes\n", sizeof ( fpVar ) );
     printf( "The sizeof \"dpVar\"  is %d bytes\n", sizeof ( dpVar ) );
}
```

On an engineering workstation, the program output is

```
The sizeof "cpChar" is 4 bytes
The sizeof "ipVar"  is 4 bytes
The sizeof "fpVar"  is 4 bytes
The sizeof "dpVar"  is 4 bytes
```

Here we see that four bytes are needed for pointers to each basic data type. Pointers are usually the size of the natural word size on the particular machine.

8.9.3 Pointers to Pointers

We have already seen that we can define pointers to any data type. In the development of engineering software, it often makes sense to define a pointer that will point to another pointer. In this section, we simply demonstrate the concept and show how indirect values apply a pointer to a pointer.

Computer Program. Program 8.6 defines an integer `iValue`, an integer pointer `ipPtrToInt`, and `ippPtrToPtrToInt`, a pointer to a pointer of type int. Then we print the value of `iValue` using each data type.

PROGRAM 8.6: DEMONSTRATE POINTER TO POINTER CONSTRUCT

```
/*
 *  ================================================
 *  Demonstrate use of pointer to pointer
 *  ================================================
 */

#include <stdio.h>   /* for printf() prototype */

int main ( void ) {
int iValue = 10;
int *ipPtrToInt        = &iValue;
int **ippPtrToPtrToInt = &ipPtrToInt;

    printf (" Direct Access           : iValue = %4d\n",            iValue );
    printf (" Via *ipPtrToInt         : iValue = %4d\n",       *ipPtrToInt );
    printf (" Via **ippPtrToPtrToInt : iValue = %4d\n", **ippPtrToPtrToInt );
}
```

The program output is

```
Direct Access          : iValue =   10
Via *ipPtrToInt        : iValue =   10
Via **ippPtrToPtrToInt : iValue =   10
```

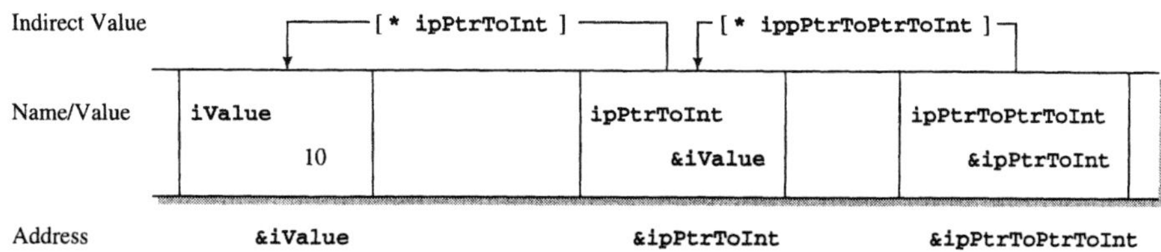

FIGURE 8.14 Layout of memory for `iValue`, `ipPtrToInt`, and `ippPtrToPtrToInt`.

Notice how we use one level of indirection to access the value of `iValue` from `ipPtrToInt` and two levels of indirection from `ippPtrToPtrToInt`. The latter is defined with the `**` (double star) notation. We have initialized the variables so that `ipPtrToInt` points to `iValue` and `ippPtrToPtrToInt` points to `ipPtrToInt`. A schematic of the memory layout after the initializations is given in Figure 8.14.

We return to this topic in Chapter 10, where the pointer-to-pointer construct is used for the dynamic memory allocation of two-dimensional arrays.

8.10 POINTER ARITHMETIC

Pointer arithmetic is a convenient mechanism for changing the value of a pointer in increments of the size of its base type. In this section, we illustrate the features of pointer arithmetic by working through two examples.

Example. Consider the statement pair

```
char caName []       = "Engineering";
char * cpPtrToChar = &caName [ 0 ];
```

The first line defines and initializes a character array called `caName`. The second statement declares a pointer of type `char` and initializes its value to the base address of `caName` (i.e., `&caName [0]`). In this example, the base type of `cpPtrToChar` is `char` and the size of `char` is 1 (byte). The indirect value of `cpPtrToChar` is the first character in `Engineering` (i.e., the letter `E`). The arithmetic expression (an example of pointer arithmetic)

```
cpPtrToChar = cpPtrToChar + 1;
```

increments the character pointer by `1*sizeof(char)` or 1 byte. Now `cpPtrToChar` points to `&caName [1]` and has as its indirect value the second character in `Engineering`. The entire contents of `caName` can be accessed, character by character, by systematically incrementing `cpPtrToChar` by 1 and then taking the indirect value `*cpPtrToChar`.

Computer Program. Program 8.7 demonstrates the use of pointer arithmetic when the base type of a pointer occupies more than 1 byte.

PROGRAM 8.7: POINTER ARITHMETIC FOR FLOATS

```
/*
 *  ========================================================
 *  Illustrate pointer arithmetic with floats.
 *  ========================================================
 */

#include <stdio.h>    /* for printf() prototype */

int main ( void ) {
enum { Max = 10 };
float faArray[ Max ];
float * fpFloats = faArray;
int iCounter    = 0;

   /* [a] : Initialize each float to the square of its index */

   for( iCounter = 0; iCounter < Max; ++iCounter )
      faArray[iCounter] = iCounter * iCounter;

   /* [b] : Reset the counter , and print the values */

   iCounter = 0;
   while( iCounter++ < Max ) {
      printf( "*(%p) = %f\n", fpFloats, *fpFloats );
      fpFloats++;
   }
}
```

On an engineering workstation, the program output looks similar to the following:

```
*(f7fff618) = 0.000000
*(f7fff61c) = 1.000000
*(f7fff620) = 4.000000
*(f7fff624) = 9.000000
*(f7fff628) = 16.000000
*(f7fff62c) = 25.000000
*(f7fff630) = 36.000000
*(f7fff634) = 49.000000
*(f7fff638) = 64.000000
*(f7fff63c) = 81.000000
```

Points to note are as follows:

1. In the opening sections of the program, pointer `fpFloats` is initialized to the base address of array `faArray`. The first loop initializes the array elements to the square of their index.
2. When we write (in the second loop)

```
fpFloats  = fpFloats + 1;
```

or `fpFloats++`, a compiler will generate low-level code to increase the address referred to by `fpFloats` by `sizeof(float)` bytes, namely

```
fpFloats  = fpFloats + 1 * sizeof( float );
```

Pointer arithmetic makes `fpFloats` point to the next float and not to the next byte. The latter would be only 1 byte away. Luckily, we do not have to keep track of these kinds of details.

8.11 RELATIONSHIP BETWEEN POINTERS AND ARRAYS

Pointers and arrays are used in *almost* the same way to access memory. While a pointer is a variable that takes addresses as values, an array name is a compile-time constant that can never be modified. When an array name is used in a reference, the expression evaluates to the address of zeroth index element in the array. The array subscripting operator will behave the same whether it is used with an array or a pointer. The two exceptions to this behavior are

1. When the array name is the argument of `sizeof` or the `&` operator
2. When an array is used as a literal string initializer for an array of characters

Consider the integer pointer and array of integers in the following fragment of code:

```
enum { MaxTabs = 4 };
int iaArray [ MaxTabs ];
int *ipTab = iaArray;
```

When an array is declared, the compiler allocates a base address and sufficient memory to contain the elements of the array. The base address of an array is a compile-time constant. You can access it at run-time but, unlike a pointer, you cannot modify its value. The statement `iaArray++` is meaningless. The statements

```
       ipTab = iaArray;

and    ipTab = &iaArray [0];
```

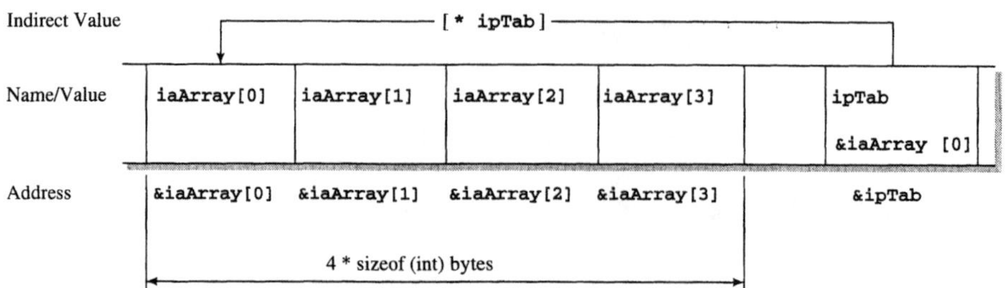

FIGURE 8.15 Layout of memory for `iaArray` and `ipTab`.

are equivalent. Here we see how the pointer `ipTab` is initialized to point to the base address of `iaArray` (or first integer in the `iaArray`) at run-time.

Figure 8.15 is a schematic of memory layout for the integer array and pointer of type int. All the attributes of the pointer variable are explicitly shown in the memory diagram. The address of `ipTab` is `&ipTab`. Remember that `ipTab` is a variable and is stored at a specific address, just like any other variable. The indirect value of `ipTab` is the integer `ipArray[0]` (or equivalently `*ipTab`). The four elements of `iaArray` can be accessed using 16 different ways.

C Code	*Access Method*	*C Code*	*Access Method*
`iaArray [ 0 ] ====>`	`*(iaArray + 0)`	`ipTab [ 0 ] ====>`	`*(ipTab + 0)`
`iaArray [ 1 ] ====>`	`*(iaArray + 1)`	`ipTab [ 1 ] ====>`	`*(ipTab + 1)`
`iaArray [ 2 ] ====>`	`*(iaArray + 2)`	`ipTab [ 2 ] ====>`	`*(ipTab + 2)`
`iaArray [ 3 ] ====>`	`*(iaArray + 3)`	`ipTab [ 3 ] ====>`	`*(ipTab + 3)`

The first and third columns demonstrate use of index notation to access array elements. The second and fourth columns demonstrate array access via pointer arithmetic and indirect values. The low-level details of accessing the fourth element of `iaArray` are as follows:

1. `iaArray [3]`: The compiler generates code that uses the address of the array (which only it knows) as a pointer and adds an offset of three base element types (int) to the address to access the integer stored there.
2. `ipTab [3]`: The compiler generates code to retrieve the value of the pointer `ipTab` (which happens to be the address of the first integer in the array `iaArray`), then it adds an offset of three base element types (int) to the address to access the integer stored there.

Both methods employ bracket operators to dereference a pointer. In the first case, this is the array name. Array index notation is effectively converted to pointer notation by the compiler. This is why we have connected the first column to the second, and the third to the fourth.

Computer Program: Program 8.8 demonstrates how pointer notation and a one-dimensional character array can be used.

PROGRAM 8.8: EXERCISE POINTERS AND CHARACTER ARRAYS

```
/*
 * =====================================================================
 * ptrcls2.c -- first of a series of examples to illustrate pointers and
 *              arrays at work and their relationships.
 * =====================================================================
 */

#include <stdio.h>   /* for printf() prototype */
#include <string.h>  /* for strlen()           */

int main( void ) {
static char caArray[] = "character array";
char* cpChar = caArray;                       /* pointer to character array */
int iCnt;                                     /* counter for indexing       */

  /* [a] : Show some things like size of each, values, etc. */

  printf( "The value of \"caArray\" is %x\n", caArray );
  printf( "The value of \"cpChar\"  is %x\n", cpChar );
  printf( "The size of \"caArray\"  is %d\n", sizeof( caArray ) );
  printf( "The size of \"cpChar\"   is %x\n", sizeof( cpChar ) );
  printf( "The address(&) of \"caArray\" is %x\n", &caArray );
  printf( "The address(&) of \"cpChar\"  is %x\n", &cpChar );

  /* [b] : Manipulate character array */

  printf("\n");
  for( iCnt = 0; iCnt < strlen(caArray); ++iCnt ) {
    printf( "\ncaArray[%-2d] = %c\tcpChar[%-2d] = %c %-2d[cpChar] = %c"
            "\t *(cpChar + %-2d) = %c",
            iCnt, caArray[iCnt], iCnt, cpChar[iCnt],
            iCnt, iCnt[cpChar], iCnt, *(cpChar+iCnt) );
  }

  /* [c] : Now use the pointer as the variable */

     printf("\n\nUsing pointer incrementing for caArray = ");
     for( iCnt = 0; iCnt < strlen( caArray ); ++iCnt )
          putchar( *cpChar++ );
     puts(" ");
}
```

Program 8.8 generates two blocks of output:

```
The value of "caArray" is 40d8
The value of "cpChar"  is 40d8
The size of "caArray"  is 16
The size of "cpChar"   is 4
The address(&) of "caArray" is 40d8
The address(&) of "cpChar"  is f7fff7dc

caArray[ 0] = c cpChar[ 0] = c  0 [cpChar] = c *(cpChar +  0) = c
caArray[ 1] = h cpChar[ 1] = h  1 [cpChar] = h *(cpChar +  1) = h
caArray[ 2] = a cpChar[ 2] = a  2 [cpChar] = a *(cpChar +  2) = a
caArray[ 3] = r cpChar[ 3] = r  3 [cpChar] = r *(cpChar +  3) = r
caArray[ 4] = a cpChar[ 4] = a  4 [cpChar] = a *(cpChar +  4) = a
caArray[ 5] = c cpChar[ 5] = c  5 [cpChar] = c *(cpChar +  5) = c
caArray[ 6] = t cpChar[ 6] = t  6 [cpChar] = t *(cpChar +  6) = t
caArray[ 7] = e cpChar[ 7] = e  7 [cpChar] = e *(cpChar +  7) = e
caArray[ 8] = r cpChar[ 8] = r  8 [cpChar] = r *(cpChar +  8) = r
caArray[ 9] =   cpChar[ 9] =    9 [cpChar] =   *(cpChar +  9) =
caArray[10] = a cpChar[10] = a 10 [cpChar] = a *(cpChar + 10) = a
caArray[11] = r cpChar[11] = r 11 [cpChar] = r *(cpChar + 11) = r
caArray[12] = r cpChar[12] = r 12 [cpChar] = r *(cpChar + 12) = r
caArray[13] = a cpChar[13] = a 13 [cpChar] = a *(cpChar + 13) = a
caArray[14] = y cpChar[14] = y 14 [cpChar] = y *(cpChar + 14) = y

Using pointer incrementing for caArray = character array
```

Points to note are as follows:

1. The program execution begins with the initialization of `caArray`

   ```
   static char caArray[] = "character array";
   ```

   and the assignment

   ```
   char * cpChar = caArray;
   ```

   In the first two lines of output we see that `caArray` and `cpChar` have equal values (i.e., `40d8`), thereby demonstrating that when the array name `caArray` is used in an expression, it evaluates to the address of the first element in the character array. The only subtlety here is that the compiler fills in the value/address of `caArray` while the running program fills in the value of `cpChar` (since it is actually stored at run-time).
2. The third line of output prints the "size of" `caArray` as `16`. The compiler calculates and generates code to print it since it is known at compile time (it had to know this because it allocated the space for the actual array after

calculating its size from the initialization string `"character array"`). On the next line, the `sizeof (cpChar)` is printed, which is the size pointer `cpChar`, 4 bytes, and not the size of the character array that is referred to. To actually print the size of the character string, we need to use the string library function `strlen`.

3. The last two lines of the first block print the addresses of `caArray` and `cpChar` using the address of operator `&`. It is important to remember here that when an array name is used as an argument to the address of operator, the array name will evaluate to the address of the first element, as always. In the second case, a run-time entity `cpChar` is the argument to the address of operator. It prints the actual run-time storage location of the pointer `f7fff7dc`. This location contains the address of the actual character array, `40d8`, because we initialized it to that value.
4. Block `[b]` shows the various ways characters in an array can be printed. Of course, we can use the standard (most intuitive) array indexing methods, as in `caArray[0]`. We can also use the pointer to access these elements, as in `cpChar[0]`. As explained in the section on pointers and arrays, when the compiler sees the expression `cpChar[0]`, it retrieves the value of `cpChar`, then it adds the offset in the brackets (times the size of each element, which is `1` byte here), then it dereferences that address. We could have simply written `*(cpChar + 0)`. The next output value just switches the order of the address and index `iCnt[cpChar]`, which is admittedly obscure. The switching works because `*(cpChar + 0)` is the same as `*(0 + cpChar)`. Finally, we add the index to the pointer (whose arithmetic ensures that we move by the base element type) before dereferencing it with the `*` operator. The last version is effectively what happens in each of the output versions.

8.11.1 Pointers and Two-Dimensional Arrays

In multidimensional arrays there are intermediate levels of type "array," and this is a case where a pointer to an array makes sense. The simplest example is for a two-dimensional array of rows and columns. Consider the definition

```
int iaaArray[ NoRows ][ NoCols ];
```

In this case, `iaaArray` evaluates to the address of the first element of iaaArray's base type, which is array of ints. An array pointer (or pointer to array) can be useful in this situation for stepping over the individual rows of the array. Because each row is an array of `NoCols` ints, a pointer to the row will refer to arrays of `NoCols` ints.

Computer Program: These principles are explored in Program 8.9, where a (4 × 2) array is allocated and initialized with

```
int iaaTest[ NoRows ][ NoCols ] = {{ 1, 2},
                                   { 3, 4},
                                   { 5, 6},
                                   { 7, 8}};
```

and then pointer notation is used to access and print the elements of the array in a number of ways.

PROGRAM 8.9: PRINT TWO-DIMENSIONAL ARRAY

```
/*
 *  ===================================================================
 *  Demonstrate use of array index and pointer notation for accessing
 *  and printing elements of a two-dimensional matrix.
 *  ===================================================================
 */

#include <stdio.h>

enum { NoRows = 4, NoCols = 2 };

int main ( void ) {
int iaaTest[ NoRows ][ NoCols ] = {{ 1, 2},
                                    { 3, 4},
                                    { 5, 6},
                                    { 7, 8}};
int ii, ij;
int *ipPtrToInt;

  /* [a] : Use pointer notation to access and print array contents */

     for (ii = 0 ; ii < NoRows; ii = ii + 1) {
          ipPtrToInt = *(iaaTest + ii);
          for (ij = 0 ; ij < NoCols; ij = ij + 1) {
               printf(" %4d", *(ipPtrToInt + ij ));
          }
          printf("\n");
     }
}
```

Program 8.9 generates the output

```
1  2
3  4
5  6
7  8
```

Figure 8.16 is a schematic of the layout of memory in array `iaaTest`. Points to note are as follows:

1. When we dereference the array name once, as in `iaaTest [0]` and `iaaTest [1]`, the result is a pointer to the beginning of the first and second rows,

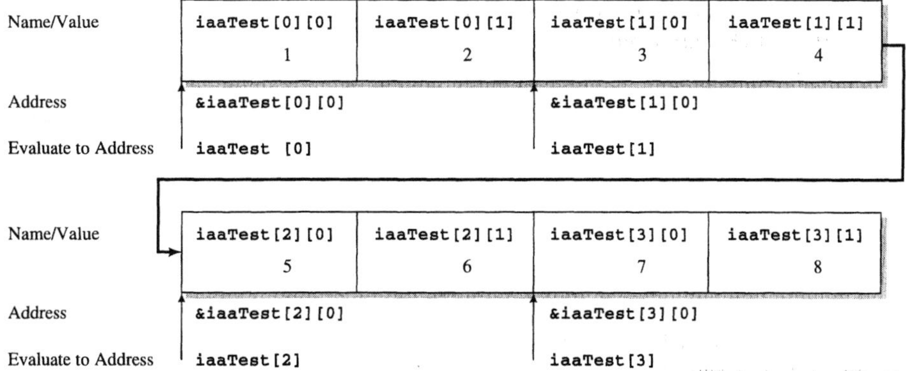

FIGURE 8.16 Layout of memory in (4 × 2) array.

respectively. Two expressions that are equivalent to `iaaTest[ ii ] [ ij ]` are

```
*(   iaaTest [ ii ] + ij )
*((*(iaaTest + ii)) + ij )
```

An examination of the assembly code for Program 8.9 will reveal that the computer treats `iaaTest[ ii ] [ ij ]` as if it were written

```
*( &iaaTest[0][0] + NoCols*ii + ij )
```

The latter is simply the dereferenced contents of memory at offset distance

```
(NoCols*ii + ij) * sizeof (int)   bytes
```

from the base address of `iaaTest`. Notice that the offset calculation depends on the number of columns in the matrix but is independent of the total number of rows in `iaaTest`.

2. The statement

```
ipPtrToInt = *(iaaTest + ii);
```

assigns to `ipPtrToInt`, the starting address of row `ii+1` in `iaaTest`. The same address in array index notation is given by

```
ipPtrToInt = &iaaTest [ii];
```

An alternative strategy of implementation for Program 8.9 is to declare the pointer as

```
int (*ipPtrToInt) [ NoCols ] = iaaTest;
```

Now `ipPtrToInt [ii][ij]` is equivalent to `iaaTest [ii][ij]`.

FURTHER INFORMATION

1. Experience indicates that the random number generator defined by Equation 8.16 gives a much longer cycle of random numbers than many similar implementations. Detailed discussions of this algorithm may be found in Chapter 10 of Weiss [6], in the second edition of *Numerical Recipes in C* [4], and the original paper of Schrage [5].

REVIEW QUESTIONS

1. What are common uses for arrays?
2. Why might the Hungarian notation be useful when using arrays? Can you always (at least in your mind) tell the type of a variable when using Hungarian notation?
3. Why does C not check array bounds automatically? Can you compensate if necessary?
4. What are the essential features of character arrays in C?
5. What does NaN mean?
6. How is a multidimensional array supported in C if it only intrinsically supports single-dimensioned arrays?
7. What does the name of an array evaluate to when used in an expression?
8. Why are pointers important in C? For what purposes might you use them?
9. What are the attributes of all variables in C? What additional attribute does a pointer have?
10. How can Hungarian notation help you when dereferencing pointers?
11. How is a void pointer useful?
12. How are arrays and pointers related?

8.12 PROGRAMMING EXERCISES

Problem 8.1 (Beginner): Write a function

```
void printInts( int iaArray[] , int iNoValues ) {

        .... details removed ....
}
```

that will print each element in an integer array `iaArray` separated by tabs and arrange the arrays contents into five columns. Write a test program that will call `printInts()` to print the contents of

```
int iaArray[] = { 1, 2, 3, 4, 5, 6, 7, 8 };
```

Your output should look something like:

```
1       2       3       4       5
6       7       8
```

Problem 8.2 (Beginner): Write a test program and function

```
/*
 *  ==============================================================
 *  arrayAverage() : Compute average value of elements in
 *                   a two-dimensional array.
 *
 *  Input   : float faaArray[][] -- two-dimensional array of floats.
 *          : int   iNoRows      -- no of rows in the array.
 *          : int   iNoCols      -- no of columns in the array.
 *  Output  : float              -- average value of the elements.
 *  ==============================================================
 */

float arrayAverage ( float faaArray[][ NoRows ], int iNoRows, int iNoCols ) {

      .... details removed ....

}
```

to calculate and print the average value of elements in a two-dimensional array of floats.

Problem 8.3 (Beginner): Write a function that will fill an array of ints with random integer numbers. Pass the function the array to fill, the size of the array, and two ranges for the random values: a low value and a high value. Arrange for the random numbers to be within these low and high limits.

Your test program should print the two-dimensional array of random integer numbers.

Problem 8.4 (Beginner): Figure 8.17 is a schematic of an irregular polygon having seven sides. Suppose that the *x* and *y* vertex coordinates are stored as two columns of information in the array

```
enum { Sides = 7, Cols = 2 };
float faaPolygon [ Sides ][ Cols ] = { { 1.0 1.0 },
                                       { 1.0 5.0 },
                                       { 6.0 5.0 },
                                       { 7.0 3.0 },
                                       { 4.0 3.0 },
                                       { 3.0 2.0 },
                                       { 3.0 1.0 }};
```

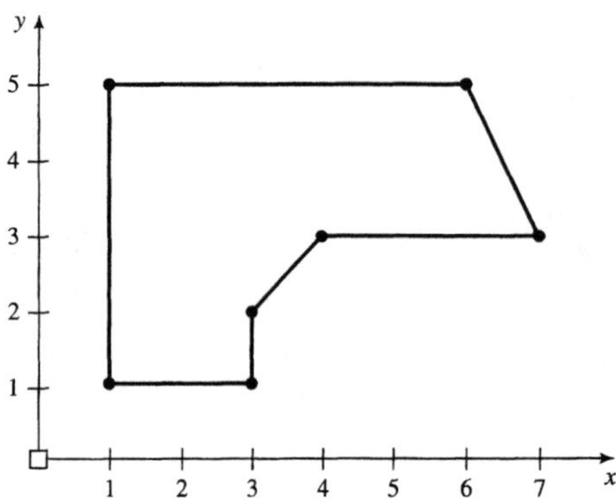

FIGURE 8.17 Seven-sided irregular polygon.

Write a C program that will compute and print

1. The minimum and maximum polygon coordinates in both the x and y directions.
2. The minimum and maximum distance of the polygon vertices from the coordinate system origin.
3. The perimeter and area of the polygon.

Note. For Parts 1 and 2, use the `max()` and `min()` macros described in Chapter 11. In Part 3, use the fact that the vertices have been specified in a clockwise manner.

Problem 8.5 (Intermediate): Monte Carlo methods solve problems by experiments with random numbers on a computer and have been around since about the mid-1940s. A relatively straightforward way of estimating π is to conduct an experiment where darts are randomly thrown at a square board of side length `D`, as shown in Figure 8.18.

Given that the area of the circle $A_{circle} = [\pi D^2/4]$ and the area of the square $A_{square} = D^2$, then

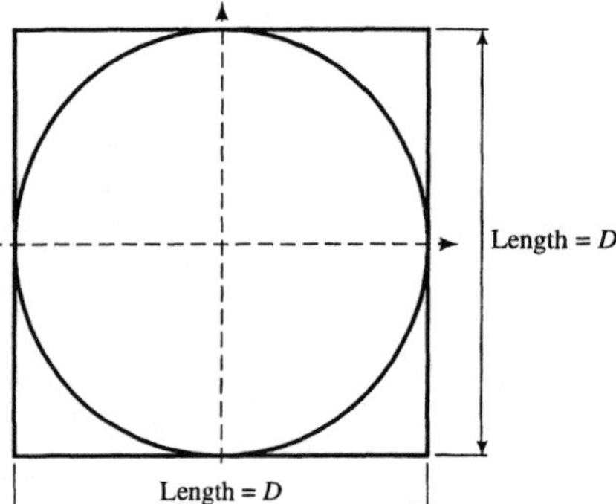

FIGURE 8.18 Estimating π via integration.

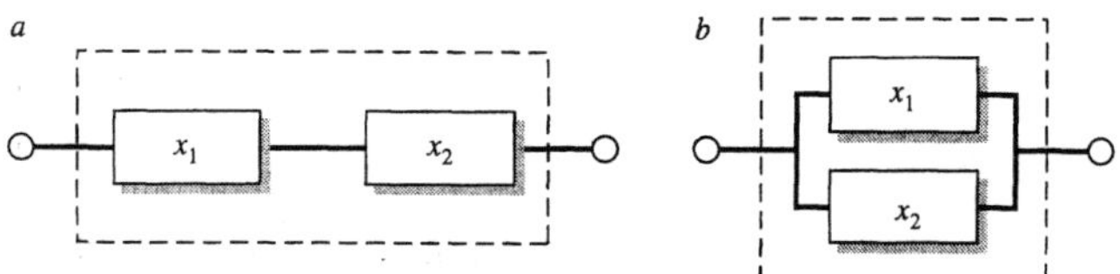

FIGURE 8.19 Reliability of (*a*) series and (*b*) parallel systems.

$$\pi = 4 \cdot \left[\frac{A_{\text{circle}}}{A_{\text{square}}}\right] \tag{8.30}$$

In the Monte Carlo experiment, N darts are thrown at the board. Let $P_i = (x_i, y_i)$ be the coordinate point of the ith dart ($i = 1, 2, 3 \ldots N$). Point P_i is inside the circle if

$$x_i^2 + y_i^2 \leq \left[\frac{D^2}{4}\right] \tag{8.31}$$

If at the conclusion of the experiment, X darts have landed inside the circle ($X \leq N$), then a Monte Carlo estimate of π is

$$\pi \sim 4 \cdot \left[\frac{X}{N}\right] \tag{8.32}$$

Write a computer program to simulate this experiment. Your computer program should generate pairs of uniformly distributed random numbers, one for the x-coordinate and a second for the y-coordinate. The random numbers should be scaled so that they cover the interval `[-D,D]`. Calculate whether each data point P_i lies inside the circle. At the conclusion of the experiment, sum the number of darts that lie inside the circle and evaluate Equation 8.32.

The output from your program should include (1) the total number of trials in the experiment (N), (2) the total number of trial points inside the circle (X), and (3) the Monte Carlo estimate of π.

Problem 8.6 (Intermediate): The left-hand side of Figure 8.19 shows a simple system consisting of two components in series, and the right-hand side shows a simple system consisting of two components in parallel. In both the series and parallel models, the system will work if there is a pathway of working components from the left- to the right-hand side of the system. Series systems models are appropriate for engineering systems that work only when all its components work. Conversely, a parallel systems model is appropriate for engineering systems where all the pathways of working components must fail before the system fails [20].

In computing the overall reliability of the system, we assume that each component works or it has failed completely. The state of a system containing n components can be represented by $x = [x_1, x_2, \ldots, x_n]$, with the state of component i being

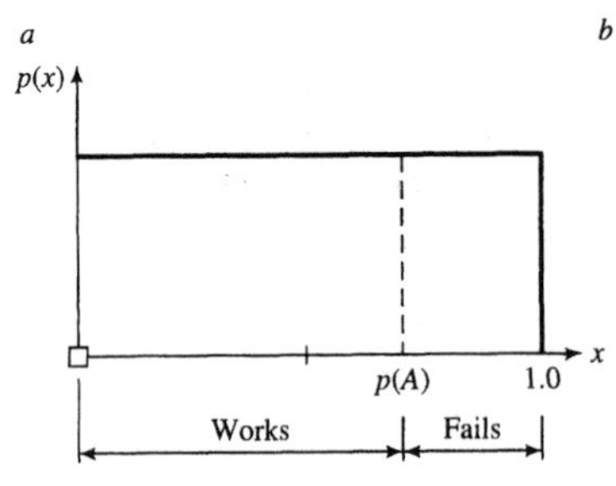

b

Trial No.	Comp. A	Comp. B	System
1	Fails	Works	Fails
2	Fails	Works	Fails
3	Works	Fails	Fails
4	Works	Works	Works
5	Works	Fails	Fails
⋮			
N	Works	Works	Works

X system components work

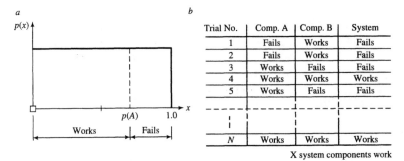

FIGURE 8.20 Numerical experiment for (*a*) Component and (*b*) system reliability.

$$x_i = \begin{cases} 1 & \text{if component } i \text{ works} \\ 0 & \text{if component } i \text{ has failed} \end{cases}$$

for $i = 1, 2, \ldots n$. We define the structure function for the system, $\Phi(x)$, as

$$\Phi(x) = \begin{cases} 1 & \text{if the system works with state vector } x \\ 0 & \text{if the system fails with state vector } x \end{cases}$$

For the series system, the state function is given by

$$\Phi(x) = \begin{cases} 1 & \text{if the system works with state vector } x \\ 0 & \text{if the system fails with state vector } x \end{cases}$$
$$= \min(x_1, x_2, \ldots, x_n)$$

In other words, the series system will work if and only if all the components x_1, $x_2, \ldots, x_n$ work. For the parallel system, the state function is given by

$$\Phi(x) = \begin{cases} 1 & \text{if the system works with state vector } x \\ 0 & \text{if the system fails with state vector } x \end{cases}$$
$$= \max(x_1, x_2, \ldots, x_n)$$

In other words, the parallel system will work when one or more of the components works.

Write a C program that will use Monte Carlo techniques to estimate the reliability of the simple series and parallel systems. The Monte Carlo method can be set up as `N` trial experiments. For each trial in the experiment, the state of a component i can be simulated by generating a random number uniformly distributed between `[0,1]` and comparing its value to $p(x_i)$, the probability that component x_i works. The component will be deemed to work when the random number is less than $p(x_i)$. Otherwise, component i has failed. A summary of this process is shown on the left-hand side of Figure 8.20.

Conduct numerical experiments for $p(x_1) = p(x_2) = 0.50$ and $p(x_1) = p(x_2) =$

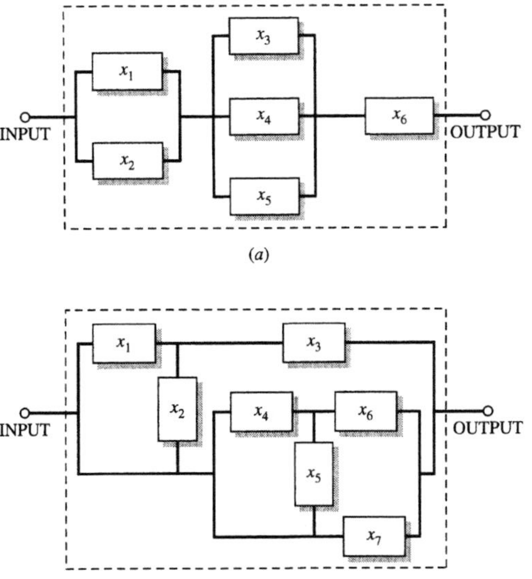

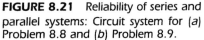

FIGURE 8.21 Reliability of series and parallel systems: Circuit system for *(a)* Problem 8.8 and *(b)* Problem 8.9.

0.90. Theoretical considerations indicate that a working pathway for the series circuit will occur with probability

$$\text{Probability of working pathway} = p(x_1) \cdot p(x_2) \tag{8.33}$$

and for the circuit with components in parallel, a working pathway will occur with probability

$$\text{Probability of working pathway} = 1 - [1 - p(x_1)] \cdot [1 - p(x_2)] \tag{8.34}$$

For example, if $p(x_1) = p(x_2) = 0.5$, then the series system will work 25% of the time and the parallel system will work 75% of the time.

Compare the system reliability computed via simulation to the theoretical values. Do you need the same number of trial circuits to get a reasonable estimate of the system reliability?

Problem 8.7 (Intermediate): Write a C program to simulate the reliability of the network shown in Figure 8.21a. Assume that $p(x_1) = p(x_2) = \cdots = p(x_6) = 0.95$.

What is the overall reliability of the system? Can you derive a formula for the system reliability?

Problem 8.8 (Advanced): Write a C program to simulate the reliability of the network shown in Figure 8.21b.

This problem can be simplified by noting that components $\{x_4, x_5, x_6, \text{and } x_7\}$ are connected with the same topology as components $\{x_1, x_2, x_3, \{x_4, x_5, x_6, \text{and } x_7\}\}$. Carefully write down all the pathways that will lead to a working system and implement C code for the equivalent parallel system.

Assuming that $p(x_1) = p(x_2) = \cdots = 0.50$, what is the overall reliability of the system? Derive a formula for the system reliability.

Problem 8.9 (Intermediate): The stress due to torsion in a solid elastic cylinder of square cross-section defined by the lines $x \pm 1$ and $y \pm 1$ is given by the solution to

$$\frac{\partial^2\sigma(x, y)}{\partial x^2} + \frac{\partial^2\sigma(x, y)}{\partial y^2} + 2 = 0 \tag{8.35}$$

subject to the boundary condition $\sigma(\cdot) = 0$ along all surfaces. Derive a finite difference stencil for Equation 8.35, assuming that the mesh is square. Write a computer program to solve for the internal stresses. Use MATLAB, or some other graphics package, to plot the distribution of stresses inside the cylinder.

Problem 8.10 (Intermediate): In statistics, the normal distribution (or Gaussian distribution) has the probability density function

$$p(y) = \frac{1}{\sqrt{2\pi}} e^{-y^2/2} \tag{8.36}$$

If u_1 and u_2 are two random numbers selected from a uniform distribution `[0,1]`, then a pair of normally distributed random numbers, y_1 and y_2, can be obtained with the transformation

$$y_1 = \sqrt{-2.0 \cdot \log_e(u_1)} \cdot \cos(2\pi u_2) \tag{8.37}$$

$$y_2 = \sqrt{-2.0 \cdot \log_e(u_1)} \cdot \sin(2\pi u_2) \tag{8.38}$$

Equations 8.37 and 8.38 are the Box-Muller transformation. Write a C function `Normal()` that returns a normally distributed random number generated by the Box-Muller method.

You should use the `Random()` function presented in Section 8.5 to obtain u_1 and u_2, and the `static` attributes of C to save one of the two values of y_1 and y_2 between function calls to `Normal()`. The random number sequence should be initialized with a second C function called `InitNormal()`.

Write a test program that will generate an ensemble of normally distributed numbers. Calculate the mean and standard deviation of the normal deviates. Use MATLAB to construct a histogram of normal deviates.

Problem 8.11 (Intermediate): Figure 8.22 shows the cross-section of a long conducting metal box with a detached lid. The sides and bottom of the box are at 100 Volts potential, and the lid is at ground (0 V) potential. The box is assumed to extend to infinity in the z direction (so that there are no "edge effects" to consider). The static distribution of voltage $V = V(x, y)$ inside the metal box is given by solutions to Laplace's equation

$$\frac{\partial^2 V(x, y)}{\partial x^2} + \frac{\partial^2 V(x, y)}{\partial y^2} = 0 \tag{8.39}$$

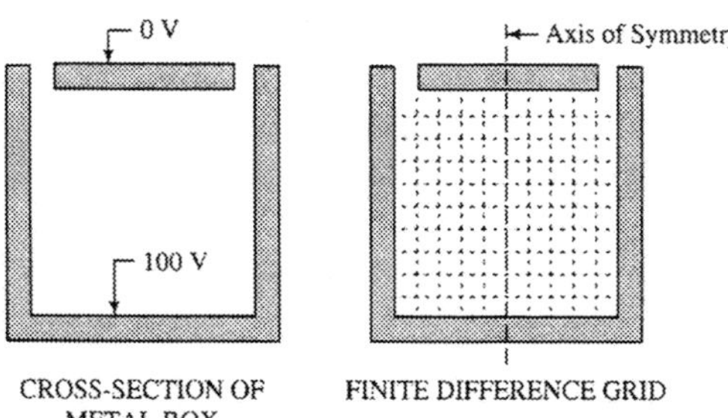

FIGURE 8.22 Cross-section of tall (infinite) metal box.

with boundary conditions $V = 0$ V on the top or lid of the box and $V = 100$ V along both sides and the bottom of the box.

1. Use the method of finite differences outlined in Sections 8.5 and 8.7 to find the voltage distribution inside the box. Use a suitable plotting package to plot the potential.
2. Change the potential on the walls and lid of the box relative to each other and show how the voltage distribution changes.

Problem 8.12 (Advanced): The classic example of what we now call the Monte Carlo method is that of Buffon, who pointed out that π could be experimentally determined by throwing an ensemble of needles onto a ruled surface and then counting the number of needles that intersect a line (see Figure 8.23).

If the parallel lines are spaced distance `1` apart and the needle has length `L`, with $[L < 1]$, then the probability that a needle will cross a line is $\frac{2L}{\pi}$. Buffon showed that if a needle is dropped `N` times, then the number of line crossings X will be approximately $\frac{2NL}{\pi}$. It follows that $\frac{2NL}{X}$ is a Monte Carlo estimate of π.

Write a C program that will simulate the Buffon experiment without using π itself. You should observe that the only thing that matters in the experiment is

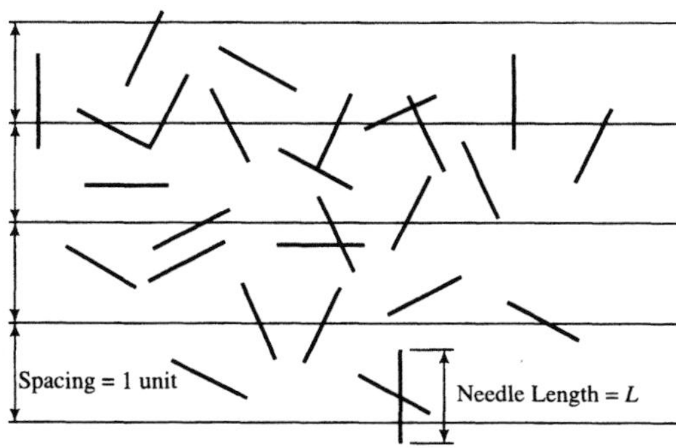

FIGURE 8.23 Schematic of Buffon needle problem.

whether a particular needle crosses a horizontal line. This can be determined by the vertical position of the needle and its orientation alone. The horizontal position of the needle is irrelevant, and it should be left out of the problem formulation. Moreover, Buffon's experiment assumes that the needle orientations will be uniformly distributed between $[0, 2\pi]$.

The hard part of this problem is devising a scheme for generating angles uniformly distributed over the interval $[0, 2\pi]$ without using π itself. For a hint, see Figure 8.18.

Print any information that you think is important, including the number of trial points, crossings, and Monte Carlo estimate of π.

9

FUNCTIONS II

9.1 INTRODUCTION

This chapter explains some advanced but very useful features of functions in C. We begin with a quick review of concepts discussed in Chapter 7. When arguments are passed to a function, a copy of the argument is sent to the function being called. When the program execution jumps to the function being called, the function's data space is accessed for values of the function arguments and local variables. The memory needed for the function data space is temporary and is lost once the function returns. This multistep procedure is the *call-by-value* mechanism in C, and it applies to function arguments of all data types.

In Section 9.2, we show how pointers as function arguments can be used to access memory that is nonlocal to a function and, in Section 9.3, we show how pointer constants (i.e., array names) can be used to pass one- and multidimensional arrays as function arguments. They are smaller and faster to pass than the array itself. We conclude this chapter with an examination of string functions.

9.2 POINTERS AS FUNCTION ARGUMENTS

This section investigates the use of pointers as function arguments, and shows how they can be used to access and change the value of variables that are nonlocal to a function. This feature of C is useful when you want to write a function that will change the value of variables declared in the calling function. Although we did not

```
int main( void ) {                    int main( void ) {
float faaWork [ 20 ] [ 20 ];          float fXCoord, fYCoord;

    InitArray( .. faaWork .. );         GetCoordinates( .. &fXCoord, &fYCoord .. );

}                                     }

void                                  void
InitArray( ... faaWork ... ) {        GetCoordinates( ... *fXCoord, *fYCoord ... ) {

    faaWork[1][1] = .. ;                  *fXCoord = ....;
    faaWork[2][1] = .. ;                  *fYCoord = ....;
}                                     }
==================================================================================
Pass Array to Calling Function       Pass Multiple Variables to Calling Function
```

FIGURE 9.1 Schematics of functions that access nonlocal memory.

mention it in Chapter 3, the standard library function `scanf(...)` makes use of this feature when it reads input from the keyboard, and assigns values to variables declared in the calling function.

Figure 9.1 contains schematics of two applications where variables are declared in one function and values of the same variables are assigned in a separate function:

1. In the left-hand schematic, memory for `faaWork [20][20]` is declared in `main()`. The purpose of `InitArray()` is to initialize the contents of an array specified in the function argument.
2. In the right-hand schematic, floating point variables `fXCoord` and `fYCoord` are declared in `main()`. The purpose of function `GetCoordinates()` is to initialize the coordinate values.

For each application, the question we want to answer is "how should the function arguments be constructed so that after the function call is complete, assignments to the nonlocal variables remain intact?" We study this problem by working step by step through the development of a short function to swap two variables.

9.2.1 Function to Swap Two Variables

The following script of code is a reasonable, albeit incorrect, first cut at a function for swapping two integer values:

```
/*
 *  ==============================================================
 *  SwapInts () : Naive (and incorrect) implementation of
 *                swap function
 *
 *  Input   : int iVal1 -- first integer argument to be swapped.
 *          : int iVal2 -- second integer argument to be swapped.
```

```
 *  Output : void.
 *  ==============================================================
 */

void SwapInts( int iVal1, int iVal2 ) {
   int iTemp;
   iTemp = iVal1;
   iVal1 = iVal2;
   iVal2 = iTemp;
}
```

SwapInts() has two integer arguments iVal1 and iVal2. We have been careful enough to use an intermediate value, iTemp, to hold one of the variables while the other is overwritten (this strategy is like trying to exchange the contents of two drinking glasses; you need a third glass). Although the values of iVal1 and iVal2 are, in fact, swapped inside SwapInts(), our implementation fails because the swapped values are lost when the function returns.

PROGRAM 9.1: USE POINTERS TO SWAP VARIABLES

```
/*
 *  ==========================================================
 *  SwapInts() : Swap two integers. Correct implementation.
 *
 *  Input  : int *ipVal1 -- pointer to first integer
 *                          argument to be swapped.
 *         : int *ipVal2 -- pointer to second integer
 *                          argument to be swapped.
 *  Output : void.
 *  ==========================================================
 */

void SwapInts( int *ipVal1, int *ipVal2 ) {
int iTemp;

  iTemp   = *ipVal1;
  *ipVal1 = *ipVal2;
  *ipVal2 = iTemp;
}

int main( void ) {
int iVal1 = 100;
int iVal2 = 200;

  SwapInts( &iVal1, &iVal2 );
}
```

Program 9.1 contains the complete details of a calling function and correct implementation for SwapInts(). We changed the arguments to SwapInts() from the integer variables iVal1 and iVal2 to two integer pointers to the same variables. As such, the calling function, main(), passes the addresses of the two integer variables to be swapped.

```
SwapInts( &iVal1, &iVal2 );
```

Creating temporary pointers (using the & operator) produces clear code and corresponds directly with the logic of the situation. The same results could have been obtained with

```
int main( void ) {
int iVal1 = 100;
int iVal2 = 200;
int * ipPtrToVal1 = & iVal1;
int * ipPtrToVal2 = & iVal2;

    SwapInts( ipPtrToVal1, ipPtrToVal2 );
}
```

Here we explicitly use pointers for the arguments to SwapInts(). In both cases, however, the addresses of iVal1 and iVal2 are copied to the stack (i.e., a block of computer memory) before the function call commences.

Figure 9.2a is a schematic of the memory layout before SwapInts() is called. The data space for main() is defined with memory allocated for variables iVal1 and iVal2. Figures 9.2b to 9.2d show the data spaces for main() and SwapInts() immediately after each of the three executable statements in SwapInts().

The values of iVal1 and iVal2 in the calling routine are swapped by systematically dereferencing the addresses of iVal1 and iVal2, and temporarily storing the value of iVal1 in iTemp. This strategy of passing the address of variables and pointers to a function is called pass-by-reference because variable values are obtained by dereferencing the function arguments.

9.2.2 Need for the const Keyword

There are two important problems with the pass-by-reference style of programming. First, the syntax of SwapInts() is ugly and error prone. When a programmer looks at an individual line of code, it is not always clear whether a * is being used to dereference a pointer or to multiply two numbers.

The second and more serious drawback is that we have allowed the SwapInts() function to access and change variables that it does not own. When functions are allowed to change the value of nonlocal variables, this behavior violates the idea of data encapsulation. Behavior of this type is called a "side effect," and it makes computer programs much harder to debug. For example, in the script of code

```
iVal1 = Function2( iCount );
```

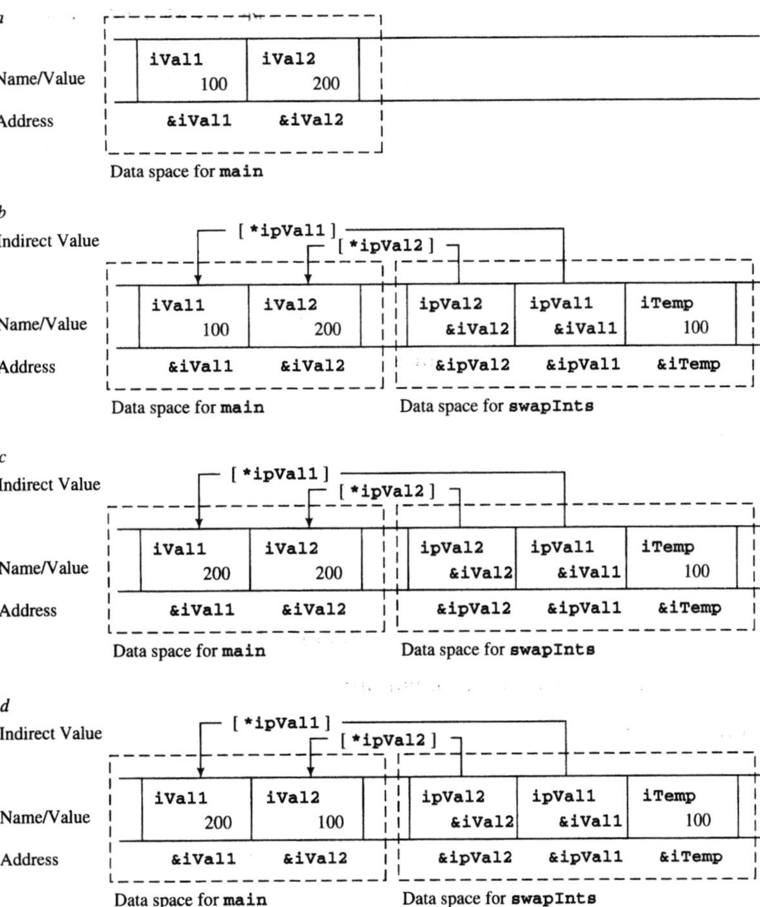

FIGURE 9.2 Schematics of memory layout in Program 9.1: (a) layout of memory before function call, (b) after iTemp = *ipVal1, (c) after ipVal1 = *ipVal2, and (d) after *ipVal2 = iTemp.

it is very clear that `iVal1` will be changed by the return value from `Function2()`. If, however, the script of code is changed to

```
iResult = Function2( &iVal1 , iCount );
```

and details of function `Function2()` are

```
int Function2 ( int *ipIntPtr ) {
    *ipIntPtr = 2;
}
```

then you cannot tell by looking at the first block of code whether `iVal1` is changed by `Function2()` or, in fact, by any function `Function2()` happens to call.

The C programming language provides the keyword `const` as a mechanism for avoiding this oversight. We can specify that the values "referred to" are to be considered constants. Then the compiler will not allow us to change them indirectly through pointers that are passed as function arguments. For example,

```
int Function3 ( const int *ipIntPtr ) {
    *ipIntPtr = 2;    <==== compiler flags an error here !!
}
```

`const int *ipIntPtr` is `const` and cannot be assigned to. Since pass-by-reference is potentially dangerous, you should always pass pointers to `const` objects unless you really intend to change the objects in the function.

9.3 ARRAYS AS FUNCTION ARGUMENTS

This section describes techniques for passing one- and multidimensional arrays as function arguments. These techniques must be computationally efficient and contain enough information so that array elements can be accessed by the function being called. Rather than pass a copy of the entire contents of an array to a function, we simply refer to an array with a pointer and pass the pointer to the function. This pointer will take as its value the address of the array in memory. We demonstrate this feature of C by working through two computer programs.

Computer Program. Program 9.2 allocates memory for a one-dimensional array `iaArray` in its main function and then calls a function `ArrayZero` to zero the array's contents.

PROGRAM 9.2: PASSING ONE-DIMENSIONAL ARRAYS TO FUNCTIONS

```
/*
 *  ============================================================
 *  Demonstrate passing of one-dimensional array to functions
 *  ============================================================
 */

#include <stdio.h>

enum { MaxArray = 10 };

int ArrayZero( int iaArr[] ) {
int iCnt;
```

```
    for( iCnt = 0; iCnt < MaxArray; ++iCnt )
        iaArr[iCnt] = 0;

    return;
}

int main( void ) {
int iaArray[MaxArray];

  ArrayZero( iaArray );

}
```

Points to note are as follows:

1. When we set up a function call to `ArrayZero`

   ```
   ArrayZero( iaArray );
   ```

   the array name argument evaluates to the address of the zeroth index element in the array. An equivalent statement is

   ```
   ArrayZero( &iaArray[ 0 ] );
   ```

   In both cases, the value of the function argument inside `ArrayZero()` is the address of zeroth element in `iaArray`. It is very important to note that

   - When statements of code inside function `ArrayZero()` change the value of elements in `iaArray`, we are actually updating elements of the array declared in the calling function.
   - When the function `ArrayZero()` returns, only the temporary copy of the address of the zeroth element in `iaArray` is lost. The changes that we made to `iaArray` persist.

2. From a practical standpoint, pointers and array names are almost the same. The only important distinction is that you cannot treat an array name as a modifiable variable. An array name is a pointer constant.

9.3.1 Passing Multidimensional Arrays to Functions

Multidimensional arrays are stored by default in a row-wise contiguous block of memory (see, for example, Figures 8.8 and 8.16). When we use multidimensional arrays, the array contents are accessed in the standard mathematical and intuitive way. For example,

```
enum { NoRows = 5, NoCols = 5 };
int iaaFirst[ NoRows ][ NoCols ];
```

```
iaaFirst[0][0]  = 0;
iaaFirst[2][3]  = 100;

..... etc .....
```

When iaaFirst is passed to a function, we call it ArrayDetails(), the function arguments are declared as

```
int ArrayDetails( int iaaFirst [ NoRows ][ NoCols ] );
```

Here we see that iaaFirst is an array of integers having NoRows rows and NoCols columns. It is a good idea to provide a complete description of the array details in the function declaration because it enhances readability of the program source code.

It is also important to realize that this level of detail is somewhat redundant. Because two-dimensional arrays are really "arrays of arrays," which are defined at compile-time, the compiler will know the total number of bytes stored in the array. The arrays contents will be stored row-wise by default. With this information in place, the layout of memory in a multidimensional array can be determined uniquely with an array declaration containing all the array dimensions, except the first (i.e., the leftmost). The number of rows is redundant information, and this is reflected in the second declaration.

```
int ArrayDetails( int iaaFirst [][ NoCols ] );
```

We specify the number of columns in the array being referenced so that function ArrayDetails will know how big each array in the "array of arrays" is. The number of rows is not important to the function because array bounds checking is not done. Indeed, it is the programmer's responsibility to ensure that only valid array indices are used within the function.

When function ArrayDetails is called (as opposed to declared), all that is normally supplied as an argument is the array name. The script of code

```
iVal = ArrayDetails( iaaFirst );
```

is a typical example of ArrayDetails use. Recall that when the array's name is used without any brackets, the name of the array evaluates to the address of the first element of the array (i.e., a pointer constant). In this particular case, the name iaaFirst evaluates to the address of an array of arrays of ints (the type prefix is iaa or int array). This is what we pass to the function.

Computer Program. Program 9.3 demonstrates how function arguments lists may be used to pass multidimensional arrays from one function to another.

PROGRAM 9.3: PASSING MULTIDIMENSIONAL ARRAYS TO FUNCTIONS

```
/*
 *  ============================================================
 *  Demonstrate passing of multidimensional arrays to functions
 *  ============================================================
 */

#include <stdio.h>

enum { NoRows = 3, NoCols = 2 }; /*  sizes/limits  */

/*  Print message and details of array */

void
PrintArrayDetails( char *cpMessage,
                   const float faaVals [] [ NoCols ] ) {

int ii, ij;

    printf("\n");
    for( ii = 0; ii < NoRows; ii = ii + 1 ) {
        printf("*** %s \t:", cpMessage );
        for( ij = 0; ij < NoCols; ij = ij + 1 ) {
             printf(" faaVals[%2d][%2d] = %5.1f ", ii, ij,
               faaVals[ii][ij]);
        }
        printf("\n");
    }
}

/* Print array and update contents */

void TestFunction( float faaVals [] [ NoCols ] ) {

   PrintArrayDetails("In TestFunction()", faaVals );

   faaVals[2][0] = 100;
   faaVals[2][1] = 200;
}

/*
 *  ============================================================
 *  Test program for passing multidimensional arrays to functions
 *  ============================================================
 */
```

```
int main( void ) {
static float faaVals[ NoRows][ NoCols ] = { { 1.0, 2.0 },
                                            { 3.0, 4.0 },
                                            { 5.0, 6.0 } };

    PrintArrayDetails("In main()", faaVals );

    TestFunction( faaVals );

    PrintArrayDetails("Back in main()", faaVals );
}
```

Program 9.3 is the composition of three functions. The function `main()` initializes an array called `faaVals` and then makes a series of function calls to `PrintArrayDetails()` and `TestFunction()`. The purpose of `PrintArrayDetails()` is to print the details of a message header and the contents of a two-dimensional array. Both quantities are defined in the function argument list. `TestFunction()` calls `PrintArrayDetails()` to print the contents of `faaVals` and then updates the arrays contents. Together these operations generate the output

```
*** In main()    : faaVals[ 0][ 0] =   1.0  faaVals[ 0][ 1] =   2.0
*** In main()    : faaVals[ 1][ 0] =   3.0  faaVals[ 1][ 1] =   4.0
*** In main()    : faaVals[ 2][ 0] =   5.0  faaVals[ 2][ 1] =   6.0

*** In TestFunction()    : faaVals[ 0][ 0] =   1.0  faaVals[ 0][ 1] =   2.0
*** In TestFunction()    : faaVals[ 1][ 0] =   3.0  faaVals[ 1][ 1] =   4.0
*** In TestFunction()    : faaVals[ 2][ 0] =   5.0  faaVals[ 2][ 1] =   6.0

*** Back in main()       : faaVals[ 0][ 0] =   1.0  faaVals[ 0][ 1] =   2.0
*** Back in main()       : faaVals[ 1][ 0] =   3.0  faaVals[ 1][ 1] =   4.0
*** Back in main()       : faaVals[ 2][ 0] = 100.0  faaVals[ 2][ 1] = 200.0
```

which is conveniently partitioned into three blocks. Points to note are as follows:

1. You can prevent a function from modifying value of array elements passed in function arguments by adding the qualifier `const` to the argument declaration. An example is

   ```
   PrintArrayDetails( .... const float faaVals[][ NoCols ] )
   ```

   Now the compiler will not let the programmer accidentally modify the value elements of `faaVals[][]` inside `PrintArrayDetails()`. You can, however, still access the array elements, which in the case of `PrintArrayDetails()` is all that we want to do anyway.

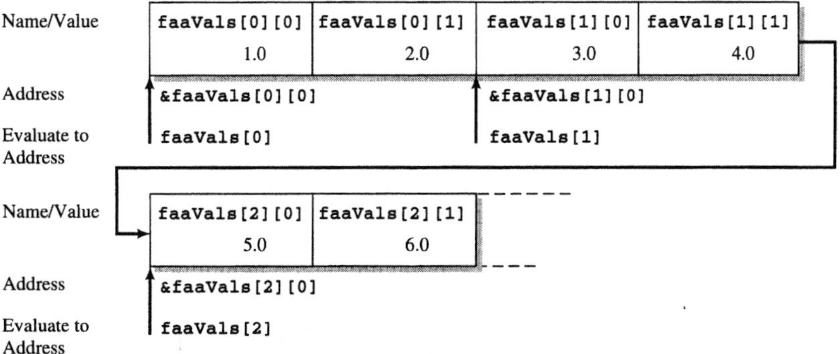

FIGURE 9.3 Schematic of array `faaVals`.

2. The declaration

```
enum { NoRows = 3, NoCols = 2 };
static float faaVals[ NoRows ][ NoCols ] = { { 1.0, 2.0 },
                                             { 3.0, 4.0 },
                                             { 5.0, 6.0 }};
```

allocates at compile time, a (3 × 2) array called `faaVals`. It contains 6 × 4 = 24 bytes of memory, as shown in Figure 9.3. The expression `faaVals [0]` evaluates to the starting address of the first row in `faaVals`, and expressions `faaVals [1]` and `faaVals [2]`, to the starting addresses for the second and third rows, respectively.

3. The contents of `faaVals` are printed in the first block of program output.

4. When the function `TestFunction()` is called, the address of the first item of `faaVals` is passed as an argument. Also notice that the argument declaration in `TestFunction()` is

```
void TestFunction( float faaVals[][ NoCols ] ) {
```

thereby indicating that the memory for array `faaVals` is arranged in two columns. The compiler can easily deduce that since the total number of bytes in `faaVals` is 24, and each element is a float (4 bytes), `faaVals` has three rows. We do not need to pass the number of rows to the function.

The second block of program output corresponds to the contents `faaVals`, as printed from within `TestFunction()`. After the contents of `faaVals [2][0]` and `faaVals [2][1]` are assigned values `100` and `200`, respectively, and the program control returns to main, the contents of `faaVals` are printed for a third time. The important point to note is that the array value modifications remain intact. This occurs because the array arguments are pointers, and the array modification updates the contents of memory located outside the scope of `TestFunction()`.

5. There is an important difference between passing the member of an array as a function argument:

```
Dummy ( faaVals [ 1 ][ 1 ] );        <== pass a float
```

and passing an array

```
Dummy ( faaVals [][ NoCols ] );      <== pass a pointer
                                         of type float
```

Function arguments containing the member of an array pass to the function the value of the member in the array. Function arguments that are an array name pass to the function a pointer to the first member of the array.

9.4 STRING FUNCTIONS

One task that crops up repeatedly in C programming for engineering applications is the need to manipulate text and character strings. Most of the string functions that you will need are provided as part of the standard library. The standard library contains string functions for copying, concatenating (i.e., appending one string to the end of another), comparing, locating substrings, and basic memory management. We highly recommend that you take time to familiarize yourself with the capabilities of these functions and then use them. This strategy of programming will save time because the standard library string functions have already been written and debugged by the compiler writers.

Appendix 2 contains a complete listing of the standard library functions dedicated to manipulation of strings, and Table 9.1 contains a summary of the string functions that we use in Programs 9.4 and 9.5.

Table 9.1 shows that string functions often have one or more argument(s) that are null-terminated strings. String arguments to functions are handled as `char` pointers. The pointer will take the starting address of the corresponding string as

TABLE 9.1 String Functions Used in Programs 9.4 and 9.5

Function	*Header*	*Description*
`atoi(...)`	`stdlib.h`	Converts alphabetic string to integer.
`sprintf(cpS, kcpF.. )`	`stdio.h`	Copies output to cpS, using format kcpF.
`strcat(cpS,kcpE)`	`string.h`	Concatenates kcpE onto the end of cpS.
`strchr(kcpS,c)`	`string.h`	Finds and returns reference character c in kcpS.
`strcmp(kcp1,kcp2)`	`string.h`	Compares kcp1 to kcp2, returns <0, 0, >0 value.
`strcpy(cp1,kcp2)`	`string.h`	Copies string referred to by kcp2 to location cp1.
`strlen( kcp1 )`	`string.h`	Computes length of string referred to by kcp1.
`tolower(int iC)`	`ctype.h`	Converts and returns iC in lowercase.

its value. The same strings will be terminated by the \0 character. These so-called "string characteristics" play a central role in the construction of algorithms for operations on strings. Strings can be any length. To compute the length of a string, for example, the `strlen()` library function simply counts the number of characters as it moves along a string until it reaches the literal \0 character.

We now exercise the most commonly used string functions by working through the details of two computer programs.

Computer Program. Program 9.4 explores two techniques for generating two-part file names. The program uses the string function `strcpy()` to copy the contents of a string from one block of memory to another; `strcat()` to concatenate, or join, the contents of two strings; and `strlen()` to compute the number of characters in a given string.

PROGRAM 9.4: ALLOCATION OF STRING FUNCTION ARGUMENTS

```
/*
 *  ==================================================
 *  argalloc.c -- demonstrate use of string functions
 *  ==================================================
 */

#include <stdio.h>
#include <string.h>

int main( void ) {
enum   { MaxString = 20 };                 /* allocate enough for long string */
char   caString[MaxString] = "myfile";     /* compile-time allocation         */
char*  cpStringExt = ".dat";               /* point to extension              */
char   caNewExtension[MaxString];          /* read in at run time             */
char*  cpNew;                              /* assigned dynamically below      */

   /* [a] : copy the extension referred to by cpStringExt onto the end of   */
   /*       the string contained in (ultimately referred to by) caString    */

   strcat( caString, cpStringExt );
   printf( "\nThe concatenated file name is %s\n", caString );

   /* [b] : reset caString to its original state ("myfile") */

   strcpy( caString, "myfile" );
```

```
    /* [c] : dynamically request a new file extension */

    printf( "\nEnter another file extension (<20 characters long):" );
    scanf( "%s", caNewExtension );

    /* [d] : dynamically allocate the necessary space at run time */

    cpNew = (char*) malloc( strlen(caString) + strlen(caNewExtension) + 1 );
    if( NULL == cpNew ) { /* allocation failure */
        print("\n");
        printf("Memory allocation failure in file %s, line %i\n",
                __FILE__, __LINE__);
        return 1;
    }

    /* [e] : copy in source string and concatenate the extension */

    strcpy( cpNew, caString );
    strcat( cpNew, caNewExtension );
    printf( "\nThe concatenated file name is %s\n", cpNew );

    return 0;
}
```

Suppose that Program 9.4 has been compiled into an executable program called `TestString`. The following script records a typical session of input/output (I/O) for the program's execution:

```
prompt >> TestString
The concatenated file name is myfile.dat
Enter another file extension (<20 characters long): .input
The concatenated file name is myfile.input
prompt >>
```

Points to note are as follows:

1. The C preprocessor directives

```
#include <stdio.h>
#include <string.h>
```

ensure that Program 9.4 is provided with the appropriate function declarations for I/O and for the text processing of strings [i.e., the functions beginning with `str..()` in Table 9.1].

2. The first half of Program 9.4 makes use of the array declarations

```
enum  { MaxString = 20 };
char  caString[MaxString] = "myfile";
char* cpStringExt = ".dat";
```

The declaration for `caString` is composed of two parts. First, memory is allocated for an array of `MaxString = 20` characters. Its contents are then initialized by copying the character string `"myfile"` into the first six elements of `caString` (i.e., array elements `caString[0]` to `caString [5]`). `cpStringExt` is a character pointer, which takes as its value the address of a character array containing the string `.dat`. After these arrays have been declared and their contents initialized, the layout of memory is as shown in the upper half of Figure 9.4a.

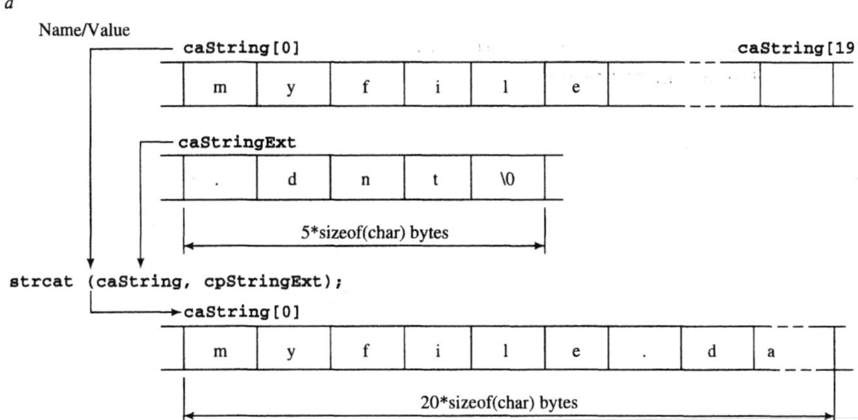

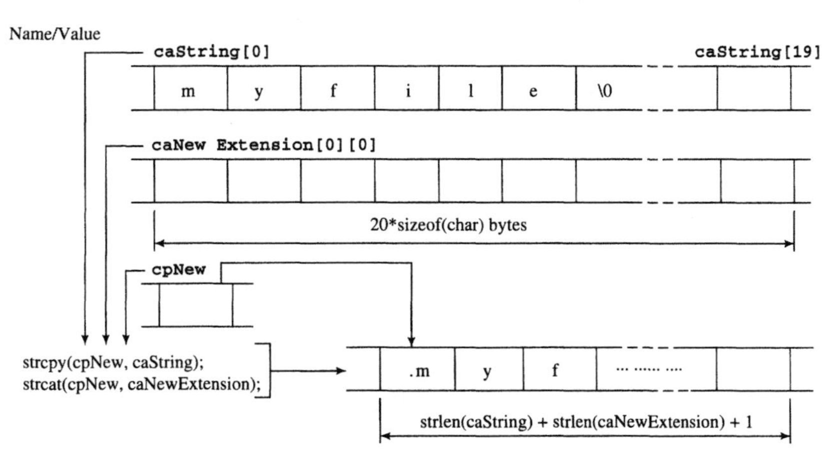

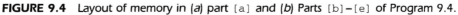

FIGURE 9.4 Layout of memory in (*a*) part `[a]` and (*b*) Parts `[b]`–`[e]` of Program 9.4.

3. In Section `[a]` of Program 9.4, the function call

```
strcat( caString, cpStringExt );
```

appends the contents of character string `cpStringExt` to the end of the occupied contents of character array `caString`. The result of this string operation is stored in `caString`, as shown in the lower half of Figure 9.4a.

4. The string functions assume that a programmer has allocated enough memory for the string operation and the results of the operation to be stored. For example, in the setup work for the string operation

```
strcat( caString, cpStringExt );
```

memory is allocated for 20 elements in `caString`. This strategy of memory allocation is conservative. When `.dat` is appended to `myfile`, only 11 of the 20 array elements are occupied (do not forget that one extra element is needed for the end-of-string sentinel).

When a programmer fails to provide a string function with adequate working memory, the error will most often show up as unpredictable run-time behavior of the program. Sometimes the computer program will let you know something is wrong by crashing via a segmentation fault (do not complain; at least you know an error exists, and its approximate location). Sometimes the same program will crash later in its execution. Finding programming errors in the second situation can be very difficult because, most likely, you will be looking for coding errors in the wrong place.

5. In many practical engineering applications, memory requirements for strings will vary widely from one problem to the next. A key problem with compile-time allocation of arrays is the burden it places on programmers to estimate upper bounds on array sizes. If the array dimensions are carefully selected, then the allocated memory will be more than is actually used, but not much more.

6. With item [5] in mind, Sections `[b]` through `[e]` of Program 9.4 prompt the user for the name of a new file extension. They use dynamic memory allocation techniques to compute and allocate memory for the occupied contents of `caString`, plus the new file name extension at run-time.

Figure 9.4b is a schematic of the `caString` and `caNewExtension` arrays, the `cpNew` character pointer, and in the lower right-hand corner, the dynamically allocated array for the concatenated string.

7. The statement

```
cpNew  = (char *) malloc( strlen(caString) + strlen(caNewExtension) + 1 );
```

allocates memory for the concatenated string while the program is running and assigns, to `cpNew`, a pointer to the starting address of the allocated memory. The ability of a program to request memory at run-time is called dynamic memory allocation, and we cover this topic in detail in Chapter 10. At this point we simply mention that malloc() is a function in the standard library that takes care of the memory allocation. strlen() is a string function that returns the length of the occupied contents of its character string argument. Therefore, the line of code evaluates to

```
cpNew = (char *) malloc( strlen(caString) +
                         strlen(caNewExtension) + 1);
      = (char *) malloc( 6 + 4 + 1 );
      = (char *) malloc( 11 );
```

Memory is allocated for 11 bytes, the length of the original string and the string extension, plus one space for the end-of-string sentinel.

8. In Section [e], the occupied contents of caString are copied to the memory block referenced by cpNew. The occupied contents of caNewExtension are then appended to the contents of the memory block referenced by cpNew. The concatenated file name is printed to the screen.

Computer Program. Suppose that as part of a research program, you need to collect and store a large quantity of experimental data. The data will be stored in an ensemble of files that share a common first name, and have numerical extensions that begin at some integer M and increase by one to some general number N. For example, the sequence of file names could be

```
data.101 , data.102 , data.103 , data.104, ........  data.N
```

The storage of experimental data in file data.101 will take three steps:

1. File data.101 is opened;
2. The experimental data is written to data.101;
3. File data.101 is closed.

The three-step procedure will be repeated for each of the files: data.102, data.103, and so forth. We cover the mechanics of opening and closing files, and writing data to files in Chapter 12.

Program 9.5 handles a small component of this process. The program (1) prompts the user for a character string that begins the sequence of file names (e.g., data.201), and (2) takes care of the string operations needed to increment the file name. Item 2 is more complicated than one might initially assume. We need to take apart the string that represents the file name, convert the extension to an integer, increment that integer, and then convert it back to a string and append it to the original file name base (data in this case). Although the individual steps are simple, the concepts at work here are very important. This may not be the only way to do this type of string manipulation, but it does seem to be a fairly straightforward and efficient method.

PROGRAM 9.5: EXERCISE STRING FUNCTIONS IN STANDARD LIBRARY

```
/*
 *  ==========================================================================
 *  strings.c -- Exercise String and Character Functions
 *
 *  The program design is as follows:
 *
 *     Read a string that represents a file name prefix (e.g., "data")
 *     Read in a string that represents a file name in the form prefix.N
 *     Convert the file name to lower case
 *     Find the . before N (beginning of string in the form .123)
 *     Check that the file name actually starts with the prefix string
 *     Copy and Convert N, still a char string, to an integer
 *     Increment the integer form of N
 *     Convert the integer N back into a string
 *     Append the new incremented N to a copy of the file prefix
 *     Print the new filename
 *
 *  ==========================================================================
 */

#include <stdio.h>
#include <string.h>
#include <ctype.h>   /* for tolower decl. */
#include <stdlib.h>  /* for atoi decl. */

int main( void ) {
enum { MaxString  20 };          /* allocate strings needed */
                                 /* for this program        */
char  caPrefix[ MaxString ];
char  caFilename[ MaxString ];
char* cpToSuffix;
char  caSuffix[ MaxString ];
char  caNewCopy[ MaxString ];
int iCount, iSuffix;

   /* [a] : Read a string that represents a file name */
   /*       prefix (e.g., "data")                     */

   printf( "\n" );
   printf( "Enter the lower case prefix for the " );
   printf( "data file names (e.g., \"data\"):" );
   scanf( "%s%*c", caPrefix );
```

```
/* [b] : Read in a string that represents a file name */
/*       in the form prefix N.                        */

printf( "Enter the filename (e.g., \"data.122\"):" );
scanf( "%s%*c", caFilename );

/* [c] : Convert the file name to lower case */

for( iCount = 0; iCount < strlen(caFilename); iCount++ )
   caFilename[iCount] = tolower(caFilename[iCount] );

/* [d] : Find the . before N (beginning of string in the form .123) */

cpToSuffix = strchr( caFilename, '.' );

/* [e] : 0 terminate prefix, save pointer to suffix */

*cpToSuffix++ = 0;

/* [f] : Check that the file name actually starts with */
/*       the prefix string.                            */

strcpy( caNewCopy, caFilename );
if( strcmp( caNewCopy, caPrefix ) ! 0 ) {
   printf( "\nImproper suffix error.  Aborting.\n" );
   return 1;
}

/* [g] : Copy and Convert N, still a char string, to an integer */

strcpy( caSuffix, cpToSuffix );
iSuffix = atoi( caSuffix );

/* [h] : Increment the integer form of N */

iSuffix += 1;

/* [i] : Convert the integer N back into a string */

sprintf( caSuffix, "%i", iSuffix );

/* [j] : Append the new incremented N to a copy of the file prefix */

strcat( caNewCopy, "." );
strcat( caNewCopy, caSuffix );
```

```
    /* [k] : Print the new filename */

    printf( "\nThe new filename is %s\n", caNewCopy );
    return 0;
}
```

The I/O from Program 9.5 in a typical run is

```
Enter the lower case prefix for the data file names (e.g., "data"):data
Enter the filename (e.g., "data.122"): DaTa.123
The new filename is data.124
```

Points to note are as follows:

1. The C preprocessor directives

```
#include <stdio.h>
#include <string.h>
#include <ctype.h>    /* for tolower decl. */
#include <stdlib.h>   /* for atoi decl. */
```

ensure that Program 9.5 is provided with the appropriate function declarations for I/O and text processing of strings. The header file `ctype.h` is included because it contains `tolower()`, a character mapping function that converts uppercase characters to lowercase (if applicable). We include `stdlib.h` because it contains the string-to-number functions `atoi()`, `atof()`, and `atol()`.

2. Sections `[a]` and `[b]` prompt the user for a lowercase base name (i.e., a prefix for the file name), followed by a character string representing the file name in the form `prefix.N`. In the first two lines of the I/O script shown here, `data` is entered as the base name, and `DaTa.123` is entered as the name of the first file in the file sequence.

   The file name is stored in character array `caFileName`, as shown in Figure 9.5a.

3. String comparisons are case sensitive and, therefore, `DaTa` will not evaluate as equal to `data`. Hence, this program converts the file name to all lowercase letters so that a comparison of names will not be affected.

   With this goal in mind, Section `[c]` illustrates use of the `ctype.h` declared function `tolower()`. The for looping construct

```
for( iCount = 0; iCount < strlen(caFilename); iCount++ )
     caFilename[ iCount ] = tolower( caFilename[ iCount ] );
```

walks along the `caFilename` array and converts each character in the entered file name from uppercase to lowercase (when applicable). For our script of

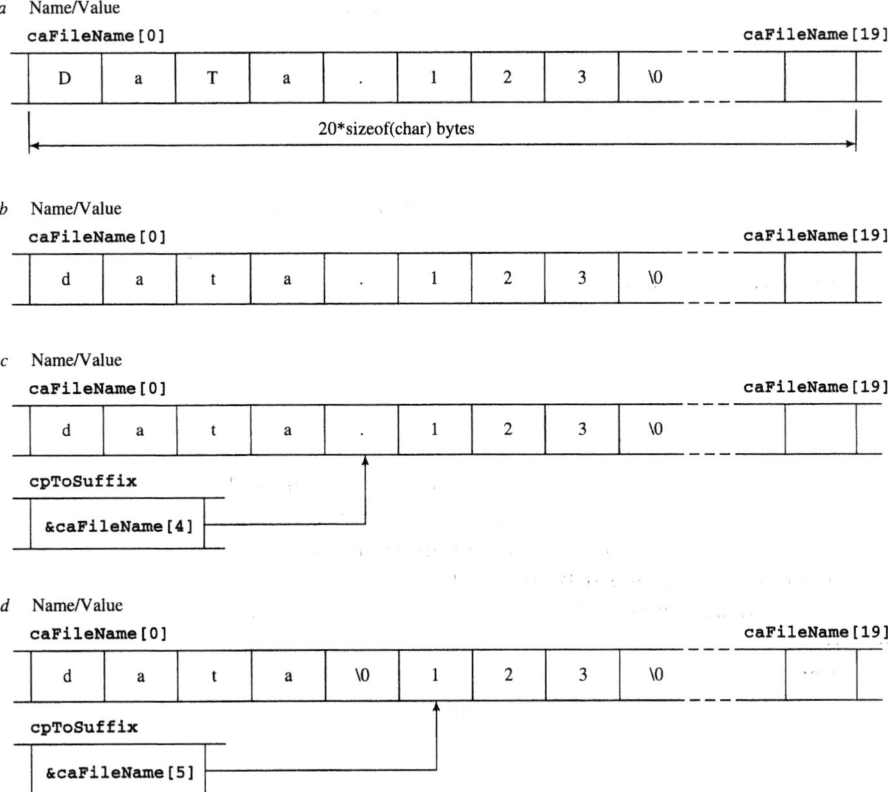

FIGURE 9.5 Layout of memory *(a)* at the end of Section `[b]`, *(b)* of Section `[c]`, *(c)* of Section `[d]`, and *(d)* of Section `[e]` of Program 9.5.

I/O, `DaTa.123` is converted to `data.123`. Now the contents of `caFileName` are as shown in Figure 9.5b.

4. Section `[d]` uses `strchr()` to find the period in the file name separating the prefix from the extension. This position in memory is assigned to the character pointer `cpToSuffix` (see Figure 9.5c).
5. The single line of code

```
*cpToSuffix++ = 0;
```

replaces the dot character in the file name by an end-of-string sentinel, and then increments the character pointer by 1 byte so that it addresses the beginning of the numerical extension. The layout of memory for `caFileName` and `cpToSuffix` is shown in Figure 9.5d.

6. Sections `[f]` through `[k]` are relatively straightforward. In Section `[f]`, we use `strcmp()` to make sure that the file name prefix stored in `caPrefix` and the first block of contents in `caFileName`—up to the end-of-string sentinel—are

identical. In Section [g], the filename extension is copied to caSuffix. atoi() converts the string to an integer. Now that the extension is in integer form it can be incremented directly (see Section [h]). Finally, Sections [i] through [k] demonstrate the use of sprintf() to convert the integer back into a string, and successive applications of strcat() to reassemble a new copy of the file name with the incremented numerical extension.

REVIEW QUESTIONS

1. Why are pointers required to swap values using a function?
2. Why can an array name's value be changed inside a function?
3. What are two problems associated with the pass-by-reference style of programming?
4. Suppose that a two-dimensional array of floats, faaArray, is passed to a function ArrayDetails(). Which of the following lines is a valid function declaration

```
enum { NoRows = 5, NoCols = 10 };

int ArrayDetails( faaArray[][] );
int ArrayDetails( faaArray[ NoRows ][        ] );
int ArrayDetails( faaArray[        ][ NoCols ] );
int ArrayDetails( faaArray[ NoRows ][ NoCols ] );
```

   for ArrayDetails()?
5. What is the purpose of the const keyword?
6. What is the difference between a character pointer and a string?
7. Why is the C string library fairly extensive? What would you use strings for?

9.5 PROGRAMMING EXERCISES

Problem 9.1 (Beginner): Modify Program 7.1 so that a user is prompted for the quadratic equation coefficients by a function readCoefficients(). The structure of readCoefficients() should look similar to the following:

```
/*
 *  ==========================================================
 *  readCoefficients () -- read coefficients from keyboard.
 *
 *  Input  : float *fpA -- pointer to coefficient "a".
 *         : float *fpB -- pointer to coefficient "b".
 *         : float *fpC -- pointer to coefficient "c".
```

```
 *  Output : void.
 *  ===========================================================
 */

void readCoefficients ( float *fpA, float *fpB, float *fpC ) {

     .... add details here .....

}
```

In addition to filling in the body of `readCoefficients()` and adjusting `main()`, you will need to make an appropriate function declaration for `readCoefficients()` so that the program will compile.

Problem 9.2 (Beginner): Write a function `countblanks()` to count the number of blanks in a character string. The function specifications should look similar to the following:

```
/*
 *  ===========================================================
 *  countblanks() : Count blanks in a character string.
 *
 *  Input  : char *cpString -- pointer to character string.
 *  Output : int            -- number of blanks in the
 *                             character string.
 *  ===========================================================
 */

int countblanks( char *cpString ) {

     .... add details here .....

}
```

Write a test program that allocates memory for the character string

```
"This string contains four blanks"
```

prints the message, and then computes and prints the number of blanks in the character string.

Problem 9.3 (Beginner): Write a function

```
void DateToString( char *cpDate , int iDay,
                         int iMonth, int iYear );
```

that converts the three integer arguments for the day, month, and year into a character array accessed by the pointer `cpDate`. The character array representation for the date should follow the format

```
day-month-year
```

The `DateToString()` should check that the input data is well defined (e.g., the month is within the range 1 through 12) before proceeding with the string conversion. Simply assume that a leap year occurs when the year is divisible by 4.

Test your implementation of `DateToString()` with the script of code

```
enum  { LengthOfDate = 50 };   /* Length of array for date */
char caDate[ LengthOfDate ];   /* Character array for the date */

DateToString( caDate, 25, 12, 98 );

printf("Christmas Day is : %s \n", caDate );
```

It should produce

```
Christmas Day is : 25-December-1998
```

Problem 9.4 (Beginner): The fragment of code

```
int main( void ) {
float fX = 12.3;
float fY = -1.3;
float fZ =  2.0;

    printf("The floats are : fX = %8.3f\n", fX );
    printf("               : fY = %8.3f\n", fY );
    printf("               : fZ = %8.3f\n", fZ );

    sortfloats ( &fX, &fY, &fZ );

    printf("The ordered floats are : fX = %8.3f\n", fX );
    printf("                       : fY = %8.3f\n", fY );
    printf("                       : fZ = %8.3f\n", fZ );
}
```

is a test program for a function

```
void sortfloats( float *, float *, float * );
```

that rearranges three floating point variables so that they are numerically ordered. For example, the fragment of test code generates

```
The floats are : fX =   12.300
               : fY =   -1.300
               : fZ =    2.000
The ordered floats are : fX =  -1.300
                       : fY =   2.000
                       : fZ =  12.300
```

Fill in the details of function `sortfloats()`.

Hint. An efficient way of rearranging the variables is with the `max(a,b)` and `min(a,b)` macros given in Chapter 11.

Problem 9.5 (Intermediate): Write a function that will print a menu and request a choice from the user. The function should check that the choice is valid and return it to the calling routine. When an invalid choice is made, the function should state that it is invalid, display the valid choices, and request a new selection.

The function will be passed an array of pointers to character strings. Each entry in the array is another choice for the menu. If the function is passed the array of char pointers (the menu)

```
char* cpaTheMenu [] = { "Startup", "Process", "Stop", "Quit" };
```

for example, the function should print the menu

```
Select from the following:
Choice  Value
------  -----
0     : Startup
1     : Process
2     : Stop
3     : Quit

Your choice -->
```

and if the choice is not 0 to 3, then print an error message, and loop for a new selection/choice.

10

DYNAMIC ALLOCATION OF MEMORY

10.1 NEED FOR DYNAMIC MEMORY ALLOCATION

The need for dynamic memory allocation is best motivated by first returning to the style of programming adopted in Chapter 8 and noting that array declarations of the type

```
enum { NoRows = 4 , NoCols = 2 };

int myFunction( void ) {
float faaMatrix[ NoRows ][ NoCols ];

        faaMatrix [0][0] = faaMatrix [1][1] = 2.0;
}
```

fix the dimensions of `faaMatrix` at compile time and produce a conceptual layout of memory as shown in Figure 8.16. Recall that, by definition, C stores consecutive elements of an array along its rows. When `myFunction()` is entered at run-time, memory for `faaMatrix` will be assigned on the process stack and will be available while the program executes within `myFunction()`. This space will be discarded once the program control leaves `myFunction()`—that is, of course, unless we prefix the array declaration with the storage class specifier `static`.

From the viewpoint of developing engineering software, which may need to run in a multitasking environment such as UNIX, this style of programming has several limitations:

1. Declarations of the above-mentioned type assume general ($m \times n$) matrices that may or may not have special structure. If a matrix is symmetric, for example, then storage requirements are halved. This observation is important for engineering applications such as finite element analysis, where matrices often contain tens of thousands of elements, and where solutions to sets of equations $[A] \cdot \{x\} = \{b\}$ typically consume 50% to 90% of total computational work.
2. For many engineering problems, storage requirements for many matrices will not be known at compile time and, indeed, may vary significantly from problem to problem. Program performance could be improved if the data could respond to the demands of a specific problem. A naive solution is to "allocate more storage for arrays and other data structures than you'll ever use." In the days of FORTRAN, this was a standard way of avoiding the problem of unknown storage requirements.
3. What do you do when several people want to run similar programs having large arrays on a multitasking operating system such as UNIX? For the operating system to accommodate several programs at once, it time shares the central processor between each of the tasks. This means that each task or program will get a small slice of time when the central processor works one specific program. For this program to work, both the processor's time and the memory of the computer must be partitioned or swapped to accommodate all the programs. If the actual hardware of the machine does not have sufficient memory for the programs, then it may be forced to employ `virtual memory`. Virtual memory is created and handled by the operating system to make it look like the machine actually has more memory than it does by using hard disk space to store part of the memory. The drawback to virtual memory is slow speed caused by memory being swapped to and from the disk drive.

These items point to the need for flexible self-adjusting data structures and procedures that engineers can employ for using as much of the computer system memory as is available, and for returning resources to the computer when they are no longer needed. C provides the necessary power to solve these problems.

This chapter describes and demonstrates use of the dynamic memory allocation functions `malloc()`, `calloc()`, and `realloc()`. Memory will be deallocated with the function `free()`. We write our own functions for dynamic memory allocation that includes error checking and demonstrate their use by working through a series of problems involving dynamic allocation of one- and two-dimensional arrays.

10.2 MEMORY ALLOCATION WITH malloc(), calloc(), and realloc()

The `malloc()` function obtains the `n` bytes of memory and returns a pointer to this memory. Its declaration in `<stdlib.h>` is

```
void * malloc( size_t size );
```

Function calls to `malloc()` must provide the size of the memory block (in bytes)

Short Summary of Functions in `<stdlib.h>`

`malloc(n)`	The `malloc()` function obtains the `n` bytes of memory and returns a pointer to this memory. In ANSI C, `malloc()` returns a generic pointer of type void (i.e., `void *`), which is automatically cast to `char *` when an assignment is made.
`calloc(m,n)`	The `calloc()` function allocates memory for arrays of bytes (instead of a single block of bytes with `malloc()`). The first function argument `m` is the number of cells in the array. The second argument `n` is the number of bytes required for each cell.
`realloc(p,m)`	The `calloc()` function changes the size of an object pointed to by `char *p` to size `m` bytes. Contents of the new object will be unchanged up to the original size of the object; if the new size is larger than the old size, then the new space is uninitialized.
`exit(n)`	The `exit(n)` function terminates a program with cleanup activities. `n = 0` indicates successful program termination. Nonzero values of `n` indicate unsuccessful program termination.
`free(p)`	The `free()` function deallocates memory previously obtained by either the `malloc()` or `calloc()` functions. The function argument, `p`, is a pointer to the space. Once a block of memory has been marked as free, it may be used by a program for other purposes.

Note. The functions `malloc()` and `realloc()` contain "garbage" unless explicitly initialized. Use of the function `calloc(m,n)` is equivalent to `p = malloc(m*n)` followed by `memset(p,0,m*n)`, with `memset()` setting all the bits in the block of memory to zero.

to be allocated. The `size_t` type is the type returned by sizeof, and it is normally an `unsigned int`. Unsigned integers are predictable and portable because `n` bits are always stored in straight binary notation, with values ranging 0 to $2^n - 1$. When the requested memory is available, `malloc()` will return a generic pointer of type void (i.e., `void *`), which is automatically cast to `char *` when an assignment is made.

The `calloc()` function dynamically allocates memory for an array of objects. Its declaration in `<stdlib.h>` is

```
void * calloc( size_t nitems, size_t size);
```

Function calls to `calloc()` must contain two arguments: the number of objects to be allocated (nitems) and the size of each of them (size). Unlike `malloc()` and `realloc()`, `calloc()` initializes the allocated memory to 0.

The `realloc()` function has the declaration

```
void * realloc( void * , size_t size );
```

and is useful for situations where memory requirements change during a program's execution and where the contents of a previously allocated array need to be expanded. One approach would be to simply `malloc()` a larger array, copy the smaller of the two arrays into the new larger one, and then free the first array. A key problem with this strategy is that there may not be enough memory to allocate another complete array, and we may only want to extend the first one by a few

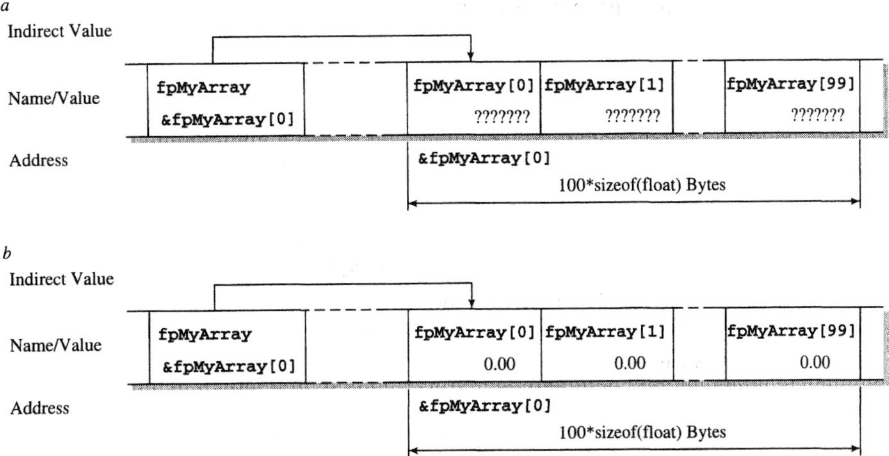

FIGURE 10.1 Memory contents with (*a*) `malloc()` and (*b*) `calloc()`.

elements. The `realloc()` function mitigates this problem by reallocating an existing array to a new dimension, while preserving any data in the current array.

The `malloc()`, `calloc()`, and `realloc()` functions will return a NULL pointer when the requested memory is not available. In such cases, an error message should be printed and the program execution terminated.

Example. The script of code

```
float *fpMyArray;
fpMyArray = (float *) malloc( 100*sizeof(float) );
```

shows the essential details of code needed to allocate an array of 100 floats. The argument to `malloc()`, `100*sizeof(float)` defines the number of bytes needed for the array. An equivalent block of memory would be obtained with the function call

```
float *fpMyArray;
fpMyArray = (float *) calloc( 100, sizeof(float) );
```

In both cases, the void pointer returned by `malloc()` or `calloc()` is cast to a pointer of type float. Figures 10.1a and 10.1b show the layout of memory and memory contents when `malloc()` and `calloc()` are used for dynamic memory allocation. It is important to note that in both methods, the pointer `*fpMyArray` will occupy a separate block of memory than the array itself. Moreover, `malloc()` allocates memory but does not initialize its contents—hence, use of the question marks in Figure 10.1a. Memory allocated by `calloc()` will have its contents set to 0.

Example. Suppose that an array of 100 characters has been dynamically allocated with the block of code

```
cpString = (char *) calloc( 100,  sizeof(char) );
if( cpString == (char *) NULL ) {
    fprintf( stderr, "ERROR : calloc() failed !" );
    exit (1);
}
```

and now we find that we want to extend the array to 150 characters. One approach would be to allocate a new array of 150 characters, copy the contents of the first array to the second, and then free the first array. A better approach is to simply use `realloc()`, as in

```
cpString = (char *) realloc( cpString, 150 );
if( cpString == (char *) NULL ) {
    fprintf( stderr, "ERROR : realloc() failed !" );
    exit (1);
}
```

Note that `cpString` may change location in this call to `realloc()`. We can be assured, however, that if new memory is allocated, the previous values (up to the lesser of the two array sizes) will be copied into the new memory locations.

10.3 DEALLOCATING MEMORY WITH free()

Generally speaking, it is good programming practice to keep track of memory usage and to return it to the operating system pool when it is no longer needed. Releasing memory is particularly important for programs that embed memory allocation functions inside looping control structures. Otherwise left unchecked, the size of an executable program will grow monotonically until hardware limitations are exceeded.

We use the function `free()` to deallocate memory previously allocated with `malloc()`, `calloc()`, or `realloc()`. Its declaration in `<stdlib.h>` is

```
void free ( void * );
```

The memory allocated in the previous two examples can be deallocated with

```
free ( fpMyArray );
free ( cpString );
```

The size of the block to be freed is not included as a function argument because the `malloc()` and `free()` package remembers the size of each block when it was allocated. On many computer systems, `free()` does not actually return memory to the operating system. Instead, it merely makes the memory available for future `malloc()` calls in the same process.

10.4 DYNAMIC ALLOCATION OF CHARACTER STRINGS

Our first application is development of `saveString()`, a function for the dynamic allocation of character strings.

PROGRAM 10.1: ALLOCATION OF CHARACTER STRINGS WITH saveString()

```
/*
 *  ========================================================
 *  Test dynamic allocation of memory for character strings
 *  ========================================================
 */

#include <stdio.h>
#include <stdlib.h>

int main( void ) {
char *saveString( char * );
char *cpName;

   /* [a] : Allocate memory for character string */

   cpName = saveString("My test string");

   /* [b] : Print contents of character string */

   printf("TEST STRING : \"%s\"\n", cpName );

   /* [c] : Free character string memory */

   free( cpName );

}

/*
 *  ===============================================================
 *  Version 1 of saveString() : Safe allocation of character strings
 *
 *  Input  :  char *cpName     -- pointer to character string.
 *  Output :  char *cpTemp     -- pointer to allocated memory.
 *  ===============================================================
 */
```

```
char *saveString( char *cpName ) {
char *cpTemp;

    cpTemp = (char *) malloc( (unsigned) (strlen( cpName ) + 1) );
    if( cpTemp == (char *) NULL) {
        fprintf(stderr,"saveString(): malloc failed\n");
        exit(1);
    }
    strcpy( cpTemp, cpName );

    return cpTemp;
}
```

Program 10.1 contains Version 1 of `saveString()` and a short test program. The program output is simply

```
TEST STRING : "My test string"
```

Points to note are as follows:

1. Memory of the character string is allocated by

```
cpTemp = (char *) malloc( (unsigned) (strlen( cpName ) + 1) );
```

   The number of characters in the string pointed to by `cpName` is computed by the string function `strlen( cpName )`. One extra character of memory is allocated for the end-of-string sentinel. For example, in Program 10.1, `strlen("My test string")` will return 14 and memory will be allocated for 15 characters.

2. In `saveString()`, we check that requests for dynamic memory allocation are successful before trying to use the memory (this principle applies to all instances of dynamic memory allocation). The header file `<stdlio.h>` is included because it contains the definition for `NULL`. The script of code

```
if(cpTemp == (char *) NULL) {
   fprintf(stderr,"ERROR : malloc failed in saveString()\n");
   exit(1);
}
```

   will be executed when `malloc()` has failed. First, the terse error message

```
ERROR : malloc() failed in saveString()
```

will be printed. We use the file print function `fprintf(.....)` with the standard error file descriptor `stderr` so that an error message will be directed to the engineer's screen, even if the program's output is being redirected to a file. The program's execution will then be terminated with the function call `exit(1)`.

3. The line of code

```
strcpy( cpTemp, cpName );
```

copies the contents of string pointed to by `cpName` into the block of memory pointed to by `cpTemp`.

4. Before the program execution is terminated, memory for the character string is deallocated (i.e., released to the system) by calling `free ( cpName )`. We do not need to cast the argument to `free()`.

10.5 GENERIC FUNCTIONS FOR DYNAMIC MEMORY ALLOCATION

In this section, we develop a family of generic functions for dynamic memory allocation. The need for these functions is motivated in part by the observation that five lines of code

```
cpTemp = (char *) malloc( (unsigned) uiSize );
if (cpTemp == (char *) NULL) {
    fprintf(stderr, "ERROR : Unable to allocate sufficient memory\n");
    exit (1);
}
```

are required just to allocate one block of memory and check for errors. Allocating 20 blocks of memory would require 100 lines of source code. A second problem with our previous code is that error messages of the type

```
ERROR : Unable to allocate sufficient memory
```

tell the user why the program failed, but not where the failure took place. A large engineering program may allocate tens, or possibly hundreds, of memory blocks during its execution, and an engineer would like to know precisely where the memory allocation failed and why. If the memory allocation occurs near the beginning of a program's execution, then perhaps the program is simply too large for the computer's resources. However, if the memory allocation failure occurs near the end of the program's execution, then several strategies are available for obtaining more memory. On a multitasking engineering workstation, more memory can often be obtained by simply removing other programs (e.g., do not run `Netscape`, `xrn`, and the application program at the same time). More memory resources can also be obtained by releasing previously allocated memory that is no longer needed.

These drawbacks are mitigated with the functions safeMalloc() and safeCalloc(). The details of safeMalloc() are as follows:

```
void *safeMalloc( unsigned int uiSize, char cpFileName, int iLineNo ) {
void *vpTemp;

   vpTemp = malloc( uiSize );
   if (vpTemp == (void *) NULL) {
       fprintf( stderr, "ERROR : malloc() failed in safeMalloc()\n");
       fprintf( stderr, "ERROR : safeMalloc called in file %s : line %d\n",
               cpFileName, int iLineNo );
       exit (1);
   }

   else
       return( vpTemp );
}
```

The function safeMalloc() has three arguments. uiSize is the number of bytes of memory that malloc() will be requested to allocate. The current file name and line of source code from which safeMalloc() was called is recorded in cpFileName and iLineNo. Like malloc(), safeMalloc() returns a void pointer that will be cast to the appropriate data type. The benefit of this approach is that now one block of memory can be requested in one statement of code:

```
float *fpTemp1 = (float *) safeMalloc( 20*sizeof (float),
                                       --FILE--, --LINE-- );
float *fpTemp2 = (float *) safeMalloc( 50*sizeof (float),
                                       --FILE--, --LINE-- );
```

and a descriptive error message will be printed when malloc() fails. Here, --FILE-- and --LINE-- are predefined macros in ANSI C that give the name of the current source file (expressed as a character string) and the line number of the current source program line (expressed as a decimal integer). Further details on --FILE-- and --LINE-- may be found in Chapter 11.

10.6 A FILE OF MISCELLANEOUS FUNCTIONS

In this section, we put our generic memory allocation functions safeMalloc() and safeCalloc() in a miscellaneous functions file called miscellaneous.c. We write a header file, miscellaneous.h, which will contain function declarations and will act as an interface between the miscellaneous functions and an engineering application program.

A schematic of the package and an engineering application program is shown in Figure 10.2. In addition to safeMalloc() and safeCalloc(), the miscellaneous

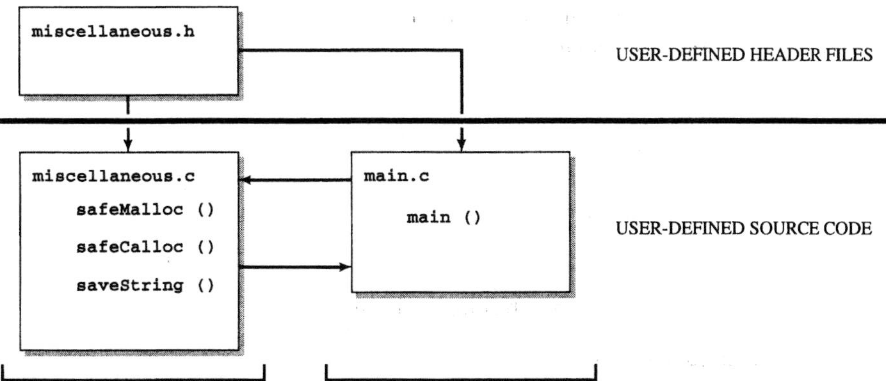

FIGURE 10.2 Engineering program and miscellaneous functions.

functions file will contain a revised version of `saveString()`. The details of `miscellaneous.h` are as follows:

```
/*
 *  ========================================
 *  Header file for Miscellaneous Routines
 *  ========================================
 */

#ifndef MISCELLANEOUS_H
#define MISCELLANEOUS_H

/* Generic allocation functions */

void * safeMalloc( unsigned int , char * , int );
void * safeCalloc( unsigned int, unsigned int, char * , int );

/* Miscellaneous functions */

char * saveString( char * , char *, int );

#endif /* end case MISCELLANEOUS_H */
```

The block of code bounded by `#ifndef MISCELLANEOUS_H` and `#endif` uses the existence of `MISCELLANEOUS_H` (or lack thereof) to ensure that the function declarations are included at the top of a file once at most. The use of these macros simplifies the detection of errors in macro definitions when they exist. We have included functions declarations for ANSI-compliant compilers, where type checking on function arguments takes place.

The contents of `miscellaneous.c` are contained in Program 10.2.

PROGRAM 10.2: C FUNCTIONS FOR DYNAMIC MEMORY ALLOCATION

```
#include "miscellaneous.h"

/*
 *  ============================================================
 *  safeMalloc : Safe memory allocation with malloc().
 *
 *  Input :   unsigned int uiSize -- no of bytes to be allocated.
 *            char *cpFileName    -- pointer to file name.
 *            int iLineNo         -- line number.
 *  Output :  void *vpTemp        -- pointer to allocated memory.
 *  ============================================================
 */

void *safeMalloc( unsigned int uiSize, char *cpFileName, int iLineNo ) {
void *vpTemp;

     vpTemp = malloc( uiSize );
     if (vpTemp == (void *) NULL) {
         fprintf( stderr, "ERROR : malloc() failed in safeMalloc()\n");
         fprintf( stderr, "ERROR : safeMalloc called in file %s : line %d\n",
                  cpFileName, iLineNo );
         exit (1);
     }
     else
        return( vpTemp );
}

/*
 *  ===============================================================
 *  safeCalloc : Safe memory allocation with calloc().
 *
 *  Input :   unsigned int uiNoItems -- no array elements.
 *            unsigned int uiSize    -- bytes in each array element.
 *            char *cpFileName       -- pointer to file name.
 *            int iLineNo            -- line number.
 *  Output :  void *vpTemp           -- pointer to allocated memory.
 *  ===============================================================
 */

void *safeCalloc( unsigned int uiNoItems, unsigned int uiSize,
                          char *cpFileName,        int iLineNo ) {
void *vpTemp;

     vpTemp = calloc( uiNoItems, uiSize );
```

```
    if (vpTemp == (void *) NULL) {
        fprintf( stderr, "ERROR : calloc() failed in safeCalloc()\n");
        fprintf( stderr, "ERROR : safeCalloc called in file %s : line %d\n",
                 cpFileName, iLineNo );
        exit (1);
    }
    else
       return( vpTemp );
}


/*
 *  ==========================================================
 *  saveString : Safe allocation of character strings
 *
 *  Input :   char *cpName     -- pointer to character string.
 *            char *cpFileName -- pointer to file name.
 *            int iLineNo      -- line number.
 *  Output :  char *cpTemp     -- pointer to allocated memory.
 *  ==========================================================
 */
char *saveString( char *cpName, char cpFileName, int iLineNo ) {
char *cpTemp;


    cpTemp = (char *) safeMalloc((unsigned)(strlen( cpName ) + 1),
                                  cpFileName, iLineNo );
    strcpy(cpTemp, cpName);


    return cpTemp;
}
```

Points to note are as follows:

1. The header file `miscellaneous.h` is included at the top of `miscellaneous.c` because it contains the function declarations for `safeMalloc()`, `safe-Calloc()`, and `saveString()`. With the function declarations in place, the source code for each of these functions can be presented in any order.
2. It is important to remember that `safeCalloc()` sets all the bits of the allocated memory to zero, and `safeMalloc()` leaves the array contents uninitialized. Sometimes programmers incur a high price for overlooking this point. In the coding of numerical applications, for example, an algorithm may not work unless the contents of a particular matrix (or vector) are identically zero. To avoid unexpected catastrophe, always use `safeCalloc()`.

3. Notice that we have rewritten `saveString()` to take advantage of `safe-Malloc()`.

10.7 DYNAMIC ALLOCATION OF ONE-DIMENSIONAL ARRAYS

In this section, we demonstrate dynamic memory allocation by developing an application program that uses one-dimensional arrays for the storage of three-dimensional vectors.

By definition, a row vector is simply a (1 × n) matrix, and a column vector is a (n × 1) matrix. The geometry of vectors is most evident for problems that occur in three-dimensional space, as shown in the left-hand schematic of Figure 10.3.

If `i`, `j`, and `k` are unit vectors along the `x`, `y`, and `z` axes, respectively, then a general vector `A` may be written

$$\mathtt{A} = a_1\mathtt{i} + a_2\mathtt{j} + a_3\mathtt{k} \tag{10.1}$$

Here a_1 is the magnitude of `A` along the `x` axis, a_2 the magnitude of `A` along the `y` axis, and a_3 the magnitude of `A` along the `z` axis. The mathematical operations of vector addition and subtraction are defined by

$$A + B = \langle a_1, a_2, \ldots, a_n\rangle + \langle b_1, b_2, \ldots, b_n\rangle \tag{10.2}$$

$$= \langle a_1 + b_1, a_2 + b_2, \ldots, a_n + b_n\rangle \tag{10.3}$$

and

$$A - B = \langle a_1, a_2, \ldots, a_n\rangle - \langle b_1, b_2, \ldots, b_n\rangle \tag{10.4}$$

$$= \langle a_1 - b_1, a_2 - b_2, \ldots, a_n - b_n\rangle \tag{10.5}$$

When the dimension of a vector is two or three, as shown in Figure 10.3, the sum (or composition) of two vectors corresponds to the diagonal of a parallelogram formed by the two vectors as sides. Vector subtraction is the addition of a vector directed in the opposite sense. The sum of two vectors must be commutative (i.e., the order of summation must not affect the result).

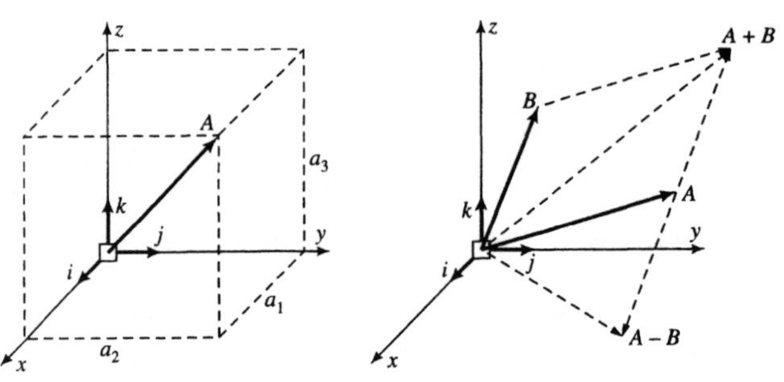

FIGURE 10.3 Vector geometry and arithmetic operations.

TABLE 10.1 A Shopping List of Basic Vector Operations

Vector Function	*Purpose*
`vecPrint()`	Print contents of the vectors.
`vecCopy()`	Make a copy of a vector.
`vecAdd()`	Compute sum of two vectors.
`vecSub()`	Compute difference of two vectors.
`vecDotProduct()`	Compute dot product of two vectors.
`vecCrossProduct()`	Compute cross product of two vectors.
`vecLength()`	Compute length (or magnitude) of a vector.

Although vectors are a subset of matrices (from a mathematical point of view), in practical computer implementations, functions for vector arithmetic are implemented separately from functions for matrix arithmetic. With this point in mind, Table 10.1 contains a shopping list of functions for vector operations. Function names begin with the abbreviated keyword `vec....`, followed by a one- or two-part word that describes the function's purpose. Functions are provided for dynamic allocation of memory for vectors (i.e., `vecAlloc`), printing vectors (i.e., `vecPrint`), vector arithmetic (i.e., `vecAdd`, `vecSub`), and the dot product and cross product.

10.7.1 Dynamic Allocation of Vectors

Computer Program. We now develop a vector test program that will dynamically allocate memory for two vectors

$$A = [1, 2, 3] \quad B = [-3, 4, 5] \tag{10.6}$$

and compute and print the sum `A + B`. Here is the program source code.

PROGRAM 10.3: EXERCISE VECTOR FUNCTIONS

```
/*
 *  ===========================================================
 *  Dynamically allocate, print, and add three-dimensional vectors
 *  ===========================================================
 */

#include <stdio.h>
#include "miscellaneous.h"

/* Declarations for vector functions */

void   vecPrint( char *, float *, int );
float *vecAdd( float *, float *, int );
```

```
int main( void ) {
enum { VectorLength = 3 };
float *fpA, *fpB, *fpC;

  /* [a] : Allocate and initialize vectors "A" and "B" */

  fpA = (float *) safeCalloc( VectorLength, sizeof(float) ,
                              __FILE__, __LINE__ );

  fpA [0] =  1; fpA [1] = 2; fpA [2] = 3;

  fpB = (float *) safeCalloc( VectorLength, sizeof(float) ,
                              __FILE__, __LINE__ );

  fpB [0] = -3; fpB [1] = 4; fpB [2] = 5;

  /* [b] : Compute "A + B" */

  fpC = vecAdd( fpA, fpB , VectorLength );

  /* [c] : Print contents of vectors */

  vecPrint( "A",   fpA , VectorLength );
  vecPrint( "B",   fpB , VectorLength );
  vecPrint( "A+B", fpC , VectorLength );

  /* [d] : Free vector memory */

  free ( fpA );
  free ( fpB );
  free ( fpC );

}

/*
 *  ================================================================
 *  vecAdd() : Addition of two vectors
 *
 *  Input :   float  *fpA -- pointer to float array
 *            float  *fpB -- pointer to float array
 *            int iLength -- length of float array
 *  Output :  float *fpC  -- pointer to array containing vector sum
 *  ================================================================
 */

float *vecAdd( float *fpA, float *fpB, int iLength ) {
```

```
float *fpC;
int   iRow;

     fpC = (float *) safeCalloc( iLength, sizeof(float) ,
                                 __FILE__, __LINE__ );

     for(iRow = 0 ; iRow < iLength; iRow++ )
         fpC [ iRow ] = fpA [ iRow ] + fpB [ iRow ];

     return ( fpC );
}

/*
 * ==========================================================
 *  vecPrint() : Naive Implementation of Vector Print
 *
 *  Input :   char *cpMessage -- pointer to vector message.
 *            float *fpVector -- pointer to float array
 *            int     iLength -- length of float array
 *  Output :  void.
 * ==========================================================
 */

void vecPrint( char *cpMessage , float *fpVector , int iLength ) {
int iRow;

    if(cpMessage != (char *) NULL)
       printf("\nVECTOR \"%s\" \n\n", cpMessage );
    else
       printf("\nVECTOR : \"UNTITLED\" \n\n");

    for(iRow = 1; iRow <= iLength; iRow++)
       printf(" %3d   %16.5e\n", iRow, fpVector[ iRow-1 ]);

}
```

The output generated by Program 10.3

```
VECTOR "A"

   1         1.00000e+00
   2         2.00000e+00
   3         3.00000e+00
```

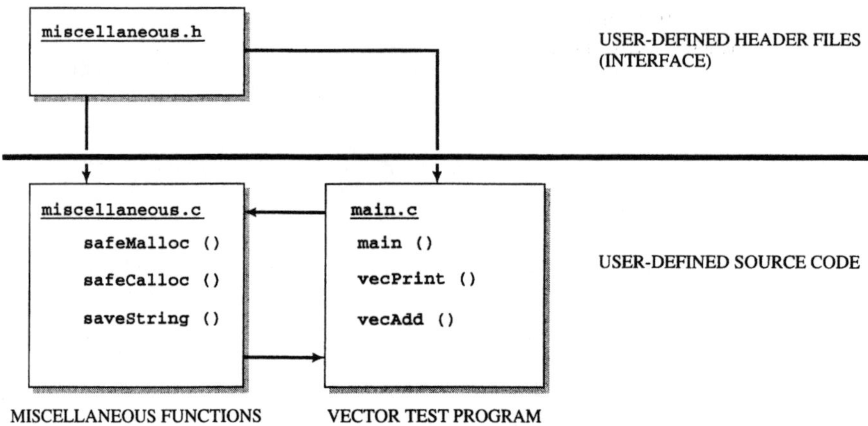

FIGURE 10.4 Architecture of vector test program.

```
VECTOR "B"

   1        -3.00000e+00
   2         4.00000e+00
   3         5.00000e+00

VECTOR "A+B"

   1        -2.00000e+00
   2         6.00000e+00
   3         8.00000e+00
```

is composed of three parts, vectors `A` and `B`, and the vector sum, `A + B`.

Points to note are as follows:

1. Figure 10.4 is a schematic of the user-defined header files and program source code files that will participate in Program 10.3. The header file `miscellaneous.h` acts as an interface between `miscellaneous.c` and our matrix test program located in `main.c`. The contents of `miscellaneous.h` and `miscellaneous.c` are as described in the previous sections.
2. Program 10.3 contains three functions, `main()`, `vecPrin()`, and `vecAdd()`. The fragment of code

```
fpA = (float *) safeCalloc( VectorLength, sizeof(float) ,
                            __FILE__, __LINE__ );
fpA [0] = 1; fpA [1] = 2; fpA [2] = 3;
```

within `main()` dynamically allocates memory for the vector `fpA` and initializes the element values to 1, 2, and 3, respectively. An identical procedure is used for vector `fpB`. The vectors are added together by simply writing

```
fpC = vecAdd( fpA, fpB, VectorLength );
```

Memory for the result of the vector summation is dynamically allocated inside `vecAdd()`. When the summation computation is complete, `vecAdd()` returns a float pointer to the calling function.

10.8 DYNAMIC ALLOCATION OF TWO-DIMENSIONAL ARRAYS

From a mathematical point of view, a matrix (or array) of order m by n is simply a set of numbers arranged in a rectangular block of horizontal m rows and n vertical columns. We say

$$A = \begin{bmatrix} a_{11} & a_{12} & \cdots & a_{1n} \\ a_{21} & a_{22} & \cdots & a_{2n} \\ \vdots & \vdots & \ddots & \vdots \\ a_{m1} & a_{m2} & \cdots & a_{mn} \end{bmatrix} \tag{10.7}$$

is a matrix of size (m × n). Sometimes we say "matrix A has dimension m rows by n columns," or simply that "A is an m-by-n matrix." The numbers that make up the array are called the `elements` of the matrix; they could be integers, real numbers, complex numbers, or even polynomials. In the double subscript notation a_{ij}, the first subscript i denotes the row number, and the second subscript j denotes the column number.

10.8.1 Allocation of Small Matrices

Computer Program. To see how dynamic memory allocation of matrices works, we look at the details of a small computer program that allocates memory for two matrices, initializes their contents to skew-symmetric matrices, and prints the following contents to the screen:

```
MATRIX "A"

     0.00000       -1.00000       -2.00000       -3.00000
     1.00000        0.00000       -1.00000       -2.00000
     2.00000        1.00000        0.00000       -1.00000
     3.00000        2.00000        1.00000        0.00000
```

```
MATRIX "B"

        0.00000       -1.00000       -2.00000       -3.00000
        1.00000        0.00000       -1.00000       -2.00000
        2.00000        1.00000        0.00000       -1.00000
        3.00000        2.00000        1.00000        0.00000
```

Two strategies of matrix allocation are presented. Matrix "A" is allocated in such a way that the entire matrix is located in a single contiguous (or sequential) block of computer memory. We call the storage pattern for matrix "B" indirect because each row of the matrix will be stored in its own block of memory. Here is the program source code.

PROGRAM 10.4: ALLOCATE AND PRINT SMALL MATRIX

```
/*
 *  ==============================================================
 *  Program to dynamically allocate and print two small matrices
 *  ==============================================================
 */

#include <stdio.h>
#include "miscellaneous.h"

/* function declarations */

void      matPrint( char *, double **, int , int );
double ** matAllocSequentialDouble( int , int );
double ** matAllocIndirectDouble( int , int );

int main( void ) {
enum { NoRows = 4, NoColumns = 4 };
double   **dppA;
double   **dppB;
int iRow, iCol;

   /* [a] : Allocate memory for small 4 × 4 matrices */

   dppA = matAllocSequentialDouble( NoRows , NoColumns );
   dppB = matAllocIndirectDouble( NoRows ,  NoColumns );
```

```
   /* [b] : Initialize matrix element values */

   for( iCol = 1; iCol <= NoColumns; iCol++ )
        for( iRow = 1; iRow <= NoRows; iRow++ ) {
             dppA [ iRow - 1 ][ iCol - 1 ] = iRow - iCol;
             dppB [ iRow - 1 ][ iCol - 1 ] = iRow - iCol;
        }

   /* [c] : Print matrix */

   matPrint( "A", dppA, NoRows, NoColumns);
   matPrint( "B", dppB, NoRows, NoColumns);
}

/*
 *  ===================================================================
 *  matAllocSequentialDouble() : Memory allocation of matrices with
 *                               sequential storage pattern.
 *
 *  matAllocIndirectDouble() : Memory allocation of matrices with
 *                             indirect storage pattern.
 *
 *  Input :   int iNoRows      -- number of rows in matrix.
 *            int iNoColumns   -- number of columns in matrix.
 *  Output :  double **dppM    -- pointer to pointer to allocated matrix.
 *  ===================================================================
 */

double ** matAllocSequentialDouble( int iNoRows , int iNoColumns ) {
double **  dppM;
int        iRow;

   dppM     = (double **) safeMalloc( iNoRows * sizeof(double *),
                                      __FILE__, __LINE__ );
   dppM [0] = (double *)  safeMalloc( iNoRows * iNoColumns *
                                      sizeof(double), __FILE__, __LINE__ );
   for( iRow = 1; iRow < iNoRows; iRow++ )
        dppM [ iRow ] = dppM [ 0 ] + (iRow * iNoColumns);

   return ( dppM );
}

double ** matAllocIndirectDouble( int iNoRows , int iNoColumns ) {
double **  dppM;
int        iRow;
```

```
   dppM = (double **) safeMalloc( iNoRows * sizeof(double *),
                                  __FILE__, __LINE__);
   for( iRow = 0; iRow < iNoRows; iRow++ )
        dppM [ iRow ]  = (double *) safeMalloc( iNoColumns * sizeof(double),
                                                 __FILE__, __LINE__ );
   return ( dppM );
}

/*
 *  ======================================================================
 *  matPrint() : Naive implementation of matrix print
 *
 *  Input :    char *cpMatrixName -- pointer to matrix name.
 *             double **dppM      -- pointer to pointer to allocated matrix.
 *             int iNoRows        -- number of rows in matrix.
 *             int iNoColumns     -- number of columns in matrix.
 *  ======================================================================
 */

void matPrint( char *cpMatrixName , double **dppM , int iNoRows , int
iNoColumns ) {
int iRow, iCol;

    printf("\n\"MATRIX %s\"\n\n", cpMatrixName);
    for( iRow = 1; iRow <= iNoRows; iRow++ ) {
         for( iCol = 1; iCol <= iNoColumns; iCol++ )
              printf(" %12.5f ", dppM [ iRow - 1 ][ iCol - 1 ] );
         printf("\n");
    }
}
```

Points to note are as follows:

1. The matrix test program has three user-defined matrix functions, `matAllocSequentialDouble()`, `matAllocIndirect()`, and `matPrint()`. The block of declarations:

   ```
   void      matPrint( char *, double **, int ,  int );
   double ** matAllocSequentialDouble( int , int );
   double ** matAllocIndirectDouble( int , int );
   ```

   tells the compiler that functions `matAllocSequentialDouble()` and `matAllocIndirectDouble()` will accept two integer arguments, and return a pointer-to-a-pointer of data type `double`. `matPrint()` has four arguments; a character pointer for the matrix name, a pointer-to-a-pointer for the base

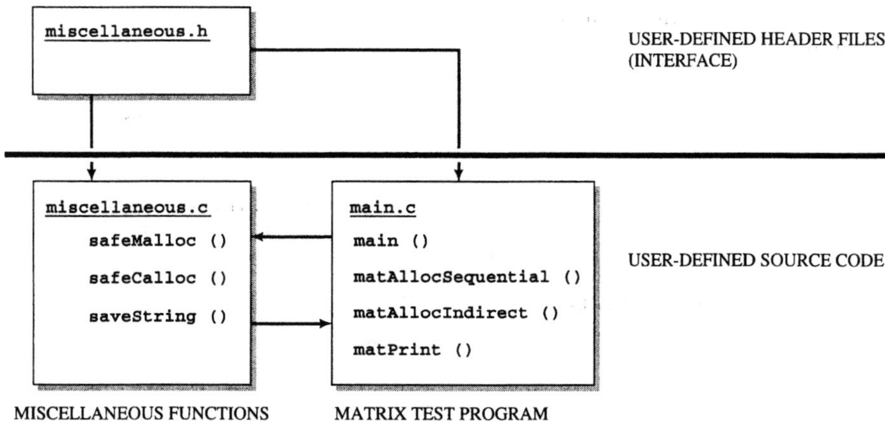

FIGURE 10.5 Architecture of matrix test program.

address of the matrix, and two integers for the number of rows and columns to be printed.

2. Figure 10.5 is a schematic of the user-defined header files and program source code files that make up Program 10.4. The header file `miscellaneous.h` acts as an interface between `miscellaneous.c` and our matrix test program located in `main.c`. The contents of `miscellaneous.h` and `miscellaneous.c` are as described in the previous sections.
3. Our implementation of the matrix print function assumes that all of the matrix elements will fit inside the width of a single page. This assumption is naive—a better implementation of matrix print would automatically divide large matrices into blocks of columns for printing, and label all rows and columns.

10.8.2 Allocating Matrices with Sequential Storage Pattern

The function `matAllocSequentialDouble()` in Program 10.4 generates a pattern of row-wise contiguous (or sequential) matrix storage similar to that shown in Figure 10.6. In Figure 10.6, we use dashed lines to denote an address reference and solid lines to connect sequential memory locations. The three-step procedure for matrix allocation is

1. The C statement

```
dppM = (double **) safeMalloc( iNoRows * sizeof(double *),
                               --FILE--, --LINE-- );
```

allocates a one-dimensional array of pointers of data type `double`, and assigns to `dppM`, a pointer to the array of pointers. Once again, we use `safeMalloc()` instead of `malloc()` because the former function takes care of error checking.

For our matrix test problem, `iNoRows = 4`. Figure 10.6a shows the layout

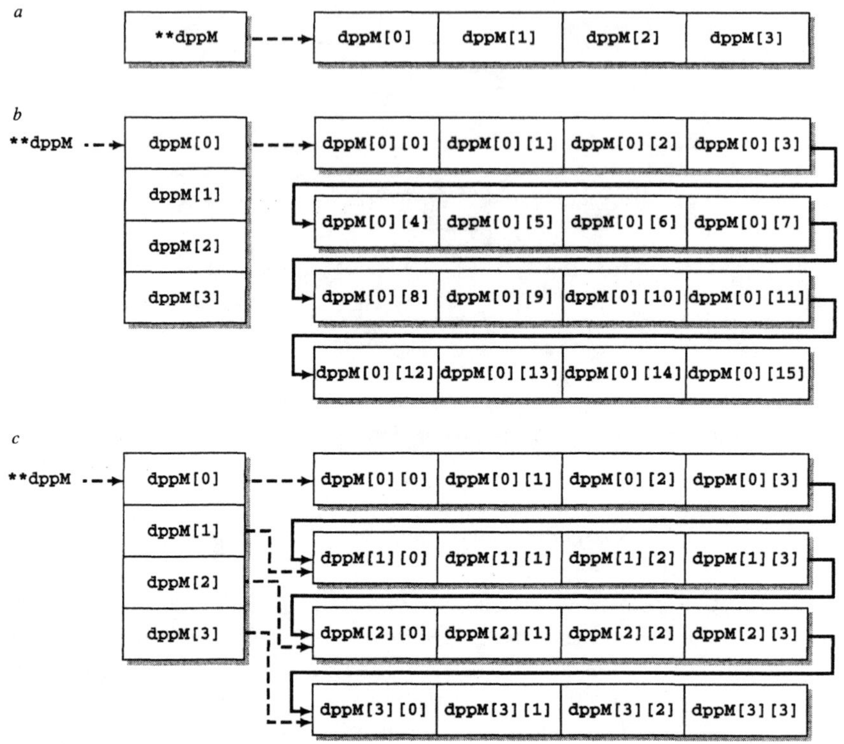

FIGURE 10.6 Sequence of assembly for sequential matrix storage: Layout of memory after *(a)* Step 1, *(b)* Step 2, and *(c)* Step 3.

of memory for `dppM` at the end of Step 1. The array of pointers occupies `iNoRows` × `sizeof(double *)` bytes of memory.

2. The C statement

```
dppM [0] = (double *) safeMalloc( iNoRows * iNoColumns * sizeof(double),
                                   __FILE__, __LINE__ );
```

allocates (`iNoRows` × `iNoColumns` × `sizeof(double)`) bytes of memory and assigns the base address to `dppM [0]`. The layout of memory is as shown in Figure 10.6b. At this point, there is no concept of multiple rows in a two-dimensional matrix. Rather we simply have one row of memory that ranges from `dppM [0][0]` to `dppM [0][15]`.

3. The C statement block

```
for( iRow = 1; iRow < iNoRows; iRow++ )
     dppM [ iRow ] = dppM [ 0 ] + (iRow * iNoColumns);
```

uses pointer arithmetic to assign the base address of matrix rows `2,3 ... (iNoRows1)` to pointers `dppM [1]`, `dppM [2]`, `... dppM [iNoRows-1]`. Figure 10.6c shows the layout memory, with adjusted pointers, for the fully allocated (4 × 4) test matrix.

10.8.3 Allocating Matrices with Indirect Storage Pattern

We use the term `indirect storage` to describe matrices whose contents are not stored in a single contiguous block of memory. The two-step procedure for dynamic memory allocation of matrices with indirect storage patterns is

1. The C statement

```
dppM = (double **) safeMalloc( iNoRows * sizeof(double *),
                                  __FILE__, __LINE__);
```

   allocates a one-dimensional array of pointers of data type `double`, and assigns to `dppM`, a pointer to the array of pointers. For our skew-symmetric matrix test problem, `iNoRows = 4`, and Figure 10.7a shows the layout of memory for `dppM` at the end of Step 1.

2. The block of C statements

```
for( iRow = 0; iRow < iNoRows; iRow++ )
   dppM[ iRow ]=(double *)safeMalloc(iNoColumns*sizeof(double),
                          __FILE__, __LINE__ );
```

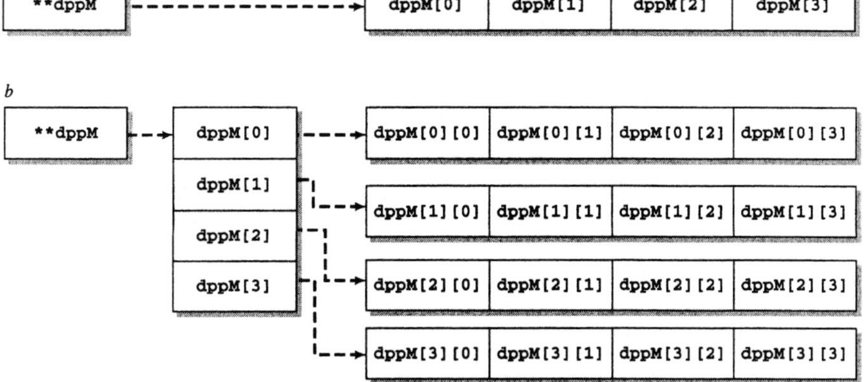

FIGURE 10.7 Sequence of assembly for indirect matrix storage: Layout of memory after (*a*) Step [1] and (*b*) Step [2].

iterates through the loop iRow = 0 to iRow = iNoRows - 1 allocating block of memory of length (iNoColumns×sizeof(double)) bytes. The base address of each memory block is assigned to dppM [iRow].

Figure 10.7b shows the layout of memory for matrix "A" at the completion of Step 2. Again, we use dotted lines to denote an address reference and solid lines to connect sequential memory locations.

Remark 10.1

Functions matAllocSequentialDouble() and matAllocIndirectDouble() may be rewritten with safeCalloc() instead of safeMalloc(). A revised code version of matAllocSequentialDouble() is

```
double **matAllocSequentialDouble( int iNoRows , int iNoColumns ) {
double **dppM;
int       iRow;

   dppM    = (double **) safeCalloc( 1, iNoRows * sizeof(double *),
                                    __FILE__,  __LINE__ );
   dppM[0] = (double *)  safeCalloc( 1, iNoRows * iNoColumns * sizeof(double),
                                    __FILE__,  __LINE__ );

      for( iRow = 1; iRow < iNoRows; iRow++ )
           dppM[ iRow ]  = dppM[ 0 ] + (iRow*iNoColumns);

   return (dppM);
}
```

The safeMalloc() and safeCalloc() versions of matAllocSequential-Double() generate identical layouts of matrix memory. The benefit of using safe-Calloc() is that the matrix contents will be automatically initialized to zero.

Remark 10.2

In both the safeMalloc() and safeCalloc() versions of matAllocSequen-tialDouble(), array elements can be accessed via the array index notation dppM [iRow][iCol] or via

```
*( dppM + NoColumns * iRow + iCol )
```

the dereferenced contents of memory at offset distance

```
( NoColumns*iRow + iCol ) * sizeof( double )
```

bytes from the base address of dppM.

In both the `safeMalloc()` and `safeCalloc()` versions of `matAllocIndirectDouble()`, matrix elements are accessed with two steps of indirection (i.e., pointer arithmetic). To the base address of `dppM`, we add `iRow`, take the value thus addressed as the new address, and add `iCol`. The matrix element corresponds to the dereferenced contents at this new address.

Notice that the dimensions of `dppM [][]` do not enter into this calculation at all. In fact, the number of assembly code lines generated by the compiler is constant because there is no multiplication, just an additional indirection.

10.8.4 Deallocating Matrix Memory

You may have noticed that Program 10.4 does not release (or free) the memory for matrices `A` and `B`, and so in Program 10.5, we present two functions for freeing matrix memory.

Algorithms that free matrix memory are, generally speaking, mirror images of those used to allocate memory. Matrix memory is released in the opposite order (or sequence) in which it was allocated. With these points noted, we now add the statements

```
double ** matAllocSequentialDouble( int , int );
void      matFreeSequentialDouble( double ** );
void      matFreeIndirectDouble( double ** , int );

int main( void ) {

   ..... source code deleted .....

   /* [c] : Print Matrices */

   ..... source code added later .....

   /* [d] : Free Matrix Memory */

   matFreeSequentialDouble( dppA );
   matFreeIndirectDouble( dppB , NoRows );
}
```

to the header and lower sections of Program 10.4, and write two functions for the deallocation of sequential and indirect matrix storage patterns. The function names are `matFreeSequentialDouble()` and `matFreeIndirectDouble()`, respectively.

PROGRAM 10.5: FREE MATRIX MEMORY

```
/*
 * ===============================================================
 * matFreeSequentialDouble() : Deallocate memory for matrices
 *                             with sequential storage pattern.
 *
 * matFreeIndirectDouble()  : Deallocate memory for matrices
 *                            with indirect storage pattern.
 *
 * Input  :  double **Matrix -- pointer to allocated matrix.
 *        :  int iNoRows     -- number of rows in matrix.
 * Output :  void
 * ===============================================================
 */

void matFreeSequentialDouble( double **dppM ) {

   free ( dppM [0] );
   free ( dppM );
}

void matFreeIndirectDouble( double **dppM, int iNoRows ) {
int iRow;

   for( iRow = 0; iRow < iNoRows; iRow++ )
        free ( dppM [ iRow ]);

   free ( dppM );
}
```

Matrices with an indirect storage pattern may be deallocated in two steps:

1. The block of C statements

   ```
   for( iRow = 0; iRow < iNoRows; iRow++ )
        free ( dppM [ iRow ]);
   ```

   walks from `iRow = 0` to `iRow = iNoRows - 1` and systematically releases memory in matrix rows `dppM [ 0 ]` to `dppM [ iNoRows-1 ]`.
2. The single C statement

   ```
   free ( dppM );
   ```

   releases memory for the array of pointers of type double. Also note that because `malloc()` remembers the size of allocated memory blocks, there is no need to size information as a function argument to `free()`.

For our matrix test problem, Step 1 changes the layout of the matrix memory from Figure 10.7b back to Figure 10.7a, and Step 2, from Figure 10.7a back to the single variable `**dppM`.

Remark 10.3

Not only are fixed-size arrays used in a different way than sequential and indirect arrays, but also the machine code generated by fixed-size array declarations is quite different from the code generated by sequential and indirect array declarations. From a user point of view, the main distinction is with function declarations.

Suppose, for example, that we want to pass a (4 × 4) array called `M` from `main()` to a function called `myFunction()`. The following script of code shows appropriate function declarations for fixed-size and sequential and indirect array declarations. We put the scripts side by side for ease of comparison.

```
enum { NoRows = 4; NoCols = 4};

int main( void )                               int main( void )
{                                              {
double daaM[ NoRows ][ NoCols ];               double **dppM =
                                                       matAllocIndirectDouble(....);

   myFunction( daaM );                            myFunction( dppM );

}                                              }

myFunction( double daaMatrix[][ NoCols ] )     myFunction( double **dppM )
{                                              {

   daaM[1][2] = 3;                                dppM[1][2] = 3;

}                                              }
===========================================   ====================================
MATRIX SIZE FIXED AT COMPILE TIME              DYNAMIC ALLOCATION OF MATRICES
===========================================   ====================================
```

The left-hand column shows array and function declarations for fixed-size arrays. The right-hand column shows the corresponding array declarations, memory allocation, and function declarations for arrays having an indirect storage pattern.

Review Questions

1. Why is dynamic memory allocation important if C is designed to support operating system code?

2. What is virtual memory? When is it used?

3. How are the functions `malloc()`, `calloc()`, and `realloc()` related? How are they different?

4. Draw and label a diagram showing the layout of memory for the script of code

```
float *fpMyArray;
fpMyArray = (float *) malloc( 5*sizeof(float) );
```

   What can you say about the contents of array `fpMyArray` after this block of code has finished executing?

5. What happens when a dynamic memory allocation request fails? How can you test for a failure?

6. Why are the functions `safeMalloc()` and `safeCalloc()` useful?

7. What does the abbreviated block of code

```
#ifndef MISCELLANEOUS_H
#define MISCELLANEOUS_H

    .... contents removed .....

#endif /* end case MISCELLANEOUS_H */
```

   do?

8. Why is it important to deallocate memory that you have allocated? When do you do this?

9. Is there anything wrong with freeing the same block of memory more than once?

10. Explain the step-by-step procedure for allocating a (5 × 4) array of floats having a sequential storage pattern.

11. Explain the step-by-step procedure for allocating a (5 × 4) array of floats having an indirect storage pattern.

12. Suppose `fppA` is a (5 × 4) array having an indirect storage pattern. Explain the step-by-step procedure for retrieving an array element (e.g., `fppA [3][2]`).

10.9 PROGRAMMING EXERCISES

Problem 10.1 (Beginner): Rewrite Program 10.3 so that it allocates and deallocates memory within two new functions

```
/*
 * ================================================================
 * vecAlloc() : dynamically allocate vector.
 *
 * Input  : int iLength   -- length of the vector to be allocated.
 * Output : float *fpX    -- pointer to allocated memory.
 * ================================================================
 */

float *vecAlloc ( int iLength ) {

    .... fill in details here ...
}

/*
 * ================================================================
 * vecFree() : free vector memory.
 *
 * Input  : float *fpX -- pointer to vector memory.
 * Output : void.
 * ================================================================
 */

void vecFree ( float * ) {

    .... fill in details here ...
}
```

The function `vecAlloc()` should have one argument for the vector length to be allocated. The function `vecFree()` should have one argument of type float pointer containing the base address of the vector memory to be released.

Problem 10.2 (Beginner): The length (or magnitude) of a n-dimensional vector X is given by

$$|X| = \left[\sum_{i=1}^{n} x_i^2 \right]^{1/2} \tag{10.8}$$

Write C code and a test program for

```
/*
 * =======================================================
 * vecLength() : Compute length of a vector "X".
 *
 * Input  :  float    *fpX    -- pointer to vector X.
 *           int    iNoRows   -- no of rows in vector X.
 * Output :  float fLength    -- length of vector X.
 * =======================================================
 */
```

```
float vecLength ( float *fpX , int iNoRows ) {
float fLength;

    .... fill in details of vector length calculation here ...

    return (fLength);
}
```

Function `vecLength()` should return a float containing the vector length. The first argument to `vecLength()` should be a pointer to the vector whose length is being computed, and the second argument, an integer for the vector length.

If you have already solved Problem 10.1, then by all means use the functions `vecAlloc()` and `vecFree()` in your solution.

Problem 10.3 (Beginner): Engineers and scientists can often simplify problems by transforming a vector $V = [v_x, v_y]$ from a coordinate system $x - y$ to a second system $x' - y'$. If the coordinate systems are related by the coordinate system transformation shown in Figure 10.8, then the components of $V' = [v_x', v_y']$ in the new coordinate system are given by

$$\begin{bmatrix} v_x' \\ v_y' \end{bmatrix} = \begin{bmatrix} \cos(\theta) & \sin(\theta) \\ -\sin(\theta) & \cos(\theta) \end{bmatrix} \cdot \begin{bmatrix} v_x \\ v_y \end{bmatrix} \tag{10.9}$$

Develop a test program that will dynamically allocate memory for the vector V and the (2×2) transformation matrix, prompt the user for components of the vector and the transformation angle, and compute and print the components of V in the new coordinate system.

Use your test program to demonstrate that

1. When $\theta = \pm 90$ degrees, the dot product $V \cdot V' = 0$, irrespective of the components in V.
2. The rotational transformation does not change the length of the vector.

Problem 10.4 (Beginner): Let X and Y be n-dimensional vectors. The dot product of two vectors X and Y is a scalar defined by

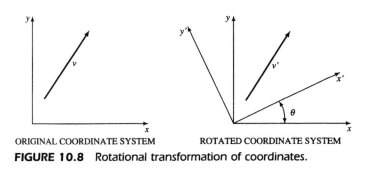

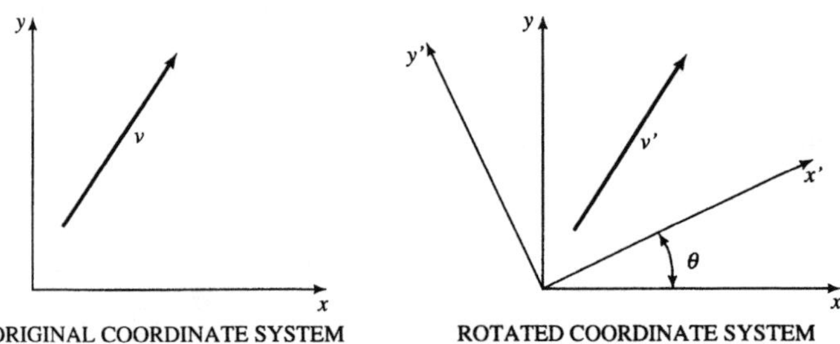

FIGURE 10.8 Rotational transformation of coordinates.

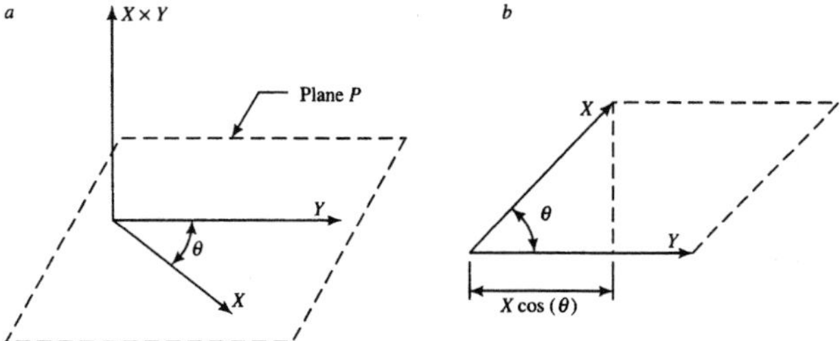

FIGURE 10.9 Interpretation of *(a)* cross- and *(b)* vector dot products.

$$\text{X} \cdot \text{Y} = |X||Y| \cos(\theta) \tag{10.10}$$

with θ being the angle formed between the tails of X and Y as shown on the right-hand side of Figure 10.9. If Y is a unit vector in an arbitrary direction, then the dot product operation computes the component of X along the direction of the unit vector.

Computation of the dot product $X \cdot Y$ is given by

$$X \cdot Y = \sum_{i=1}^{n} x_i \cdot y_i = x_1 y_1 + x_2 y_2 + x_3 y_3 + \cdot \cdot \cdot + x_n y_n \tag{10.11}$$

Write a function

```
/*
 * ===================================================================
 * vecDotProduct() : Compute dot product of vectors "X" and "Y"
 *
 * Input  :  float *fpX        -- pointer to vector X.
 *           float *fpY        -- pointer to vector Y.
 *           int iNoRows       -- number of rows in vectors "X" and "Y".
 * Output :  float fDotProduct -- result of X.Y calculation.
 * ===================================================================
 */

float vecDotProduct ( float *fpX , float *fpY , int iNoRows ) {
float fDotProduct;

    .... fill in details of dot product calculation here ...

    return (fDotProduct);
}
```

to compute the dot product of two vectors.

Develop a test program that will dynamically allocate and instantiate vectors X and Y, and exercise the `vecDotProduct()` function. Demonstrate by example that for arbitrarily chosen X and Y, $X \cdot Y - Y \cdot X = 0$.

Problem 10.5 (Beginner): Let two vectors X and Y lie in a plane P, as shown in the left-hand schematic of Figure 10.9. The vector cross product of X and Y is

$$X \times Y = \det \begin{vmatrix} i & j & k \\ x_1 & x_2 & x_3 \\ y_1 & y_2 & y_3 \end{vmatrix} \tag{10.12}$$

$$= (x_2 \cdot y_3 - y_2 \cdot x_3)i - (x_1 \cdot y_3 - y_1 \cdot x_3)j + (x_1 \cdot y_2 - y_1 \cdot x_2)k \tag{10.13}$$

The magnitude of the cross product equals the area of the parallelogram shown on the right-hand side of Figure 10.9 (i.e., the product of the length of one of the vectors times the projection of the second vector onto a line perpendicular to the first vector).

Write a function

```
/*
 * ===========================================================================
 * vecCrossProduct() : Compute cross product of vectors "X" and "Y"
 *
 * Input  : float *fpX             -- pointer to vector X.
 *          float *fpY             -- pointer to vector Y.
 *          int iNoRows            -- number of rows in vectors "X" and "Y".
 * Output : float *fpCrossProduct  -- result of cross product calculation.
 * ===========================================================================
 */

float *vecCrossProduct ( float *fpX , float *fpY , int iNoRows ) {
float *fpCrossProduct;

     .... fill in details of dot product calculation here ...

     return (fpCrossProduct);
}
```

to compute the cross product of vectors X and Y.

Develop a test program that will dynamically allocate and instantiate vectors X and Y, and exercise the `vecCrossProduct()` function. Demonstrate by example that for arbitrarily chosen X and Y, $X \times Y + Y \times X = 0$.

Problem 10.6 (Intermediate): If A is a $(m \times n)$ matrix and B is a $(r \times p)$ matrix, then the matrix sum $C = A + B$ is defined only when $m = r$ and $n = p$. The matrix sum is a $(m \times n)$ matrix C whose elements are

$$c_{ij} = a_{ij} + b_{ij} \tag{10.14}$$

for $i = 1, 2, \cdots m$ and $j = 1, 2, \cdots n$. Extend the functionality of Program 10.4 with a new function:

```
/*
 * ==================================================================
 * matAdd() : Compute matrix sum "A + B"
 *
 * Input  :  double **dppA    -- pointer to pointer to allocated matrix A.
 *           double **dppB    -- pointer to pointer to allocated matrix B.
 *           int iNoRows      -- number of rows in matrices A and B.
 *           int iNoColumns   -- number of columns in matrices A and B.
 * Output :  double **dppC    -- pointer to pointer to matrix C = A + B.
 * ==================================================================
 */

double **
matAdd( double **dppA , double **dppB, int iNoRows , int iNoColumns ) {
     .... fill in details of matrix addition code here ....

}
```

Modify the `main()` function in Program 10.4 to show that if $A = \begin{bmatrix} 2 & 1 \\ 4 & 6 \end{bmatrix}$ and $B = \begin{bmatrix} 4 & 2 \\ 0 & 1 \end{bmatrix}$, then $C = A + B = \begin{bmatrix} 2 & 1 \\ 4 & 6 \end{bmatrix} + \begin{bmatrix} 4 & 2 \\ 0 & 1 \end{bmatrix} = \begin{bmatrix} 6 & 3 \\ 4 & 7 \end{bmatrix}$.
You should use `matAllocIndirectDouble()` to dynamically allocate memory for matrices A and B, `matAdd()` to compute the matrix sum, and `matPrint()` to print the result of the matrix addition. `matAdd()` should call `matAllocIndirectDouble()` to dynamically allocate memory for matrix C.

Problem 10.7 (Advanced): Three-dimensional arrays may be viewed as rectangular blocks of memory. With this view in mind, write and test two functions

```
/* Allocate block of memory */

float *** blockAlloc ( int, int, int );

/* Print block of memory    */

void      blockPrint ( float ***, int, int, int );
```

for the allocation and printing of small three-dimensional blocks of memory. The function `blockAlloc ()` should return a pointer to a pointer of type float. The three arguments to `blockAlloc ()` should define the number of rows, columns, and layers in the block of memory. The first argument to `blockPrint ()` should contain the base address of the allocated memory block, with the remaining arguments defining the number of rows, columns, and layers in the block.

11

THE C PREPROCESSOR

11.1 COMPILING MULTIPLE FILE C PROGRAMS

In this chapter, we describe in detail the C preprocessor's general capabilities and the role it plays in the compilation of a multifile C program.

Figure 11.1 is a schematic of files and libraries in a generic multiple file C program. The C program is composed of `M` header files (i.e., `file1.h, ..... fileM.h`), `N+1` source code files (i.e., `main.c, .... fileN.c`), `N+1` object code files (i.e., `main.o, file1.o, .. fileN.o`), a number of software library archive files, and an executable file for the compiled program. A software library is simply a group of object modules that have been compiled in advance and stored in an archive format. All our C programs will call functions in the standard library because it contains, among others, functions to handle input and output (I/O), and functions to manipulate strings and handle dynamic memory allocation. Figure 11.1 also shows that our engineering program will call functions in `math.a`, an archive library of mathematical functions, and `X11.a`, an archive of functions for writing C programs, which will interact with the X window system. Each library will usually have one or more header files containing function declarations (and other information) needed for a successful program compilation.

With this overall picture of a C program's components in place, the next question to ask is how should such a program be compiled? Most C compilers are actually a collection of software tools designed to handle different components of the compilation process. As depicted in Figure 11.1, the compilation of a C program will progress from left to right and will typically contain four steps:

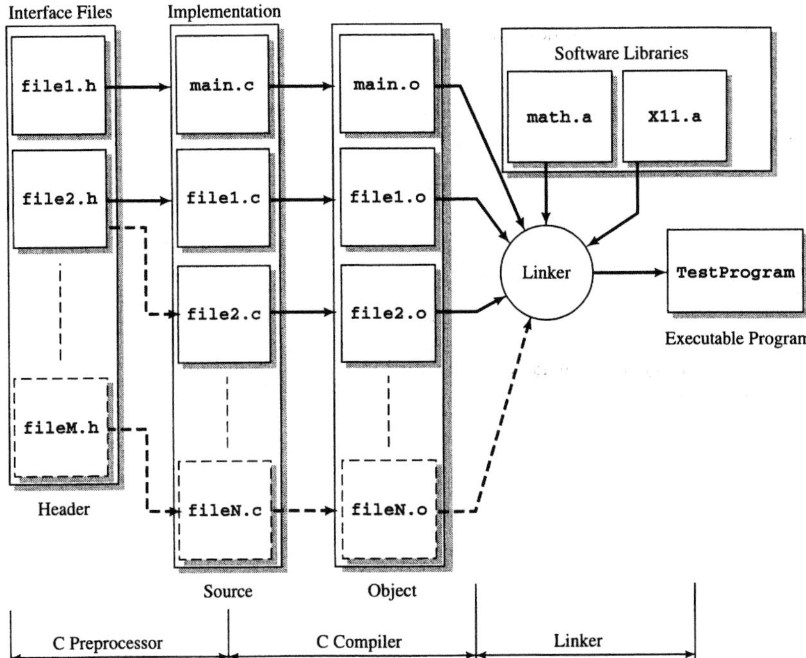

FIGURE 11.1 Compilation of a multiple file C program.

1. *C Preprocessor.* The C preprocessor reads and modifies C source code before it is passed to the C compiler. In addition to removing all comment statements from C source code, the preprocessor scans the C source code files for directive commands composed of a # character followed by a keyword for the type of action to be taken. Preprocessor actions include macro substitution, conditional compilation of machine-dependent features, and the inclusion of other source files. The specification of these actions is covered in Section 11.2.
2. *C Compiler.* For each `.c` source code file, the compiler will generate a corresponding `.o` machine code (or object) file. The object file will contain executable code for the functions defined in the source code file, and a list of names and addresses of external variables and functions defined in other files (see also Step 3).
3. *Linker.* The linker ties the program code together. It combines the program object files, connects the program code to functions in the external libraries, and tries to find declarations for the variables and functions unresolved at Step 2 of the compilation. All C programs will be linked to the standard library by default. The linker can be told to search through any number of previously developed libraries for declarations as well.
4. *Executable Program File.* Finally, the object module files and external library code are converted into an executable program form.

In our engineering computer program, the `math.a` and `X11.a` archives can be linked to a C program by appending `-lm` and `-lX11` to the compilation command:

```
gcc -c main.c file1.c file2.c -lm -lX11 -o TestProgram
```

Some "dumb" linkers will automatically include all the object code in the entire library; this makes the resultant executable much larger, even though some of the code is never called! Smart linkers will search the library archive and extract only those functions that match unresolved references.

In practice, the distinction between the compiler and linker can be somewhat transparent because the compiler will automatically invoke the linker, unless it is explicitly instructed not to. The linker will fail if:

1. It cannot resolve all function and variable references,
2. An entry point into the program is not defined (i.e., you write a program that does not have a `main()` function), or
3. Two or more functions are found with the same name. This is one of the harder bugs to find at compile time because the linker phase fails, and the corresponding error messages tend not to be particularly informative.

11.2 CAPABILITIES OF THE C PREPROCESSOR

Lines of C code that begin with a # character are called preprocessor directives. Preprocessor directives are followed by a keyword for the type of action to be taken. Table 11.1 contains a summary of the C preprocessor directives along with a description of their use. The C preprocessor has commands for macro substitution, conditional compilation of machine-dependent features, and the inclusion of other source files.

TABLE 11.1 C Preprocessor Directives and Their Use

Directive	Use
`#include`	Include text from a file.
`#define`	Define a macro.
`#undef`	Undefine a macro.
`#line`	Give a line number for compilation message.
`#if`	Test if a compile-time condition holds.
`#ifdef`	Test if a symbol is defined.
`#ifndef`	Test if a symbol is not defined.
`#else`	Indicate alternatives for a test failing.
`#elif`	Combination of `else` and `if`.
`#endif`	End a preprocessor conditional.

11.2.1 File Inclusion

To see how these features are implemented, we start with file inclusion and the small script of code

```
#include <stdio.h>
#include "solve.h"
#include "defs.h"

int main( void ) {

     .... contents of main program deleted ....
}
```

The first three lines are called inclusion directives, and instruct the C preprocessor to process the source text of the named files before the compiler begins to parse the source program. For example, the line

```
#include <stdio.h>
```

tells the C preprocessor to read the header file for the standard I/O library, and insert it into the program at the appropriate point as if it were originally part of the program text. Placing angled brackets <> around the file name tells the preprocessor to look for the file in a directory other than the current working directory. In UNIX environments, the list of places that the preprocessor will look is described by the `path` variable located in your `.cshrc` file (or sometimes your `.login` file). A file name inserted between `"..."`

```
#include "solve.h"
#include "defs.h"
```

initiates a search first in the directory of the original source file, followed by the sequence of directories listed in the path variable. The `printenv` command

```
prompt >> printenv
... many details of environmental variables removed ...
PATH = /users/austin/bin: /lib/: /include: /usr/bin:
       /usr/etc: /usr/games:
       /isr/X11R5/mit/lib/X:
       /isr/X11R5/mit/include/X:.
```

displays the list of directories in your path variable, along with the current setting of all other variables in the shell environment.

As already mentioned, it is good programming practice to put all globally defined variables, program definitions, and external function declarations into a few header files and use the preprocessor to include their contents at the top of

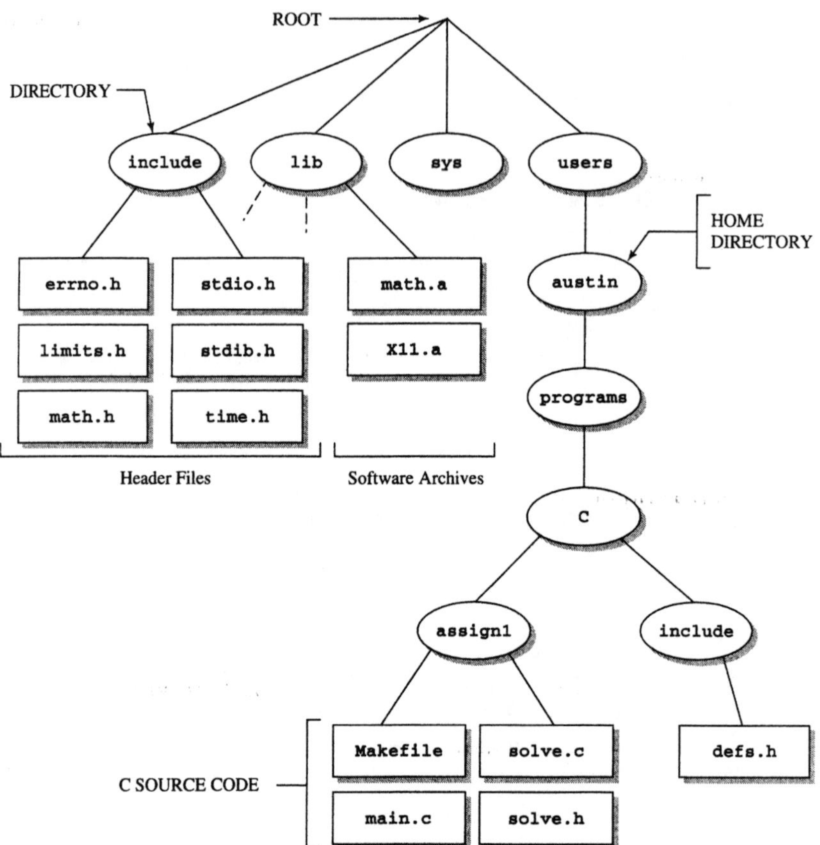

FIGURE 11.2 Extended file system hierarchy.

every relevant file. Consistency among global variable and function declarations is thereby assured. In our example, the file `stdio.h` makes the declarations for the standard I/O file descriptors. The preprocessor removes all definition command lines from the source file and makes additional transformations to the source file as directed by the commands. It is a good idea to place all these definitions in a single header file. In this case, the header file is called `defs.h` and is shown in the lower box of Figure 11.2.

11.2.2 Using the `-I` and `-L` Compiler Options

We strongly discourage use of preprocessor statements with path names hard coded into the source code, for example,

```
#include "/users/austin/programs/C/include/defs.h"
```

because they lack portability. A better programming approach is to use simple preprocessor declarations

```
#include "defs.h"
```

and use of compiler option -I that will tell the compiler which directories to search through for defs.h. A complete command might look like

```
gcc -I/users/austin/programs/C/include main.c solve.c -o SOLVE
```

Similarly, the -L option provides the compiler with a list of additional directories that may contain relevant software libraries. If we wanted to include the X11.a archive, then the above-mentioned compilation command would be extended to

```
gcc -I/users/austin/programs/C/include -L/lib main.c solve.c -o SOLVE -lX11
```

11.2.3 Macro Substitution and Templates

Names in #define cause an identifier to be defined as a macro to the preprocessor. When the name of the macro is recognized in the program source text, the name is effectively replaced by a copy of the body. So, for example, the declaration

```
#define NDOF 3
```

causes the identifier NDOF to be replaced by the number 3. The judicious use of #defines can vastly improve program clarity. By convention, all identifiers that are changed by the preprocessor are written in capital letters.

11.2.4 Macros with Arguments

The #define facility may be used to write macros containing one or more arguments. For example, the macro declarations:

```
#define max(a, b) ((a) > (b) ? (a) : (b))
#define min(a, b) ((a) < (b) ? (a) : (b))
#define sign(a) ( a > 0 ?  1 : -1)
```

have a name and list of formal parameters contained within parentheses. The max(a,b) and min(a,b) macros return the maximum and minimum values of arguments a and b, respectively. The sign(a) macro returns the value 1 for positive argument a and -1 otherwise. These three macros would form an essential component of the defs.h header file.

The C preprocessor substitutes and expands macro definitions into the source code before compilation begins. Hence, the block of code

```
if( fNewTemp > fOldTemp )
    fTempValue = fNewTemp;
else
    fTempValue = fOldTemp;
```

can now be simply written

```
fTempValue = max( fNewTemp, fOldTemp );
```

The `max(..)` macro source code is not only shorter than the former version, but in our opinion, it is also more readable. Now a word of caution. You should remember that the preprocessor does not know C, and strange things can happen if `#define` macros are taken too far. Suppose, for example, that we execute

```
iMax = max( iCnt++, iVal );
```

What is surprising is that the value of `iCnt` will be incremented once (or twice) depending on the result of the comparison. Because preprocessor macro substitutions are literal, the previous statement expands to

```
iMax = ((iCnt++)>(iVal) ? (iCnt++):(iVal))
```

Variable `iCnt` will always be incremented at least once due to the `++` in the comparison. For those cases where `iCnt` is greater than `iVal`, however, `iVal` will be incremented for a second time.

11.2.5 Predefined Preprocessor Names

Predefined preprocessor names are used by a program to determine its environment and adjust environmental-dependent features accordingly. These features include, for example, the machine name, the number of bits in a character, or perhaps, the size of an `unsigned int`.

Most preprocessors predefine the names `__FILE__` and line `__LINE__` for the current file and line number in the source code. Most often we use these names to inform users of an error in the code. For example, in the dynamic memory allocation routine

```
/*
 * ============================================================
 * safeMalloc : Safe memory allocation with malloc().
 *
 * Input :    unsigned int uiSize -- no of bytes to be allocated.
 *            char *cpFileName    -- pointer to file name.
 *            int iLineNo         -- line number.
 * Output : void *vpTemp          -- pointer to allocated memory.
 * ============================================================
 */

void * safeMalloc( unsigned int uiSize, char *cpFileName, int iLineNo ) {
void * vpTemp;
```

```
    vpTemp = malloc( (unsigned) uiSize );
    if (vpTemp == (void *) NULL) {
        fprintf( stderr, "ERROR : malloc() failed in safeMalloc()\n");
        fprintf( stderr, "ERROR : safeMalloc called in file %s : line %d\n",
                 cpFileName, iLineNo );
        exit (1);
    }
    else
        return( vpTemp );
}
```

the file name and line number at which the error occurred will be printed in an error message when memory for a character string cannot be allocated. The function call

```
enum {ArraySize = 10000000};
double *dpExpData = (double *) safeMalloc( ArraySize*sizeof(double),
                                           __FILE__, __LINE__ );
```

could generate the error message

```
ERROR : malloc() failed in safeMalloc()\n");
ERROR : safeMalloc called in file data_analysis.c : line 235
```

The identifier `__STDC__` is the decimal constant 1 and indicates whether a particular implementation of C conforms to the ANSI C standard.

```
/*
 *  ==========================================================
 *  miscellaneous.h : Header file for Miscellaneous Routines
 *  ==========================================================
 */

#ifndef MISCELLANEOUS_H
#define MISCELLANEOUS_H

/* Declarations for Miscellaneous Functions */

#if __STDC__                         /* Start case STDC    */

void * safeMalloc( unsigned int , char * , int );
void * safeCalloc( unsigned int , unsigned int , char * , int );

#else /* case not STDC */

void * safeMalloc();
```

```
void * safeCalloc();

#endif /* end case STDC */
#endif /* end case MISCELLANEOUS_H */
```

The header file `miscellaneous.h` (for details, see Chapter 10) contains two levels of preprocessor commands. The outer block is bounded by `#ifndef MISCELLANEOUS_H`. The second instance of `#endif` uses the existence of constant `MISCELLANEOUS_H` (or lack thereof) to ensure that miscellaneous data structure and function declarations are included at most once at the top of a file. In other words, `miscellaneous.h` can be included multiple times without an error occurring. A second level of preprocessor commands uses the predefined symbol `__STDC__` to separate compilers that support standard C from those that do not (e.g., the classic K&R compiler).

Review Questions

1. Briefly describe the four stages a C program will pass through when it is being compiled.
2. Why are the macros `__FILE__` and `__LINE__` called predefined preprocessor names?
3. Why are preprocessor statements of the type

```
#include "/users/austin/programs/C/include/defs.h"
```

considered to be poor programming style? What is a good way of overcoming these limitations?

12

INPUT AND OUTPUT

12.1 BASIC CONCEPTS

In this chapter, we take a detailed look at C's capabilities for handling input and output (I/O). This opening statement is a bit of a misnomer because, strictly speaking, I/O are not part of the C language per se. C handles I/O through a set of functions provided by the standard C library. The beauty of putting I/O in the standard library, and providing programmers with the mechanisms to call functions in external libraries, is that it leaves you, the programmer, free to concentrate on development of code for problem solving.

Until this point (and with only one or two exceptions), our computer programs have used the `scanf()` function for program input from the keyboard and `printf()` for program output to the computer screen. This mode of operation works well for programs that require at most one channel (or stream) of input and that will generate at most one channel of output. This chapter begins with an introduction to the concept of streams. We see how the streams concept applies to standard I/O, and I/O from and to files. Then we see how to write engineering applications that can read engineering datasets from one or more devices other than the keyboard (e.g., files) and direct output to one or more devices (e.g, the screen and files).

12.1.1 Streams

The standard C library maintains what are called streams. A *stream* is a source or destination of data that may be associated with a computer disk or other peripheral device (e.g., files, tapes, screen, sockets). We note:

TABLE 12.1 Standard Streams

File Pointer	*Name*	*Description*
`stdin`	Standard input	Connected to the keyboard
`stdout`	Standard output	Connected to the screen
`stderr`	Standard error	Connected to the screen

1. Streams must be opened before I/O can be performed. The actions needed to open a device are device dependent. For example, opening a file for I/O requires different actions than setting up I/O to and from a screen.
2. The library routine returns a pointer to a block of information needed for performing I/O on the stream. This information is stored in a data object of type `FILE`, which is defined in `<stdio.h>`.
3. A stream must be closed after a program is finished with it.

C recognizes text and binary streams. A *text stream* is a sequence of bytes organized into lines, each ending with a newline character. *Binary streams* are sequences of unprocessed bytes. If a program writes a binary stream to a file and then reads it back, the contents will match exactly.

Table 12.1 shows that the keyboard is the device for standard input, and that the computer screen is the device for standard output and errors. When we call `printf()` to deliver a character stream to the computer screen, we are using the standard output file. Similarly, when `scanf()` reads character input from the keyboard, we are using the standard input file. `stderr` is a special file descriptor for sending error messages to the computer screen. When a C program begins execution, the three streams—`stdin`, `stdout`, and `stderr`—will be automatically opened.

12.2 USING `printf()` FOR BUFFERED OUTPUT

`printf()` is a versatile function for accessing the terminal screen and producing formatted output. The capabilities of `printf()` include

1. Automatic formatting of numerical output when no other specification is given.
2. The ability to accept a variable number of arguments.
3. The ability to determine output formats at run-time (e.g., `%*.*f`).
4. The ability to return the number of bytes that have been printed.

The function declaration for `printf()` is

```
int printf ( const char * kcpFormat [, argument(s), ... ]);
```

TABLE 12.2 Format Specifiers for `printf()` Function

Character	*Description*
d, i	A signed decimal (integers). Arguments should be of type `int`, `short`, or `long`.
f, e, g	Floating point numbers (g is most flexible, and makes the best choice of representation). If no modifier is used, then `double` is assumed. Arguments of type `float` are automatically converted to type `double`. By default, conversion specifications for floats (e.g., written as `%f`) will be written with six digits of precision.
E, G	The same as `e` and `g` but put `E` for exponent.
o	An unsigned octal `int`, `short`, or `long`.
x, X	An unsigned hexadecimal `int`, `short`, or `long`.
u	An unsigned `int`, `short`, or `long`.
c	The argument is printed as a character. Precision specifications are not relevant to the c conversion.
s	Character string. The argument should be of type `char *`. If a precision specification is not given, then the converted value will be a sequence of characters up to the terminating null character. If a specification of *p* characters is given, then a string will be printed that is the shorter of its actual length and *p*.

The leftmost part of the declaration is the keyword `int`, indicating that `printf()` will return an integer value (for the number of bytes printed). The arguments to `printf()` are specified between the brackets `()`. The first argument is a control character string containing a specification for what the output will look like. Zero or more arguments (specified with the ellipsis . . .) may be required to follow the first argument. Table 12.2 contains a brief description of character type options.

`printf()` is called by giving the function name followed by a list of arguments enclosed within parentheses. The scripts of code

```
Basic printf() statements                          Output
=====================================================================
printf("One String");                              One String
printf("Two"); printf("Strings\n");                TwoStrings
printf("Two = %d\n", 2 );                          Two = 2
printf("Two = %d Twelve = %d\n", 2 , 12 );         Two = 2 Twelve = 12
=====================================================================
```

demonstrate the use of `printf()` with a variable number of arguments. The first two cases contain one and two character string arguments, respectively. Notice that in the second example, the strings will be positioned immediately adjacent to one another. The third and fourth examples demonstrate basic use of *conversion specifications*. Conversion specifications begin with a percent sign (`%`), and are followed by one or more formatting options for output including left/right justification, numeric signs, size specification, precision specification, decimal points, and padded zeros. One argument value must be added to the argument list of `printf()` for every field with a `%` specifier in the string constant. The conversion specification `%d` simply tells `printf()` to output the contents of `Two` and `Twelve` as a sequence of digits. This sequence of digits will be kept as short as possible but not shorter than a specified precision. We explain the details on how to specify precision in a moment. Now consider the variable declarations

```
int    iInt       =          1001;
float  fFloat     =     3.1415926;
double dDouble    = M_PI*100000.0;
char   cChar      =           'a';
char   sString[]  = "Test String";
```

and the use of `printf()` for their basic output:

```
Basic printf() statement                          Output
=========================================================================
printf( "iInt (int)    = %d\n", iInt );        iInt (int)    = 1001
printf( "iInt (hex)    = %x\n", iInt );        iInt (hex)    = 3e9
printf( "iInt (oct)    = %o\n", iInt );        iInt (oct)    = 1751
printf( "fFloat        = %f\n", fFloat );      fFloat        = 3.141593
printf( "fFloat        = %g\n", fFloat );      fFloat        = 3.14159
printf( "dDouble       = %f\n", dDouble );     dDouble       = 314159.265359
printf( "dDouble       = %g\n", dDouble );     dDouble       = 314159
printf( "cChar (char) = %c\n", cChar );        cChar (char) = a
printf( "cChar (int)   = %d\n", cChar );       cChar (int)   = 97
printf( "sString       = %s\n", aString );     sString       = Test String
=========================================================================
```

In each statement `\n` is an escape character that forces output onto a new line.

12.2.1 Use of Escape Characters in Output

Table 12.3 contains a list of *escape character* sequences for I/O. We have already seen many examples where the escape character `\n` forces output onto a new line.

TABLE 12.3 Escape Sequences for `printf()` Function

\a	alert (bell)	\b	backspace
\f	form feed,	\n	newline
\r	carriage return	\t	horizontal tab
\v	vertical tab	\0	character with binary value 0
\"	double quote (literal)	\ooo	octal number
\xhh	hexadecimal number		

Horizontal tabs are useful for generating output arranged into aligned columns. For example, the following script

```
printf( "\nOutput without tabs formatting\n");
printf( "fFloat  = %f dDouble = %f\n",  fFloat, dDouble );
printf( "sString = %s cChar   = %c\n", sString, cChar );

printf( "\nOutput with tabs formatting\n");
printf( "fFloat  = %f \t dDouble = %f\n",  fFloat, dDouble );
printf( "sString = \"%s\" \t cChar   = %c\n", sString, cChar );
```

shows output for `fFloat`, `dDouble`, `sString`, and `cChar`, arranged into two-by-two arrays.

```
Output without tabs formatting
fFloat  = 3.141593 dDouble = 314159.265359
sString = Test String cChar   = a

Output with tabs formatting
fFloat  = 3.141593        dDouble = 314159.265359
sString = "Test String"   cChar   = a
```

The first block of output uses the standard basic conversion specifications without tabs. In the second block of output, conversion specifications for the first and second columns are separated by the tab escape character `\t`, thereby forcing the output for the second column to be aligned with the tab boundary.

The escape sequence `\"` is useful for putting quotation marks around a character string, as demonstrated in the second block of output.

12.2.2 Formatting Options for Conversion Specifications

Conversion specifications begin with a percent sign (`%`), and are followed by one or more formatting options for output, including left/right justification, numeric signs, size specification, precision specification, decimal points, and padded zeros. Figure 12.1 is a graphic of the six components in a conversion specification (the

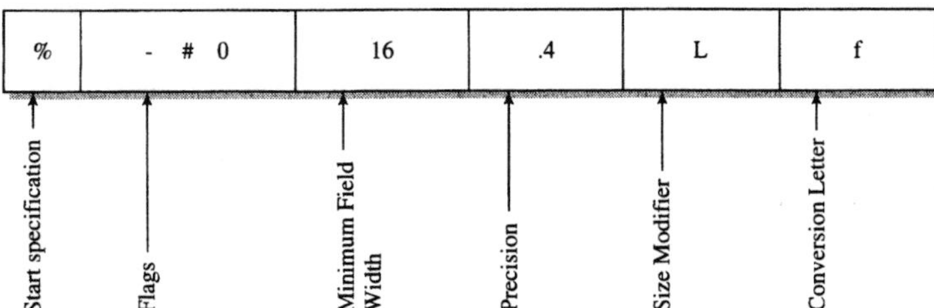

FIGURE 12.1 Conversion specifications for formatted output.

example is `%-16.4Lf`). For those of you familiar with regular expressions, an equivalent format is

```
% [ flags ] [ width ] [ .precision ] [ F | N | h | l | L ] type_char
```

where the entries between brackets [] are optional and the vertical bars | mean "choose one among these options." The details of each specifier are as follows

1. *Flags.* Flags handle the justification of the output. A minus (-) means left justify the output field. A plus (+) means always put + or − sign. The # flag forces the result to be converted to an alternate form, the details of which depend on the conversion character. For example, the # causes trailing zeros to be printed in the `g` and `G` conversions. This flag only applies to the `e`, `E`, `f`, `g`, `G`, `o`, `x`, and `X` conversion operations.

   A `blank` implies that the output should begin with a blank if positive and a minus sign (−) if negative. By default, formatted output will be right justified.
2. *Width.* The width specifier sets the minimum number of characters to print. Additional characters are padded with blanks or zeros. This can be specified in two different ways. Most often a digit string specifies the field width; alternatively, the width can be specified with a `*`, where the actual value is given in the argument list.
3. *Precision.* The precision modifier is for the maximum number of characters to print after a decimal point.
4. *Input.* The input size modifier is given by `[h|l|L]` (and `[F|N]` on DOS machines). `h` is used for short values, `l` is for long values, and `L` for long double values.
5. *Type_char.* A summary of character type options is given in Table 12.2. For the `d`, `i`, `o`, and `u` conversions, the converted value will be a sequence of decimal digits representing the absolute value of the argument. The sequence will be as short as possible but not shorter than the specified precision. If required, leading zeros will be inserted to satisfy precision specifications. The `+`, `space`, `#` flags and precision specifications are not relevant to the character (`c`) and string (`s`) options.

Thus, the conversion specification `%-16.4Lf` in Figure 12.1 represents a long floating point number, printed with a maximum of 16 characters (including the decimal point), and with four decimal places of accuracy to the right-hand side of the decimal point. Use of the minus sign left justifies the output.

Example. The following script demonstrates the use of conversion specifications with formatted options. The variables `iInt`, `fFloat`, `dDouble`, and so forth, are as previously defined.

```
Modified printf() statement                         Formatted Output
================================================================================

printf( "\nOptions for Integers\n");               Options for Integers
printf( "iInt (int)    = %d\n",   iInt );          iInt (int)    = 1001
printf( "iInt (int)    = %8d\n",  iInt );          iInt (int)    =     1001
printf( "iInt (int)    = %-8d\n", iInt );          iInt (int)    = 1001
printf( "iInt (int)    = %08d\n", iInt );          iInt (int)    = 00001001

printf( "\nOptions for Floats\n");                 Options for Floats
printf( "fFloat        = %f\n",     fFloat );      fFloat        = 3.141593
printf( "fFloat        = %g\n",     fFloat );      fFloat        = 3.14159
printf( "fFloat        = %6.2f\n",  fFloat );      fFloat        =   3.14
printf( "fFloat        = %-6.2f\n", fFloat );      fFloat        = 3.14

printf( "\nOptions for Doubles\n");                Options for Doubles
printf( "dDouble       = %f\n",      dDouble );    dDouble       = 314159.265359
printf( "dDouble       = %g\n",      dDouble );    dDouble       = 314159
printf( "dDouble       = %16.8f\n",  dDouble );    dDouble       =  314159.26535898
printf( "dDouble       = %-16.8f\n", dDouble );    dDouble       = 314159.26535898
printf( "dDouble       = %16.8e\n",  dDouble );    dDouble       =   3.14159265e+05
printf( "dDouble       = %-16.8e\n", dDouble );    dDouble       = 3.14159265e+05

printf( "\nOptions for Characters\n");             Options for Characters
printf( "cChar (char) = %c\n",   cChar );          cChar (char) = a
printf( "cChar (char) = %5c\n",  cChar );          cChar (char) =     a
printf( "cChar (char) = %-5c\n", cChar );          cChar (char) = a

printf( "\nOptions for Character Strings\n");      Options for Character Strings
printf( "sString       = %s\n",      sString );    sString       = Test String
printf( "sString       = %14s\n",    sString );    sString       =    Test String
printf( "sString       = %-14s\n",   sString );    sString       = Test String
printf( "sString       = %.8s\n",    sString );    sString       = Test Str
printf( "sString       = %14.6s\n",  sString );    sString       =         Test S
printf( "sString       = %-14.6s\n", sString );    sString       = Test S
================================================================================
```

The floating point specifications e and E tell printf() to output the floating point number in exponential format. Unless the floating point number to be printed equals zero, then the number before the letter e will represent a value between 1.0.. and 9.99... The two-digit part after the e represents an exponent value expressed as a signed decimal integer. The floating point number will be approximately equal to the first component multiplied by 10 raised to value of the exponent. The total number of digits in the output field should be at least seven larger than the number of digits appearing after the decimal point.

The floating point specifications g and G tell printf() to select the better of the f or e formats. Although the rules for selecting the format are implementation dependent, as a general guideline, if the number to be printed falls within the range of conversion specification, then use of the f format is likely. Otherwise, the floating point number will be printed in exponential format. These examples also show how the output is left justified by inserting a minus (-) at the front of the conversion specification.

Remark 12.1

A word of warning: When the number to be formatted will not fit within the specified field (e.g., if π happened to be greater than 10^7), then `printf()` just outputs the whole value. This is the only logical thing to do that will not result in a loss of information.

12.3 USING scanf() FOR BUFFERED INPUT

The `scanf()` function scans and reads an arbitrary number of arguments from standard input. The function declaration for `scanf()` is

```
int scanf( const char * kcpFormat [, address, ...] );
```

The first argument is a control character string that contains a description of the expected form of the input. A typical description will contain one or more conversion specifications, and provide for white space character and "other special character" input. The arguments following the first argument are the addresses of memory locations where the scanned items are to be assigned. As with `printf()`, one additional argument to `scanf()` must be added for each conversion specification in the control character string. A summary of format specifiers for `scanf()` is located in Table 12.4. These ideas are best illustrated with an example. Consider the script

```
int   iValue;
float fValue;

   scanf("%d %f", &iValue, &fValue );
```

The first argument is a control string containing conversion specifications for an integer (given by `%d`) and a float (given by `%f`). Characters in the input stream are converted to values defined by the control specification and placed at the addresses given by the corresponding address values in the `scanf()` parameter list. If the numbers `4` and `4.5` are typed at the keyboard, then the value of `4` would be positioned at the memory address `&iValue` and `4.5` at the address `&fValue`.

`scanf()` returns an integer for the number of conversion specifications that are successful. In our simple example shown, `scanf()` will return the integer 2, corresponding to two successful conversions.

`scanf()` will terminate reading when an unexpected character is read (i.e., the

TABLE 12.4 Format Specifiers for `scanf()` Function

Format	*Description*
d	A signed decimal conversion is performed. A value of int, short, or long is assigned depending on the size specification.
u	An unsigned decimal conversion is performed. Again, the value unsigned, unsigned short, or unsigned long is made depending on the size specification.
o	An unsigned octal conversion is performed. Modifications are as for `%u`.
x	An unsigned hexadecimal conversion is performed. Modifications are as for `%u`.
f, e, g	A signed floating point conversion is performed.
lf	A conversion to type double is performed.
Lf	A conversion to long double is performed.
c	A character (including white space).
s	A string of non-white space characters is read and assigned. The string is terminated by appending an end-of-string sentinel.

input does not match the description given in the control string), or the scan width is exhausted, whichever comes first.

12.3.1 Scanning Multiple Lines of Input

Chapter 7 contains a computer program that prompts the user multiple times for lines of input from the keyboard. Because we were just learning the basics of C at that point, some of the subtle points of scanning formatted input were glossed over. It is now appropriate to revisit the topic of scanning multiple lines of formatted input and fill in the missing details.

In a first-cut implementation of these programs, it would have been tempting to simply write

```
enum {BufferSize = 24 };
char caBuffer [ BufferSize ];

printf("\nWould you like to input a quadratic equation (yes/no/quit)  : ");
scanf("%s", caBuffer);
```

The character array `caBuffer` stores the keyboard input provided in response to the prompt. If we type `yes` after the prompt and then hit the <Enter> key, as in

```
Would you like to input a quadratic equation (yes/no/quit)  : yes
```

then the contents of the input buffer will look similar to the following:

```
yes<CR>
```

`scanf()` will transfer the first three characters from the input buffer, `y`, `e` and `s`, into the first three elements of character array `caBuffer` and leave the carriage return `(<CR>)` in the input buffer.

Now suppose that we want to prompt a user for multiple lines of input. The lines of input could be your first name followed by your family name. The script of code

```
enum { BufferSize = 24 };
char caFirstName[ BufferSize ], caFamilyName[ BufferSize ];

printf("\nPlease type your first name : ");
scanf("%s", caFirstName);
printf("\nPlease type your family name : ");
scanf("%s", caFamilyName);
```

shows the essential details of a preliminary implementation. The first half of the script will behave exactly as described, with a carriage return being left in the buffer after your first name is transferred into the character array `caFirstName`. The shortcomings of this implementation show up only in the second half of the script where the user is prompted for his or her family name. For the purposes of discussion, assume that the family name is `smith`. The contents of the input buffer after the <Enter> key is hit for the second time will be

```
<CR>smith
```

The heart of the problem lies with the carriage return remaining in the input buffer when the `scanf()` function is called for the second time. Instead of transferring the family name `smith` to character array `caFamilyName`, some computers will transfer `<CR>` instead. This is not what you want. An easy way of safeguarding against this possibility is to use the `%*c` format

```
printf("\nPlease type your first name : ");
scanf("%s%*c", caFirstName);
printf("\nPlease type your family name : ");
scanf("%s%*c", caFamilyName);
```

which reads the input string and discards the carriage return character. The format specifier `%*c` means "one or more characters."

12.3.2 Flushing the `stdin` and `stdout` Buffers

The standard library enhances the run-time performance of program output by first writing output to a file buffer and then sending a complete block of output to `stdout` (or an appropriate device). The file buffer plays a similar role in reading input from `stdin`.

On some computer systems, output will be written to the file buffer and sent to the screen when the buffer is full and/or when an end-of-line character is encountered. There are practical situations, however, where we may want the output to appear on the screen even if one of the conditions listed here is not met. Generating a prompt for the user to supply command input is one such situation.

```
Flushing Output Buffers          Flushing Input Buffers
===========================================================
printf("prompt >> ");            fflush( stdin );
fflush( stdout );                scanf("..." , ... );
===========================================================
```

Problems of this type can be solved with the `fflush()` function. The `fflush()` function takes an output/input stream as its argument and forces any internal buffers to be emptied (or flushed) to the destination device.

12.4 FILE INPUT/OUTPUT

Even before we could write our first C program, we needed to learn how to deal with files. Files are, after all, where the source code for our C programs preside. You should think of a file as simply a contiguous stream of bytes. A file always has a name. In UNIX operating system environments, information is also stored on the size and directory location of the file, who owns the file, and who can read it.

The five operations a C programmer can conduct on a file are

1. Open it for reading, writing, or appending.
2. Close it.
3. Read from it at the current position.
4. Write to it at the current position.
5. Reposition the place where the next file I/O operation will take place.

Files need to be opened before they can be written to, read from, or appended to. When you have finished writing to the file, it should be closed.

A large number of stream-related functions for file I/O are handled by `FILE` structures and pointers to `FILE` structures. The details of the identifier `FILE` are defined in `stdio.h`. To get started, all that you need to know is that `FILE` pointers are defined with statements of the type

```
FILE * FpStream;
```

and that `stdio.h` must be included before the first use of `FILE`. For the most part, thereafter, programmers do not need to concern themselves with the internal details of `FILE`.

12.4.1 Opening and Closing Files

The function `fopen()` opens files, and the function `fclose()` closes files. The relevant function prototypes are

```
FILE * fopen( const char * cpFilename, const char * cpMode );
int    fclose ( FILE * FpStream );
```

TABLE 12.5 Modes of I/O

Mode of I/O	*Description*
r	Read mode. Open file for reading.
w	Create file for writing. If the file already exists, overwrite it.
a	Append mode. Write to the end of a file if it exists. Create a new file if it does not exist.
r+	Update mode. Open existing file for read or write.
w+	Create/update mode. Create a new file for update (read or write). If the file already exists, then overwrite it.
a+	Append mode. Open for update at end of file. Create a new file if it does not already exist.

The first argument to `fopen()` is a character string containing the name and location of the file. The second argument to `fopen()` is a character string that encodes the direction of data flow (i.e., read, write, append) that will take place once the file is opened. Table 12.5 contains a list of file options.

Example. To see how these concepts work in practice, the following fragment of code uses these functions to open a file for writing.

```
FILE * FpOut:                           /* define file structure pointer        */
char * cpFilename = "FFTData.dat";      /* character string for file name       */
char * cpMode     = "w";                /* character string for mode of I/O     */

/* [a] : open file for writing */

FpOut = fopen( cpFilename, cpMode );
if( NULL == FpOut ) {
    printf( "Error: Cannot open %s in %s mode for writing",
             cpFilename, cpMode );
    exit(1);
}

/* [b] : write data to file */

   ..... details of source code removed .....

/* [c] : close file */

fclose ( FpOut );
```

The name of the file is `FFTData.dat`, and the mode of I/O is `w`. C programs should always check that the return value from `fopen()` is not equal to `NULL` before proceeding to communicate with the file. Two ways in which `fopen()` may fail to return a valid file pointer for reading are if

1. The file does not exist.
2. The file permission does not permit reading or writing by the user.

Upon learning that `fopen()` has returned a `NULL` pointer, a computer program should print an error message and either terminate the program execution or prompt the user for another file name. Our short example takes the former course of action. The function call

```
exit (1);
```

returns a status of 1 to the host environment, thereby triggering termination of the computer program execution. Cleanup activities include the flushing of buffers (with the function `fflush()`) and closing of I/O streams. Files are closed by calling the `fclose()` function.

For computer systems that have the capability of distinguishing between text and binary modes, the "mode of I/O" specification can include a second character suffix. On UNIX and DOS systems, for example, the "mode of I/O" specification can be modified to

```
char * cpMode = "w+t";     /* character string for mode of
                              I/O   */
```

for writing to a text file and to

```
char * cpMode = "w+b";     /* character string for mode of
                              I/O   */
```

for writing to a binary file. The reason binary and text modes of I/O need to be distinguished is so that special characters can be identified and handled accordingly. For example, a `CTRL-z` is taken as the end-of-file (EOF) character in text mode. In the case of carriage return-line feed (CR-LF) sequences, a `CR-LF` sequence is translated into a LF on input, and a LF is translated into a CR-LF on output. These translations can be suppressed if the `b` suffix is used, rather than the `t` suffix.

12.4.2 Functions `fprintf()` and `fscanf()`

The functions `fprintf()` and `fscanf()` are the file counterparts of `printf()` and `scanf()`. The function prototypes are

```
int fprintf( FILE* FpStream, const char * kcpFormat [, argument, ... ] );
int fscanf(  FILE* FpStream, const char * kcpFormat [, address, ...]   );
```

where `FpStream` is a file pointer to the I/O stream. `fscanf()` scans input from the stream `FpStream` using the same specified formats and arguments as for `scanf()`. Similarly, `fprintf()` prints to `FpStream` using the same formats and arguments as for `printf()`.

12.4.3 Functions `fgetc()` and `fputc()`

Standard C also provides a family of macros and functions for I/O of individual characters from and to file streams. For example, the function

```
int fgetc( FILE * FpStream );
```

reads and returns the next character from the designated file stream. `fgetc()` returns `EOF` when an EOF is encountered. A second function

```
int fputc( int c, FILE * FpStream );
```

converts the argument `c` to an unsigned char and writes it to the file associated with `FpStream`. I/O of character strings is handled by the functions

```
char * fgets( char * cpString, int iNChars, FILE * FpStream );
int    fputs( const char * kcpString, FILE* FpStream );
```

In the argument list for `fgets()`, `iNChars` characters are read from `FpStream` into a string pointed to by `cpString`. Similarly, for `fputs()`, the string `kcpString` is printed onto the stream `FpStream`. `fgets()` reads and retains newline characters and appends a terminating `NULL` character to the end of the string. In contrast, `fputs()` does not append a newline character, and the terminating `NULL` is not output.

12.5 PROGRAM 12.1: STATISTICS OF WEEKLY RAINFALL

This case study problem uses a one-dimensional array of floats to store rainfall measurements recorded over a 1-week period. We demonstrate how computer output may be sent to a file and how MATLAB graphics may be used to enhance interpretation of a computer program's output.

12.5.1 Problem Statement and Source Code

Program 12.1 prompts a user for measured rainfall, r_i, for each day in a particular week. The average value of the weekly rainfall is computed with the formula

$$\text{Average } \bar{r} = \frac{1}{7}\sum_{i=1}^{7} r_i \tag{12.1}$$

and printed. Finally, we call the function `fileOut()` to output the daily rainfalls and the average values into a file called `RAIN.TXT`. The daily rainfalls and average values are read by MATLAB and plotted in a histogram format.

PROGRAM 12.1: STATISTICS OF WEEKLY RAINFALL

```
/*
 *  ===================================================================
 *  rainfall.c : The purposes of this C program are:
 *
 *    (a) To read daily rainfalls for one week, and compute the maximum
 *        daily rainfall and the average daily rainfall.
 *    (b) Demonstrates use of one-dimensional arrays, and output to a file.
 *  ===================================================================
 */

#include <stdio.h>

#define max(a, b) ((a) > (b) ? (a) : (b))

void fileOut( float faRainfall[], float fAv );

enum { MaxDays = 7 };

int main( void ) {
float faRainfall[ MaxDays ];      /* store the daily rainfall     */
float fSum = 0.0;                 /* store sum of daily rainfalls */
float fMax = 0.0;                 /* store maximum rainfall       */
float fAv  = 0.0;                 /* store average rainfall       */
int iDay;                         /* day counter                  */

   /* [a] : Initialize the rainfall for each day to zero */

   for( iDay = 1; iDay <= MaxDays; iDay = iDay + 1 )
        faRainfall[ iDay-1 ] = 0.0;

   /* [b] : Prompt the user for the rainfall for each day: */

   for( iDay = 1; iDay <= MaxDays; iDay = iDay + 1 ) {
        printf( "Enter the rainfall (in inches) for day %d -->", iDay );
        scanf( "%f%*c", &faRainfall[ iDay-1 ] );
   }
```

```
   /* [c] : Print the maximum and average rainfall for the week: */

   for( iDay = 1; iDay <= MaxDays; iDay = iDay + 1 )  {
        fMax = max( fMax, faRainfall[ iDay-1 ] );
        fSum += faRainfall[ iDay-1 ];
   }

   fAv = fSum/MaxDays;
   printf("\nThe maximum amount of rain this week was %f inches\n", fMax );
   printf(  "The average daily rainfall this week was %f inches\n", fAv );

   /* [d] : Write details of rainfall to output file  */

   fileOut( faRainfall, fAv);
}

/*
 *  ====================================================================
 *  fileOut() : Write rainfall data to a file called RAIN.TXT
 *
 *  Input :  float faRainfall[] -- array of daily rainfall measurements.
 *           float fAv          -- average daily rainfalls for week.
 *  Output : void
 *  ====================================================================
 */

void fileOut( float faRainfall[], float fAv ) {
FILE *FpRain;          /* typedef struct, defined in stdio.h */
int     iDay;          /* day counter                        */

    FpRain = fopen("RAIN.TXT", "w");
    if(FpRain == NULL) {
       printf("ERROR >> File RAIN.TXT could not be opened\n");
       exit(1);
    }

    for ( iDay = 1; iDay <= MaxDays; iDay = iDay + 1 )
        fprintf( FpRain, "%f %f \n", faRainfall[ iDay-1 ], fAv );

    fclose( FpRain );
}
```

Suppose that Program 12.1 has been compiled into an executable file called RAINFALL. The following script of I/O demonstrates a typical session:

```
prompt >>
prompt >> RAINFALL
```

```
Enter the rainfall (in inches) for day 1 --> 0.1
Enter the rainfall (in inches) for day 2 --> 1.0
Enter the rainfall (in inches) for day 3 --> 0.0
Enter the rainfall (in inches) for day 4 --> 0.2
Enter the rainfall (in inches) for day 5 --> 3.56
Enter the rainfall (in inches) for day 6 --> 0.0
Enter the rainfall (in inches) for day 7 --> 0.0

The maximum amount of rain this week was 3.560000 inches
The average daily rainfall this week was 0.694286 inches
prompt >> exit
```

The contents of RAIN.TXT are

```
0.100000 0.694286
1.000000 0.694286
0.000000 0.694286
0.200000 0.694286
3.560000 0.694286
0.000000 0.694286
0.000000 0.694286
```

12.5.2 Histogram of the Rainfall Data

Figure 12.2 is a histogram of the weekly rainfall, generated with the visualization package MATLAB and the contents of RAIN.TXT. The commands needed to generate this figure are left as an exercise (see Problem 14.1).

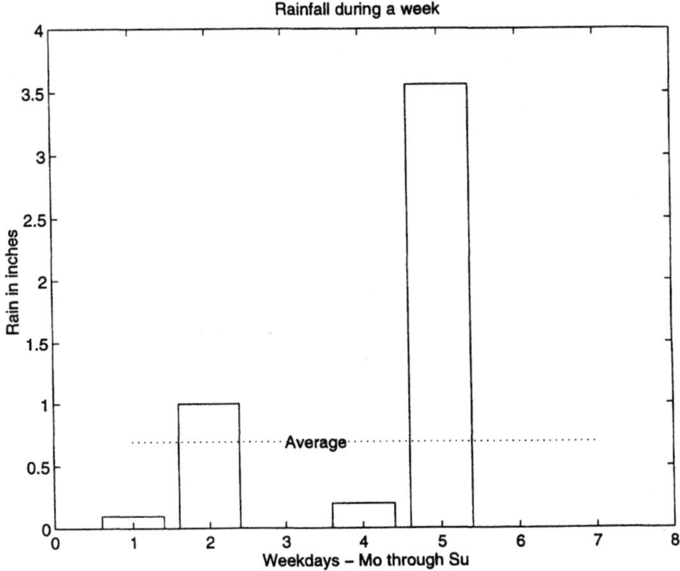

FIGURE 12.2 Histogram of weekly rainfall.

12.5.3 Storing the Rainfall Data

The `main()` function of Program 12.1 stores the weekly rainfall measurements in an array elements `faRainfall[ 0 ]` through `faRainfall[ 6 ]`. `fSum` stores the sum of the daily rainfalls, `fMax` the maximum of the daily rainfalls, and `fAv` the average daily rainfall for the week.

12.5.4 Sending the Program Output to a File

The line of code

```
void fileOut( float faRainfall[], float fAv );
```

is a declaration that provides the compiler with details on the function `fileOut()`, our user-defined function for printing information on the weekly rainfall to file `RAIN.TXT`. Function `fileOut()` has two arguments, an array of floats called `faRainfall`, and a float called `fAv`, the average daily rainfall for the week of recording. `fileOut()` prints the daily rainfall measurements and the average daily rainfall as two columns of output in the file `RAIN.TXT`. The line of code

```
FILE *FpRain;
```

declares the variable `FpRain` to be a pointer of type FILE. The standard library function `fopen()` with the arguments `"RAIN.TXT"` and `"w"` opens a file called `RAIN.TXT` with "write" permission. The looping construct

```
for ( iDay = 1; iDay <= MaxDays; iDay = iDay + 1 )
    fprintf( FpRain, "%f %f \n", faRainfall[ iDay-1 ], fAv );
```

creates two columns of output in `RAIN.TXT`. The first column contains the daily rainfall measurements, and the second column contains the average daily rainfall. The `"RAIN.TXT"` file is closed by `fclose()`.

12.6 READING DATASETS FROM AN INPUT FILE

Now that we have seen how a C program can send formatted output to a file, the next problem to consider is reading datasets into a C program from a file. For all but the smallest engineering datasets, this approach to C programming is the only way to efficiently handle datasets. The three steps needed to read a formatted dataset from a file are

1. Open the data file.
2. Read the contents of the formatted dataset file into the C program.
3. Close the data file.

Steps 1 and 3 are rather straightforward and have already been described in the previous sections. Step 2 is complicated by the multitude of strategies needed to read and store datasets. One source of complication occurs when a computer program needs to read and store multiple datasets. Sometimes they will be located in separate files; other times they will be stored sequentially within one dataset file. Experimental datasets are seldom perfect, and very sophisticated procedures may be needed to handle missing data values and comment statements arbitrarily positioned within the dataset.

Despite the potential for these complications, our discussion in this tutorial is limited to the simplest and most common cases. Variations on these themes are left as exercises.

12.6.1 Reading Datasets of Known Size

Perhaps the most straightforward scenario occurs when the number of data points is known before reading begins. A simple, effective solution is to simply insert the number of data points at the top of the dataset file and have the computer program read this number immediately before the dataset is read. For example, five data points can be read from a file

```
5
3.2
3.5
4.5
5.5
4.3
```

by placing an integer at the top. The fragment of code

```
FILE  *FpData;                /* Pointer to dataset file        */
float *fpData;                /* Pointer to floating point array */
int iNoDataPoints, iCount ;   /* Counters                       */

/* Read in no of data points : 5 !!  */

fscanf ( FpData, "%d*c", &iNoDataPoints );

/* Allocate memory and read in data points */

fpData = (float *) safeMalloc( iNoPoints*sizeof (float ),
                               --FILE--, --LINE-- );

for ( iCount = 0; iCount < iNoDataPoints; iCount++ )
      fscanf ( FpData, "%d*c", &fpData[ iCount ] ) ;
```

reads and stores the expected number of dataset rows in `iNoDataPoints`. After a block of memory has been dynamically allocated for the dataset, a `for()` loop can systematically read and store the dataset's contents in `fpData`.

Of course, if the dataset contains more than one column of input, then the first row of the dataset file should contain the number of rows and columns in the dataset (see Problem 12.3).

12.6.2 Reading Datasets of Unknown Size

A second scenario that is common, but still relatively straightforward to handle, occurs when the quantity of data is unknown, yet, the nature of the problem is such that a line of data can be read and processed immediately by the program. In other words, storage of the complete dataset within the program is not required. The standard way of handling this problem is with the programming construct

```
float fpDataValue;
while ( fscanf ( FpData, "%d*c", &fpDataValue ) != EOF ) {

         .... source code for processing the line of data.

}
```

The `while()` loop will continue reading lines of data until the integer returned from `fscanf()` equals `EOF`. On many systems, `EOF` will take the value -1.

12.6.3 Reading Datasets via Standard Input

Instead of receiving input from the keyboard, UNIX systems allow computer program input to be redirected from a file with a command of the form

```
myProg < inputFile
```

Of course, the executable program `myProg` can use either of the reading strategies just outlined.

This strategy of program input is popular because it is often easier and more reliable to set up a chain of commands in a file than manually type the commands at the keyboard. This technique is limited, however, in the sense that only one stream of program input can exist (i.e., program input from multiple file sources is not possible).

12.7 PROGRAM 12.2: MEMORY REALLOCATION FOR DATASETS

12.7.1 Problem Statement and Source Code

In this section, we look at the more interesting problem of reading and storing an unknown quantity of data. Problems of this type crop up in a variety of engineering applications. For example, a computer program written to analyze experimental data might not know ahead of time how many data points were recorded. Similar difficulties arise in the long-term monitoring of engineering systems, where analysis of the collected data is likely to proceed before the testing is complete.

In both of these scenarios, computer programs are needed for the storage and efficient handling of datasets having unknown sizes. A key component of the solution procedure is estimating how much memory will be needed (past experience would be useful here), as well as being prepared to dynamically reallocate memory when more data arrives than expected. With this background in mind, our dataset for this exercise

```
1
2
3
4
5
6
7
```

contains only seven data points. However, we assume that three data points are likely. Should the actual quantity of data exceed initial estimates, a reallocation procedure will be triggered where the available memory to store the dataset will be incremented by two elements (obviously, a lot of memory reallocation strategies are possible here). C's `realloc()` function is ideal for this purpose.

PROGRAM 12.2: MEMORY REALLOCATION FOR DATASETS

```
/*
 *  ===================================================================
 *  This program reads and stores an unknown one-dimensional stream of
 *  data from an input file.
 *
 *  Written By : Mark Austin                              September 1997
 *  ===================================================================
 */

#include <stdio.h>
#include "miscellaneous.h"

void vecPrint( char *, float *, int );     /* declaration for vector */
                                           /* function               */

int main( void ) {
enum { InitialLength = 3, Increment = 2 };
float     *fpData;
float  fDataPoint;
int iNoPoints = 0;
int iVectorLength;
```

```
    /* [a] : Allocate and print initial data vector */

    fpData = (float *) safeCalloc( InitialLength, sizeof (float),
                                   __FILE__, __LINE__);

    iVectorLength = InitialLength;

    vecPrint( "Initial data vector", fpData , iVectorLength );

    /* [b] : Read data from standard input until an EOF is obtained */

    while ( scanf( "%f%*c", &fDataPoint ) != EOF ) {

        iNoPoints = iNoPoints + 1;
        if( iNoPoints > iVectorLength ) {

            iVectorLength += Increment;

            fpData = (float *) realloc( fpData , iVectorLength*sizeof
              (float) );
            if(fpData == NULL) {
               printf("ERROR >> Memory Reallocation Failure\n");
               exit(1);
            }

            vecPrint( "Reallocated Data Vector", fpData , iVectorLength );
        }

        fpData[ iNoPoints - 1 ] = fDataPoint;
    }

    vecPrint( "Final Data Vector", fpData , iVectorLength );

    /* [c] : Free vector memory */

    free( fpData );
}

/*
 *  ==============================================================
 *  vecPrint() : Naive Implementation of Vector Print
 *
 *  Input :   char *cpMessage -- pointer to vector message.
 *            float *fpVector -- pointer to float array
 *            int     iLength -- length of float array
 *  Output :  void.
 *  ==============================================================
 */
```

```
void vecPrint( char *cpMessage , float *fpVector , int iLength ) {
int iRow;

    if(cpMessage != (char *) NULL)
       printf ("\nVECTOR \"%s\" \n\n", cpMessage );
    else
       printf("\nVECTOR : \"UNTITLED\" \n\n");

    for(iRow = 1; iRow <= iLength; iRow++)
       printf(" %3d   %16.5e\n", iRow, fpVector[ iRow-1 ]);

}
```

12.7.2 Program Architecture

Figure 12.3 is a schematic of the file and function architecture for Program 12.2. Program 12.2 employs the safe memory allocation routines from Chapter 10. An interface between our test program and the memory allocation routines located in `miscellaneous.c` will be provided by the `miscellaneous.h` header file. The heart of our dataset storage program is contained in `main()`. The function `vecPrint()` prints the dataset as a vector, and as we soon see, `vecPrint()` will be called whenever a key change in the storage capabilities of the dataset takes place.

12.7.3 Running the Program

Program 12.2 assumes that its data will be provided via standard input [hence, the use of `scanf()`]. If the contents of our dataset are stored in `expt.data` and the

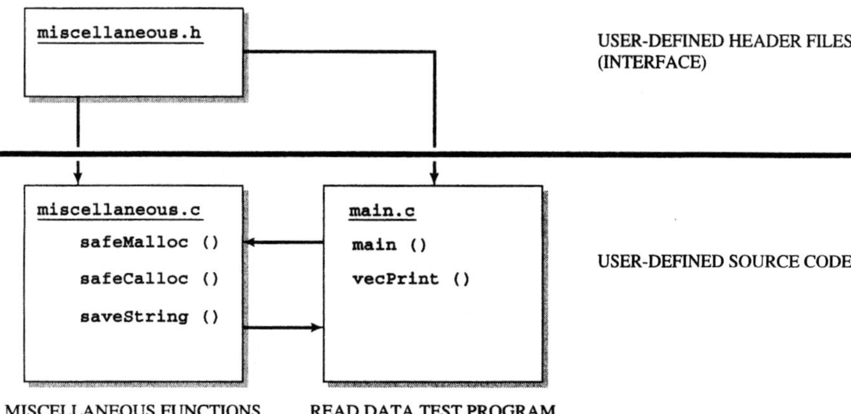

FIGURE 12.3 Architecture of read data test program.

executable program file is called `myProg`, redirection of keyboard input to file input is easily accomplished with the UNIX command

```
prompt >> myProg < expt.data
```

The program output is

```
VECTOR "Initial data vector"

   1        0.00000e+00
   2        0.00000e+00
   3        0.00000e+00

VECTOR "Reallocated Data Vector"

   1        1.00000e+00
   2        2.00000e+00
   3        3.00000e+00
   4        0.00000e+00
   5        0.00000e+00

VECTOR "Reallocated Data Vector"

   1        1.00000e+00
   2        2.00000e+00
   3        3.00000e+00
   4        4.00000e+00
   5        5.00000e+00
   6        0.00000e+00
   7        1.70622e-41

VECTOR "Final Data Vector"

   1        1.00000e+00
   2        2.00000e+00
   3        3.00000e+00
   4        4.00000e+00
   5        5.00000e+00
   6        6.00000e+00
   7        7.00000e+00
```

composed of four parts. The `"Initial data vector"` has length three. The second component of the program's output is generated immediately after the fourth number has been read. At this point, the allocated memory contains only three items. Thus, `realloc()` increases the available memory from three to five and transfers the original contents to the new array. The reallocation process is repeated after the sixth element is read. Notice that in the output, the seventh array element is `1.70622e-41` and not exactly zero. `realloc()` does not set the bits of the newly allocated array to zero. Part four of the program's output contains the complete vector of seven elements.

12.7.4 Reading and Storing the Dataset File

As mentioned in the problem statement, we initially allocate memory for a dataset containing three items. The block of code

```
fpData = (float *) safeCalloc( InitialLength, sizeof (float),
                               __FILE__, __LINE__ );
iVectorLength = InitialLength;
```

allocates the required memory for array `fpData` and initializes `iVectorLength` to 3. The latter is used to keep track of the current length of array `fpData`.

The heart of the memory allocation/reallocation strategy is contained within block `[b]` of the program source code. The outermost `while( ... )` loop will read data until `scanf()` encounters an EOF. After a new data point has been read, `iNoPoints`, the number of data points, will be incremented by 1. The relational expression

```
iNoPoints > iVectorLength
```

will evaluate to `false` when `fpData` still has room to store the new data point. The program execution will simply jump to

```
fpData[ iNoPoints - 1 ] = fDataPoint;
```

where the new data element is assigned to the appropriate location in `fpData`. The need to increase the dimensions of `fpData` occurs when `iNoPoints > iVectorLength` evaluates to `true`. The pair of statements

```
iVectorLength += Increment;
fpData = (float *) realloc( fpData ,
                            iVectorLength*sizeof (float) );
```

increment the available storage by `Increment` (i.e., 2) elements, without discarding the array's contents. Choosing an appropriate `Increment` value obviously requires some engineering judgment and, in some sense, should be related to the size of the dataset. After reading 1,000 data values, for example, a reasonable increment value might be `200-300`.

FURTHER INFORMATION

1. A summary of I/O functions in the standard library can be found in Appendix 2 of this text. For a good discussion of the standard library and its implementa-

tion, see Plauger [31]. Similarly, a complete discussion on file I/O for UNIX environments can be found in Stevens [41].

2. One problem with I/O is that the details of implementation tend to be operating system dependent. In this chapter, we focus on I/O for UNIX operating systems such as SunOS and Berkeley UNIX. For details of I/O implementation on Windows 95/98 and System V computers, consult your computer manual.
3. In this chapter, we introduce the concept of streams and then show how they apply to standard I/O and file I/O. Because of the rapid expansion in client/server computers in many sectors of business and engineering, socket-based I/O is now playing a key role in communication of information between processes on the same computer and between processes on different computers. A good introduction to network-based computing and Berkeley Sockets can be found in Stevens [40].

Review Questions

1. What is a standard stream?
2. What is the difference between a text stream and a binary stream?
3. What are the four main capabilities of the `printf()` function?
4. List four uses of escape characters in formatting program output.
5. What happens when a number to be printed will not fit within the specified format?
6. What are two situations where `scanf()` will terminate the reading of standard input prematurely?
7. For the generation of floating point output from engineering applications programs, what are the advantages of the `%g` format compared to the `%f` format?
8. What is the purpose of the `%*c` format?
9. List two ways in which `fopen()` may fail? How should C programs be written to guard against these possibilities?

12.8 PROGRAMMING EXERCISES

Problem 12.1 (Beginner): Modify Program 12.1 so that the rainfall measurements (in inches) for days one through seven are read from a file `RAIN.DATA`. The modified program should open the file `RAIN.DATA`, read the contents, and then close the file (it should not read the contents of `RAIN.DATA` by simply redirecting standard I/O).

Problem 12.2 (Beginner): Modify Program 12.2 so that the program input is read directly from a dataset file `MATRIX.DATA`. The modified program should open the file `MATRIX.DATA` and read its contents until an `EOF` is encountered. The `MATRIX.DATA` file should be closed before the program execution terminates.

Problem 12.3 (Beginner): Suppose that a matrix of floating point numbers is stored in a dataset file as follows:

```
   5     3
 1.0   2.0    3.0
 4.0   5.0    6.0
 7.0   8.0    9.0
10.0  11.0   12.0
13.0  14.0   15.0
```

The first row of the data file contains the number of rows and columns in the dataset, respectively. Write a C program that will

1. Read the first line of the data file and then dynamically allocate memory for the matrix.
2. Read and store the contents of the dataset in the matrix.
3. Print the contents of the matrix to the screen.

Problem 12.4 (Intermediate): One way of enhancing the readability of a dataset file is to place a block of comment statements in the header explaining the file's contents. For example, the dataset file

```
This file contains a matrix of floating point numbers.
Data : January 30, 1998.

Number of Rows    = 3
Number of Columns = 5
   1.0   2.0    3.0
   4.0   5.0    6.0
   7.0   8.0    9.0
  10.0  11.0   12.0
  13.0  14.0   15.0
```

is a lot more descriptive than in Problem 12.3. Write a C program that will skip over the header comments, and read the number of rows and columns in the dataset. The contents of the dataset should then be read and stored, and printed once the reading process is complete.

Problem 12.5 (Intermediate): An experiment is conducted on 36 specimens to determine the tensile yield strength of `A36` steel. The experimental results are as follows:

```
42.3    42.1    41.8    42.4    47.7    41.4
40.5    38.7    40.8    39.6    42.4    37.5
39.9    45.3    41.6    36.8    45.4    44.8
39.2    40.7    38.5    40.1    42.8    42.5
43.1    36.2    46.2    41.5    38.3    40.2
41.9    40.4    39.1    38.6    46.3    39.5
```

Write a C program that will

1. Read the experimental test results from a file named `experimental.data`.
2. Compute the maximum, minimum, average, and median tensile strengths.
3. Generate a histogram of "observations" versus "yield stress."
4. Construct a bar graph or stair plot of "cumulative frequency" versus "yield stress."

In Steps 3 and 4, format your program output so that MATLAB, or some other graphics package, can easily read and produce the required plots.

Note. The average value of the experimental results can be computed using formulae presented in Section 8.5. After the experimental results have been numerically sorted, the median value is the midvalue (if the number of data points is odd) or the average of the two middle values (if the number of data points is even). The "cumulative frequency" versus "yield stress" is given by

$$\text{Cumulative frequency(y)} = \int_0^y p(x)\,dx \tag{12.2}$$

where $p(x)$ is the probability distribution of tensile yield strengths.

PART 3

MATLAB PROGRAMMING TUTORIAL

MATLAB is a great programming language for solving problems that can be conveniently represented by matrices, that lend themselves to a solution with operations from linear matrix algebra and that can be presented using relatively simple two- and three-dimensional graphics. Computing the solution to a family of linear equations and representing, manipulating, and displaying engineering data are perhaps the two best examples of problems for which MATLAB is ideally suited.

As we soon see, not only is the MATLAB programming language exceptionally straightforward (almost every data object is assumed to be an array), but also MATLAB program code will be much shorter and simpler than an equivalent implementation in C, FORTRAN, or Java. MATLAB is, therefore, an ideal language for creating prototypes of software solutions to engineering problems, and using them to validate ideas and refine project specifications. Once these issues have been worked out, the MATLAB implementation can be replaced by a C or Java implementation that enhances performance and allows for extra functionality (e.g., a fully functional graphical user interface that perhaps communicates with other software package over the Internet).

Chapter 13 is an introduction to programming in MATLAB Version 5.0 and includes all the basic concepts you need to know. Topics include variables and variable arithmetic, matrices and matrix arithmetic, control structures, built-in matrix functions, M-files, and so forth. Four engineering applications are solved at the end of Chapter 13. Where appropriate, pointers are given to equivalent or similar implementations of these problems in C and Java. A brief introduction to MATLAB graphics is contained in Chapter 14. Many other texts weave MATLAB graphics into the introductory sections of MATLAB programming. However, in an effort to keep the tutorial length short, we separate graphics from programming. Chapter 15 covers the solution of linear matrix equations in MATLAB. We demonstrate the power of MATLAB by working step by step through the formulation and solution of a variety of engineering applications involving families of matrix equations and, where applicable, MATLAB graphics.

13

INTRODUCTION TO MATLAB

13.1 GETTING STARTED

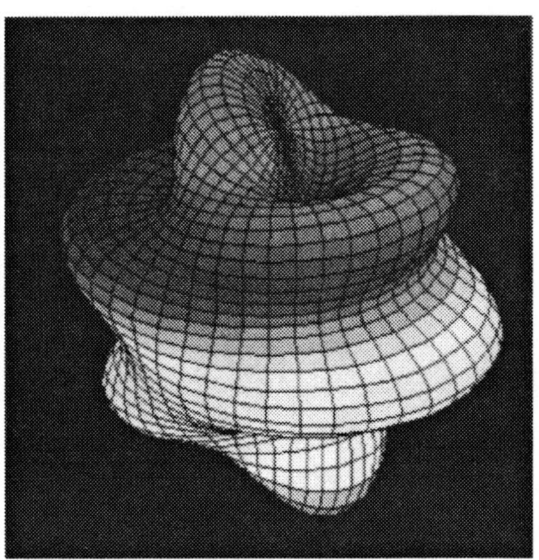

The MATrix LABoratory program (MATLAB) was initially written with the objective of providing scientists and engineers with interactive access to the numerical computation libraries LINPACK and EISPACK. These libraries are carefully tested, high-quality programming packages for solving linear equations and eigenvalue problems [8, 38]. MATLAB enables scientists and engineers to use matrix-based techniques to solve problems without having to write programs in traditional languages such as C and FORTRAN.

Currently, MATLAB is a commercial matrix laboratory package that operates as an interactive programming environment with graphical output. The MATLAB programming language is exceptionally straightforward to use since almost every data object is assumed to be an array. MATLAB is available for many different computer systems, including Macintosh, PC, and UNIX platforms.

The purposes of this tutorial are two-fold. In addition to helping you get started with MATLAB, we want you to see how MATLAB can be used in the solution of engineering problems. The latter objective is achieved through the presentation of a series of engineering application problems. Throughout this tutorial, we assume that you

1. Will read a few sections and then go to a UNIX workstation or PC/Macintosh to experiment with MATLAB
2. Are familiar with the operating system on your computer
3. Have access to supplementary material on matrices, matrix arithmetic/operations, and linear algebra

13.1.1 Professional and Student Versions of MATLAB

Professional and student editions of MATLAB Version 5.0 are available. The functionality of the student edition of MATLAB is limited in the following way: Each matrix is limited to 16,384 elements, large enough to study problems having 128-by-128 matrices. From this point on, we assume that you have installed (follow the instructions accompanying the software disks) the student version of MATLAB on your computer.

13.1.2 Entering and Leaving MATLAB

The procedure for entering and leaving MATLAB on UNIX and Mac/PC platforms is as follows.

UNIX Platform

A MATLAB session may be entered by simply typing

```
prompt >> matlab
```

Here `prompt >>` is the operating system prompt. A window should open and start MATLAB. When you run MATLAB under the window system, whether you start from the menu or a system prompt, a small MATLAB logo window will appear while the program is loading and disappear when MATLAB is ready to use. MATLAB will present the (double arrow) prompt

```
>>
```

You are now in MATLAB. From this point on, individual MATLAB commands may be given at the program prompt. They will be processed when you hit the "return" key. A MATLAB session may be terminated by simply typing

```
>> quit
```

or by typing `exit` at the MATLAB prompt.

Macintosh and PC Platforms

Click on the icon for MATLAB or STUDENT-MATLAB. Most of your interaction with MATLAB will take place in a Command window, where you will be presented with the prompt

```
EDU>>
```

The procedure for leaving MATLAB is the same as any other program operating on these platforms.

Both PC and Macintosh platforms come with a variety of programming and application development tools. For example, the PC platform supports an integrated M-file editor, a visual M-file editor, and performance profiler. The Macintosh platform comes with an M-file debugger and Workspace browser.

13.1.3 Online Help

Online help is available from the MATLAB prompt, both generally (listing all available commands)

```
>> help
[a long list of help topics follows]
```

and specifically

```
>> help demo
[a help message on MATLAB's demo program follows]
```

The `version` command will tell you which version of MATLAB you are using. The `helpdesk` command

```
>> helpdesk
```

will initiate the execution of a World Wide Web (WWW) browser for MATLAB Online Reference Documentation. Check it out.

13.2 VARIABLES AND VARIABLE ARITHMETIC

MATLAB supports a variety of data types for the desktop solution of engineering computations. Some problems will require the representation of `scalar` numbers or variables whose values are scalar numbers. Other types of computations require the use of complex numbers containing real and imaginary components. Moreover, solutions to a range of engineering problems may be expediently computed through the use of one-dimensional arrays and/or multidimensional matrices of scalars and complex numbers. This section explains how variables work in MATLAB.

The names and (data) types of MATLAB variables do not need to be declared because MATLAB does not distinguish between integer, real, and complex values. In fact, any variable can take integer, real, or complex values. Like most programming languages, variable names in MATLAB should be chosen so that they do not conflict with function or subroutine names, command names, or the names of certain values. However, name conflicts are bound to occur, and we deal with this topic below in the subsection entitled "Handling Name Conflicts."

13.2.1 Defining Variables

The equality sign is used to assign values to variables:

```
>> x = 3

  x =

         3

>>
```

As we soon see, variable names can be assigned to scalars, vectors (i.e., one-dimensional matrices), and matrices. Generally speaking, variable names will be a mixture of letters, digits, and the underscore character. The first character in a variable name must be a letter. Although variable names can be of any length, MATLAB Version 5.0 requires that they be unique within the first 31 characters. It is also important to bear in mind that variable names in MATLAB are case sensitive, meaning that variables `x` and `X` are distinct. Indeed, at this point, `X` is not even defined.

Table 13.1 shows some of the special built-in variable names and numbers used in MATLAB. The following script shows how you can learn their values from the MATLAB interpreter.

TABLE 13.1 Special Variable Names and Numbers in MATLAB

Variable Name	*Meaning*	*Value*
ans	Represents a value computed in an expression but not stored in a variable name.	
eps	Represents the floating point precision for the computer being used. It is the smallest amount with which two values can differ in the computer.	2.2204 e-16
"i" and "j"	Imaginary unit in a complex number.	sqrt(-1)
pi	$\pi = 3.141\ldots$	3.1415926 ..
NaN	Represents "not a number." NaNs crop up in undefined expressions (e.g., division by zero) and in matrix elements where data is missing.	
inf	Infinity typically results from a division by zero or an arithmetic overflow.	(∞)
clock	The current time is represented in a six-element row vector containing year, month, day, hour, minute, and seconds.	
date	The current date is represented in a character string format.	
flops	Floating point operations count.	

```
>> eps
  eps =

        2.2204e-16

>> pi
  ans =

        3.1416

>> help pi

  PI      3.1415926535897....
          PI = 4*atan(1) = imag(log(-1)) = 3.1415926535897....
>>
```

Points to note are

1. The machine's round-off, the smallest distinguishable difference between two numbers as represented in MATLAB, is denoted eps.
2. The variable ans keeps track of the last output that was not assigned to another variable. You can use this property in a sequence of calculations where the output of one computation is used in the following calculation.

Program output can be suppressed by simply appending a semicolon (;) to command lines, as in

```
>> x = 3;
>> x

  x =

        3

>>
```

More than one command may be entered on a single line if the commands are separated by commas or semicolons. To see how MATLAB handles these cases, try typing the command sequence

```
>> x = 3, y = 4; z = 5   % define and initialize variables x, y, and z.
```

In MATLAB, the % symbol indicates the beginning of a comment and, as such, the MATLAB interpreter will disregard the rest of the command line.

13.2.2 Arithmetic Expressions

Table 13.2 summarizes the meaning and order of evaluation of MATLAB operators in arithmetic expressions involving scalars and variables. With the exception of the

TABLE 13.2 Meaning and Precedence of Arithmetic Operators

Operator	*Meaning*	*Example*
^	Exponentiation of "a" raised to the power of "b"	`2^3 = 2*2*2 = 8`
*	Multiply "a" times "b"	`2*3 = 6`
/	Right division (a/b) of "a" and "b"	`2/3 = 0.6667`
\	Left division (a\b) of "a" and "b"	`2\3 = 3/2 = 1.5`
+	Addition of "a" and "b"	`2 + 3 = 5`
-	Subtraction of "a" and "b"	`2 - 3 = -1`

Precedence of Arithmetic Expressions

Operators	*Precedence*	*Comment*
( )	1	Innermost parentheses are evaluated first.
^	2	Exponentiation operations are evaluated right to left.
* /	3	Multiplication and right division operations are evaluated left to right.
\	3	Left devision operations are evaluated right to left.
+ -	4	Addition and subtraction operations are evaluated left to right.

left division operator, arithmetic expressions in MATLAB follow a fairly standard notation. The MATLAB commands

```
>> 2+3;           % Compute the sum "2" plus "3"
>> 3*4;           % Compute the product "3" times "4"
>> 4^2;           % Compute "4" raised to the power of "2"
```

are examples of basic arithmetic operations. The lower half of Table 13.2 shows the precedence and order of operator evaluation for arithmetic expressions. Operators having the highest precedence (i.e., a low precedence number) are evaluated first. So, for example, power operations are performed before division and multiplication, which are done before subtraction and addition. For example,

```
>> 2+3*4^2;
```

generates `ans = 50`. That is,

```
    2 + 3*4^2     <== exponent has the highest precedence.
==> 2 + 3*16      <== then multiplication operator.
==> 2 + 48        <== then addition operator.
==> 50
```

Arithmetic expressions involving operators of equal precedence are evaluated left to right. Of course, parentheses may be used to group terms or to make them more readable. For example,

```
>> (2 + 3*4^2)/2
```

generates `ans = 25`. That is,

```
    (2 + 3*4^2)/2    <== evaluate expression within
                         parentheses. Exponent has
                         highest precedence.
==> (2 + 3*16)/2     <== then multiplication operator.
==> (2 + 48)/2       <== then addition operator inside
                         parentheses.
==> (50)/2           <== then division operator
==> 25
```

Even though the addition operator has lower precedence than the divide operation, the order of evaluation can be easily altered with the use of parentheses. The second key use of parentheses is for function calls, that is, a function name followed by parentheses containing zero or more arguments. In this case, the function calls associated with a set of parentheses will be evaluated; innermost levels of parentheses first. For example, the step-by-step order of evaluation for

```
>> 4.0*sin( pi/4 + pi/4 )
```

is

```
    4*sin( pi/4 + pi/4 )        <== begin evaluation of left-hand
                                    side multiplication
==> 4*sin(pi/4 + pi/4 )         <== evaluate expression within
                                    function parentheses, starting
                                    with leftmost division.
==> 4*sin( 0.7854 + pi/4)       <== evaluate right-hand side
                                    division.
==> 4*sin( 0.7854 + 0.7854 ) <== evaluate sum.
==> 4*sin( 1.5708)              <== sin(pi) function call.
==> 4*1.0                       <== finish evaluation of left-hand
                                    side multiplication.
==> 4.0
```

In this example, `sin(x)` is a function call to compute the sine of angle `x` measured in radians.

MATLAB has a `flops` function for counting the number of floating point operations needed to complete a MATLAB command or block of MATLAB commands. We can easily verify, for example, that five floating point operations are needed to evaluate the arithmetic expression

```
>> 4*sin( pi/4 + pi/4 );
>> flops

ans =

     5

>>
```

13.2.3 Numerical Precision of MATLAB Output

All arithmetic is done to double precision, which for 32-bit machines means to about 16 decimal digits of accuracy. MATLAB automatically prints integer values as integers and floating point numbers to four decimal digits of accuracy, with blank lines being inserted between textual lines of output. Exponential format is automatically used when the value of a number falls outside the range of numbers that can be printed using the default format.

A summary of formatting options for the printing of the variable

```
>> a = 20.12345678901234
```

is shown in Table 13.3. Two useful commands are `format long`, which instructs MATLAB to display floating point numbers to 16 digits of accuracy, and `format compact`, which instructs MATLAB to abbreviate its output by removing all blank lines. Consider, for example, the script of code

TABLE 13.3 Formatting Options for MATLAB Output

MATLAB Command	*Meaning*	*Example*
`format short`	Default—4 decimal places	`20.1235`
`format long`	Output printed to 14 decimal places	`20.12345678901234`
`format short e`	Exponential format with 4 decimal places	`2.0123e+01`
`format long e`	Exponential format with 14 decimal places	`2.012345678901234e+01`

```
>> x = 2.345                    % define variable "x"

x =

    2.3450

>> format compact               % "compact" version of output.
>> format long                  % "double precision" output.
>> x^30
ans =
     1.271409381050112e+11
>>
>> format short                 % switch back to "default" output.
```

To save space in this tutorial, all our calculations from this point on are conducted with the `format compact` in place.

13.2.4 Built-In Mathematical Functions

MATLAB has a platter of built-in functions for mathematical and scientific computations (see Table 13.4). You should remember that the arguments to trigonometric functions are given in radians. Also bear in mind that MATLAB has functions to round floating point numbers to integers: They are `round`, `fix`, `ceil`, and `floor`.

Example. Verify that

```
sin(x)^2 + cos(x)^2 = 1.0
```

for some arbitrary values of x. The MATLAB code is

```
>> x = pi/3;
>> sin(x)^2 + cos(x)^2 - 1.0
ans =
     0
>>
```

Alternatively, we can write the arithmetic expression in terms of the ans variable storing the angle.

```
>> pi/4;
ans =
     0.7854
>> sin(ans)^2 + cos(ans)^2 - 1.0
ans =
     0
>>
```

Active Variables

When you want to know the active variables, you can use who. For example,

```
>> who
  Your variables are:
  ans      x
>>
```

The command whos gives a detailed listing of the active variables, together with information on the number of elements and their size in bytes.

The command clear removes an item from the active variable list. For example, try typing clear x.

13.2.5 Program Input and Output

Throughout this tutorial, we employ a variety of techniques for input and output of MATLAB variables and matrices. We see, for example, that variables and matrices can be defined explicitly, with built-in functions, and using data that are loaded into MATLAB from an external file. In this section, we are concerned only with I/O of variables and introduce other features of I/O as needed.

MATLAB has two functions for the basic input of variables from the keyboard and for formatted output of variables.

Input of Variables from the Keyboard

MATLAB has a built-in function "input" that enables the value of variables to be specified at the keyboard. For example, the command

```
A = input('Please type the value of Coefficient A :');
```

will print the message

```
Please type the value of Coefficient A :
```

TABLE 13.4 Common Trigonometric and Mathematical Functions

Function	*Meaning*	*Example*
Trigonometric Functions		
`sin (x)`	Compute the sine of x (x is in radians).	`sin(pi) = 0.0`
`cos (x)`	Compute the cosine of x (x is in radians).	`cos(pi) = 1.0`
`tan (x)`	Compute the tangent of x (x is in radians).	`tan(pi/4) = 1.0`
`asin (x)`	Compute the arcsine of x. Complex results are obtained if `abs(x) > 1` for some elements.	`asin(pi/2) = 1.0`
`acos (x)`	Compute the arccosine of x. Complex results are obtained if `abs(x) > 1` for some elements.	`acos(pi/2) = 0.0`
`atan (x)`	Compute the arctangent of the elements of x.	`atan ( [ 0.5 1.0 ] ) = 0.4636 0.7854`
`atan2 (x,y)`	Compute the four-quadrant inverse tangent of the real parts of x and y. This function returns an angle between −pi and pi.	`atan2 (1,2) = 0.4636`
`exp (x)`	Compute `e^x` where e is the base for natural logarithms.	`exp(1.0) = 2.7183`
`log (x)`	Compute the natural logarithm of x to the base e.	`log(2.7183) = 1.0`
`log10 (x)`	Compute the logarithm of x to the base 10.	`log10(100.0) = 2.0`
Mathematical Functions		
`abs(x)`	Return absolute value of x.	`abs( -3.5 ) = 3.0`
`ceil(x)`	Round x toward positive infinity.	`ceil (-3.8) = -3`
`fix(x)`	Round x toward the nearest integer toward zero.	`fix (-3.8) = -3`
`floor(x)`	Round x toward minus infinity.	`floor (-3.8) = -4`
`rem(x,y)`	Return the remainder of x/y. In C, this function is implemented as the modulo operator.	
`round(x)`	Round x to the nearest integer.	`round(3.8) = 4`
`sign(x)`	Return −1 if x is less than 0, 0 if x equals zero, and 1 if x is greater than zero.	`sign(3) = 1`
`sqrt(x)`	Compute the square root of x.	`sqrt(3) = 1.7320...`

enclosed between single quotes on the computer screen. MATLAB will then wait for a numerical value to be typed at the keyboard, followed by the return key. In this particular case, the result of the numerical input will be assigned to variable `A`.

Formatted Output of Variables

MATLAB uses the function `fprintf` for formatted output of messages and numbers. The general syntax for this function is

```
fprintf( format , matrices or variables )
```

The first argument contains the text and format specifications to be printed, and it is followed by zero or more matrices and variables. MATLAB's format argument operates in an almost identical manner to formatted output in the C programming language. For example, the specification `%f` is used for floating point numbers, and `%e` is used for exponential notation. The command

```
fprintf( 'Volume of sphere = %f\n' , 3.4 )
```

generates the output

```
>> fprintf( 'Volume of sphere = %f\n' , 3.4 )
Volume of sphere = 3.400000
>>
```

The only difference in the MATLAB and C versions of `fprintf` is MATLAB's use of single quotes and C's use of double quotes to enclose the message. Of course, format specifications can contain information on the total width and number of decimal places to be printed. You can find the relevant details in Chapters 3 and 12.

Saving and Restoring Variables

To save the value of the variable `x` to a plain text file named `x.value` use

```
>> save x.value x -ascii
```

To save all variables in a file named `mysession.mat` in reloadable format, use

```
>> save mysession
```

To restore the session, use `load mysession`. PC and Macintosh versions also come with a `File` menu for saving and retrieving data.

13.3 MATRICES AND MATRIX ARITHMETIC

A matrix (or array) of order m by n is simply a set of numbers arranged in a rectangular block of m horizontal rows and n vertical columns. We say

$$A = \begin{bmatrix} a_{11} & a_{12} & \cdots & a_{1n} \\ a_{21} & a_{22} & \cdots & a_{2n} \\ \vdots & \vdots & \ddots & \vdots \\ a_{m1} & a_{m2} & \cdots & a_{mn} \end{bmatrix} \tag{13.1}$$

is a matrix of size (m × n). Sometimes we say "matrix A has dimension (m × n)." The numbers that make up the array are called the `elements` of the matrix and, in MATLAB, no distinction is made between elements that are real numbers and complex numbers. In the double subscript notation a_{ij} for matrix element `a(i,j)`, the first subscript i denotes the row number, and the second subscript j denotes the column number.

By definition, a row vector is simply a (1 × n) matrix and a column vector is a (m × 1) matrix. The ith element of a vector

$$V = [v_1 \quad v_2 \quad v_3 \quad v_4 \cdots v_n] \tag{13.2}$$

is simply denoted v_i. The MATLAB language has been designed to make the definition and manipulation of matrices and vectors as simple as possible.

13.3.1 Definition and Properties of Small Matrices

Matrices can be introduced into MATLAB by explicitly listing the elements through the use of built-in matrix functions and by M-files and external data files. We explain how matrices are defined in M-files and external files in a moment. For now, consider the statements

```
>> A = [1 2 3 4; 5 6 7 8; 9 10 11 12; 13 14 15 16 ];
```

and

```
>> A = [ 1  2  3  4
         5  6  7  8
         9 10 11 12
        13 14 15 16 ]
```

Both statements create a four-by-four matrix and assign its contents to a variable A. In the explicit declaration of matrices, a matrix is entered in row-major order, meaning all the first row, then all the second row, and so forth. Matrix rows are separated by a semicolon or a new line, and the elements within a row of a matrix may be separated by commas as well as a blank. The elements of a matrix are enclosed by brackets. Matrix elements that are floating point numbers are specified in the usual way (e.g., 3.1415926). Blank spaces must be avoided when listing a number in exponential form (e.g., 2.34e-9).

Row and column vectors are declared as matrices having either one row or column, respectively.

Accessing Matrix Elements

The matrix element located in the *i*th row and *j*th column of `A` is referred to in the usual way:

```
>> A(1,2), A(2,3)
ans =
        2
ans =
        7
>>
```

Similarly, the elements in a row or column vector may be accessed by simply typing the vector name followed by the index number inserted between brackets. For example,

```
>> V = [ 5 4 3 2 1 ];     % declare a row vector having 5
elements
>> V (2)                  % access the second element in vector V
ans =
      4
>>
```

The elements of vectors and matrices may be easily modified with statements of the form

```
>> A(2,3)  = 10;         % modify matrix element A (2,3)
>> V(2)    = 10;         % modify vector element V (2)
```

Size of a Matrix

The MATLAB function `size` returns a one-by-two matrix containing the number of rows and columns in a matrix. The script of code

```
>> size ( [ 1 2 3 4 5; 6 7 8 9 10; 11 12 13 14 15 ] )
ans =
     3     5
>>
```

shows how the `size` function returns the number of rows and columns in a three-by-five matrix.

Equal Matrices

Two matrices A and B are equal if they have the same number of rows and columns, and all the corresponding elements are equal (i.e., $a_{ij} = b_{ij}$ for $i = 1 \cdots m$ and $j = 1 \cdots n$. In MATLAB, a copy of the matrix

```
>> A = [ 1 2 3; 4 5 6 ];
```

can be made by simply writing

```
>> B = A
B =

     1     2     3
     4     5     6

>>
```

Square Matrices

If a matrix has the same number of rows as columns (i.e., m = n), then we say that it is square and that the matrix is of order n. The group of elements $a_{11}, a_{22} \cdots a_{nn}$ are called the principal diagonal elements.

Empty Matrices

MATLAB allows for the definition of matrices where one or more dimensions of the matrix may be empty, that is, contain no matrix elements. For example, the statement

```
>> A = [];
```

defines an empty matrix A. The MATLAB function isempty() can be used to test whether a matrix is empty (see Table 13.7 for more details on calling this function).

Defining Matrices with Built-In MATLAB Functions

Table 13.5 shows that MATLAB has a variety of built-in functions for the definition of small matrices. The script of code

```
>> eye (3,4)
ans =
     1     0     0     0
     0     1     0     0
     0     0     1     0

>>
```

shows, for example, how a matrix of three rows and four columns with 1s along the matrix diagonal is generated by the function call eye(3,4).

TABLE 13.5 Defining Small Matrices with MATLAB Functions

Function	*Meaning*	*Example*
`eye (n)`	Returns a n-by-n identity matrix.	`eye (3)`
`eye(m,n)`	Returns a m-by-n matrix of ones along the matrix diagonal and zeros elsewhere.	`eye (3,4)`
`zeros(n)`	Returns a n-by-n matrix of zero elements.	`zeros (3)`
`zeros(m,n)`	Returns a m-by-n matrix of zero elements.	`zeros (3,4)`

Diagonal Matrix

A square matrix A whose elements $a_{ij} = 0$ for all $i \neq j$ is called a `diagonal` matrix. We write `A = diag(`$a_{11}, a_{22}, a_{33}, \cdots, a_{nn}$`)`. A diagonal matrix whose elements on the principal diagonal are all 1 is called the `unit matrix` or `identity matrix`. This special matrix has notation I.

Let `X` be a row or column vector containing n elements. `diag(X)` is the $(n \times n)$ diagonal matrix with the elements of `X` placed along the diagonal. Consider, for example,

```
>> X = [ 4 3 2 1 ];
>> diag(X)
ans =
     4     0     0     0
     0     3     0     0
     0     0     2     0
     0     0     0     1

>>
```

Conversely, if `A` is a square matrix then `diag(A)` is a vector containing the diagonal elements of `A`. Consider, for example,

```
>> A = [ 1 2 3; 4 5 6; 7 8 9 ];
>> diag (A)
ans =

     1
     5
     9

>>
```

Lower and Upper Triangular Matrices

A lower triangular matrix `L` is one where $a_{ij} = 0$ for all entries above the diagonal. An upper triangular matrix `U` is one where $a_{ij} = 0$ for all entries below the diagonal.

That is,

$$L = \begin{bmatrix} a_{11} & 0 & \cdots & 0 \\ a_{21} & a_{22} & \cdots & 0 \\ \vdots & \vdots & \ddots & \vdots \\ a_{m1} & a_{m2} & \cdots & a_{mn} \end{bmatrix} \quad U = \begin{bmatrix} a_{11} & a_{12} & \cdots & a_{1n} \\ 0 & a_{22} & \cdots & a_{2n} \\ \vdots & \vdots & \ddots & \vdots \\ 0 & 0 & \cdots & a_{mn} \end{bmatrix}$$

The MATLAB functions `triu` and `tril` extract the upper and lower sections of a matrix, respectively. For example, the script

```
>> U = triu(A)
U =
        1     2     3
        0     5     6
        0     0     9
>> L = tril(A)
L =
        1     0     0
        4     5     0
        7     8     9
>>
```

extracts the upper and lower triangular sections of matrix `A` defined in the previous section. The function calls `triu(A,k)` and `tril(A,k)` generate square matrices of values from `A` with zeros below/above the `k-th` diagonal. For example, the script of code

```
>> U1 = triu(A, 1);
>> U2 = triu(A,-1);
```

generates the matrices

$$U1 = \begin{bmatrix} 0 & 2 & 3 \\ 0 & 0 & 6 \\ 0 & 0 & 0 \end{bmatrix} \quad \text{and} \quad U2 = \begin{bmatrix} 1 & 2 & 3 \\ 4 & 5 & 6 \\ 0 & 8 & 9 \end{bmatrix}$$

Building Matrices from Blocks

Large matrices can be assembled from smaller matrix blocks. For example, with matrix `A` in hand, we can enter the following commands:

```
>> C = [A; 10 11 12];      <== generates a (4X3) matrix
>> [A; A; A];              <== generates a (9X3) matrix
>> [A, A, A];              <== generates a (3X9) matrix
```

As with variables, use of a semicolon with matrices suppresses output. This feature can be especially useful when large matrices are being generated. If A is a three-by-three matrix, then

```
>> B = [ A, zeros(3,2); zeros(2,3), eye(2) ];
```

will build a certain five-by-five matrix. Try it.

13.3.2 Reading and Saving Datasets

Suppose that the array of numbers

```
 1    10.0
 2    15.0
 3    14.0

.... data items removed from file ...

28     9.0
29     4.0
30     0.0
```

is stored in a file `rainfall.dat` and that each row of the file corresponds to the date and daily rainfall measurement (in mm) for one calendar month. The command

```
>> load rainfall.dat
```

will read the contents of `rainfall.dat` into an array called `rainfall`, having 30 rows and 2 columns. The command

```
>> save rainfall.dat rainfall -ascii
```

will save the contents of array `rainfall` in the data file `rainfall.dat`. The array elements will be written in ASCII using eight digits of accuracy. The command

```
>> save
```

will save array `rainfall`, and all the other matrices and variables in the MATLAB workspace, in a nonreadable `mat` file called `matlab.mat`. The contents of `matlab.mat` can be reloaded into MATLAB at a later date by simply reissuing the `load` command. For an extensive list of `save` and `load` command options, see the online documentation.

13.3.3 Application of Mathematical Functions to Matrices

In your high school mathematics classes, you probably learned that `sin(x)` is the sine of an angle x measured in radians. A typical MATLAB command could be

```
>> x = pi/4;
>> sin ( x )
ans =
        0.7071
>>
```

MATLAB makes an important departure from traditional mathematics in the way it deals with matrices and the mathematical and trigonometric functions listed in Table 13.4. Instead of only allowing for the computation of mathematical formulae on a single variable (as demonstrated in the previous example), MATLAB enables mathematical formulae to be computed on the entire contents of a matrix by writing only one line of code. So how does this work? When we write the statement

```
>> x = pi/4;
```

we naturally think of x as being a variable. However, MATLAB treats x as if it were a matrix containing only one element. The same numerical result can be obtained by writing

```
>> sin ( [ pi/4 ] )
ans =
        0.7071
>>
```

If the dimensions of the input matrix are expanded to something like

```
>> x = [ 1 2 3 4 5; 6 7 8 9 10]
x =
       1       2       3       4       5
       6       7       8       9      10
>>
```

then the command

```
>> sin(x)
ans =
      0.8415    0.9093    0.1411   -0.7568   -0.9589
     -0.2794    0.6570    0.9894    0.4121   -0.5440
>>
```

generates a two-by-five matrix containing the sine computations for each of the matrix elements in x. In other words, MATLAB systematically walks through all the elements in x and computes the sine of the corresponding matrix element.

We will soon see that this feature of MATLAB applies to nearly all the functions listed in Table 13.4. The true benefit of this feature lies in the development of MATLAB software for the solution of problems requiring repetitive calculations. Because the need for looping constructs can be eliminated in many cases, the complexity of user-written code needed to implement a numerical algorithm in MATLAB can be significantly simpler than counterpart implementations in C and Java, for example.

13.3.4 Colon Notation

A central part of the MATLAB language syntax is the "colon operator," which produces a list. For example,

```
>> -3:3
  ans =
       -3     -2     -1     0     1     2     3
>>
```

The default increment is by 1 but that can be changed. For example,

```
>> x = -3 : .3 : 3
  x =
    Columns 1 through 7
     -3.0000   -2.7000   -2.4000   -2.1000   -1.8000   -1.5000   -1.2000
    Columns 8 through 14
     -0.9000   -0.6000   -0.3000         0    0.3000    0.6000    0.9000
    Columns 15 through 21
      1.2000    1.5000    1.8000    2.1000    2.4000    2.7000    3.0000
>>
```

In this particular case you may think of x as a list, a vector, or a matrix, which begins at −3 and whose entries increase by .3, until 3 is surpassed. Generally speaking, the colon operator can be used anywhere in MATLAB code where a generated list is appropriate. Consider, for example, the block of statements for generating a table of sines

```
>> x = [0.0:0.1:2.0]' ;
>> y = sin(x);
>> [x y]
```

The first command generates a column vector of elements ranging from zero to two in increments of 0.1. You should note that because sin operates entrywise, the second command generates a column vector y from the vector x. The third command takes the x and y column vectors and places them in a 21-by-2 matrix table. Go ahead, try it.

Colon notation can also be combined with the earlier method of constructing matrices. For example, the command

```
>> A = [1:6 ; 2:7 ; 4:9];
```

generates a 3-by-3 matrix A.

13.3.5 Submatrices

Any matrix obtained by omitting some rows and columns from a given matrix A is called a "submatrix" of A. A very common use of the colon notation is to extract rows, or columns, as a sort of "wild card" operator, which produces a default list. For example,

```
>> A(1:4,3)
```

is the column vector consisting of the first four entries of the third column of A. A colon by itself denotes an entire row or column. So, for example,

```
>> A(:,3)
```

is the third column of A, and `A(1:4,:)` is the first four rows of A. Arbitrary integral vectors can be used as subscripts. For example, the statement

```
>> A(:,[2 4])
```

generates a two-column matrix containing columns 2 and 4 of matrix A. This subscripting scheme can be used on both sides of an assignment statement. The command

```
>> A(:,[2 4 5]) = B(:,1:3)
```

replaces columns 2, 4, and 5 of matrix A with the first three columns of matrix B. Note that the entire altered matrix A is printed and assigned. Try it.

13.3.6 Matrix Arithmetic

The following matrix operations are available in MATLAB:

```
Operator     Description          Operator     Description
============================================================
      +      addition                   '      transpose
      -      subtraction                \      left division
      *      multiplication             /      right division
      ^      power
============================================================
```

These matrix operations apply, of course, to scalars (one-by-one matrices) as well. If the sizes of the matrices are incompatible for the matrix operation, an error message will result, except in the case of scalar-matrix operations (for addition, subtraction, and division as well as for multiplication) in which case each entry of the matrix is operated on by the scalar.

Matrix Transpose

The transpose of a $m \times n$ matrix A is the $n \times m$ matrix obtained by interchanging the rows and columns of A. For example, the matrix transpose of

$$A = \begin{bmatrix} 1 & 2 & 3 & 4 \\ 5 & 6 & 7 & 8 \end{bmatrix} \quad \text{is} \quad A^T = \begin{bmatrix} 1 & 5 \\ 2 & 6 \\ 3 & 7 \\ 4 & 8 \end{bmatrix}$$

The matrix transpose is denoted A^T. In MATLAB, the transpose of a matrix is computed by following the matrix name with the single quote [apostrophe]. For example,

```
>> A = [ 1 2 3 4; 5 6 7 8 ];
>> A'
ans =
     1     5
     2     6
     3     7
     4     8
>>
```

We say that a square matrix A is "symmetric" if A = A^T, and it is "skew-symmetric" if A = $-A^T$.

Matrix Addition and Subtraction

If A is a $(m \times n)$ matrix and B is a $(r \times p)$ matrix, then the matrix sum C = A + B is defined only when $m = r$ and $n = p$ (see Figure 13.1a). The matrix sum is a $(m \times n)$ matrix C whose elements are

$$c_{ij} = a_{ij} + b_{ij} \tag{13.3}$$

for $i = 1, 2, \cdots m$ and $j = 1, 2, \cdots n$. For example, if

$$\text{A} = \begin{bmatrix} 2 & 1 \\ 4 & 6 \end{bmatrix}$$

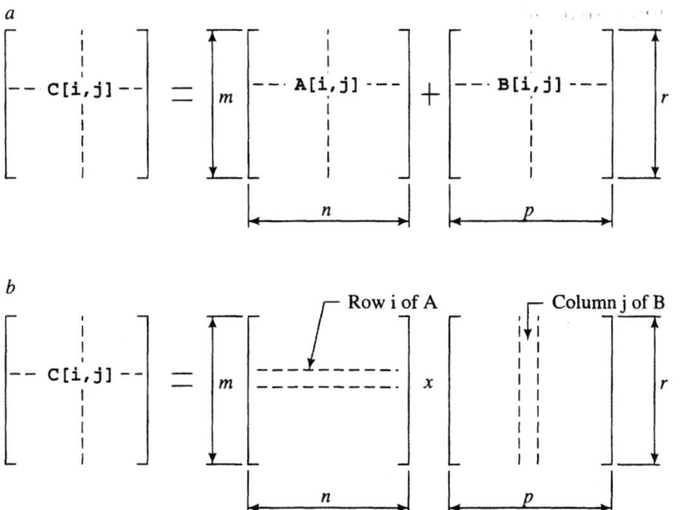

FIGURE 13.1 Schematics of (a) matrix addition and (b) matrix multiplication.

and

$$B = \begin{bmatrix} 4 & 2 \\ 0 & 1 \end{bmatrix}$$

then

$$C = A + B = \begin{bmatrix} 2 & 1 \\ 4 & 6 \end{bmatrix} + \begin{bmatrix} 4 & 2 \\ 0 & 1 \end{bmatrix} = \begin{bmatrix} 6 & 3 \\ 4 & 7 \end{bmatrix}$$

The MATLAB commands for this computation are

```
>> A = [ 2 1; 4 6 ];
>> B = [ 4 2; 0 1 ];
>> C = A + B
C =
      6     3
      4     7
>>
```

Matrix subtraction is identical to matrix addition, except that $c_{ij} = a_{ij} - b_{ij}$ for $i = 1, 2, \cdots m$ and $j = 1, 2, \cdots n$. The matrix addition and matrix subtraction operations require mn floating point operations (flops).

Dot Product

Let

$$X = [x_1 \quad x_2 \quad x_3 \quad \cdots \quad x_n]$$

be a row vector containing n elements and

$$Y = \begin{bmatrix} y_1 \\ y_2 \\ y_3 \\ \vdots \\ y_n \end{bmatrix}$$

be a column vector containing the same number of elements. The dot product, also sometimes called the scalar product or inner product, is a special case of matrix multiplication (see the next section) and is defined by

$$X * Y = \sum_{i=1}^{n} x_i \cdot y_i$$

For example, the dot product of row vector `X = [ 1, 2, 3, 4, 5 ]`, with its matrix transpose, can be computed in MATLAB by simply typing

```
>> X = [ 1, 2, 3, 4, 5 ];
>> Y = X';
>> X*Y
   ans =
        55
>>
```

The results of this computation can be easily verified by hand

```
X*Y = [ 1 2 3 4 5 ]*[ 1 2 3 4 5 ]'
    = 1*1 + 2*2 + 3*3 + 4*4 + 5*5
    = 1 + 4 + 9 + 16 + 25
    = 55
```

The dot product operation on two vectors containing n elements requires n floating point operations (flops).

Matrix Multiplication

Let `A` and `B` be $(m \times n)$ and $(r \times p)$ matrices, respectively. The matrix product $A \cdot B$ is defined only when interior matrix dimensions are the same (i.e., $n = r$).

The matrix product C = A · B is a $(m \times p)$ matrix whose elements are

$$c_{ij} = \sum_{k=1}^{n} a_{ik} b_{kj} \tag{13.4}$$

for $i = 1, 2, \cdots m$ and $j = 1, 2, \cdots n$. From a geometric point of view, c_{ij} is the dot product of the ith row of A with the jth column of B (see Figure 13.1b). Assuming that matrices A and B are as defined in the previous section:

$$\mathrm{C} = \mathrm{A} \cdot \mathrm{B} = \begin{bmatrix} 2 & 1 \\ 4 & 6 \end{bmatrix} \cdot \begin{bmatrix} 4 & 2 \\ 0 & 1 \end{bmatrix} = \begin{bmatrix} 2 \cdot 4 + 1 \cdot 0 & 2 \cdot 2 + 1 \cdot 1 \\ 4 \cdot 4 + 6 \cdot 0 & 4 \cdot 2 + 6 \cdot 1 \end{bmatrix} = \begin{bmatrix} 8 & 5 \\ 16 & 14 \end{bmatrix}$$

The MATLAB commands for this operation are

```
>> A = [ 2 1; 4 6 ];
>> B = [ 4 2; 0 1 ];
>> C = A*B
C =
       8     5
      16    14
>>
```

Computation of the matrix product requires $2mnp$ flops. When the dimensions of the matrices are approximately equal, then computational work is $2n^3$ flops.

Because the number of rows equals the number of columns in square matrices, square matrices can always be multiplied by themselves. The triple matrix product of

```
>> A = [ 2 1; 4 6 ];
```

can be evaluated by writing

```
>> A*A*A
ans =
      48    56
     224   272
>>
```

or by simply writing

```
>> A^3
ans =
      48     56
     224    272
>>
```

Example. A magic square is a square matrix that has equal sums along all its rows and columns. For example,

```
>> magic(4)
ans =
    16     2     3    13
     5    11    10     8
     9     7     6    12
     4    14    15     1
>> magic(4)
```

In this particular case, the elements of each row and column sum to 34. Now we can use matrix multiplication to check the "magic" property of magic squares:

```
>> A = magic(4);
>> b = ones(4,1);
>> A*b;              <== (4×1) matrix containing row sums.
>> v = ones(1,4);
>> v*A;              <== (1×4) matrix containing column sums.
```

Scalar Multiplication of Matrices

Scalars multiply matrices on an element-by-element basis. For example, with matrix `A` in place

```
>> 2*A                    % multiply elements of matrix "A" by "2".
ans =
     4     2
     8    12
>> A/4                    % right division of "A" by "4".
ans =
    0.5000    0.2500
    1.0000    1.5000
>> 4/A                    % left division of "A" by "4".
and =
    0.5000    0.2500
    1.0000    1.5000
>>
```

Matrix Division

Left and right division of matrices is a generalization of left and right division in variable arithmetic. Let `A` and `B` be two matrices. Right division of two matrices, written

```
>> A/B
```

corresponds to the solution of the linear matrix equations `A.X = B`. Similarly, left division of two matrices is written

```
>> A\B
```

and corresponds to the solution of the linear matrix equations `X.A = B`. We discuss the nature of these solutions in more detail in Chapter 15.

Matrix Inverse

The inverse of a square matrix `A`, denoted A^{-1}, is given by the solution to the matrix equations

$$A \cdot A^{-1} = A^{-1} \cdot A = I$$

In MATLAB, A^{-1} can be computed with `inv(A)`.

Arithmetic on Submatrices

MATLAB provides for the computation of arithmetic operations on submatrices. Suppose that matrix `A` is

```
>> A = [  1   2   3   4   5   6;
          7   8   9  10  11  12;
         13  14  15  16  17  18;
         19  20  21  22  23  24  ];
>>
```

Columns 2 and 4 of `A` can be multiplied on the right by the two-by-two matrix `[1 2;3 4];`

```
>> A(:,[2,4]) = A(:,[2,4])*[1 2;3 4]
A =
     1    14     3    20     5     6
     7    38     9    56    11    12
    13    62    15    92    17    18
    19    86    21   128    23    24
>>
```

Matrix `A` is altered and printed.

13.3.7 Matrix Element Level Operations

MATLAB has a special convention whereby a dot positioned in front of the arithmetic operations listed in the upper half of Table 13.2 will force entry-by-entry computation of the matrix operation. By definition, the matrix addition and matrix subtraction operations are already computed on an element-by-element basis; matrix operations such as multiplication and left and right matrix division, however, are not. The best way of seeing how this works is to simply walk through a couple of examples.

Example. We start with

```
>> [1,2,3,4].*[1,2,3,4]
  ans =
         1      4      9     16
>>
```

Here the expression `[1,2,3,4].*[1,2,3,4]` evaluates to

```
[1,2,3,4].*[1,2,3,4]  ==>  [ 1*1 ,2*2 ,3*3 ,4*4 ]
                      ==>  [   1 ,  4 ,  9 , 16 ].
```

The same result can be obtained with `[1,2,3,4].^2`. Similarly, the expression

```
>> [1,2,3,4]./[1,2,3,4]
ans =
      1      1      1      1
>>
```

evaluates to a vector of 1s.

Example. Suppose that we wish to verify $\sin(x)^2 + \cos(x)^2 = 1$ for a variety of argument values x. The block of code

```
>> x = [ -pi : pi/4 : pi ];
```

creates a one-by-nine array x containing values that range from $-\pi$ to π in increments of $\pi/4$. The command

```
>>  sin(x).^2 + cos(x).^2
```

generates the output

```
ans =
      1     1     1     1     1     1     1     1     1
>>
```

The order of evaluation is as follows. First, one-by-nine matrices are computed for $\sin(x)$ and $\cos(x)$. Element-level operations square each element in $\sin(x)$ and then each element in $\cos(x)$. The output is simply the sum of the latter two matrices.

13.4 CONTROL STRUCTURES

Control of flow in the MATLAB programming language is achieved with logical expressions, branching constructs for the selection of a solution procedure pathway, and a variety of looping constructs for the efficient computation of repetitious operations.

13.4.1 Logical Expressions

In MATLAB, a logical expression involves the use of relational and logical operands for the comparison of variables and matrices of the same size. Table 13.6 summarizes the six relational operators and three logical operators in the MATLAB programming language.

Relational operators allow for the comparison of variables, and matrices of the same size. In the case of variable comparisons, the outcome will be 1 if the comparison is true, and 0 otherwise. Indeed in MATLAB, as in other languages such as C and Java, true is represented by a nonzero integer (usually one) and false is represented by zero. To see how this works in practice, we look at the script of code

```
>> 3 < 5
  ans =
        1
>> a = 3 == 5
    a =
        0
>>
```

TABLE 13.6 Summary of Relational and Logical Operators

Relational Operators

Operator	*Description*
<	Less than
>	Greater than
<=	Less than or equal
>=	Greater than or equal
==	Equal
~=	Not equal

Logical Operators

Operator	*Description*	*Precedence*
^	Not	1
&	And	2
|	Or	3

In the first example, 3 is less than 5, so the result of the relational expression is true (i.e., 1). The second example contains both an assignment "=" operator and an equality "==" operator. Because the precedence of evaluation for the "==" operator is higher than the assignment operator, the relational comparison is made first, and then the result is assigned to variable a. In this particular case, 3 is not equal to 5, and so variable a assumes a value of 0 (i.e., false).

When relational operands are applied to matrices of the same size, as in

```
>> A = [ 1 2; 3 4 ];
>> B = [ 6 7; 8 9 ];
>> A == B
  ans =
         0     0
         0     0
>> A < B
  ans =
         1     1
         1     1
>>
```

the result will be a matrix of 0s and 1s giving the value of the relationship between corresponding entries.

Logical expressions can be combined by using the logical operands, and, or, and not (see the lower half of Table 13.6). The following table shows how the logical operators can be combined.

A	B	A & B	A | B	~A
True	True	True	True	False
True	False	False	True	False
False	True	False	True	True
False	False	False	False	True

Logical operands also apply to matrices of the same size. In the script

```
>> A = [ 1 2; 3 4 ];
>> B = [ 6 7; 8 9 ];
>> A & B
ans =
     1     1
     1     1
>>
```

all the matrix elements in ans evaluate to 1 because matrices A and B contain only nonzero matrix elements.

MATLAB also has an ensemble of built-in functions for the evaluation of

TABLE 13.7 Logical Functions in MATLAB

Function	*Description*
`any(x)`	For vector arguments `x`, `any(x)` returns 1 if any of the elements of `x` are nonzero. Otherwise, `any(x)` returns 0. When `x` is a matrix argument, `any(x)` operates on the columns of `x`, returning a row vectors of 1s and 0s.
`all(x)`	For vector arguments `x`, `all(x)` returns 1 if all the elements of the vector are nonzero. Otherwise, it returns 0. For matrix arguments `x`, `all(x)` operates on the columns of `x`, returning a row vector of 1s and 0s.
`find (x)`	This function finds the indices of the nonzero elements of `x`. The function argument can be combined with logical and relational expressions.
`isnan (x)`	`isnan(x)` returns is where the elements of `x` are `NaN`s and 0s where they are not. Recall that `NaN` means "Not a Number."
`finite (x)`	`finite(x)` returns is where the elements of `x` are finite and 0s where they are not.
`isempty(x)`	In MATLAB, an empty matrix has a zero size in at least one dimension. `isempty(x)` returns 1 if `x` is an empty matrix and 0 otherwise.

logical expressions involving matrices. A summary of their capabilities is given in Table 13.7.

13.4.2 Selection Constructs

Generally speaking, a selection construct enables the details of a program's problem-solving procedure to be tied to the evaluation of one or more logical expressions. The following diagram shows the syntax for three commonly used selection constructs in the MATLAB programming language:

```
If-end construct
================
if < condition1 >,
   < program1 >
end;
```

```
If-else-end construct
=====================
if < condition1 >,
   < program1 >
else
   < program2 >
end;
```

```
If-elseif-end construct
=======================
if < condition1 >,
   < program1 >
elseif < condition2 >,
   < program2 >
elseif < condition3 >
   < program3 >

.....

elseif < conditionN >
   < programN >
end;
```

In each of these constructs, the block of statements `<program1>` will be executed when the logical expression `<condition1>` evaluates to true. Otherwise, the program control moves to the next program construction. For the leftmost construct, this means the end of the selection construct. For the if-else-end construct, the block of statements <program2> will be executed when <condition1> evaluates to false. For example, in the block of statements

```
>> a = 2; b = 1;
>> if a < b,
      c = 3;
   else
      c = 4;
   end;
>> c
   c =
        4
>>
```

the logical expression a $<$ b evaluates to false, thereby causing the second block of program statements to be executed.

Another variation is the "if-elseif-end" construct. MATLAB will systematically evaluate the sequence of logical expressions <condition1>, <condition2> · · · <conditionN> until one evaluates to true. After the corresponding block of <program> statements has been executed, the program control will jump to the end of the "if-elseif-end" construct.

13.4.3 Looping Constructs

MATLAB provides a number of looping constructs for the efficient computation of similar calculations. The syntax for the `while` and `for` looping constructs is

```
While-loop construct                 For-loop construct
====================                 ==================

while < condition1 >,                for i = <array of values>
    < program1 >                           < program1 >
end                                  end
```

In the while looping construct, the block of statements <program1> will be executed while the logical expression <condition1> evaluates to true. For example, the following script

```
A "while looping" construct          Iteration No   i     i < 4     y
===========================          ==================================

>> i = 2;                                       1   2      true     8
>> while ( i < 4 ),                             2   3      true    12
      y = 4*i,                                  3   4     false
      i = i + 1,
   end
>>
```

shows a simple while loop and an analysis of the values involved in the looping construct.

In the for looping construct, the block of statements `<program1>` will be executed for each of the vectors `i` defined by the column elements in `<array>`. For example, the looping construct

```
A "for looping" construct            Iteration No     i      c
=========================            =========================

>> for i = [2,4,5,6,10],                        1      2      4
       c = 2*i                                  2      4      8
   end                                          3      5     10
>>                                              4      6     12
                                                5     10     20
```

executes five times. The values for the variable `i` during execution are successively `2`, `4`, `5`, `6`, and `10`. When `<array>` is a two-dimensional matrix, the values of `i` will be vectors corresponding to the matrix columns of `<array>`. For example, an extension of our previous example is

```
A "for looping" construct        Iteration No        i           c
=========================        ===================================

>> for i = [ 2 4 5 6 10;
             1 2 3 4  5 ],                 1   [  2 1]'    [ 4    2 ]'
       c = 2*i                             2   [  4 2]'    [ 8    4]'
   end                                     3   [  5 3]'    [ 10   6 ]'
>>                                         4   [  6 4]'    [ 12   8 ]'
                                           5   [ 10 5],    [ 20 10 ]'
```

Looping constructs may be nested of course. Here is an example of the contents of a matrix being initialized inside a nested for loop:

```
MATLAB source code                i       j                A(i,j)
======================         ======================================

>> for i=1:2,                     1       1       A(1,1)  = 1/1 = 1.0
      for j=1:2,                  1       2       A(1,2)  = 1/2 = 0.5
          A(i,j)  = i/j;          2       1       A(2,1)  = 2/1 = 2.0
      end                         2       2       A(2,2)  = 2/2 = 1.0
   end
>>
```

There are actually two loops here, with one nested inside the other; they define A(1,1), A(1,2), A(2,1), and A(2,2) in that order.

Programming Tip. Looping constructs in the MATLAB programming language need to be used with care. The first potential problem is with `while` loops and the implicit danger of the program control becoming trapped inside a loop because `<condition1>` never evaluates to false.

A second important issue is performance. Generally speaking, MATLAB code written with the `for` and `while` looping constructs will execute much slower than if MATLAB's implied looping constructs are employed. For example, the block of MATLAB code

```
>> x = [ 0 : 0.1 : 2.0 ];
>> y = zeros(1,21);
>> for i = 1:21,
         y(i) = sin(x(i));
   end
>>
```

will have faster execution if it is simply written

```
>> x = [ 0 : 0.1 : 2.0 ];
>> y = sin(x);
```

This is because the former looping constructs are interpreted, and MATLAB's implied looping constructs are executed as a low-level compiled code.

13.5 GENERAL-PURPOSE MATRIX FUNCTIONS

MATLAB has an ensemble of built-in matrix functions that are useful for general-purpose engineering and scientific computations.

13.5.1 Sorting the Contents of a Matrix

When `x` is a matrix, `sort(x)` sorts each column of `x` in ascending order. For example,

```
>> x = [  1   3   4;
          5  -4  16;
         -4  -8 -10 ];
>> sort(x)
ans =
    -4    -8   -10
     1    -4     4
     5     3    16
>>
```

sort(x) also returns an index matrix i, containing a mapping between elements in the x matrix and the y (sorted) matrix. For example,

```
>> [ y, i ] = sort(x)
y =
    -4    -8   -10
     1    -4     4
     5     3    16
i =
     3     3     3
     1     2     1
     2     1     2
>>
```

In colon notation y(:,j) = x(i(:,j),j). Hence, by walking down the first column of the index matrix i, we see that matrix elements x(3,1), x(1,1), and x(2,1) have increasing values.

13.5.2 Summation of Matrix Contents

When x is a vector, sum(x) returns the sum of the elements of x. When x is a matrix, sum(x) returns a row vector with the sum over each column. For example,

```
>> sum ( [  1   3   4;
            5  -4  16;
           -4  -8 -10 ] )
ans =
            2  -9  10
>>
```

Watch out for this function being used in statistical analysis of experimental data and least squares analysis.

13.5.3 Maximum/Minimum Matrix Contents

The MATLAB function max(A) returns the maximum element in vector A, and min(A) returns the minimum element in vector A. When A is a matrix, max(A) will return a row vector containing the maximum value in each column of A. Similarly, min(A) will return a row vector containing the minimum value in each column of A. For example, the script of code

```
>> A = [ 1 2 3 4; 5 6 7 8 ];
>> max (A)
ans =
     5     6     7     8
```

```
>> min (A)
ans =
     1     2     3     4
>>
```

shows how the maximum and minimum values of each column of A are computed.

Some MATLAB functions can return more than one value. In the case of max, the interpreter returns the maximum value and also the column index where the maximum value occurs. For example, the script of code

```
>> [m, i] = max(A)
m =
     5     6     7     8
i =
     2     2     2     2
>>
```

shows how the maximum value in each column of A is located at index 2.

13.5.4 Random Numbers

The MATLAB function rand returns numbers and matrices of numbers containing elements that are uniformly distributed between zero and one. Theoretical considerations indicate that the average value of these elements should be close to 0.5.

For example, the function call rand(3) will return a three-by-three matrix with random entries. The function call

```
>> A = rand(10,30);
```

generates a 10-by-30 matrix of elements uniformly distributed between zero and one, and assigns the result to matrix A. The average value of the matrix elements can be computed by simply writing

```
>> average = sum(sum(A))/300
average =
    0.5059
>>
```

In the nested function call sum(sum(A)), the sum of the elements in each matrix column is computed, and then the sum of the matrix column sums is evaluated. In the previous example, the number of elements in matrix A is 300.

The function randn generates matrices with elements chosen from a normal distribution with mean 0.0 and variance 1.0.

The mean value and scatter of uniform and normally distributed random numbers may be adjusted by multiplying the contents of rand and randn by suitable linear transformations. For example, to obtain a 3-by-5 matrix of elements uniformly distributed between −1 and 1, we can simply write

```
>> B = 2*rand(3,5) - ones(3,5)
B =
   -0.1650    0.8609   -0.8161    0.4024   -0.4751
    0.3735    0.6923    0.3078    0.8206   -0.9051
    0.1780    0.0539   -0.1680    0.5244    0.4722
>>
```

Sequences of random numbers will be generated when the functions `rand` and `randn` are called repeatedly. Sequences of random numbers that are repeatable—in other words, the same sequence of random numbers will be the same each time the MATLAB program is executed—can be generated by initializing a seed number. The syntax is

```
>> rand  ('seed', n );
>> randn ('seed', n );
```

where `n` is the seed number (greater than unity). Further information on initializing sequences of random numbers in MATLAB can be obtained by typing `help rand`.

13.6 PROGRAM DEVELOPMENT WITH M-FILES

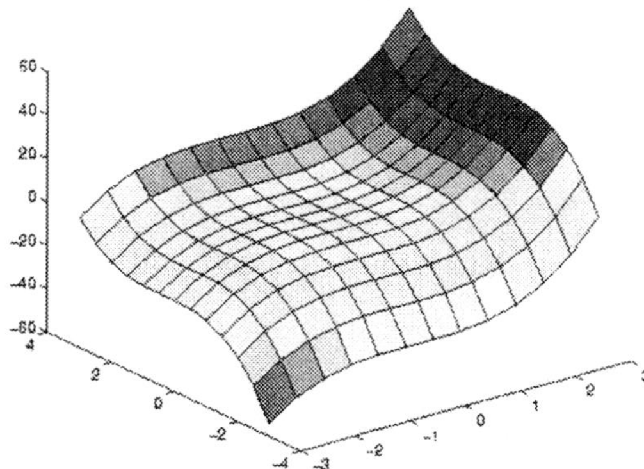

We have so far assumed in this tutorial that all MATLAB commands will be typed in at the keyboard. Practical considerations dictate that this mode of operation is suitable only for the specification of the smallest problems, perhaps a handful of MATLAB commands or less. A much better problem-solving approach is to use a text editor to write the commands in an M-file, and then ask MATLAB to read and execute the commands listed in the M-file.

This section describes two types of M-files. Script M-files correspond to a main program in programming languages such as C. Function M-files correspond to a subprogram or user-written function in programming languages such as C. An M-file can reference other M-files, including referencing itself recursively.

13.6.1 M-File Preparation

UNIX Platforms

In a UNIX environment, a standard text editor can be used to prepare the contents of an M-file. The M-file should be located in the same directory as the MATLAB program. After the M-file has been created and saved, the list of commands inside the M-file can be executed by moving to the MATLAB window and typing the M-file name without the `.m` extension. To be more precise, suppose that we create a program file

```
myfile.m
```

in the MATLAB language. The commands in this file can be executed by simply typing the command `myfile` at the MATLAB prompt. The MATLAB statements will run like any other MATLAB function. You do not need to compile the program since MATLAB is an interpretative (not compiled) language.

UNIX commands can be invoked from inside the MATLAB environment by preceding the command by a `!` (e.g., `!ls` will list the files located in the current working directory).

Macintosh and PC Environments

An M-file can be prepared in a Mac/PC environment by clicking on `new` in the file menu. A new window will appear. After the list of commands has been typed into the file, it can be saved by clicking on `save as` in the edit menu. The file can be executed from the command window by typing the M-file name without the `.M` extension. A second pathway in the Macintosh environment is to click on `save and go` in the file menu.

13.6.2 Script M-Files

Suppose that we use our favorite text editor to create a file called `sketch.m`, containing

```
[x y] = meshgrid(-3:.5:3, -3:.5:3);
z = x.^3 + y.^3 + x.^2 - y.^2
surf(x,y,z);
```

Without getting into too many details on MATLAB graphics at this point, the first two lines generate a rectangular grid of `x,y,z` points in a format suitable for a three-dimensional MATLAB plot. The function call `surf(x,y,z)` asks MATLAB to generate a surface plot. The simple command

```
>> sketch
```

will force MATLAB to open the file `sketch.m` and systematically execute the sequence of commands within. The result, shown at the top of Section 13.6, will be the same as if you had entered the three lines of the file at the prompt.

13.6.3 Function M-Files

Function files provide extensibility to MATLAB by allowing you to create new problem-specific functions having the same status as other built-in MATLAB functions. Unlike some other traditional programming languages, each function file contains one function. Functions are like scripts, but for the purposes of enhancing computational speed, are compiled into a low-level bytecode when called for the first time.

Square Root Calculation

In this section, we develop a MATLAB function file called `sqroot.m` to compute the square root of a positive number `N` via the recursive relationship

$$x_{n+1} = \frac{1}{2} \cdot \left[x_n + \frac{N}{x_n} \right] \tag{13.5}$$

A good initial estimate of the square root is $x_o = N/2$. The program uses the criterion

$$\left| \frac{x_{n+1} - x_n}{x_n} \right| \le \varepsilon \tag{13.6}$$

for a test on convergence, where ε is a very small number. In our implementation, ε is taken as `eps`, the floating point precision for the computer being used (see Table 13.1).

PROGRAM 13.1: SQUARE ROOT CALCULATION

```
function sqroot(x)
% SQROOT Compute square root by Newton's method

% Check that value of function argument is greater or equal to zero.

  if x <= 0,
     error('In sqroot() : argument x must be positive');
  end;
```

```
% Initial guess

  xstart = x/2;

% Iteration loop to compute square root

  for i = 1:100
      xnew = ( xstart + x/xstart)/2;      % new estimate of square root.
      disp(xnew);                         % print xnew.
      if abs(xnew - xstart)/xnew < eps,   % check convergence of iterations.
         break,
      end;
         xstart = xnew;                   % update estimate of square root.
 end
```

When MATLAB executes a function M-file for the first time, it will open the appropriate text M-file and compile the function into a low-level representation that will be stored within MATLAB. For those cases where an M-file function references other M-file functions, they will also be compiled and placed in MATLAB's memory.

The command sequence

```
>> format long
>> format compact
>> sqroot(20)
```

loads the contents of `sqroot.m` into MATLAB memory and then computes the square root of 20 by iteration

```
>> sqroot(20)
     6
    4.66666666666667
    4.47619047619048
    4.47213779128673
    4.47213595499996
    4.47213595499958
    4.47213595499958
>>
```

A function M-file will terminate its execution when either a `return` statement is encountered or, as is the case in this example, an end-of-file (EOF) is reached.

The first line of Program 13.1 contains declarations for the function name, `sqroot`, and its input argument(s). Without this line the file would simply be a script file. MATLAB requires that M-file functions be stored in files having the same name (i.e., the function `sqroot` must be stored in an M-file called `sqroot.m`).

Your MATLAB programs should contain lots of comments telling the reader in plain English what is occurring. Some day that reader will be you, and you will wonder what you did. Comment lines up to the first noncomment line in a function M-file are the help text returned when you request online help. For Program 13.1, this means

```
>>  help sqroot

   SQROOT Compute square root by Newton's method
>>
```

We also urge you to use the indented style that you have seen in the previous programs. It makes the programs easier to read, the program syntax easier to check, and forces you to think in terms of building your programs in blocks.

Matrices and variables in a function file have scope that is local by default. The `sqroot` function is simple enough that all the relevant details can be handled with `x`, `xstart`, and `xnew`. The statement `disp( xnew )` displays the matrix `xnew` as text, without printing the matrix name.

Error messages play an important role in nearly all computer programs since they help you debug future programs. Because the algorithm in Program 13.1 can only compute the square root of positive floating point numbers, we need to check that `sqroot()` is called with a positive argument. The block of MATLAB code

```
if x <= 0,
   error('In sqroot() : argument x must be positive');
end;
```

prints an error message when argument `x` is negative. For example, the script of code

```
>> sqroot(-4)
Error using ==> sqroot
In sqroot() : argument x must be positive
>>
```

tries to compute the square root of −4. The function `error()` displays the message enclosed within single quotes and causes an exit from the M-file to the keyboard.

Variations on Standard Use

It is also important to bear in mind that our implementation of `sqroot()` is very minimal. As already demonstrated, function calls of the type `sqroot(20)` are possible. However, we want the ability to integrate function calls into expressions involving matrices. This can be done by changing the function declaration to

```
function [y] = sqroot(x)
```

Now expressions of the type

```
>> x = 3.5 * sqroot ( 10000 )
x =
        350
>>
```

are possible.

Statistics of Experimental Data

In this example, we show how the mean and standard deviation of an array of experimental data can be computed inside a single MATLAB function. Suppose that

$$x = [x_1, x_2, x_3, \cdot\ \cdot\ \cdot\ x_N]^T \tag{13.7}$$

is a column vector of data points collected in an experiment. The mean value of the data points is given by

$$\mu_x = \frac{1}{N}\left[\sum_{i=1}^{N} x_i\right] \tag{13.8}$$

and the standard deviation by

$$\sigma_x = \left[\sum_{i=1}^{N} \frac{[x_i - \mu_x]^2}{N}\right]^{1/2} = \left[\frac{1}{N}\sum_{i=1}^{N} [x_i^2] - \mu_x^2\right]^{1/2} \tag{13.9}$$

For the case where an experiment generates a two-dimensional array of experimental data, Equations 13.8 and 13.9 can be applied to each column in the two-dimensional matrix.

PROGRAM 13.2: STATISTICS OF EXPERIMENTAL DATA

```
function  [mean, stdev] = stat(x)

% STAT  Mean and standard deviation
%       For a vector x, stat(x) returns the
%       mean and standard deviation of  x.
%       For a matrix x, stat(x) returns two row vectors containing,
%       respectively, the mean and standard deviation of each column.

 [m   n] = size(x);

if m == 1
   m = n;      % handle case of a row vector
end

mean   = sum(x)/m;
stdev  = sqrt(sum(x.^ 2)/m - mean.^2);
```

The first line of Program 13.2 tells MATLAB that function `stat` will accept an array argument and return a one-by-two matrix containing the mean and standard deviation of the experimental data points. Notice that `mean` and `stdev` are both computed inside the function body.

As indicated in the documentation for Program 13.2, when `x` is a row or column vector, `stat(x)` returns the mean and standard deviation of `x`. For a general matrix `x`, `stat(x)` returns two row vectors containing, respectively, the mean and standard deviation of each column. With Program 13.2 placed in the M-file `stat.m`, the MATLAB commands

```
>> y = [1:10];
>> [ym, yd] = stat(y)

  ym =
         5.5000
  yd =
         2.8723
>>
```

compute the mean and standard deviation of the integers 1 through 10. The mean and standard deviation of the entries in the vector `y` are assigned to `ym` and `yd`, respectively.

Variations on Standard Use

Two variations on the standard use of `stat.m` are possible. First, single assignments can also be made with a function having multiple output arguments. For example,

```
>> xm = stat(x)
```

(no brackets needed around `xm`) will assign the mean of `x` to `xm`. In this case, the standard deviation of `x` will be lost. Second, when `x` is a two-dimensional matrix, `stat(x)` will return the matrices containing mean and standard deviation of each column in `x`. For example, when

```
>> x = [ 1 2; 3 4; 5 6 ];
```

`stat(x)` gives

```
>> [ xm, xstd ] = stat(x);
>> xm
xm =
     3     4
>> xstd
xstd =
    1.6330    1.6330
>>
```

Programming Tip Generally speaking, function M-files are more difficult to debug than script M-files because you cannot use MATLAB to print the value of variables inside the function. We therefore suggest that you develop function files first as script files and then once the script file works properly, encapsulate the script inside a function declaration with appropriate arguments and comment statements.

13.6.4 Handling Name Conflicts

Suppose that we do not know `sum` is a built-in function and type the MATLAB statement

```
>> x = 1;
>> y = 2;
>> z = 3;
>> sum = x + y + z;
```

with the intent of using `sum` to represent the sum of values stored by the variables `x`, `y`, and `z`. The name `sum` now represents a variable and MATLAB's built-in `sum` function is hidden (you can check this with the command `who`).

When a name is typed at the prompt or used in an arithmetic expression, the MATLAB interpreter evaluates the name by systematically walking through four steps

1. It looks to see if the name is a variable.
2. It looks to see if the name is a built-in function.
3. It looks in the current directory to see if the name matches a script file (e.g., `sum.m`).
4. It looks in the MATLAB search path for a script file matching the name (e.g., `sum.m`). Clearing the variable `sum` (i.e., by typing `clear sum`) reactivates the built-in function `sum`.

13.7 ENGINEERING APPLICATIONS

Now that we are familiar with MATLAB's matrix and M-file capabilities, we work step by step through the design and implementation of four programs. They are

1. A MATLAB program that computes and plots the relationship between Fahrenheit and Celsius temperature. This program is the graphical counterpart of Problem 3.2 in the C tutorial and is similar to Program 19.3 in the Java tutorial.
2. A MATLAB program that computes and plots the time–history response (i.e., "displacement versus time" and "velocity versus time") of an undamped single degree of freedom (SDOF) oscillator. This example is similar to Program 19.4 in the Java tutorial.
3. A MATLAB program that will prompt a user for the coefficients in a quadratic

equation, and then compute and print the roots. Functionally equivalent implementations of this problem in C and Java can be found in Programs 7.1 and 18.3, respectively.

4. A MATLAB program that reads experimental data from a data file, and then computes and plots a histogram of the data. The mean and standard deviation of the experimental data are computed with `stat.m` (see Section 13.6). This program is similar to Program 12.1 in the C tutorial (also see Problem 12.5).

A key issue in the design of almost every MATLAB program is the problem of finding a good balance among the use of user-defined code and built-in MATLAB library functions. The advantages of user-defined functions are that they enable the development of customized problem-solving procedures. However, writing and testing user-defined code can be a very time-consuming process. Library functions have the benefit of enabling reuse of code that has already been written and thoroughly tested. A judicious use of library functions can result in significant reductions in the time and effort needed to write and test MATLAB programs.

Obtaining a good balance in the use of user-defined code and library functions requires experience and, to some extent, is an art. This means that novice MATLAB programmers must place a priority on becoming familiar with the availability and purposes of library functions.

13.7.1 Temperature Conversion Program

Problem Statement

The relationship between temperature measured in Fahrenheit (T_f) and temperature Celsius (T_c) is given by the equation

$$T_f = \frac{9}{5} T_c + 32 \tag{13.10}$$

Write an M-file that computes and plots the temperature conversion relationship for the range −50 through 100 degrees Celsius.

In addition to having a suitable title, the vertical and horizontal axes of your graph should be properly labeled. See, for example, Figure 13.2.

Pseudocode

We begin our implementation with the observation that Equation 13.10 is linear. It follows that the temperature conversion relationship can be plotted by simply drawing a straight line between the (T_c, T_f) coordinates evaluated at $T_c = -50$ and $T_c = 100$. The pseudocode for this problem is

```
allocate two-by-one arrays to hold the Celsius and
Fahrenheit temperatures.

set the Celsius array values to -50 and 100 degrees.
compute the Fahrenheit temperatures.
```

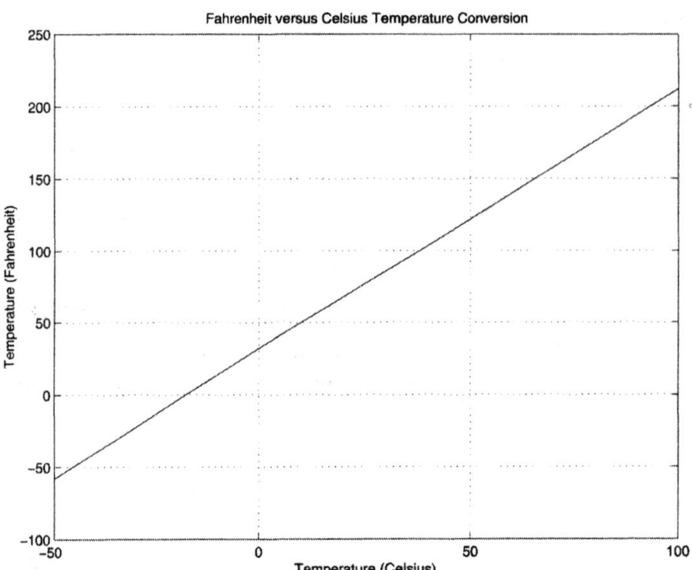

FIGURE 13.2 Fahrenheit versus Celsius.

```
plot the array values.
label the horizontal/vertical axes.
add a plot title.
```

Program Source Code

Here is the program source code.

PROGRAM 13.3: TEMPERATURE CONVERSION PROGRAM

```
% =====================================================================
% temperature.m -- Compute and plot a graph of Celsius versus Fahrenheit
%                  for the range -50 through 100 degrees Celsius.
%
% Written By : Mark Austin                                   March 1997
% =====================================================================

% Allocate arrays for Celsius and Fahrenheit temperatures.

  tempC = zeros(2);
  tempF = zeros(2);

% Compute temperatures at graph end-points.

  tempC(1)  = -50; tempF(1)  = 9*tempC(1)/5 + 32;
  tempC(2)  = 100; tempF(2)  = 9*tempC(2)/5 + 32;
```

```
% Plot and label the graph

  plot( tempC, tempF );
  grid;
  xlabel('Temperature (Celsius)');
  ylabel('Temperature (Fahrenheit)');
  title ('Fahrenheit versus Celsius Temperature Conversion');
```

Running the Program

As indicated in the block of comment statements at the top of the source code, Program 13.3 is stored in the M-file `temperature.m`. The command

```
>> temperature
```

executes the script file and generates Figure 13.2.

Program Architecture

Table 13.8 shows how key tasks in the problem statement have been mapped to user-defined MATLAB code and function calls in MATLAB. As already mentioned, all the user-defined MATLAB code is located in the script M-file `temperature.m`. A variety of built-in MATLAB functions are employed for the matrix allocation and to generate the graph.

Analysis of the MATLAB Code

The Celsius and Fahrenheit temperature values are stored in the arrays `tempC` and `tempF`, respectively. Once array `tempC` has been initialized, the contents of `tempF` are evaluated via Equation 13.10. The command

```
plot( tempC, tempF );
```

TABLE 13.8 Mapping of Tasks to MATLAB Code

Tasks	*	*User-Defined Code*	*MATLAB Library*
Define arrays `tempC` and `tempF`.	*	In `temperature.m`	`zeros()`
	*		
Initialize `tempC`.	*	In `temperature.m`	
Compute `tempF`.	*	In `temperature.m`	
	*		
Plot `tempF` versus `tempC`.	*	In `temperature.m`	`plot()`
Add a grid to the plot.	*		`grid`
Label the horizontal axis.	*		`xlabel()`
Label the vertical axis.	*		`ylabel()`
Add a plot title.	*		`title()`

creates a linear plot of array `tempF` versus `tempC`. The contents of `tempC` are the data points along the horizontal axis. The data points along the vertical axis are stored in `tempF`. The command `grid` adds a grid to the plot. Labels along the horizontal and vertical axes, and a plot title, are added to the figure with the three commands

```
xlabel('Temperature (Celsius)');
ylabel('Temperature (Fahrenheit)');
title('Fahrenheit versus Celsius Temperature Conversion');
```

13.7.2 Free Vibration Response of Undamped Single Degree of Freedom System

Problem Statement

The free vibration response of an undamped single degree of freedom (SDOF) oscillator is given by

$$y(t) = y(0)\cos(wt) + \frac{v(0)}{w}\sin(wt) \tag{13.11}$$

where t is time (seconds), and m and k and the mass and stiffness of the system, respectively. $y(t)$ and $v(t)$ are the displacement and velocity of the system at time t. By definition, $w = \sqrt{(k/m)}$ is the circular natural frequency of the system.

Write an M-file that will compute and plot the "displacement versus time" [i.e., $y(t)$ versus t] and "velocity versus time" [i.e., $v(t)$ versus t] for the time interval 0 through 10 seconds when mass, $m = 1$ and stiffness, $k = 10$. The initial displacement and velocity are $y(0) = 10$ and $v(0) = 10$, respectively. To ensure that your plot will be reasonably smooth, choose an increment in your displacement and velocity calculations that is no larger than 1/20th of the system period $T = 2\pi\sqrt{(m/k)}$.

Pseudocode

We begin our analysis by noting that $v(t)$ is simply the derivative of the displacement with respect to time. Hence, in mathematical terms,

$$v(t) = \frac{dy(t)}{dt} = -y(0)w\sin(wt) + v(0)\cos(wt) \tag{13.12}$$

Since neither $y(t)$ nor $v(t)$ are linear functions, we implement our solution in three stages. First, a two-dimensional array will be allocated for the system response storage. Components of the system response [i.e., $y(t)$ and $v(t)$] will then be computed and stored in the array columns. Finally, the array contents will be plotted. The pseudocode for this problem is

```
define number of points, ''npoints'', for plotting.

setup array response (npoints,3) for storing t, y(t), and v(t).
    column 1 will store the time values
    column 2 will store the system displacement
    column 3 will store the system velocity
```

```
define problem parameters
    sdof mass "m"
    sdof stiffness "stiff"
    time increment 'dt' for plotting purposes.
    initial displacement "x0"
    initial velocity "v0"

for i = 1 to npoints
    column 1 of array = time t = (i-1)*dt;
    column 2 of array = y(t)
    column 3 of array = v(t)
end loop

plot y(t) versus t for t = 0 to 10 seconds.
hold the plot.
plot v(t) versus t for t = 0 to 10 seconds.

add a grid to the plot.
label the horizontal/vertical axes.
add a plot title.
```

Notice how certain statements have been indented to show the structure of the eventual program. Once preliminary ideas are written this way the steps can be refined until the pseudocode is very close to the target language.

The fidelity of the system response evaluation is controlled by the variable `npoints`. In addition to using several arrays for storage and plotting purposes, the pseudocode employs a looping construct for the systematic evaluation of the system response at regular intervals between $t = 0$ and $t = 10$ seconds.

Program Source Code

Here is the program source code.

PROGRAM 13.4: FREE VIBRATION RESPONSE OF UNDAMPED SDOF SYSTEM

```
% ===================================================================
% sdof.m -- Compute dynamic response of sdof system.
%
% Written By: Mark Austin                                 March 1997
% ===================================================================

% Setup array for storing and plotting system response

  nopoints = 501;
  response = zeros(nopoints,3);
```

```
% Problem parameters and initial conditions

  mass  = 1;
  stiff = 10;
  w     = sqrt(stiff/mass);
  dt    = 0.02;

  disp10     =  1;
  velocity0 = 10;

% Compute displacement and velocity time history response

  for i = 1 : nopoints
      time = (i-1)*dt;
      response(i,1) = time;
      response(i,2) =  disp10*cos(w*time)    + velocity0/w*sin(w*time);
      response(i,3) = -disp10*w*sin(w*time) + velocity0*cos(w*time);
  end

% Plot displacement versus time

  plot(response(:,1), response(:,2));
  hold;

% Plot velocity versus time

  plot(response(:,1), response(:,3));

  grid;
  xlabel('Time (seconds)');
  ylabel('Displacement (m) and Velocity (m/sec)');
  title('Time-History Response for SDOF Oscillator');
```

Running the Program

Assume Program 13.4 is stored in the script M-file `sdof.m`. The command

```
>> sdof
```

generates the curves shown in Figure 13.3.

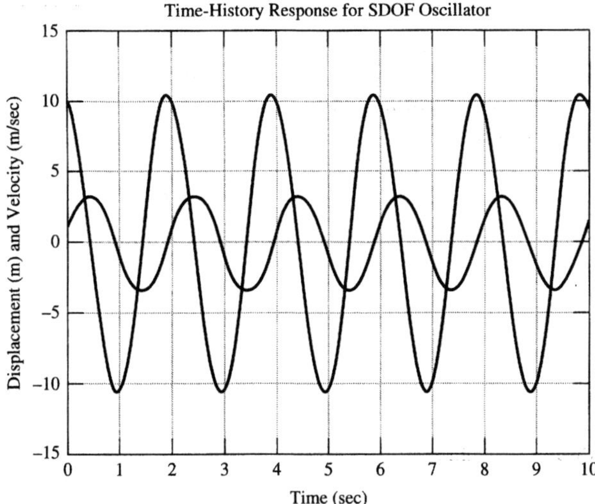

FIGURE 13.3 Time–history response of SDOF oscillator.

How do we know that these graphs are correct? From a mathematical viewpoint, we expect that the natural period of this system will be

```
T = 2*pi*sqrt(m/k) = 6.282/sqrt(10) = 2.0 seconds
```

A quick visual inspection of Figure 13.3 reveals that both $y(t)$ and $v(t)$ oscillate with a natural period of 2 seconds (the time-step increment, $dt = 0.02$ sec, easily satisfies the stated criteria for a smooth graph). The second point to notice is that at $t = 0$ seconds, the displacement and velocity graphs both match the stated initial conditions. Moreover, you should observe that because the initial velocity is greater than zero, we expect the $y(t)$ curve to initially increase. It does. A final point to note is the relationship between the displacement and velocity. When the oscillator displacement is at either its maximum or minimum value, the mass will be at rest for a short time. In mathematical terms, peak values in the displacement curve correspond to zero values in the velocity curve.

Program Architecture

The left- and right-hand sides of Table 13.9 show how key tasks in the SDOF problem statement have been mapped to user-defined MATLAB code and calls to MATLAB functions. Once again, because this problem is relatively straightforward, all the user-defined source code is located within one M-file, `sdof.m`.

Built-in MATLAB functions are used for the response array allocation, the `sin()` and `cos()` trigonometric calculations, and the square root calculation. Of course, we could have substituted `sqrt()` in the MATLAB library with the `sqroot()` function from Program 13.1. Both implementations give the same numer-

TABLE 13.9 Mapping of Tasks to MATLAB Code

Tasks	*	*User-Defined Code*	*MATLAB Library*
Setup array response (npoints,3).	*	In sdof.m	zeros()
Compute circular natural freq w.	*		sqrt()
	*		
Compute $y(t)$ and $v(t)$.	*	In sdof.m	sin()
	*		cos()
	*		
Plot $y(t)$ and $v(t)$ versus t.	*	In sdof.m	plot()
Hold the graphics.	*		hold
Label the horizontal axis.	*		xlabel()
Label the vertical axis.	*		ylabel()
Add a grid to the plot.	*		grid
Add a plot title.	*		title()

ical result. However, use of the sqroot() function requires that MATLAB automatically locate and compile sqroot.m after it has been referenced from sdof.m.

Analysis of the MATLAB Code

The variables disp10 and velocity0 store the SDOF displacement and velocity at time, $t = 0$. The looping construct

```
for i = 1 : nopoints
    time = (i-1)*dt;
    response(i,1) = time;
    response(i,2) =  disp10*cos(w*time)    + velocity0/w*sin(w*time);
    response(i,3) = -disp10*w*sin(w*time) + velocity0*cos(w*time);
end
```

systematically walks along the rows of the response array and evaluates the time t, displacement $y(t)$, and velocity $v(t)$ for columns 1 through 3 of response. The execution speed will be rather slow because the looping construct is interpreted. The command

```
plot( response(:,1), response(:,2) );
```

draws the contents of column 2 in array response versus column 1. In other words, a plot of $y(t)$ versus t is drawn. The graph of $v(t)$ versus t is generated with

```
plot(response(:,1), response(:,3) );
```

A far more efficient way of computing and storing the system response is with the commands

```
time     =  0.0:0.02:10;
displ    =  displ0*cos(w*time)     + velocity0/w*sin(w*time);
velocity = -displ0*w*sin(w*time) + velocity0*cos(w*time);
```

The first statement generates a (1×501) matrix called `time` having the element values 0, 0.02, 0.04 . . . . 10.0. The dimensions of matrices `displ` and `velocity` are inferred from the dimensions of `time` with the values of the matrix elements given by the evaluation of formulae on the right-hand side of the assignment statements. The required plots can be generated with

```
plot(time, displ);
hold;
plot(time, velocity);
```

The first statement creates a plot of vector `displ` versus vector `time`. The `hold` command places a hold on the current plot and all axis properties so that subsequent graphing commands may be added to the existing graph. The third statement creates the plot of $v(t)$ versus t.

Of course, the benefits of "fast evaluation of the SDOF formulae" and "convenient storage of the results in array response" can be combined. The block of code

```
time = [ 0:0.02:10 ]';
response(:,[1]) =  time;
response(:,[2]) =  displ0*cos(w*time)     + velocity0/w*sin(w*time);
response(:,[3]) = -displ0*w*sin(w*time) + velocity0*cos(w*time);
```

defines a (501×1) matrix called `time`, and then uses the second technique to compute (501×1) matrices of $x(t)$ and $v(t)$. The results of these calculations are assigned to the columns of response with submatrix notation

```
response(:,[k])
```

for the kth column of response.

13.7.3 Compute Roots of Quadratic Equation

Problem Statement

It is well known that the roots of a quadratic equation are given by solutions to

$$p(x) = ax^2 + bx + c = 0 \tag{13.13}$$

A number of solution cases exist. For example, when both $a = 0$ and $b = 0$, we consider the equation to be `extremely degenerate` and leave it at that. When

$a = 0$ and $b \neq 0$, we consider the case `degenerate`; in this situation, the equations reduce to $p(x) = bx + c = 0$, which has one root. Otherwise, we have

$$\text{Roots} = \left[\frac{-b \pm \sqrt{b^2 - 4ac}}{2a}\right] \tag{13.14}$$

The term $b^2 - 4ac$ is known as the discriminant of the quadratic equation.

Write a program that will interactively prompt a user for the equation coefficients a, b, and c at the keyboard, and then compute and print its roots along with an appropriate message for the type of solution. Appropriate messages are `extremely degenerate`, `degenerate`, `two real roots`, and `two complex roots`. For example, if $a = 1$, $b = 2$, and $c = 3$, the computer program should print

$$\text{Two complex roots: Root 1} = -1.0000 + 1.414214\,i \tag{13.15}$$

$$\text{Root 2} = -1.0000 - 1.414214\,i \tag{13.16}$$

Pseudocode

Because this problem contains numerous details and types of solutions, we refine our pseudocode over several iterations of development.

Iteration 1. A first draft pseudocode version for this task might look similar to the following:

```
announce the quadratic equation solving program
request a, b, and c from the user

calculate the discriminant
if the discriminant is >= 0 then the roots are real:
   compute and print real roots x1 and x2
else the roots are complex
   the real part is -b/2a
   the imaginary part is the square root of (the negative of
   the discriminant) / 2a

print the results
```

Iteration 2. Using successive refinement we can develop this pseudocode further into

```
print 'quadratic equation solving program'
print 'Enter the coefficients a, b, and c'
read the coefficients

discriminant = b^2 - 4ac
if the discriminant is >= 0 then equation has real roots x1, x2.
   x1 = -b/2a - sqrt( discriminant) / 2a
   x2 = -b/2a + sqrt( discriminant) / 2a
```

```
else, the discriminant is < 0, and roots are complex numbers
   (re, im) with
   re = -b/2a
   im = sqrt( - discriminant) / 2a
   print 'Complex roots'
```

Iteration 3. Iteration 2 still does not look like MATLAB code so at least one more stage of development is desirable

```
print 'quadratic equation solving program'
print 'Enter the coefficients a, b, and c'

input coefficients dA, dB, dC
if( dA equal to zero )
    compute roots to determinate equations
    exit

discriminant = b^2 - 4ac
if (discriminant >= 0.0)     % The roots are real
   root1 = -b/2a - sqrt( discriminant )/2a
   root2 = -b/2a + sqrt( discriminant )/2a
   print 'The first  root is ' root1
   print 'The second root is ' root2
else                         % The roots are complex
   re = -b/2a
   im = sqrt( -discriminant )/2a
   print 'The first  complex root is', re, im
   print 'The second complex root is', re, -im
```

This version of pseudocode is very close to MATLAB, and we are ready to begin writing the MATLAB code for our quadratic equation solver.

Program Source Code

The source code for Program 13.5 is contained in two files, a script M-file called `quadratic.m` and a function M-file called `discriminant.m`. Here are the details.

PROGRAM 13.5: COMPUTE ROOTS OF QUADRATIC EQUATION

```
% ===========================================================================
% quadratic.m -- Coefficients are read in from keyboard
%                Roots of Quadratic are printed to screen.
%
% Note : Naive implementation of quadratic equation solver. This algorithm
%        does not take into account possible loss of accuracy when two
%        floating point numbers of almost equal size are subtracted.
%
% Written By : Mark Austin                                          July 1997
% ==========================================================================
```

```
% Print Welcome Message

  disp('Welcome to the Quadratic Equation Solver (Version 1)\n');
  disp('=====================================================\n');

% Prompt User for Coefficients of Quadratic Equation

  disp('Please enter coefficients for equation a.x^2 + b.x + c\n');
  A = input ('Enter coefficient a : ');
  B = input ('Enter coefficient b : ');
  C = input ('Enter coefficient c : ');

% Print Quadratic Equation to Screen

  fprintf('Equation you have entered is : %g.x^2 + %g.x + %g\n', ...
          A, B, C);

% Compute Roots of simplified equations : A equals zero

  RootsFound = 0;
  if A == 0 & B == 0,
     fprintf('Cannot solve extremely degenerate equation' );
     fprintf('%14.8g = 0.0\n', C );
     RootsFound = 1;
  end;

  if A == 0 & B ~= 0 & RootsFound == 0,
     Root1 = - C/B;
     fprintf('Degenerate root : Root = %14.8g\n', Root1 );
     RootsFound = 1;
  end;

% Compute Roots of Quadratic Equation : A not equal to zero

  if RootsFound == 0,
  Discriminant = discriminant(A,B,C);     % Compute discriminant of
                                          % quadratic equation.
  if Discriminant >= 0,                   % Case for two real roots

     Root1 = -B/2.0/A - sqrt( Discriminant )/2.0/A;
     Root2 = -B/2.0/A + sqrt( Discriminant )/2.0/A;

     fprintf('Two Real Roots : Root1 = %14.8g\n', Root1 );
     fprintf('               : Root2 = %14.8g\n', Root2 );
  else                                 % Case for complex roots
```

```
      fprintf('Two Complex Roots : Root1 = %14.8g + %14.8g i\n', ...
                    -B/2.0/A,  sqrt( -Discriminant )/2.0/A);
            fprintf('                   : Root2 = %14.8g + %14.8g i\n', ....
                    -B/2.0/A, -sqrt( -Discriminant )/2.0/A);
   end;
end;
```

```
function   [ discrim ] = discriminant( A, B, C )

% DISCRIMINANT : Compute discriminant in quadratic equation.
%

discrim = B*B - 4*A*C;
```

Running the Program

The following script of code

```
>> quadratic
Welcome to the Quadratic Equation Solver (Version 1)
====================================================
Please enter coefficients for equation a.x^2 + b.x + c

Enter coefficient a : 1.2

Enter coefficient b : 3.4

Enter coefficient c : 5.6
Equation you have entered is : 1.2.x^2 + 3.4.x + 5.6
Two complex roots : Root1 =      -1.4166667 +      1.6308655 i
                  : Root2 =      -1.4166667 +     -1.6308655 i
```

shows a typical session of I/O for Program 13.5. You should verify that this solution is correct by substituting $a = 1.2$, $b = 3.4$, and $c = 5.6$ into Equation 13.14.

Although this example does not demonstrate it, a key limitation of this program is the absence of checking for loss of numerical accuracy that occurs when two floating point numbers of almost equal size are subtracted. Situations of this type arise, for example, when $a = 1.0$, $b = 1000000.0$, and $c = 1.0$. An algorithm for overcoming this problem is explained in Problem 7.8 of the C tutorial.

Program Architecture

Table 13.10 shows how key tasks in the quadratic equation solution procedure have been mapped to user-defined MATLAB code and MATLAB function calls. Other than the discriminant computation in `discriminant.m`, the heart of our quadratic equation solver is contained in `quadratic.m`. When MATLAB executes `quadrat-`

TABLE 13.10 Mapping of Tasks to MATLAB Code

Tasks	*	*User-Defined Code*	*MATLAB Library*
Announce quadratic program.	*	In `quadratic.m`	`disp()`
Read equation coefficients.	*	In `quadratic.m`	`input()`
	*		
Compute discriminant.	*	In `discriminant.m`	
Compute square root	*	In `quadratic.m`	`sqrt()`
Solve quadratic equation.	*	In `quadratic.m`	
Print roots of quadratic equation.	*		`fprintf()`
	*		

`ic.m` for the first time and encounters the reference to a function `discriminant`, the function M-file `discriminant.m` will be located and compiled into MATLAB's memory.

The MATLAB function `disp()` displays messages enclosed within single quotes. `fprintf()` displays messages containing formatted output. The function `input()` prompts a user for keyboard input (there is no point in reinventing the wheel). Finally, we employ the MATLAB function `sqrt()` for the square root calculation in Equation 13.14.

Analysis of the MATLAB Code

The script M-file, `quadratic.m`, contains the commands needed to compute and print the roots of the quadratic equation. The function M-file, `discriminant.m`, contains the function

```
function [ discrim ] = discriminant( A, B, C )
```

accepting three matrix arguments and returning a matrix

```
discrim = B*B - 4*A*C;
```

containing the equation discriminant. We implicitly assume in this function declaration that `A`, `B`, and `C` will be one-by-one matrices. The execution of `discriminant` is terminated by an EOF.

13.7.4 Statistical Analysis of Experimental Data

Problem Statement

Suppose that the concentration of spores of pollen per square centimeter are measured over a 15-day period and stored in a data file `expt.dat`.

```
 1  12
 2  35
 3  80
 4  120
 5  280
 6  290
 7  360
 8  290
 9  315
10  280
11  270
12  190
13  90
14  85
15  66
```

The first and second columns of `expt.dat` store the "day of the experiment" and the "measured pollen count," respectively.

Write a MATLAB program that will read the contents of the data file into an array and create and label a two-dimensional bar plot showing the "pollen count" versus "day." The program should then compute the mean and standard deviation of the pollen count, and plot and label dashed lines for the mean pollen count and the mean pollen count ± one standard deviation.

Pseudocode

We begin our analysis by noting that the mean and standard deviation of the experimental data can be computed by the function `stat()` in Program 13.2. Hence, the pseudocode for this problem is

```
read the contents of file expt.dat into the array expt.

draw and label the bar chart.

call the function stat() to compute the mean and standard
deviation of the experimental data.

construct a working array of coordinate points for plotting the
dashed lines -- horizontal lines are required for:
    mean value - 1 standard deviation.
    mean value alone.
    mean value + 1 standard deviation.
```

PROGRAM 13.6: STATISTICAL ANALYSIS OF EXPERIMENTAL DATA

```
% =======================================================
% expt.m -- Statistical analysis of experimental data.
%
% Written By : Mark Austin                     July 1997
% =======================================================

% Store experimental results in array

  load expt.dat

% Generate bar plot of experimental results

  bar(expt(:,1), expt(:,2),'b')
  xlabel('Day of Expt');
  ylabel('Pollen Count');

% Compute terms from experimental results.

  [xm, xd] = stat(expt(:,2))

% Create and display mean value of pollen count

  mean_minus = xm(1,1) - xd(1,1);
  mean_plus  = xm(1,1) + xd(1,1);

  data = [  1, xm(1,1), mean_minus, mean_plus;
           15, xm(1,1), mean_minus, mean_plus ];
  hold;
  plot (data(:,1), data(:,2), 'b');
  plot (data(:,1), data(:,3), 'b:');
  plot (data(:,1), data(:,4), 'b:');

  text(1,   xm(1,1) + 10,'Mean Pollen Count');
  text(1,mean_minus + 10,'Mean - Std');
  text(1, mean_plus + 10,'Mean + Std');
```

Running the Program

The script of code

```
>> format compact
>> expt
```

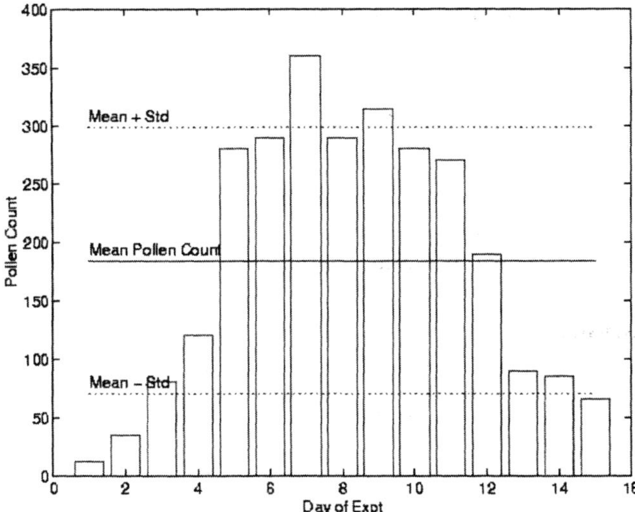

FIGURE 13.4 Pollen count versus day of experiment.

```
    xm =
       184.2000
    xd =
       114.2309
>>
```

shows the command needed to run Program 13.6 and the textual output that is generated.

Figure 13.4 shows the bar chart of pollen count measurements and mean/standard deviation statistics. Solid- and dashed-line summaries of the mean data value and the mean value ± one standard deviation are then superimposed on the bar chart.

Program Architecture

Table 13.11 shows how tasks in the problem statement have been mapped to user-defined MATLAB code and calls to built-in MATLAB functions.

After the script M-file `expt.m` has loaded the contents of `expt.dat` into an array `expt` containing two columns and created a bar chart of the data, the function M-file `stat.m` is called to compute the mean and standard deviation of the experimental data.

Analysis of the MATLAB Code

The command

```
load expt.dat;
```

loads the content of data file `expt.dat` into the array `expt`. Then the command

```
[xm, xd] = stat( expt(:,2) )
```

TABLE 13.11 Mapping of Tasks to MATLAB Code

Tasks	*	*User-Defined Code*	*MATLAB Library*
File holding the experimental data.	*	`expt.data`	
Read the file expt.dat into an array "expt".	*	In `expt.m`	`load`
Draw the bar chart.	*	In `expt.m`	`bar()`
Label the horizontal axis.	*		`xlabel()`
Label the vertical axis.	*		`ylabel`
Compute the mean and std of the experimental data.	*	In `stat.m`	
Hold the graphics.	*	In `expt.m`	`hold`
Draw the dashed horizontal lines.	*		`plot()`
Label the dashed lines.	*		`text()`

calls the user-defined function `stat` defined in `stat.m` to compute the mean and standard deviation of data values stored in the second column of `expt`. The mean and standard deviation are represented by `xm` and `xd`, both one-by-one matrices. A two-by-four array, `data`, holds the coordinate values of the solid- dashed-line segments for plotting purposes.

Otherwise, Program 13.6 relies on a variety of function calls to the MATLAB graphics library to draw and label the bar chart. A detail description of these functions and their capabilities are found in Chapter 14.

FURTHER INFORMATION

The MATLAB program comes with a lot of M-file examples. To find their location on your computer, type the MATLAB command `path`. This will lead you to some really nifty demos.

REVIEW QUESTIONS

1. What does the `helpdesk` command do?
2. What is the maximum array size supported by the student edition of MATLAB Version 5?
3. MATLAB output can be rather lengthy. What is an easy way of shortening the length of the output?

4. What is the purpose of the `eps` constant?

5. What does the `input` function do?

6. Briefly explain how "precedence of arithmetic operators" works in MATLAB.

7. Explain step by step how the arithmetic expression

```
>> 1/2*( 2 + 3*4^2 )
```

is evaluated in MATLAB.

8. Consider the script of code

```
>> ix = 1;
>> ij = 2*ix;
>> ik = 2*(ix==1) + (3*ij ~= 6);
```

What is the value of `ik`?

9. By default, MATLAB prints floating point numbers to four decimal places of accuracy. How would you adjust this option?

10. What are the three ways of defining a matrix in MATLAB?

11. What is the output generated by the MATLAB commands?

```
>> A = [ 1 2; 3 4 ];
>> B = [ A 2*A ]
```

12. What is the output generated by the sequence of commands?

```
>> x = [ 1, 2, 3; 4, 5, 6 ];
>> sin(2*x);
```

13. What does the command

```
>> x = -10.0: 0.2: 10.0
```

do?

14. What is the output generated by the sequence of commands?

```
>> x = [ -pi : pi/2 : pi ];
>> sin(x).^2 + cos(x).^2
```

15. If `A` is a $(m \times n)$ matrix and `B` is a $(r \times p)$ matrix, what restrictions must exist on m, r, n, and p for the matrix sum `C` = `A` + `B` to be defined?

16. If `A` is a $(m \times n)$ matrix and `B` is a $(r \times p)$ matrix, what restrictions must exist on m, r, n, and p for the matrix product `C` = `A` · `B` to be defined?

17. Suppose that

```
>> y = [ 1 2 3 ; 4 5 6; 7 8 9 ];
```

How would you use the `for` looping construct to compute the sum of the elements in matrix `y`?

How would you use the `sum()` function to sum the matrix elements in `y` (a one line answer will suffice)?

18. Why does the fragment of code

```
>> y = zeros(1:1000);
>> for i = 1:1000
       y(i) = 2*sin(i);
   end
```

execute slower than

```
>> y = 2*sin([1:1000]);
```

19. Suppose that a matrix `data` contains

```
data = [ 1.5  1.0  3.0;
         6.5 -1.2 12.4;
         2.5 -1.0  3.8;
         2.4  8.1  5.8 ];
```

How would you use MATLAB to compute the maximum matrix element value in each row and column of matrix `data`?

13.8 PROGRAMMING EXERCISES

Problem 13.1 (Beginner): Figure 13.5 shows a mass m resting on a frictionless surface. The mass is connected to two walls by springs having stiffnesses k_1 and k_2. The natural period of the mass-spring system is

$$T = 2\pi\sqrt{\frac{m}{k_1 + k_2}} \tag{13.17}$$

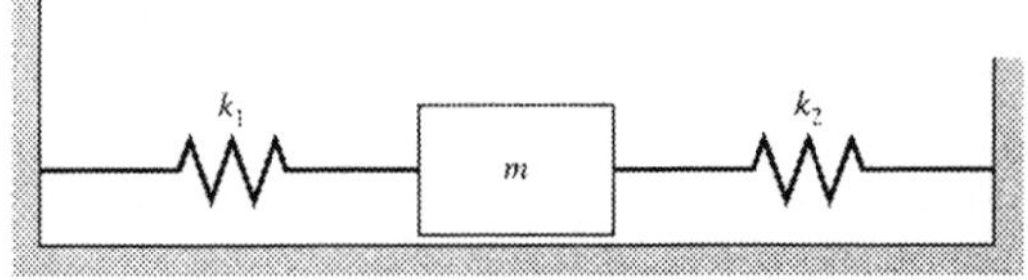

FIGURE 13.5 Mass-spring system.

Write a MATLAB program that will prompt a user for m, k_1, and k_2, check that the supplied values are all greater than zero, and then compute and print the natural period of the mass-spring system.

Problem 13.2 (Beginner): Suppose that during squally conditions, regular one second wind gusts produce a forward thrust on a yacht sail corresponding to

$$F(t) = \begin{cases} 4 + 15 \cdot t - 135 \cdot t^3 & 0.0 \leq t \leq 0.3, \\ (731 - 171t)/140 & 0.3 < t \leq 1.0 \end{cases} \tag{13.18}$$

$F(t)$ has units kN. Write a MATLAB program that computes and prints $F(t)$ for $0 \leq t \leq 3$ seconds. The program output should look something like the following:

```
      Time            Thrust
   (seconds)            (kN)
   ==========================
      0.00              4.00
      0.25              5.64
      0.50              4.61
      0.75              4.31
      1.00              4.00
      1.25              5.64
      1.50              4.61
      1.75              4.31
      2.00              4.00
      2.25              5.64
      2.50              4.61
      2.75              4.31
      3.00              4.00
```

Problem 13.3 (Beginner): The adjacent figure shows a triangle defined by the vertex coordinates (x_1, y_1), (x_2, y_2), and (x_3, y_3).

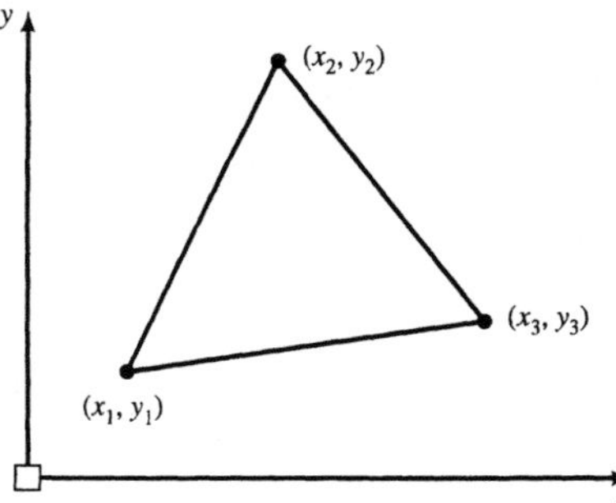

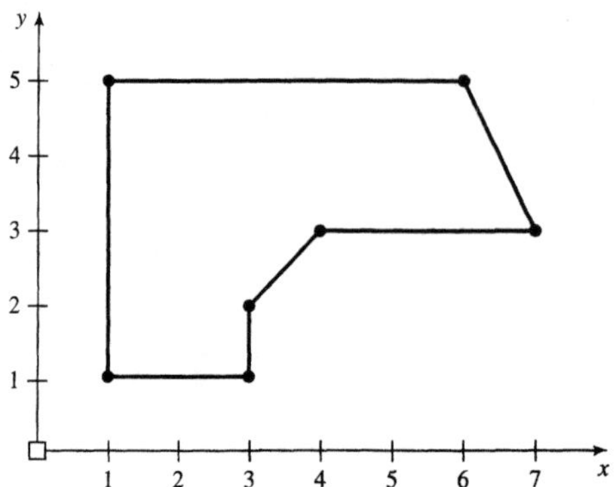

FIGURE 13.6 Seven-sided irregular polygon.

Write a MATLAB program that will

1. Interactively prompt a user for x and y coordinates at each of the triangle vertices.
2. Print the triangle vertices in a tidy table.
3. Compute and print the area of the triangle (make sure that it is positive) and its perimeter.

Problem 13.4 (Beginner): Figure 13.6 is a schematic of an irregular polygon having seven sides. Suppose that the x and y vertex coordinates are stored as two columns of information in the file `polygon.dat`.

```
1.0  1.0
1.0  5.0
6.0  5.0
7.0  3.0
4.0  3.0
3.0  2.0
3.0  1.0
```

Write a MATLAB script file that will read the contents of `polygon.dat` into an array `polygon`, and then compute and print

1. The minimum and maximum polygon coordinates in both the x and y directions
2. The minimum and maximum distance of the polygon vertices from the coordinate system origin
3. The perimeter and area of the polygon

Note. You should use the `max()` and `min()` functions provided by MATLAB for Part 2. In Part 3, you should use the fact that the vertices have been specified in a clockwise manner.

Problem 13.5 (Beginner): An efficient way of computing the cube root of a number N is to compute the root of

$$f(x) = x^3 - N = 0 \tag{13.19}$$

with the method of Newton Raphson, namely,

$$x_{n+1} = x_n - \left[\frac{f(x_n)}{f'(x_n)}\right] \tag{13.20}$$

Substituting Equation 13.19 into Equation 13.20 and rearranging terms gives the recursive relationship

$$x_{n+1} = \frac{1}{3} \cdot \left[\frac{2x_n^3 + N}{x_n^2}\right] \tag{13.21}$$

Write a MATLAB program that will

1. Prompt the user for a number N, and compute the cube root of N via Equation 13.21. The details of the cube root calculation should be contained within a function M-file called cuberoot. A suitable function declaration is

```
[ answer ] = cuberoot ( N )
```

Your M-file function should use Equation 13.6 for a test on convergence.

2. Print the number N, its cube root, and the number of iterations needed to compute the result.

Hint. Your solution to this problem should be similar to Program 13.1.

Problem 13.6 (Intermediate): Write and test a function M-file `matadd.m` for the element-by-element addition of matrices A and B using Equation 13.3. An appropriate function declaration is

```
[ matrixsum ] = matadd ( A, B )
```

After your M-file function has checked that matrices A and B have compatible sizes, Equation 13.3 should be evaluated inside a set of two nested for loops.

Write a test program to allocate and initialize matrices A and B, and compute their sum using the `matadd` function and MATLAB's built-in library for matrix addition. What is the relative speed of these two approaches?

Problem 13.7 (Intermediate): Repeat the experiment described in Problem 13.6 but for the multiplication of two matrices A and B. An appropriate function declaration is

```
[ matrixproduct ] = matmult ( A, B )
```

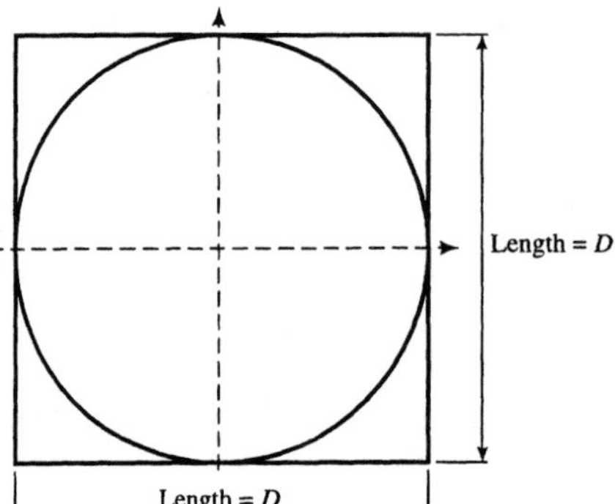

FIGURE 13.7 Estimating π via integration.

Again, the matrix multiplication should be computed with a set of two nested for loops.

Problem 13.8 (Intermediate): Monte Carlo methods solve problems by experiments with random numbers on a computer. They have been around since about the mid-1940s. A relatively straightforward way of estimating π is to conduct an experiment where darts are randomly thrown at a square board of side length `D`, as shown in Figure 13.7.

Given that the area of the circle $A_{circle} = [\pi D^2/4]$ and the area of the square $A_{square} = D^2$, then

$$\pi = 4 \cdot \left[\frac{A_{circle}}{A_{square}} \right] \tag{13.22}$$

In the Monte Carlo experiment, N darts are thrown at the board. Let $P_i = (x_i, y_i)$ be the coordinate point of the ith dart ($i = 1, 2, 3 \ldots N$). Point P_i is inside the circle if

$$x_i^2 + y_i^2 \leq \left[\frac{D^2}{4} \right] \tag{13.23}$$

If at the conclusion of the experiment X darts have landed inside the circle ($X \leq N$), then a Monte Carlo estimate of π is

$$\pi \sim 4 \cdot \left[\frac{X}{N} \right] \tag{13.24}$$

Write a MATLAB program that will

1. Simulate this experiment by generating pairs of uniformly distributed random numbers, one for the x-coordinate and a second for the y-coordinate. The random numbers should be scaled so that they cover the interval `[-D,D]`. Calculate whether each data point P_i lies inside the circle. At the conclusion

of the experiment, sum the number of darts that lie inside the circle and evaluate Equation 13.24.

2. Print the total number of trials in the experiment (N), the total number of trial points inside the circle (X), and the Monte Carlo estimate of π.
3. Draw Figure 13.7 together with the (x, y) coordinates of the dart throwing experiment.

14

MATLAB GRAPHICS

Graphics are an indispensable part of engineering education and professional practice because they provide insight into the complicated relationships that exist between multidimensional scientific and engineering phenomena. One of the neat features of MATLAB is its graphics capabilities. Using only a few simple MATLAB commands, two- and three-dimensional plots and subplots can be created, with labels and titles, axes, and grids.

14.1 SIMPLE TWO-DIMENSIONAL PLOTTING

MATLAB has an ensemble of functions for the simple two-dimensional plotting of functions and data that take the form (x_i, y_i), $i = 1, 2, 3, \cdots, n$. They are

`plot(x,y)`	Draws a linear plot of vector `y` versus vector `x`.
`semilogx(x,y)`	Draws a plot of vector `y` versus vector `x`, using a logarithmic scale for `x` and a linear scale for `y`.
`semilogy(x,y)`	Draws a plot of vector `y` versus vector `x`, using a logarithmic scale for `y` and a linear scale for `x`.
`loglog(x,y)`	Draws a plot of vector `y` versus vector `x`, using logarithmic scales for both `x` and `y` axes.

In each of these function calls, the contents of `x` are the data points along the horizontal axis of the plot. The data along the vertical axis of the plot is stored in a second vector `y`. Vectors `x` and `y` should have the same length. If `x` or `y` is a matrix, then the vector is plotted versus the rows or columns of the matrix, whichever line up.

By default, MATLAB will plot each data point pair on a set of axes scaled to cover the range of values in x and y, and connect the marked data points with straight line segments. The latter helps to highlight trends implied by the sequence of data point pairs.

For function calls that involve logarithmic transformations, it is important to remember that the logarithm of x is undefined for negative x. MATLAB will handle these accidental oversights by printing an error message indicating that data points have been omitted from a plot.

Coordinate labels, plot titles, grid, and textual messages can be added to simple two-dimensional plots with

`grid on`	Add grid lines to a plot. The command `grid off` takes them off. The command `grid` by itself toggles the grid state.
`xlabel('x axis label')`	Add text beside the x axis on the current axis.
`ylabel('y axis label')`	Add text beside the y axis on the current axis.
`title('title of plot')`	Add text at the top of the current axis.
`text(x,y,'text')`	Add 'text' string to a plot where (x, y) is the coordinate of the center left edge of the character string taken from the plot axes.
`gtext('text')`	Activate the use of the mouse to position a cross-hair on the graph at which the 'text' will be placed when any key is pressed.

Example. Draw the graph of

$$y(x) = \left[\frac{\sin(2x)}{2x}\right] \quad \text{for} \quad -10 \leq x \leq 10 \tag{14.1}$$

The sequence of MATLAB commands

```
>> x = -10 : 0.2 : 10;
>> y = 1/2*sin(2.*x)./x;
Warning: Divide by zero
>> plot(x,y)
>> grid
>> xlabel('x')
>> ylabel('sin(2x)/2x')
```

generates Figure 14.1.

Vector x is a (1×101) matrix holding the coordinates of domain [-10,10] partitioned into intervals of 0.2, and y is a vector of the same length giving the values of $y = \sin(2x)/2x$ within the partition. Equation 14.1 is evaluated successfully for each of the elements in matrix x except x(51) = 0, where a "divide by zero" occurs. Does this make sense? By writing a Taylors series

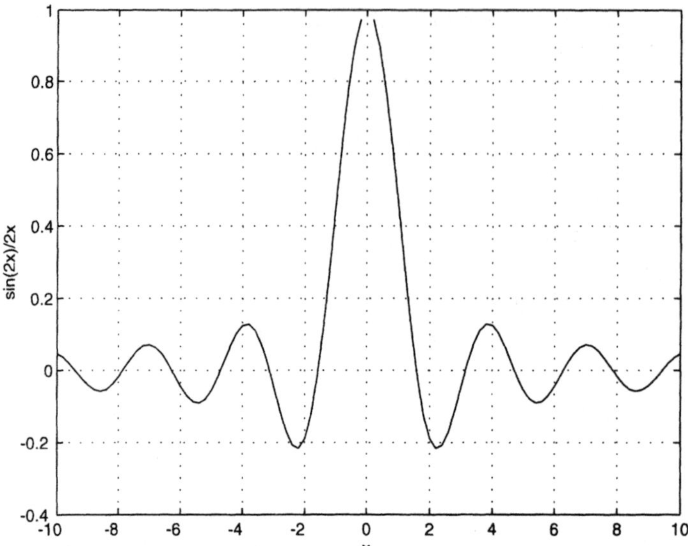

FIGURE 14.1 $y = \sin(2x)/2x$ for $-10 \le x \le 10$.

expansion for sin($2x$) and dividing through by $2x$, it is relatively easy to show that $y(0) = \sin(0)/0 = 1$. MATLAB does not pick up on this point. Instead, the element of vector `y` corresponding to $x = 0$ is assigned `NaN`, and the `plot()` function treats the array element $y(51)$ as missing data (see the upper sections of Figure 14.1).

Note. One way of "mitigating" this problem is to replace the zero element(s) in matrix `x` with `eps`, that is,

```
>> x = -10 : 0.2 : 10;
>> x = x + (x==0)*eps
```

In the second MATLAB command, a component of matrix `x` will be incremented by `eps` when the logical expression `(x==0)` evaluates to true. Otherwise, the components of `x` remain unchanged. Now the `y` matrix is generated without error, and `sin(0)/0` evaluates to `1`.

Axes of Plots

In Figure 14.1, MATLAB has automatically fixed the range of x and y values so that the plotted function fills the space that is available [i.e., $x$min = min(x), $x$max = max(x). In doing so, the "missing data item" at $y(0)$ has been unintentionally hidden by the border of Figure 14.1. Perhaps it would be more evident if the range of y values in Figure 14.1 were rescaled to cover the interval `[ -0.4 , 1.2]`?

MATLAB provides the function `axis` to control the scaling and appearance of axes in a plot. In this tutorial, we make frequent use of the function call

`axis( [xmin, xmax, ymin, ymax ] )`	Set the range of x and y values in the current plot to `[ xmin, xmax]` and `[ ymin, ymax]`, respectively.

In addition, the command `axis('equal')` changes the current axis box size so that equal tick mark increments on the x- and y-axis are equal in size. Similarly, the command `axis('off')` turns off all axis labeling and tick marks. Axis labeling and tick marks is turned back on again with `axis('on')`.

Thus, the sequence of MATLAB commands

```
>> x = -10 : 0.2 : 10;
>> x = x + (x==0)*eps;
>> y = 1/2*sin(2.*x)./x;
>> plot(x,y)
>> axis([ -10 10 -0.4 1.2 ])
>> grid;
>> xlabel('x')
>> ylabel('sin(2x)/2x')
```

generates a graph nearly identical to Figure 14.1, in this case with the range of x and y values covering `[-10,10]` and `[-0.4,1.2]`, respectively, and with the correct evaluation of $\sin(2x)/2x$ at $x = 0$.

Parametrically Defined Curves

Plots of parametrically defined curves can also be made. For example, a plot of the parametric curve

$$[x(t), y(t)] = [\cos(3t), \sin(2t)] \text{ for } 0 \le t \le 2\pi \tag{14.2}$$

can be created with the MATLAB commands

```
>> t = 0: 0.02: 2*pi;
>> plot( cos(3*t), sin(2*t) )
>> grid
>> axis('equal')
```

The result is shown in Figure 14.2. Notice how we have used the `axis('equal')` command to equalize the scales in the x- and y-axis directions. This makes the parametric plot take its true shape instead of an oval.

Setting Line and Mark Types, and Colors

As already demonstrated in Figures 14.1 and 14.2, MATLAB will automatically connect the data points in a plot by solid lines. When the data points are closely

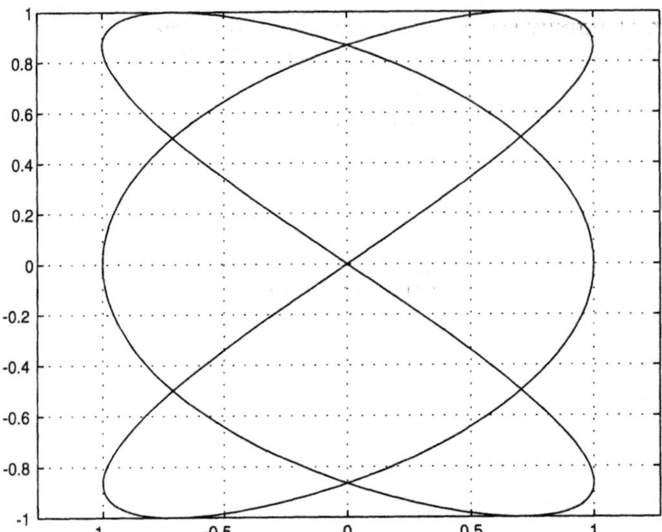

FIGURE 14.2 Parametric contour $(x, y) = [\cos(3t), \sin(2t)]$.

spaced, this gives the appearance of a smoothly drawn curve. Table 14.1 contains the line and mark types, and color options, that can be used in MATLAB plots. For example, the script

```
>> t = 0: 0.04: 2*pi;
>> plot( t.*cos(3*t), 2.*t.*sin(2*t), 'o')
>> grid
```

generates the pathway of `'o'` points shown in Figure 14.3. In this case, we have deliberately omitted the `axis('equal')` command so that the horizontal and vertical axes can be independently scaled to fill the rectangular space available on a page.

Combinations of line and mark types, and color settings, can be specified by simply bundling the combined settings into a text string enclosed by single quotes. For example, the command

```
>> plot( t.*cos(3*t), 2.*t.*sin(2*t), 'og' )
```

tells MATLAB to plot Figure 14.3 with green circles.

TABLE 14.1 Summary of Line Types and Line Colors

Line type	`solid (-), dashed (-), dotted (:), dashdot (-.)`
Mark type	`point (.), plus (+), star (*), circle (o), x-mark (x)`
Color	`yellow (y), magenta (m), cyan (c), red (r), green (g), blue (b), white (w), black (k)`

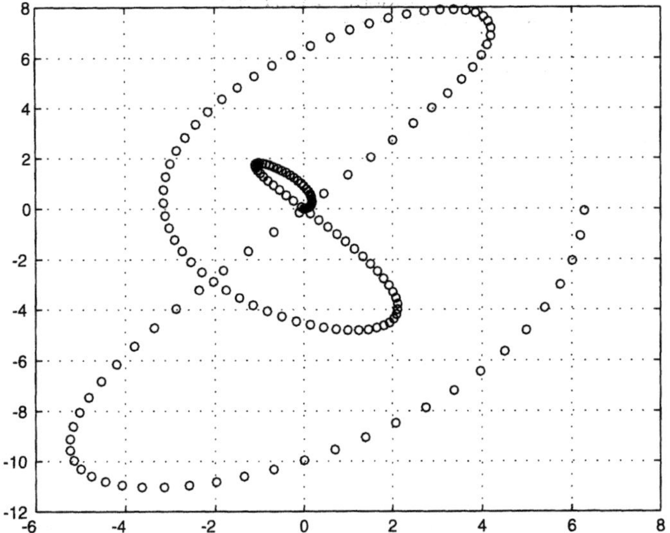

FIGURE 14.3 Parametric contour $(x, y) = [t*\cos(3t), 2t*\sin(2t)]$.

Clearing Plots

The command `clf` deletes all objects from the current figure. The command `cla` deletes all objects (e.g., lines, text) from the current axes.

14.1.1 Histograms, Bar Charts, and Stem Diagrams

The function specifications that follow are a subset of MATLAB functions available for plotting histograms, bar charts, stair-step plots, and stem diagrams:

`bar(x,y)`	Draws a bar graph of the elements of vector `y` at locations specified in vector `x`. The *x* values must be ascending order.
`hist(x,y)`	Plot a histogram of the values in vector `y` using the bins specified in vector `x`.
`stairs(x,y)`	A stair-step graph is a bar graph without internal lines. This function call draws a stair-step graph of the elements of vector `y` at locations specified in vector `x`.
`stem(x,y)`	Plots the data sequence `y` as stems from locations specified in `x`. Each stem is terminated by a circle positioned at the data value.

For a complete list of options for each function, type

```
>> help function_name
```

(e.g., help bar) within MATLAB.

Example. The block of MATLAB code

```
>> x = 1:6;
>> y = zeros(1,6);
>> for i = 1:600
       ii       = ceil( 6*rand(1) );
       y(1,ii)  = y(1,ii) + 1;
   end,
>> bar(x,y)
>> axis([0, 8, 0, 125 ]);
>> grid
>> xlabel('Number on Dice (1 through 6)');
>> ylabel('Number of scores in Experiment');
```

simulates an experiment where a regular die is thrown 600 times and the total number of scores, `1` through `6`, is counted and plotted as a bar chart (see Figure 14.4). You should observe that the sum of column heights 1 through 6 is 600 and that the average column height is 100.

Figure 14.5 is a graphical representation of the same die-throwing experiment, but in this case, the grid has been removed and the frequency of die scores is displayed as a stem chart.

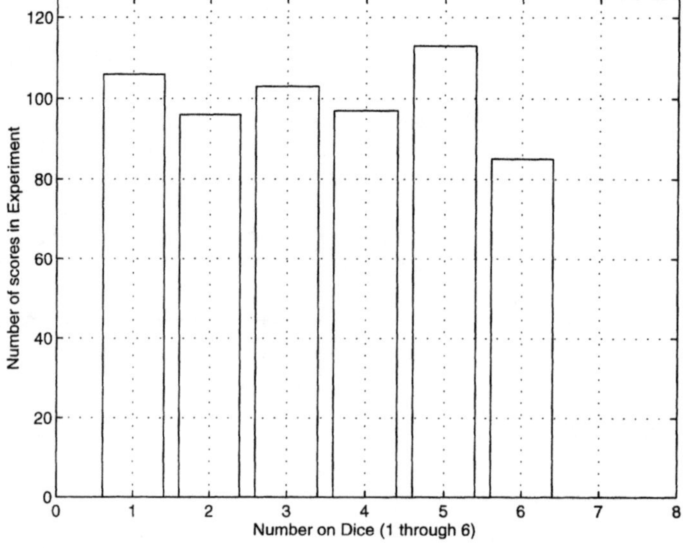

FIGURE 14.4 Bar chart of scores in die-throwing experiment.

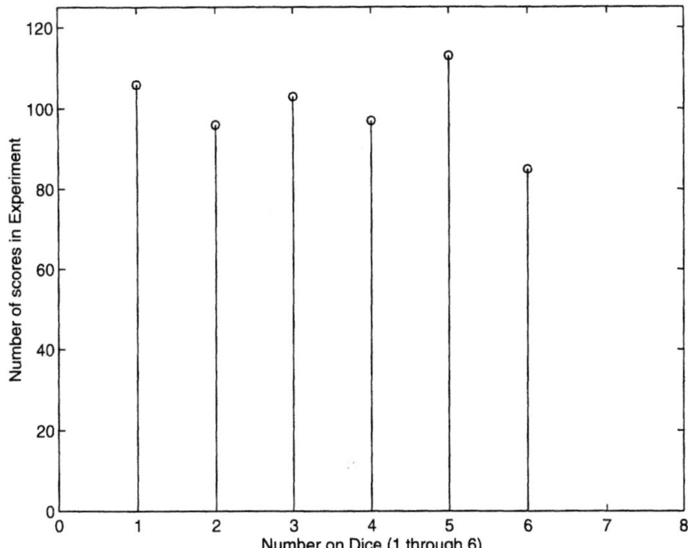

FIGURE 14.5 Stem chart of scores in die-throwing experiment.

14.1.2 Multiple Plots

A straightforward way of plotting multiple curves on the same graph is with the command

`plot(x,y,w,z, ... )`	Opens a graphics window and draws a linear plot of vector y versus vector x, and vector w versus vector z on the same graph. Again, if x, y, w or z is a matrix, then the vectors are plotted versus the rows or columns of the matrix, whichever line up.

MATLAB will plot the data set y versus x first, then w versus z and so forth. This strategy of implementation means that the length of vectors x and y need not be the same as w and z.

The following examples illustrate three ways of making multiple plots on a single graph, as shown in Figure 14.6.

Example. Consider the script of code

```
>> x = 0 : .01 : 2*pi;
>> y1 = sin(x);
>> y2 = sin(2*x);
>> y3 = sin(4*x);
>> plot( x, y1 ,'--', x, y2, ':', x, y3,'+' )
>> grid
>> title ('Dashed, line, and dotted line graph')
```

Three plots are drawn with one call to `plot()`. Here we use a dashed line and dotted line for the first two graphs, while a + symbol is placed at each node for the third.

Example. When one of the arguments to `plot` is a vector and the other is a matrix, `plot` will graph each column of the matrix versus the vector. For example,

```
>> x = 0 : .01 : 2*pi;
>> y = [ sin(x)', sin(2*x)', sin(4*x)' ];
>> plot(x,y)
```

`x` is an array having one row and 629 columns. `y` is a matrix having 629 rows and 3 columns.

Holding Figures

So far in this tutorial we have generated all our figures, including those with multiple plots, with one call to `plot`. Another way of generating figures with multiple plots is with the command `hold`, which freezes the current graphics screen so that subsequent plots are superimposed on it.

For example, Figure 14.6 can also be generated with the sequence of commands

```
>> x  = 0 : .01 : 2*pi;
>> plot( x,   sin(x), '--' )
>> hold
```

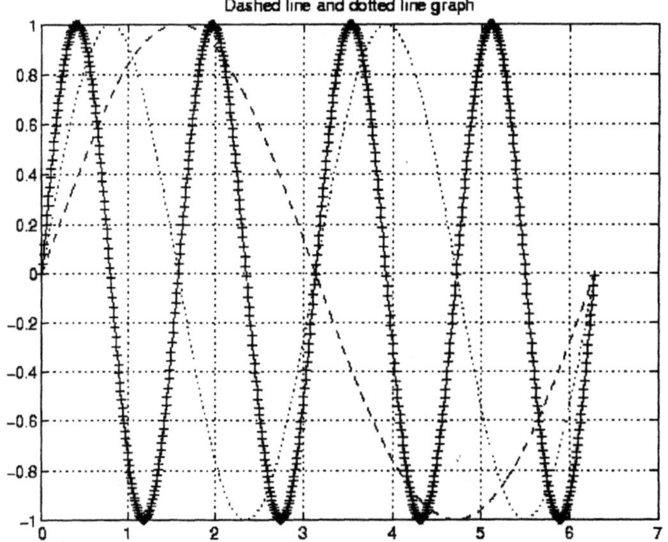

FIGURE 14.6 Overriding default line and point types.

```
>> plot( x, sin(2*x), ':' )
>> plot( x, sin(4*x), '+' )
>> grid
>> title ('Dashed, line, and dotted line graph')
```

The "hold" can be released by entering `hold` again. The command `hold on` holds the current plot and all axis properties so that subsequent graphing commands add to the existing graph. Conversely, the command `hold off` returns to the default mode whereby `plot` commands erase the previous plots and reset all axis properties before drawing new plots.

14.2 THREE-DIMENSIONAL PLOTS

MATLAB uses the function `plot3`, the three-dimensional counterpart of `plot`, to display arrays of data points (x_i, y_i, z_i), $i = 1, 2, 3, \cdots, n$ in three-dimensional space. The syntax is

`plot3(x,y,z)` When `x`, `y`, and `z` are vectors of the same length, this function plots a line in three-dimensional space through the points whose coordinates are the elements of `x`, `y`, and `z`.

There are many variations on this function's use, and we simply recommend you type `help plot3` for a list of options.

Example. Suppose that eight experimental measurements (x, y, z) are stored in the rows of a matrix called `data`:

```
>> data = [ 2.5  1.3  0.0;
            0.0  2.0  0.0;
            1.0  3.0  0.0;
            2.5  3.5  4.0;
            3.0  1.0 -2.0;
            2.0 -1.0 -2.0;
            3.5  4.0 -2.5;
            0.0  1.0  0.0 ];
>>
```

The block of MATLAB commands:

```
>> plot3 ( data(:,1), data(:,2), data(:,3), 'o' )
>> axis([ -1 4 0 5 -5 5 ])
>> grid
>> xlabel('x'), ylabel('y'), zlabel('z')
```

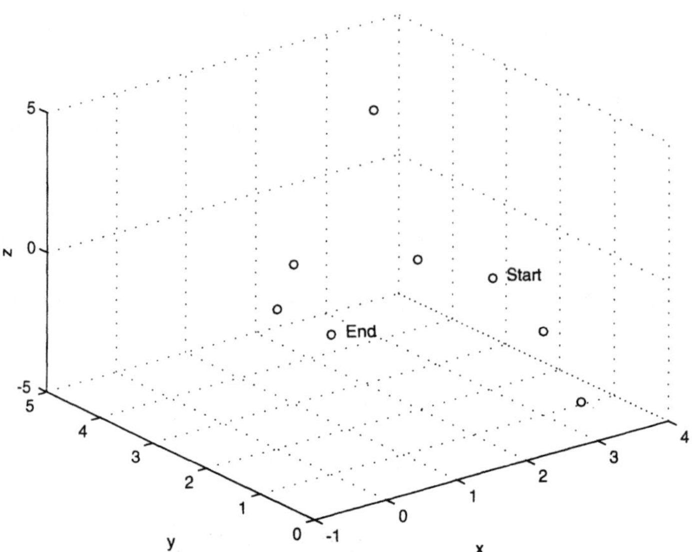

FIGURE 14.7 Three-dimensional plot of experimental data points.

generates the data points, grid, and axes in Figure 14.7. The first thing that you should notice about this script is how we have used colon notation (e.g., `data(:,1)`) to extract the vectors `x`, `y`, and `z` from `data`. This script also demonstrates that many of the optional features we have used with `plot`, such as line and mark types, grid, and axis settings, can also be used with `plot3`.

Now we add the labels `Start` and `End` to the first and last points in array `data`. The block of MATLAB code

```
>> a = size ( data )
>> text( data(       1,1) + 0.2, data(       1, 2), 'Start' );
>> text( data( a(1,1),1) + 0.2, data( a(1,1), 2), 'End' );
```

uses the function `size` to obtain the number of rows and columns in array data—`a(1,1)` contains the number of rows in `data`, and `a(1,2)` the number of columns. The `text` function then adds the desired labels at the coordinates of the first and last data points.

14.3 MESH AND SURFACE PLOTTING

MATLAB provides a suite of functions for creating three-dimensional mesh and surface plots of functional relationships

$$z = f(x, y) \tag{14.3}$$

above a rectangular region defined in the (x-y) plane. MATLAB represents $z = f(x, y)$ as an array of data points above a regular grid of points lying in the (x-y) plane

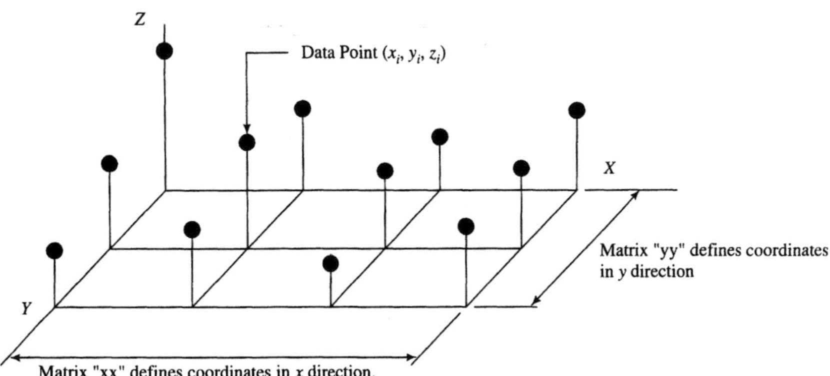

FIGURE 14.8 Three-dimensional mesh above regular grid of points in $(x$-$y)$ plane.

(see Figure 14.8). The surface shape (or mesh shape) is highlighted by connecting the neighboring data points by straight-line segments, with the result in many cases looking like a fishing net.

Three steps are needed to create a mesh or surface plot:

1. **Generate Two-Dimensional Grid in (*x*-*y*) Plane.** A rectangular grid of points in the $(x$-$y)$ plane is generated by defining vectors xx and yy for the coordinate positions of the nodes along the x- and y-axes. Then, the function call

```
[ x, y ] = meshgrid ( xx, yy )
```

   transforms the domain into rectangular arrays x and y for the efficient evaluation of $z = f(x, y)$. The rows of the output array x are copies of the vector xx, and the columns of the output array y are copies of the vector yy.

2. **Compute *z* values at (*x*,*y*) Coordinates of Grid.** Now that matrices x and y of coordinates in the $(x$-$y)$ domain are in place, we can systematically evaluate Equation 14.3 for each (x, y) coordinate pair. The results are stored in a rectangular array z.

   We soon see that by writing $f(x, y)$ in terms of matrix element level operations, in many cases, the entire evaluation of (x, y) coordinate pairs can be achieved with only one MATLAB statement.

3. **Draw Mesh and Surface Plots.** Three-dimensional mesh and surface plots may be produced with the functions

`mesh(z)`	Creates a three-dimensional mesh plot of the elements of matrix z. If z is an m-by-n matrix, then the x- and y-axes will cover the ranges 1 through m and 1 through n, respectively.
`surf(z)`	Draws a three-dimensional surface plot of the elements of matrix z. Otherwise, it is the same as `mesh(z)`.
`mesh(x,y,z)`	Creates a three-dimensional mesh plot of the elements of matrix

z, the x- and y-axes labeled to cover the range of values in matrices xx and yy.

`surf(x,y,z)` Creates a three-dimensional surface plot of the elements of matrix z, the x- and y-axes labeled to cover the range of values in matrices xx and yy.

The `mesh` and `surf` functions can also be used with various color options, and we refer you to the online MATLAB documentation for the relevant details.

Example. Suppose that we want to create a three-dimensional plot of the function

$$z = f(x, y) = [x^2 + y^2] \cdot \frac{\sin(y)}{y} \tag{14.4}$$

over the domain $-10 \leq x \leq 10$ and $-10 \leq y \leq 10$.

The block of MATLAB code

```
>> xx = -10: 0.4: 10;
>> yy = xx;
>> yy = yy + (yy==0)*eps
>> [x,y] = meshgrid(xx,yy);
```

generates matrices xx and yy containing coordinates of $-10 \leq x \leq 10$ and $-10 \leq y \leq 10$ divided into intervals of 0.4. The third statement moves points along the

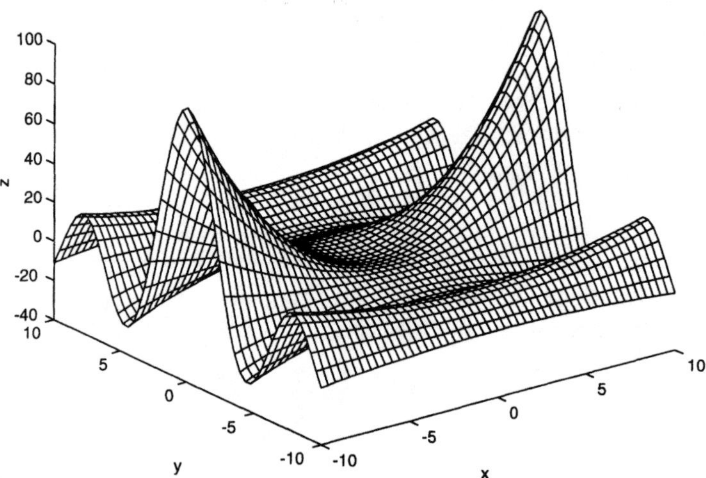

FIGURE 14.9 Three-dimensional mesh.

line $y = 0$ to $y =$ eps so that MATLAB will not generate a "divide by zero" in its evaluation of Equation 14.4. Finally, the `meshgrid` function returns (51 × 51) matrices `x` and `y` containing the x- and y-coordinates in the rectangular domain. The command

```
>> z = (x.^2 +  y.^2).*sin(y)./y
```

systematically evaluates z, a (51 × 51) matrix, for each of the (x-y) coordinate pairs in the rectangular domain. Finally, the commands

```
>> mesh(xx,yy,z)
>> xlabel('x'), ylabel('y'), zlabel('z')
```

generate a three-dimensional mesh plot, with the x- and y-axes scaled to cover the range of points contained in matrices `xx` and `yy`. The result is shown in Figure 14.9.

14.4 CONTOUR PLOTS

A contour plot is an elevation map containing families of lines connecting regions of equal elevation. Sometimes it is convenient to think of a contour as a slice of a region at a particular elevation.

In MATLAB, contour plots are generated from three-dimensional elevation data:

`contour(z)`	Generates a contour plot of matrix z where the matrix elements are treated as heights above the (x-y) plane.
`contour(x,y,z)`	Generates a contour plot where `x` and `y` are vectors specifying coordinates on the x- and y-axes. Again, `z` is a matrix whose elements are treated as heights above the (x-y) plane.
`contour(x,y,z,v)`	Matrices `x`, `y`, and `z` are as previously defined. Vector `v` tells contour to draw `length (v)` contour lines at the elevations specified in the elements of `v`.

Three-dimensional mesh and surface plots may be drawn with a contour diagram lying in the (x-y) plane. The relevant function specifications are

`meshc(x,y,z)`	This function is the same as `mesh`, except that a contour plot is drawn beneath the mesh.
`surfc(x,y,z)`	This function is the same as `surf`, except that a contour plot is drawn beneath the surface.

Example. With matrices xx, yy, x, y, and z in place for Figure 14.9, a two-dimensional contour map can be drawn and labeled with

```
>> contour(xx,yy,z)
>> xlabel('x'), ylabel('x')
```

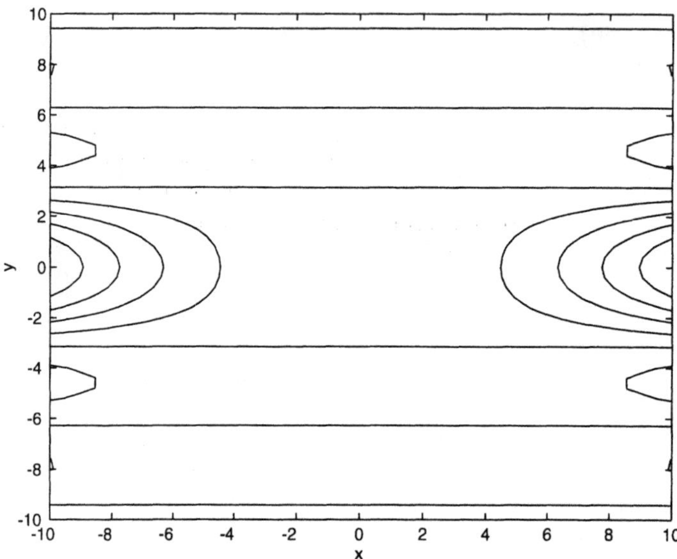

FIGURE 14.10 Contour plot.

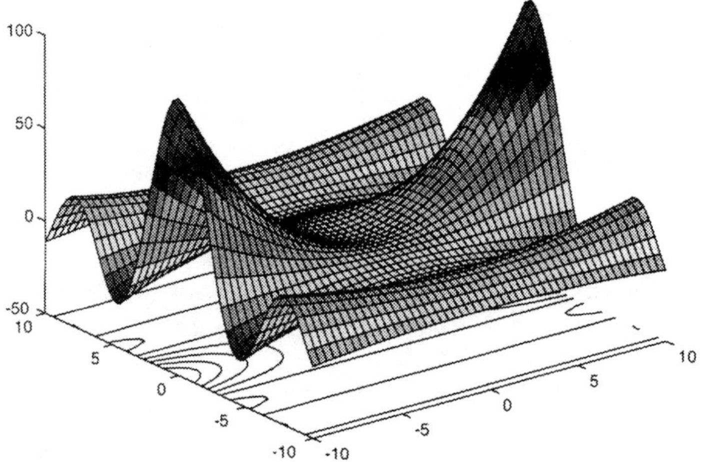

FIGURE 14.11 Combined surface and contour plot.

Similarly, a three-dimensional surface plot with a contour map drawn beneath can be generated with the command

```
>> surfc(xx,yy,z)
```

The results are shown in Figures 14.10 and 14.11.

14.5 SUBPLOTS

MATLAB graphics windows will contain one plot by default. The `subplot` command can be used to partition the graphics screen so that either two or four plots are displayed simultaneously. Two subwindows can be displayed either "side by side" or "top and bottom." When the graphics window is partitioned into four subwindows, two are on the top and two are on the bottom.

The syntax for setting up a `subplot` is

`subplot(i,j,k)` The subplot function takes three integer arguments `i`, `j`, and `k`. Integers `i` and `j` specify that the graphics window should be partitioned into an *i*-by-*j* grid of smaller windows. The subwindows are numbered from left to right, top to bottom. Integer `k` specifies the *k*th subplot for the current graphics window.

Example. The sequence of commands that follow generates the array of subplots shown in Figure 14.12.

```
% Define array of temperatures in chimney cross section

  temp = [ NaN    NaN    NaN    NaN   200.0  147.3  96.5  47.7  0.0 ;
           NaN    NaN    NaN    NaN   200.0  146.9  96.0  47.4  0.0 ;
           NaN    NaN    NaN    NaN   200.0  145.2  93.9  46.1  0.0 ;
           NaN    NaN    NaN    NaN   200.0  140.4  88.9  43.2  0.0 ;
         200.0  200.0  200.0  200.0   200.0  128.2  78.8  37.8  0.0 ;
         147.3  146.9  145.2  140.4   128.2   94.3  60.6  29.6  0.0 ;
          96.5   96.0   93.9   88.9    78.8   60.6  40.2  19.9  0.0 ;
          47.7   47.4   46.1   43.2    37.8   29.6  19.9  10.0  0.0 ;
           0.0    0.0    0.0    0.0     0.0    0.0   0.0   0.0  0.0 ];

% Generate contour and surface subplots.

  subplot(2,2,1);
  contour( temp )
  title('Contour Plot');
  subplot(2,2,2);
  mesh( temp )
```

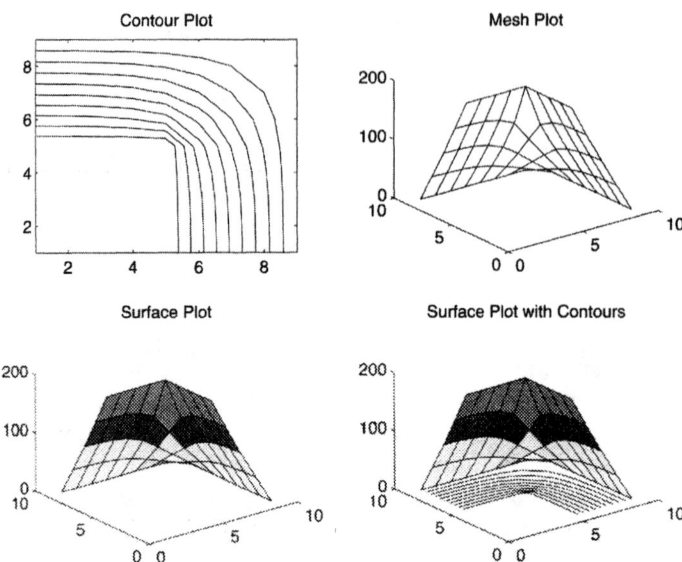

FIGURE 14.12 Temperature profiles in chimney cross-section.

```
  title('Mesh Plot');
  subplot(2,2,3);
  surf( temp )
  title('Surface Plot');
  subplot(2,2,4);
  surfc( temp )
  title('Surface Plot with Contours');

% ================================================
% The End !
```

In the function calls `contour( temp )`, `mesh( temp )`, `surf( temp )`, and `surfc( temp )`, the elements of matrix `temp` are treated as elevations above the (x-y) plane.

You may recognize array `temp` from the C tutorial, where we computed the distribution of temperatures in one fourth of a chimney cross-section. The chimney interior is represented by the block of `NaN`s. The zero elements along the right-hand side and bottom of `temp` represent the outside temperature. The row and column of 200 elements are the temperature along the inside wall of the chimney.

14.6 HARD COPIES OF MATLAB GRAPHICS

To create a black-and-white postscript file of a MATLAB figure, just type

```
>> print name-of-figure.ps
```

Color postscript files can be generated with

```
>> print -dpsc name-of-figure.ps
```

Similarly, to create a color `jpg` file (i.e., Joint Photographic Experts Group file), try the following command

```
>> print -djpeg name-of-figure.jpg
```

Online information can be obtained by typing `help print`.

14.7 PREPARING MATLAB GRAPHICS FOR THE WORLD WIDE WEB

The UNIX tool `xv` can then be used to convert the postscript file into a "gif" file format, suitable for reading by WWW browsers.

REVIEW QUESTIONS

1. How can the axes in a two-dimensional plot be constrained to retain the true shape of a figure?
2. How does MATLAB handle the plotting of
$$f(x) = \frac{(x-2)}{(x-2)}$$
at $x = 2$? What is a good way of avoiding the "divide-by-zero" scenario?
3. What does the `hold` command do?
4. How would you draw a three-dimensional surface together with a contour plot of elevation levels?

14.8 PROGRAMMING EXERCISES

Problem 14.1 (Beginner): Suppose that column 1 in the following file, `RAIN.TXT`, contains the daily rainfall for 1 week, and the second column contains the average rainfall for the week.

```
0.100000 0.694286
1.000000 0.694286
0.000000 0.694286
0.200000 0.694286
3.560000 0.694286
0.000000 0.694286
0.000000 0.694286
```

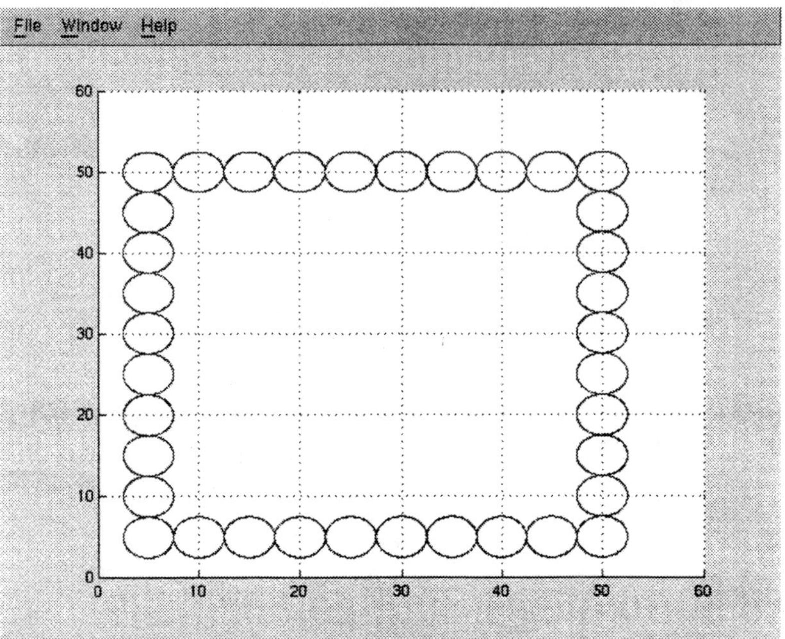

FIGURE 14.13 Rectangular layout of circles.

Write a MATLAB program that will

1. Read the contents of `RAIN.TXT` into MATLAB.
2. Plot a histogram of the daily rainfall measurements and a horizontal line for the average weekly rainfall.

Problem 14.2 (Beginner): The fragment of MATLAB code

```
>> t = 0:0.01:2*pi;
>> plot( sin(t), cos(t) )
```

plots a circle of radius 1 centered at the origin.

1. Write a function file `circle.m` that will plot a circle of radius r centered at coordinate (x, y). A suitable function declaration is

```
function circle ( x, y, r )
```

2. With your `circle` function in hand, write a short M-file that will generate the rectangular layout of circles shown in Figure 14.13. The circles are positioned along the x coordinates $x = 5$ and $x = 50$ and the y coordinates $y = 5$ and $y = 50$. Each circle should have a radius 2.5.

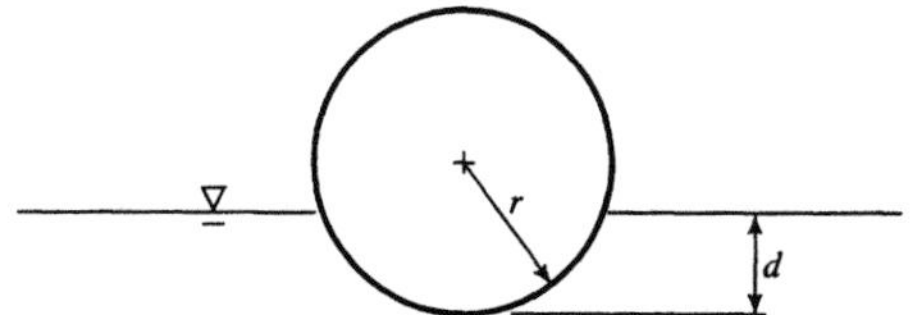

FIGURE 14.14 Sphere floating in water.

Problem 14.3 (Beginner): Write a MATLAB script file that will plot and label the function:

$$z = f(x, y) = [e^{-x^2-y^2} \cdot \sin(y) \cdot \sin(y)] \qquad (14.5)$$

over the domain $-2 \leq x \leq 2$ and $-2 \leq y \leq 2$.

Problem 14.4 (Beginner): Write a MATLAB script file that will plot and label the function:

$$z = f(x, y) = \text{int}\,[4.0 \cdot \sin^3(x) \cdot \sin^3(y) + 0.5] \qquad (14.6)$$

for the domain $-10 \leq x \leq 10$ and $-10 \leq y \leq 10$. In Equation 14.6, `int` is a function that truncates the fractional part of a floating point number.

Problem 14.5 (Intermediate): Figure 14.14 shows a sphere of radius r and density ρ floating in water. The weight of the sphere will be $4/3\rho\pi r^3$. The volume of the spherical segment displacing water is $1/3\pi(3rd^2 - d^3)$.

1. Show that the depth of the sphere floating in water is given by solutions to

$$f(x, \rho) = x^3 - 3 \cdot x^2 + 4 \cdot \rho = 0 \qquad (14.7)$$

   where $x = d/r$ is a dimensionless quantity.
2. Write a MATLAB program that will compute the depth to which a sphere will sink as a function of its radius for $\rho = 0$ to $\rho = 1$ in increments of 0.1.
3. Use MATLAB to plot and label the results.

Note. Perhaps the most straightforward way of solving this problem is to write a numerical procedure that computes the root of the cubic equation. This is not as hard as it might seem since $f(0, \rho)$ is always greater than zero and $f(2, \rho)$ is always less than zero. Only one solution to Equation (14.7) lies within the interval $f([0, 2], \rho)$, and so standard root finding techniques such as bisection and Newton Raphson will work. A more elegant way of solving this problem is with the `contour` function.

Problem 14.6 (Intermediate): Write a block of MATLAB code that will evaluate and plot Equation 14.1 without error and without moving the `x = 0` coordinate to `x = eps`.

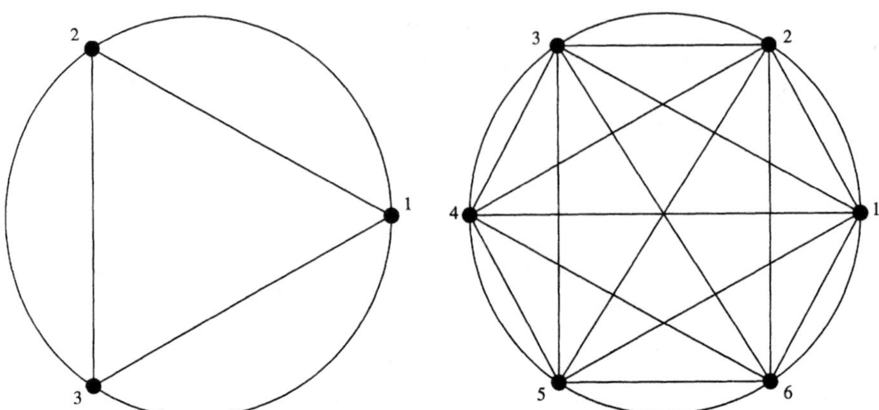

FIGURE 14.15 Partitioned circles.

Problem 14.7 (Intermediate): Write a MATLAB script file that will plot and label the family of ellipses defined by

$$[x(t), y(t)] = [A \sin(t), B \cos(t)] \tag{14.8}$$

for $0 \leq t \leq 2\pi$, $A = 1$, and $B = 1, 2, \cdots 5$.

Problem 14.8 (Intermediate): Write a MATLAB program that will draw a circle, and partition and label its perimeter into n equal segments. Line segments should then be drawn to connect all the points lying on the circle perimeter. The left- and right-hand sides of Figure 14.15 demonstrate the required partitioning and labeling for $n = 3$ and $n = 6$, respectively.

Devise an algorithm that requires no more than $n(n - 1)/2$ function calls to draw all the line segments. This is not as hard as it seems—simply observe, for example, that once a line segment has connected points 1 and 6, there is no need to draw a second line connecting points 6 and 1.

Problem 14.9 (Intermediate): An experiment is conducted on 36 specimens to determine the tensile yield strength of `A36` steel. The experimental results are as follows:

```
42.3   42.1   41.8   42.4   47.7   41.4
40.5   38.7   40.8   39.6   42.4   37.5
39.9   45.3   41.6   36.8   45.4   44.8
39.2   40.7   38.5   40.1   42.8   42.5
43.1   36.2   46.2   41.5   38.3   40.2
41.9   40.4   39.1   38.6   46.3   39.5
```

Write a MATLAB program and appropriate M-files that will

1. Read the experimental test results from a file `experimental.data`.
2. Compute the maximum, minimum, average, and median tensile strengths.
3. Generate a histogram of "observations" versus "yield stress."
4. Construct a bar graph or stair-step graph of "cumulative frequency" versus "yield stress."

Note. The average value of the experimental results can be computed using formulae presented in Section 8.5. After the experimental results have been sorted numerically, the median value is the midvalue (if the number of data points is odd) or the average of the two middle values (if the number of data points is even). The "cumulative frequency" versus "yield stress" is given by

$$\text{Cumulative frequency}(y) = \int_0^y p(x)\,dx \tag{14.9}$$

where $p(x)$ is the probability distribution of tensile yield strengths.

15

SOLUTION OF LINEAR MATRIX EQUATIONS

15.1 SYSTEMS OF LINEAR MATRIX EQUATIONS

In this chapter, we learn how MATLAB can be used to solve engineering problems involving linear systems of matrix equations. Linear systems of equations arise in many areas of engineering including structural mechanics, circuit simulation, control of electrical and mechanical devices, and finite element analysis. Moderate to large families of equations commonly represent the state of a system (e.g., equations of equilibrium, energy and momentum conservation).

15.1.1 Definition of Linear Matrix Equations

We begin with the basics. In expanded form, a system of m linear equations with n unknowns may be written

$$\begin{array}{ccccccccccc} a_{11}x_1 & + & a_{12}x_2 & + & a_{13}x_3 & + & \cdots & + & a_{1n}x_n & = & b_1 \\ a_{21}x_1 & + & a_{22}x_2 & + & a_{23}x_3 & + & \cdots & + & a_{2n}x_n & = & b_2 \\ a_{31}x_1 & + & a_{32}x_2 & + & a_{33}x_3 & + & \cdots & + & a_{3n}x_n & = & b_3 \\ \vdots & & \vdots & & \vdots & & & & \vdots & & \vdots \\ a_{m1}x_1 & + & a_{m2}x_2 & + & a_{m3}x_3 & + & \cdots & + & a_{mn}x_n & = & b_m \end{array} \tag{15.1}$$

The constants a_{11}, a_{21}, a_{31}, $\cdots$ a_{mn} and b_1, b_2, $\cdots$ b_m are called the equation coefficients. Most often the coefficients will be real numbers, but they could also be complex numbers. The variables $x_1, x_2, \cdots x_n$ are the unknowns in the system of equations. The matrix equivalent of Equation 15.1 is $[A] \cdot \{X\} = \{B\}$, where

$$[A] = \begin{bmatrix} a_{11} & a_{12} & \cdots & a_{1n} \\ a_{21} & a_{22} & & \vdots \\ \vdots & & & \vdots \\ a_{m1} & \cdots & \cdots & a_{mn} \end{bmatrix}, \{X\} = \begin{Bmatrix} x_1 \\ x_2 \\ \vdots \\ x_n \end{Bmatrix}, \text{ and } \{B\} = \begin{Bmatrix} b_1 \\ b_2 \\ \vdots \\ b_m \end{Bmatrix} \quad (15.2)$$

Equations 15.2 are said to be homogeneous when the right-hand side vector `{B}` = 0. A system of equations is said to be under-determined when there are more unknowns than equations (i.e., `m` < `n`). Conversely, a system of equations is termed over-determined when there are more equations than unknowns (i.e., `m` > `n`). Over-determined systems of equations arise in linear optimization methods, and in the problem of finding the best fit of a low-order equation to experimental data. A well-known name for the latter application is least squares analysis.

15.1.2 Geometry of Two- and Three-Dimensional Systems

Linear algebra plays a central role in the development of numerical equation solvers because it allows for the classification solutions to Equation 15.2. Indeed, before the development of numerical equation solvers can proceed, we need to understand under what circumstances a system of equations will have a unique solution. For those cases where a system of equations has more than one solution, we also need to know how many solutions there will be and how they can be characterized.

A good way of gaining insight into these issues is to study systems of equations whose solutions are simple enough to be graphically displayed. This will occur for two- and three-dimensional problems (i.e., when $m = n = 2$ and $m = n = 3$).

Two-Dimensional Example

When $m = n = 2$, the matrix equations $[A] \cdot \{X\} = \{B\}$ can be interpreted as a pair of straight lines in the (x_1, x_2) plane. That is,

$$a_{11}x_1 + a_{12}x_2 = b_1 \quad (15.3)$$

$$a_{21}x_1 + a_{22}x_2 = b_2 \quad (15.4)$$

The pair of Equations 15.3 and 15.4 may be interpreted as a linear transformation from two-dimensional coordinate space (x_1, x_2) into a two-dimensional right-hand side vector space (b_1, b_2) (see Figure 15.1).

The problem of finding solutions to Equations 15.3 and 15.4 is equivalent to finding points $X = (x_1, x_2)$ in the (X_1, X_2) plane that will be mapped via the transformation $A \cdot X$ into the (B_1, B_2) plane.

As we soon see, this problem is complicated by three types of solutions, namely, (1) no solutions to `A.X = B`, (2) a unique solution to `A.X = B`, or (3) an infinite number of solutions to `A.X = B`.

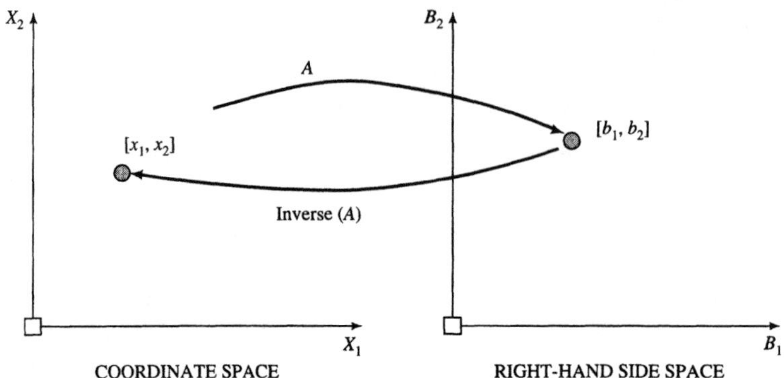

FIGURE 15.1 Matrix transformations.

15.1.3 Hand Calculation Procedures

There are two hand calculation procedures for computing a solution(s) to the system of equations. In the `graphical method`, plots of lines in two dimensions are constructed. Solutions to the system of equations correspond to points where the lines intersect. An example of such a solution is shown in the left-hand schematic of Figure 15.2, labeled Unique Solution.

In the second method, the equations are premultiplied by constants in such a way that when they are combined *variables will be eliminated.* For example, if Equation 15.3 is multiplied by a_{21} and Equation 15.4 is multiplied by a_{11}, then we have the system of equations

$$a_{21} \cdot a_{11} \cdot x_1 + a_{21} \cdot a_{12} \cdot x_2 = a_{21} \cdot b_1 \tag{15.5}$$

$$a_{11} \cdot a_{21} \cdot x_1 + a_{11} \cdot a_{22} \cdot x_2 = a_{11} \cdot b_2 \tag{15.6}$$

Subtracting Equation 15.5 from Equation 15.6 gives

$$x_2 = \left[\frac{a_{11} \cdot b_2 - a_{21} \cdot b_1}{a_{11} \cdot a_{22} - a_{12} \cdot a_{21}} \right] \tag{15.7}$$

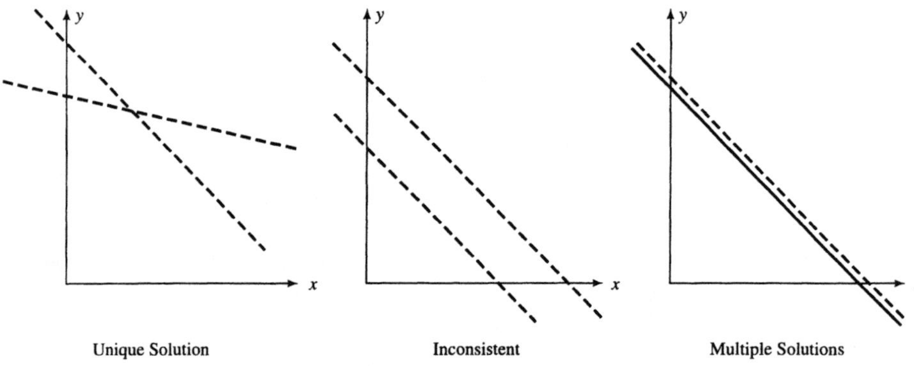

FIGURE 15.2 Types of solutions to matrix equations.

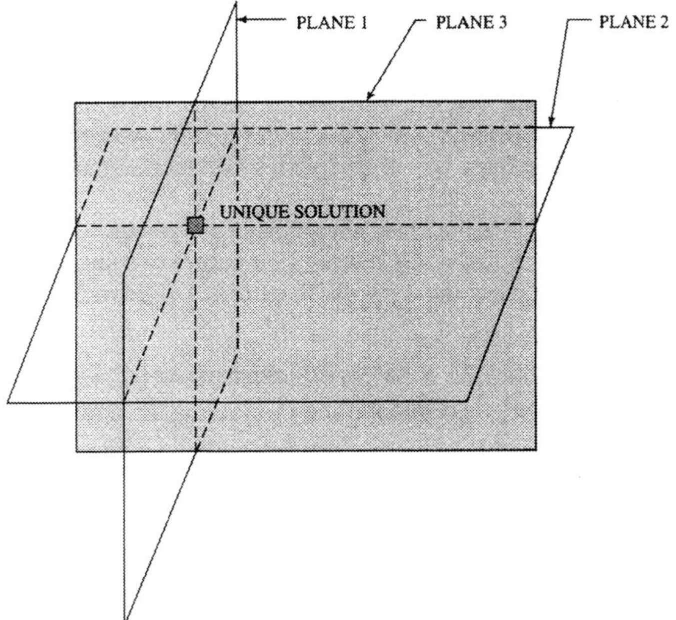

FIGURE 15.3 *Intersection of planes in three-dimensional space.*

Now x_2 can be back-substituted into either Equation 15.3 or Equation 15.4 for the corresponding value of x_1. You may have noticed that this procedure is not unique. If Equation 15.3 is multiplied by a_{22} and Equation 15.4 is multiplied by a_{12}, subtraction of equations gives

$$x_1 = \left[\frac{a_{22} \cdot b_1 - a_{12} \cdot b_2}{a_{11} \cdot a_{22} - a_{12} \cdot a_{21}}\right] \tag{15.8}$$

and x_1 can be back-substituted into either Equation 15.3 or 15.4 for the corresponding value of x_2.

15.1.4 Types of Solutions for Systems of Linear Matrix Equations

We observe that the denominators of Equations 15.7 and 15.8 are the same, and correspond to the determinant of a (2×2) matrix, namely,

$$\det(A) = \det\begin{bmatrix} a_{11} & a_{12} \\ a_{21} & a_{22} \end{bmatrix} = a_{11} \cdot a_{22} - a_{12} \cdot a_{21} \tag{15.9}$$

The same principles apply to families of equations containing three unknowns (i.e., $m = n = 3$). When the equations are written in the form $[A] \cdot \{X\} = \{B\}$, A is a (3×3) matrix. From a geometric point of view, each equation describes a plane in three-dimensional space, as shown in Figure 15.3. The solution to the system of equations corresponds to those points in three-dimensional space that lie in all three planes. There will only be one such point when det(A) $\neq$ 0. The mathematical condition det(A) = 0 occurs when two or more planes are parallel. As with the two-dimensional case, there will be either an infinite number of solutions or no solutions. An infinite number of solutions occurs when all three planes have the same equation (or a nonzero constant multiplied by the same equations). No solutions occur when at least two of the planes are parallel but do not have the same equation.

When problem sizes increase above three unknowns, we can no longer rely on graphical methods to find a solution(s). The nature of solutions to linear equations is given instead by theoretical results from linear algebra. The results are

1. A unique solution $\{X\} = [A^{-1}] \cdot \{B\}$ exists when $[A^{-1}]$ exists (i.e., det$[A] \neq 0$).
2. The equations are inconsistent when $[A]$ is singular and rank$[A \mid B] \neq$ rank$[A]$.
3. If rank $[A|B]$ equals rank$[A]$, then there are an infinite number of solutions.

For the case of a unique solution, $[A^{-1}]$ is the inverse of matrix `A`, and such a matrix will exist when the determinant of `A` is nonzero. An equivalent way of detecting a unique solution is with the rank of matrix `A`, that is, the number of linearly independent rows in matrix `A`. In a nutshell, a unique solution to the matrix equations will exist when the `rank(A)` equals the number of rows or columns in `A`. In cases 2 and 3 above, the notation $[A \mid B]$ stands for the matrix `A` juxtaposed with matrix `B`.

The MATLAB function `inv (A)` will return the inverse $[A^{-1}]$ of matrix `A` when it exists. The MATLAB function `det (A)` will return the determinant of a square matrix `A`. The MATLAB function `rank (A)` will return the rank of `A`, otherwise known as the number of linearly independent rows (or columns) in `A`.

15.2 CASE STUDY PROBLEM: THREE LINEAR MATRIX EQUATIONS

Suppose that the following three equations describe the equilibrium of a simple structural system as a function of external loads and computed displacements.

$$\begin{aligned} 3x_1 - 1x_2 + 0x_3 &= 1 \\ -1x_1 + 6x_2 - 2x_3 &= 5 \\ 0x_1 - 2x_2 + 10x_3 &= 26 \end{aligned} \tag{15.10}$$

This family of equations can be written in the form `A.X = B` where

$$[A] = \begin{bmatrix} 3 & -1 & 0 \\ -1 & 6 & -2 \\ 0 & -2 & 10 \end{bmatrix}, \{X\} = \begin{Bmatrix} x_1 \\ x_2 \\ x_3 \end{Bmatrix}, \text{ and } \{B\} = \begin{Bmatrix} 1 \\ 5 \\ 26 \end{Bmatrix} \tag{15.11}$$

In a typical application, matrices `A` and `B` will be defined by the parameters of the engineering problem, and the solution matrix X will need to be computed. In this particular case, the solution matrix

$$\{X\} = \begin{Bmatrix} 1 \\ 2 \\ 3 \end{Bmatrix} \quad (15.12)$$

makes the left- and right-hand sides of matrix Equation 15.11 equal. The following script of MATLAB code

```
>> A = [ 3 -1 0; -1 6 -2; 0 -2 10 ];
>> B = [ 1; 5; 26 ];
>> X = A\B
```

defines matrices A and B, and computes and prints the solution to A.X = B, namely,

```
>> X = A\B
X =
     1.0000
     2.0000
     3.0000
>>
```

Of course, this solution can be verified by first computing the inverse of A, and then premultiplying it by B. The relevant details of MATLAB code are

```
>> Ainv = inv(A)
Ainv =
     0.3544     0.0633     0.0127
     0.0633     0.1899     0.0380
     0.0127     0.0380     0.1076
>> X = Ainv*B
X =
     1.0000
     2.0000
     3.0000
>>
```

We use MATLAB to check that this result is consistent with the rank and determinant of matrix A. First, the script of code

```
>> rank (A)
ans =
       3
>>
```

shows that the matrix rank is equal to 3, the number of rows and columns in matrix

A. We therefore expect that the matrix equations will have a unique solution. A second indicator of the solution type is the matrix determinant. The script of code

```
>> det (A)
ans =
   158
>>
```

shows that the matrix determinant is nonzero, again indicating the presence of a unique solution to the matrix equations.

15.3 SINGULAR SYSTEMS OF MATRIX EQUATIONS

A family of matrix equations A is said to be singular when the individual equations are dependent. That is, one or more of the matrix equations can be written as a linear combination of the remaining equations. For example, matrix

```
>> A = [ 1 2 3;
         2 4 6;
         4 5 6 ];
```

is singular because the elements of the second row are simply two times those in the first row. For a general matrix A, such a relationship may be far from evident, and so we must rely on the rank and determinant functions to identify singular systems. In this case, the function call

```
>>  rank (A)
ans =
     2
>>
```

highlights the presence of a singular system because the `rank(A) = 2` is less than 3, the number of rows and columns in A. Consequently, the inverse of A will not exist. If this is accidentally overlooked in an engineering computation, MATLAB will display an error message and return a solution vector containing NaNs or $\pm\infty$, depending on the values elements in matrix A. Consider, for example,

```
>> Ainv = inv(A)
Warning: Matrix is singular to working precision.

Ainv =
   Inf   Inf   Inf
   Inf   Inf   Inf
   Inf   Inf   Inf
>>
```

The error condition `Inf` will be propagated to all subsequent arithmetic computations involving `Ainv`.

Generally speaking, if a matrix determinant is computed to be exactly zero, then there is no difficulty in identifying the three types of matrix solutions mentioned in the previous section. But what about matrices that are nearly singular? Many practical implementations are complicated by factors such as round-off error, finite precision, and limited ranges of numbers that may be stored in a computer (i.e., underflow and overflow of numbers). Perhaps matrix A is singular and a nonzero calculation is due to numerical problems, or perhaps it is not singular. Resolving these issues is far from a trivial matter.

15.4 ENGINEERING APPLICATIONS

Now that we are familiar with MATLAB's matrix and graphics capabilities, this section works step by step through the design and implementation of four engineering applications that require the solution of linear matrix equations.

They are

1. A MATLAB program for the structural analysis of a cantilever truss.
2. A MATLAB program for the electrical analysis of a circuit containing resistors and batteries.
3. A MATLAB program that computes a least squares analysis of experimental data.
4. A MATLAB program that computes and plots the distribution of temperature in a chimney cross-section. This problem is also solved in Section 8.7 of the C tutorial.

Each problem description is accompanied by a brief discussion of the theory needed to set up the relevant matrix equations.

15.4.1 Structural Analysis of a Cantilever Truss

Problem Statement

In the design of highway bridge structures and crane structures, engineers are often required to compute the member forces and support reactions in planar truss structures. The analysis of cantilever truss structures is governed by the following principles:

1. At each joint, the sum of internal and external forces in the horizontal and vertical directions must equal zero.
2. The sum of external forces and support reactions in the horizontal and vertical directions must equal zero.
3. For the entire structure and all possible substructures, the sum of moments must equal zero.

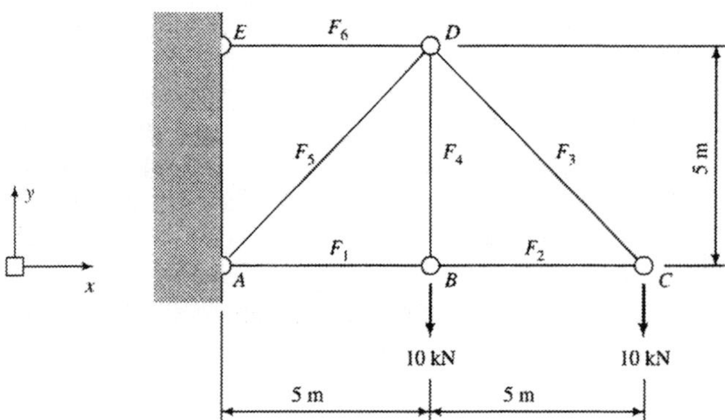

FIGURE 15.4 Six-bar cantilever truss.

Figure 15.4 shows a six-bar cantilever truss carrying `10 kN` loads at joints `B` and `C`. The analysis begins with the arbitrary assignment of element numbers in the truss, numbers for the joints, and reaction components.

We assume that

1. The truss elements can only carry axial forces, with tensile axial forces being positive and compressive axial forces being negative.
2. All the joints are pinned (in other words, the joints cannot transfer moments; only axial forces from the truss elements).

The forces $F_1, F_2, \cdots F_6$ represent the axial forces in truss members `1` through `6`, and R_{ax}, R_{ay}, R_{ex}, and R_{ey} the support reactions at joints `A` and `E`.

The cantilever truss is "statically determinate" in the sense that axial forces in the elements and the support reactions can be computed without a knowledge of material properties. Equations of equilibrium in the horizontal and vertical directions are written for each of the five joints. The equations are then expressed in matrix form, and solved for the member axial forces and horizontal and vertical reaction components. For example, the forces acting on joint `A` are

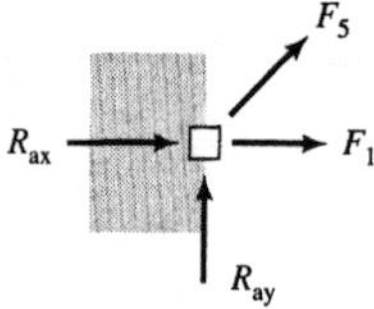

The equations of equilibrium in the horizontal and vertical directions are

$$\sum F_x = F_1 + \frac{F_5}{\sqrt{2}} + R_{ax} = 0 \qquad \sum F_y = \frac{F_5}{\sqrt{2}} + R_{ay} = 0 \tag{15.13}$$

The equations of equilibrium for joint B are

$$\sum F_x = F_1 - F_2 = 0 \qquad \sum F_y = F_4 - 10 = 0 \tag{15.14}$$

The equations of equilibrium for joint C are

$$\sum F_x = F_2 + \frac{F_3}{\sqrt{2}} = 0 \qquad \sum F_y = \frac{F_3}{\sqrt{2}} - 10 = 0 \tag{15.15}$$

The equations of equilibrium for joint D are

$$\sum F_x = \frac{F_3}{\sqrt{2}} - \frac{F_5}{\sqrt{2}} - F_6 = 0 \qquad \sum F_y = F_4 + \frac{F_3}{\sqrt{2}} + \frac{F_5}{\sqrt{2}} = 0 \tag{15.16}$$

and, for joint E, the equations of equilibrium are

$$\sum F_x = F_6 + R_{ex} = 0 \qquad \sum F_y = R_{ey} = 0 \tag{15.17}$$

Equations 15.13 to 15.17 are solved in two steps. First, we put Equations 15.14 to 15.16 in matrix form and solve for the member forces $F_1, F_2, \cdots F_6$. Then we back-substitute the member forces into Equations 15.13 and 15.17 to get the support reactions. In matrix form, equations 15.14 to 15.16 are

$$\begin{bmatrix} 1 & -1 & 0 & 0 & 0 & 0 \\ 0 & 0 & 0 & 1 & 0 & 0 \\ 0 & 1 & 1/\sqrt{2} & 0 & 0 & 0 \\ 0 & 0 & 1/\sqrt{2} & 0 & 0 & 0 \\ 0 & 0 & 1/\sqrt{2} & 0 & -1/\sqrt{2} & -1 \\ 0 & 0 & 1/\sqrt{2} & 1 & 1/\sqrt{2} & 0 \end{bmatrix} \cdot \begin{Bmatrix} F_1 \\ F_2 \\ F_3 \\ F_4 \\ F_5 \\ F_6 \end{Bmatrix} = \begin{Bmatrix} 0 \\ 10 \\ 0 \\ 10 \\ 0 \\ 0 \end{Bmatrix} \tag{15.18}$$

In step two, the support reactions are given by

$$\begin{Bmatrix} R_{ax} \\ R_{ay} \\ R_{ex} \\ R_{ey} \end{Bmatrix} = \begin{Bmatrix} -1 & 0 & 0 & 0 & -1/\sqrt{2} & 0 \\ 0 & 0 & 0 & 0 & -1/\sqrt{2} & 0 \\ 0 & 0 & 0 & 0 & 0 & -1 \\ 0 & 0 & 0 & 0 & 0 & 0 \end{Bmatrix} \cdot \begin{Bmatrix} F_1 \\ F_2 \\ F_3 \\ F_4 \\ F_5 \\ F_6 \end{Bmatrix} \tag{15.19}$$

Program Source Code

Program 15.1 allocates memory for matrix Equations 15.18 and 15.19, initializes the nonzero matrix element values, and computes a solution to Equations 15.18 and 15.19. It prints matrices of axial forces in the truss members and components of reaction at joints A and E.

PROGRAM 15.1: STRUCTURAL ANALYSIS OF CANTILEVER TRUSS

```
% ======================================================================
% truss.m : Compute internal forces and reactions in cantilever truss structure.
%
% Matrices : Truss     = Represents truss geometry and element connectivity.
%          : Load      = External forces acting on the truss nodes.
%          : Force     = Internal member forces acting in truss elements.
%          : Support   = Relationship between truss and support reactions.
%          : Reactions = Matrix of support reaction forces.
% ======================================================================

% Define problem parameters

  NoElmts     = 6;
  NoReactions = 4;

% Setup matrix for "truss connectivity"

  Truss = zeros( NoElmts, NoElmts );
  Truss( 1 , 1 ) =  1;
  Truss( 1 , 2 ) = -1;

  Truss( 2 , 4 ) =  1;

  Truss( 3 , 2 ) =  1;
  Truss( 3 , 3 ) =  1/sqrt(2);

  Truss( 4 , 3 ) =   1/sqrt(2);

  Truss( 5 , 3 ) =   1/sqrt(2);
  Truss( 5 , 5 ) =  -1/sqrt(2);
  Truss( 5 , 6 ) =  -1;

  Truss( 6 , 3 ) =   1/sqrt(2);
  Truss( 6 , 4 ) =   1;
  Truss( 6 , 5 ) =   1/sqrt(2);

% Setup matrix for "external loads" on truss nodes

  Load = zeros( NoElmts, 1 );
  Load( 2 , 1 ) =  10;
  Load( 4 , 1 ) =  10;
```

```
% Print matrices for "truss connectivity" and "external loads"

  Truss
  Load

% Solve equations and print "internal member" forces

  Force = Truss\Load

% Setup matrix for "support reactions"

  Support = zeros( NoReactions, NoElmts );

  Support( 1 , 1 ) = -1;
  Support( 1 , 5 ) = -1/sqrt(2);
  Support( 2 , 5 ) = -1/sqrt(2);
  Support( 3 , 6 ) = -1;

% Compute and print "support reactions"

  Reactions = Support*Force

% ================================================================
% the end!
```

Running the Program

Assume that Program 15.1 is contained the M-file `truss.m`. The script of input/output (I/O):

```
>> format compact
>> truss
Truss =
    1.0000   -1.0000         0         0         0         0
         0         0         0    1.0000         0         0
         0    1.0000    0.7071         0         0         0
         0         0    0.7071         0         0         0
         0         0    0.7071         0   -0.7071   -1.0000
         0         0    0.7071    1.0000    0.7071         0
Load =
     0
    10
     0
    10
     0
     0
```

```
Force =
  -10.0000
  -10.0000
   14.1421
   10.0000
  -28.2843
   30.0000
Reactions =
    30
    20
   -30
     0
>>
```

shows the command needed to run the program (i.e., `truss`) and the output that is generated by the analysis.

For programming convenience, we define the variables `NoElmts` and `NoReactions` for the number of frame elements and reactions, respectively. The matrices in Equations 15.18 and 15.19 are defined by first allocating memory for zero matrices of the appropriate size and then filling in the nonzero matrix elements.

Validating the Results

The member `"Forces"` matrix contains the axial forces in elements `1` through `6`. A quick examination of the matrix reveals that $F_1 = F_6 = -10$ kN (i.e., compression) and that $F_4 = 10$ kN (i.e., tension). Element `6` carries a tensile force of 30 kN. If you take moments about joint `A`, then you will see that the axial force in element `6` times a lever arm of `5 m` is balanced by the 10 kN loads at lever arms `5 m` and `10 m`.

The `"Support"` reactions matrix contains the horizontal and vertical support reactions at joints `A` and `E`. Two points should be noted. First, because the horizontal component of externally applied loads is zero, we expect that the sum of the horizontal reactions at joints `A` and `E` will be zero. They are. Second, you should also note that truss element 2 transfers all the externally applied vertical loads to support `A`. The vertical reaction at support `A` is 20 kN, which is the sum of the two externally applied loads.

15.4.2 Analysis of an Electrical Circuit

Problem Statement

The analysis of electrical networks composed of resistance and voltage supplies is governed by three basic principles:

1. **Ohm's Law.** The drop in voltagê across a resistor R in the direction of an assumed current is proportional to the current. In other words, $V = I \cdot R$.

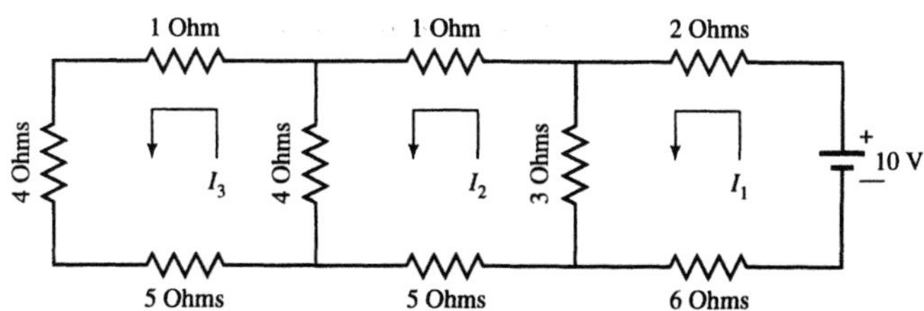

FIGURE 15.5 Three-loop voltage-resistance circuit.

2. **Kirchoff's Law.** The sum of all currents entering and exiting a node must equal zero.
3. **Kirchoff's Voltage Law.** The sum of voltage drops around any closed loop must sum to zero.

Consider the circuit shown in Figure 15.5, consisting of three loops, nine resistors, and one battery.

The analysis begins with the arbitrary assignment of current directions in each of the three loops. The current in each loop will be deemed to be positive when it flows in the direction shown. For loop 1, a positive voltage change occurs between the negative and positive battery terminals. The voltage drops across the upper and lower resistors in loop one are $2I_1$ and $6I_1$, and $3 \cdot (I_1 - I_2)$ in the left-most resistor. Applying Kirchoff's Voltage law to loop 1 gives

$$6 \cdot I_1 + 2 \cdot I_1 + 3 \cdot (I_1 - I_2) = 10 \text{ V} \tag{15.20}$$

For loop 2, Kirchoff's voltage law gives

$$I_2 + 5 \cdot I_2 + 3 \cdot (I_2 - I_1) + 4 \cdot (I_2 - I_3) = 0 \text{ V} \tag{15.21}$$

and for loop 3, Kirchoff's Voltage Law gives

$$I_3 + 4 \cdot I_3 + 5 \cdot I_3 + 4 \cdot (I_3 - I_2) = 0 \text{ V} \tag{15.22}$$

Putting Equations 15.20 to 15.22 in matrix form gives

$$\begin{bmatrix} 11 & -3 & 0 \\ -3 & 13 & -4 \\ 0 & -4 & 14 \end{bmatrix} \cdot \begin{Bmatrix} I_1 \\ I_2 \\ I_3 \end{Bmatrix} = \begin{Bmatrix} 10 \\ 0 \\ 0 \end{Bmatrix} \tag{15.23}$$

Program Source Code

Program 15.2 defines and initializes matrix Equation 15.23, and solves and prints the solution to the currents in each of the three loops.

PROGRAM 15.2: ANALYSIS OF AN ELECTRICAL CIRCUIT

```
% ======================================================================
% electrical.m -- Compute currents in an electrical circuit
%
% Matrices : Resist  = Rows represents resistors in each loop.
%          : Voltage = Voltage gain in each loop provided by battery.
%          : Current = Current in each loop.
%
% ======================================================================

% Setup matrix for "resistances in circuit loops"

  Resist = [ 11  -3   0;
             -3  13  -4;
              0  -4  14 ]

% Setup matrix for "voltage gains" in circuit loops

  Voltage = [ 10; 0; 0 ]

% Solve equations and print currents

  Current = Resist\Voltage

% ==========================================================
% the end!
```

Running the Program

Assume that Program 15.2 is stored in `electrical.m`. The MATLAB script

```
>> format compact
>> electrical
Resist =
    11    -3     0
    -3    13    -4
     0    -4    14
Voltage =
    10
     0
     0
Current =
    0.9765
    0.2471
    0.0706
>>
```

shows the command needed to execute the program and the output that is generated. A (3 × 3) matrix of system resistances is explicitly defined and initialized in one MATLAB statement. A (3 × 1) matrix of system voltages is defined in a second statement. With these matrices in place, solutions to Equation 15.23 are computed and printed by simply writing

```
>> Current = Resist\Voltage
```

Of course, we could have computed the currents in each loop of the circuit by writing `inv(Resist)*Voltage`.

Validating the Results

You should verify that the solution is correct by multiplying `Resist*Current` and checking that the result is equal to `Voltage`.

15.4.3 Least Squares Analysis of Experimental Data

Problem Statement

Engineers are often faced with the practical problem of having to model complex physical processes and phenomena that are not fully understood. The lack of understanding may be due to the overwhelming size of the system, or perhaps, because information about the system is missing. In an effort to better understand system behavior, many engineers design and conduct laboratory experiments, and use the experimental data in the construction of simplified empirical models. The simplified models will be based on numerous assumptions in behavior and may contain parameters that can be adjusted or modified to provide a "best fit" to the experimental data.

Figure 15.6 is a plot of experimental data points $(x_1, y_1), (x_2, y_2), \cdots (x_N, y_N)$, and a dashed-line polynomial $y = p(x)$ of best fit that has been drawn by hand. The polynomial might predict, for example, the relationship between an input signal, x, and an output signal, $y = p(x)$. Notice that approximately half of the data points deviate from the line in a positive direction (i.e., are above the line) and approximately half the data points are below the line (i.e., negative deviation).

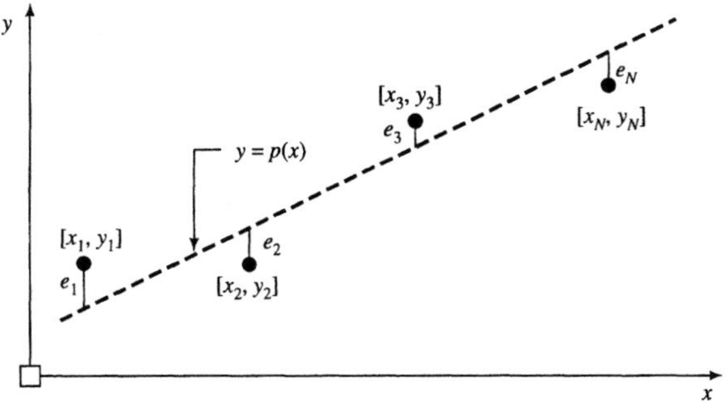

FIGURE 15.6 Experimental data points and line of best fit.

Although it is certainly possible to find a high-order polynomial that will interpolate the data points exactly, in many engineering applications, theoretical considerations and good engineering judgment indicate that a low-order polynomial (or simpler curve) will provide a good approximation to the data. Unfortunately, there are no hard-and-fast rules for selecting a best functional form. An engineer should look for obvious trends, such as a linear, quadratic, cubic polynomial, for symmetries and antisymmetries in the data, and for periodic behavior, suggesting functional forms containing `sin()` and `cos()` terms.

Derivation of Discrete Least Squares Equations

In this section, we formulate a mathematical procedure for fitting a polynomial curve

$$p(x) = a_o + a_1 \cdot x + a_2 \cdot x^2 + \cdots + a_n \cdot x^n \tag{15.24}$$

of degree n through N data points (x_1, y_1), (x_2, y_2), $\cdots$ (x_N, y_N), where $(N > n + 1)$. To avoid mathematical difficulties with positive/negative distances in error deviations, the objective of discrete least squares is to minimize the sum of the squares of the distance between the y values of the data and $y = p(x)$. In mathematical terms, we want to minimize

$$\sum_{i=1}^{N} e_i^2 = \sum_{i=1}^{N} [y_i - p(x)]^2 \tag{15.25}$$

or

$$S(a_o, a_1, \cdots, a_n) = \sum_{i=1}^{N} [y_i - a_o - a_1 \cdot x_i \cdots a_n x_i^n]^2 \tag{15.26}$$

The optimal parameter settings are given by the solution to the linear equations

$$\frac{\partial S}{\partial a_0} = 0, \frac{\partial S}{\partial a_1} = 0, \cdots \frac{\partial S}{\partial a_n} = 0 \tag{15.27}$$

The partial derivatives of Equations 15.27 are

$$\left[\sum_{i=1}^{N}\right] \cdot a_o + \left[\sum_{i=1}^{N} x_i\right] \cdot a_1 + \cdots + \left[\sum_{i=1}^{N}\right] \cdot a_n = \sum_{i=1}^{N} y_i \tag{15.28}$$

$$\left[\sum_{i=1}^{N} x_i\right] a_o + \left[\sum_{i=1}^{N} x_i^2\right] a_1 + \cdots + \left[\sum^{N} x_i^{n+1}\right] a_n = \sum_{i=1}^{N} y_i \cdot x_i \tag{15.29}$$

$$\left[\sum_{i=1}^{N} x_i^n\right] a_o + \left[\sum_{i=1}^{N} x_i^{n+1}\right] a_1 + \cdots + \left[\sum^{N} x_i^{n+m}\right] a_n = \sum_{i=1}^{N} x_i^n \cdot y_i \tag{15.30}$$

The family of $n + 1$ Equations 15.28 through 15.30 is linear in the parameters a_o, a_1, $\cdots$ a_n. In matrix form, the equations may be written

$$\begin{bmatrix} N & \sum_{i=1}^{N} x_i & \cdots & \sum_{i=1}^{N} x_i^n \\ \sum_{i=1}^{N} x_i & \sum_{i=1}^{N} x_i^2 & \cdots & \sum_{i=1}^{N} x_i^{n+1} \\ \vdots & \vdots & \ddots & \vdots \\ \sum_{i=1}^{N} x_i^n & \sum_{i=1}^{N} x_i^{n+1} & \cdots & \sum_{i=1}^{N} x_i^{2n} \end{bmatrix} \cdot \begin{bmatrix} a_0 \\ a_1 \\ \vdots \\ a_n \end{bmatrix} = \begin{bmatrix} \sum_{i=1}^{N} y_i \\ \sum_{i=1}^{N} x_i \cdot y_i \\ \vdots \\ \sum_{i=1}^{N} x_i^n \cdot y_i \end{bmatrix} \tag{15.31}$$

Example Analysis of Experimental Data. Suppose that you have been asked to formulate an engineering model to describe the force-displacement relationship for the simple spring shown on the left-hand side of Figure 15.7. The purpose of the model is to describe the functional relationship between an applied force `F` and a measured displacement `x`.

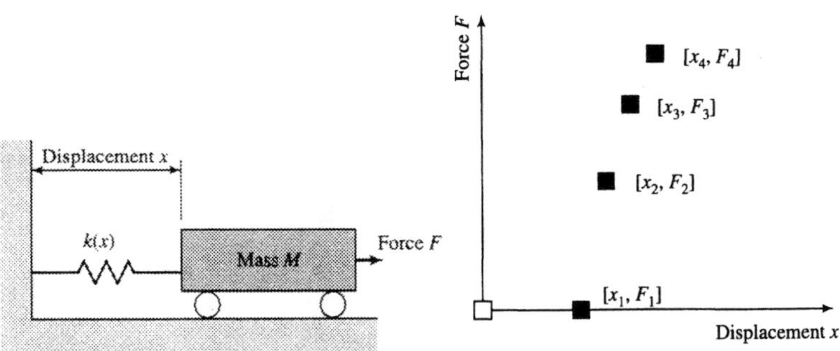

FIGURE 15.7 Force-displacement experiment for mass-spring system.

The force-displacement model is calibrated by conducting a displacement-controlled experiment, where displacement of the mass is increased to a prescribed level and the force is measured. The experimental results are

Data Point	Displacement (cm)	Force (N)
1	5.0	0.0
2	5.5	47.5
3	6.0	90.0
4	6.5	127.5
5	7.0	160.0
6	7.5	187.5
7	8.0	210.0

A schematic of coordinate pairs (measured displacement, applied force) is plotted on the right-hand side of Figure 15.7. Theoretical considerations indicate that the force-displacement relationship is mildly nonlinear and is closely approximated by the quadratic:

$$\text{Force}(x) = a_o + a_1 \cdot x + a_2 \cdot x^2 \tag{15.32}$$

where a_o, a_1, and a_2 are coefficients to be determined via experiment and least squares analysis. When $n = 2$, Equation 15.31 takes the form

$$\begin{bmatrix} N & \sum_{i=1}^{N} x_i & \sum_{i=1}^{N} x_i^2 \\ \sum_{i=1}^{N} x_i & \sum^{N} \cdot x_i^2 & \sum_{i=1}^{N} x_i^3 \\ \sum_{i=1}^{N} \cdot x_i^2 & \sum^{N} x_i^3 & \sum_{i=1}^{N} x_i^4 \end{bmatrix} \cdot \begin{bmatrix} a_0 \\ a_1 \\ a_2 \end{bmatrix} = \begin{bmatrix} \sum_{i=1}^{N} y_i \\ \sum_{i=1}^{N} x_i \cdot y_i \\ \sum_{i=1}^{N} x_i^2 \cdot y_i \end{bmatrix} \tag{15.33}$$

Program Source Code

Program 15.3 stores the experimental data in a matrix `data` and then assembles and solves the matrix Equation 15.33.

PROGRAM 15.3: LEAST SQUARES ANALYSIS OF EXPERIMENTAL DATA

```
% ======================================================================
% leastsq.m -- Compute least squares polynomial fit on experimental data
%
% Experiment : x = displacement of spring (cm).
%              f = force in spring (N).
%
% Least squares fit : p(x) = a + b.x + c.x^2
% ======================================================================

% Store force-displacement relationship in matrix "data"
data = [ 5.0    0.0;
         5.5   47.5;
         6.0   90.0;
         6.5  127.5;
         7.0  160.0;
         7.5  187.5;
         8.0  210.0 ];

% Compute terms in least squares matrix and right-hand vector

N = 7;
sumx   = sum(data(:,1));
sumy   = sum(data(:,2));
sumxy  = sum(data(:,1).*data(:,2));

sumx2  = sum(data(:,1).*data(:,1));
sumx2y = sum(data(:,1).*data(:,1).*data(:,2));
sumx3  = sum(data(:,1).*data(:,1).*data(:,1));
sumx4  = sum(data(:,1).*data(:,1).*data(:,1).*data(:,1));

A = [     N   sumx   sumx2
       sumx  sumx2   sumx3
      sumx2  sumx3   sumx4 ]

B = [ sumy; sumxy; sumx2y]
```

```
% Compute and print constants a,b,c

Coefficients = A\B

% ======================================================================
% the end!
```

Running the Program

Assume that Program 15.3 is contained in the M-file `leastsq.m`. The script of MATLAB I/O

```
>> format compact
>> leastsq
A =
   1.0e+04 *
    0.0007    0.0046    0.0303
    0.0046    0.0303    0.2059
    0.0303    0.2059    1.4282
B =
   1.0e+04 *
    0.0823
    0.5836
    4.1891
Coefficients =
 -750.0000
  200.0000
  -10.0000
>>
```

shows the commands used to run the program and the output that is generated. Matrices `A` and `B` represent Equation 15.33. The matrix `Coefficients` contains the results of the least squares analysis, that is, the values for a_o, a_1, and a_2 that provide the best fit of Equation 15.32 to the experimental data.

Assembling the Least Squares Matrix Equations

Program 15.3 stores the system displacements and applied forces in columns 1 and 2 of matrix `data`. The most straightforward and, admittedly, inefficient way of computing the matrix element terms in Equation 15.33 is with blocks of MATLAB code that look similar to the following:

```
sumx2 = 0.0;
for i = 1:N
    sumx2 = sumx2 + data(i,1)*data(i,1);
end,
```

Here sumx2 holds the sum of x_i^2 terms needed for matrix elements $A(1,3)$, $A(2,2)$, and $A(3,1)$. Evaluation of this looping structure in MATLAB will be slow because it is interpreted. The same numerical result can be obtained in much less time with the single statement

```
sumx2   = sum( data(:,1).*data(:,1) );
```

Now the MATLAB function sum is applied to matrix element-level multiply operations on all the items in column one of matrix data. The .* syntax signifies matrix element-level multiply operations, and the colon (:) operation implies all the items within a column of matrix data.

It is possible, in fact, to completely eliminate the sumx2-type terms from the calculation and to form the (3 × 3) least squares matrix in one statement block involving matrix element-level multiplies on data. Similar expressions can be written for matrix B.

Validating the Results

The polynomial coefficients $a_o = -750$, $a_1 = 200$, and $a_2 = -10$ define the force-displacement relationship

$$\text{Force}(x) = -750 + 200 \cdot x - 10 \cdot x^2 \tag{15.34}$$

$$= -10 \cdot (x - 5) \cdot (x - 15) \tag{15.35}$$

The sum of deviations

$$\sum_{i=1}^{N} e_i^2 = \sum_{i=1}^{N} [y_i - p(x)]^2 = 0.0 \tag{15.36}$$

indicating that our second-order polynomial passes through the seven data points exactly (okay, we confess—we set it up that way).

15.4.4 Distribution of Temperature in Chimney Cross-Section

Problem Statement

In this example, we use a finite difference approximation of Laplace's equation to compute the distribution of temperature in a chimney cross-section. A detailed description of the chimney geometry, Laplace's equation, and a suitable finite difference approximation may be found in Chapter 8 (of the C tutorial).

Program Source Code

Our solution to this problem uses the "method of iteration" to compute the steady-state temperature profile at the internal nodes. Once the temperature profile is known we create a two-dimensional color contour plot of the temperature distribution inside the chimney wall.

PROGRAM 15.4: DISTRIBUTION OF TEMPERATURE IN CHIMNEY CROSS-SECTION

```
% =====================================================================
% chimney.m -- Compute and displace profiles of temperature in chimney
%              cross section.
% =====================================================================

%  Setup working array and boundary conditions along
%  internal/external walls.

 T = zeros(9,9);

 for i = 5:9;
     T(i,5) = 200;
 end;
 for i = 1:5;
     T(5,i) = 200;
 end;
 for i = 6:9;
 for j = 1:4;
     T(i,j) = NaN;
 end;
 end;

% Loop over internal nodes and compute new temperatures

 counter   = 0;
 maxchange = 200;
    while (maxchange > 1)
        counter = counter+1;
        maxchange = 0;
        k=5;
        l=4;
        for c = 6:8;
            newtemp    = 0.25*(2*T(l+1,c)+2*T(l,c+1));
            tempchange = newtemp - T(l,c);
            maxchange  = max(maxchange,abs(tempchange));
            T(l,c)=newtemp;
           for r=k:8
               newtemp    = 0.25*(T(r,c-1)+T(r,c+1)+T(r-1,c)+T(r+1,c));
               tempchange = newtemp - T(r,c);
               maxchange  = max(maxchange,abs(tempchange));
               T(r,c)= newtemp;
           end
           newtemp    = 0.25*(T(9,c-1)+T(9,c+1)+2*T(8,c));
           tempchange = newtemp - T(9,c);
           maxchange  = max(maxchange,abs(tempchange));
```

```
            ,c)=newtemp;
            l=l-1;
            k=k-1;
         end
         counter;
         maxchange;                 % to view counter or maxchange remove
    end

% Compute reflected temperature

  for i = 2:4
      for j = 1: 11-i
          T(i,j) = T(10-j,10-i);
      end
  end

% Print Temperature array.

T

% Plot temperature contours.

contour(T)
hold;

% Now overlay perimeter of chimney section on contours.

perim = [ 1 , 1;
          9 , 1;
          9 , 9;
          5 , 9;
          5 , 5;
          1 , 5;
          1 , 1 ];

plot(perim(:,1),perim(:,2),'w');
text(1.1,5.3,'Temp = 200.0');
text(7.0,1.3,'Temp = 0.0');

% =====================================================
% The End!
```

Running the Program

Assume that Program 15.4 is contained in the M-file `chimney.m`. The abbreviated script of I/O:

```
>> format compact
>> chimney

   .... lots of program output removed ....

T =

  Columns 1 through 7

         0          0          0          0          0          0          0
   47.9527    47.4495    45.9241    42.8111    37.2518    28.7560    19.0375
   96.9120    96.1208    93.6699    88.3435    77.7632    59.1105    38.4899
  147.6536   147.0166   144.9543   139.9098   127.2653    92.5014    59.1105

  200.0000   200.0000   200.0000   200.0000   200.0000   127.2653    77.7632
       NaN        NaN        NaN        NaN   200.0000   139.9098    88.3435
       NaN        NaN        NaN        NaN   200.0000   144.9543    93.6699
       NaN        NaN        NaN        NaN   200.0000   147.0166    96.1208
       NaN        NaN        NaN        NaN   200.0000   147.6536    96.9120

  Columns 8 through 9

         0          0
    9.3215          0
   19.0375          0
   28.7560          0
   37.2518          0
   42.8111          0
   45.9241          0
   47.4495          0
   47.9527          0
>>
```

shows the commands needed to run the chimney analysis and compute the distribution of temperatures throughout the chimney cross-section. Figure 15.8 is two-dimensional contour plot of chimney temperature.

Computational Procedure

The first block of code sets up a (9 $\times$ 9) matrix for modeling one fourth of the chimney cross-section. The temperature along the interior and exterior walls is set to 200 and 0 degrees, respectively. In MATLAB the interior region of the chimney

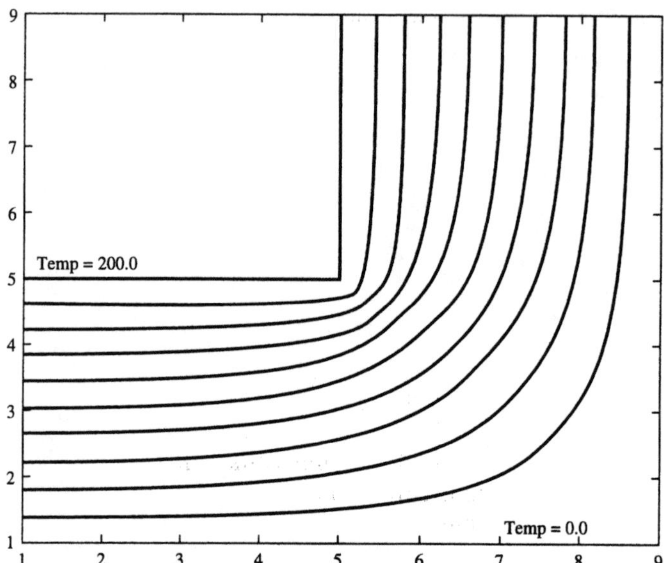

FIGURE 15.8 Temperature profile in chimney.

can be represented with NaNs, that is, a missing data item. At this point in the program execution, the contents of matrix T are

```
T =
     0     0     0     0     0     0     0     0     0
     0     0     0     0     0     0     0     0     0
     0     0     0     0     0     0     0     0     0
     0     0     0     0     0     0     0     0     0
   200   200   200   200   200     0     0     0     0
   NaN   NaN   NaN   NaN   200     0     0     0     0
   NaN   NaN   NaN   NaN   200     0     0     0     0
   NaN   NaN   NaN   NaN   200     0     0     0     0
   NaN   NaN   NaN   NaN   200     0     0     0     0
```

The main block of code walks along columns 6 through 8 and evaluates the finite difference stencils for

```
Column No            Row Nos
==========================
        6      4 through 9
        7      3 through 9
        8      2 through 9
==========================
```

For example, after the algorithm has walked along column 6 for the first time, the contents of T are

```
T =

  Columns 1 through 7

        0         0         0         0         0         0         0
        0         0         0         0         0         0         0
        0         0         0         0         0         0         0
        0         0         0         0         0         0         0
 200.0000  200.0000  200.0000  200.0000  200.0000   50.0000         0
      NaN       NaN       NaN       NaN  200.0000   62.5000         0
      NaN       NaN       NaN       NaN  200.0000   65.6250         0
      NaN       NaN       NaN       NaN  200.0000   66.4062         0
      NaN       NaN       NaN       NaN  200.0000   83.2031         0

  Columns 8 through 9

        0         0
        0         0
        0         0
        0         0
        0         0
        0         0
        0         0
        0         0
        0         0
```

Bear in mind that the temperature at stencil $T(4,6)$ is still zero because all the neighboring stencils are initially zero. The three-line block of code

```
newtemp    = 0.25*(T(9,c-1)+T(9,C+1)+2*T(8,c));
tempchange = newtemp - T(9,c);
maxchange  = max(maxchange,abs(tempchange));
```

computes the new temperature estimate at the node, the change in node temperature from the previous iteration, and the maximum change in temperature occurring over rows 6 through 8 for the current iteration.

The outermost loop of the algorithm will iteratively refine the temperature profile until satisfactory convergence occurs. For this example, we stop refining the temperature profile when the maximum change in temperature over rows 6 through

8 is less than 1 degree. At the conclusion of the main block of code, the temperature profile is

```
T =

  Columns 1 through 7

         0          0          0          0          0          0          0
         0          0          0          0          0          0          0
         0          0          0          0          0          0    38.4899
         0          0          0          0          0    92.5014    59.1105
  200.0000   200.0000   200.0000   200.0000   200.0000   127.2653    77.7632
       NaN        NaN        NaN        NaN   200.0000   139.9098    88.3435
       NaN        NaN        NaN        NaN   200.0000   144.9543    93.6699
       NaN        NaN        NaN        NaN   200.0000   147.0166    96.1208
       NaN        NaN        NaN        NaN   200.0000   147.6536    96.9120

  Columns 8 through 9

         0          0
    9.3215          0
   19.0375          0
   28.7560          0
   37.2518          0
   42.8111          0
   45.9241          0
   47.4495          0
   47.9527          0
```

The final temperature profile is obtained by reflecting the temperatures along the line $y = x$.

Of course, the temperature profile may also be computed by writing and solving the finite difference equations in matrix form (see Problem 15.7).

Review Questions

1. Explain how a system of m linear equations containing n unknowns can be represented in matrix form.
2. What are the three types of solutions matrix equations can have?
3. What role does the matrix determinant play in determining whether a family of matrix equations will have a unique solution?
4. Let A be a $(n \times n)$ matrix and B be a $(n \times 1)$ matrix. Under what conditions will the solution to $A \cdot X = B$ have an infinite number of solutions? How would you use MATLAB to detect this situation?

5. Suppose that a family of three equations, each having three unknowns, is graphed in three-dimensional space and that it is immediately apparent that one of the equations is a linear combination of the remaining two. If the equations are written in matrix form, what can you say about (1) the matrix rank, (2) the matrix determinant, and (3) the matrix inverse?

15.5 PROGRAMMING EXERCISES

Problem 15.1 (Beginner): Suppose that the cable profile of a small suspension bridge carrying a uniformly distributed load corresponds to the solution of the differential equation

$$\frac{d^2w}{dx^2} = 1.0 \tag{15.37}$$

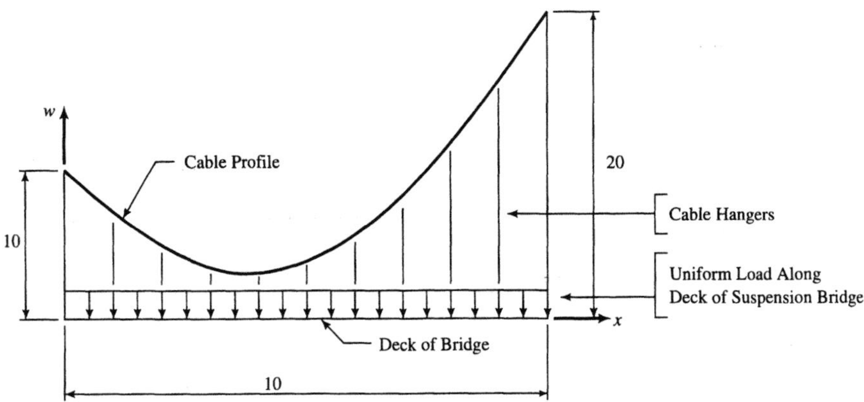

with the boundary conditions $w(0) = 10$ and $w(10) = 20$. It is easy to show that the analytic solution to the cable profile is

$$w(x) = \frac{1}{2}x^2 - 4x + 10 \tag{15.38}$$

Now solve Equation 15.37 via the method of finite differences.

1. What is a suitable finite difference approximation to Equation 15.37?
2. If the cable profile is divided into five regions along the x-axis, with four internal nodes, write down the family of finite difference equations that you would solve for the cable profile (do not try to find a solution to these equations).
3. Write a MATLAB program to solve the family of equations by the "method of iteration."
4. Write down the family of linear matrix equations corresponding to this finite difference problem. Write a MATLAB program that computes the solution to

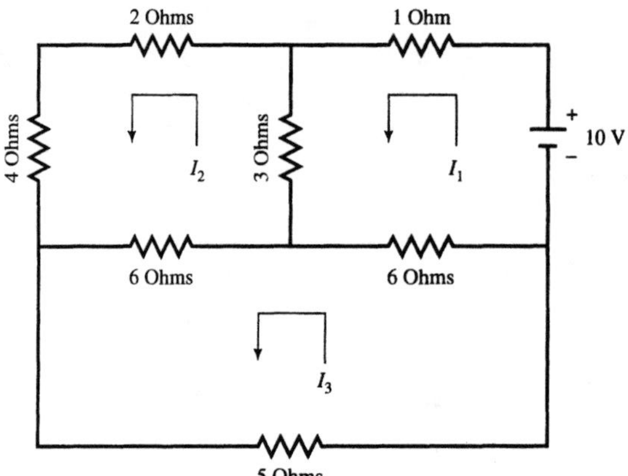

FIGURE 15.9 Three-loop voltage-resistance circuit.

these equations, and then displays the numerical solution and Equation 15.38 on the same graph.

Problem 15.2 (Beginner): Figure 15.9 shows a three-loop voltage-resistance circuit, containing one battery and seven resistors. Write a MATLAB program to compute and print the magnitude of current flows in each of the three loops. For each loop, assume that anticlockwise current flow is positive.

Problem 15.3 (Intermediate): In the solution of many fluid mechanics and chemical engineering problems, conservation of mass is a central principle. Briefly stated, conservation of mass accounts for all sources and sinks of a material that pass in and out of a control volume (see the left-hand side of Figure 15.10).

For a specified interval of time, the accumulation of substance is simply the sum of the inputs minus the sum of the outputs. When the sum of the inputs equals the sum of the outputs, accumulations are zero, and the mass within the volume

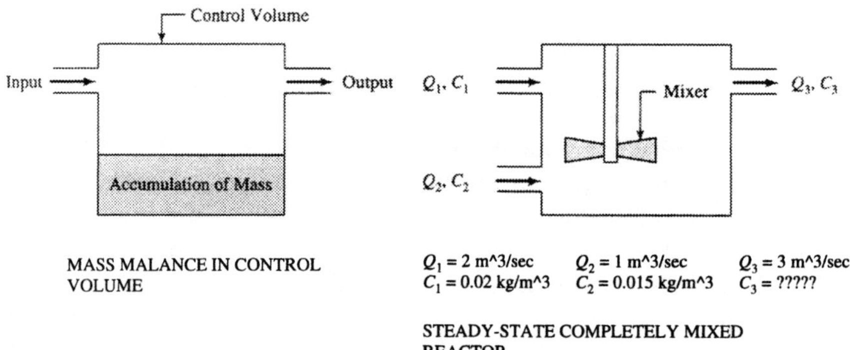

FIGURE 15.10 Conservation of mass in fully mixed reactor.

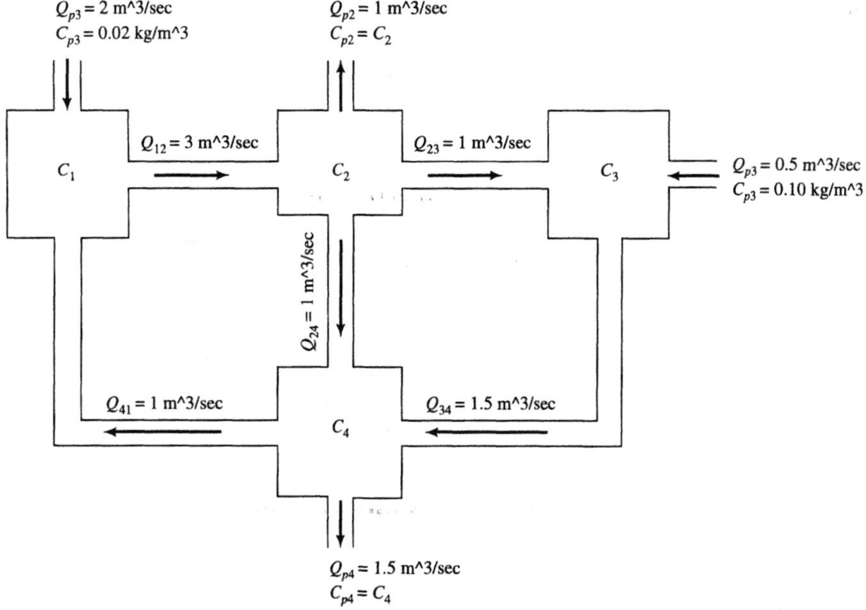

FIGURE 15.11 Network of four fully mixed reactors.

will be constant. Since the mass within the volume does not change with time, we say that such a system is in steady state.

The principle of conservation of mass can be used to determine the concentrations of substances in system of coupled fully mixed reactors. To see how the analysis proceeds, first look at the single fully mixed reactor shown on the right-hand side of Figure 15.10. The reactor has one input pipe and two output pipes. You should observe that the concentration at the output pipe is not shown because it can be computed via the principle of conservation of mass.

The mass of substance passing through each pipe is simply the flow rate, Q (m^3/sec), multiplied by the concentration of substance C (kg/m^3). For a system in steady state (where the mass does not increase or decrease due to chemical reactions), conservation of mass requires

$$C_1 \cdot Q_1 + Q_2 \cdot C_2 = Q_3 \cdot C_3 \tag{15.39}$$

Hence, the concentration of mass in the output pipe is

$$C_3 = \left[\frac{(Q_1 \cdot C_1 + Q_2 \cdot C_2)}{Q_3}\right] = \left[\frac{0.055}{3}\right] \text{kg/m}^3 \tag{15.40}$$

Exactly the same principles can be used to compute the concentration of substances in the network of fully mixed reactors shown in Figure 15.11. The concentrations of mass in reactors 1 through 4 are denoted by the symbols C_1, C_2, C_3, and C_4. Because there are four reactors, four simultaneous mass-balance equations are needed to describe the distribution of substance concentrations.

1. Show that the mass-balance equations may be written

$$\begin{bmatrix} Q_{12} & 0 & 0 & -Q_{41} \\ Q_{12} & -Q_{12} & 0 & 0 \\ 0 & -Q_{23} & Q_{34} & 0 \\ 0 & Q_{24} & Q_{34} & -(Q_{p4}+Q_{41}) \end{bmatrix} \cdot \begin{Bmatrix} C_1 \\ C_2 \\ C_3 \\ C_4 \end{Bmatrix} = \begin{Bmatrix} Q_{12} \cdot C_{p1} \\ 0 \\ Q_{p3} \cdot C_{p3} \\ 0 \end{Bmatrix} \tag{15.41}$$

2. Develop a MATLAB program to solve Equation 15.41 for the concentrations in each reactor.

Problem 15.4 (Intermediate): In the design of highway bridge structures and crane structures, engineers are often required to compute the maximum and minimum member forces and support reactions due to a variety of loading conditions.

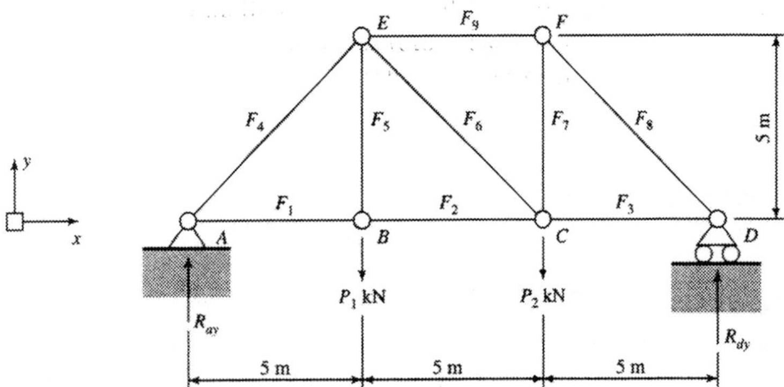

FIGURE 15.12 Front elevation of pin-jointed bridge truss.

Figure 15.12 shows a nine-bar pin-jointed bridge truss carrying vertical loads P_1 kN and P_2 kN at joints B and C. The symbols F_1, F_2, · · · F_9 represent the axial forces in truss members 1 through 9, and R_{ay} and R_{dy} are the support reactions at joints A and D. (Notice that because support D is on a roller and there are no horizontal components of external loads, horizontal reactions will be zero.)

Write down the equations of equilibrium for joints B through F and put the equations in matrix form. Now suppose that a heavy load moves across the bridge and that, for engineering purposes, it can be represented by the sequence of external load vectors.

$$\begin{bmatrix} P_1 \\ P_2 \end{bmatrix} = \begin{bmatrix} 10 \\ 0 \end{bmatrix}, \begin{bmatrix} P_1 \\ P_2 \end{bmatrix} = \begin{bmatrix} 5 \\ 5 \end{bmatrix}, \begin{bmatrix} P_1 \\ P_2 \end{bmatrix} = \begin{bmatrix} 0 \\ 10 \end{bmatrix} \tag{15.42}$$

Develop a MATLAB program that will solve the matrix equations for each of the external load conditions, and compute and print the minimum and maximum axial forces in each of the truss members.

Problem 15.5 (Intermediate/Advanced): In the detailed stages of a petroleum refinery design, an experiment is conducted to determine the empirical relationship between solubility weight (%) of n-butane in anhydrous hydrofluoric acid at high pressures and temperature. A plot of the experimental data

Data Point	Temperature (C)	Solubility (%)
1	25	2.5
2	38	3.3
3	85	7.1
4	115	11.0
5	140	19.7

on semilog graph paper indicates that solubility and temperature follow the nonlinear relationship

$$\text{Solubility } s(t) = a_o e^{a_1 \cdot t} \tag{15.43}$$

where a_o and a_1 are parameters to be determined. A linear least squares problem can be obtained by applying the transformation $\log_e[s(t)] = \log_e(a_o) + a_1 \cdot t$.

1. Show that the least squares estimate of parameters a_o and a_1 is given by solutions to the matrix equations

$$\begin{bmatrix} N & \sum_{i=1}^{N} t_i \\ \sum_{i=1}^{N} t_i & \sum_{i=1}^{N} t_i^2 \end{bmatrix} \cdot \begin{bmatrix} \log_e(a_o) \\ a_1 \end{bmatrix} = \begin{bmatrix} \sum_{i=1}^{N} \log_e(s_i) \\ \sum_{i=1}^{N} t_i \cdot \log_e(s_i) \end{bmatrix} \tag{15.44}$$

2. Write a MATLAB program to compute parameters a_o and a_1 by solving matrix Equation 15.44.

Problem 15.6 (Intermediate): Figure 15.13 is a three-dimensional view of a 2 by 2 km site that is believed to overlay a thick layer of mineral deposits. To create a model of the mineral deposit profile and establish the economic viability of mining the site, a preliminary subsurface exploration consisting of 16 bore holes is conducted. Each bore hole is drilled to approximately 45 m, with the upper and lower boundaries of mineral deposits being recorded. The bore hole data is as follows:

```
Borehole     [ x, y ] coordinate          [ upper, lower ]  mineral surfaces
===========================================================================
       1     [    10.0 m,    10.0 m ]     [ -30.5 m,   -40.5 m ]
       2     [   750.0 m,    10.0 m ]     [ -29.0 m,   -39.8 m ]
       3     [ 1250.0 m,     10.0 m ]     [ -28.0 m,   -39.3 m ]
       4     [ 1990.0 m,     10.0 m ]     [ -26.6 m,   -38.5 m ]
       5     [    10.0 m,   750.0 m ]     [ -34.2 m,   -41.4 m ]
       6     [   750.0 m,   750.0 m ]     [ -32.8 m,   -40.6 m ]
       7     [ 1250.0 m,    750.0 m ]     [ -31.8 m,   -40.1 m ]
       8     [ 1990.0 m,    750.0 m ]     [ -30.3 m,   -39.4 m ]
       9     [    10.0 m,  1250.0 m ]     [ -36.7 m,   -42.0 m ]
```

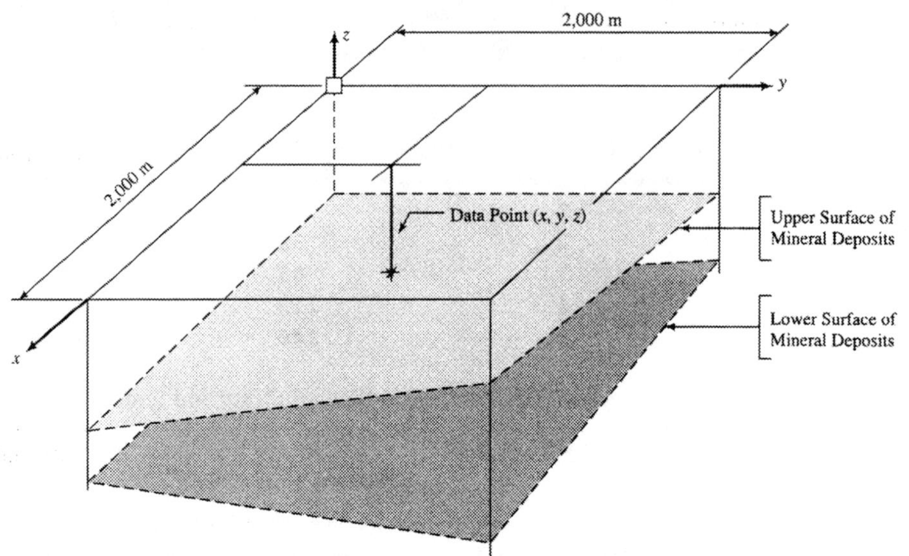

FIGURE 15.13 *Three-dimensional view of mineral deposits.*

10	[750.0 m, 1250.0 m]	[-35.2 m, -41.2 m]
11	[1250.0 m, 1250.0 m]	[-34.2 m, -40.7 m]
12	[1990.0 m, 1250.0 m]	[-32.8 m, -40.0 m]
13	[10.0 m, 1990.0 m]	[-40.4 m, -42.8 m]
14	[750.0 m, 1990.0 m]	[-39.0 m, -42.1 m]
15	[1250.0 m, 1990.0 m]	[-38.0 m, -41.6 m]
16	[1990.0 m, 1990.0 m]	[-36.5 m, -40.9 m]

With the bore hole data collected, the next step is to create a simplified three-dimensional computer model of the site and subsurface mineral deposits. The mineral deposits will be modeled as a single six-sided object. The four vertical sides are simply defined by the boundaries of the site. The upper and lower sides are to be defined by a three-dimensional plane

$$z(x, y) = a_o + a_1 \cdot x + a_2 \cdot y \tag{15.45}$$

where coefficients a_o, a_1, and a_2 correspond to minimum values of

$$S(a_o, a_1, a_2) = \sum_{i=1}^{N} [z_i - z(x_i, y_i)]^2 \tag{15.46}$$

Things to do:

1. Show that minimum value of $S(a_o, a_1, a_2)$ corresponds to the solution of the matrix equations

$$\begin{bmatrix} N & \sum_{i=1}^{N} x_i & \sum_{i=1}^{N} y_i \\ \sum_{i=1}^{N} x_i & \sum^{N} x_i^2 & \sum_{i=1}^{N} x_i \cdot y_i \\ \sum_{i=1}^{N} y_i & \sum^{N} x_i \cdot y_i & \sum_{i=1}^{N} y_i^2 \end{bmatrix} \cdot \begin{bmatrix} a_o \\ a_1 \\ a_2 \end{bmatrix} = \begin{bmatrix} \sum_{i=1}^{N} z_i \\ \sum_{i=1}^{N} x_i \cdot z_i \\ \sum_{i=1}^{N} y_i \cdot z_i \end{bmatrix} \tag{15.47}$$

2. Write an M-file that will create three-dimensional plots of the bore hole data at the lower and upper surfaces. See the MATLAB function `griddata()`.
3. Write an M-file that will set up and solve the matrix equations derived in part 1 for the upper and lower mineral planes.
4. Compute and print the average depth and volume of mineral deposits enclosed within the site.

Note. The least squares solution corresponds to the minimum value of function $S(a_o, a_1, a_2)$. At the minimum function value, we will have

$$\frac{dS}{da_o} = \frac{dS}{da_1} = \frac{dS}{da_2} = 0 \tag{15.48}$$

Equation 15.47 is simply the three equations (15.48) written in matrix form. You should find that the equation of the upper surface is close to `z(x,y) = -30.5 + x/500 - y/200` and the lower surface is close to `z(x,y) = -40.5 + x/1000 - y/850`.

Problem 15.7 (Intermediate): Repeat the "chimney temperature" problem using the following problem-solving procedure:

1. Write an M-file that sets up the finite difference equations in matrix form and then computes a solution by solving $A.T = B$, where T is the temperature at the internal nodes of the chimney.
2. Create a three-dimensional mesh (or surface) plot of the temperature distribution in one fourth of the chimney cross-section.

Problem 15.8 (Intermediate): Figure 15.14 shows the cross-section of a long conducting metal box with a detached lid. The sides and bottom of the box are at 100 Volts potential, and the lid is at ground (0 V) potential. Laplace's equation and the method of finite differences can be used to compute the distribution of potential inside the box. The solution procedure is almost identical to the chimney problem described in the chapter, but with temperature changed to voltage.

The box is assumed to extend to infinity in the z direction (so that there are no "edge effects" to consider). This simplifies the problem to two dimensions (x

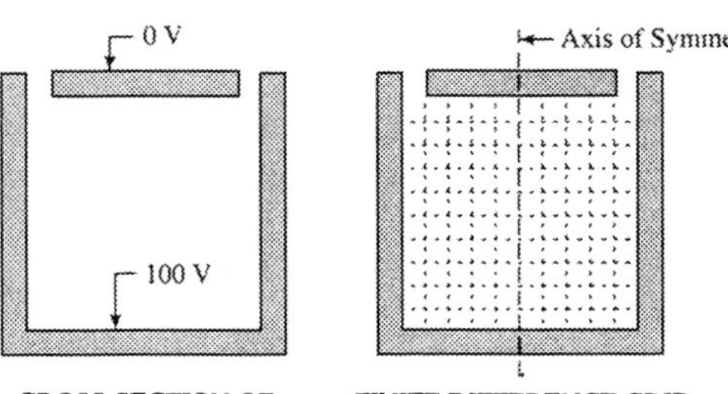

FIGURE 15.14 Cross-section of tall (infinite) metal box.

and y). The static distribution of voltage, $V = V(x, y)$, inside the metal box is given by solutions to Laplace's equation

$$\frac{\partial^2 V(x,y)}{\partial x^2} + \frac{\partial^2 V(x,y)}{\partial y^2} = 0 \tag{15.49}$$

with boundary conditions $V = 0$ V on the top or lid of the box and $V = 100$ V along both sides and the bottom of the box. Write a MATLAB program that will

1. Compute the voltage distribution inside the box via the method of finite differences described in Chapter 8 of the C tutorial.
2. Plot a contour map of the voltage potential.
3. *Optional:* Change the potential on the walls and lid of the box relative to each other and show how the voltage distribution changes.

PART 4

JAVA PROGRAMMING TUTORIAL

This Java tutorial is for engineers who are familiar with C and who want to learn how to program stand-alone Java applications and Java applet programs that can be displayed by a web browser. There are two reasons we are requiring a knowledge of C as a prerequisite. First, many syntactic details of Java, such as the syntax for arithmetic expressions, and looping and branching constructs, have been borrowed from C. We refer readers to the C tutorial for detailed coverage of topics that are common to both languages. The second reason for the prerequisite is that Java is often described in terms of features it does not support. For example, many of the language constructs C programmers have difficulty with, such as pointers and pointer arithmetic, dynamic allocation and reallocation of memory, have either been removed from Java or are automatically handled by it.

We see that although Java was originally designed for applications programming in the consumer electronics industry, the language has most recently captured the attention of the software community because its features enable the development of applications that can run anywhere on the Internet and the World Wide Web. Java is an architecture-neutral object-oriented language that can process multiple tasks simultaneously. Each of these terms will be fully explained in this tutorial. From a user's point of view, whether the software is object-oriented or not does not change anything. You run a program and you do not care if it has been written with an object-oriented language. But if you are accustomed to programming in conventional languages such as C and MATLAB, "object-oriented" means major adjustments to the way applications are planned and implemented. This adjustment is probably the hardest part in learning Java.

In this tutorial, we illustrate the process of designing and implementing object-oriented programs in Java for temperature conversion, computing the roots to a quadratic equation, and computing and plotting the time-history response of a single degree of freedom oscillator. Further engineering applications are found in the exercises section of Chapter 19.

16

INTRODUCTION TO JAVA

16.1 JAVA—A LITTLE HISTORY

Java started its life under a different name and for a different purpose than it is used for today. The original "Oak" programming language was written for the development of small multimedia applications embedded within consumer electronics devices, such as toasters, microwave ovens, and personal digital assistants (PDAs). These so-called intelligent consumer devices have their own peculiar tasks to perform, and their day-to-day performance must be very reliable.

In the early 1990s, the introduction of microprocessors to everyday life objects, such as TVs and VCRs, was seen by many people as a new-age revolution. To address this issue, Sun Microsystems funded an internal research project code-named "Green." The small "Green" team, headed by James Gosling, needed software that would be small, fast, and very reliable. They quickly realized that languages such as C and C++ were not well suited to the range of tasks "consumer devices" needed to perform. One major problem that they anticipated was the difficulty in providing software for new devices. Every time a new chip was developed for a new device, you would have to recompile the program written in C or C++ for this particular chip. The complexity of C and C++ meant that it would be extremely difficult to write reliable software.

In mid-1991, Gosling and coworkers started working on the design and implementation of a new language tailored to the needs of the consumer devices domain. Gosling named the language "Oak" after an oak tree outside his window at Sun. He designed this new language to be small, reliable, and architecture independent.

The development team was soon incorporated into a new company named FirstPerson. Unfortunately, FirstPerson ran into a lot of difficulties mainly because the marketplace for intelligent consumer electronic devices was not developing as Sun had anticipated.

It was the release of NCSA Mosaic and the explosion of the World Wide Web (WWW) in 1993 (for further details, see Tutorial 1) that saved the project. The developers of Oak realized that an architecture-neutral language would be ideal for programming interactive applications on the Web because a program accessed within a web page could run anywhere and without having to be installed. Accordingly, the developers added a lot of functionality to the language for networking tasks. They also changed the name "Oak" to "Java." The Web took the Internet by storm, and before long Java would take the Web by storm.

Sun formally announced Java at the SunWorld conference in May 1995. Java generated immediate interest in the business community because it was neither an academic language like Pascal nor a language designed by one person (or a small group) for their own local use like C or C++. Java was instead designed for commercial reasons. Enormous interest in Java was generated in the business community because of another Internet-related development, the World Wide Web.

16.2 THE "FAMOUS" JAVA BUZZWORDS

The folks at Sun Microsystems describe Java as follows [43]:

> Java: A simple, object-oriented, network-savvy (distributed), interpreted, robust, secure, architecture neutral, portable, high-performance, multithreaded and dynamic language.

Sun acknowledges that this description is more like a list of buzzwords than anything else. But the truth is that each word represents a feature of the Java language. Although many of these features can be used to describe other programming languages, this combination is unique to Java and its programming environment. It is therefore important to capture their full meaning, and so it makes sense to explain each buzzword one by one.

16.2.1 Simple

Simplicity in a programming language means leaving out features that are not needed and making the supported features work in a clear concise way. Simple certainly does not mean poor. The Java language was designed so that it could be easily learned by a programmer. Experience in the development of other languages, such as C, indicates that a good way of achieving this goal is to keep the set of language structures and reserved words small. As a case in point, Table 16.1 shows that Java Version 1.0 has only 47 reserved keywords.

Once the concept of object-oriented programming and a few other Java-specific concepts are understood, it will take you just a few days before you can write useful Java applications. The Java learning curve is quite gentle because, generally

TABLE 16.1 Reserved Keywords in Java 1.0

abstract	default	if	private	throw
boolean	do	implements	protected	throws
break	double	import	public	transient
byte	else	instanceof	return	try
case	extends	int	short	void
catch	final	interface	static	volatile
char	finally	long	super	while
class	float	native	switch	
const	for	new	synchronized	
continue	goto	package	this	

speaking, there are only a small number of clear ways to accomplish a given task with Java. That is what makes Java simple and powerful. Java deviates from a lot of programming languages where the ability to write something in a thousand different ways is considered a feature; a good example of this is Perl. Although a large suite of features provides a programmer with considerable freedom, too often the result is source code that is unnecessarily complex and hard to understand. For software packages that are developed in teams and used for many years, the result can be excessive life cycle maintenance costs. By keeping things simple, Java makes software easier to maintain.

16.2.2 Object-Oriented

The need for object-oriented software is motivated by the economic benefits of software reuse, and the opportunity it affords for improvements in the design and maintenance of large software systems. New programming languages and operating systems are object-oriented. If you want to be "à la mode" in the computer world, you need to be object-oriented.

Rather than looking at the actions your application will perform, an object-oriented problem solution focuses on the problem data and the operations that can manipulate the data. This adjustment is probably the hardest part in learning Java. Bertrand Meyer, creator of the Eiffel language, states the situation quite succinctly [24]:

> When laying out the architecture of a system, the software designer is confronted with a fundamental choice—should the structure be based on the actions or on the data? In the answer to this question lies the difference between traditional design methods and the object-oriented approach.

A key advantage Java has over other languages, such as C++, is that it was designed from scratch. Java is not a derivate of another language with object-type language extensions that enable application of the object-oriented model/paradigm. Java was instead built on the combined experience of object developments over the past few years and was shaped to include all the fundamental concepts in a clean way. Patrick Naughton [25], a member of the Java development team at Sun, says about Java,

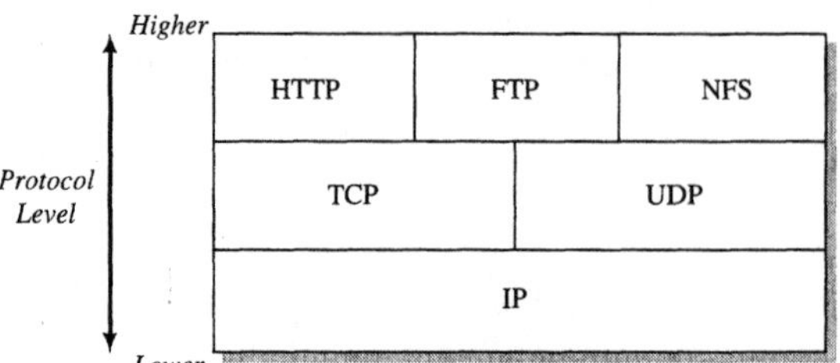

FIGURE 16.1 The protocol stack.

"it's a nice balance between the purist, 'everything is an object' model, and the hacker's, 'stay out of my way' model." We think it's a success.

16.2.3 Network Savvy (Distributed)

Java comes with a complete library for network applications, making it easy for a programmer to deal with low-level protocols such as TCP/IP (Transport Control Protocol and Internet Protocol) and higher-level protocols such as HTTP (Hyper Text Transfer Protocol) and FTP (File Transfer Protocol). The relationship among these protocols is shown in Figure 16.1.

As experienced C programmers can attest, at least three or four different function calls are usually needed before you can open a network connection between two computers. Java streamlines this process by requiring only one function call to make client/server connections and access remote objects on the Internet. In fact, opening a specified Uniform Resource Locator (URL) on the Web is no more difficult than opening a local file on the computer (see Figure 16.2).

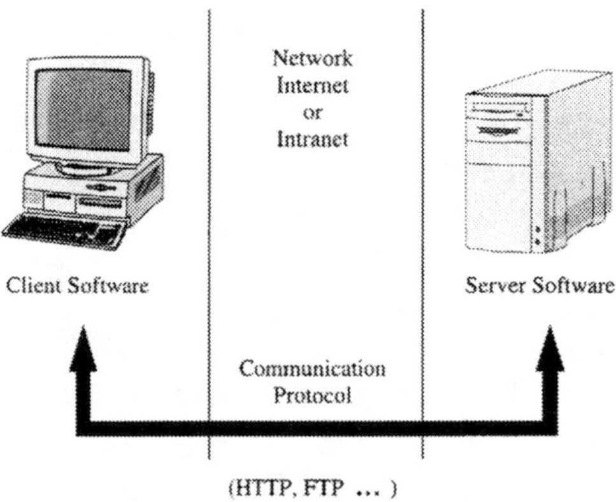

FIGURE 16.2 The client/server architecture.

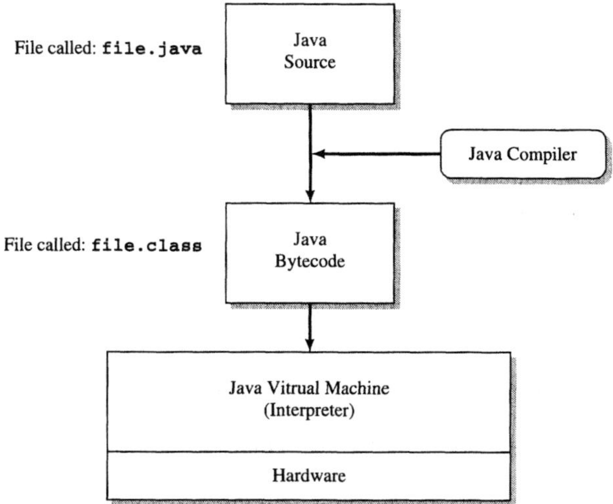

FIGURE 16.3 *The Java compiling and running scheme.*

16.2.4 Interpreted

Java programs are compiled and interpreted in the two-step sequence shown in Figure 16.3. With the source code file `file.java` as its input, the Java compiler generates a low-level bytecode file `file.class`. The bytecode file is then passed to the Java interpreter for execution. The Java compiler is called `javac`, and the name of the Java interpreter is `java`.

Bear in mind that three steps are needed to compile and run programs written in traditional languages such as C. First, the program source code is compiled into object files. The object files are then linked together with external libraries and an executable program file is generated. Finally, the program file is actually run/executed. Java is therefore a good language for rapid prototyping, easy experimentation, and concept testing because the time-consuming "link phase" of the traditional program development cycle has been removed.

The next issue to address is that of a *bytecode*—what is it? The concept of bytecode is not specific to Java. In related work, network protocols have been developed to address the problem of communication of information over heterogeneous hardware platforms. By developing systems that rely on network protocols to specify the order in which data must be sent over a network, users are assured that computers on both sides of a connection will be able to communicate properly and avoid problems of data/information corruption.

An emerging technique (well, it has been around for a while) for distributing applications is based on the concept of a *mobile code.* A mobile code is a low-level language that does not depend on the machine architecture, unlike assembly languages for example. Therefore, mobile codes can be transmitted across the network and executed on the other end, regardless of the computer type.

The Java bytecode is one example of a mobile code. Other languages that rely

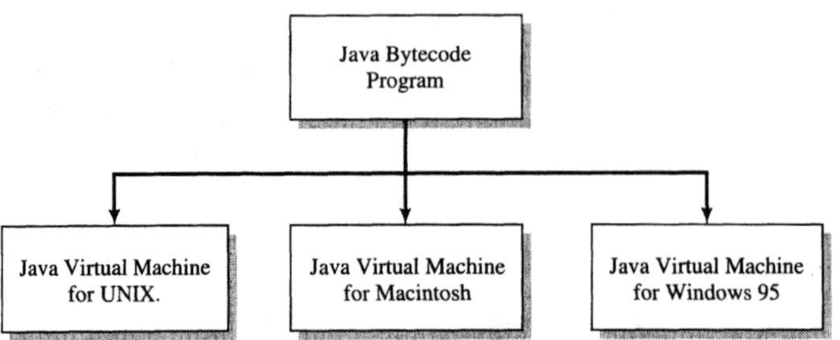

FIGURE 16.4 Execution of Java bytecodes on various platforms.

on mobile code or some sort of bytecode include Safe-Tcl, Penguin-Perl5, Python, Caml Special Light, scheme48, Guile, and Obliq. All these languages are human readable. Java bytecodes, in contrast, are not human readable. The Java language has been designed for efficient interpretation and for fast download over a network. Although these features make Java unique, it is equally important to note that there is nothing technically sacred about the relationship between Java source code and Java bytecode. Java programs can be compiled into native machine language, and other programming languages (e.g., Perl, FORTRAN) can be compiled into a Java bytecode.

The *bytecode interpreter*, also known as the Java Virtual Machine, simulates a computer with a chip that understands Java. The key advantage in this approach to program development, as shown in Figures 16.3 and 16.4, lies in the fact that the Virtual Machine has already been ported to a variety of hardware platforms. Thus, any Java program that you may write can run on any of those Virtual Machines without any changes. When a new piece of computer hardware is released to the marketplace, all that Java application programs need is for someone to develop a new Virtual Machine (based on Sun specifications) for that specific hardware. This strategy of program development completely bypasses the need to port application software to a variety of hardware platforms.

The main difference between the execution of a program compiled into native machine language and the execution of a bytecode is that the latter transforms the code as many times as needed during the execution, perhaps three, four, or more times. This can result in run-times that are much slower than equivalent applications compiled into native machine code. Future versions of the Java Virtual Machine will mitigate this problem by being able to transform the bytecode into native language for your machine on the fly.

16.2.5 Robust

In our short section on the history of Java, we mentioned that Java was designed to execute on consumer electronics products such as televisions and toasters. Above all other considerations, consumers expect their devices to work reliably. You do not want your toaster to pop the message

```
Syntax error, line 17283, offset 0x172a, reprogram'
```

while you are eating your breakfast. Because of this, Java has features that help programmers write software that will be reliable and robust. A key feature is early checking by the Java compiler for possible problems. Generally speaking, the earlier in the development process you are able to detect possible problems, the easier it will be to write robust software.

Java is what we call a "strongly typed" language. You do not have implicit declarations as in C++, and you cannot mix data types like you can in C (e.g., `int letter_num = 'a' -mychar`). The benefit of making a language like Java strongly typed is that the compiler can perform early checks for potential type mismatch problems, thereby protecting programmers from their own mistakes.

16.2.6 Secure

Java was designed to run in a *network environment*, meaning that you can download an application from anywhere on the Internet and have it run on your local machine. This sounds pretty much like letting anybody run anything on your computer. To prevent that "anybody" installing and running a virus on your machine, Java comes with a number of security features. At run-time, for example, the Java run-time system (interpreter) uses a *code verification* mechanism to ensure that the code loaded over the network (bytecode) does not violate any Java language restrictions. A second security feature is that these programs are prohibited from writing to your disk space.

Of course, Java is not 100% safe, and there is always a tradeoff between functionality and security. Java offers a reasonable middle ground between ignoring the security problem and being paralyzed by it. The net is a dangerous environment after all.

16.2.7 Architecture Neutral

In a physical sense, the Internet is a catch-all phrase to describe millions of interconnected PCs, Macs, and UNIX boxes, each having their own operating system and window management system. Java was developed with the goal of allowing applications programs to run on any of these platforms without having to port and recompile the code. For this reason, when you compile a Java source program, the result is not native machine code but a low-level architecture-neutral bytecode language that represents data in a format independent of the target machine.

The Java interpreter (also called the Java Virtual Machine) can later read this bytecode and translate it into machine-dependent system calls. This combination of features is the reason Java applications can run on any computer that implements a Java Virtual Machine.

In addition to the obvious benefit of enabling the spread of Java applications over the network, there are important economic advantages to this approach to applications program development and distribution. Today's software market is obliged to create multiple versions of a software package for different platforms: UNIX, PC, Mac, and so forth. With multiple "flavors" of UNIX and Windows (95, 98, and NT) now in wide use, the task of producing software for all possible platforms is becoming increasingly difficult. With Java, you write your application once and it will run on any machine that implements the Java Virtual Machine. This could be the end of the "religious war" between PCs and Macs.

16.2.8 Portable

Being *architecture neutral* is one big part of being portable, but Java goes further. As mentioned in Tutorial 1, computer hardware has been providing approximately 25% more power per dollar per year since the mid-1980s. Following up on these advances with software developments that exploit the hardware potential is rapidly becoming a very difficult problem because, in part, a program that you write today for a certain chip is not guaranteed to run tomorrow.

The Java designers made several hard decisions in the Java language and the Java run-time system to ensure that Java would really be platform independent. Thus, you can truly "write once, run anywhere, anytime, forever." In the long run, this approach will save the software industry enormous amounts of money because there will no longer be a need to port software to a menagerie of platforms. Now you can understand the interest companies have in Java.

16.2.9 High Performance

Due to the fact that it is an interpreted language, today's Java is a little slow. So why should we call it high performance?

A good way of understanding this issue is to classify existing programming languages according to the scale shown in Figure 16.5. The left-hand side represents high-level, fully interpreted scripting languages such as Perl, UNIX shell, and Tcl. Scripting languages are portable and are great for prototyping applications, but they are also very slow. The right-hand side of the scale represents traditional languages like FORTRAN and C. They have high performance at run-time but suffer in terms of reliability and portability.

Java sits in the middle of this scale. Without compromising the benefits of language simplicity and program portability, Java bytecodes execute at speeds

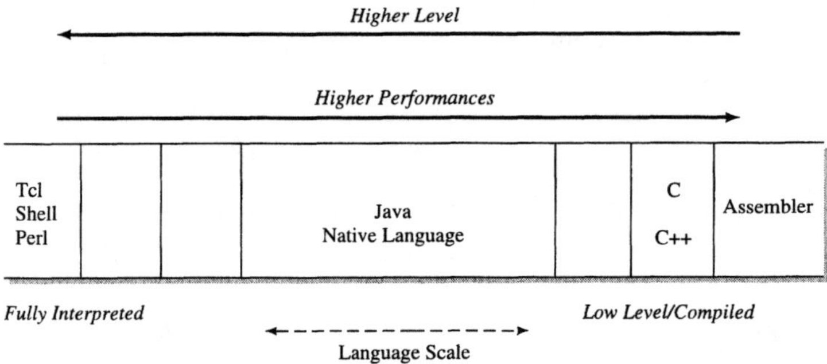

FIGURE 16.5 Java language scale.

much faster than high-level scripting languages. In an effort to move the run-time performance of Java programs closer to that of traditionally compiled programs, the Java designers are also working on "just-in-time compilers," which will translate Java bytecodes into native machine code at run-time. Estimates are that "just-in-time compilers" will increase the performance of already existing Java applications by a factor of 20. What is really neat is that the Java bytecode format was designed by Sun with this idea in mind, so the development of "just-in-time compilers" is fairly simple. The resulting product is fast.

16.2.10 Multithreaded

Many present-day application programs allow users to do multiple things at the same time. Consider, for example, a modern PC running a web browser. You can download a document and scroll a page while listening to your latest "Garbage" CD (easily the best CD of 1995!). The capability of running multiple processes (lightweight processes) at the same time is called *multithreading*. Each thread is able to handle a single task at a time.

So how does multithreaded programming compare to standard programming? When you do standard programming on a single-processor machine, all the instructions in your program are executed in serial. You cannot start task T_2 before task T_1 has finished. This style of programming is like having a single thread (see Figure 16.6).

However, if you are running your program on a multiprocessor machine, two tasks (like T_{21} and T_{22}) can run (or execute) at the same time. Each task running in parallel is called a thread and will run on its own processor (see Figure 16.7). Even if you are running Java on a single-processor machine, you can still program

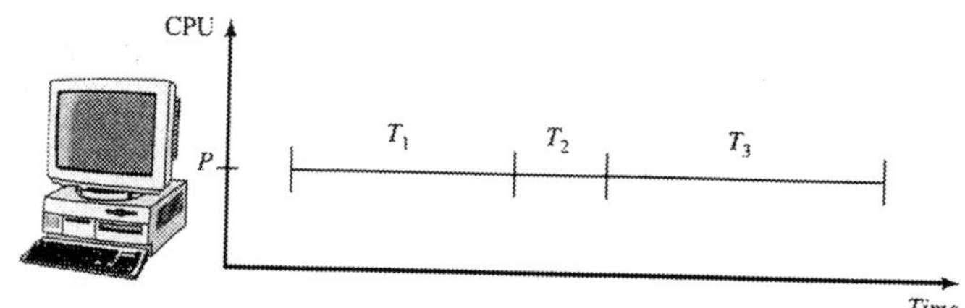

FIGURE 16.6 Single processor, single thread.

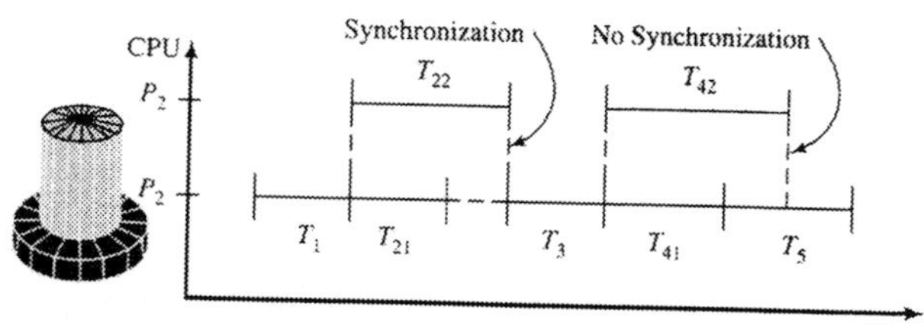

FIGURE 16.7 Multiprocessors, multithreads.

using threads because most of today's modern operating systems (e.g., UNIX, Windows 95/98) can simulate multiprocessor machines, thereby allowing you to run multiple processes at the same time.

The main problem programmers face when writing C or C++ code that deals with multitasking is making sure that the participating threads can run separate tasks concurrently. In operating system circles, this is a well-known and difficult problem. You want to obtain locks on shared resources (so a certain process is the only one accessing the resource at a certain time) and then release them. Any error in this procedure can easily lead to deadlock situations, where all processes are waiting for some resources to be freed.

The Java language supports multithreading. The Java libraries (details given as follows) come with primitive methods to start a thread, run a thread, stop a thread, and get the current status of a running thread. The libraries also offer a set of synchronization primitives, which are based on the monitor and condition paradigm, a widely used synchronization scheme.

16.2.11 Dynamic

Java is a dynamic language because it can adapt to a changing and evolving environment. Because Java is not compiled with static information, part of the application can be loaded locally or over the network when needed at run-time.

Two new features in Java 1.1 are "Object Serialization" and "Reflection." These features allow Java objects to discover information about other objects at run-time.

16.3 JAVA AND THE INTERNET

In this tutorial, we learn how to design and write stand alone Java application programs that operate locally on your computer, and Java applet programs that can be downloaded over the Internet to your computer and then executed. Of course, most of the initial excitement over Java is due to its relationship with the Internet and the Web. In the long term, however, longevity of the Java language will depend on the development of significant application programs that reside locally on your computer.

16.3.1 Java Applet Programs

An applet is simply a Java miniprogram that runs within a web browser or viewer and is usually part of an HTML (HyperText Markup Language) page. Standard HTML pages contain text and static images. Java programs add interactive content to the Web with a level of functionality that is almost the same as a stand-alone Java program.

What is really neat is that because Java bytecodes are architecture neutral, they can be transported over a network and executed by a Web browser that contains a Java Virtual Machine (i.e., a Java-enabled browser). The ability of a

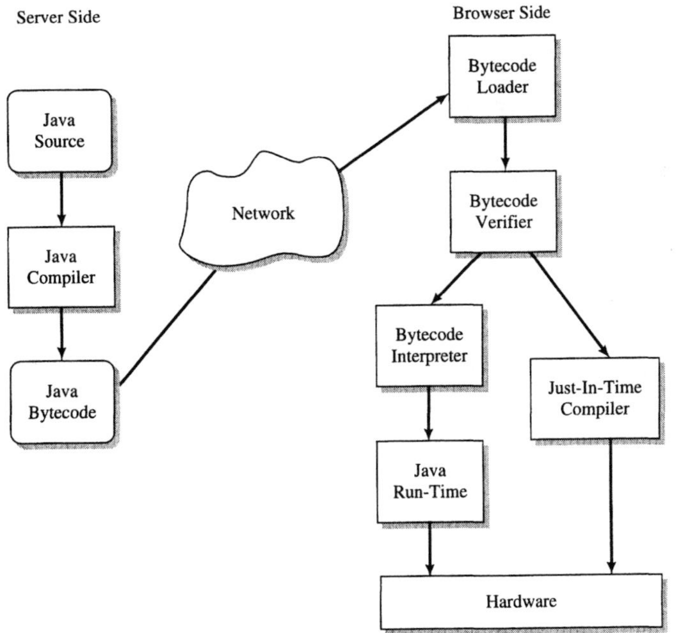

FIGURE 16.8 Compiling, downloading, and executing a Java applet.

bytecode to travel across a network and then operate on a variety of computational platforms is the heart of Sun Microsystem's write once/run anywhere computing model. It is this model that is causing all the excitement over Java.

16.3.2 Java Applets and HTML Documents

As mentioned in the first tutorial, the Web is simply a global network of web browsers and web servers. When a typical web user accesses a certain page on the Web, a chain of low-level activities is set in place. The browser will send a request to the server of the site and ask for a document. The server will respond to this request by sending back to the browser the document using HTML, a layout language for web pages containing text and images.

When your web browser finds an `<applet>` HTML tag in the document you have requested, it will automatically contact the server mentioned in the `<applet>` specification and retrieve the bytecode corresponding to that applet. The bytecode will travel across the network from the server to the browser and pass through the sequence of activities shown on the right-hand side of Figure 16.8.

16.3.3 Applet Tags and Parameters

For a browser to display an applet on a web page, the document that the browser is displaying must contain the name of the applet, its size, and its location on the

TABLE 16.2 Commonly Used Applet Tags

Required Applet Tags	
`code '=' 'AppletFile'`	This attribute lists the name of the file that contains the compiled applet subclass. The file name is listed relative to the base URL of the applet.
`width '=' pixels`	The initial width of the applet display area in pixels
`height '=' pixels`	The initial height of the applet display area in pixels
Optional Applet Tags	
`codebase '=' codebaseURL`	This attribute lists the base URL of the applet—that is, the directory containing the applet code. When this parameter is not specified, the document URL will be used by default.
`'<' parameter name '=' appletattribute 'VALUE' = 'value' '>'`	
This tag enables applet-specific parameters to be specified. Applets employ the `getParameter()` method to access their attributes.	

Internet. An applet tag has the form

```
<applet
  code   = < name of class >
  width  = < width of applet in pixels >
  height = < width of applet in pixels >

>
[ <parameter name = <parameter1> value = <value1> ]
[ <parameter name = <parameter2> value = <value2> ]

............
</applet>
```

The applet specification begins with `< applet...` and ends with the `< /applet >` tag. The items within <> represent programmer-supplied identities. Entities within `[]` brackets are optional. Table 16.2 contains a description of these parameters.

16.3.4 Application Safety

One problem with Java-enabled browsers that automatically download and execute applets on a web page is the door that they open for malicious behavior. A rogue programmer could, for example, write an applet that would delete the files and directories of the user viewing the web page. To prevent incidents of this type from occurring, most web browsers place severe restrictions on the applets they execute.

One of the main differences between a standard Java application and an applet is that applets do not have privileges to access your local file system for reading or writing. Java applets only have network access to the host computer from which the applet code was imported. These various levels of security are implemented through Java's networking packages, which provide interfaces to standard networking protocols such as HTTP and FTP (see Figures 16.1 and 16.2).

The second line of defense is the bytecode loader and a bytecode verifier. These packages make sure that the applet you have just downloaded over the network does not contain any malicious code. Once the bytecode verifier has ensured that the applet is virus free and will not corrupt your machine memory or destroy any files on your file system, it is executed using one of the two pathways shown on the right-hand side of Figure 16.8:

1. The standard method involves a bytecode interpreter and a Java run-time or Virtual Machine. In this configuration the code is evaluated as often as needed. A piece of code can be used multiple times, in which case it will be evaluated every single time, thus making the applet execution slower.
2. A just-in-time compiler will execute a first pass on the bytecode and compile it into machine-native code. This phase is time consuming but the execution can then be up to 20 times faster, giving the applet a very good overall performance.

It is important to note that these security restrictions are imposed by the Java Virtual Machine within the web browser, not by the Java language.

Further Information

1. You can find more about Java on the JavaSoft web server. The URL is

   `http://www.javasoft.com/`

   You can also find a list of major milestones in the Java history at the following address:

   `http://ils.unc.edu/blaze/java/javahist.html.`

2. For more details on Java's security mechanisms and how security is achieved at a low level, we refer you to "Low Level Security in Java" by Frank Yellin. The URL is

   `http://www.w3.org/pub/Conferences/WWW4/Papers/197/40.html.`

3. You will find more references about mobile codes on the server of the W3Consortium at

   `http://www.w3.org/pub/WWW/MobileCode.`

Review Questions

1. What choice in the Java language design made it attractive for businesses?
2. Java has many important features. Why are the features "architecture neutral" and "portable" of particular importance to companies?
3. What are the main differences in the development cycles of C and Java programs?
4. What features of the Java program development cycle are important for the applications programs development?
5. What are the advantages of interpreted programs over native-code programs?
6. What is a just-in-time compiler?
7. Why do browsers place security restrictions on Java applets?
8. What is a bytecode verifier?

17

OBJECT-ORIENTED PROGRAM DESIGN

17.1 FUNDAMENTAL CONCEPTS

In real-world engineering environments, computer program source codes that are hundreds of thousands, and sometimes millions, of lines long are now commonplace. Many of these computer programs are capable of solving problems that are so complex, even the best human minds cannot simultaneously comprehend all the program's working details. It is therefore vitally important that the design and implementation of large computer programs be based on systematic procedures for software development, including attention to program specification and design, organization, coding, testing, and maintenance of software [4]. Careful planning of these activities is needed because large programs are most often written by programming teams and developed within the constraints of limited budgets and short time-to-market schedules.

This chapter introduces and describes several tenets of computer program development that facilitate this process.

17.1.1 Principle of Abstraction

The principle of *abstraction* plays a key role in the design and implementation of large software projects. Practicing abstraction means picking out the essential attributes of a system and putting the remaining details aside. For example, rather than view a helicopter as a large collection of mechanical parts, most of us deal with an abstract, reliable, idealized notion of a helicopter and its behavior (see

FIGURE 17.1 A helicopter.

Figure 17.1). This notion of abstraction allows us to go for a joy ride in a helicopter without becoming overwhelmed by the complexities of how the engine, navigation and control systems work. We can, of course, inquire about the mechanical workings at a later point.

A second well-known technique for reducing the complexity of large systems is to organize them into hierarchies, together with mechanisms for examining layers in the hierarchy at will. The two most common types of hierarchal abstraction in computer programming circles are procedural abstraction and data abstraction.

1. *Procedural Abstraction.* The "procedural" approach to problem solving is based on the idea that software can be developed in a stepwise refinement of a system's function. The process begins with a topmost statement, or function representing the task to be accomplished and is followed by a step-by-step refinement of the function into functions that accomplish more basic tasks Computer programs written in Pascal, Ada, and C tend to follow this style of program development.
2. *Data Abstraction.* In the "data" approach to problem solving, programmers focus on the problem data and the operations that can be applied to the data Objects and object operations are an equivalent way of looking at the problem An object can be a concept, an abstraction, or a thing with crisp boundaries and meaning for the problem domain at hand. This is the object-oriented paradigm.

17.1.2 Need for Software Reuse

The success of large-scale software development can be measured from at least two viewpoints. Software customers are looking for programs that are easy to use and, of course, produce correct results in the shortest possible time. Software developers, on the other hand, want computer programs that are easy to understand, maintain, and extend. Economic considerations usually dictate that, whenever possible, new software systems should be assembled from previously developed software components and frameworks. Software modules should be designed so that they can be easily adapted to the changing requirements of ongoing development and employed for multiple projects. This is software reuse.

17.2 OBJECT-ORIENTED SOFTWARE DEVELOPMENT

The aims of object technology and object-oriented programming techniques are to deliver cost-effective high-quality software to the customer, and it is through "software reuse" that object technology delivers its economic benefits [23]. Object-oriented technology provides mechanisms for explicitly dealing with information hiding through encapsulation and communication among objects with message passing. The principles of encapsulation, inheritance, and polymorphism enable systems of objects and their behavior to be represented in a manner that is efficient and amenable to software reuse. Do not worry if some of these terms seem a little unfamiliar at this point, we define them in this chapter.

Object-oriented program development involves analysis, design, and programming. The analysis phase takes a "real-world entity" apart, and understands and identifies its key components. Object-oriented analysis includes identification of (1) the objects, (2) the operations on the objects, and (3) how the objects interact (see Figure 17.2).

Object-oriented design is the act of reassembling the components into hierarchies of interconnected computer-world objects. These hierarchies should have the capability to answer questions about the real-world system's behavior and be responsive to change in the real world.

Object-oriented programming is the process of translating the computer-world objects into source code called "classes" in Java. Although it is certainly feasible

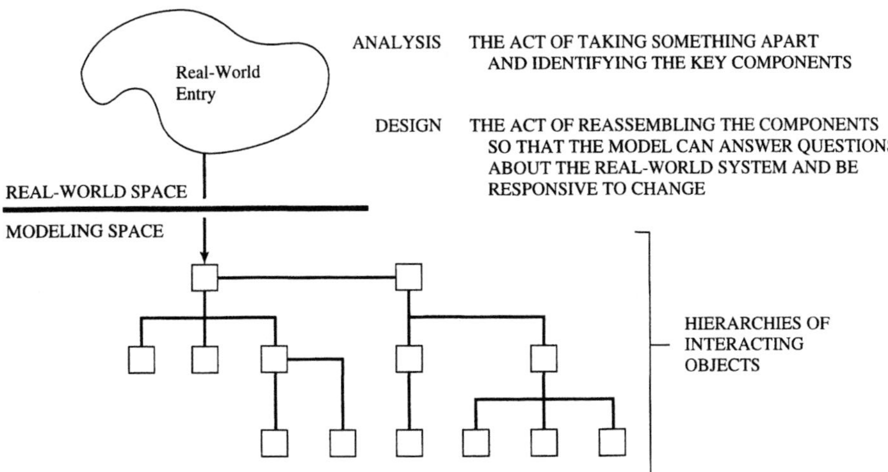

FIGURE 17.2 Object-oriented analysis and design.

to implement objects of code in traditional programming languages such as C, object-oriented programming languages contain additional features that encourage a programmer to follow the principles of object-oriented design. In fact, to be object-oriented, a programming language must support (1) encapsulated objects, (2) inheritance between objects, and (2) polymorphism. In other words,

Object-oriented = Objects + Inheritance + Polymorphism

At this point, some of you may be thinking that object-oriented programming languages are a necessary component for software reuse. They are not. Many of the most widely used software packages in engineering are not object-oriented. Moreover, an object-oriented programming language by itself cannot guarantee a good program design. The language can only encourage it. As we soon see, the real challenge in object-oriented software development lies in the design of object-structure hierarchies that reduce the complexity of large software systems and deliver maximum information with minimal cognitive effort on the part of the software designer.

17.2.1 Encapsulation

Encapsulation is the process of "bundling related data and functions" into wrapped objects. It is the key to object-oriented program design, especially when it is enforced by the programming language. The data and functions may belong together because they have similar properties, or perhaps common behavior. When the tenet of encapsulation is combined with that of "information hiding," the result is individual software modules that serve a cohesive well-defined purpose. The software modules and their interfaces will reveal as little as possible about the module's inner workings to the outside world. The object wrapping protects the object code from unintended access by other code. A detailed discussion of these principles is located in Tutorial 1.

In object-oriented terminology, and particularly in Java, the wrapper object is called a *class,* the functions inside the class are called *private methods,* and the data inside the class are *private variables. Public methods* are the interface functions for the outside world to access your private methods. A class may also contain public variables, but their use is often considered to be a bad programming habit. Figure 17.3 is a graphical representation of a class.

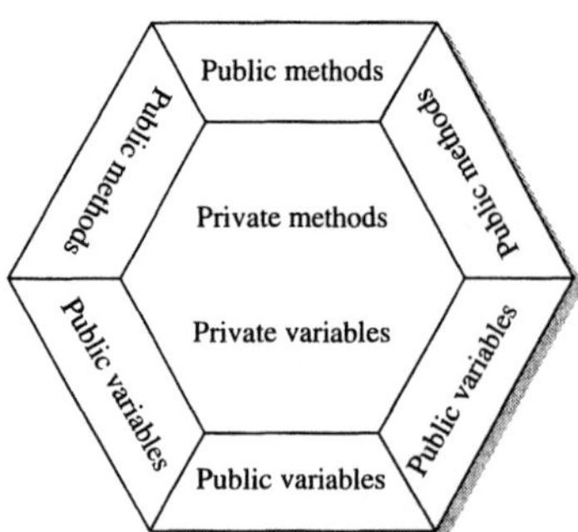

FIGURE 17.3 Graphical representation of a class.

17.2.2 Relationships Among Classes

Object-oriented software packages are assembled from collections of classes and class hierarchies that are related in three fundamental ways:

1. *Use:* Let `A` and `B` be two classes. Class `A` uses Class `B` if a method in `A` sends a message to an object of type `B`, or alternatively, a method of `A` creates, receives, or returns objects of type `B`.

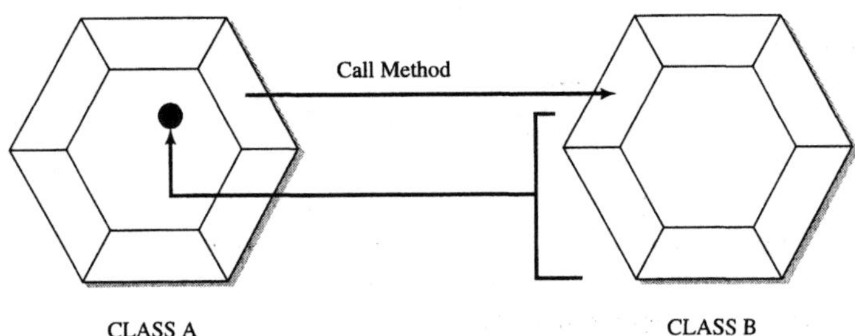

2. *Containment (Has a):* An object of type `A` contains (or has a) object(s) of type `B`. Clearly, containment is a special case of use (i.e., see Item 1).

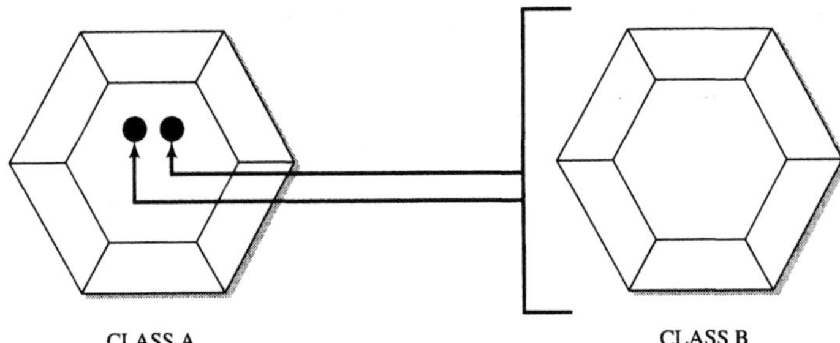

3. *Inheritance (Is a):* In everyday life, we think of inheritance as something that is received from a predecessor or past generation. The physical features we inherit from our ancestors are perhaps the best example of inheritance.

   Object-oriented programming languages employ inheritance as a means of allowing similar attributes or properties in a group of objects to be stored in a base or parent class, which other subclasses, or children, can subsequently inherit. In the adjacent diagram Class `B` extends (or inherits) the data and methods from Class `A`. Class `B` will add its own specialized methods.

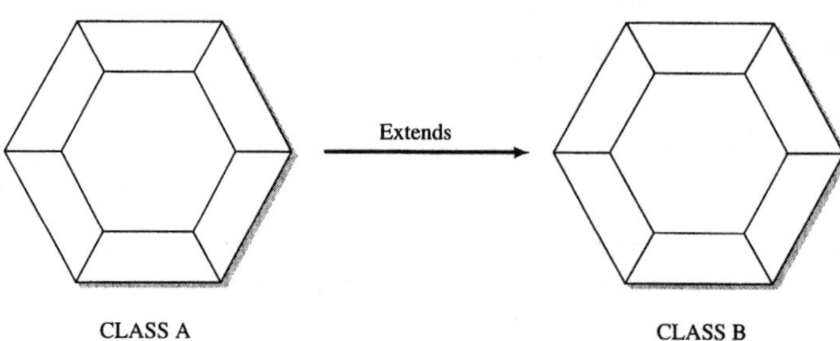

The challenge in designing a class hierarchy lies in the identification of similar attributes or properties in a group of objects that can be stored in a base or parent class. Because the common attributes and operations in a class are only implemented once, inheritance facilitates the efficient storage of data/information. Inheritance also enables "programming by extension." Several examples of this programming technique are presented in Chapters 18 and 19.

17.2.3 Engineering Example

Now we try to understand this important principal by looking at an example from the design and analysis of civil engineering structures (see Figure 17.4). Civil engineering structures are often modeled as an assembly of nodes and elements. We assume

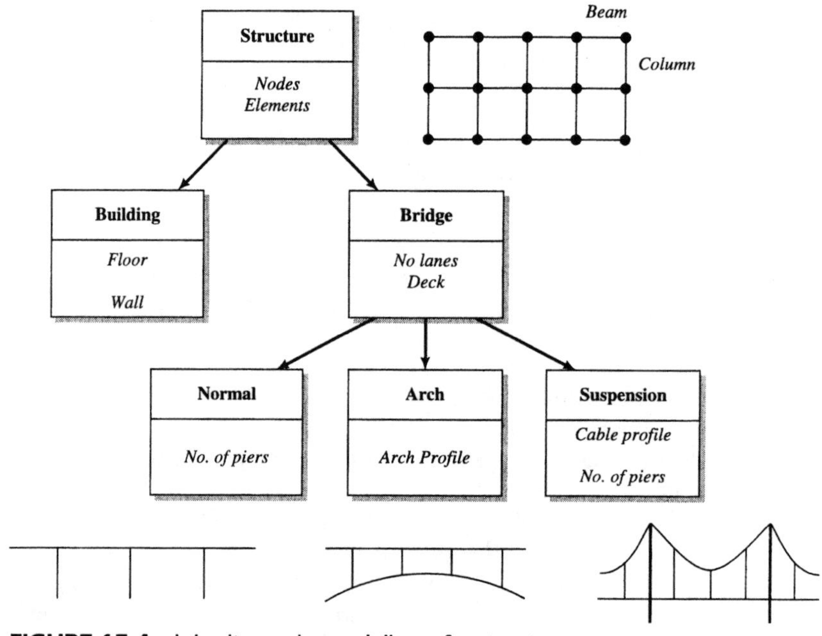

FIGURE 17.4 Inheritance in modeling of a structure.

that this idealization is the most general, or abstract, way of describing a structure, and we define a `Structure` class for that object. Remember that class is the Java name for an object. The `Structure` class will be the uppermost (or root) object in the hierarchy. In a typical Java implementation of this class, its characteristics would be implemented as public methods and public variables.

With the `Structure` object in place, the next issue to consider is how can we define the model for highway bridge? Our notion of a structure and highway bridge are similar in the sense that their models both have nodes and elements. However, they are also distinct in the sense that a highway bridge has a deck and a certain number of lanes for the cars. An efficient way of capturing both the similarities and differences of these systems is to view a bridge as "a kind of" structure with "a little more" added on.

A class that extends the properties and attributes of another class is called a *subclass.* The subclass will have the same attributes (i.e., public methods, public variables) as the class, plus some others of its own. In our case study problem, for example, `Bridge` is a subclass of `Structure`. The `Bridge` class will inherit all the attributes of the `Structure` class and add a few properties of its own. The analogy can be continued of course, with `Normal`, `Arch`, and `Suspension` bridges being subclasses of `Bridge`. They inherit properties from both the `Structure` and `Bridge` classes, and add attributes unique to their respective classes.

17.2.4 Polymorphism

Polymorphism is the ability of an object or object operation to assume different forms. Polymorphism is an important tenet of object-oriented programming because it enhances the flexibility of methods and classes within a class hierarchy (note that "poly" means "many" and "morph" means "form").

In the case of Java, polymorphism is the ability of methods and operators to have meanings that depend on the context in which they are used. Polymorphism comes in two flavors:

1. *Overloading:* In classical programming languages, separate tasks are nearly always implemented with separate functions. But sometimes situations arise where two tasks are very similar and perhaps only differ in the function arguments they use. You want to give them the same function name and let the computer use the correct one based on the type of the arguments you give. That is exactly what overloading is about.

   Suppose, for example, that we want to define a "mean" function that will work for both integer and float arguments. Using the C programming language, this problem would be solved with two functions:

   ```
   int   meanInt(int a, int b);
   float meanFloat(float a, float b);
   ```

In Java, you still have to define two functions with separate source codes, but you can give them the same name:

```
int   mean(int a, int b);
float mean(float a, float b);
```

At run-time, if you call the function "mean" with integer arguments, the first function will be called. If you call the function with floats as arguments, then the second function will be called. Overloading is also a feature of C++.

2. *Overriding:* Recall that in the principal of inheritance, objects are a subclass of other objects and inherit all their attributes. More precisely, an object will inherit all the public methods and public variables specified in objects higher in the object hierarchy. But what if the public method of the superclass of a certain object is not exactly as you want it to be? Well, you can redefine the method for that object and still keep the same name.

   Suppose that in our civil engineering example, the way in which the object `Bridge` calculates the number of lanes is not really appropriate for the number of lanes in an arch bridge. You still want the "arch bridge" object to be a subclass of `Bridge`, however. Java allows you to define `Arch` as a subclass of `Bridge`, and then override the number of lanes calculation in the "Arch" class with a new function having the same name as in "Bridge," but with different details of calculation. This is overriding.

17.3 IS JAVA OBJECT-ORIENTED?

So how does Java measure up to these criteria? The Java language provides mechanisms to create objects and methods, and to design interfaces for those objects to communicate. It also provides mechanisms to enforce the object-oriented model by defining encapsulation, inheritance, and polymorphism. So we can say that Java is an object-oriented language.

REVIEW QUESTIONS

1. What three principles enforce the object-oriented paradigm in a computer language?

2. What is the general principle behind the object-oriented concept? Briefly explain it.

3. What is encapsulation, inheritance, and polymorphism?

4. Function polymorphism comes in two forms: overloading and overriding. What is an example of overloading? What is an example of overriding? How might you replicate overloading in C?

5. How does the principle of "programming by extension" work?

6. Let `A` and `B` be two classes in a program. In terms of Classes `A` and `B`, briefly explain the meaning of the class relationships `use`, `contain`, and `inheritance`.

7. From a software engineering standpoint, what is the main disadvantage of public variables?

17.4 REVIEW EXERCISES

Problem 17.1 (Beginner): Design a class hierarchy for clocks. All clocks should store the hour (1–24), minute (1–60), and second (1–60), and a flag for `AM` and `PM`. The class hierarchy should have separate methods for digital and analog displays. A `stop clock` should contain an ensemble of methods for timing events.

Problem 17.2 (Beginner): Design a class hierarchy for bicycles. The class hierarchy should distinguish single rider and tandem machines. Information on the material type, shape, and size of the bicycle, including the wheels, should be represented. What kinds of methods will be needed to compute the weight of a bicycle?

Problem 17.3 (Intermediate): How would you adapt the class hierarchy of bridge and building structures shown in Figure 17.4 to represent a large building that contains a foot bridge?

18
THE JAVA LANGUAGE

18.1 GETTING STARTED

Java is a small programming language designed specifically for reliable run-time performance in a networked environment. Its design deliberately incorporates the best features of a number of languages, notably C, and omits the worst features from a number of languages, notably C and C++. To highlight the similarities and differences of C and Java, the left-hand side of Table 18.1 summarizes the features of C that have been omitted to create Java. The right-hand side of Table 18.1 summarizes the features added to C to create Java. This table is a combination of ideas initially presented by van der Linden [45]. A key purpose of this chapter is to explain why certain features have been added to and removed from C to create Java.

Java is identical to many other programming languages in the sense that data and instructions are the two basic building blocks of a computer program. Variables and data types are the heart of a program's data. Control structures and methods are essential components of a program's instructions. C programmers have a head start in learning the Java basics because the syntax, data types, and control structures of both languages are almost the same. By only briefly mentioning the syntactic details of the language, this tutorial quickly gets to the features of Java that distinguish it from C. The ability to write bug-free graphical software that will operate in a secure manner in a networked environment is perhaps the most important feature of Java. Before we can get to that point, however, we need to see how object-oriented program design and analysis works in practice, and how the basic

TABLE 18.1 Comparison of Features in Java and C

Features Omitted from C to Create Java	*Features Added to C to Create Java*
`goto` statement	Classes and object-oriented programming
`typedef`	Uniform data types
Pointer arithmetic	Threads
Structures, unions, and enums	Automatic management of dynamic memory
Global variables	Exceptions
Automatic type conversion	Java application programming interfaces
Nonuniform data types	

structure of Java programs (i.e., classes, methods) work. These points are illustrated by seeing how the principles of encapsulation, inheritance, and polymorphism can be applied to the solution of elementary engineering problems.

18.1.1 Java Platform Requirements

Before we can start working with Java, we need to answer the question, "What platforms support Java?" There are two answers to this question:

1. *WWW Surfer.* For someone who simply wants to surf the Web, access to Java is provided through a Java Virtual Machine embedded within a web browser. The two most widely used browsers that include the Java Virtual Machine are Netscape 3.0 and up and Microsoft Internet Explorer 3.0 and up. Versions of these browsers exist for `Windows95/98`, `WindowsNT`, `MacOS`, `SunOS`, `Solaris`, and most UNIX Operating Systems (OS). With a Java-enabled web browser in hand, web surfers can download and execute Java applets (a special form of Java application described in Chapter 16) on any of those platforms.
2. *Java Developer.* Life is a little different for the Java program developer. In addition to having the capability of running Java programs, developers need to compile Java program source code into a program bytecode. The association of a Virtual Machine (or running environment) and a compiler, an editor, and so forth is called a "Development Environment." The first of these environments was the Java Development Kit (JDK) created by Sun Microsystems. The JDK is freely available for `Sparc` and X86 `Solaris`, `WindowsNT`, and `Windows95/98` platforms. Since then many other companies have released development kits for Java program development on many different platforms, including PCs and Macs.

Note. One of the most difficult problems in porting the Java Virtual Machine to different platforms is getting the multithreading ability of Java to work. To allow different threads to run at the same time, the Java Virtual Machine relies heavily on the underlying operating system to handle these tasks. The Java Virtual Machine is not supported on Windows 3.11 because the underlying operating system does not easily support multitasking.

18.1.2 Java Development Kit

Sun Microsystems has created an ensemble of Java libraries and development tools for Java applications development, and bundled them into a package called the JDK. The most important tools in this package are

1. **`javac`:** The `javac` program compiles Java source code files into bytecode files. The Java source code file names must end with `.java`. For each class found in the source code, `javac` will create a separate class file named `name-of-the-class.class`.
   Syntax: `javac source-file.java`
2. **`java`:** The name of the Java bytecode interpreter is `java`, and it accepts as its input argument, the name of the bytecode file you want to run without the `.class` extension. The interpreter will execute the main method of that class.
   Syntax: `java class-name`
3. **`jdb`:** The Java debugger is a Java application that allows you to follow step by step all the details of execution in a Java program.
   Syntax: `jdb class-name`
4. **`javadoc`:** The Java document generator generates HTML documents for a list of Java source files specified on the command line. This program employs the 'doc' comments to create the output file.
   Syntax: `javadoc filenames.java`
5. **`appletviewer`:** The Java applet viewer reads HTML files passed as arguments. It downloads all the applets referenced in each document by an `<applet>` and displays them, each in their own window.
   Syntax: `appletviewer files.html`

We assume in the remainder of this tutorial that the JDK has been downloaded and correctly installed on your system.

Java WorkShop

Java WorkShop is an integrated Java development environment that helps you to organize and develop large projects containing many source code files, create user interfaces, and incorporate them into web pages. The Java WorkShop tools include a Portfolio Manager, a Project Manager, a Source Editor, a Build Manager, a Source Browser, a Debugger, and an Applet tester.

18.2 PROGRAM 18.1: "PEACE ON EARTH" STAND-ALONE PROGRAM

In this section we jump right into Java by working step by step through the process of writing, compiling, running, and analyzing a small stand-alone Java application program. Like computer programs written in C, Java programs are developed using a write–compile–run cycle that continues until the program works correctly. All that you need to write Java source code is a "standard ASCII text" editor (a fancy editor is not required).

18.2.1 Problem Statement and Source Code

Program 18.1 simply prints `Peace on Earth!` to the computer screen.

PROGRAM 18.1: PEACE ON EARTH STAND-ALONE PROGRAM

```
/*
 * ==============================================================
 * The 'Peace On Earth' Java application example
 *
 * Written By : David Chancogne                    October 1996
 * ==============================================================
 */

 class Peace {
     public static void main (String[] args) {
        System.out.println("Peace on Earth!");
     }
}       // end of class Peace.
```

The source code for Program 18.1 should be located in a file called `Peace.java`, that is, a file name beginning with the same name as the class defined in that file, plus the `.java` extension.

18.2.2 Compiling and Running the Program

Java programs are compiled and executed in two steps. First, the Java source code is compiled into a low-level bytecode. The bytecode is interpreted by a program called the Java Virtual Machine. If some of these terms seem a little unfamiliar at this point, do not panic—the concepts of a class and bytecode will be described soon (a description of the terms *bytecode* and *Java Virtual Machine* are also in Chapter 16).

The name of the Java compiler is `javac`, and the name of the Java interpreter is `java`. The command line

```
prompt >> javac Peace.java
```

invokes the compiler with file name `Peace.java` as input. The list of program files before and after compilation is

Files before Compilation	*Files after Compilation*
Peace.java	Peace.java
	Peace.class

TABLE 18.2 Types Comments in Java

Type of Comment Statement	*Interpretation in Java*
`// Single-line comment`	All text following `//` up to the end of the line is considered as comment. There is no limit to the number of characters in the line.
`/* This is the classical C comment. It can be on multiple lines */`	All text between `/*` and `*/` is ignored by the compiler.
`/** This is a 'doc' comment. It can be on multiple lines */`	All comments between `/**` and `*/` are intended to describe declarations. A tool called `javadoc` extracts those comments and creates HTML documentation out of them.

You should find that the Java compiler has created a `Peace.class` file in your current directory. The script of code

```
prompt >> java Peace
Peace on Earth!
prompt >>
```

shows how the bytecode for Program 18.1 is executed. The Java interpreter expects a class name (in this case, `Peace`) as an argument. Remember that Java and UNIX are case sensitive, thus you have to use a capital "P" for the class name.

18.2.3 Comment Statements

Comments in Java are simply words or lines of text that you put in your Java code to document its purpose. Java treats comment statements as white space. Table 18.2 briefly summarizes the three types of comments recognized by the Java compiler; they are single-line comments, block comments, and documentation comments. Short inline comment statements begin with two forward slashes (//); the Java compiler will ignore the rest of the line.

Program 18.1 also uses multiline comment statements with which C programmers will be familiar; that is, a comment statement begins with the two-character sequence `/*` and ends with the first occurrence of the character pair `*/`. In both C and Java, you cannot place a `/* ... */` comment inside another `/* ... */` comment.

18.2.4 Identifiers and Reserved Words

An identifier is a user-defined name given to classes, methods, and variables. Identifier names in Java may be constructed from sequences of letters and digits, underscores (_), and the dollar ($) sign of unlimited length. The first character in a variable name must be a letter, however. Identifier names in Java are case sensitive, so if you accidentally type "peace" when you really meant "Peace," Java will not be able to reconcile the mistake.

Java programmers have created a defacto standard of beginning class names with a capital letter, a convention we will adopt for this tutorial. We also begin each syllable in a long identifier name with a capital letter. The names of constants and variables for basic data types (details given below) will be prefixed with Hungarian notation (described in the C tutorial).

Like most programming languages, Java has a family of reserved words that are defined as part of the programming language itself. For example, the Java keywords are used to define the basic data types, and for the basic branching and looping constructs. Table 16.1 shows the keywords in Java 1.0. These keywords must not be used for user-identified information in a program (e.g., as the name of a variable).

18.2.5 Layout of Program Source Code

Java is a free-format programming language, meaning that it treats tabs, spaces, line feeds, and carriage returns as white space. Sequences of white space are treated as a single white space. It follows that the program layouts

```
class Peace {
    public static void main ( String[] args ) {
        System.out.println("Peace on Earth!");
    }
}
```

and

```
class Peace
{
    public static void main ( String[] args )
    {
        System.out.println("Peace on Earth!");
    }
}
```

are functionally equivalent. The style you choose to use is really an issue of personal taste. For this tutorial, we employ the former layout because it uses less paper. Notice how we indent the blocks of source code to reflect the hierarchy of methods within classes, and blocks of computational code within the methods.

18.2.6 Objects and Classes

Java is an object-oriented programming language, and the concept of a class is the pathway to object creation. Every Java program will contain at least one class definition, and each class definition will contain at least one method definition (a method in Java is just like a function in C). Although the main purpose of this tutorial is to teach you how to program your own Java classes, we rely on the classes and methods located within the Java libraries for much of our Java program functionality. The block of code

```
class Peace {       <=== Definition and opening brace for class "Peace".

}                   <=== Closing brace for class "Peace".
```

defines a class called `Peace`. All the methods for the class Peace are contained within the matched braces following the class definition.

18.2.7 The `main()` Method

Every stand-alone Java program must contain a class with the method `main`, as with programs written in C, this is where the execution of a Java program begins. The block of code

```
public static void main (String[] args) {
   System.out.println("Peace on Earth!");
}
```

defines the method `main` for our first Java program. The keyword `public` specifies the method access (i.e., who or which groups have access to the method), and the keyword `static` indicates that `main` will be a class method rather than an instance method. The distinction between these method types will become important when we start to build more substantial application programs. The keyword `void` indicates that the main method will not return a value.

The text enclosed in parentheses following the `main` method name is called a parameter specification. Our first Java program has only one argument

```
String[] args
```

an array `args` of instances of objects from the class `String`. An alternative syntax that C programmers will be familiar with is `String args[]`. In either case, the argument list is not used by the application program because the program is so simple.

18.2.8 Output with `System.out.println()`

Java employs the methods `println` and `print` for displaying sequences of information enclosed within parentheses. For example, the statement

```
System.out.println("Peace on Earth!");
```

tells the `println` method to display "Peace on Earth" on your computer screen. Java and C are similar in that character strings are a sequence of characters surrounded by double quotation marks, and statements are terminated by a semicolon. The `println` method automatically appends a newline character to the output stream (the `print` method does not).

Java programs use a "dot" notation as a means of referring to objects in Java (e.g., `System.out.println`). The `System.out` part of the display statement indicates that information should be sent to the computer screen/display.

18.3 PROGRAM 18.2: "PEACE ON EARTH" JAVA APPLET PROGRAM

As mentioned in Chapter 16, an applet is simply a Java program that runs within a web browser or viewer and is usually part of a Hypertext Markup Language (HTML) page. The strong appeal of Java applet programs stems from their ability to be downloaded over the Internet to your local computer and then executed. In other words, a Java applet program need only be written once and can then be executed anywhere on the Internet.

18.3.1 Problem Statement and Program Source Code

In this example, we simply write `Peace on Earth!` as text on a graphical display. Figure 18.1 is a typical screen dump of the "Peace on Earth" applet. Our implementation is composed of two parts. First, we write and examine the Java program source code. We then develop an HTML file that will load the applet into a web browser or viewer.

18.3.2 Program Source Code

The source code for the Java applet program is on page 498.

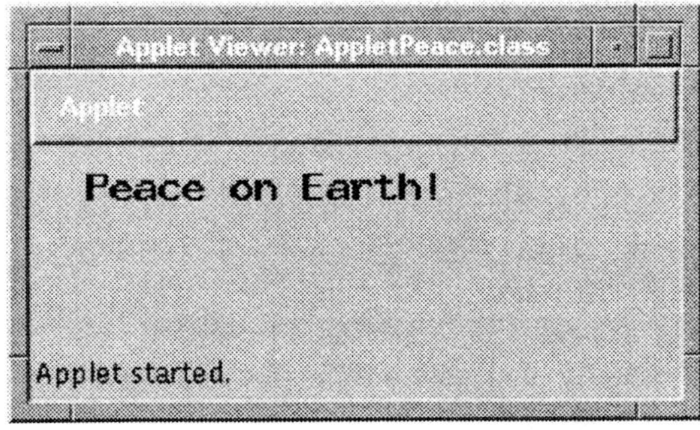

FIGURE 18.1 Screen dump of "Peace on Earth" applet.

PROGRAM 18.2: "PEACE ON EARTH" APPLET

```
/*
 * ==============================================================
 * File : AppletPeace.java
 *
 * This is the applet version of our first Java program
 * ==============================================================
 */

import java.applet.*;
import java.awt.*;

public class AppletPeace extends Applet {
    public void paint (Graphics g) {

        // Set the font for the graphic context

        g.setFont(new Font("Courier", Font.ITALIC, 18));

        // Draw the appropriate String.

        g.drawString("Peace on Earth!", 25, 25);
    }
}
```

This short program uses many of the concepts you need to be familiar with to write simple applet programs. Of course, the concepts of comments, identifiers and reserved words, and classes and objects described in Section 18.2 also apply to Java applets.

C and Java programs are similar in that they both make extensive use of external packages (or libraries) for adding functionality to a program. The import statement

```
import java.applet.*;
import java.awt.*;
```

indicate that you will use classes from the `java.applet` and `java.awt` packages. The applet is created with classes from the `java.applet` package. Graphical elements in the applet are created with classes from the `java.awt` package. Both packages contain a hierarchy of classes, a topic that is described in depth in Chapter 19. The asterisk is a "wild card" character that indicates multiple classes are to be imported.

Every Java program is composed of at least one class definition, and most Java programs are constructed from hierarchies of classes. The line

```
public class AppletPeace extends Applet {

    ...... details of code removed .....
}
```

begins an applet class definition for the `AppletPeace` class. The keyword `class` introduces the class definition and is immediately followed by `AppletPeace`, the name of the class for our program.

Java applet programs are never created from scratch. Instead, we use Java's inheritance mechanism to build on, or extend, the functionality provided by methods in the `Applet` class. The phrase `... AppletPeace extends Applet ...` declares that the class `AppletPeace` will inherit all the methods and properties available with `Applet`, and then add some of its own. The ability of Java programs to inherit and override methods is the "programming-by-extension" mechanism mentioned in Chapter 17.

The browser or viewer in which we run the program is actually responsible for creating an instance of the `AppletPeace` class. The keyword `public` gives the browser permission to create and execute the applet. The line

```
public void paint (Graphics g) {
```

introduces the `paint()` method. The keyword `public` gives the browser permission to call the `paint()` method. The keyword `void` indicates that this method will not return a value after it has finished its execution. The parameter list for `paint()` contains `Graphics g`, which is a graphics object named `g` associated with the applet component. The browser will automatically call the `paint()` method whenever the applet needs to be drawn or redrawn on the HTML page. The latter situation will occur, for example, when the applet window has been uncovered or moved. The line

```
g.setFont(new Font("Courier", Font.ITALIC, 18));
```

calls the `setFont()` method associated with the graphics object `g`. The `setFont()` parameter list indicates that the font should be changed to an Italic Courier style, size 18. The line

```
g.drawString("Peace on Earth!", 25, 25);
```

calls the `drawString()` method to print the text enclosed in quotation marks. Printing of the text begins at pixel coordinate $(x, y) = (25, 25)$. The origin of the pixel coordinate system is located at the top left-hand corner of the applet. The x coordinate represents the number of pixels from the left-hand edge of the applet, and the y coordinate represents the number of pixels measured downward from the top of the applet. It is important to remember that because the size and number of pixels on a graphics display is hardware dependent, the visual layout of text in an applet will also be hardware dependent.

18.3.3 The init() Method

We have already seen that stand-alone Java programs begin their execution in the method main(). Java applet programs begin their execution in a method called init(). Program 18.2 simply inherits the init() method from the Applet class. In Chapter 19, we encounter applet programs containing user-defined init() methods.

18.3.4 The HTML File

A browser displays an applet on a web page by reading an HTML file containing the applet specification. Here is a simple HTML document that embeds the applet

```
<!-- File AppletPeaceOnEarth.html -->

<html>
<head>
<title> Peace on Earth </title>
</head>
<body>

<applet
 code = "AppletPeace.class" width = 200 height = 50>
</applet>

</body>
</html>
```

within a file AppletPeaceOnEarth.html.

HTML files contain tags that mark the elements of a file for your browser or viewer to read. Elements include heads, titles, paragraphs, lists, and so forth. HTML tags consist of a left angle < bracket, a tag name, and a right angle > bracket. Tag items are usually paired (e.g., <title> and </title>) to indicate the beginning and end of the pair. The elements <html>, <head>, <body>, and their corresponding end tags are required by nearly every HTML document. The <html> tag tells your browser that the file contains HTML-coded information. The <head> tag identifies the first part of the HTML-coded document containing the page title. The <title> tag contains the document title.

The applet specification begins with <applet ... and ends with the </applet> tag. The line code = "AppletPeace.class" tells the browser to load the bytecode AppletPeace.class. The second and third arguments specify the width and height of the applet on the HTML page in pixels.

18.3.5 Compiling and Running the Program

Program 18.2 should be compiled into a bytecode file called `AppletPeace.class`. The list of program files before and after compilation is

Files before Compilation	*Files after Compilation*
AppletPeaceOnEarth.html	AppletPeaceOnEarth.html
AppletPeace.java	AppletPeace.java
	AppletPeace.class

The command

```
prompt >> appletviewer AppletPeaceOnEarth.html
```

invokes the applet viewer with the HTML file `AppletPeaceOnEarth.html` as an argument. Of course, you can also use a Java-enabled web browser to download and display the contents of `AppletPeaceOnEarth.html`.

18.4 PRIMITIVE DATA TYPES

The word `data` is used to describe any type of information that may be manipulated by a computer. In Java, a binary digit, or bit, is the smallest unit of information a computer can manipulate.

Table 18.3 contains a summary of the eight basic data types in Java, their size, default values, and precision and range of values that can be stored. The data types

TABLE 18.3 Data Types in Java

Type	*Contains*	*Default Value*	*Size*	*Range and Precision*
boolean	True or false	false	1 bit	
char	Unicode character	\u0000	16 bits	\u0000/\uFFFF
byte	Signed integer	0	8 bits	−128/127
short	Signed integer	0	16 bits	−32768/32767
int	Signed integer	0	32 bits	−2147483648/2147483647
long	Signed integer	0	64 bits	−9223372036854775808/9223372036854775807
float	IEEE 754 floating point	0.0	32 bits	± 13.40282347E+38 / ± 11.40239846E−45
	Floating point numbers are represented to approximately 6 to 7 decimal places of accuracy.			
double	IEEE 754 floating point	0.0	64 bits	± 11.79769313486231570E+308/ ± 14.94065645841246544E−324
	Double precision numbers are represented to approximately 15 to 16 decimal places of accuracy.			

`byte`, `short`, `int`, and `long` store integers covering a variety of ranges. The data types `float` and `double` store floating point numbers. The data type `char` holds a single character. The data type `boolean` holds logical information and assumes a value of either true or false. All the numerical values in Java are signed. The basic data types are also called primitive data types because they are the smallest items of data from which Java programs can be built.

Compared to C, Java is very strict in the range of sizes and values a primitive data type can take. As a case in point, an `int` in C can be 8, 16, or 32 bits, depending on the compiler and the underlying computer architecture. An `int` in Java is always 32 bits wide. Along with its use of the Java Virtual Machine, the strict enforcement of data sizes is one of the key ways Java achieves its platform independence. Java and C also differ in their treatment of uninitialized variables. In C, uninitialized variables should be assumed to contain garbage. Uninitialized Java variables take the default standardized values shown in Table 18.3.

The primitive data types in Java have been defined in accordance with a number of standards that ensure error conditions will be properly handled and that the language will be suitable for internationalization. As shown in Table 18.3, for example, the `float` and `double` data types have been defined in accordance with the IEEE 754 Standard for Binary Floating Point Arithmetic [11, 42]. This standard includes not only positive and negative sign-magnitude numbers, but also positive and negative zeros, positive and negative infinites, and a special Not-a-Number (usually abbreviated NaN). The NaN value is used to represent the result of certain operations such as dividing zero by zero.

The goals of software internationalization are to support software that can work in many countries, having their own languages, currencies, formats for dates, and so forth. The Unicode Worldwide Character Standard is a character coding system designed to support the interchange, processing, and display of the written texts of the diverse languages of the modern world. In addition, it supports classical and historical texts of many written languages. In its current version (2.0), the Unicode standard contains 38,885 distinct coded characters derived from 25 supported scripts. These characters cover the principal written languages of the Americas, Europe, the Middle East, Africa, India, Asia, and the Pacific.

18.5 JAVA VARIABLES

A *variable* is simply a block of memory whose value can be accessed with a name or identifier. A variable contains either the contents of a primitive data type or a reference to an object. The object may be an instance of a class, an interface, or an array.

The scope of a variable is the range over which it is defined and, in the case of Java, is tied to the class hierarchy of a program. Java supports three types of variables:

1. *Local Variables.* These are variables whose scope is limited to a block of code. Local variables are defined within the current block of code and have meaning for the time that the code block is active.

2. *Instance Variables.* These variables hold data for an instance of a class. Instance variables have meaning from the time they are created until there are no more references to that instance.
3. *Class Variables.* These variables hold data that can be shared among all instances of a class. Class variables have meaning from the time that the class is loaded until there are no more references to the class.

Sometimes we also use the term *reference-type variable* for variables that refer to objects and arrays, as opposed to those variables that simply provide a name for a small block of memory storing one of the basic data types. The importance of this distinction will become clear when we get to the sections on creating objects and passing data types and objects to methods.

18.5.1 Declaring a Variable

A variable can only be used in a Java program after it has been declared. Variable declarations introduce the name and data type of a variable to a program and most often follow the syntax

```
variable-type name-of-variable(s);
```

and

```
variable-type name-of-variable = expression;
```

Java variables can be declared for the basic data types and instances of a particular class. The amount of memory used to store each variable is determined by its data type (for more details, see Table 18.3).

Java is a strongly typed language, meaning that each variable in Java must hold the same type of data for which it was declared. For example, the declarations

```
float fRadius;
float fArea     = 3.4;
String myString = "This is a String";
```

instruct the computer to assign 4 bytes of memory for each of the variables `fRadius` and `fArea`, and to assign the value of `3.4` to `fArea`. The layout of memory for `fRadius` and `fArea` should be thought of as

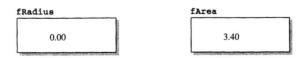

You should notice that, because `fRadius` represents a primitive data type, it automatically assumes the default value `0.0`.

TABLE 18.4 Variable Modifiers

Type of Modifier	*Interpretation in Java*
`public`	The variable can be accessed by any class.
`private`	The variable can be accessed only by methods within the same class
`protected`	The variable can also be accessed by subclasses of the class.
`static`	The variable is a class variable.

Character strings in Java are instances of the class `String`. They are no primitive data types. Their use is so common that string literals may be enclosed within quotes, and the Java compiler will automatically create a `String` object Hence, in the third example, an instance of the class `String` is assigned to `myString` with the contents `"This is a String"`. The layout of memory should be though of as something like

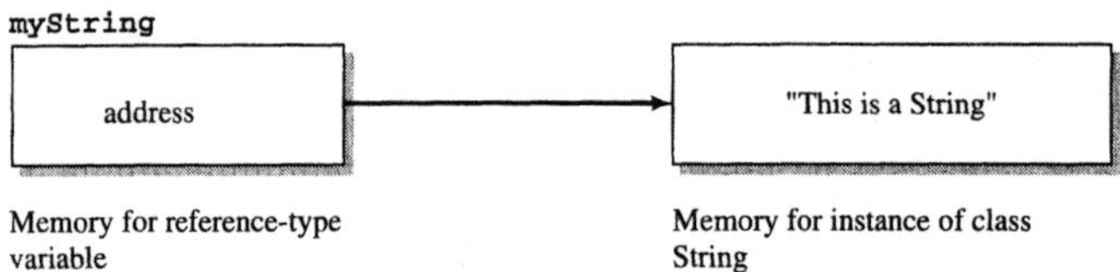

We say that `myString` is a reference-type variable because it holds the address o (or refers to) an instance of the class `String`. Java programmers are not allowed to access the address, however.

18.5.2 Variable Modifiers

The scope of a Java variable can be controlled with a variable modifier. A summary is found in Table 18.4.

18.5.3 Constants

Java does not support `#define` or `enumerated` constants in the same way as C. Instead, Java provides similar functionality with the variable modifier `final` indicating the value of the variable will not change. Suppose, for example, that we wrote

```
#define PROBLEM_SIZE  12
```

in C. Similar functionality in Java can be accomplished with

```
public final static int PROBLEM_SIZE = 12;
```

Use of the keyword `static` indicates that `PROBLEM_SIZE` is a class variable. We suggest that you use capital letters for the names of constants.

18.5.4 No Global Variables

In a programming language such as C, a variable is considered global if it can be accessed and referred to from anywhere in the program. Java does not support global variables. Every variable is declared within a class and forms part of that class. This is a fundamental tenet of object-oriented programming, where everything has to be part of a class. Class variables are the closest thing Java has to global variables.

18.5.5 Casting of Variables

Unlike C, Java does not allow casting between arbitrary variables. Only casts between numerical values and subclasses and superclasses of the same object are allowed.

18.6 EXPRESSIONS

An expression in Java computes a value that can be used in a variety of ways. Values are often assigned to variables, for example, and combined with other variables to form more complicated arithmetic, logical, and relational expressions.

18.6.1 *Arithmetic Expressions*

The arithmetic operators in Java—unary plus (+) and unary minus (−), multiply (*) and divide (/), add (+) and subtract (−), and assignment (=)—have the same syntax, precedence hierarchy, and associativity as those in C. Java also supports the operators ++ and -- to increment and decrement variables in shorthand form.

Operators having a high level of precedence will be evaluated before those with a low level of precedence, and operators with equal precedence will be evaluated using the rules for associativity (i.e., right-to-left or left-to-right evaluation). Of course, the order of evaluation in arithmetic expressions can be altered with parentheses.

Type Conversion

Java automatically converts the type of a variable to an appropriate form when it is used in binary arithmetic. The rules for promotion of operators in binary arithmetic are

1. If either operand is of type `double`, the other is converted to `double`.
2. If either operand is of type `float`, the other is converted to `float`.
3. If either operand is of type `long`, the other is converted to `long`.
4. Otherwise, both operands are converted to type `int`.

Suppose, for example, that an integer `iA` is added to a float `fB`:

```
fB + iA
```

Java temporarily converts `iA` to data type `float` before adding its value to `fB`. C and Java deviate on the use of type conversions in function (or method) calls. Rather than automatically converting an argument to a required type for a function call, Java provides multiple implementations of mathematical and trigonometric functions for a variety of function argument types:

```
Math.abs ( int a    )  // return absolute value of integer 'a'.
Math.abs ( long a   )  // return absolute value of long 'a'.
Math.abs ( float a  )  // return absolute value of float 'a'.
Math.abs ( double a )  // return absolute value of double 'a'.
```

We elaborate on these features later in this chapter.

18.6.2 Relational Expressions

Logical and relational operators are used to test the relationship between two or more values. Expressions involving logical and relational operators will evaluate to a nonzero value when the relationship is `true`. Otherwise, the relationship is `false`. However, unlike C, you cannot use integers (0 and nonzero) to represent true and false.

Java supports the same set of logical and relational operators as C. For a detailed discussion, please see the relevant sections of the C tutorial.

18.7 CONTROL STATEMENTS

Java is very similar to C in that both languages contain features that allow the flow of program execution to be controlled by the outcome of logical and relational expressions evaluated at run-time. The key features are as follows.

18.7.1 Selection Constructs

A *selection construct* enables the pathway of execution in a Java program to be controlled by the results of conditional statements. In many cases, these conditional statements are constructed from expressions involving logical and relational operators.

`if-else`

Branching constructs allow a program to decide on two or more pathways of program execution depending on the outcome of a logical expression. The `if-else` construct is the most basic form of conditional flow control.

```
Syntax of if-else construct      Example
===========================      ===========================

if (boolean-expression) {        if ( iValue == 0 ) {
    statement1;                     fResult = 0;
    statement2;                  } else {
    ..........                      fResult = MAX/value;
} else {                         }
    statement3;
    ..........
}
```

When the boolean condition evaluates to true, `statement1` will be executed, followed by `statement2`, and so forth. Otherwise, `statement3` will be executed and so on. In both cases, the use of braces ({· · ·}) groups zero or more statements into a statement block. The `else` part of this branching construct is optional.

In the example, the logical expression `iValue == 0` evaluates to true when `iValue` equals zero.

switch

A switch statement evaluates an integer expression and then uses its value to jump to an appropriate case label among those listed inside the following switch block. When a matching case is found, program control is transferred to the first statement following the case label. However, when the result of the integer expression is not matched by a case label, the program control jumps to the first statement following the `default` label. If this default label is not found, the entire switch statement will be skipped.

```
Syntax of switch construct         Example
============================       ============================

switch ( Integer-expression ) {    int SMALL  = 0;
    case Integer-value1:           int MEDIUM = 1;
         statement1;               int LARGE  = 2;
    case Integer-value2:
         statement2;               switch (size) {
                                       case SMALL:
    .......                                 System.out.println("Small");
                                            break;
    default:                           case MEDIUM:
         default-statement;                 System.out.println("Medium");
}                                           break;
                                       case LARGE:
                                            System.out.println("Large");
                                            break;
```

```
        default:
            System.out.println("Make a
            choice!");
            break;
    }
```

As with C, the keyword `break` causes Java to exit the current case. In fact, a break statement can be used to exit any block; most often this will be a loop.

18.7.2 Looping Constructs

Looping constructs enable a Java program to iterate, or loop, over one or more statements of code, while a conditional statement evaluates to true.

`while` and `do-while`

Looping constructs are useful when a task has to be repeated multiple times. The `while` and `do-while` looping constructs are exactly the same as in C. In the `while` loop the boolean expression is evaluated and, if the result is true, the following block is executed until the condition becomes false. Note that if the condition is false in the first place, the block is never executed.

```
Syntax of while constructs        Example
============================      ===========================

while ( boolean-expression )      int iValue = 10;
   statement1;
                                  while ( iValue > 0) {
or                                    System.out.println("Count : " + iValue );
                                      iValue--;
while ( boolean-expression ) {    }
   statement2;
   statement3;

   ......
}

Syntax of do-while construct      Example
============================      ===========================

do                                int iValue = 10;
   statement1;
while ( boolean-condition )       do {
                                      System.out.println("Count : " + iValue );
or                                    iValue--;
                                  } while ( iValue > 10)
```

```
do {
   statement2;
   statement3;

   .......
} while ( boolean-condition );
```

In the case of a do-while loop, the block is executed at least once before the boolean condition is evaluated. Then if the result turns out to be true, the block is executed until the condition evaluation is false.

for

The for loop statement is used to loop over a range of values from beginning to end. Typically, the loop is used to iterate a variable over a range of values until some logical end to that range is reached.

```
Syntax of for loop construct                      Example
============================                      ==================================
for ( init-expr; boolean-expr; incr-expr )        init iExpr;
      statement1;                                 for  ( int i = 0 ; i < 8; i++ ) {
                                                          iExpr = iExpr*2;
or                                                }

for ( init-expr; boolean-expr; incr-expr ) {
      statement2;
      statement3;
      ......
}
```

In the for loop syntax, init-expr is one or more expressions that are executed before the loop is entered for the first time. boolean-expr is usually a relational expression that will evaluate to either true or false. The for looping construct will continue cycling over the block of statements for as long as boolean-expr evaluates to true. incr-expr is zero or more statements that will be executed at the conclusion of each cycle in the loop.

18.7.3 Exception-Handling Constructs

An *exception* is a programming feature that simplifies error handling immediately after an abrupt interrupt in programming processing. Common problems include running out of memory, trying to open a file that might not be present, and trying to make a network connection when the network is down.

Exceptions do not reduce the amount of error handling a program should do—rather, they simply allow all the blocks of code that handle errors to be assembled in one place. They also allow for the program control to be directed to that place when something goes wrong. Every exception is a Java class.

try-catch and try-catch-finally

Java facilitates built-in exception handling with the try-catch and try-catch-finally programming constructs.

```
try {
     ...  Java statements .....
}

catch ( ExceptionType1 exceptionVariable1 ) {

      ... Java statements .....
}

catch ( ExceptionType2 exceptionVariable2 ) {

      ... Java statements .....
}
```

The try clause contains statements that may cause an exception. The catch clauses permit likely exception types to be caught and dealt with in an appropriate manner. Last, the finally clause

```
finally {

      ... Java statements .....
}
```

contains code that will be executed regardless of whether an exception occurs within the try clause. The finally clause is optional.

18.8 CLASSES AND OBJECTS

A class is a specification or blueprint for a software object containing data and an ensemble of operations for inspecting and manipulating the data. In Java, these operations are computed by bodies of executable code called methods. Methods contain step-by-step instructions for computing a specific task and are the object-oriented counterpart of functions in C. Programming with classes and methods is strongly encouraged because it enables complex problems to be efficiently represented as hierarchies of simpler tasks.

18.8.1 Class and Method Definitions

The syntax for making a class definition in Java is

```
modifier class name-of-class {  <=== beginning of the
                                     class body.

      ... variables and methods  ....

}                               <=== end of the
                                     class body.
```

and the syntax for making a method definition in Java is

```
modifier return-type name-of-method ( parameter-list ) {

      ... executable statements ....

}                               <=== end of the
                                     method body.
```

In both cases, `modifier` establishes the class or method type and its scope (i.e., what other methods can call it). A summary of class and method modifiers is located in Table 18.5. Some of our Java methods use more than one modifier.

TABLE 18.5 Summary of Class and Method Modifiers

Modifier	*Interpretation in Java*
Class Modifiers	
`abstract`	The class contains methods that are unimplemented. An abstract class cannot be instantiated.
`final`	The class cannot be subclassed.
`(none)`	A nonpublic class is accessible only in its package.
`public`	The class can be accessed by any class.
`static`	This is a top-level class (not an inner class).
Method Modifiers	
`abstract`	The method is provided without a body; the body will be provided by a subclass.
`final`	The method may not be overridden.
`native`	The method is implemented in C or in some other platform-dependent way. No body is provided.
`private`	The method is only accessible within the class that defines it. You should use this keyword for methods that are only of concern to the internal details of the class.
`public`	The method is accessible anywhere the class is accessible.
`static`	Only one instance of a static member will be created, no matter how many instances of the class are created. These member functions may be accessed through the same class name.

The return-type specifies the type of information the method will return. Methods that do not return anything should use the return type `void`. Finally, methods have a `parameter-list` containing zero or more arguments.

The code for each class will usually be stored in a separate file called `classname.java`. Defining an object of a certain class is called creating an instance of that class. When you want to work with a particular object, you create an instance of that class.

Example: Circle Class. We illustrate these concepts by defining a class to represent circles. A circle can be described by the `x` and `y` position of its center and by its `radius`. There are numerous things we can do with circles—compute their circumference or perimeter, compute their area, check whether points are inside them, and so forth. Although each circle is a particular object with its own `(x,y)` coordinate and `radius`, circle is a general concept that can be captured in a "class definition."

```
class Circle {
      public double dX, dY;
      public double dR;

      public double perimeter() {
         return 2 * 3.1415 * dR ;
      }

      public double area() {
         return 3.1415 * dR * dR ;
      }

}
```

The first line of source code uses the keyword `class` to define the class. The name used for the class must be the same as the one used for the file name. In our example, the file would be called `Circle.class`.

The body of `Circle` contains three public instance variables, `dX`, `dY`, and `dR`, and two public methods, `perimeter()` and `area()`. Our use of the keyword `public` makes the variables and methods accessible from outside of the class. Our use of the keyword `double` serves a dual purpose. First, it specifies that variables `dX`, `dY`, and `dR` will be of type `double`. Second, it indicates that `perimeter()` and `area()` will both return a `double`. The methods `perimeter()` and `area()` do not have any arguments.

18.8.2 Creating an Object

Now that we have created a class to represent circles, we want to be able to work with it. To be able to work with an actual object `Circle`, we need to create an

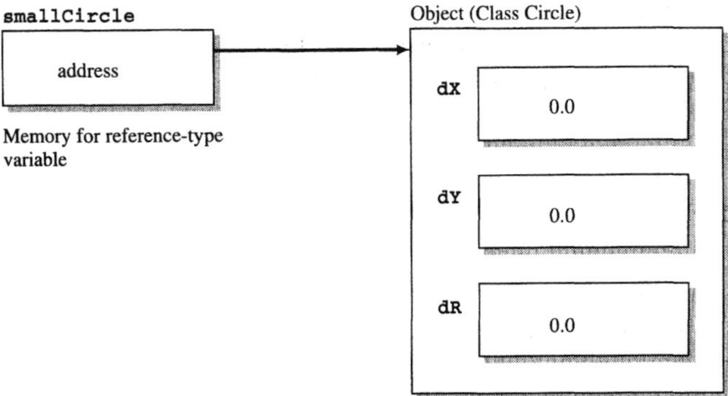

FIGURE 18.2 Layout of memory for circle object.

instance of that class. The creation of an object requires two steps: declaration and creation.

```
Circle smallCircle;
smallCircle = new Circle();
```

The first line is a declaration of a variable `smallCircle` that can reference an object of type `Circle`. In the second step, the `new` operator creates an instance of class `Circle` and a reference to the object is assigned to `smallCircle`. This two-step procedure can be shortened into one step of course:

```
Circle smallCircle = new Circle();
```

After a computer has executed these steps, the layout of memory looks similar to Figure 18.2. `smallCircle` is an abstract identifier that holds a reference to (or the address in memory of the object location) an object of type `Circle`. `smallCircle` does not hold the object itself. Otherwise, creating an instance of a class is like creating a copy of the code defined in the class. The copy will have its own values for the instance variables `dX`, `dY`, and `dR`. Access will also be provided to the methods defined in the class.

No Pointers

We know that some of you will look at `smallCircle` and think "Hey, that's a pointer." It is not. Java has no pointers. Although the Java run-time system may treat the reference as a pointer or handle, or perhaps a pointer to a pointer, all these details are implementation dependent and deliberately hidden from the Java programmer. All that a Java programmer needs to know is that the run-time system will take care of the details of referencing objects. There are two important reason for these restrictions:

1. Elimination of pointers simplifies the language and eliminates many notoriou sources of bugs.
2. Pointers and pointer arithmetic could be used to sidestep Java's run-time check and security mechanisms. Removing pointers allows Java to provide the securit guarantees that it does.

18.8.3 Accessing Object Data

Now that we have created an object, we can use its data fields. The dot operato (.) is used to access the different public variables of an object. For example,

```
Circle smallCircle = new Circle();

/* Initialize the circle to have center (2,2) and radius 1.0 */

smallCircle.dX = 2.0;
smallCircle.dY = 2.0;
smallCircle.dR = 1.0;
```

sets the variables `dX`, `dY`, and `dR` to 2.0, 2.0, and 1.0, respectively.

18.8.4 Accessing Object Methods

This is where things get interesting. To access the methods of an object, we us the same syntax as accessing the data of the object: the dot operator (.).

```
Circle smallCircle = new Circle();
double dArea;

smallCircle.dR  = 2.5;
dArea = smallCircle.area();
```

Take a look at the last line. We did not write

```
dArea = area( smallCircle );
```

But instead, we wrote

```
dArea = smallCircle.area();
```

This is why Java is called an object-oriented language. The object is the focus, no the function call. This is probably the single most important feature of the object oriented paradigm.

By calling smallCircle.area() the syntax itself implies that the object we are working on is smallCircle. If you remember, this object is a copy of the code of the class Circle, which is going to calculate the area of the circle based on its own value of the radius dR.

18.8.5 Passing Arguments to Methods

Java passes all primitive data type variables and reference data type variables to a method by value. A copy of the variable's value is used by the method being called. To see how this principle works in practice, the following script of code is a Java implementation of the tryChange program from the C tutorial. The script of Java code

```
class TryChange {
    public static void main( String args[] ) {
    int iValue = 3;

        System.out.println("In main()        : iValue = " + iValue );
        changeValue( iValue );
        System.out.println("In main()        : iValue = " + iValue );

    }   // end main().

    static void changeValue( int iValue ) {
        System.out.println("In tryChange() : iValue = " + iValue );
        iValue = iValue + 100;
        System.out.println("In tryChange() : iValue = " + iValue );
    }
}
```

generates the output

```
prompt >> java TryChange
In main()       : iValue = 3
In tryChange()  : iValue = 3
In tryChange()  : iValue = 103
In main()       : iValue = 3
prompt >>
```

The important point to note here is that a copy of the value of iValue is passed to changeValue(). Even though the value of iValue is changed inside changeValue(), this change is not propagated back to main(). In fact, as the last line of output clearly shows, the value of iValue in main() remains unaffected by the operations of changeValue().

When an object is passed to a method, it is a copy of a reference to that object that is actually passed and not a copy of the object itself. This means that a method can change the value of data in an external object in much the same way that "pointers as function arguments" enable C functions to access blocks of memory outside their immediate scope (for more details, see Chapter 9). Consider, for example, an array created by using the `new` keyword to return an object referring to an array in memory.

```
double RotMatrix[][] = new double[4][4];
Structure.applyTransformation(RotMatrix);
```

Passing the array object to a method/function is like passing a reference of that array to the function.

18.8.6 Using Constructor Methods for Object Creation

If we have another look at the object creation code,

```
Circle smallCircle = new Circle();
```

it looks like we are calling a function named `Circle()`. Well, guess what, you are exactly right. Every Java class comes with at least one method called the *constructor method,* which has the same name as the class itself. The purpose of that constructor method is to perform any necessary initialization for the new object. This method is called every time you create an instance of the class.

If you do not specify any constructor method when you write the code of a class, Java provides a default one for you that takes no arguments and performs no special initialization. We could define our own constructor method by writing

```
class Circle {
      public double dX, dY, dR;       // Center and radius

      // Our constructor method

      public Circle( double dX, double dY, double dR ) {
         this.dX = dX;
         this.dY = dY;
         this.dR = dR;
      }

      public double perimeter() {
         return 2 * 3.1415 * dR ;
      }

      public double area() {
         return 3.1415 * dR * dR ;
      }
}
```

With this new constructor method, the initialization becomes part of the object creation step

```
Circle smallCircle = new Circle( 2.0, 2.0, 1.0 );
```

Note how we used the keyword `this` to refer to the current object. `this.dX` refers to the `dX` coordinate for the current instance of the object, whereas `dX` just refers to the variable passed as an argument. There are two important notes about naming and declaring constructor methods:

1. The constructor method name is always the same as the class name.
2. The return type is implicitly an instance of the class. No return type is specified in a constructor declaration nor is the `void` keyword used. The `this` object is implicitly returned. A constructor method should not use a return statement to return a value.

18.8.7 Subclass and Inheritance

As mentioned in our introduction to object-oriented development in Chapter 17, one of the major benefits of this problem-solving approach is the ability to extend or subclass the behavior of an existing class, and to continue to use the code written for the original class.

When you extend a class to create a new class, the new extended class inherits all the fields and methods of the class that was extended. The original class on which the extension is based is known as the superclass.

If the class does not specifically override the behavior of the superclass, then the subclass inherits all the behavior from its superclass because, as we said, the extended class inherits the fields and methods of its superclass. In Java, you extend a class by using the keyword `extends` in the class declaration. To see how this works in practice, let us build on the previous `Circle` class by adding a color attribute to `Circle`.

```
class ColoredCircle extends Circle {
      private Color color;  // The color of the circle.

      // Constructor method for this class.

      public ColoredCircle() {
         super(); // Call the superclass constructor method
         this.color=Color.black;
      }

      // Set the color for the current circle.

      public void setColor(Color c) {
         color=c;
      }

}
```

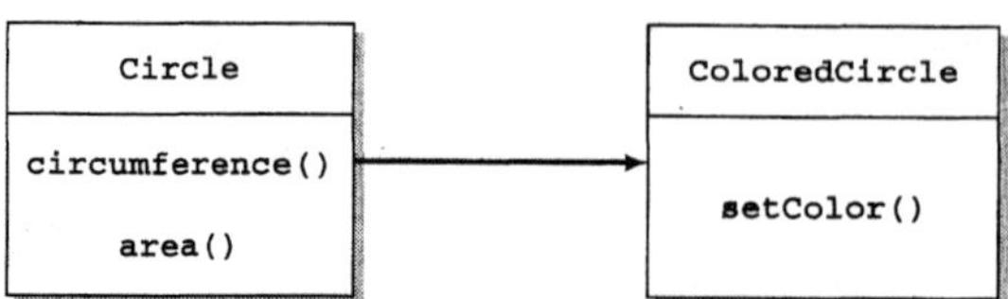

FIGURE 18.3 `Circle` class and `ColoredCircle` subclass.

Now let us see how it works. First we declare the class `ColoredCircle` as extending the class `Circle` by using the keyword `extends`. We then declare a public variable for the class named `color` and of type `Color` to handle the color of the circle. The class hierarchy is shown in Figure 18.3.

Two public methods are defined for this class:

1. `setColor`. This method takes a color as its argument and assigns this value to the color of the circle.
2. `ColoredCircle`. This method has the same name as the class itself; it is a constructor method. We first use the keyword `super`. This keyword refers to the superclass of the current class (just like `this` refers to the current class). Function calls of the type `super.method()` call the implementation of the method in the superclass. By just calling `super()`, we invoke the constructor method of the superclass [the method `Circle()` in that case]. The next line uses the keyword `this` to refer to the public variable `color` of the current class.

Note. One of the main differences between C++ and Java is that Java does not allow multiple inheritance (i.e., a class cannot extend more than one class). Multiple inheritance allows a designer to mix attributes from disparate classes in the class hierarchy. This restriction in Java is justified by the need to keep the language and program design simple. However, Java employs the `interface` construct to simulate multiple inheritance, and an example of its use can be found in Chapter 19.

18.8.8 Abstract Methods and Classes

Suppose we have a bundle of classes that contain similar methods and properties but for which the details of implementation are class dependent. By representing these common methods and properties as placeholder methods and properties in an abstract class, and leaving the details of implementation to the subclasses of the abstract class, often the collective implementation of these classes can be simplified.

Figure 18.4 shows, for example, three classes for different types of geometric shapes. Rather than write separate blocks of Java code for the `Circle`, `Rectangle`, and `Triangle` classes, their collective implementation can be simplified if each class is viewed as a specialized case of the abstract class `Shape` containing the methods `area()` and `perimeter()`. The abstract methods `area()` and `perimeter()` in `Shape` are merely placeholders (i.e., their bodies are empty/unimplemented). All the nonabstract descendants of `Shape` must contain versions of these methods that are implemented. From a programming point of view, the collective

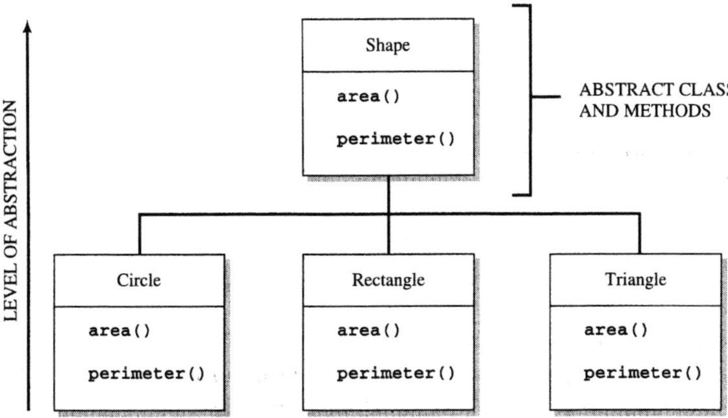

FIGURE 18.4 Hierarchy of geometric shapes.

implementation of these classes is simplified because high-level Java source code can be written in terms of the abstract methods `area()` and `perimeter()` in `Shape`. Then when the program is compiled and executed, the Java run-time system will call the appropriate method for a specific circle, triangle, or rectangle shape.

This is one good example of inheritance of methods at work. In Chapter 19, we encounter abstract classes for window and graphics operations and applets.

18.8.9 Scoping

The scope of a method or variable is the portion of the program code in which the method or variable can be referenced. For example, variables defined in a class are available to all the methods in that class.

Variables defined in a method are local to the method and cannot be accessed out of this method. In the same method, two variables cannot have the same name. Within a method, however, if you declare a variable with the same name as a `public` or `private` variable of the class, then this name will hide the class variable and refer to the method variable instead. To access the class variable, use the keyword `this` to refer explicitly to the current class.

Example. The class definition

```
class Scope {

   public int x;        // A public variable for the class 'Scope'

   public void main() {

         int x;         // We define a new variable 'x' which will
         int i;         // hide the previous defined 'x'.
         int k;
```

```
            x = 3;      // Here 'x' refers to the method variable
                        // The second 'x' declared.

            this.x = 2; // To access the class variable you need
                        // to use the keyword 'this'.


            // Here's a block of code that is WRONG! There is
            // already a variable 'i' in the 'main()' method.

            for (int i=0; i<1; i++) {
                 A a = new A();
                 a.M1();
            }

            // Declare a new variable 'j' in the method 'main()'.

            for (int j=0; j<1; j++) {
                 int j;       // WRONG! Variable 'j' already exists.
            }
      }
}
```

demonstrates a variety of situations where variables with the same name are declared within a class. As indicated by the comments, some of the declarations are legal. Others are not.

18.8.10 Object Destruction

In standard C programming, memory management must be done (and done carefully) by the programmer. Calls to functions like `malloc()` reserve some memory for future uses. A programmer needs to remember to free this memory when it is no longer needed by the program.

In Java, you never do any explicit memory reservation with `malloc()` because creating a new object with the `new` keyword takes care of the details of memory allocation for you. Also, once a block of memory is no longer needed by a program, the Java run-time system will automatically take care of its release to the operating system.

The Garbage Collector

Java uses a technique called *garbage collection* to automatically detect objects that are no longer being used and to free them. An object is no longer in use when there are no more references to it. Remember that even though Java programmers do not use pointers, the Java system does. In a nutshell, the garbage collector uses the scope of variables and classes to determine if an object is still in use and can be released to the system. The garbage collector runs as a low-priority process and does most of its work when nothing else is going on (i.e., idle time while waiting for user input).

Example. In the previous example, the scope of `A` is restricted to the body of the `for` loop. When a program has finished executing the `for` loop, variable `A` will be made available for garbage collection because it is no longer referenced.

18.9 CLASS LIBRARIES AND METHODS

Generally speaking, there are two clear and distinct ways of implementing a feature in a programming language. One option is to build the feature into the language itself. The `while` looping construct is a feature of the Java language, for example. The second and better way of implementing a new feature is to support it through an application library. This strategy of development expands the range of applications for which the programming language can be easily used, while keeping it small and easy to learn. This approach to software development has been wildly successful for C and C++, and so Java simply follows in their footsteps.

All the Java development environments contain a well-defined set of libraries that constitutes the core of the Java language. These classes are documented through their Application Program Interface (API), usually consisting of a list of public methods and public variables for that class. Some third-party vendors are also developing their own libraries. Many of these libraries are freely available to the public.

18.9.1 Package and Import Statements

Every class is part of a *package,* and every package is identified by its name. Packages provide a high-level layer of access protection and name-space management for collections of Java classes, interfaces, exceptions, and errors. Packages reduce the likelihood of name clashes because class and interface names are evaluated with respect to the package to which they belong. A package may include other packages (i.e., subpackages).

An *interface* is somewhat akin to a stripped-down class. It specifies a set of methods that an instance of a class may handle but omits inheritance relations and method implementations. Examples of interface implementations are found in Section 19.7, event handling in the Abstract Windowing Toolkit.

Core Packages in Java 1.1

Version 1.1 of the JDK contains 538 classes within 24 core packages. Figure 18.5 shows a small part of the Java Class Library Hierarchy that we focus on in this tutorial.

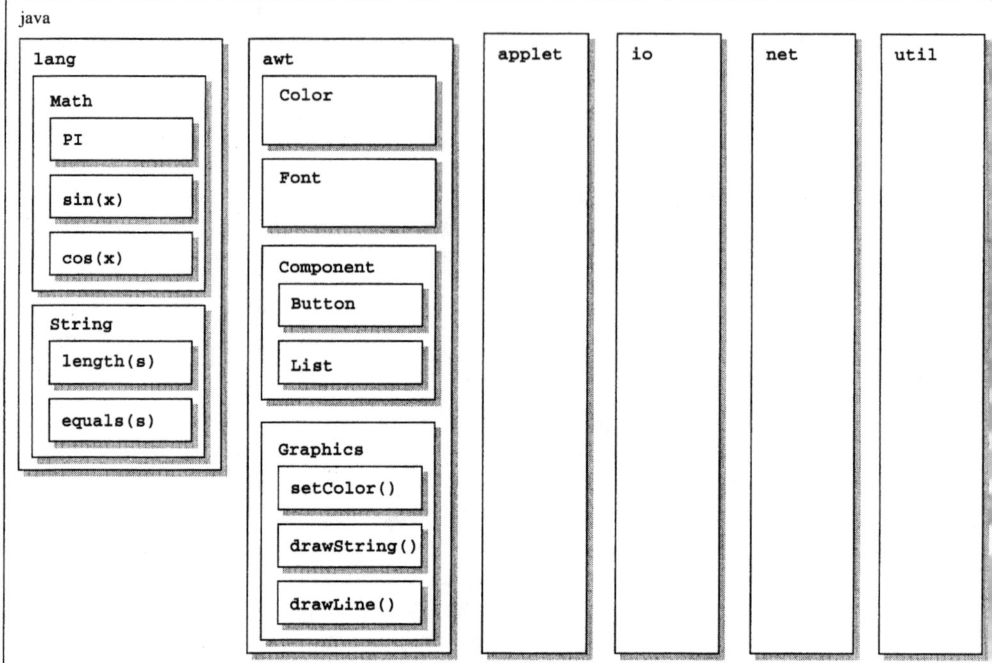

FIGURE 18.5 Class Library Hierarchy in Java 1.1.

The entire API is implemented as one large package called `java`, which contain a number of subpackages, the most prominent of them being

1. `java.lang`. The Java Language Package contains the basic declarations o objects and classes needed by most Java programs, including threads, exceptions, and a variety of other fundamental types. This package is automaticall imported by the compiler into all Java programs.
2. `java.io`. The Java Input/Output Package contains classes for program input output (I/O) with files and streams. Roughly speaking, this package is th equivalent of the standard I/O library available on most UNIX platforms.
3. `java.net`. The Java Networking Package contains classes that enable communication via HTTP, FTP, Telnet, sockets, and other networking protocols.
4. `java.util`. The Java Utilities Package contains classes for date and tim manipulations, storage and processing of large quantities of information, manipulation of strings, and generation of random numbers.
5. `java.applet`. The Java Applet Package contains classes for the creation an control of small Java application programs known as applets (for more information, see Chapter 19).
6. `java.awt`. The Java Abstract Window Toolkit contains classes for the creatio of graphical user interface components such as buttons, canvases, fonts, an

colors. It contains classes for the handling of window events. This library is used by developers to build graphical user interfaces that execute across X Windows, Microsoft Windows, and Mac desktops (for more information, see Chapter 19).

7. `java.awt.event`. The Java Abstract Window Toolkit Event-Handling Package contains classes and interfaces for the Java 1.1 event-handling model. Facilities are provided for the representation and listening of events. We come back to this topic in Chapter 19.

Subpackage names are assembled from individual names separated by periods. Although this naming scheme implies a hierarchy of packages, subpackages are really completely different packages. A class in a subpackage has no more access to a class in the parent package (or vice versa) than it would to a class in a completely different package.

Classes that belong to a package may be referenced by their fully qualified name. For example,

```
java.awt.Font
```

tells the Java compiler that the class `Font` belongs to the `java.awt` package. Because the fully qualified name is rather cumbersome, we obviously require a mechanism to refer to `java.awt.Font` as simply `Font`.

18.9.2 Import Statements

An *import statement* makes Java classes available to a program under an abbreviated name. Import statements come in two forms:

```
import package.class;
import package.*;
```

The first form allows a class to be referred to by its class name alone. The asterisk `(*)` in the second form references all the classes in the named package. Since importing all the classes associated with a package neither increases the compile time nor the code size, there is little reason not to do it. For example, after the statement

```
import java.awt.*;
```

has been encountered, `java.awt.Font` can simply be referred to as `Font`. A Java program may contain any number of `import` statements. The `java.lang` package is so fundamental to Java programming that it is automatically imported into every Java program.

At this point, it is important to note that although package names are hierarchical, their import declarations are not. To import classes from the packages `java.awt.event` and `java.awt.image`, for example, we must explicitly write

```
import java.awt.*;
import java.awt.event.*;
import java.awt.image.*;
```

A Java program can only import multiple packages if their class names are unique

No Preprocessor

In the first phase of the compilation of a C program, the source code is parsed by a preprocessor. The preprocessor is responsible for transforming all `#include`, `#define`, and `#ifdef` directives into equivalent C expressions/statements. Java does not have this kind of preprocessor because, in fact, you do not really need one.

The `#include` directive is not needed because Java uses the keyword `import` to specify where to look for additional references to classes. Note that the import statement does not include the file, it just tells the compiler where to look for class references. Moreover, unlike C and C++, Java does not distinguish between declaring a function and defining the function. Java does not use the C-style header files where you include the declaration of the function at the top of a file. Each Java class file acts as both the interface declaration and the implementation of the object.

The `#define` directive is used in C to define global constants. In Java, every constant must be declared as `public final` within a class. The constant π is defined as `java.lang.Math.PI`.

Given that Java is platform independent, there is no real need for the `#ifdef` and/or `#if` directives, which are used for conditional compilation of programs (usually based on platform dependencies).

18.9.3 Class Libraries in Development

Many other class libraries are available and/or are currently under development:

1. *JDBC:* A library developed by SunMicrosystems that you can use to create applications that communicate with databases. This library has classes to handle different database formats such as Oracle and SQL. Since the release of Java 1.1, the JDBC library is part of the standard distribution. More information on JDBC can be found at the JavaSoft web server:

   `http://java.sun.com/products/jdbc`

2. *LiquidReality:* A library developed by DimensionX for three-dimensional graphics programming. DimensionX has been acquired by Microsoft recently.

LiquidReality supports the most recent version of VRML (2.0). For further information on LiquidReality, point your browser to the Microsoft web server:

```
http://www.microsoft.com/dimensionx/lr
```

3. *IFC:* This is the Internet Foundation Classes developed by Netscape. The library includes utility classes such as drag and drop. Have a look at Netscape IFC at

```
http://developer.netscape.com/library/ifc/index.html
```

4. *Sun Products and API:* Javasoft, the division of Sun specializing in development and promotion of Java, offers a variety of APIs, from JavaCard (for using Java on smart cards) to JavaTel (which allows you to control telephony over Java). Some of these libraries are still at the proposal stage. For a closer look at the constantly increasing number of products, go to

```
http://java.sun.com/products/index.html
```

18.9.4 Using Class Methods

A *class method* is a method that does not require an object to be invoked. Class methods are called in the same manner as instance methods except that the name of the class is substituted for the instance name. Two of the most commonly used class methods are `System` and `Math` and, in this section, we briefly describe them.

System Class Methods

The `System` class is part of the `java.lang` package. Its methods provide low-level platform-independent functionality to the Java run-time system, including standard I/O, getting the current date and time, copying arrays, and so forth.

We have already encountered methods from the `System` class in a number of places. For example, in Program 18.1, the line

```
System.out.println("Peace on Earth!");
```

uses the `System` class's `println()` method to display the `"Peace on Earth!"` string argument followed by a new line.

`System.out` by itself is a class variable that references the standard output stream. `System.in` and `System.err` are class variables that reference the standard input stream and the standard error stream, respectively.

Math Class Methods

In this tutorial, we make extensive use of the methods for computing mathematical functions and obtaining mathematical constants.

TABLE 18.6 Mathematical Constants and Methods in Java

Function	*Meaning*	*Example*
Mathematical Constants		
`Math.PI`	Get pi = 3.1415926....	`Math.PI`
`Math.E`	Get e = 2.171...	`Math.E`
Trigonometric and Mathematical Methods		
`Math.sin (x)`	Compute the sine of `x` (in radians).	`Math.sin(pi) = 0.0`
`Math.cos (x)`	Compute the cosine of `x` (in radians).	`Math.cos(pi) = 1.0`
`Math.tan (x)`	Compute the tangent of `x` (in radians).	`Math.tan(pi/4) = 1.0`
`Math.exp (x)`	Compute `e^x` where `e` is the base for natural logarithms.	`Math.exp(1.0) = 2.7183`
`Math.log (x)`	Compute the natural logarithm of `x` to the base `e`.	`Math.log(2.7183) = 1.0`
`Math.abs(x)`	Return absolute value of `x`.	`Math.abs( -3.5 ) = 3.0`
`Math.pow(x,y)`	Return `x` raised to the power of `y`.	`Math.pow( 2, 3 ) = 8.0`
`Math.random()`	Return a random number uniformly distributed between 0 and 1.	`Math.random() = 0.4315.`
`Math.round(x)`	Round `x` to the nearest integer.	`Math.round( 4.9) = 5`
`Math.sqrt(x)`	Compute square root of `x`.	`Math.sqrt(3) = 1.7320..`

Table 18.6 contains an abbreviated summary of commonly used mathematical methods and constants from the class `java.lang.Math`. This class is the equivalent of the C `<math.h>` functions. The constants and mathematical functions in this class have a compound name that begins with the prefix `Math`. To compute `3.0` raised to the power of `4.5`, for example, we would write

```
fValue = Math.pow ( 3.0, 4.5 );
```

Most of the functions in Table 18.6 require an argument to be of type `double`.

String Class Methods

Java represents strings of characters with the built-in type `String`. Unlike the eight basic data types shown in Table 18.3, `String` is a class from which objects can be instantiated and methods can be invoked (see Table 18.7).

TABLE 18.7 String Methods in Java

Method	*Meaning*
`s1.length ()`	Compute the number of characters in string `s1`.
`s1.compareTo(s2)`	This method makes a lexicographic comparison of strings `s1` and `s2`. The returned value will be zero if the strings are equal; −1 when `s1` is less than `s2`, and 1 otherwise.
`s1.equals(s2)`	This boolean method returns true if the sequence of characters in `s1` is exactly the same as `s2`.
`s1.toUpperCase()`	This string valued function returns a string with all the lowercase characters in `s1` converted to uppercase.

Strings do not work well with the basic family of relational operators. Instead, you should use the `String` methods to compute operations on string objects. For example, the script

```
String s1 = new String("Here is a short string");
String s2 = new String("This string is a little bit longer");

if( true == s1.equals(s2) ) {
    System.out.println("Strings s1 and s2 are the same!");
} else {
    System.out.println("Strings s1 and s2 are different!");
}
```

instantiates two strings `s1` and `s2`, and then makes a test to see if the string's contents are identical. Instead of testing equality with the relational expression `s1 == s2`, we write `true == s1.equals(s2)`. The output is

```
Strings s1 and s2 are different!
```

18.10 ARRAYS

In Java, an array is simply a sequence of numbered items of the same type. Permissible types include the primitive data types and instances of a class. In either case, individual items in the array are referenced by their position number in the array.

Java arrays are also objects; you create an array using the `new` keyword. Like the objects we created in the previous sections, variables do not hold an array. They can only refer to an array. For example, the left-hand side of the statement

```
float[] faBuffer = new float [5];
```

creates a variable `faBuffer` of type `float []` (you can also write `float faBuffer []`). Initially the value of `faBuffer` is null. The right-hand side of the statement creates a new array of five floats and assigns the result to `faBuffer`. The layout of memory in the array object is

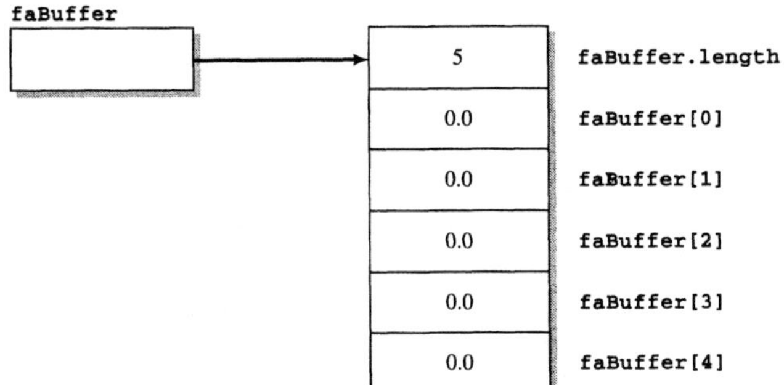

The first and last elements in the array are `faBuffer[0]` and `faBuffer[4]`, and like newly instantiated primitive data types, the array elements take a default value of 0.0. You can use the syntax `.length` to query the size of an array:

```
int iBufferSize = faBuffer.length;
```

Multidimensional arrays are considered as arrays of arrays and are created by putting as many pairs of `[]` as of dimensions in your array:

```
double daaMat[][] = new double[4][4]; // This is a 4x4 matrix
```

Multidimensional arrays are considered as arrays of arrays, so you can query the different dimensions with the following syntax:

```
array.length;           // Length of the first dimension.
array[0].length;        // Length of the second dimension.
array[0][0].length;     // Length of the third dimension.
.... etc ...
```

For example, the number of rows and columns in `daaMat` can be computed with

```
int iNoRows    = daaMat.length;
int iNoColumns = daaMat[0].length;
```

Arrays are like primitive data types in the sense that their elements can be used just like any other primitive data type. For example, the contents of `daaMat` can be printed by systematically looping over the rows and columns.

```
for (int y = 0; y < daaMat.length; y++ ) {
    for (int x = 0; x < daaMat[y].length; x++ ) {
        System.out.print( daaMat[x][y] + " ");
    }
    System.out.print("\n");
}
```

The expression `daaMat.length` corresponds to the number of matrix rows, and `daaMat[y].length` is the number of columns in matrix row $y + 1$.

Programming Tip. Object-oriented programs should not attempt to pass complete arrays from one class to another. Rather, the classes should be designed so that arrays are part of the class data and the methods operate on that data.

18.11 PROGRAM 18.3: COMPUTE ROOTS OF QUADRATIC EQUATION

18.11.1 Problem Statement

It is well known that the roots of a quadratic equation are given by solutions to

$$p(x) = ax^2 + bx + c = 0 \tag{18.1}$$

A number of solution cases exist. For example, when both $a = 0$ and $b = 0$, we consider the equation to be `extremely degenerate` and leave it at that. When $a = 0$ and $b \neq 0$, we consider the case `degenerate`; in this situation, the equations reduce to $p(x) = bx + c = 0$, which has one root. Otherwise, we have

$$\text{Roots} = \left[\frac{-b \pm \sqrt{b^2 - 4ac}}{2a} \right] \tag{18.2}$$

The term $b^2 - 4ac$ is known as the discriminant of the quadratic equation.

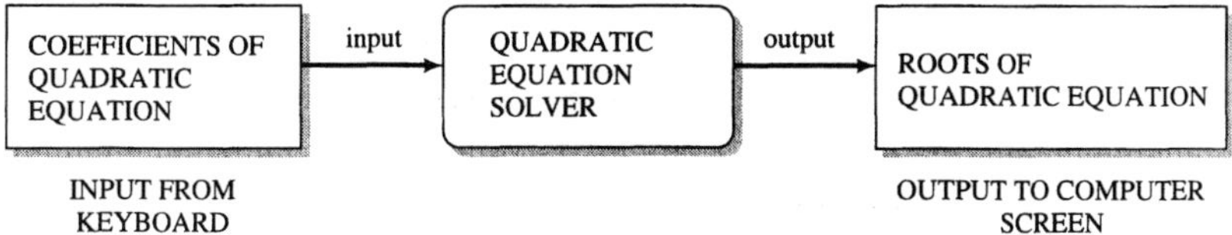

FIGURE 18.6 Quadratic equation solution procedure.

Figure 18.6 is a high-level schematic of the problem-solving procedure that will be followed. The program will begin its execution by prompting a user for the equation coefficients a, b, and c. After the coefficients have been specified at the keyboard and read by the computer program, the roots of the quadratic equation will be computed and printed to the computer screen along with an appropriate message for the type of solution. Appropriate messages are `Extremely degenerate`, `Degenerate`, `Two real roots`, and `Two complex roots`. For example, if 1, 2, and 3 are real for a, b, and c, the computer program will print

$$\text{Two complex roots} \quad \text{Root 1} = -1.0000 + 1.414214\,i \tag{18.3}$$

$$\text{Root 2} = -1.0000 - 1.414214\,i \tag{18.4}$$

As a first cut, the Java code will be implemented in the most straightforward fashion possible, thereby highlighting similarities with the C implementation in Chapter 7 and the MATLAB, implementation in Chapter 13. Refinement of the program object design will be left as an exercise (see Problem 18.6).

18.11.2 Program Modules and Class Hierarchy

Suppose that after a few iterations of development, the pseudocode for our Java program looks like

```
define variables for a, b, c, discriminant

println "quadratic equation solving program"
println "Enter the coefficients a, b, and c"
```

```
read coefficient 'a' from the keyboard
read coefficient 'b' from the keyboard
read coefficient 'c' from the keyboard

if( a equal to zero )
    compute roots to determinate equations
    exit

discriminant = b^2 - 4ac
if (discriminant >= 0.0)    // The roots are real.
   root1 = -b/2a - sqrt( discriminant )/2a
   root2 = -b/2a + sqrt( discriminant )/2a
   println "The first  root is " root1
   println "The second root is " root2
else
                            // The roots are complex.
   re = -b/2a
   im = sqrt( -discriminant )/2a
   println "The first  complex root is", re, im
   println "The second complex root is", re, -im
```

A key issue in the design of almost every Java program is the problem of finding a good balance in the use of user-defined classes and methods, and library classes and methods. The advantage of user-defined methods is that they enable the development of customized problem-solving procedures. However, writing and testing user-defined code can be a very time-consuming process. The benefits of class libraries are that they enable reuse of code that has already been written and thoroughly tested. The judicious use of class libraries can result in significant reductions in the time and effort needed to write and test Java programs.

Obtaining a good balance in the use of user-defined code and library functions requires experience and, to some extent, is an art. This means that novice Java programmers must place a priority on becoming familiar with the availability and purposes of library methods, particularly those in the JDK.

With these points in mind, Table 18.8 shows the mapping of "Tasks to Java

TABLE 18.8 Mapping Tasks to Methods and Class Libraries

Task	* *User-Defined* * *Methods*	*Java Class Libraries*
Solve quadratic equation.	* `main()`	
Compute discriminant.	* `fdiscriminant()`	
Read coefficients.	* `keyboardInput()`	
	*	
Standard output to screen	*	`System.out.println()`
Standard input from keyboard	*	`System.in.readLine()`
Square root computation	*	`Math.sqrt()`

Methods and Java Class Libraries" that are implemented in Program 18.3. The heart of our quadratic equation solution procedure will be contained in three user-defined methods: `main()`, `fdiscriminant()`, and `keyboardInput()`. The overall program implementation will be kept as simple as possible by putting all three of these methods in the user-defined class `Quadratic`.

We employ methods from the `System` class library, `System.out.println()` and `System.in.readLine()`, to handle formatted output and input, respectively. Evaluation of Equation 18.2 requires a square root calculation, and this will be handled by the method `Math.sqrt()` located in the `Math` class library.

18.11.3 Program Source Code

Here is the program source code.

PROGRAM 18.3: Compute Roots of Quadratic Equation

```
/*
 * ======================================================================
 * This Java Program prompts a user for coefficients in a quadratic equation,
 * and computes and prints the roots of the equation.
 *
 * Written By : Nathan Blattau and Mark Austin                   July, 1997
 * =======================================================================
 */

import java.lang.Math;
import java.util.*;
import java.io.*;

class Quadratic {

    public static void main( String args[] ) {

    float fA,fB,fC;
    float fRoot1, fRoot2;
    float fDiscriminant;
    String sLine;

        // Print welcome message.

        System.out.println("Welcome to The Quadratic Equation Solver");
        System.out.println("----------------------------------------");
```

```
// Prompt user for coefficients in quadratic equation...

System.out.println("Please enter coefficients for equation");
System.out.println("a.x^2 + b.x + c");

System.out.println("Coefficient a : " );
sLine = keyboardInput();
fA    = Float.valueOf(sLine).floatValue();

System.out.println("Coefficient b : ");
sLine = keyboardInput();
fB    = Float.valueOf(sLine).floatValue();

System.out.println("Coefficient c : ");
sLine = keyboardInput();
fC    = Float.valueOf(sLine).floatValue();

// Print details of quadratic equation to screen.

System.out.println("The equation you have entered is : ");
System.out.println(+fA+".x^2 + "+fB+".x + "+fC);

// Check for Degenerate roots (i.e., fA = fB = zero).

if ( fA==0 && fB==0 ) {
    System.out.println("Cannot solve " + fC +" = 0.0");
    return;
}

if ( fA==0 && fB !=0 ) {
    fRoot1 = -fC/fB;
    System.out.println("Degenerate root : Root = "+ fRoot1);
    return;
}

// Compute discriminant of quadratic equation.

fDiscriminant = fdiscriminant(fA,fB,fC);

// Case for two real roots.

if ( fDiscriminant >= 0.0 ) {

    fRoot1 = (float)(-fB/2.0/fA-(float)Math.sqrt(fDiscriminant)/
                     2.0/fA);
    fRoot2 = (float)(-fB/2.0/fA+(float)Math.sqrt(fDiscriminant)/
                     2.0/fA);
```

```
            System.out.println("Two real roots : Root1 : " + fRoot1);
            System.out.println("                         Root2 : " + fRoot2);
            return;
        }

        // Two complex roots

        fRoot1 = (float) (-fB/2.0/fA);
        fRoot2 = (float) (Math.sqrt(-fDiscriminant)/2.0/fA);

        System.out.println("Two complex roots'');
        System.out.println("Root1 : " + fRoot1 + "+" + fRoot2 + "i");
        System.out.println("Root2 : " + fRoot1 + "-" + fRoot2 + "i");

}

/*
 * ==========================================================
 * Method fdiscriminant() : compute discriminant of quadratic
 *
 * Input  : fA, fB, and fC -- coefficients in quadratic equation
 * Output : float fReturn -- discriminant of quadratic equation
 * ==========================================================
 */

static float fdiscriminant(float fA, float fB, float fC) {
float fReturn;

   fReturn= (float)(fB*fB-4.0*fA*fC);
   return fReturn;
}

/*
 * ==========================================================
 * Method keyboardInput() : Get line of input from keyboard
 *
 * Input : None.
 * Output : String sLine -- character string of keyboard input
 * ==========================================================
 */

static String keyboardInput() {
String sLine;
```

```
        DataInputStream in = new DataInputStream(System.in);
        try{
            sLine = in.readLine();
            return sLine;
         }
         catch (Exception e){
             return "error";
         }
    }
}
```

Compared to the Java programs presented at the beginning of this chapter, Program 18.3 is a lot more representative of simple Java programs that you are likely to write. It is our first program containing floating point variables, arithmetic expressions, assignment statements, and branching constructs for flow of program control. It also employs methods in the Java Library for I/O and a method in the math library for a square root calculation.

18.11.4 Compiling and Running the Program

Program 18.3 is stored in a file called `Quadratic.java` because Java requires a file name prefix corresponding to the class it contains. The command line

```
prompt >> javac Quadratic.java
```

asks the Java compiler `javac` to compile the program `Quadratic.java` into a bytecode file called `Quadratic.class`. The list of program files before and after compilation is

Files before Compilation	*Files after Compilation*
Quadratic.java	Quadratic.java Quadratic.class

The command

```
prompt >> java Quadratic
```

asks the Java interpreter (actually it is the Java Virtual Machine) to run the `Quadratic` program. The script

```
prompt >> java Quadratic
Welcome to The Quadratic Equation Solver
----------------------------------------
Please enter coefficients for equation
a.x^2 + b.x + c
```

```
Coefficient a :
1.0
Coefficient b :
2.0
Coefficient c :
1.0
The equation you have entered is :
1.x^2 + 2.x + 1
Two real roots : Root1 : -1
                 Root2 : -1
prompt >>
```

shows the program I/O for a = 1.0, b = 2.0, and c = 1.0. When the exercise is repeated for $a = 1.0$, $b = 1.0$, and $c = 1.0$, the computed roots are

```
prompt >>

..... details of program input/output removed .....

Two complex roots
Root1 : -0.5+0.866025i
Root2 : -0.5-0.866025i
prompt >>
```

These two examples are the same as those in the C tutorial and, of course, the programs give the same answer.

18.11.5 Program Architecture

Figure 18.7 is an abbreviated class hierarchy diagram for Program 18.3. Each class in this program inherits directly from the class `Object`. The `Object` class is special in a number of ways. First, it is the only Java class that does not have a superclass. All variables can be assigned to a variable of type `Object`, and all methods can invoke the methods of `Object`.

Program 18.3 employs classes and methods from three packages. The user-defined code consists of three methods contained within the class `Quadratic`. The user-defined methods call the `sqrt()` method located in the `Math` class (i.e., the `java.lang` package). Program I/O is handled by classes and methods in the `java.io` package, as shown on the right-hand side of Figure 18.7.

18.11.6 Import Statements

Java programs derive much of their functionality from classes located in the Java class libraries. The import statements

```
import java.lang.Math;
import java.util.*;
import java.io.*;
```

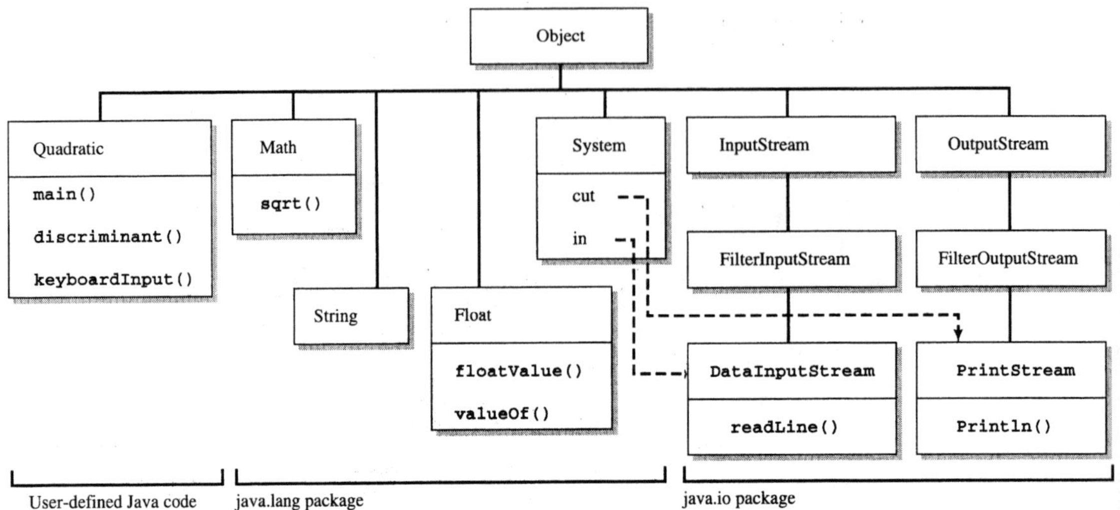

FIGURE 18.7 Class hierarchy for Program 18.3.

tell Java that it may be required to execute code available from the listed class libraries. The `java.lang.Math` class contains an assortment of mathematical functions and mathematical constants. The `java.util` package contains a host of utility packages. A hierarchy of classes for program I/O is defined in `java.io`. The asterisk is a "wild card" character that indicates multiple classes are to be imported.

18.11.7 String Objects

Java supports instances of objects corresponding to user-defined classes and Java library classes. For example, the declaration

```
String sLine;
```

makes `sLine` an instance of `String`, a Java class for storing and manipulating sequences of characters, otherwise known as character strings.

18.11.8 Scope of Variables

When a variable is declared inside a method, its scope is restricted to the body of the method itself. Hence, in Program 18.3 variables `fA`, `fB`, `fC`, and `sLine` will only be known to the method `main` within the class `Quadratic`. Communication to other methods in the class is handled via passing of parameters as part of the method call.

18.11.9 Handling Input from the Keyboard

Within the method `main()`, the line

```
sLine = keyboardInput();
```

calls the method keyboardInput to read a stream of characters supplied as keyboard input and assigns the result to sLine. The method definition for keyboardInput is

```
static String keyboardInput() {  <== Definition and opening
                                      brace for method
                                      "keyboardInput"

}                                <== Closing brace for
                                      method "keyboardInput"
```

The keyword static indicates that keyboardInput will be a class method, and the keyword String indicates that keyboardInput will return an instance of an object of type String (i.e., a character string). You should notice that Java does not require the details of a method be given before it is actually called.

8.11.10 Converting Strings to Numbers

The pair of statements

```
sLine = keyboardInput();
fA    = Float.valueOf(sLine).floatValue();
```

converts the stream of characters contained in sLine to a floating point number and assigns the result to fA. Float is a class within the java.lang package that provides a family of methods for manipulating information associated with the float primitive data type. The details of the string to instance of Float conversion are handled by the method valueOf(). The method floatValue() converts an instance of Float to a primitive float data type. Similar families of methods exist for the int and double primitive data types.

Notice that this program only checks to see that input has been supplied. It does not actually check that a floating point number has been typed. If you supply garbage as input, the class libraries for string to floating point number conversion will print some sort of error message and terminate the program execution.

8.11.11 Arithmetic Expressions

In the case of double real roots, the individual roots are computed with the arithmetic expression

```
fRoot1 = (float)(-fB/2.0/fA-(float)Math.sqrt(fDiscriminant) /
                  2.0/fA);
fRoot2 = (float)(-fB/2.0/fA+(float)Math.sqrt(fDiscriminant) /
                  2.0/fA);
```

The expression (float) Math.sqrt casts the result of the square root calculation to a constant of type float. Otherwise, the remainder of this statement is a standard arithmetic expression with assignment of the results to fRoot1 and fRoot2.

18.11.12 Input and Output Streams

Program I/O is handled by the classes `DataInputStream` and `PrintDataStrea` To see how this works, we need to look at the definition of the `System` class:

```
public final class System extends Object {

        // Constants
        public static final InputStream  in;
        public static final PrintStream out;

        // Class methods ....

        ..... details of class definition removed ...
}
```

Here we see that `in` is a public class variable of type `InputStream` and `out` is public class variable of type `OutputStream`. The modifier `final` prevents t value of `in` and `out` from being changed. Hence, when we write

```
System.out.println( .... )
```

we are invoking the `println()` method located in the `java.io` package. Th relationship between these constants and methods is indicated by the dashed lir in Figure 18.7.

18.11.13 Overloading the + Operator

Before the roots of the quadratic equation are printed, the numerical value of th root is converted to a character string and concatenated (or joined) to a strir explaining the details of the result. Java facilitates this process with the + operato

```
System.out.println("Two complex roots");
System.out.println("Root1 : " + fRoot1 + "+" + fRoot2 + "i");
System.out.println("Root2 : " + fRoot1 + "-" + fRoot2 + "i");
```

where one or more of the operands is a character string. Its purpose takes on completely new meaning. The remaining operands—in this case, the floating poi numbers represented by `fRoot1` and `fRoot2`—are converted to a string, and th strings are concatenated together.

18.12 PROGRAM 18.4: POINT AND LINE SEGMENT OPERATIONS

18.12.1 Problem Statement

Figure 18.8 shows a line segment in a (xy) coordinate frame. The segment is define as a straight line joining two endpoints at coordinates (x_1, y_1) and (x_2, y_2).

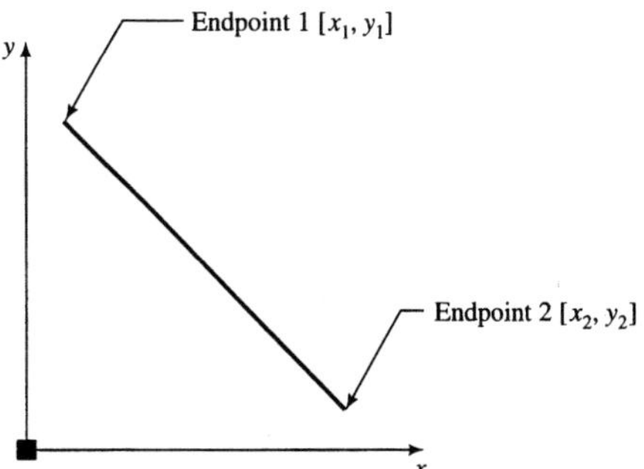

FIGURE 18.8 Line segment in (x-y) coordinate frame.

The following program is developed in two stages. First, we write a class `Point` for the definition and positioning of (x, y) coordinates. Then with the `Point` class in place, we write a class for defining and computing operations on line segments. Test programs are written to exercise the capabilities of both classes.

18.12.2 Program Modules and Class Hierarchy

The point and line segment operations are

Point	*Line Segment*
Allocate a new point.	Allocate a new line segment.
Set (x, y) coordinates.	Set coordinates of line segment endpoints.
Get x coordinate.	Get endpoint 1.
Get y coordinate.	Get endpoint 2.
Print coordinates.	Print endpoints of line segment.
	Compute and print equation of line segment (not implemented in program).
	Compute intersection of two line segments (not implemented in program).
Exercise methods in `Point` class.	Exercise methods in `LineSegment` class.

The `Point` class should contain methods for constructing instances of a `point`, setting the (x, y) coordinate values, retrieving the x and y coordinates, and printing the coordinates as a string. Each of these methods can be exercised by a test program included as part of the `Point` class.

Similarly, the `LineSegment` class should contain methods for constructing instances of a line `segment`, setting the coordinate values of the endpoints, retrieving endpoints 1 and 2, and printing the details of the line segment. An advanced implementation (these details are not included in the program) might also compute and print the equation of the line segment, and compute the intersection of two line segments (see, for example, Problem 18.8). Each of these methods can be exercised by a test program included as part of the `LineSegment` class.

18.12.3 Program Source Code

The source code for Program 18.4 is partitioned into two parts. The first half contains the user-written code for the `Point` class. The second part of the source code contains details of the `LineSegment` class.

Program 18.4: POINT AND LINE SEGMENT APPLICATIONS

```
/*
 * ====================================================================
 * Definition of class Point : A point is represented by its
 *                             (x,y) coordinates.
 *
 * Written By : Mark Austin                                October 1997
 * ====================================================================
 */

public class Point {
   protected double dX, dY; // (x,y) coordinates of the Point

   // Constructor method : just create instance of class.

   public Point() { }

   // Create instance of class and set (x,y) coordinates.

   public Point( double dX, double dY ) {
      setPoint( dX, dY );
   }

   // Set x and y coordinates of Point.

   public void setPoint( double dX, double dY ) {
      this.dX = dX;
      this.dY = dY;
   }

   // Get x and y coordinates.

   public double getX() { return dX; }
   public double getY() { return dY; }

   // Convert the point into a String representation.

   public String toString()
      { return "[" + dX + ", " + dY + "]"; }
```

```
   // Exercise methods in point class.

   public static void main( String args[] ) {
   double dX, dY;

      System.out.println("Point test program");
      System.out.println("================================");

      // Create two new points.

      Point point1 = new Point();
      point1.setPoint( 1.0, 1.0 );
      Point point2 = new Point( 1.5, 4.5 );

      // Print (x,y) coordinates of points.

      System.out.println("Point 1 : " + point1.toString() );
      System.out.println("Point 2 : " + point2.toString() );

      // Get x and y coordinates.

      dX = point1.getX(); dY = point1.getY();
      System.out.println("Point 1 : X coordinate = " + dX );
      System.out.println("          Y coordinate = " + dY );
      dX = point2.getX(); dY = point2.getY();
      System.out.println("Point 2 : X coordinate = " + dX );
      System.out.println("          Y coordinate = " + dY );

      System.out.println("================================");
      System.out.println("End of Point test program");
   }
}
```

```
/*
 * ==================================================================
 * Definition of class LineSegment:
 *
 * A line segment is defined by the (x,y) coordinates of
 * its two end points.
 *
 * Written By : Mark Austin                            October 1997
 * ==================================================================
 */

public class LineSegment {
   protected Point p1, p2; // points defining the LineSegment

   // Constructor method : just create instance of class.

   public LineSegment() { }
```

```
    // Create instance of class and set (x,y) coordinates.

    public LineSegment( double dX1, double dY1,
                        double dX2, double dY2 ) {

       setLineSegment( dX1, dY1, dX2, dY2 );
    }

    // Set x and y coordinates of LineSegment.

    public void setLineSegment( double dX1, double dY1,
                                double dX2, double dY2 ) {
       p1 = new Point( dX1, dY1 );
       p2 = new Point( dX2, dY2 );
    }

    // Get end points 1 and 2.

    public Point getPoint1() { return p1; }
    public Point getPoint2() { return p2; }

    // Print details of line segment.

    public void printSegment() {

       System.out.println("Line Segment");
       System.out.println("Point 1 : (x,y) = " + p1.toString() );
       System.out.println("Point 2 : (x,y) = " + p2.toString() );
    }

    // Compute length of line segment.

    public double segmentLength() {
       double dLength;
    dLength = (p1.getX() - p2.getX())*(p1.getX() - p2.getX()) +
              (p1.getY() - p2.getY())*(p1.getY() - p2.getY());

    return ((double) Math.sqrt(dLength));
 }

 // Exercise methods in line segment class.

 public static void main( String args[] ) {
 double dX, dY;

    System.out.println("LineSegment test program");
    System.out.println("===============================");
```

```
    // Create two new line segments.

    LineSegment s1 = new LineSegment();
    s1.setLineSegment( 1.0, 1.0, 4.0, 5.0 );
    LineSegment s2 = new LineSegment( 1.5, 1.5, 1.5, 4.5 );

    // Print details of line segments.

    s1.printSegment();
    s2.printSegment();

    // Compute length of line segments.

    System.out.println("Segment1 has length : " + s1.segmentLength());
    System.out.println("Segment2 has length : " + s2.segmentLength());

    // End of exercise.

    System.out.println("==============================");
    System.out.println("End of LineSegment test program");
  }
}
```

18.12.4 Compiling and Running the Program

Program 18.4 contains the source code for two classes: `Point.java` and `LineSegment.java`. The `Point` class is compiled by typing

```
>> javac Point.java
```

and the `LineSegment` class is compiled by typing

```
>> javac LineSegment.java
```

The Java compiler is pretty smart and, when the `LineSegment` class is being compiled, will determine the dependency of the `LineSegment` and `Point` classes and automatically compile `Point.java` into a bytecode file if it does not already exist. The list of program files before and after compilation is

Files before Compilation	*Files after Compilation*	
Point.java	Point.java	Point.class
LineSegment.java	LineSegment.java	LineSegment.class

The Point and LineSegment classes both have test programs located inside their main() methods. Typing

```
>> java Point
```

generates the output

```
Point test program
=================================
Point 1 : [1.0, 1]
Point 2 : [1.5, 4.5]
Point 1 : X coordinate = 1.0
          Y coordinate = 1.0
Point 2 : X coordinate = 1.5
          Y coordinate = 4.5
=================================
End of Point test program
```

The Point class test program creates and initializes two new points, the first using the default constructor and the setPoint() method, and the second with the Point() constructor containing two arguments. The point coordinates are then printed by calling the toString() method to create a character string. Finally, the getX() and getY() methods are used to retrieve and print the individual x and y point coordinates.

Similarly, the LineSegment test program generates

```
LineSegment test program
=================================
Line Segment
Point 1 : (x,y) = [1.0, 1]
Point 2 : (x,y) = [4, 5.0]
Line Segment
Point 1 : (x,y) = [1.5, 1.5]
Point 2 : (x,y) = [1.5, 4.5]
Segment1 has length : 5.0
Segment2 has length : 3.0
=================================
End of LineSegment test program
```

The line segment test program begins its execution by creating two new line segments—for simplicity of implementation, the endpoint coordinates are specified in the program source code. After the details of each line segment have been printed the length of each line segment is computed and printed.

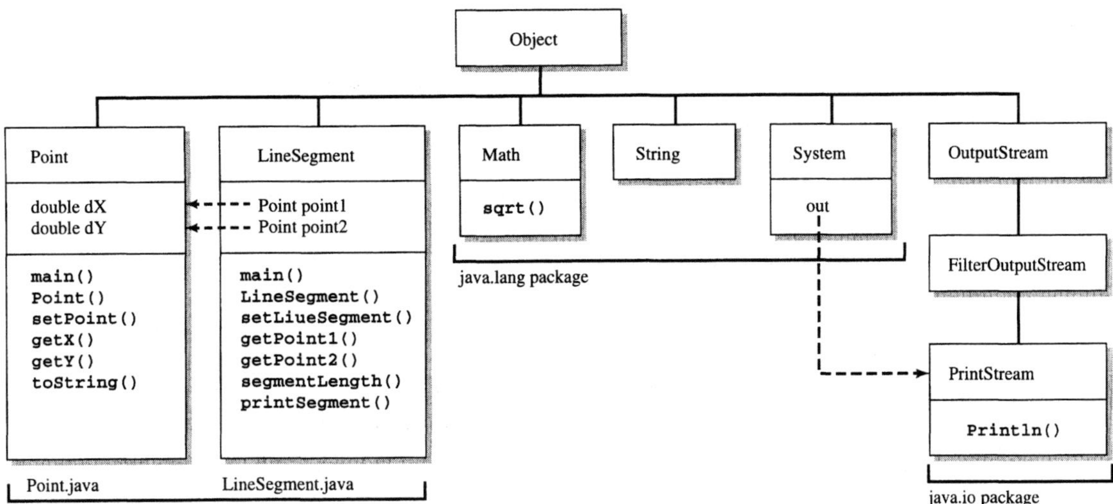

FIGURE 18.9 Class hierarchy for Program 18.4.

18.12.5 Program Architecture

Figure 18.9 shows the class hierarchy of user-defined Java code and classes from the JDK that make up Program 18.4. Programs 18.3 and 18.4 employ essentially the same hierarchy of classes for simple mathematical computations and program output. What is new in Program 18.4 is its use of two classes of user-defined Java code. A line segment endpoint is defined by the skeleton class

```
public class Point {
    protected double dX, dY;

    ..... methods for class Point...
}
```

and the line segment by

```
public class LineSegment {
    protected Point p1, p2;

    ..... methods for class LineSegment...
}
```

The connectivity between these classes is indicated by the dashed arrows in Figure 18.9.

18.12.6 Constructor Methods

Both the `Point` and `LineSegment` classes support multiple constructor methods. We look at the former in detail. As demonstrated in the `Point` test program, `Point` objects can be created using either of the methods:

```
// Constructor method : just create instance of class.

public Point() { }

// Create instance of class and set (x,y) coordinates.

public Point( double dX, double dY ) {
   setPoint( dX, dY );
}
```

The default constructor (i.e., `public Point() {}`) must be explicitly listed when more than one constructor is used in a class.

FURTHER INFORMATION

1. For more information about Unicode, check out the Unicode web site at

   `http://www.unicode.org.`

2. On the JavaSoft web server, you will find the JDK API User's Guide with a complete description of all the classes available in a standard distribution. At the time of writing, the lastest version is JDK 1.1.5:

   ```
   http://java.sun.com/products/jdk/1.1/docs/api/
     API_users_guide.html
   ```

3. Cafe (`http://cafe.symantec.com/`) is another Java development environment from Symentec (`http://www.symantec.com`). It comes with a Java source code editor, a Java compiler, a debugger, and tools to organize projects and manage code. Other Java development environments include

   ```
   Borland Latte          http://www.borland.com/internet/latte
   Microsoft Visual J++   http://www.microsoft.com/visualj
   Asymetrix' SuperCede   http://www.asymetrix.com/nettools/ide
   ```

4. At the time of writing, the latest version of the JDK is 1.1.5, and you can download it directly from the Sun server at

   `http://www.javasoft.com/products/jdk/1.1/index.html`

5. Finally, you can download an evaluation version of Java WorkShop for a 30-day trial period at

```
http://shop.sun.com
```

Review Questions

1. What are the two different "types" in Java?
2. What is the main difference between "objects" and "classes"?
3. What is the procedure for creating an instance of a class?
4. What does the "dot" notation do?
5. What are the three types of variables in Java?
6. Why does the concept of a "global variable" not make any sense in Java?
7. Consider the statement

```
public final static int iMyExamScore = 100;
```

   What is the purpose of the keywords public, final, static?

8. What are the advantages of "no pointers" and "garbage collection" in Java?
9. What is the purpose of `this` and `super()`?
10. Suppose that the fragment of code

```
class FooBar {
      int iA;

      public void FooBar() {
            int iA = 7;
      }
}
```

   is followed by

```
FooBar f = new FooBar();
String s = "Value of iA = " + f.iA;
```

   What is the contents of `s`?

11. What is the difference between a class method and an instance method?
12. What is an abstract class? Why is it useful?
13. What is an abstract method? Why is it useful?

14. What is an object reference? What kinds of information are provided to the Java Virtual Machine by a reference-type variable?

15. Can a Java program have more than one `main()` method?

16. Suppose that a particular Java program is made up of five classes—`Location`, `Shape`, `Circle`, `Rectangle`, and `TestShape`—all contained within the file `TestShape.java`. What command would you give to compile this program? What files will exist after the compilation?

18.13 PROGRAMMING EXERCISES

Problem 18.1 (Beginner): The volume of a sphere of radius r is

$$\text{Volume} = \frac{4}{3}\pi r^3 \tag{18.5}$$

Write a Java program that will prompt the user for a sphere's radius, and then compute and print the volume of the sphere. You should use the `Math.pow()` method in the math class library to compute r^3.

Problem 18.2 (Beginner): The area of a triangle having side lengths a, b, and c is

$$\text{Area} = \sqrt{s(s-a)(s-b)(s-c)} \tag{18.6}$$

where $s = (a + b + c)/2$. Write a Java program that will prompt the user for the three side lengths of the triangle, and then compute and print the area of the triangle via Equation 18.6.

Note. To ensure that the triangle is well defined, your program should check that all side lengths are greater than zero and that the sum of the shorter two side lengths exceeds the length of the longest side.

Problem 18.3 (Beginner): Extend the test program for Program 18.4 so that a user is interactively prompted for the (x, y) coordinate positions of the line segments.

Problem 18.4 (Intermediate): Create a triangle class containing three `Point` objects and methods for moving a point, and computing the area and centroid of the triangle.

Problem 18.5 (Intermediate): This question does not involve programming per se but tests your knowledge of classes and inheritance. The following Java program

```
/*
 * =============================================
 * Test Program for Rectangle and Circle Shapes.
 * =============================================
 */

import java.lang.Math;
```

```
// Location of a point ( dX, dY ).

class Location {
      double dX, dY;
}

// Class of Shapes.

class Shape {
      Location c = new Location();

      public String toString() { return ""; }
      public double perimeter() { return 0.0; }
}

// Class of Rectangles.

class Rectangle extends Shape {
      double dSide1, dSide2;

      public Rectangle ( double dSide1, double dSide2,
                         double dX, double dY ) {
            this.dSide1 = dSide1;
            this.dSide2 = dSide2;

            c.dX = dX;
            c.dY = dY;
      }

      public String toString() {
            return "Rectangle : Side1 = " + dSide1 +
                              " Side2 = " + dSide2 ;
      }

      public double perimeter() {
            return 2.0*(dSide1 + dSide2);
      }
}

// Class of Circles.

class Circle extends Shape {
      double dDiameter;

      public Circle ( double dDiameter, double dX, double dY ) {
            this.dDiameter = dDiameter;
            c.dX = dX;
            c.dY = dY;
      }
```

```
        public String toString() {
              return "Circle : Diameter = " + dDiameter + "
                     [x,y] = ["+ c.dX + "," + c.dY + "]";
        }

        public double perimeter() {
              return Math.PI*dDiameter*dDiameter/4.0;
        }
}

public class TestShape {

public static void main ( String args[] ) {

        Shape s[] = new Shape [2];

        s[0] = new Rectangle( 2.0, 2.0, 2.0, 2.0 );
        s[1] = new Circle( 2.0, 2.0, 2.0 );

        // Print details of the array of shapes


        for (int ii = 1; ii <= s.length; ii = ii + 1) {
             System.out.println(  s[ii-1].toString() );
             System.out.println( "Perimeter = " +
                                 s[ii-1].perimeter() );
        }
   }
}
```

contains five classes: Location, Shape, Circle, Rectangle, and TestShape. Th compiled program generates the output (yes, it works!)

```
Rectangle : Side1 = 2.0 Side2 = 2.0
Perimeter = 8.0
Circle : Diameter = 2.0 [x,y] = [2.0,2.0]
Perimeter = 3.141592653589793
```

Please examine the source code carefully and answer the following questions:

1. List the variables and methods available to the class Circle.
2. List the variables and methods available to the class Rectangle.
3. Draw and label a diagram showing the layout of memory resulting from th statement

```
Shape s[] = new Shape [2] ;
```

4. What is the relationship between the classes Shape and Location?

5. Draw and label a diagram showing the relationship among the five classes.
6. Briefly explain (in terms of the classes and methods called) the sequence of activities generated by the looping construct?

```
for (int ii = 1; ii <= s.length; ii = ii + 1) {
     System.out.println( s[ii-1].toString() );
     System.out.println( "Perimeter = " + s[ii-1].perimeter() );
}
```

Problem 18.6 (Intermediate): A key problem with the implementation of Program 18.3 is lack of flexibility. An improved implementation would separate the storage and solution of the quadratic equation from the test program.

Quadratic	TestQuadratic
Quadratic(fA, fB, fC)	main()
rootsOfQuadratic ()	keyboardInput()
fdiscriminant (fA, fB, fC)	

With this observation in mind, rewrite Program 18.3 so that all the details associated with the storage and solution of the quadratic equation are contained within a class `Quadratic`. The method `Quadratic()` should initialize the quadratic equation, and the method `rootsOfQuadratic()` should compute and print the equation roots. The method `fdiscriminant()` should compute the equation discriminant. The test program details should be contained within a second `TestQuadratic` class.

Problem 18.7 (Intermediate): Complex variables and complex variable arithmetic are used in the solution of many types of engineering problems. In electrical engineering, for example, complex numbers are a staple of circuit analysis. In structural dynamics, complex variables can be used to formulate models of damping.

This question develops a small Java class for complex number arithmetic and a corresponding test program. Starting with the skeleton class library

```
/*
 * ==========================================================
 * Complex : Class library for complex number arithmetic.
 * ==========================================================
 */

public class Complex {
    protected double dReal, dImaginary;

    // Constructor methods

    public Complex() {}
```

```
    public Complex( double dReal, double dImaginary ) {
        this.dReal       = dReal;
        this.dImaginary = dImaginary;
    }

    ...... details of methods for complex arithmetic go here ..
}
```

develop a suite of methods for complex number arithmetic. Methods should b written for

Method	*Description*
`Complex();`	Create new instance of complex number.
`Negate();`	Compute -ve of complex number.
`Abs();`	Compute absolute value of complex number.
`Add();`	Add two complex numbers.
`Sub();`	Subtract two complex numbers.
`Mult();`	Multiply two complex numbers.
`Div();`	Divide complex numbers.
`Scale();`	Scale complex number by real number.
`Conjugate();`	Compute complex conjugate.
`Sqrt();`	Compute square root of complex number.
`toString();`	Convert a complex number to a string.

You should develop a test method `main()` within the `Complex` class to exercis each of the class methods. Now we use the library to solve a simple problem. If a, b, and c are complex numbers, show that solutions to

$$a \cdot x^2 + b \cdot x + c = 0 \tag{18.7}$$

are given by

$$x = \frac{-b \pm \sqrt{b^2 - 4ac}}{2a} \tag{18.8}$$

Use your library of functions and Equation (18.8) to show that solutions to

$$(2.00 + 2.00i)x^2 + (3.00 + 3.00i)x + (3.00 + 5.00i) = 0.0 \tag{18.9}$$

are $x_1 = -0.5445 - 1.2164i$ and $x_2 = -0.9555 + 1.2164i$. Check that x_1 and x_2 ar in fact solutions to Equation (18.9) by evaluating each term, and arranging re and complex components in a table of output. Your output could look like

```
Verification of Root1
a.x^2 = -5.015884447523356+0.2827825704493987i
b.x   = 2.015884447523357-5.282782570449398i
c     = 3.0+5.0i
=====================================================
sum   = 8.881784197001252E-16+8.881784197001252E-16i
```

```
Verification of Root2
a.x^2 = 3.5158844475233577-5.782782570449397i
b.x   = -6.515884447523357+0.782782570449398i
c     = 3.0+5.0i
=================================================================
```

Problem 18.8 (Intermediate/Advanced): Write and test a function `segmentIntersection()` that takes as its input two line segments and computes the intersection of the line segments.

Figure 18.10 shows that three types of line intersection exist. If the line segments are parallel, then they may also overlap (as shown in the left-hand diagram). The results of the intersection calculation is a line segment. Otherwise, the lines may intersect at a single point or not at all.

To accommodate these three cases within a single function, you should assume that

```
Segment segmentIntersection ( Segment line1, Segment line2 );
```

takes as its input two line segments and returns a single line segment as its output. A single-point intersection may be thought of as a line segment with its two endpoints at the same location—such a line segment will have zero length. For those cases where two line segments do not intersect, `segmentIntersection()` should return a single node with `NaN` coordinates.

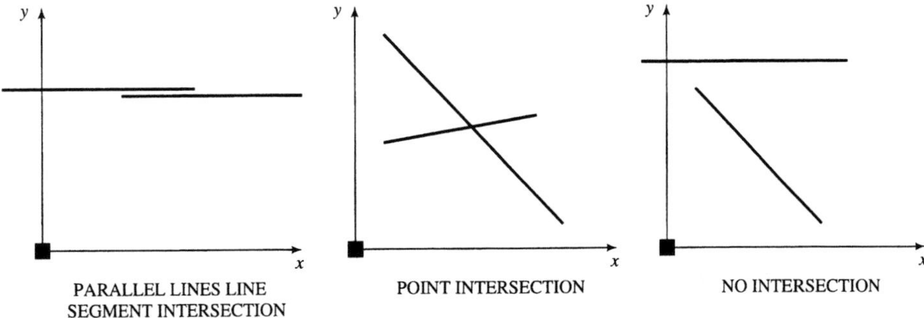

FIGURE 18.10 Intersection of line segments.

19

JAVA GRAPHICS

19.1 INTRODUCTION

A graphical user interface (GUI) is simply a pictorial interface to a comput program. GUIs play an important role in the development of modern comput programs because they allow for a level of human–computer interaction that is lot more descriptive than is possible with interfaces that are purely textual (i.e character only).

19.1.1 Developing a Java GUI

Suppose that you have been asked to develop a GUI front-end to an engineerir applications program written in Java. The step-by-step development procedure roughly as follows:

1. Create a sketch of the GUI showing the desired layout of components ar their intended connectivity to the applications program.
2. Create a skeleton of GUI components. Two issues to consider are as follow "how do you want the components to look on the screen?," and "how shoul the components respond when a user moves or resizes the interface?"
3. For each major interface component, design and write Java code to interce critical events.
4. Hook the applications code to the GUI.

Most of the work in Steps 1 and 2 lies in the definition of rectangular windows with a variety of attachments (e.g., text areas, buttons, menus, scroll bars, and canvases for painting arbitrary data on a screen). A knowledge of the different layout managers will be needed for the "intelligent packing" of subwindows. Step 3 is concerned with the detection and handling of events (e.g., mouse clicks, keystrokes). An in-depth knowledge of the Java event model will be required at this point. Step 4 is where details of the event-handling code are connected to the applications program. Because the GUI, event-handling methods, and applications code are likely to exist in separate classes/packages, an understanding of how Java integrates classes and packages is necessary.

With this brief introduction to GUI development in mind, this chapter has three purposes. First, we introduce the basic features of the Java Abstract Windowing Toolkit, including graphics (e.g., window coordinates, color, fonts), components (e.g., buttons, text, canvases), and layout managers. The Java 1.1 event model is the second main topic for this chapter. Finally, these concepts are demonstrated in Section 19.8 where we work step by step through the development of three engineering applications with simple GUIs.

19.2 THE JAVA ABSTRACT WINDOWING TOOLKIT

The Java Abstract Windowing Toolkit (AWT) contains a large number of classes and methods for the development of platform-independent GUIs. By platform independent, we mean that these GUI interfaces will operate across X windows platforms, Microsoft windows, and Mac desktops, a feature that is made possible by the pathway of development shown in Figure 19.1. Beginning at the left-hand side of Figure 19.1, an engineer writes a Java application program that calls a generalized set of classes in the AWT. These classes have been carefully designed to operate without concern for platform-dependent windowing issues. The latter

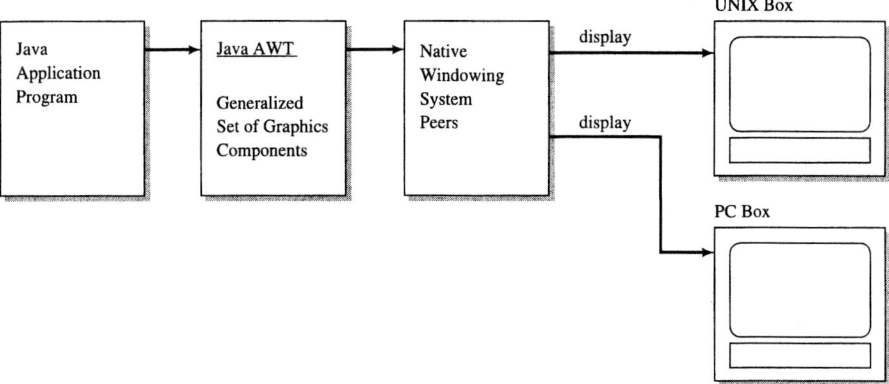

FIGURE 19.1 Creating and displaying an AWT component.

are taken care of instead by a set of AWT classes known as peers. A peer is a native windowing component that can manage the display of stand-alone applications and applets. Most of the work associated with displaying and managing a component on the computer screen is handled by the peer classes at run-time. Suppose, for example, that we want to display a button on the screen. The peer classes associated with a UNIX box might present a button having an X Windows/Motif look and feel. A Windows 95 button peer might display a button having a Windows 95 look and feel. The peer approach to GUI development side steps the need for software development in native windowing components (a key economic benefit), and gives stand-alone application and applet programs the same look and feel as native windowing components. All the details of the peer classes are hidden from the Java programmer, of course.

19.2.1 AWT Packages

The AWT is composed of six packages:

AWT package	*Description*
`java.awt`	Classes for basic component functionality.
`java.awt.datatransfer`	Classes for clipboards and data transfer.
`java.awt.event`	Classes for handling AWT events.
`java.awt.image`	Classes for fundamental image manipulation.
`java.awt.peer`	Classes for peer interfaces for component peers.
`java.awt.test`	A single applet that tests a limited subset of AWT functionality.

In this chapter, we are mainly concerned with classes in the `java.awt` and `java.awt.event` packages.

19.2.2 AWT Class Hierarchy

Broadly speaking, the AWT packages contain four important sections:

1. *Graphics.* The graphics classes contain methods for defining colors and fonts drawing lines and text, and displaying images.
2. *Components.* The component classes contain methods for the definition of GU components. Buttons, labels, lists, check boxes, text fields, text areas, and scrol bars are examples of GUI components.
3. *Layout Managers.* The layout manager classes control the layout of component within their container objects.
4. *Handling Events.* Whenever a user clicks on a mouse, drags and drops or resize a window, or types on the keyboard, the operating system will generate a

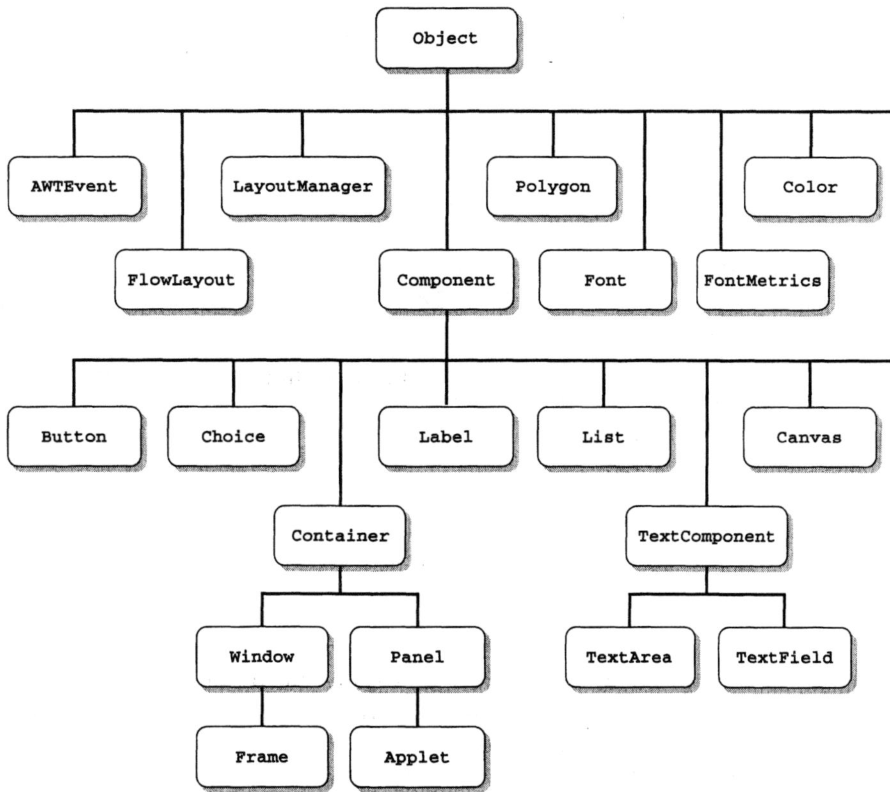

FIGURE 19.2 *AWT class hierarchy.*

event. The event-handling classes allow a programmer to specify actions that a program should take in response to these events.

Figure 19.2 shows the important parts of the AWT class hierarchy that are covered in this tutorial (the AWT is huge, and a complete explanation of its capabilities is beyond our resources). For a well-written explanation of the complete AWT class hierarchy, we recommend that you see *Java in a Nutshell* [10].

Each class in the AWT class hierarchy inherits directly from `Object`, the root class in Java. The classes `Canvas`, `Color`, `Polygon`, `Font`, and `FontMetrics` define methods for performing graphical and textual operations in a `Component`. The `AWTEvent` class contains methods for detecting and handling events. The `FlowLayout` and `LayoutManager` classes contain methods for the management of component widgets within containers.

The AWT class hierarchy structure has been carefully designed so that its methods can be used without editing. Customized classes with special properties are created by programming subclasses that contain the relevant content/modifications to the original class(es). This is what we call *programming by extension.*

19.3 AWT COMPONENTS AND CONTAINERS

Most of the action in a GUI can be traced back to interactions between AWT components, containers, and layout managers.

Component

Approximately half of the classes in the `java.awt` package are associated with the abstract class `Component`. The subclasses of `Component` represent all the visual elements from which a GUI can be constructed. A brief description of these components and their functionality is found in the upper-half of Table 19.1. Each component element has a graphics object, a native peer, and information on the component's location and size; foreground and background colors; fonts; and maximum, minimum, and preferred component sizes. Collectively, these attributes define the behavior and look and feel of an element in its native environment (see, for example, the right-hand side of Figure 19.1).

Container

A container object is simply a general-purpose component that may itself contain multiple components. `Container` is an abstract class that is meant to be subclassed. As shown in Figure 19.2, the three most commonly used `Container` subclasses are `Frame`, `Panel`, and `Applet`. Every container object comes equipped with a layout manager for the positioning of multiple components within the container. A brief description of the most commonly used container classes is located in the

TABLE 19.1 Component Subclasses and Methods

Component Subclasses	*Description*
`Button`	A textual button for triggering an action.
`Canvas`	A canvas for painting graphics.
`Choice`	A pop-down menu of textual entries.
`Label`	A component that displays a string.
`List`	A scrollable list of textual entries.
Component Methods	*Description*
`getFont()`	Get the "named font" from the system properties.
`getGraphics()`	Get the Graphics object associated with a particular component.
`getSize()`	Get the size of the current component.
`setBackground()` `setForeground()`	Set the background and foreground colors.
`setFont()`	Set the font.
`paint()`	A method that is invoked when the component and its contents need to be drawn

TABLE 19.2 Container Subclasses and Container Methods

Container Subclasses	*Description*
`Applet`	Applet is the superclass of all applet programs.
`Frame`	A top-level window with a titlebar and optional menubar.
`Panel`	A panel is a container that does not have its own window—instead, it is contained inside another container.
`TextField`	A single-line component for entering text.
`Window`	A borderless window with no title.
Container Methods	*Description*
`add()`	Add a component to a container.
`setLayout()`	Set the layout of components within a container.
`paint()`	A method that is invoked when the container and its contents need to be drawn.

lower-half of Table 19.2. In practical terms, all that you have to do is add a component to a container, specify the desired layout of components in the program, and the system will pretty much take care of itself. When a user interacts with one or more components in a way that requires some sort of action, the components will generate events that the program will detect and to which it will react. We see how to handle these events in Section 19.7.

19.3.1 Windows and Frames

Stand-alone Java application programs requiring a window are commonly implemented as extensions of the `Frame` class. The `Frame` class extends `Window`, which in turn extends `Container`.

A `Window` object represents an independent top-level window that is not contained within another object. The main purpose of a `Window` object is to provide window management functionality, including, for example, methods for resizing and for drag and drop of windows. Window objects have neither borders nor titles; in fact, they are not meant to be used directly.

`Frame` objects automatically inherit all the window management functionality provided by the `Window` class methods because `Frame` is a direct extension of `Window`. A `Frame` object is a window with a title bar and a border; what a `Frame` object lacks is content. Java programmers add content to a `Frame` by creating a new class that extends `Frame`, and overrides the appropriate methods with new methods containing the frame content. Once again, this approach to program development is efficient because the basic methods for handling the `Frame` behavior do not need to be reimplemented.

Frames and applets are sometimes termed top-level windows because most often they are containers and are not contained within another object.

Computer Program. Program 19.1 is a small stand-alone Java program that creates and displays a Frame that has no functionality per se but contains skeleton code for the addition of component, painting, and event-handling functionality later.

PROGRAM 19.1: A FRAME THAT HAS NO FUNCTIONALITY

```
/*
 * ============================================================
 * TestFrame.java : Create a Frame that has no functionality.
 *                  Useful, huh!
 * ============================================================
 */

import java.awt.*;

public class TestFrame extends Frame {

    // The main method creates an instance of the class.
    public static void main( String args[] ) {
       TestFrame t = new TestFrame();
    }

    public TestFrame() {                            // Define window Frame.

       /* Define I/O components */

          // Source code for I/O components goes here ....

       /* Initialize and display Frame */

       setTitle("Simple Frame Interface");         // Set Frame Title.
       setSize(400,120);                           // Set the Frame size.
       show();                                     // Display the Frame.
    }

    public void paint (Graphics g) {         // Method for painting

          // Source code for painting on the frame goes here ....

    }
}
```

```
.ass QuitListener extends MouseAdapter {

   // Source code for handling of mouse events goes here ....

lass CelListener extends KeyAdapter {

   // Source code for handling of keyboard events goes here ....
```

Figure 19.3 is a snapshot of Program 19.1 running in a `Motif` windows environment on a UNIX box. The top left- and right-hand corners contain the usual frame icons for destroying, iconifying, and resizing a frame. The iconify and resize icons work as you might expect. However, Java has disabled the skull-bones icon for destroying the window. These details must be provided by a programmer.

Our empty frame program is implemented in terms of the class `TestFrame`, which extends `Frame`. Within the `main` method, the statement

```
TestFrame t = new TestFrame();
```

declares a variable `t` of type `TestFrame` and calls the constructor `TestFrame()` to make an instance of the class. At this point, the object referenced by `t` will contain all the necessary information for the underlying window system to display a window. Frames must be sized before they are displayed, however. The block of statements

```
setSize(400,120);
show();
```

sets the window width to 400 pixels and the window height to 120 pixels. Finally, the method `show()` tells the Java Virtual Machine to display the frame using features appropriate to the environment in which the program is running. Of course, the look and feel and size of Figure 19.3 will vary across hardware platforms, and so hard-coding the dimensions of the frame height and width in pixel coordinates is rather unsatisfactory. A better implementation would query the run-time system

FIGURE 19.3 Simple Frame GUI.

for the size of the display in pixel coordinates (you can do this in Java) and si the frame accordingly. We leave the implementation of these details as an exerci for the reader.

A number of methods are available for customizing the look and feel of frame. For example, the statement

```
setTitle("Simple Frame Interface");
```

sets the frame title to `"Simple Frame Interface"`. Of course, a frame with title can also be created in one statement:

```
TestFrame t = new TestFrame("Simple Frame Interface");
```

In the following sections, we see how components can be added to a frame (ar indeed any container object) with the method `add()`, and how the method `setLay out()` can be used to control the layout of components within a frame.

We use the method `paint()` for painting content onto a canvas, and extensio of the classes `MouseAdapter` and `KeyAdapter` for the handling of mouse a keyboard events.

19.3.2 Applets

From a technical point of view, an applet is a Java program or object that belon to the class `java.applet.Applet`. Figure 19.2 shows where `Applet` fits into t AWT class hierarchy. The `Applet` class is a specialized type of `Panel`, which turn is designed to be embedded inside a container called an "applet context Two examples of applet contexts are Java-enabled browsers and Sun's apple viewer program.

The `Applet` class contains a number of methods that allow a Java program retrieve, display, and execute information from the applet context within which is operating. A summary of these methods is contained in Table 19.3. Otherwis the `Applet` class does not do much. Functionality is added to an application progra by extending the `Applet` class and overriding its methods, most notably the metho `paint()` and `init()`.

The `init()` method initializes the applet when a document containing t applet is opened. An applet's `paint()` method is automatically called by the sy tem just after the applet has been created and whenever the applet needs to b redrawn, perhaps because the applet window has been moved or uncovered.

19.4 AWT GRAPHICS

This section describes the AWT `Graphics` class. Methods are provided for t painting and filling of graphical regions, and for the drawing and positioning of te and images on graphical regions. We start with a few basic concepts.

TABLE 19.3 Applet Execution and Display Methods

Execution Methods	*Description*
`init()`	The `init()` method is called to initialize an applet when a document containing an applet is opened. An `init()` method takes the place of a constructor method in stand-alone Java applications.
`start()`	The `start()` method is called after the `init()` method. It starts the applet.
`stop()`	The `stop()` method is called when an applet no longer needs to be displayed. This could be because a browser is moving onto a new page, or perhaps because the browser has been iconified. The `stop()` method is always called before the `destroy()` method.
`destroy()`	After the `stop()` method has been called, the `destroy()` method is called to clean up any resources that are being held.
Display Methods	***Description***
`paint()`	Paint the component.
`repaint()`	Schedules a call to the components `update()` method as soon as possible. A call to `repaint()` is normally invoked when the graphics no longer accurately represent the state of a system.
`update()`	The `update()` method redraws the component. By default, this method redraws the background and then calls the `paint()` method.

19.4.1 Graphics Coordinate System

Before we can draw anything in Java, we need to understand the coordinate system employed for representing points on a graphics window. By default, the top left-hand corner of a graphics window is given the coordinate `(0, 0)` (see Figure 19.4).

The `x` coordinate axis measures distances in the left-to-right horizontal direction. The `y` coordinate axis measures distances in the vertical direction downward from the top left-hand corner. In both cases, the units of measure are pixels, the smallest units of resolution on a computer monitor. This coordinate system is needed to position text, lines, and polygons on the computer screen.

19.4.2 Graphics Objects and Methods

`Graphics` objects are used for drawing strings, characters, bytes, lines, and rectangles (see Table 19.4 for an abbreviated list of methods). The `Graphics` class is

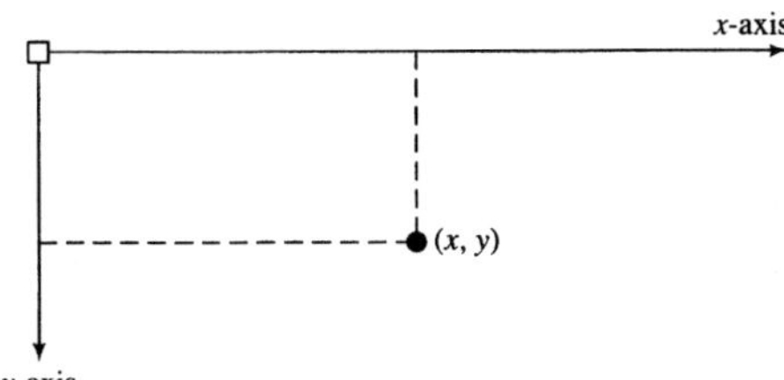

FIGURE 19.4 Graphics coordinate system.

TABLE 19.4 Graphics Methods in Java AWT

Method	*Meaning*

`public abstract void drawString (`
`   String s,    // String to be drawn.`
`   int iX,      // x coordinate.`
`   int iY,      // y coordinate.`
`)`
	Draw a text string beginning at coordinate (*iX*, *iY*).

`public abstract void drawLine (`
`   int iX1,     // x coordinate of end 1.`
`   int iY1,     // y coordinate of end 1.`
`   int iX2,     // x coordinate of end 2.`
`   int iY2,     // y coordinate of end 2.`
`)`
	Draw a line segment in the current color, beginning at pixel coordinate (*iX*1, *iY*1) and finishing at (*iX*2, *iY*2).

`public void drawRect (`
`   int iX1,      // x coordinate.`
`   int iY1,      // y coordinate.`
`   int iWidth,   // rectangle width.`
`   int iHeight,  // rectangle height.`
`)`
	Draw a rectangle having a top left-hand corner at (*iX*1, *iY*1). The width and height in pixels is `iWidth` and `iHeight`, respectively.

`public void clearRect (`
`   int iX1,      // x coordinate.`
`   int iY1,      // y coordinate.`
`   int iWidth,   // rectangle width.`
`   int iHeight,  // rectangle height.`
`)`
	Draw a rectangle in the background color. The top left-hand corner is at coordinate (*iX*1, *iY*1).

`public void drawPolygon( Polygon p );`	Draw a polygon in the current color.
`public void fillPolygon( Polygon p );`	Draw a filled polygon in the current color.

implemented as an `abstract` class (`Graphics` objects cannot be instantiated), thereby providing an avenue for portability across computer hardware platforms. Because drawing is performed differently on each platform that supports Java there cannot be one class that implements drawing capabilities on all systems. Each computer platform circumvents this problem by using a derived class of `Graphics` to take care of the drawing.

Paint Method

The `Component` class method `paint`

```
void paint ( Graphic g );
```

has a graphics object argument `g` that references an object in the system's derived `Graphic` class. The `paint()` method is automatically called after a stand-alone Java program has been instantiated or, in the case of a Java applet, the `init()` method has been called.

A well-written `paint()` method should quickly provide a graphical snapsho

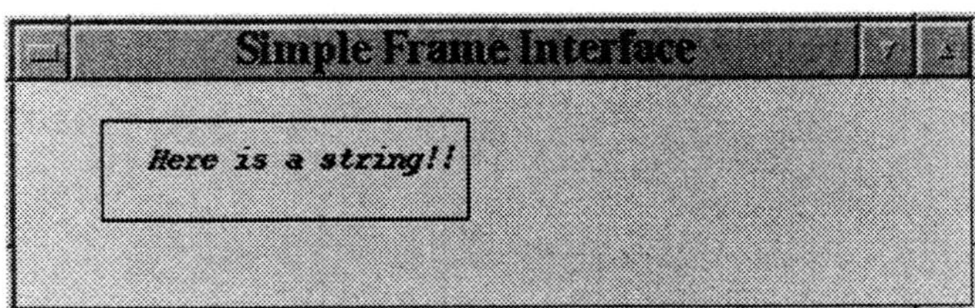

FIGURE 19.5 Frame GUI with simple graphics.

of what is happening in a program. An applications program should therefore compute the state of a system outside of the subclassed `paint()` method. It should also make the local variables essential to creating the applet graphics available to the subclassed `paint()` method.

Example. Figure 19.5 shows the GUI that is generated when the fragment of code

```
g.drawString("Here is a string!!", 60, 60);
g.drawRect( 40, 40, 150, 40);
```

is inserted into the `paint()` method of Program 19.1. The `paint()` method draws a character string `"Here is a string!!"` beginning at coordinate `(60,60)`. The second statement draws a rectangle of width 150 pixels and height 40 pixels, with the top left-hand corner positioned at coordinate `(40,40)`.

9.4.3 Polygon

A polygon is a multisided planar shape and, in Java, polygon objects are created and drawn using the methods summarized in Table 19.5 on page 567.

Example. Inserting the fragment of code

```
int iaX[] = {100, 300, 300, 250, 250, 200, 200, 100, 100};
int iaY[] = { 50,  50, 100, 100,  80,  80, 100, 100,  50};

// Create and draw polygon object.

Polygon p = new Polygon ( iaX, iaY, 9 );
g.drawPolygon( p );
```

into the `paint()` method of Program 19.1 results in the GUI shown in Figure 19.6. The x and y pixel coordinates of the polygon nodes are contained within the arrays `iaX` and `iaY`, respectively. Polygons may also be assembled incrementally. For example, the fragment of code

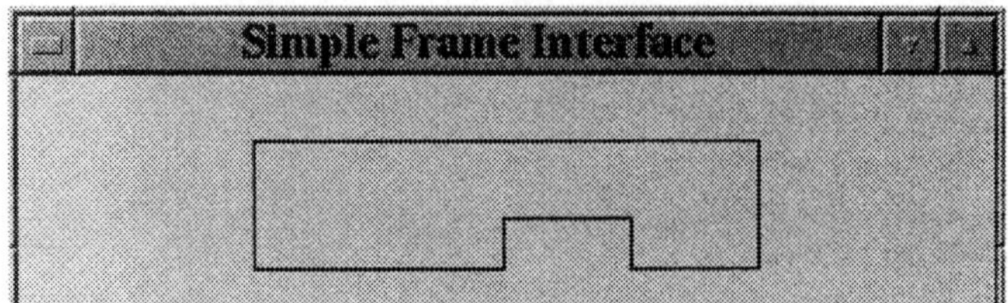

FIGURE 19.6 Frame GUI with simple polygon.

```
private Polygon p = (new) Polygon ();
for (ii = 0; ii < 5; ii = ii + 1 ) {
    p.addPoint( iaX[ ii ], iaY[ ii ] );
}
```

creates an empty polygon object referenced by `p`, and then systematically wal along the arrays `iaX` and `iaY` and adds the `(x,y)` coordinate pairs to the polyg definition with the method `addPoint()`.

19.4.4 Color

The `Color` class contains an ensemble of methods and constants for setting ar manipulating colors. Every color is treated as a (RGB) triplet. The first part of t triplet represents the amount of red in the color, the second part represents t amount of green in the color, and the third part represents the amount of blue the color. When the intensity of each part is represented by an integer (see t class definition in Table 19.6), the range of acceptable settings is `0` through `255`

Example. Let `g` be a Graphics object (details given as follows). The script of co

```
private int red   =   0;
private int green = 255;
private int blue  = 255;

Color color1 = new Color ( red, green, blue);
g.setColor( color1 );
```

calls the `Color` constructor with the red, green, and blue arguments set to 100. Th second statement sets the color to cyan for plotting. Two alternative implement tions are

```
g.setColor( new Color ( 0, 255, 255 ) );
g.setColor( Color.cyan );
```

TABLE 19.5 Polygon Methods in Java 1.1 AWT

Method	*Meaning*
`public Polygon ()`	Construct a new polygon object. The polygon will be empty.
`public Polygon ( int iaXcoord []; // x coordinates. int iaYcoord []; // y coordinates. int iNoPoints; // number of points. )`	Construct a new polygon object having `noPoints` sides. The (x,y) coordinates of the polygon nodes are given in arrays `xValues[]` and `yValues[]`.
`public void addPoint ( int iX // x coordinate. int iY // y coordinate. )`	Add a point to a polygon object.
`public boolean contains ( int iX // x coordinate. int iY // y coordinate. )`	Test whether a specified point is inside the polygon.

TABLE 19.6 Color Constants and Methods in Java AWT

Constant	*Color*	(r,g,b)
Color Constants		
`public final static Color red`	red	(255 , 0, 0)
`public final static Color green`	green	(0, 255, 0)
`public final static Color blue`	blue	(0, 0, 255)
`public final static Color black`	black	(0, 0, 0)
`public final static Color white`	white	(0, 0, 0)
`public final static Color cyan`	cyan	(0, 255, 255)
`public final static Color orange`	orange	(255, 200, 0)
`public final static Color yellow`	yellow	(255, 255, 0)
`public final static Color gray`	gray	(127, 127, 127)

Method	*Meaning*
Graphics Methods	
`public Color { int r; // 0 - 255 red constant. int g; // 0 - 255 green constant. int b; // 0 - 255 blue constant. }`	Create a color based on red, green, and blue contents.
`public abstract void setColor( Color c )`	Sets the current color for drawing with the graphics context.

Displaying Colors

Although the total number of colors that may be chosen is 256^3, in practice, most computer hardware platforms are incapable of displaying all these colors. For example, a workstation having an 8-bit color plane can only display $2^8 = 256$ distinct colors on a screen. If the system cannot return an exact color, it will return a color that is close.

19.4.5 Font and FontMetrics

The `Font` class contains an ensemble of constants and methods for setting and manipulating fonts. A summary of the font constants and methods is located in Table 19.7. The `Font` constructor takes three arguments: the font name, the font style, and the font size (e.g., 12, 14, 16, 18, 24, . . .). The font name can be any font supported by the current system. The JDK 1.1 guarantees that the fonts TimesRoman, Courier, Helvetica, Dialog, and Symbol will be available on all AWT implementations. Otherwise, the range of available fonts is system dependent.

Algorithms for positioning text on a display often need information on the size and style of the current font. The methods `getName()`, `getStyle()`, and `getSize()` return information on the name, style, and size of the current font.

TABLE 19.7 Constants and Methods in Font and FontMetrics

Constant	*Meaning*
Font Constants	
public final static int `PLAIN`	A plain font style
public final static int `BOLD`	A bold font style
public final static int `ITALIC`	An italic font style
Method	*Meaning*
Font Methods	
`public Font { Sting s; // font name. int iStyle; // font style. int iSize; // font size. }`	Creates a Font object with the specified font, style, and size.
`public abstract void setFont( Font f )`	Set the current font to the font, style, and size specified in Font.
`public int getName()`	Return current font name as a string.
`public int getStyle()`	Return an integer value indicating the current font style.
`public int getSize()`	Return an integer for the current font size.

Example. The script of code

```
Font font1 = new Font ( "Courier" , Font.PLAIN, 14 );
g.setFont ( font1 );
```

defines a new 14-point plain Courier font object called `font1` and sets the current font to `font1`. Font styles can be combined. For example, the statement

```
Font font2 = new Font ( "Courier", Font.ITALIC + Font.Bold , 14 );
```

defines a new 14-point bold italic Courier font object called `font2`. The statement

```
private int iSize = g.getSize();
```

assigns the point size of the current fold to `iSize`. Java will use the default font when a platform cannot satisfy a user's font request.

Fonts are not assigned colors. They belong to the graphical context, and so you need to set the color before drawing a font in a particular color.

19.5 AWT LAYOUT MANAGERS

The AWT comes with a handful of predefined layout managers for controlling the size and position of components in a container (e.g., frames, applets). When a user stretches or squashes the shape of a frame, a layout manager makes sure the components within a container will be arranged and presented in an appropriate manner. Instead of saying that a particular widget should be positioned in the upper left-hand corner of a display at pixel coordinate (150, 100), for example, we say things like "a widget should be positioned above or below, or to the left or right of another component." Relaxing the exact details of widget positioning enables the Java AWT to operate across hardware platforms.

The three layout managers that we use in this tutorial are

1. *Border Layout.* A border layout organizes a container into North, South, East, and West sections aligned with the container border. Each section is automatically resized to fit the size of the widgets within the container. Center is the region that remains in the center of the container.

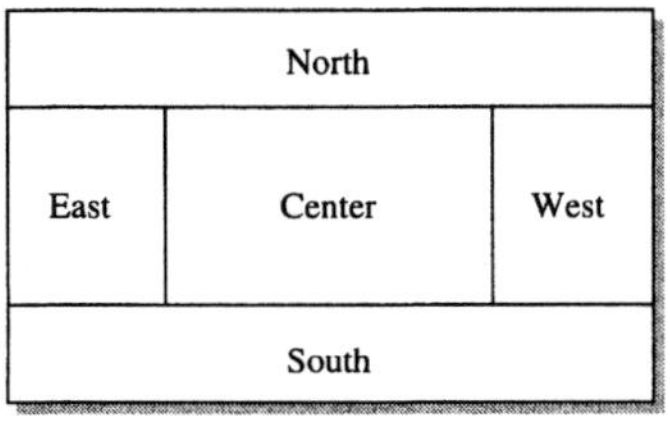

North

East Center West

South

2. *Flow Layout.* A flow layout simply lines up the components left to right without trying to be too neat about it. After laying out as many items as will fit across the container, the flow layout manager will move onto the next row. Each component gets as much space as it needs and no more. A flow layout is useful for positioning buttons on a panel. Buttons will be positioned in the center of a panel by default. However, explicit left, right, and central positioning of components on a panel may be achieved with `FlowLayout( Flowlayout.LEFT )`, `FlowLayout( Flowlayout.RIGHT )`, and `FlowLayout( Flowlayout.CENTER )`, respectively.

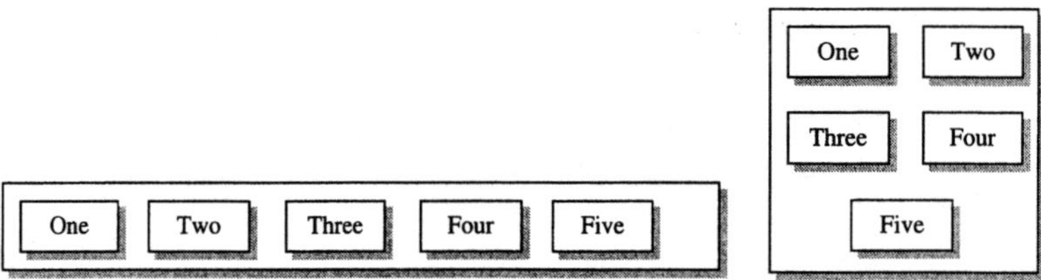

3. *Grid Layout.* A grid layout makes a bunch of components have equal size and arranges them in a rectangular grid. The adjacent diagram shows, for example, five components positioned on a three-by-two grid layout. Components are added to the cells of the layout, beginning at the top left-hand corner and moving right and down the page.

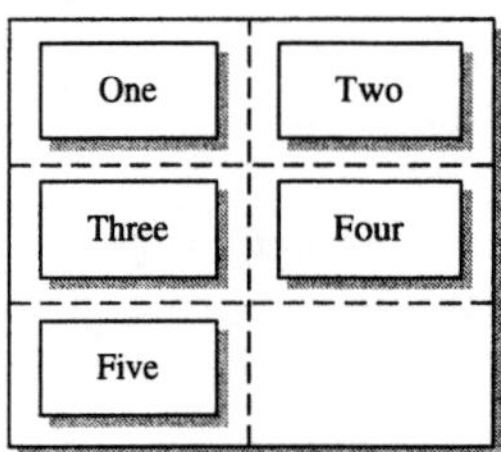

Border layout is the default manager for all `Window` objects, including `Frames` and `Dialogs`. Flow layout is the default manager for `Panel` objects. Unlike the border and flow layout schemes, components within a grid layout are sized to fit the container. The grid layout scheme is great for positioning panels but may give button components an awkward look and feel.

TABLE 19.8 Layout Manager Constructor Methods

Constructor Methods	*Description*
`FlowLayout()`	Create a new `FlowLayout` object
`BorderLayout()`	Create a new `BorderLayout` object
`GridLayout()`	Create a new `GridLayout` object

For each of these layout schemes, the details of implementation are handled by an object that acts as an interface between methods in the class `LayoutManager` and `Component` objects within a `Container`. Layout managers have constructor methods just like any other class. A summary of relevant methods is contained in Table 19.8. For example, the block of statements

```
BorderLayout border = new BorderLayout();
setLayout(border);
```

creates a `BorderLayout` object called `border`. `setLayout()` is a container method. The second statement informs a container that it should use the layout manager referenced by the variable `border`.

9.6 AWT I/O COMPONENTS

The AWT contains an ensemble of components for the I/O of information to/from a Java program. The component types include labels, buttons, choice boxes, lists, text fields, and text areas, and they should be positioned on a GUI using the layout managers described in Section 19.5. When a component object is created, it will appear on the screen having features appropriate to the environment in which the program is running.

9.6.1 Label

A `label` is an area where text can be displayed but cannot be edited. Label components are defined and manipulated by methods in the class `java.awt.Label`. A summary of `Label` methods is located in Table 19.9.

TABLE 19.9 Label Methods and Button Methods

Label Constructor Methods	*Meaning*
`public Label();`	Construct an empty label. No text is displayed.
`public Label( String s );`	Construct a label that displays the string `s`.
Button Constructor Methods	***Meaning***
`public Button();`	Construct an empty button.
`public Button( String s );`	Construct a labeled push button.
Label and Button Methods	***Meaning***
`void setText( String s )`	Set the text in the button/label to the contents of string `s`.
`public String setText()`	This method returns a string containing the string displayed on the button/label.

Example. Figure 19.7 is generated by inserting the fragment of code

```
setLayout(new GridLayout(2,1,10,10));

// Define a new label, text size and font.

Label myLabel = new Label( "This is label message 1");
Font  myFont  = new Font ( "Courier", Font.BOLD , 24 );
myLabel.setFont( myFont );

// Define a second label, then add message.

Label myLabel2 = new Label();
myLabel2.setText( "This is label message 2");

// Add labels to the frame.

add( myLabel  );
add( myLabel2 );
```

into the body of `TestFrame()` in Program 19.1. The statement

```
setLayout(new GridLayout(2,1,10,10));
```

defines a grid layout object containing two rows and one column. The third an fourth arguments to `GridLayout()` define the spacing between the rows an columns, in this case, 10 pixels.

The second block of code creates a new label object containing the string `"Thi is label message 1"` and sets the font to a bold Courier, size 24. The thi

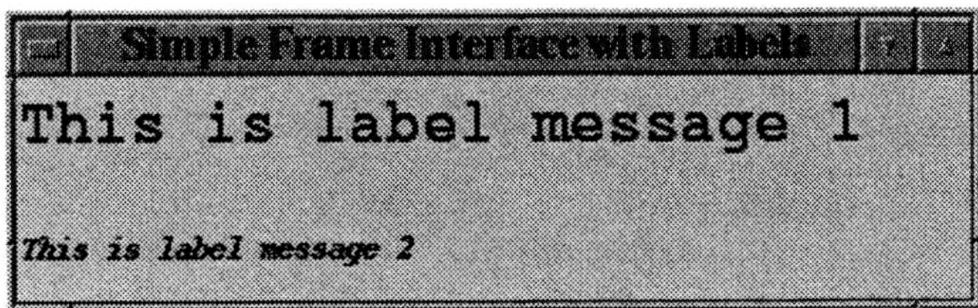

FIGURE 19.7 Simple GUI with labels.

block of code creates a second label message in the default font. Finally, the block of statements

```
add( myLabel  );
add( myLabel2 );
```

add the labels to the frame using the `GridLayout()` for the layout.

19.6.2 Button

A `button` is an area a user can click on to trigger an action. Button components are defined and manipulated by methods in the class `java.awt.Button`. A summary of `Button` methods is located in Table 19.9.

Example. Figure 19.8 is a simple GUI with six buttons obtained by inserting the script of code

```
// Define 3x2 grid for button layout.

setLayout(new GridLayout(2,3,10,10));

// Create an array of button reference variables.

Button buttons[] = new Button [6];

// Create buttons and add to the window frame.

for(int ii = 1; ii <= 6; ii++ ) {
    buttons[ii-1] = new Button ("Button" + ii);
    add( buttons[ii-1] );
}

setTitle("Simple Button Interface");    // Set Frame title.
setSize(400,120);                       // Size the Frame.
show();                                 // Display the Frame.
```

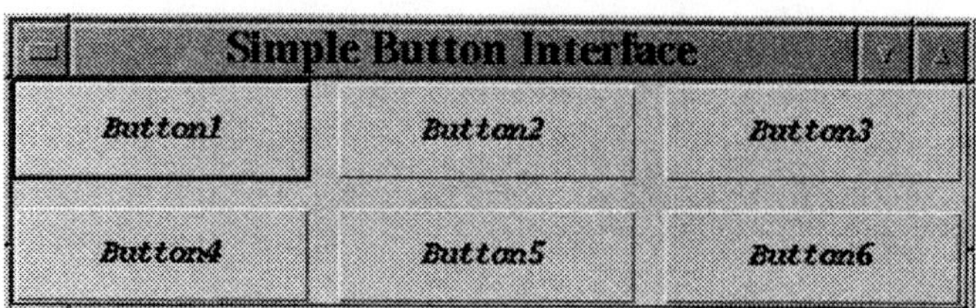

FIGURE 19.8 Simple GUI with buttons.

into `TestFrame()` in Program 19.1. We begin this example by defining a three-by-two grid layout having components spaced 10 pixels in both the vertical and horizontal directions. An array of six button reference variables is created with the statement

```
Button buttons[] = new Button [6];
```

The individual button objects are created and positioned on the three-by-two grid layout with the block of code

```
for(int ii = 1; ii <= 6; ii++ ) {
   buttons[ii-1] = new Button ("Button" + ii);
   add( buttons[ii-1] );
}
```

Unfortunately, the program corresponding to Figure 19.8 is rather useless because nothing happens when you click on the button. What is missing is the source code needed to handle button events. This topic is covered in Section 19.7.

19.6.3 Choice Boxes (Drop-Down Lists)

A choice box provides a list of items from which a selection can be made. Choice box components are ideal for representing situations where selections must be made among multiple alternatives and where the exhaustive representation of all alternatives on a computer screen would take up too much space.

Choice box components are defined and manipulated by methods in the class `java.awt.Choice`. A summary of choice box methods is located in Table 19.10.

Example. Figure 19.9 shows a stand-alone frame with a choice box containing the 10 items, `Alternative 1` through `Alternative 10`. Choice box components achieve economy of screen space by only displaying the item that has been selected from the list, in this case `Alternative 1`. To display all the choice box options on the computer screen, position the cursor over the choice box field, and press one of the mouse buttons. The complete list alternatives will drop down (hence the name drop-down list), and you can select among them. The choice box label will be updated to reflect the item that has been selected.

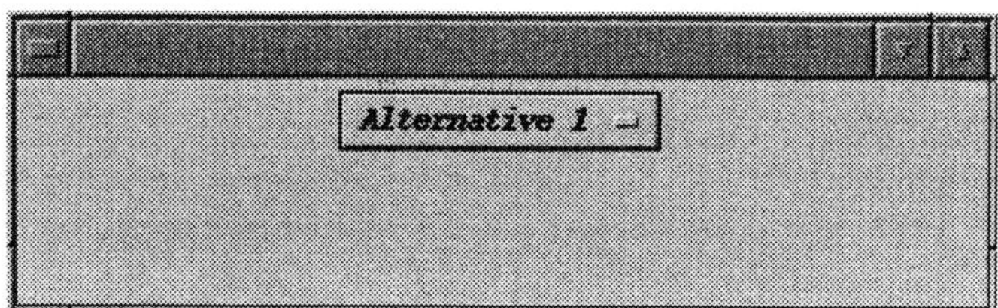

FIGURE 19.9 Simple GUI with choice buttons.

Like the previous examples in this section, Figure 19.9 has been generated by inserting the fragment of code

```
setLayout (new FlowLayout());

// Create choice buttons and add to frame

Choice choiceBox = new Choice ();

int iNoAlternatives = 10;
for(int ii = 1; ii <= iNoAlternatives; ii++ ) {
    choiceBox.addItem("Alternative " + ii);
}

add( choiceBox );

// Size and display the frame.

setTitle("Frame Interface with Choice Box");
setSize(400,120);
show();
```

into the body of method `TestFrame()` in Program 19.1. We use the `FlowLayout` component layout manager to position the choice box in the center of the frame. Recall that by default, `Frame` objects adopt a `BorderLayout` of components (see Section 19.5), and Java will position the choice box in the top left-hand corner of the frame.

A choice button is created in two steps. First, an empty choice box object is created by calling the `Choice` class constructor. Items are added to the choice box with the `addItem()` method. Hence, the block of code

```
Choice choiceBox = new Choice ();
for(int ii = 1; ii <= 6; ii++ ) {
    choiceBox.addItem("ChoiceButton" + ii);
}
```

systematically creates a choice box for items `Alternative 1` through `Alternative 10`.

TABLE 19.10 Choice Button and List Methods

Choice Box Methods	*Meaning*
`public Choice();`	Construct an empty choice button.
`public void addItem( String s )`	Add an item with string `s` to the choice box.
`public void insert ( String s; int iItemNo; )`	Insert an item with string `s` at position `iItemNo` (0 is the beginning).
`public void remove( int iItemNo )`	Remove item `iItemNo` from the choice box list.
List Methods	***Meaning***
`public List()`	Construct a list object that allows only one item to be selected.
`public List( int iItems; boolean bMs; )`	Construct a list object with `iItems` visible. Multiple items may be selected when `bMs` is true.
`public void addItem( String s )`	Add an item with string `s` to the list.
`public void remove( int iItemNo )`	Remove item `iItemNo` from the list.
Choice Box/List Methods	***Meaning***
`public String getSelectedItem()`	Return the string corresponding to the selected item.
`public String getSelectedIndex)`	Return the numerical position of the selected item.

19.6.4 Lists

A `list` is an area where a list of `String` items is displayed. When the number of list items exceeds the number of visible rows, scrollbars will automatically appear on the list component.

List components are defined and manipulated by methods in the class `java.awt.List`. A summary of `List` methods is located in Table 19.10. Because lists are created and manipulated in an almost identical step-by-step manner as choice boxes, we leave the development of a simple GUI containing a `list` component as an exercise for the reader.

19.6.5 Text Fields and Text Areas

Text field and text area components allow a user to supply textual input to a Java program. A text field component is a single-line area where textual input can be supplied from the keyboard and displayed. Text field objects are created from the class `TextField`. A text area component also provides for textual input from the keyboard but in this case over multiple lines. When the contents of a text area

TABLE 19.11 `TextComponent`, `TextField`, and `TextArea` Methods

TextComponent Methods	*Meaning*
`String getText()`	Return the text currently in the component.
`void setText( String s)`	Set the text to the contents of `s`.
`String getSelectedText()`	Return the selected text.
`void setEditable (boolean)`	Sets the ability to exit text in the component.
TextField Constructor Methods	***Meaning***
`public TextField();`	Construct a `TextField` object.

`public TextField(`
`String s,`
`int iNoColumns`
`)`
	Construct a `TextField` object having `inCol-umns` columns. Also display the string `s`.

TextArea Constructor Methods	***Meaning***
`public TextArea();`	Construct a `TextArea` object.

`public TextArea(`
`int iNoRows,`
`int iNoColumns`
`)`
	Construct a `TextField` object having `iNoCol-umns` columns. Also display the string `s`.

exceed the available text area space, horizontal and vertical scrollbars will be automatically added to the component. Text area components are created from the class `TextArea`.

Both the `TextField` and `TextArea` classes inherit many of their properties from the class `TextComponent` (see Figure 19.2). Although you cannot create an instance of `TextComponent` (it does not have a public constructor method), this class contains many of the methods defining the common functionality of `Text-Field` and `TextArea` classes. Table 19.11 summarizes the methods most relevant to this tutorial.

Example. Figure 19.10 is a four-by-two grid of label and text field component windows that prompts a user for his or her name, e-mail address, company,

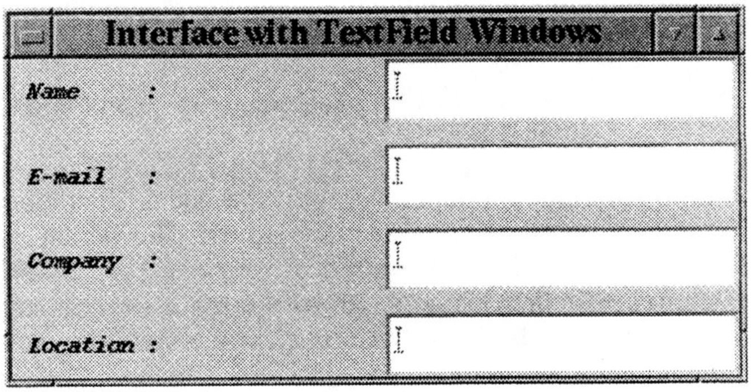

FIGURE 19.10 Simple GUI with labels and text fields.

and location. The essential details of this figure were created by the fragment of code

```
setTitle("Interface with TextField Windows");
setLayout(new GridLayout( 4, 2, 10, 10 ));

// Define four new labels.

Label myLabel1 = new Label( " Name     :" );
Label myLabel2 = new Label( " E-mail   :" );
Label myLabel3 = new Label( " Company  :" );
Label myLabel4 = new Label( " Location :" );

// Define four new text field windows

TextField myText1 = new TextField();
TextField myText2 = new TextField();
TextField myText3 = new TextField();
TextField myText4 = new TextField();

// Add labels and text fields to the frame.

add( myLabel1 ); add( myText1 );  // First row.
add( myLabel2 ); add( myText2 );  // Second row.
add( myLabel3 ); add( myText3 );  // Third row.
add( myLabel4 ); add( myText4 );  // Fourth row.
```

Because the label and text field components have been attached to a `GridLayout` component manager, their sizes will be automatically scaled to fill the available screen space.

Of course, facilities exist for creating text field components having a fixed number of columns and for initializing a text field with a string in the field. For example, the statement

```
TextField
myText4 = new TextField( "University of Maryland" , 30);
```

creates a new text field component `myText4`, which is 30 columns wide and contains the string `"University of Maryland"`. The actual width of the new text field component will be measured in terms of the character width of the font currently in use. When the length of the input stream exceeds the number of columns in the text field, the component will respond by simply scrolling the text.

The `getText()` method retrieves the contents of a text field. The contents of a text field can be changed at any time with the `setText()` method. Program 19.3 contains some examples of these methods in use.

19.6.6 Canvases

A `Canvas` is an AWT `Component` that provides a surface on which graphics and text can be drawn and mouse events can be received. `Canvas` objects by themselves do not contain features for drawing or event handling. Rather than simply create a `Canvas` object with statements of the type

```
Canvas c = new Canvas();
```

most Java programs subclass `Canvas` with a new method that overrides the `paint()` method with content that can be drawn on the canvas. When a canvas needs to be repainted, the `paint()` method in the `Canvas` subclass will ensure that its contents are redrawn correctly. Program 19.4 contains an example of this approach to program development.

19.6.7 Panels

A panel is an object contained inside a frame, another panel, or an applet (a subclass of panel) within a page in a web browser. However, unlike frame and applet objects, panel objects do not have an independent existence. You can also think of a panel as a canvas that contains other components.

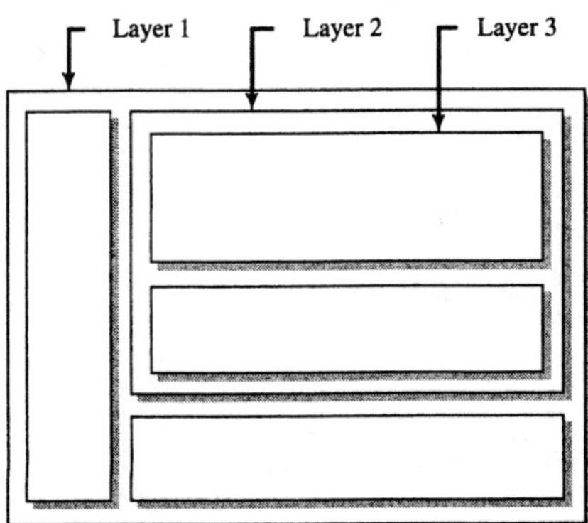

The above figure shows how panels can be nested inside one another and how a panel container can contain multiple components. In the following sections, we see how components can be added to panels and how the layout of these panels can be managed when a user resizes a window.

19.7 HANDLING AWT EVENTS

Whenever you click on a mouse, drag and drop or resize a window, or type on the keyboard, the operating system will generate an event. These events are passed to the Java run-time system for processing and response in an appropriate way.

One of the biggest differences between Java 1.0 and 1.1 is a new model for detecting and handling events. This section contains an introduction to the delegation event model contained in the JDK 1.1, released in 1997. This event model has an implementation that is both cleaner and more efficient than its predecessor.

19.7.1 Delegation Model of Event Handling

In the delegation event model, all the information associated with an event is stored in an event object. Event handling works roughly as follows

1. A listener object is an instance of a class that implements a special interface called a listener interface.
2. An event source is an object that can register listener objects and send them notifications when events occur. As we soon see, these notifications turn out to be methods of the listener interface.

The relationship between event sources and event listeners is depicted in Figure 19.11. Listener objects only register with event sources from which they are interested in receiving information. Otherwise, a listener object will not be bothered with information from event sources. More than one listener object can register with a single event source. It is conceivable, for example, that a number of listener objects might listen for actions fired by a button.

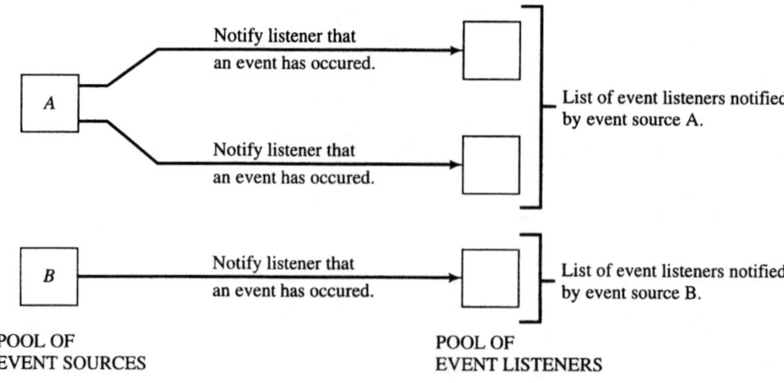

FIGURE 19.11 Model for event handling in Java 1.1.

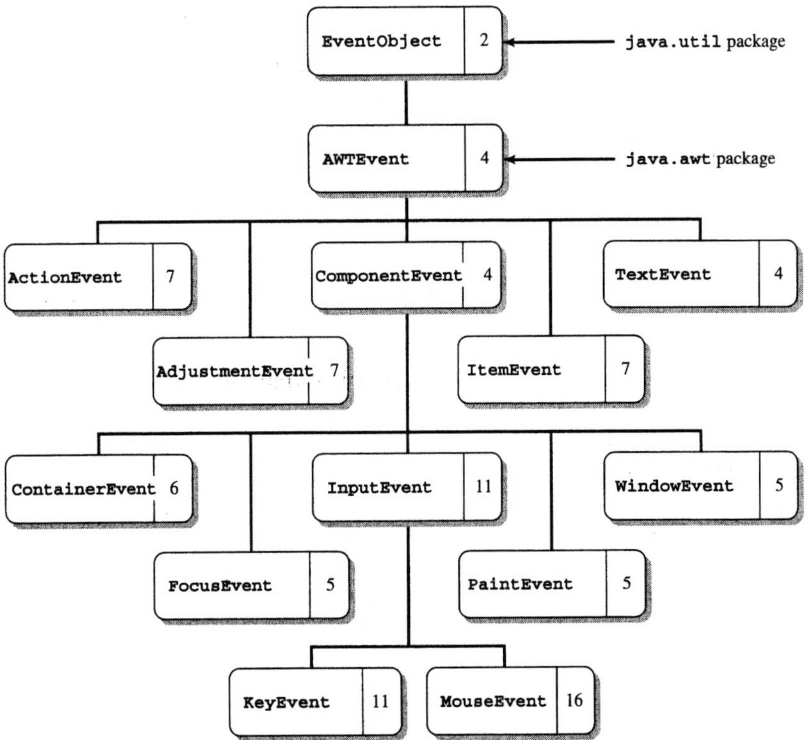

FIGURE 19.12 AWT event class hierarchy.

19.7.2 Event Class Hierarchy

Beginning with Java 1.1, events are organized into the class hierarchy shown in Figure 19.12. The root of the hierarchy is the class `java.util.EventObject` (part of the `java.util` package). The common superclass is not called `Event` because that name is already used in the Java 1.0 event model.

A variety of AWT events are handled by subclasses of `java.awt.AWTevent` (part of the `java.awt` package). Tables 19.12 and 19.13 summarize the event types generated by the AWT components and their corresponding listener registration methods. The listener methods available to each listener interface are summarized in Table 19.14.

From Table 19.12, we see that an `ActionEvent` will be generated by a button click or a double-click on a list box item, for example. `ActionEvents` employ the `ActionListener` interface, which in turn invokes the sole method `actionPerformed()`. This chain of activities among components is shown across the rows of Table 19.14.

For convenience of understanding, AWT events are partitioned into semantic and low-level event types, as indicated by the labels S and L in Tables 19.12 and 19.14. A semantic event corresponds to some form of high-level user input. Three examples are a click on a button, a double-click on a list, and pressing a return

TABLE 19.12 Events Associated with AWT Components

Component	*Events Generated*	*Semantic (S) Low-Level (L)*	*Description*
Button	ActionEvent	S	A user clicks on a button.
Choice	ItemEvent	S	A user selects or deselects an item.
Component	ComponentEvent	L	A component is moved, resized, hidden, or shown.
Container	ContainerEvent	L	A component is added or removed from a container.
List	ActionEvent	S	A user double-clicks on a list item.
	ItemEvent	S	A user selects/deselects an item.
TextComponent	TextEvent	S	A user changes text.
TextField	ActionEvent		A user finishes editing text.
Window	WindowEvent	L	A window is opened, closed, iconified, or deiconified.

key. The majority of AWT events are low level, however, and include the event types FocusEvent (i.e., a component either gains or loses focus), MouseEvent (i.e., the mouse is depressed, released, moved, or dragged), and KeyEvent (i.e., a key is either pressed or released). Semantic and low-level events are handled in exactly the same way by the Java run-time system.

TABLE 19.13 AWT Component Listener Registration Methods

AWT Class	*Listener Registration Method*
Button	void addActionListener (ActionListener);
Checkbox	void addItemListener (ItemListener);
Choice	void addItemListener (ItemListener);
Component	void addComponentListener (ComponentListener); void addFocusListener (FocusListener); void addKeyListener (KeyListener); void addMouseListener (MouseListener); void addMouseMotionListener (MouseMotionListener)
Container	addContainerListener (ContainerListener);
List	void addItemListener (ItemListener); void addActionListener (ActionListener);
MenuItem	void addActionListener (ActionListener);
TextField	void addTextListener (TextListener);
Window	void addWindowListener (WindowListener);

TABLE 19.14 Listener Interfaces and Methods

Event Class	*S/L*	*Listener Interface*	*Listener Methods*
ActionEvent	S	ActionListener	actionPerformed(ActionEvent e)
ComponentEvent	L	ComponentListener	componentHidden(ComponentEvent e) componentMoved(ComponentEvent e) componentResized(ComponentEvent e) componentShown(ComponentEvent e)
ContainerEvent	L	ContainerListener	containerAdded(ContainerEvent e) containerRemoved(ContainerEvent e)
FocusEvent	L	FocusListener	focusGrained (FocusEvent e) focusLost (FocusEvent e)
ItemEvent	S	ItemListener	itemStateChanged(ItemEvent e)
KeyEvent	L	KeyListener	keyPressed(KeyEvent e) keyReleased(KeyEvent e) keyTyped(KeyEvent e)
MouseEvent	L	MouseListener	mouseClicked(MouseEvent e) mouseEntered(MouseEvent e) mouseExited(MouseEvent e) mousePressed(MouseEvent e) mouseReleased(MouseEvent e)
		MouseMotionListener	mouseDragged(MouseEvent e) mouseMoved(MouseEvent e)
TextEvent	S	TextListener	textValueChanged(TextEvent e)
WindowEvent	L	WindowListener	windowActivated(WindowEvent e) windowClosed(WindowEvent e) windowDeactivated(WindowEvent e) windowDeiconified(WindowEvent e) windowIconified(WindowEvent e) windowOpened(WindowEvent e)

Of course, the `AWTEvent` class hierarchy contains a large number of methods for processing events. The small numbers shown on the right-hand side of each class box in Figure 19.12 indicate the number of methods available to the class. Some of these methods will be part of the class definition; the rest of these methods will be inherited.

A summary of the most commonly used methods (and all the event methods used in this tutorial) is shown in Table 19.15. Every event has a source object and a type value. The methods `getSource()` and `getID()` will retrieve the source object and type value, respectively. Event subclasses contain methods devoted to the collection of information relevant to the event type.

In the application programs that are presented at the end of this chapter, the method `getGraphics()` will be used to obtain a frame/applet graphics object. We also use the method `getKeyCode()` to detect release of the return key. Finally, the methods `getX()` and `getY()` return the *x*- and *y*-coordinates of a mouse event.

TABLE 19.15 Abbreviated List of Methods in the Event Class

Event Class	*Public Methods*	*Description*
`EventObject`	`Object getSource()`	Return the object emitted by the event.
	`String toString()`	Return string representing the object.
`AWTEvent`	`int getID()`	Return identification key for the event type.
	`paramString()`	Return the string representing the event parameters.
`ItemEvent`	`Object getItem()`	Return the object changed by the event.
`KeyEvent`	`int getKeyCode()`	Return code for the event.
	`char getKeyChar()`	Return character associated with the event.
`MouseEvent`	`int getX()`	Return *x* coordinate relative to the source object.
	`int getY()`	Return *y* coordinate relative to the source object.
`PaintEvent`	`Graphics getGraphics()`	Return `Graphics` object for the event.

19.7.3 Working with Event Listeners

An event source notifies an event listener object by invoking a method on it and passing it an event object, which is an instance of a subclass of `EventObject`. The syntax for registering a listener object with a source object is

```
eventSourceObject.addEventListener( eventListenerObject );
```

After a listener has been added to a component, methods appropriate to the listener interface will be called when events for which the listener has been registered are detected and fired by the component.

Computer Program. We now demonstrate the construction of event-handling procedures by creating the simple three-button GUI shown in Figure 19.13.

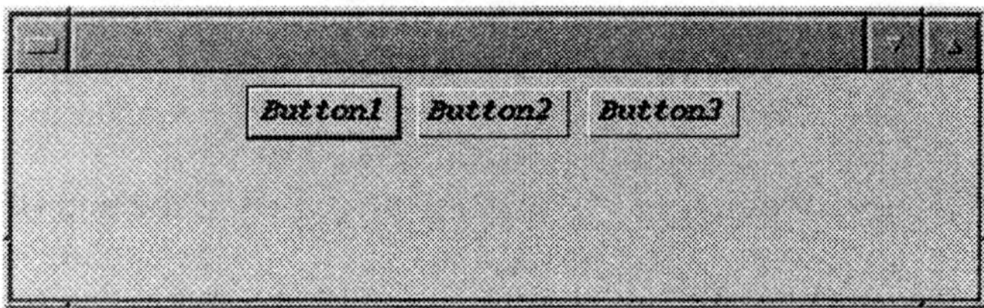

FIGURE 19.13 Simple interface with three buttons.

A listener will be registered with each of the buttons so that when a button is clicked, output corresponding to the title of the button will be printed.

```
Button1
Button2
Button3
Button2
```

Here is the program source code.

PROGRAM 19.2: DEMONSTRATE BUTTON LISTENERS

```
/*
 * ===================================================================
 * Simple GUI with three buttons connected to button listeners.
 *
 * Written By : Mark Austin                              November 1997
 * ===================================================================
 */

import java.awt.*;
import java.awt.event.*;

public class TestButton extends Frame {

    // Main method calls constructor to create instance of TestButton.

    public static void main( String args[] ) {
       TestButton t = new TestButton();
    }

    // Constructor for row of buttons.

    public TestButton() {

      // Create array of button reference variables.

      Button buttons[] = new Button [3];

      // Define flow layout manager.

      setLayout(new FlowLayout());

      // Create buttons and action and mouse listeners.

      buttons[0] = new Button ("Button" + 1);
      buttons[0].addMouseListener( new ButtonListener( buttons[0] ));
```

```
      buttons[1] = new Button ("Button" + 2);
      buttons[1].addActionListener( new ButtonAction( buttons[1] ));

      buttons[2] = new Button ("Button" + 3);
      buttons[2].addActionListener( new ActionListener() {
                public void actionPerformed( ActionEvent e ) {
                       System.out.println("Button3");
                }}
                );

      for(int ii = 1; ii <= 3; ii++ )
          add( buttons[ii-1] );

      setSize(400,120);       // Resize the Frame.
      show();                 // Display the Frame.
   }
}

/*
 * ==================================================================
 * This class listens for action events associated with the buttons.
 * ==================================================================
 */

class ButtonAction implements ActionListener {
      private Button b;

      public ButtonAction ( Button b ) {
         this.b = b;
      }

      public void actionPerformed ( ActionEvent e ) {
         String s = new String(e.getActionCommand());
         System.out.println(s);
     }
}

/*
 * ==================================================================
 * This class listens for mouse events associated with the buttons.
 * ==================================================================
 */

class ButtonListener implements MouseListener {
      private Button b;

      public ButtonListener( Button b ) {
         this.b = b;
      }
```

```
    public void mouseReleased ( MouseEvent e ) {
       String s = new String(b.getLabel());
       System.out.println(s);
    }

    public void mouseClicked ( MouseEvent e ) {};
    public void mouseEntered ( MouseEvent e ) {};
    public void mouseExited ( MouseEvent e ) {};
    public void mousePressed ( MouseEvent e ) {};
}
```

We begin our implementation by noting that a button is also an AWT component. It follows from Tables 19.12 and 19.13 that the event-handling routines can be implemented as either an `ActionListener` or a `MouseListener`. The corresponding listener methods that must be written are summarized in Table 19.14.

Program 19.2 exercises the Java 1.1 event-handling model by implementing the button listeners in three different ways.

Mouse Listener

The script of code

```
buttons[0] = new Button ("Button" + 1);
buttons[0].addMouseListener( new ButtonListener( buttons[0] ));
```

creates a button object having the label `"Button1"`. An object of type `ButtonListener` is then registered with the `buttons[0]` event source (i.e., the leftmost button). The source code for the `ButtonListener` class is located in the lower sections of Program 19.2.

The line of code

```
class ButtonListener implements MouseListener { .....
```

tells the Java compiler that the `ButtonListener` class implements the listener interface `MouseListener`. As mentioned in Chapter 18, an interface is like a stripped-down class that specifies a minimal set of methods that an instance of a class must handle before communication between two objects can occur. In addition to the class constructor method,

```
private Button b;

public ButtonListener( Button b ) {
   this.b = b;
}
```

which creates a new instance of `ButtonListener` with `Button b` as an event source, the `ButtonListener` class must contain implementations for all the `MouseListener` methods even though most of them do nothing (see Table 19.14). Only the `mouseReleased()` method contains user-defined code to retrieve and print the component label. The statement

```
String s = new String(b.getLabel());
```

creates a new string `s` having the label on button `b` (i.e., `"Button1"`).

Action Listener

The script of code

```
buttons[1] = new Button ("Button" + 2);
buttons[1].addActionListener( new ButtonAction( buttons[1] ));
```

creates a button object having the label `"Button2"`. The second statement uses the `addActionListener()` method to register an instance of `ButtonAction` with the `buttons[1]` event source (i.e., the center button). The source code details of class `ButtonAction` are simpler than `ButtonListener` because only one method, `actionPerformed()`, needs to be written. The statement

```
String s = new String(e.getActionCommand());
```

creates a new string `s`, containing the label on the component triggering the action event (i.e., in this case, `"Button2"`).

Action Listener Implemented as an Inner Class

Inner classes are defined inside another class and are a feature new to Java 1.1 They simplify the definition of small classes for local use.

The rightmost button is also implemented with an action listener but, in this case, details of the `actionPerformed()` are specified as an inner class. The script of code

```
buttons[2] = new Button ("Button" + 3);
buttons[2].addActionListener( new ActionListener() {
          public void actionPerformed( ActionEvent e ) {
                System.out.println("Button3");
          }}
          );
```

creates a button object having the label `"Button3"`. The second statement contains an unnamed instance of the inner class `ActionListener()`. `ActionListener()` has only one method, `actionPerformed()`, which simply prints `"Button3"` to the screen.

19.7.4 Adapter Classes

Table 19.14 shows that the event listener classes in Java 1.1 contain from one to seven event-handler methods. Since partial implementation of an interface is prohibited in Java, source code for all the event-handler methods must exist, even if most of the methods are empty (i.e., they do not do anything except ignore events of the corresponding type). As a convenience to programmers, the Java 1.1 AWT provides an adapter class containing default implementations for each listener interface that contains more than one method. For example, the `MouseAdapter` class

```
public class MouseAdapter implements MouseListener {
     public void mouseClicked( MouseEvent e ) { ; }
     public void mouseEntered( MouseEvent e ) { ; }
     public void mouseExited( MouseEvent e )  { ; }
     public void mousePressed( MouseEvent e ) { ; }
     public void mouseReleased( MouseEvent e ) { ; }
}
```

contains empty implementation of the five event-handling methods associated with the `MouseListener`. With this class hierarchy in place, a program can do its work by subclassing the `Adapter` class and overriding the event methods that must be handled.

Example. The following script of code

```
class ButtonListener extends MouseAdapter {
      private Button b;

      public ButtonListener( Button b ) {
         this.b = b;
      }

      public void mouseReleased ( MouseEvent e ) {
         String s = new String(b.getLabel());
         System.out.println(s);
      }
}
```

is a revised implementation of the class `ButtonListener` from Program 19.2. Now that `ButtonListener` extends `MouseAdapter`, with the latter containing empty implementations for all the methods associated with `MouseListener`, we only need to override `mouseReleased()`.

Figure 19.14 is a schematic of the revised program architecture employing the `MouseAdapter` classes, as well as the `ButtonAction` listener and the `ActionListener` inner class.

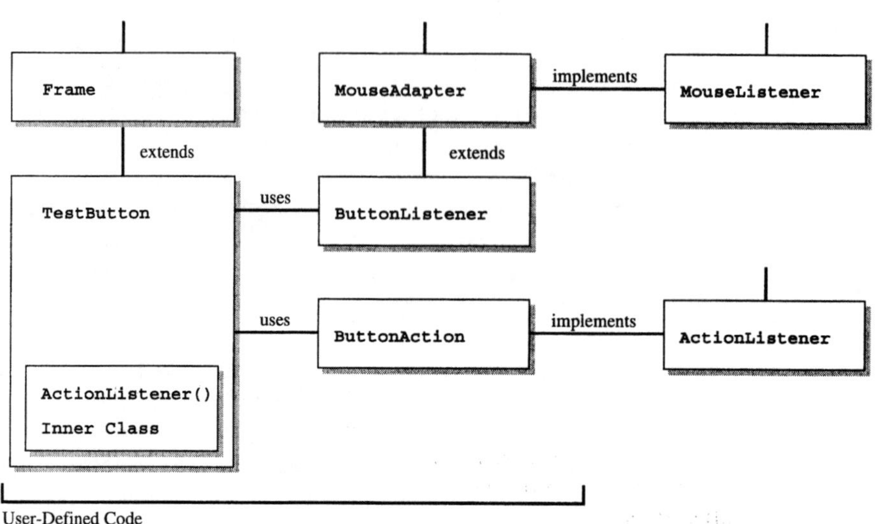

FIGURE 19.14 *Using adapter classes.*

19.8 ENGINEERING APPLICATIONS

This section demonstrates the development of GUIs and Java 1.1 event-handlin procedures by working step by step through the design and implementation of thre small engineering applications. They are

1. A stand-alone program for Fahrenheit to Celsius temperature conversion. Thi program is the graphical counterpart of Problem 3.2 in the C tutorial.
2. A stand-alone program for computing and plotting the displacement versu time for an undamped single degree of freedom (SDOF) system. This progra is similar to Program 13.4 in the MATLAB tutorial.
3. A simple drawing program implemented as an applet. The C and MATLA tutorials do not contain functionally equivalent programs.

19.8.1 Temperature Conversion Program

Problem Statement

The relationship between temperature measured in Fahrenheit (T_f) and temperatur Celsius (T_c) is given by the equation

$$T_f = \frac{9}{5} T_c + 32 \qquad (19.$$

In this example, we develop a graphically based Java program that prompts use for the temperature in either Fahrenheit (T_f) or Celsius (T_c), and then comput and displays the appropriate conversion.

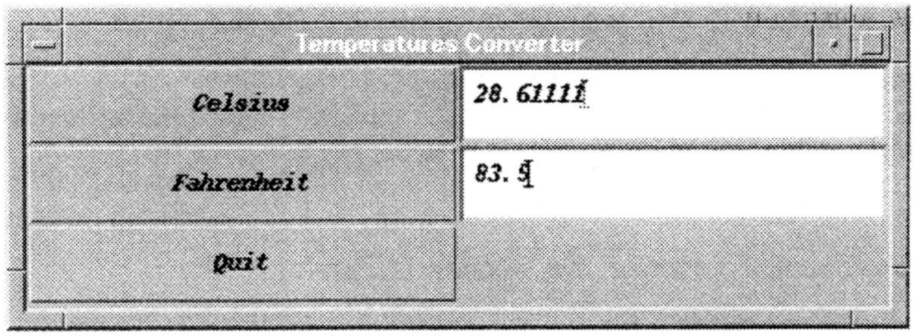

FIGURE 19.15 Interactive temperature conversion program.

Figure 19.15 is a snapshot of the interactive temperature conversion program. It shows a scenario where 83.5 degrees Fahrenheit is converted to 28.61 degrees Celsius. Fahrenheit-to-Celsius temperature conversion (or vice versa) is computed by moving the cursor to the appropriate text field and typing the temperature as input. The temperature conversion is computed and printed immediately after the return key has been pressed. A user simply clicks the `Quit` button to terminate the program execution.

Program Source Code

Here is the program source code.

PROGRAM 19.3: TEMPERATURE CONVERSION PROGRAM

```
/*
 * ==========================================================================
 * Celsius.java : Graphical version of Celsius to Fahrenheit
 *                conversion program.
 *
 * Written By : David Chancogne                              September 1997
 * ==========================================================================
 */

mport java.lang.Math;
mport java.util.*;
mport java.io.*;
mport java.awt.*;
mport java.awt.event.*;

lass TempConversion extends Frame {
extField    CelText;
extField FahrenText;
utton     CelButton;
utton  FahrenButton;
utton    QuitButton;
```

```
    // The main method just creates an instance of the class

    public static void main( String args[] ) {
       System.out.println("Celsius to Fahrenheit Converter Program");
       TempConversion p = new TempConversion();

    }

    // The constructor creates the window.

    public TempConversion() {

         setTitle("Temperatures Converter");

         CelButton    = new Button("Celsius");

         FahrenButton = new Button("Fahrenheit");
         QuitButton   = new Button("Quit");

         CelText    = new TextField(7);
         FahrenText = new TextField(7);

         // Create 3x2 grid of buttons and text fields.

         setLayout(new GridLayout(3,2));

         add(CelButton);      add(CelText);
         add(FahrenButton);   add(FahrenText);
         add(QuitButton);

         // Add listeners for the various components.

         QuitButton.addMouseListener( new QuitListener());
         CelText.addKeyListener(
                 new CelListener(CelText, FahrenText) );
         FahrenText.addKeyListener(
                 new FahrenListener(CelText, FahrenText) );

         // Set the window size and display it.

         setSize(450,150);
         show();

   }

   // The temperature conversion methods.

   public static float CelsiusToFahrenheit( float fCel ) {
       return (float)(9.0/5.0 * fCel + 32.0);
   }

   public static float FahrenheitToCelsius( float fFahrn ) {
       return (float)(5.0/9.0 * (fFahrn - 32.0) );
   }
}
```

```
/*
 * ================================================================
 * QuitListener -- this class extends the MouseAdapter class
 *                 and is attached to the "Quit" button.
 * ================================================================
 */

class QuitListener extends MouseAdapter {
    public void mouseReleased(MouseEvent e) {
       System.out.println("Thank you !");
       System.exit(0);
    }
}

/*
 * ================================================================
 * CelListener and FahrenListener -- these classes extend KeyAdapter
 * and are listening for input from the TextFields.
 * ================================================================
 */

class CelListener extends KeyAdapter {
    TextField CelText;
    TextField FahrenText;

    public CelListener( TextField c, TextField f ) {
        CelText    = c;
        FahrenText = f;
    }

    public void keyReleased(KeyEvent e) {

        // Keyboard event is release of the 'return' key

        if ( e.getKeyCode() == KeyEvent.VK_ENTER ) {
             float fTemp = 0 ; // The methods are 'static' so we can call
                               // them without an instance
             try {
                 fTemp = TempConversion.CelsiusToFahrenheit(
                         Float.valueOf(CelText.getText()).floatValue()
                     );
             } catch (Exception ex) {
                 System.out.println("Malformated number !");
             }

             FahrenText.setText(Float.toString( fTemp ));
        }

    }
```

```
class FahrenListener extends KeyAdapter {
    TextField CelText;
    TextField FahrenText;

    public FahrenListener( TextField c, TextField f ) {
        CelText    = c;
        FahrenText = f;
    }

    public void keyReleased(KeyEvent e) {

        // Keyboard event is release of the 'return' key

        if ( e.getKeyCode() == KeyEvent.VK_ENTER ) {
            float fTemp = 0;    // The methods are 'static' so we can call
                                // them without an instance
            try {
                fTemp = TempConversion.FahrenheitToCelsius(
                        Float.valueOf(FahrenText.getText()).floatValue()
                    );
            } catch (Exception ex) {
                System.out.println("Malformated number !");
            }

            CelText.setText(Float.toString( fTemp ));
        }
    }
}
```

Compiling and Running Program 19.3

The source code to Program 19.3 is contained in a file `TempConversion.java`. The list of program files before and after compilation is

Files before Compilation	*Files after Compilation*
TempConversion.java	TempConversion.java
	TempConversion.class
	QuitListener.class
	CelListener.class
	FahrenListener.class

The temperature conversion program is run by simply typing

```
>> java TempConversion
```

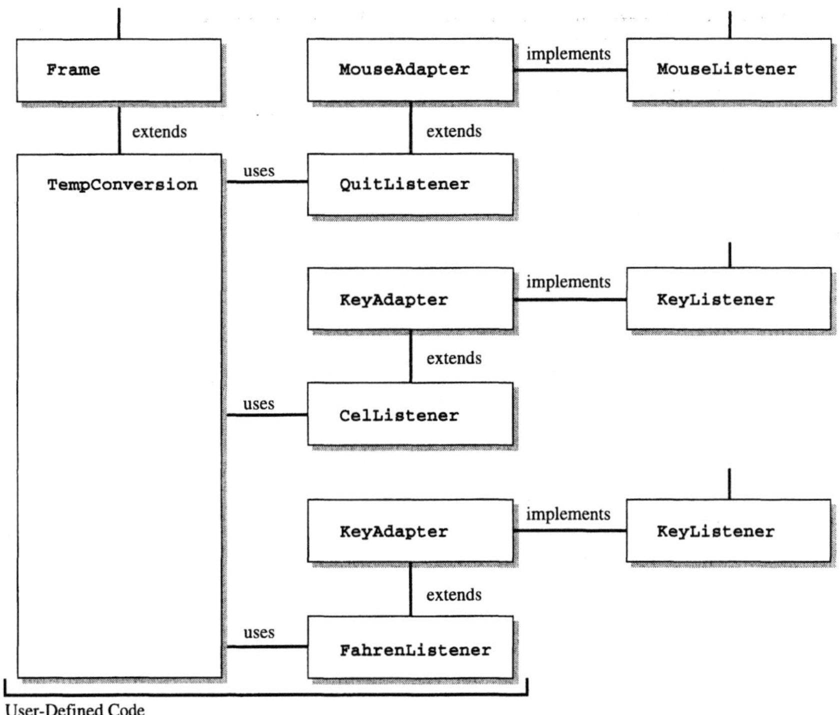

FIGURE 19.16 Architecture of classes in Program 19.3.

We execute the Java run-time system with `TempConversion` as an argument because the bytecode file `TempConversion.class` contains the method `main()`.

Program Architecture

Figure 19.16 is a schematic of the architecture of classes in Program 19.3. The program source code contains four classes—`TempConversion`, `QuitListener`, `CelListener`, and `FahrenListener`.

The heart of the GUI implementation is contained within the class `TempConversion` (details given as follows). By making `TempConversion` a subclass of `Frame`, our program automatically inherits all the window management functionality provided by `Frame`, `Window`, and their superclasses.

`TempConversion` contains four methods of its own. The method `main()` simply prints a one-line welcome message to the screen and then calls the constructor method `TempConversion()`. `TempConversion()` creates the button and text field components and attaches them to a grid layout. It also registers mouse and key listeners (details given as follows) with the `"Quit"` button and text field components. Finally, two methods

```
public static float CelsiusToFahrenheit( float fCel ) {
    return (float)(9.0/5.0 * fCel + 32.0);
}
```

```
public static float FahrenheitToCelsius( float fFahrn ) {
    return (float)(5.0/9.0 * (fFahrn - 32.0) );
}
```

are defined for the Celsius-to-Fahrenheit and Fahrenheit-to-Celsius conversio These methods are called by the listener objects registered with the text field comp nents.

Graphical User Interface Design

The GUI for Program 19.3 consists of a single stand-alone window partition into a grid of three rows and two columns. Buttons having the labels `Celsiu` `Fahrenheit`, and `Quit` are attached to cells in the first column of the grid. Tw text fields, `CelText` and `FahrenText`, are created and attached to cells in t second column of the window layout.

Recall that components within a `GridLayout` are sized to fit the contain Hence, when the graphics window in Figure 19.15 is resized, the button and te field component sizes will be adjusted to fill the new window dimensions in s equally sized subregions.

Event-Handling Procedures

Program 19.3 has three event-handling classes: `QuitListener`, `CelListener`, a `FahrenListener`. The line of code

```
QuitButton.addMouseListener( new QuitListener() );
```

tells the `QuitButton` object that an instance of the class `QuitListener` is inte ested in receiving information on mouse events. The `QuitListener` class exten `MouseAdapter` and ignores all mouse events except for when a mouse button released. In such cases, the message `Thank you !` is printed to the screen, a then the program execution is terminated. Similarly, the lines

```
CelText.addKeyListener(
        new CelListener(CelText, FahrenText) );
FahrenText.addKeyListener(
        new FahrenListener(CelText, FahrenText) );
```

tell the `CelText` and `FahrenText` text field objects that the listener objects `Cel Listener` and `FahrenListener` are interested in receiving information on ke board events. The opening sections of `CelListener` and `FahrenListener`

```
class FahrenListener extends KeyAdapter {
    TextField CelText;
    TextField FahrenText;
```

```
        public FahrenListener( TextField c, TextField f ) {
            CelText    = c;
            FahrenText = f;
        }
```

contain constructor methods that pass to the listener objects, references to the Celsius and Fahrenheit text field components. These references are subsequently used to retrieve input from the text field and to print the results of the temperature conversion in the appropriate text field box. Both listener methods employ the branching hierarchy

```
    public void keyReleased(KeyEvent e) {
        if ( e.getKeyCode() == KeyEvent.VK_ENTER ) {

             .... details of the source code removed ....
        }
    }
```

to first detect the release of a key and, more precisely, to then detect the release of the "return" key. The latter is accomplished with `KeyEvent.VK_ENTER`.

Temperature Conversion Calculations

Program 19.3 naively assumes that a user will always provide temperature input in a floating point format. Typing errors will occur, of course, and provision needs to be made for the detection of imperfect input. The try-catch block of code

```
float fTemp = 0;      // The methods are 'static' so we can call
                      // them without an instance
try {
  fTemp = TempConversion.FahrenheitToCelsius(
          Float.valueOf( FahrenText.getText() ).floatValue()
      );
} catch (Exception ex) {
  System.out.println("Malformated number !");
}
```

takes the text referred to by `FahrenText.getText()` and attempts to convert it to a floating point number, suitable as input to the method `FahrenheitToCelsius()`. The catch part of this construct will be executed when an exception occurs, perhaps because the text to floating point number conversion could not be completed. The statement

```
    CelText.setText( Float.toString( fTemp ) );
```

takes the result of the temperature conversion, stored as a floating point variable `fTemp`, converts it to a string, and then calls the `setText()` method associated with `CelText` to display the results as text in the Celsius text field component.

19.8.2 Free Vibration Response of Undamped SDOF System

Problem Statement

The free vibration response of an undamped SDOF oscillator, $y(t)$, is given by

$$y(t) = y(0)\cos(wt) + \frac{\dot{y}(0)}{w}\sin(wt) \tag{19.2}$$

where t is time (seconds), m and k and the mass and stiffness of the system, respectively. By definition, $w = \sqrt{(k/m)}$, is the circular natural frequency of the system. The natural period of the system $T = 2\pi/w$.

In this example, we develop a graphical interface for plotting the time-history displacement for the system defined by mass, $m = 1$, and stiffness, $k = 10$, for $t = 0$ seconds through $t = 10$ seconds. If the initial displacement and velocity are $y(0) = 10$ and $\dot{y}(0) = 10$, respectively, the ensuing motion will have an amplitude slightly larger than 20 with a natural period $T = 1.98$ seconds.

Figure 19.17 is a screendump of the graphical interface displaying the SDOF system response. The `Draw Graph` button scales and displays Equation 19.2 on the inner drawing area, adds a red border to the plot, and writes Equation 19.2 as a

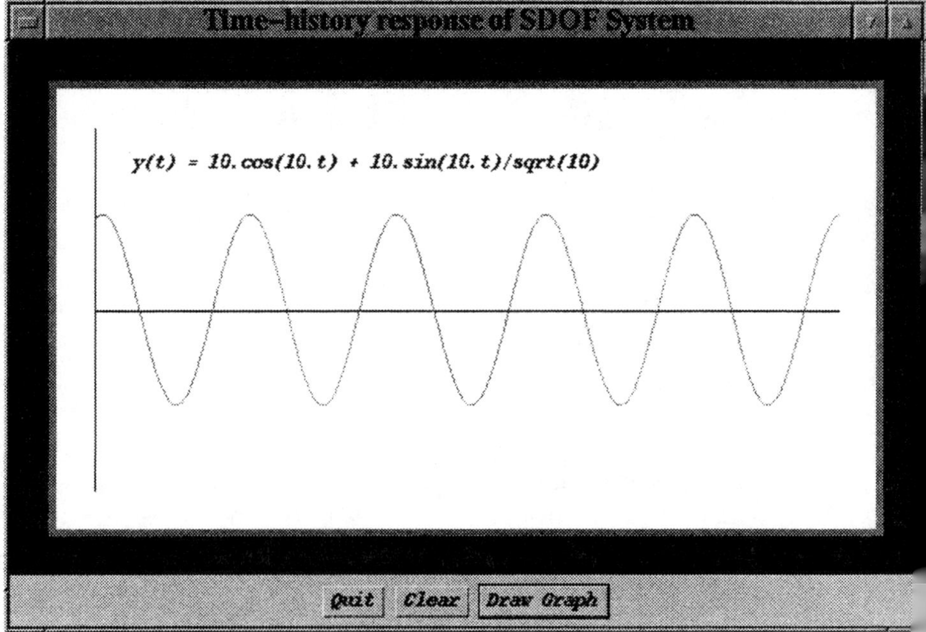

FIGURE 19.17 Graphical interface for SDOF system.

text string on the canvas. The `Clear` button erases the plot and red border, leaving a thick black perimeter and a white drawing area. Finally, the `Quit` button terminates the program execution.

Source Code

Here is the program source code.

PROGRAM 19.4: FREE VIBRATION RESPONSE OF UNDAMPED SDOF SYSTEM

```
/*
 * ===========================================================================
 * This program creates a frame with a panel and canvas, and draws a simple
 * sinusoidal graph on the canvas.
 *
 * Written By : Mark Austin                                    November 1997
 * ===========================================================================
 */

import java.awt.*;
import java.awt.event.*;

public class TestGraph extends Frame {

   // The main method creates an instance of the class.

   public static void main( String args[] ) {
      TestGraph t = new TestGraph();
   }

   // Define window frame.

   public TestGraph() {
      setLayout (new BorderLayout());
      GraphicsScreen gs = new GraphicsScreen();

      // Create lower panel and buttons.

      Panel p1 = new Panel();

      Button b1 = new Button("Quit");
      b1.addMouseListener(new ControlPanelListener(b1, gs ));
      p1.add( b1 );
```

```
        Button b2 = new Button("Clear");
        b2.addMouseListener(new ControlPanelListener(b2, gs ));
        p1.add( b2 );

        Button b3 = new Button("Draw Graph");
        b3.addMouseListener(new ControlPanelListener(b3, gs ));
        p1.add( b3 );

        // Position canvas and panel within the frame.

        add("Center", gs );
        add("South",  p1 );

        // Set frame title and size. Display the frame.

        setTitle("Time-history response of SDOF System");
        setSize(600,400);
        show();
    }
}

class GraphicsScreen extends Canvas {
    private Dimension size;
    private Graphics    gs;

    public void paint ( Graphics g ) {
        size = getSize();
        clear();
    }

    public void clear () {
        int iBorder = 25;

        // Get graphics and fill in background ....

        gs = getGraphics();
        gs.setColor( Color.black);
        gs.fillRect(  0, 0, size.width-1,       size.height-1 );

        // Draw center patch ....

        gs.setColor( Color.white);
        gs.fillRect( iBorder, iBorder, size.width-2*iBorder,
          size.height-2*iBorder );
    }
```

```
public void gsDraw () {
    int iBorder1 = 25;
    int iBorder2 = 30;
    int iScaleX  = 10; //  Maximum value of x coordinate.
    int iScaleY  = 40; //  Range of y-coordinate values.
    int iMinX    = iBorder2 + iBorder1;
    int iMinY    = iBorder2 + iBorder1;
    int iMaxX    = size.width  - iBorder2 - iBorder1;
    int iMaxY    = size.height - iBorder2 - iBorder1;
    int iDeltaX  = iMaxX-iMinX;
    int iDeltaY  = iMaxY-iMinY;

    // Get graphics and draw graph background ....

    gs = getGraphics();
    gs.setColor( Color.red );
    gs.fillRect( iBorder1, iBorder1,
                 size.width-2*iBorder1, size.height-2*iBorder1 );
    gs.setColor( Color.white );
    gs.fillRect( iBorder2, iBorder2,
                 size.width-2*iBorder2, size.height-2*iBorder2 );

    // Draw axis in black

    gs.setColor(Color.black);
    gs.drawLine( iMinX, iMinY+iDeltaY/2, iMaxX, iMinY+iDeltaY/2 );
    gs.drawLine( iMinX, iMinY, iMinX, iMaxY);

    gs.setColor(Color.red); // Change color to red for plotting

    // Calculate the original point in pixel system

    double dYorg   = FunctionToPlot(0);
    int iPrevXpt   = iMinX;
    int iPrevYpt   = (int) ((iMinY  + (iDeltaY)/2 - (iDeltaY)*dYorg/
                     iScaleY));

    // Plot function by looping over x values : problem coordinates are
    // converted to pixel coordinates for plotting.

    for (int iXpt = iMinX ; iXpt < iMaxX + 1 ; iXpt++ ) {
         double dX = (double) ((iXpt - iMinX)*((double) iScaleX/
                      (double) iDeltaX));
         double dY = FunctionToPlot( dX );
         int  iYpt = (int) (iMinY + (iDeltaY)/2 - (iDeltaY)*dY/
                      iScaleY);
```

```
                gs.drawLine( iPrevXpt, iPrevYpt, iXpt, iYpt);
                iPrevXpt = iXpt;
                iPrevYpt = iYpt;
            }

            // Print title for plot....

            gs.setColor(Color.black); // Print title of plot in black.
            gs.drawString("y(t) = 10.cos(10.t) + 10.sin(10.t)/sqrt(10)",
                          iMinX + iBorder1, iMinY + iBorder1);
        }

        // The function to plot

        public double FunctionToPlot( double dX ) {
        double dXint = 10.0;
        double dVint = 10;
        double dW    = Math.sqrt(10.0);

           return (double)( dXint*Math.cos(dW*dX) + dVint*Math.sin(dW*dX)/dW );
        }
}

class ControlPanelListener extends MouseAdapter {
        private Button button;
        private GraphicsScreen graphics;

        public ControlPanelListener( Button b, GraphicsScreen gs ) {
            graphics = gs;
            button   = b;
        }

        public void mouseReleased(MouseEvent e) {
            String s = new String(button.getLabel());

            if( s.compareTo("Quit") == 0 ) {
                System.out.println("Quit");
                System.exit(0);
            }
            if( s.compareTo("Clear") == 0 ) {
                graphics.clear();
            }
            if( s.compareTo("Draw Graph") == 0 ) {
                graphics.gsDraw();
            }
        }
}
```

Compiling and Running Program 19.4

The source code to Program 19.4 is contained in a file `TextGraph.java`. The list of program files before and after compilation is

Files before Compilation	*Files after Compilation*
`TestGraph.java`	`TestGraph.java`
	`TestGraph.class`
	`GraphicsScreen.class`
	`ControlPanelListener.class`

This program is run by simply typing

```
>> java TestGraph
```

We execute the Java run-time system with `TestGraph` as an argument because the bytecode file `TextGraph.class` contains the method `main()`.

Program Architecture

Figure 19.18 is a schematic of the architecture of classes in Program 19.4. The program source code contains three classes—`TestGraph`, `GraphicsScreen`, and `ControlPanelListener`. Most of the details of the GUI (details given as follows) are specified within the `TestGraph` and `GraphicsScreen` classes. By extending `Frame` to create `TestGraph`, this application automatically inherits all the window management methods it will need. Similarly, the methods needed to draw on a

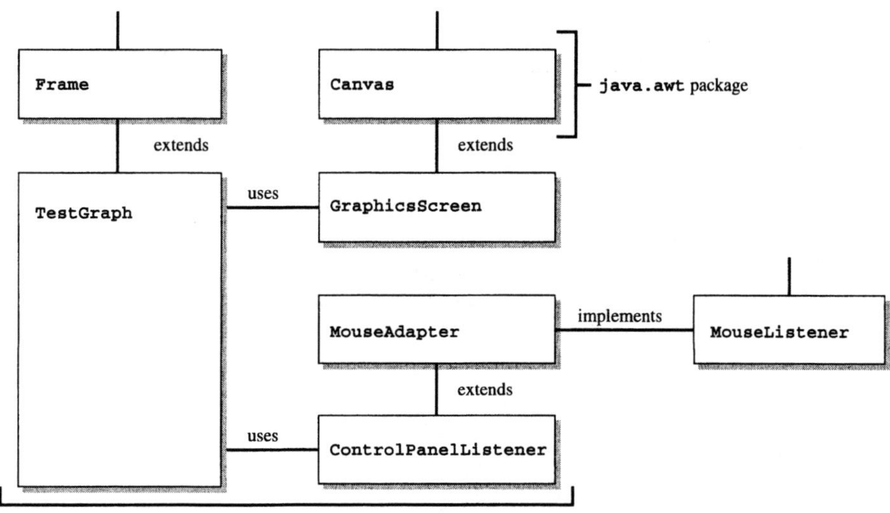

FIGURE 19.18 Architecture of classes in Program 19.4.

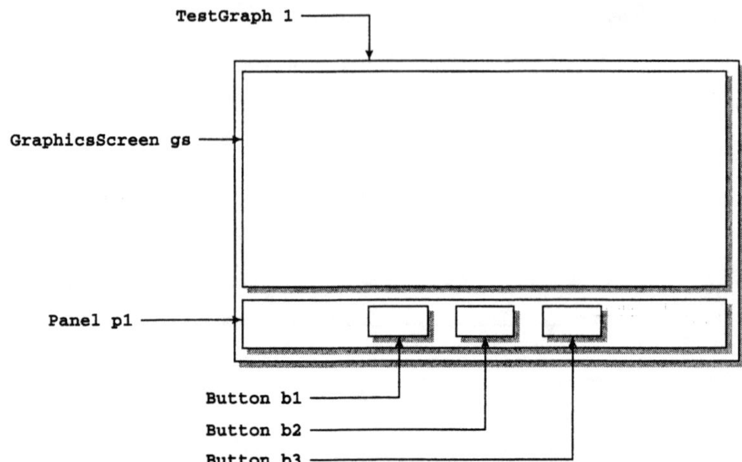

FIGURE 19.19 Schematic of GUI design for Program 19.4.

component and receive and handle events are made available to the program by subclassing `Canvas` to create `GraphicsScreen`.

Graphical User Interface Design

The GUI is composed of a frame, a canvas for plotting $y(t)$ versus t, and a pane along the lower frame border containing three control buttons. Because the frame and panel objects both subclass `Container` (see Figure 19.2), they can each have their own layout manager for the positioning of components. Keeping this poin in mind, and using the terminology presented in the program source code, Figure 19.19 shows the layout of panels, canvas, and button components inside the `TestGraph` frame. A border layout window manager is used to position `Panel p1` an `GraphicsScreen gs` inside the `TestGraph` frame. We then adopt a flow layou window manager (the default manager for panels) to center the three buttons o `Panel p1`.

All the drawing operations are handled by methods belonging to the cla `GraphicsScreen`. A high-level view of the methods is as follows:

```
class GraphicsScreen extends Canvas {
    private Dimension size;
    private Graphics    gs;

    public void paint ( Graphics g ) {
        .... Obtain size of canvas and then clear it.
    }

    public void clear () {
        .... Clear canvas and draw background patch removed
    }
```

```
        public void gsDraw () {
           .... Scale and plot the function and write title.
        }

        public double FunctionToPlot( double dX ) {
           .... Source code for function to plot.
        }
    }
```

The parameter `size` stores the `GraphicsScreen` window dimensions in pixels. This information is needed to properly map equation coordinates onto the screen pixel coordinates. The parameter `gs` stores the `Graphics` object associated with the canvas object.

The `paint()` method is automatically invoked when the `GraphicsScreen` component needs to be drawn for this first time or redrawn because the application frame has been moved or resized. After updating the parameter `size`, `paint()` calls `clear()` to fill in the background in black and then draw a white center patch. The parameter setting

```
int iBorder = 25;
```

defines a black border width of 25 pixels. The `gsDraw()` method creates a thick red border around the white drawing area, and then computes and draws the plot axes and SDOF response function.

Plotting the Function

Perhaps the most complicated part of the function plotting procedure is the mathematics needed to map Equation 19.2 onto the appropriate pixel coordinates. The parameters settings

```
public void gsDraw () {
     int iBorder1 = 25;
     int iBorder2 = 30;
     int iScaleX  = 10; //  Maximum value of x coordinate.
     int iScaleY  = 40; //  Range of y-coordinate values.
     int iMinX    = iBorder2 + iBorder1;
     int iMinY    = iBorder2 + iBorder1;
     int iMaxX    = size.width  - iBorder2 - iBorder1;
     int iMaxY    = size.height - iBorder2 - iBorder1;
     int iDeltaX  = iMaxX-iMinX;
     int iDeltaY  = iMaxY-iMinY;

     ...... details of code removed ......
```

define a black border of width 25 pixels and a red perimeter 5 pixels wide (i
`iBorder2 - iBorder1 = 5` pixels). The parameters `iScaleX` and `iScaleY`
fine the range of function values in the horizontal and vertical directions. F
example, `iScaleX = 10` because the function will be evaluated from $t = 0$ to t
10 seconds. The parameters `iMinX` through ... `iMaxY` define the minimum a
maximum pixel coordinates within which the function/axes will be displayed. `iDeltaX` and `iDeltaY` store the number of pixels in the horizontal and vertical directic
over which the function/axes will be displayed.

The looping construct

```
for (int iXpt = iMinX ; iXpt < iMaxX + 1 ; iXpt++ ) {
     double dX = (double) ((iXpt - iMinX)*((double) iScaleX/
                          (double) iDeltaX));
     double dY = FunctionToPlot( dX );
     int  iYpt = (int) (iMinY + (iDeltaY)/2 - (iDeltaY)*dY/iScaleY);

     gs.drawLine( iPrevXpt, iPrevYpt, iXpt, iYpt);
     iPrevXpt = iXpt;
     iPrevYpt = iYpt;
}
```

walks pixel by pixel along the horizontal axis and evaluates and scales the functi
value to the appropriate pixel value in the vertical direction. We then can draw
line between the previous and current point.

Notice that no provision is made to plot the function true to scale. We simp
expand the horizontal and vertical axes to fill the available drawing space.

Event-Handling Procedures

In a departure from Program 19.3, which uses separate listener classes for ea
text field and button, Program 19.4 handles "button clicks" with three instances
the same listener class. The script of code

```
String s = new String(button.getLabel());

if( s.compareTo("Quit") == 0 ) {
    System.out.println("Quit");
    System.exit(0);
}
```

```
if( s.compareTo("Clear") == 0 ) {
    graphics.clear();
}
if( s.compareTo("Draw Graph") == 0 ) {
    graphics.gsDraw();
}
```

contains the essential details of class `ControlPanelListener`. The first statement creates a string `s` containing the label of the button event source. The program control is then directed to the appropriate method in `GraphicsScreen` based on the outcome of the logical expressions. For example, `s.compareTo("Clear") == 0` evaluates to true when the button label is `"Clear"`. Communication between the listener class object and the `GraphicsScreen` object is possible because the methods `clear()` and `gsDraw()` have a `public` declaration.

19.8.3 Simple "Draw" Applet Application

Problem Statement

Our final application in this tutorial is a program that lets a user scribble on an applet. Figure 19.20 is a screendump of the draw applet running under Sun's appletviewer. Of course, the same applet can also be run as an interactive application within a web page. Lines are scribbled on the drawing area by moving the cursor to the appropriate starting point, and then moving the mouse with a button pressed. Drawing will finish when the mouse button is released. The "Clear" button erases the drawing board.

FIGURE 19.20 Screendump of draw applet.

Program Source Code

Here is the program source code.

PROGRAM 19.5: SIMPLE "DRAW" APPLET

```
/*
 * ===========================================================================
 * File : SimpleDraw.java -- This applet lets you draw with the mouse.
 *
 * Written By : David Chancogne                                 September 1997
 * ===========================================================================
 */

import java.applet.*;
import java.awt.*;
import java.awt.event.*;

public class SimpleDraw extends Applet {

      int last_x;                   // Last position of the mouse.
      int last_y;                   // Last position of the mouse.
      private Button clearButton; // This is the "Clear" Button.

      public void init() {

          // Set the background color.

          this.setBackground(Color.white);

          // Create the add 'Clear' button to applet.

          clearButton = new Button("Clear");
          this.add(clearButton);

          // Add the 3 mouse listeners

          clearButton.addMouseListener(new ClearButtonListener(this));
          this.addMouseListener(new MousePressedListener(this));
          this.addMouseMotionListener(new MouseDraggedListener(this));

      } // End of method init
}         // End of class SimpleDraw

class MousePressedListener extends MouseAdapter {
```

```
    SimpleDraw applet; // The calling applet

    public MousePressedListener(SimpleDraw a) {
        applet= a;
    }

    public void mousePressed(MouseEvent e) {

        applet.last_x = e.getX();
        applet.last_y = e.getY();

    } // End of method mousePressed
}     // End of class MousePressedListener

class MouseDraggedListener extends MouseMotionAdapter {

    SimpleDraw applet; // The calling applet

    public MouseDraggedListener(SimpleDraw a) {
        applet =a;
    }

    public void mouseDragged(MouseEvent e) {

        // Call the applet drawing method
        Graphics g = applet.getGraphics();
        g.drawLine(applet.last_x, applet.last_y, e.getX(), e.getY());
        applet.last_x = e.getX();
        applet.last_y = e.getY();

    } // End of method mouseDragged
      // End of class MouseDraggedListener

lass ClearButtonListener extends MouseAdapter {

    SimpleDraw applet; // The calling applet

    public ClearButtonListener(SimpleDraw a) {
        applet = a;
    } // End of constructor method

    public void mouseReleased(MouseEvent e) {

        // Get the graphic context
        Graphics g = applet.getGraphics();
```

```
        // Draw a rectangle with the same color as the background

        g.setColor(applet.getBackground());
        Dimension r = applet.getSize();
        g.fillRect(0, 0, r.width, r.height);

    } // End of method mouseReleased
}     // End of class ClearButtonListener
```

Compiling and Running Program 19.5

The source code to Program 19.5 is contained in a file `SimpleDraw.java`. The list of program files before and after compilation is

Files before Compilation	*Files after Compilation*
SimpleDraw.html	SimpleDraw.html
SimpleDraw.java	SimpleDraw.java
	SimpleDraw.class
	ClearButtonListener.class
	MousePressedListener.class
	MouseDraggedListener.class

The specifications for running the applet program are conveyed to a Java-enabled browser (or viewer) using the applet tag inside an HTML document. The script of code

```
<!-- File SimpleDraw.html -->
<html>
<head> <title> Simple Draw </title> </head>
<body>

<applet code="SimpleDraw.class" width=300 height=200>
</applet>

</body>
</html>
```

is a minimal HTML document, `SimpleDraw.html`, that instructs a web browser to fetch the executable applet `SimpleDraw.class` and display it on a web page as a rectangular region 300 pixels wide and 200 pixels high.

The applet program is run by simply typing

```
>> appletviewer SimpleDraw.html
```

When the `SimpleDraw.html` file is loaded into a web browser the title of the page will be `Simple Draw`.

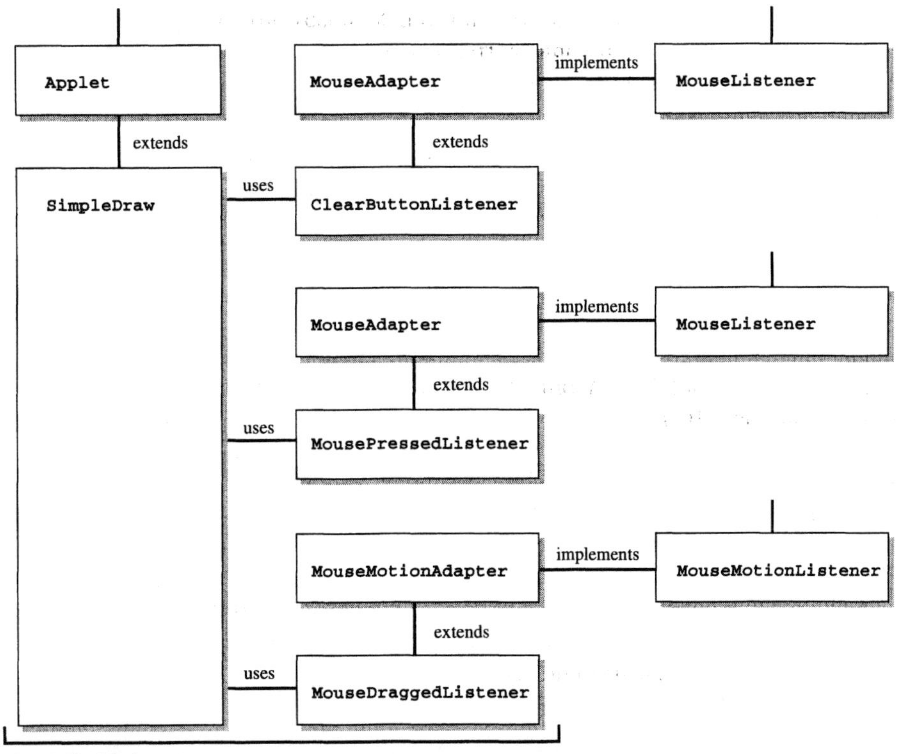

FIGURE 19.21 Architecture of Program 19.5.

Program Architecture

Figure 19.21 is a schematic of the architecture of classes in Program 19.5. The program source code contains four classes, `SimpleDraw`, `ClearButtonListener`, `MousePressedListener`, and `MouseMotionListener`. The first class establishes the general layout of components in the applet and their connectivity to the required event-handling listeners. Instances of the listener classes (details given as follows) will be executed in response to appropriate button and mouse events.

Because the executable bytecode file `SimpleDraw.class` is expected to operate inside a web browser (or appletviewer) environment, the `SimpleDraw` class is created as an extension of `java.applet.Applet`. From Figure 19.2, we recall that that `Applet` is an extension `Panel`, which is an extension of `Container`. Since all container objects come with a manager for laying out components, it follows that `SimpleDraw` will automatically inherit these capabilities. In this particular case, a flow layout manager—the default layout manager for components on `Panel` objects—positions the button on the applet.

Applet Procedures

Applet programs operate within the context of a browser/viewer environment and the AWT. After an applet bytecode file has been downloaded over the Internet to a local machine, a Java-enabled browser will automatically create an instance of the applet class and then invoke the `init()` method to initialize/build the applet's interface. You should observe that this approach to program initialization is a significant departure from stand-alone Programs 19.3 and 19.4, where constructor methods were used to initialize the details of a GUI.

The statements

```
this.setBackground(Color.white);
clearButton = new Button("Clear");
this.add(clearButton);
```

set the applet background color to white. A `"Clear"` button is then created and added to the applet.

Event-Handling Procedures

Program 19.5 is the first program in this tutorial that demands event handling beyond clicking a button or entering information into a text field component. The block of code

```
    clearButton.addMouseListener(new ClearButtonListener(this)).
    this.addMouseListener(new MousePressedListener(this));
    this.addMouseMotionListener(new MouseDraggedListener(this))
```

registers an instance of the class `ClearButtonListener` with the `clearButto` component, and instances of `MousePressedListener` and `MouseDraggedListener` with `this` (i.e., the applet component event source).

The `ClearButtonListener` class has the same relationship to `MouseAdapte` and `MouseListener` as in Program 19.3. All mouse events that occur over th `"Clear"` button will be ignored except for a mouse button being released. In suc cases, the `mouseReleased()` method will get the graphics object for the applet

```
    Graphics g = applet.getGraphics();
```

and then draw a rectangle with the same color as the background

```
    g.setColor(applet.getBackground());
    Dimension r = applet.getSize();
    g.fillRect(0, 0, r.width, r.height);
```

The `MousePressedListener` and `MouseDraggedListener` classes conta the code to handle the scribbling activities. Both classes have constructor metho that pass a reference to the `SimpleDraw` applet to an instance of the listener cla For example, the fragment of code

```
class MousePressedListener extends MouseAdapter {

    SimpleDraw applet; // The calling applet

    public MousePressedListener(SimpleDraw a) {
        applet = a;
    }

...... source code removed .....
```

stores a reference to the calling applet in `applet`. An instance of `MousePressedListener` is called by the browser when the user clicks on the applet with the mouse. Similarly, the `MousePressedListener` listener object is called by the browser when the user moves the mouse with the button down.

The JDK 1.1 generates mouse events for all mouse clicks on a multibutton mouse. The event methods are the same, irrespective of which button is clicked. An essential part of making the scribbling applet work is keeping track of the x and y pixel coordinates over which the cursor has passed. In the fragment of code

```
public void mousePressed (MouseEvent e) {

    applet.last_x = e.getX();
    applet.last_y = e.getY();

    ...... source code removed ......
```

the expressions `e.getX()` and `e.getY()` retrieve the x and y pixel coordinates measured relative to the applet object at which the mouse event occurred. The results are assigned to the SimpleDraw applet variables `last_x` and `last_y`.

FURTHER INFORMATION

For a well-written explanation of the complete AWT class hierarchy, we recommend that you see *Java in a Nutshell* [10].

REVIEW QUESTIONS

1. What are the four main steps you should work through to create and implement a GUI?
2. What is an AWT peer class? Do Java programmers access the peer classes?
3. What is the purpose of an AWT container? How is a container different from a component?
4. How are the classes `Panel`, `Applet`, `Window`, and `Frame` related to the class `Container`?
5. What is the relationship between the classes `TextComponent` and `TextField`?

6. What is the difference between the `Window` and `Frame` classes?
7. Briefly describe the advantages and disadvantages of the FlowLayout, BorderLayout, and GridLayout managers. Are these window managers implemented as objects?
8. What is the relationship between the classes `Applet` and `Container`?
9. Create a diagram showing the architecture of classes in Program 19.2 before the adapter classes are added to the source code.
10. How does the graphics coordinate system work in Java?
11. List some of the principles to which a well-implemented `paint()` method should adhere.
12. What does the script of code

```
private Button b;
String s = new String(b.getLabel());
```

do?
13. In the Java 1.1 event-handling model, what is the relationship between an event source and an event listener? How are these relationships established?
14. Why can a button listener method be implemented as either a `mouseListener` or an `actionListener`?

19.9 PROGRAMMING EXERCISES

Problem 19.1 (Beginner): Add "Print" and "Clear" buttons to Program 18.2. Hint: See Programs 19.4 and 19.5 for the appropriate source code.

Problem 19.2 (Beginner): Reimplement Program 19.3 as an applet. Hint: You should remove the `Quit` button from the applet implementation.

Problem 19.3 (Beginner): Reimplement Program 19.4 as an applet. Hint: You should remove the `Quit` button from the applet implementation.

Problem 19.4 (Intermediate): Redesign Program 19.5 so that the `Clear` button does not cover the drawing area. One possibility is to partition the GUI into two panels as shown in Figure 19.22.

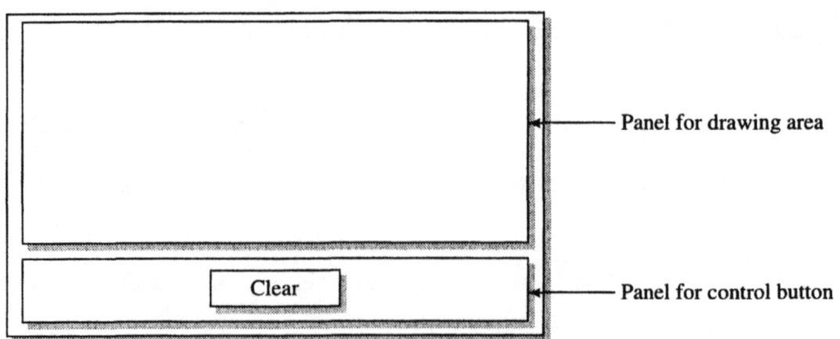

FIGURE 19.22 Schematic of modified draw interface.

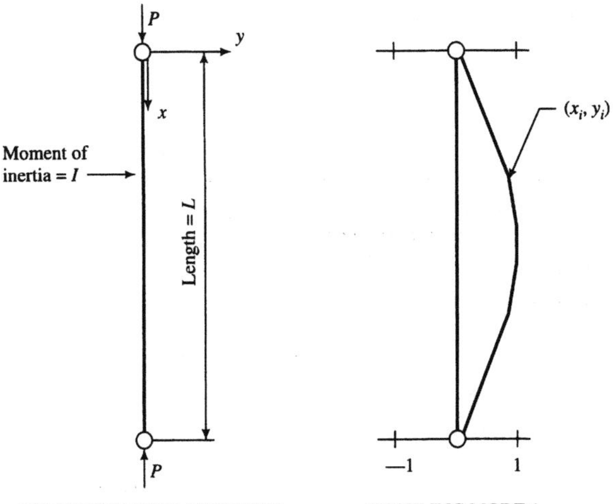

FIGURE 19.23 Elastic buckling of pin-ended column.

Problem 19.5 (Intermediate): Modify the scaling algorithm in Program 19.4 so that the horizontal and vertical axes are plotted true to scale. The shape of your plot should remain invariant to adjustments in the shape (i.e., width/height ratio) of the program window.

Problem 19.6 (Intermediate): Figure 19.23 shows a pin-ended column acted on by a central axial compressive force *P*. The column has length *L*, modulus of elasticity *E*, and constant moment of inertia *I* along its length. The theoretical buckling load is given by solutions to

$$EI \cdot \frac{d^2x}{d^2y} + P.y = 0 \tag{19.3}$$

with boundary conditions $y(0) = y(L) = 0$. Solutions to Equation 19.3 are well known and can be found in most undergraduate texts on structural mechanics. Therefore, we simply state the results here. The deformed column will be in static equilibrium and satisfy the boundary conditions, when

$$P_n = \frac{n^2\pi^2EI}{L^2} \quad \text{for } n = 1, 2, 3, \cdots \tag{19.4}$$

The mode shape $Y_n(x)$ corresponding to critical load P_n is

$$Y_n(x) = A.\sin\left(\frac{n\pi x}{L}\right) \tag{19.5}$$

Develop an applet program that will allow a user to enter *E*, *I*, and *L* in text field boxes, and then compute the lowest elastic buckling load via Equation 19.4.

Applet Viewer: ElasticRod.class
Applet
Enter Modulus of Elasticity (E) | 1000.0
Enter column inertia (I) | 20.5
Enter column length (L) | 150.0
Elastic Buckling Load | 8.992306
Applet started.

FIGURE 19.24 GUI for buckling of elastic rod computation.

Figure 19.24 shows, for example, one possible layout of components. With the parameter settings, $n = 1$, $E = 1{,}000$, $I = 20.5$, and $L = 150.0$

$$P_1 = \frac{\pi^2 EI}{L^2} = \frac{\pi^2 \cdot 1{,}000 \cdot 20.5}{150^2} \approx 8.99 \qquad (19.6)$$

Of course, your graphical interface could also include a text field entry for n.

Problem 19.7 (Intermediate): Write an applet program that will allow a user to interactively manipulate a square into any valid three- or four-sided polygon by dragging and dropping its vertex points to change the polygon's shape. Before a new vertex position is accepted, the program should check that a new polygon configuration does not have any intersecting edges. Polygon configurations that fail this test should be rejected. After a vertex has been successfully repositioned, the area of the polygon, internal angle measurements, and vertex coordinates should be calculated and displayed. The polygon area and coordinate calculations should be based on the pixel coordinate system measured within the drawing space area.

Figure 19.25 shows one possibility for the GUI. The GUI can be assembled by first defining a "results area" panel that is attached to the "East" border and a second "drawing space area" that fills the remainder of the applet region. A grid layout manager should be used to position the results output.

Problem 19.8 (Intermediate): Suppose that you have been asked to investigate the states of stress acting on a small thin-plate material element surrounding a point P. In its horizontal orientation (see Figure 19.26), the material element is acted on by two components of normal stress, σ_x and σ_y, and a shear stress, τ_{xy}. For engineering design purposes, we want to determine the planar orientations at which the maximum and minimum normal (and shear) stresses occur at P and, of course, their values.

This problem can be solved using a Mohr's circle representation for the state of plane stress acting on the element. Because the detailed derivation of Mohr's circle representation can be found in almost any undergraduate text on structur

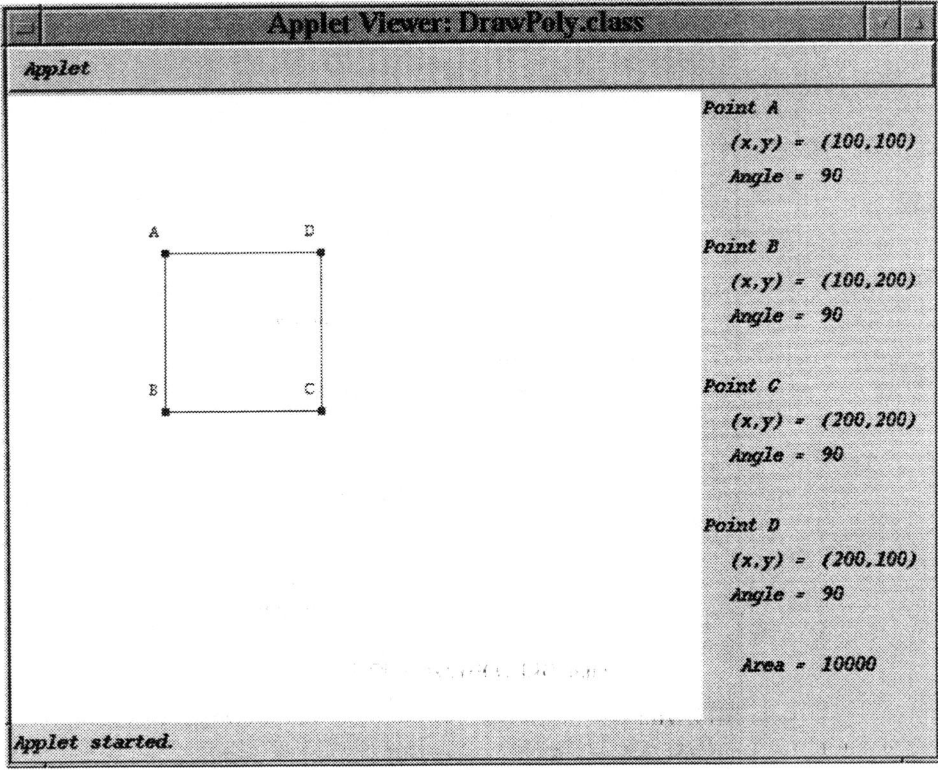

FIGURE 19.25 GUI for interactive quadralateral.

analysis/mechanics, we simply state the results. The center of Mohr's circle is positioned at

$$(\overline{\sigma}, \overline{\tau}) = \left[\frac{(\sigma_x + \sigma_y)}{2}, 0\right] \tag{19.7}$$

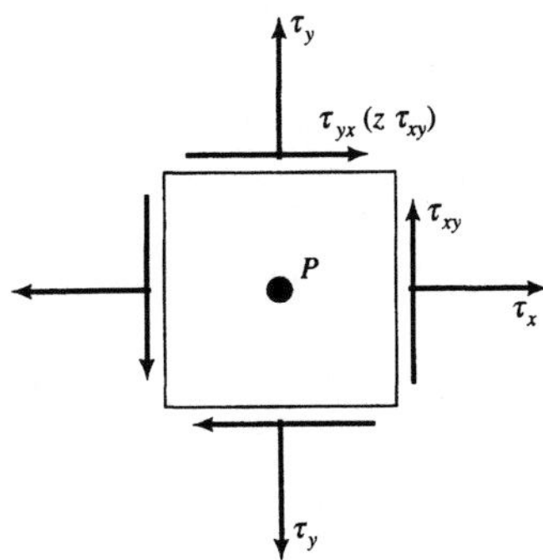

FIGURE 19.26 Plane stress element.

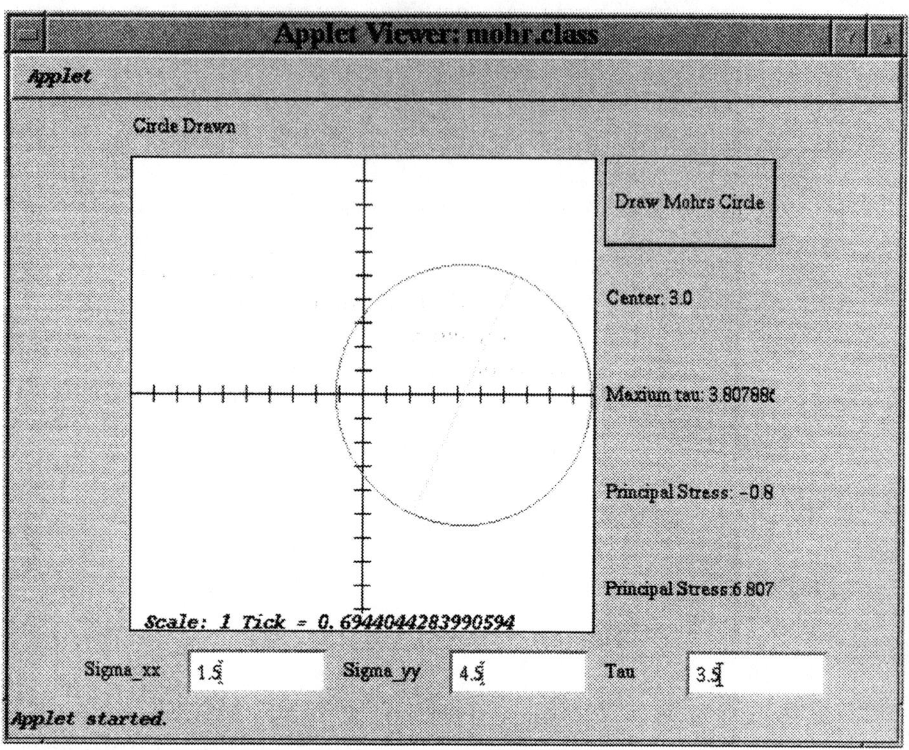

FIGURE 19.27 Mohr's circle GUI.

with radius

$$r = \sqrt{\left(\frac{\sigma_x - \sigma_y}{2}\right)^2 + \tau_{xy}^2} \quad (19.8$$

The drawing area of Figure 19.27 shows, for example, Mohr's circle correspondin to a state of plane stress given by $\sigma_x = 1.5$, $\sigma_y = 4.5$, and $\tau_{xy} = 3.5$. The norm stresses σ are plotted along the horizontal axis, with tensile stresses plotted positive to the right of the origin and compressive stresses plotted to the left of the origi Shear stresses are plotted along the vertical axis, with shear stresses that apply clockwise moment to the stressed element plotted positively above the origin.

Write an applet program that will prompt the user for the σ and τ stresses, a then calculate and display the maximum shear stress and principal stresses. Moh circle should then be drawn.

Rather than deal with the complexities of adjusting the figure axes to fit t details of a particular Mohr's circle, we suggest that you simply fix the axes a the tick marks, and adjust the interpretation of the interval represented by ea tick distance. See, for example, Figure 19.27.

Problem 19.9 (Intermediate): There are many problems in engineering whe we need to know if a point lies inside or outside of a polygon.

With this point noted, extend the functionality of Problem 19.8 so that the cursor position is tracked in real time. The extended program should display the polygon perimeter while the cursor lies outside of the polygon (and no mouse buttons are pressed) and fill the polygon with a dark color when the cursor lies inside the polygon.

The interesting part of this problem lies in determining when the cursor lies inside/outside of the polygon. One approach is to implement your own algorithm for testing if a point lies inside a polygon. Various algorithms for accomplishing this task can be found in undergraduate texts on computer science. A simpler approach is to implement the polygon as an array of points that are added to an instance of the class `Polygon`. In Java 1.1, `Polygon` has a method `contains()`, which will return `true` when a point is inside a polygon and `false` otherwise. For more information on `contains()`, see Table 19.5.

APPENDIX

1

INTRODUCTION TO UNIX

This appendix contains an introduction to the UNIX operating system. Many of the concepts that make UNIX work, such as the file system hierarchy, also apply to Windows 95 and 98™. For detailed information on the latter, we simply refer you to the appropriate operating system manuals.

DIRECTORY STRUCTURE AND FILE HANDLING

When you are beginning to learn how a new operating system works, understanding how the file system operates is the most important, and potentially confusing, first step.

File storage structures are a key component of any modern operating system because they allow users to put files and directories into well-organized groups—similar to file folders in a file cabinet. UNIX has what is called a *hierarchical file structure,* which means that the files and directories can be arranged in the form of a tree with the *root* at the base of the system (although it is normally drawn at the top of a diagram because we read from top to bottom on a printed page). You can also think of it as an inverted tree. The actual structure of the file system is then determined as you build (i.e., name and create) subdirectories in which to store files.

The root (or base) of the file system is indicated by a slash. UNIX uses a forward slash / as a type of shorthand to refer to the root. From the root, the file system grows downward, with subdirectories used to group similar files. Each

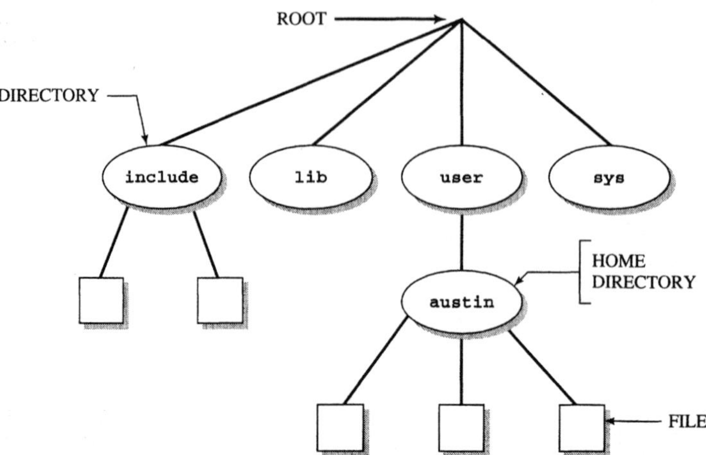

FIGURE A1.1 UNIX file system hierarchy.

subdirectory can also include other subdirectories as needed. The UNIX root / i Figure A1.1 has subdirectories `include`, `lib`, `users`, `sys`, and so forth. These ar the first and most general groupings for files in this example. Under the root, th `users` directory has other subdirectories (e.g., `austin`, `doc ....`), which can hav other subdirectories.

The `home directory` in Figure A1.1 is the location within the directory tre where a user (`austin` in this case) will be positioned when he or she first logs i The `home directory` is where you can customize "your part" of the file syste to your individual needs. You can add subdirectories and files under your logi directory, as needed, using the steps outlined in the next section. Because ther may be many users on a UNIX system, file security is important. File security mear that most users' access to certain parts of the file system will be controlled.

OPERATING SYSTEM COMMANDS

The users of an operating system communicate with the computer by typing co mands on the "command line" adjacent to the operating system prompt. In tl section, we indicate the prompt by

```
prompt >>
```

You may be surprised to learn that many of the operating system commands y are now using, or are about to use, are actually C programs. The basic comman

TABLE A1.1 Commonly Used UNIX Commands

Command	*Description*
`date`	Print current time.
`mkdir`	Make a new directory under the current, sometimes called working, directory.
`rmdir`	Remove a directory.
`ls`	Print a list of files and subdirectories.
`rm`	Remove, or delete, files.
`pwd`	Print working directory.

of interest to us are listed in Table A1.1, and we demonstrate their use by building a simple file system in UNIX.

Assembling a Simple UNIX File System

We now use the commands in Table A1.1 to construct a section of a UNIX file system. For the purposes of discussion, suppose that you have several files that you want to store on a computer's hard drive. You might naively store all the files in the same place—in a single directory (e.g., your home directory). This approach will be satisfactory if you are planning to store only a handful of files in your account. In most practical situations, however, users have hundreds of files in their accounts. If every time you list the files in the home directory, all the file names appear in one huge listing, then it is hard to wade through and understand the file information. The task of understanding the contents of your files can be vastly simplified if they are "collected" into distinct groups called subdirectories.

The three types of operations that must be supported with both files and directories are (1) create/delete/arrange, (2) edit/move/copy, and (3) list the files and directories. Users must be provided with the capability to apply these operations at any point in the file hierarchy.

For purposes of illustration, we put all our computer programs in a single directory called `programs`, and further separate computer programs into those written in `C` and those written in `MATLAB`. The hierarchy of directories is shown in Figure A1.2. The procedure for creating and naming these three directories is

```
prompt >> mkdir programs
prompt >> cd    programs
prompt >> mkdir C
prompt >> mkdir MATLAB
```

The command `mkdir` creates the new directory with the specified name, and `cd` moves the current working directory from `austin` down to `austin/programs`. It is important to note that file and directory names are case sensitive; hence, the directory name `C` is different from the lowercase `c`.

The logical extension of this hierarchy is to create separate directories for

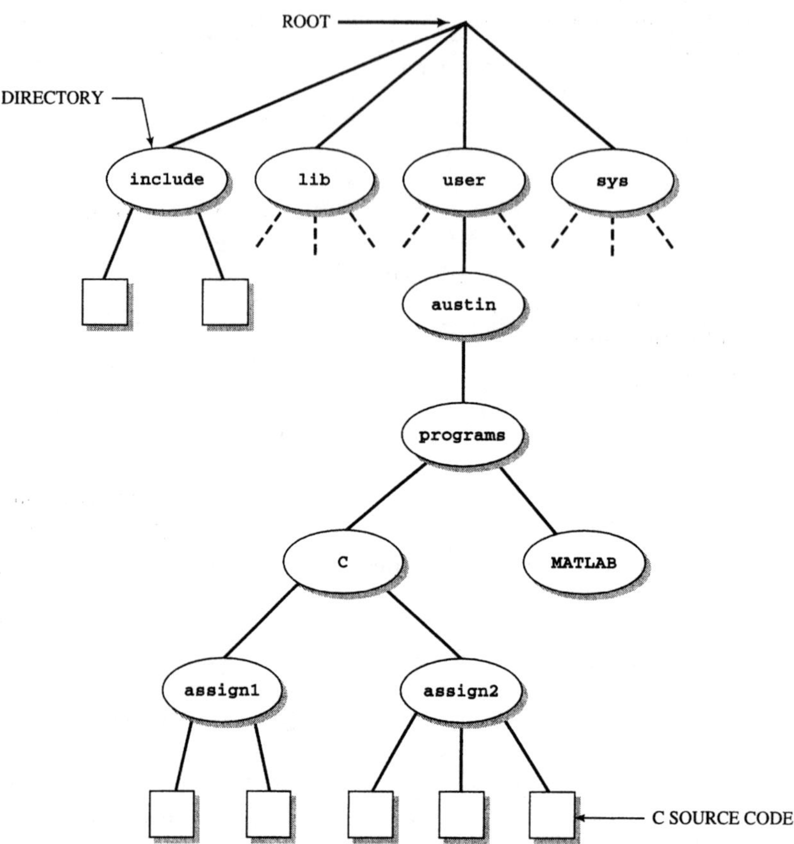

FIGURE A1.2 Extended file system hierarchy.

each class assignment. More precisely, we create the subdirectories `assign1` an assign2 under the C directory by continuing the command sequence

```
prompt >> cd    C
prompt >> mkdir assign1
prompt >> mkdir assign2
```

The layout of directories is as shown in Figure A1.2, and we are ready to crea and place the files for our first assignment in the directory named `assign1`. Fil are created and edited in a program called a text editor. Three of the most common used text editors in UNIX are `vi`, `emacs`, and `pico`. Please consult your loc documentation for a list of relevant commands.

Navigating the File System

Now that we have created the `programs` directory under the user `austin`'s log directory, with the subdirectories `C`, `MATLAB`, etc., we need the ability to change t current directory to each of these new directories. The "current working directory" should be thought of as your place marker in the file system. You can use the cd command to move the marker up and down in the file system. Theoretically, you can always refer to any directory with the absolute path name that starts at the root, as in

```
/users/austin/programs/C/assign1/file.c
```

An absolute path name always starts with a slash character. However, to save typing in diverse file systems, it is much easier to type relative path names. As the name suggests, they refer to another directory relative to the current directory. One shorthand notation that helps with this is the period . that refers to the current directory, and the other is two periods . ., which refer to the parent directory. The single dot . is seldom used since the operating system assumes that you usually want to start from the current directory. Whenever you create a subdirectory, it will be put under the current directory by default (i.e., unless you specify otherwise). To change the current working directory, we use the cd command. Given that programs is a subdirectory of austin, we can change directory from austin to programs with

```
prompt >> cd programs
```

Notice that we did not put the /users/austin/... on the beginning of the directory to which we want to change. The use of relative path names saves a lot of typing and requires less information to be remembered. After the command executes, our reference point has moved down one level in the file system. To return to the austin directory from the programs subdirectory, we could either type cd .., or

```
prompt >> cd /users/austin
```

Here it is clearly simpler to type the relative path form rather than the absolute path form. When using relative path names, you can always start from the current directory and move up or down. To move up, precede the path name with the double period. It is like you are saying, "I want to go up one level from here, wherever that may be." UNIX systems respond to cd by taking you back to your home directory.

At any point in a working session, you may need to be reminded where you are in the file system. On a UNIX system, you can execute the command pwd for print working directory to print the current directory/location (many UNIX systems can be set up to always print this information as the prompt).

Obtaining Information on Files

Suppose that we have added files to a directory. Some basic questions are how do we know they are there, when were they stored, and how big are they? We need a command that will have the operating system tell us about file information. On UNIX systems, this command is called `ls` (its name is short for `list`). If you simply type

```
prompt >> ls
```

then the operating system will print the names of the files and directories in the current directory. This is the default behavior of `ls`. Often you will also want to know the size of the files and the date on which they were created. This information is obtained by overriding the default behavior with *command options*. For example `ls` can be requested to provide a long listing of the file information by adding `-l` to the command, as in

```
prompt >> ls -l
```

The - (minus) precedes the option in this case. The long option tells `ls` to print not only the file names, but also to show the protection, ownership, size, and date of creation for each file and subdirectory.

`ls` is typical of many UNIX commands in that the default behavior can be overridden by adding options. Rather than get into the lengthy details here (some UNIX commands have a lot of options), you can find out about the options by referring to the manuals or by using the `man` facility on UNIX systems. For example to find out the `ls` options, type

```
prompt >> man ls
```

and the manual page will print. This can often be more convenient than digging out the manual to find the information.

Moving, Copying, and Removing Files/Directories

After you have a little experience with the UNIX file system, you may want to start rearranging or cleaning up your directories (e.g., deleting unnecessary or unwanted files). There are several useful commands that help with file directory management. Suppose that you want to rename a file—the `mv` command (for move) will work. To use `mv`, you specify the old file name, followed by the new file name as in

```
prompt >> mv oldName newName
```

You can also specify directories into which the files may be moved. If you have a file named `file.c` in the `/users/austin/programs/C/assign1` directory and you want to move it to the `/users/austin/programs/C/assign2` directory, you can make `assign1` the working directory by typing

```
prompt >> cd /programs/C/assign1
```

and then

```
prompt >> mv file.c ../assign2/file.c
```

Note that ../assign2/file.c specifies that the file should be moved *up one level* .. , and *down* /assign2 into the assign2 subdirectory into the file with name file.c. The final file name is optional if you want the same name; in other words, you could type the shorter form

```
prompt >> mv file.c ../assign2
```

to just move the file to the new directory. The mv command can also be used to effectively rename a file since moving a file to one with a new name is the same as renaming it. For example, the command

```
prompt >> mv file.c newfile.c
```

changes the name of the above-mentioned file.c to newfile.c. To copy files on a UNIX system, use the cp command. The operation and format is similar to the mv command. So, for example, to make a backup copy of file.c in the current directory and another copy in another directory you could type

```
prompt >> cp file.c back.c
prompt >> cp file.c ../assign2/fileback.c
```

This would make two copies of file.c: one would reside in the current directory (assumed to be assign1) in file back.c, and the other would be placed in assign2 with the name fileback.c. To delete files, use the rm (for remove) command. This is relatively simple because you just name the file to be deleted, as in

```
prompt >> rm ../assign2/fileback.c
```

In this case, we have specified the file to be deleted by using a relative path name. Similarly, to delete a directory, use the rmdir command. The named directory must have no subdirectories under it and contain no files (i.e., it must be empty). As an extended example, let us assume that the current directory is assign1. To clean out and remove the assign2 directory, we might type the following sequence of commands

```
prompt >> cd ..
prompt >> rm    assign2/*
prompt >> rmdir assign2
```

In the second command, we have used what is called a *regular expression* * to remove all the files in the assign2 directory. Use of the * infers that we want to remove all the files, regardless of their names. Any file name will match with a `*`. If we wanted to remove all the files with a `.c` extension, then we could have used

```
prompt >> rm assign2/*.c
```

because all files that have any sequence of characters followed by a `.c` will match. The `*` equates with "any character (zero or more)." Similarly, you can use another type of regular expression, the `?`, to help when selecting files, as in `rm file.?`, to delete any files that start with `file` and have a single character extension, as in `file.c`, `file.h`, `file.x`, and so forth.

One last useful UNIX system command is `date`. If you want to know the current time, you can simply type

```
prompt >> date
```

and the UNIX operating system will display the day and the time. The operating system is always maintaining this information for you. It silently updates whatever counters it needs to be able to tell the time. This is clearly an important thing for the operating system to know since it also uses this whenever you save a file. It saves the time internally along with the data so that you can remind yourself of it later when you perform a long directory listing (i.e., "is this the most recent version of this program?").

APPENDIX

2

THE STANDARD LIBRARY

The standard library interface is accessible by including various header files defined below, listed in order of their coverage within the ANSI C standard [1].

Errors—<errno.h>

<errno.h> defines several macros for reporting error conditions and an integral lvalue, `errno`, that can be modified by several other library functions. `errno` is initialized to zero at program startup and can be set to a positive value by library functions when certain errors occur.

Limits—<limits.h> and <float.h>

These header files define several macros that expand to numerical limits for the particular implementation. Using the values in these files can significantly increase portability. For example, the ranges (minimum and maximum values) for the integral and floating point types are included here. Using these values in a program, rather than "magic numbers" (e.g., `-32767`), can allow a program to be compiled and

TABLE A2.1 Listing of Constants in `<limits.h>`

Constant	*Purpose*
`CHAR_BIT`	The number of bits in a character, or byte
`SCHAR_MIN`	The minimum value for a `signed character`
`SCHAR_MAX`	The maximum value for a `signed character`
`UCHAR_MAX`	The maximum value for an `unsigned character`
`CHAR_MIN`	The minimum value for a `char`
`CHAR_MAX`	The maximum value for a `char`
`MB_LEN_MAX`	The number of bytes in a multibyte character
`SHRT_MIN`	The minimum value for a `short int`
`SHRT_MAX`	The maximum value for a `short int`
`USHRT_MAX`	The maximum value for an `unsigned short int`
`INT_MIN`	The minimum value of an `int`
`INT_MAX`	The maximum value of an `int`
`UINT_MAX`	The maximum value of an `unsigned int`
`LONG_MIN`	The minimum value of a `long int`
`LONG_MAX`	The maximum value of a `long int`
`ULONG_MAX`	The maximum value of an `unsigned long int`

executed without errors on different platforms. Table A2.1 contains a listing of th constants defined in `<limits.h>`.

Common Definitions—`<stddef.h>`

`<stddef.h>` contains a variety of types and macros, including the type `size_t` which represents the unsigned integral type that the keyword `sizeof` returns. Th header file also contains the macro `NULL`, which expands to the implementatio defined null pointer constant.

Diagnostics—`<assert.h>`

`<assert.h>` contains the `assert` macro that is useful when debugging program

```
#include <assert.h>
void assert( int iExpression );
```

Assertions are statements that are checked for a true or nonzero condition (e. to check the return value from a `malloc` call). If the assertion is true, nothing done. If the assertion is false, thereby indicating an error condition, the assert mac prints the text of the argument, the file name, and the line number where t assertion failed. The program is aborted after the error message is printed. Here is an example using an assertion:

```
#include <assert.h>
...
enum { StringMax = 100 };
char * cpString;

cpString = (char *) malloc( StringMax * sizeof( char ) );

/* make sure that cpString refers to valid memory */

assert( cpString != 0 );
```

The assert macro checks that the value of `cpString`, a `char pointer`, returned by `malloc` is not zero. If it is, `assert` prints the failed assertion and its location. It then calls `abort` to terminate the program. The `assert` macro can be deactivated by defining `NDEBUG` before `assert.h` is included (either literally, with `#define NDEBUG`, or more conveniently, with the compiler command line option `-D`, as in `-DNDEBUG`).

Assertions are often used for debugging, but they should eventually be replaced with more rigorous error-handling code. Robust, production-quality code should be designed to handle error conditions without aborting when an error occurs.

Character Handling—<ctype.h>

`<ctype.h>` declares a number of routines for testing properties of characters (e.g., Is this an uppercase letter?) and for converting characters (e.g., converting letters from upper- to lowercase). The upper section of Table A2.2 contains a listing of the character testing functions. All these functions have a declaration of the form

```
int is<Function>( int iChar );
```

where `<Function>` is the function `alpha`, `alnum`, `cntrl`, etc. The lower half of Table A2.2 contains the two macro functions supported by `<ctype.h>`. These functions return a nonzero value (i.e., `true`) if the condition is satisfied; otherwise, they return zero (i.e., `false`). An example of their use is

```
#include <ctype.h>
...
do {
    ...
} while( tolower( cpResponse ) == 'y' );
```

In this example, `cpResponse` is converted to lowercase before comparison with the character constant `'y'`.

TABLE A2.2 Character Testing and Mapping Functions in `<ctype.h>`

Function	*Purpose*
`isalpha`	Is the character alphabetic?
`isalnum`	Is the character alphanumeric?
`iscntrl`	Is the character a control character?
`isdigit`	Is the character a decimal digit?
`isxdigit`	Is the character a hex digit?
`isgraph`	Is the character a printable character (except ' ')?
`isprint`	Is the character a printable character (including ' ')?
`isspace`	Is the character a white space character?
`islower`	Is the character a lowercase letter?
`isupper`	Is the character an uppercase letter?
`ispunct`	Is the character a punctuation character (neither ' ' nor `isalnum`)?
`tolower`	Returns the lowercase value of the argument
`toupper`	Returns the uppercase value of the argument

Localization—`<locale.h>`

A growing number of programs need to be translated into other spoken languages. Components of this file make it possible to write programs that adjust for usage in different spoken languages.

Mathematics—`<math.h>`

The `<math.h>` header file contains constants and function declarations for useful mathematical calculations. All the functions are declared with `double` arguments. They return `double` values. Error conditions are handled by setting error flags (`errno` is set to `EDOM` or `ERANGE` for domain or range errors, respectively) and returning implementation-defined values.

The trigonometric functions declared in `<math.h>` are

```
double acos( double dVal );
```

Computes the arc cosine function. `dVal` should be in the range `[-1,1]` or domain error will occur.

```
double asin( double dVal );
```

Computes the arc sine function. `dVal` should be in the range `[-1,1]` or domain error will occur.

```
double atan( double dVal );
```

Computes the arc tangent function

double atan2(double dY, double dX);

`atan2()` computes the principal arc tangent of `dY/dX`, using the signs to determine the resultant quadrant. Domain errors may occur if both arguments are zero.

double cos(double dVal);

Computes the cosine of the angle `dVal` (radians)

double sin(double dVal);

Computes the sine of the angle `dVal` (radians)

double tan(double dVal);

Computes the tangent of the angle `dVal` (radians)

The hyperbolic functions declared here are

double cosh(double dVal);

Computes the hyperbolic cosine of `dVal`

double sinh(double dVal);

Computes the hyperbolic sine of `dVal`

double tanh(double dVal);

Computes the hyperbolic tangent of `dVal`

The exponential and logarithmic functions are

double exp(double dVal);

Computes `e` raised to the power `dVal`

double frexp(double dValue, int* ipExp);

Breaks down the floating point value `dValue` into a normalized fraction that it returns and into an integer power of `2` that it sets via `ipExp`

double ldexp(double dVal, int iExp);

Multiplies the floating point number `dVal` by `2` raised to the `iExp` power

double log(double dVal);

Computes the natural logarithm of `dVal`. A domain error occurs if `dVal` is negative, and a range error may occur if `dVal` is zero.

`double log10( double dVal );`

Computes the base ten logarithm of `dVal`. A domain error occurs for negative values of `dVal`, and a range error occurs with `dVal` equal to zero.

`double modf( double dVal, double* dpIntPart );`

Breaks `dVal` into integral and fractional parts. `modf()` returns the fractional part and stores the integral part indirectly via `dpIntPart`.

`double pow( double dBase, double dExponent );`

Computes and returns the value of `dBase` raised to the power `dExponent`

`double sqrt( double dVal );`

Computes and returns the square root of `dVal`, which must be nonnegative

`double ceil( double dVal );`

Computes and returns the smallest integral value not less than `dVal`

`double fabs( double dVal );`

Computes and returns the absolute value of `dVal`

`double floor( double dVal );`

Computes and returns the largest integral value not greater than `dVal`

`double fmod( double dNum, double dDenom );`

Computes and returns the remainder of the expression `dNum / dDenom`

Nonlocal Jumps—<setjmp.h>

This header file defines components (including a jump buffer type `jmp_buf`) f using nonlocal jumps in a program.

`int setjmp( jmp_buf jbEnviron );`

Saves the calling environment in the `jmp_buf` argument `jbEnviron` for la use by the `longjmp()` function. It saves the current state of the stack, a CPU registers for later use by the `longjmp()` function. When returning fr a direct invocation, zero is returned. If returning from a call to the `longjmp` function, `setjmp()` returns a nonzero value.

void longjmp(jmp_buf jbEnviron, int iVal);

Restores the environment saved previously in `jbEnviron` by a call to `setjmp()`. `longjmp()` returns to the execution point where `setjmp()` was called with a return value of `iVal`, which cannot be zero.

Signal Handling—<signal.h>

This header file defines components for handling signals during program execution. Two signal-handling functions, `signal()` and `raise()`, are declared here. `signal()` allows a program to respond to interrupts or other events in the underlying environment. `raise()` is used to manually send a signal. If a corresponding function has been defined to handle the signal, then it will respond to it.

There are several (at least six) possible signals that may be generated in a program. They include

SIGABRT Signals abnormal program termination—for instance, when the program is aborted

SIGFPE Signals a floating point exception (e.g., divide by zero)

SIGILL Signals an invalid function image (e.g., illegal instruction)

SIGINT Signals an interactive attention request

SIGSEGV Signals an invalid memory access

SIGTERM Indicates that a termination request has been sent to the program

The functions declared in `signal.h` are

void (*signal(int iSignal, void (*pFunction)(int iSig))) (int);

`signal()` is a function that is passed an integer signal number `iSignal` and a pointer to a signal-handling function called `pFunction`, which takes an integer argument `iSig`. `signal()` returns a pointer to a function that is passed an integer and returns nothing. The function argument `pFunction(int)` can be either a pointer to a user-defined signal-handling function or one of three special values that are guaranteed not to correspond (i.e., conflict) with a legal function address:

SIG_DFL Results in default handling of the signal (usually used to cancel a previously used signal handler)

SIG_ERR Represents an error condition

SIG_IGN Indicates the signal should be ignored (use with caution since something important may be ignored)

If `pFunction` is a signal-handling function, the equivalent of `signal( iSignal, SIG_DFL )` is executed so that this signal is effectively blocked. Then `(*pFunction( iSignal ))` is executed after which the program resumes at the point that execution was interrupted unless `pFunction` does not return (i.e., it may `abort` or `longjmp` out). The `signal()` function returns the value of `pFunction` for the most recent call to signal for the specified iSignal. If the request cannot be honored, SIG_ERR is returned and errno (see errno.h) is set to a positive value.

int raise(int iSignal);

Sends the signal iSignal (which effectively allows a program to manually send a signal). It returns zero if successful and nonzero otherwise.

Variable Arguments—<stdarg.h>

This header provides the components necessary for using variable argument lists in functions. Variable arguments lists are useful when the type and number of function arguments are not known at compile time (e.g., printf and scanf functions). Two important macros are required to use variable argument lists:

void va_start(va_list vaArg, parameterN);

vaArg is a type suitable for referring to the arguments (i.e., a pointer to a list of arguments) and parameterN, which is the name of the last known paramete before the variable argument list (used to initialize variable argument access). Once the va_list is initialized, each argument is retrieved using va_arg().

***type* va_arg(va_list vaArg, *type*);**

Expands to an expression with type and value of the next argument. On eac call to va_arg, vaArg is modified to return successive arguments. Finally, whe variable argument processing is complete, call va_end.

void va_end(va_list vaArg);

Modifies vaArg so that it is no longer usable

Input/Output—<stdio.h>

The <stdio.h> header file is included in almost every C program because supports standard input/output (I/O) functions. <stdio.h> declares several type macros, and functions needed for I/O.

The most important type declared in <stdio.h> is FILE, which is typically C struct that contains information necessary to control streams. Streams a logical devices (i.e., the keyboard, the screen, files) with which programs can perfo I/O. Streams can be connected to physical devices or files. Although the devic may have different characteristics, the stream handles the details so that any diff ences are hidden from the programmer. This approach enables increased portabil since the implementation details are hidden from application programmers.

Three different streams are opened by default for C programs. They are std: which is linked to the keyboard, and stdout and stderr, which are linked to terminal screen. These streams can be redirected to other devices or files if necessa

The functions supported by the standard I/O package are

int printf(const char* kcpFormat, ...);

Writes output with the format `kcpFormat` and returns the number of characters output or a negative number if an error occurred. The format string is followed by a variable number of arguments that matches the specification in the format string.

int scanf(const char* kcpfrmat, ...);

`scanf` reads input according to specifications described in the format string `kcpFormat`. The format string is followed by a list of variables that match the specification in `kcpFormat` and are passed by reference to `scanf`. `scanf` returns the number of input items that were successfully scanned and assigned (0 or more) or `EOF` on input failure. The return value is 0 when no fields are stored.

int getchar(void);

Obtains and returns the next input character (if present) from the standard input stream. It returns `EOF` when the end of file is encountered (thus the need for an `int` return value).

char* gets(char* cpString);

Reads a string of characters from `stdin` into memory referred to by `cpString` up to the newline character or end of file, and null terminates the string. Returns `cpString` if successful. If end of file is encountered and no characters have been read, then a null is returned.

int puts(const char* kcpString);

Outputs the string referred to by `kcpString` to `stdout` and appends a newline character. Returns `EOF` if a write error occurs or a nonnegative value otherwise.

int getc(FILE* FpStream);

Returns the next character from the stream or `EOF` on error or end of file

int ungetc(int iChar, FILE* FpStream);

Returns the next character from the stream or `EOF` on error or end of file. Pushes the character specified by `iChar` back into the stream `FpStream`. Returns the character pushed back or `EOF` if an error occurs.

FILE* fopen(const char* kcpFilename, const char* kcpMode);

Opens the file associated with `kcpFilename` with the specified mode. Returns a pointer to the object controlling the stream.

```
int fprintf( FILE* FpStream, const char* kcpFormat, ... );
```

Writes output to the stream `FpStream` under control of `kcpFormat`. A variable argument list follows the format with the arguments to be converted. Returns the number of characters transmitted or a negative value if an error occurred.

```
int fscanf( FILE* FpStream, const char* kcpFormat, ... );
```

Reads input from the stream `FpStream` under control of the format string `kcpFormat` into the referred to variables in the list following the format. Returns the number of input items scanned and assigned successfully or `EOF` if failure occurs before any conversion.

```
int fclose( FILE* FpStream );
```

Flushes the stream specified by `FpStream` and closes the associated file. Returns `EOF` if an error occurs.

```
int fgetc( FILE* Fpstream );
```

Gets and returns the next character from `FpStream`. If the stream is at end of file, `EOF` is returned.

```
char* fgets( char* cpString, int iMax, FILE* FpStream );
```

Reads, at most, `iMax-1` characters from the stream `FpStream` into memory specified by `cpString`. Returns `cpString` if successful or a null if end of file is encountered and no characters have been read.

```
int fputc( int iChar, FILE* FpStream );
```

Writes the character specified by `iChar` to the stream `FpStream`. Returns the character written or `EOF` if an error occurs.

```
int fputs( const char* kcpString, FILE* FpStream );
```

Writes the string pointed to by `kcpString` to the stream referred to by `FpStream`. Returns a nonnegative value or `EOF` if an error occurs.

```
int fgetpos( FILE* FpStream, fpos_t * fpPos );
```

Stores the current file position pointer for the stream `FpStream` in the object pointed to by `fpPos`. Returns zero if successful, sets `errno` on failure.

```
int fseek( FILE* FpStream, long int lOffset, int iWhere );
```

Moves the file position pointer for `FpStream` relative to the value specified by `iWhere`, which can be `SEEK_SET`, `SEEK_CUR`, or `SEED_END` to specify movement relative to the beginning of file, the current location, or the end of file, respectively.

`int fsetpos( FILE* FpStream, const fpos_t * kfpPos );`

Sets the file position for the stream `FpStream` to the value referred to by `kfpPos` (which should have been set earlier by `fgetpos`). Returns zero on success or sets `errno` on failure.

`long int ftell( FILE* FpStream );`

Obtains the current file position (number of characters from the beginning of the file) for the stream `FpStream`. Returns the current position or `-1L` on failure.

`void rewind( FILE* FpStream );`

Sets the file position to the beginning of the file

`FILE * tmpfile( void );`

Creates and returns a temporary binary file that will be removed when the file is closed or when the program terminates.

`int remove( const char* kcpFilename );`

Deletes the file referred to by `kcpFilename`. Returns zero if it succeeds or nonzero if it fails.

`int rename( const char* kcpOld, const char * kcpNew );`

Renames the file referred to by `kcpOld` to the name `kcpNew`. Returns zero if it succeeds or nonzero if it fails.

`char * tmpnam( char* cpName );`

Generates a string that is a valid name, yet not the same as an existing file name and stores it into memory referred to by `cpName` (if `cpName` is not null). If `cpName` is null, then `tmpnam` returns a pointer to a name.

`int fflush( FILE* FpStream );`

Causes all unwritten data on `FpStream` to be output. Returns `EOF` if an error occurs or zero otherwise.

`FILE* freopen( const char* kcpFile, const char* kcpMode, FILE* FpStream);`

Opens the file with name `kcpFile` with mode `kcpMode` and associates it with the stream `FpStream`. Returns null if the operation fails or the stream if it succeeds.

`void setbuf( FILE* FpStream, char* cpBuffer );`

Buffers the stream `FpStream` with the buffer `cpBuffer` with mode `_IOFBF` and size `BUFSIZ` if `cpBuffer` is not null. If `cpBuffer` is null, then the mode will be `_IONBF` (unbuffered output, see `setvbuf`). Returns zero on success or nonzero on failure.

int setvbuf(FILE* FpStream, char* cpBuffer, int iMode, size_t stSize);

Buffers the stream `FpStream` with the buffer `cpBuffer`. The mode should be set to `_IOFBF` for fully buffered I/O, `_IOLBF` for line buffered I/O, or `_IONBF` for no buffering. `stSize` specifies the size of the buffer. Returns zero on success or nonzero on failure.

int vprintf(const char* kcpformat, va_list vaArg);

`vprintf` is the same as `fprintf` with a variable argument list specified by `vaArg`

int vsprintf(char* cpString, const char* kcpformat, va_list vaArg);

`vsprintf` is the same as `sprintf` with a variable argument list `vaArg`

size_t fread(void* vpPtr, size_t stSize, size_t stNum, FILE* FpStream);

Reads up to `stNum` elements of size `stSize` into the array pointed to by `vpPtr` from the stream `FpStream`. Returns the number of elements successfully read

size_t fwrite(const void* vpPtr, size_t stSize, size_t stNum, FILE* FpStream);

Writes `stNum` elements of size `stSize` to stream `FpStream` from the array pointed to by `vpPtr`. Returns the number of elements successfully written.

void clearerr(FILE* FpStream);

Clears the end-of-file error indicators on stream `FpStream`.

int feof(FILE* FpStream);

Tests the end-of-file status on stream `FpStream`. Returns a nonzero value the end-of-file indicator is set for stream `FpStream`.

int ferror(FILE* FpStream);

Tests the error indicator for the stream. Returns a nonzero value if the err indicator is set for the stream `FpStream`.

General Utilities—`<stdlib.h>`

Several types (including `size_t`) are declared here. In addition, the followi functions are declared:

double atof(const char* kcpNum);

Converts the initial portion of the string referred to via `cpNum` into a dou value and returns it

int atoi(const char* kcpNum);

Converts the initial portion of the string referred to via `kcpNum` to an integer and returns it

long int atol(const char* kcpNum);

Converts the initial portion of the string referred to via `kcpNum` to a long int and returns it

double strtod(const char* kcpNum, char cppEnd);**

Converts the initial portion of the string referred to via `kcpNum` into a double and returns it. After conversion of the numeric part of the string, there may be remaining characters. A pointer to these is assigned to `cppEnd` so that further processing of the string can be done. For example, consider the following program

```
#include <stdlib.h>
...
char * cpNumber = "3.14rad";
char * cpNumEnd;
double dVal;
...
dVal = strtod( cpNumber, &cpNumEnd );
```

would assign `3.14` to `dVal` and set `cpNumEnd` to point to the string `"rad"`.

long strtol(const char* kcpNum, char cppEnd, int iBase);**

Converts `kcpNum` to a `long` value using the arithmetic base or radix `iBase` and returns it, and assigns a pointer to the end of the converted string to `cppEnd`

unsigned long int strtoul(const char* kcpNum, char cppEnd, int iBase);**

Converts `kcpNum` to an unsigned long integer using radix `iBase` and returns it, and assigns a pointer to the end of the converted string to `cppEnd`

int rand(void);

Returns a pseudorandom number in the range `0` to `RAND_MAX` (which is at least `32767` and is also defined in this header file)

void srand(unsigned int iSeed);

Uses `iSeed` as a seed for the random number generator. Each new seed will give a different set of pseudorandom numbers when `rand()` is called.

`void * calloc( size_t sNumElem, size_t sSize );`

Allocates memory for `sNumElem` objects, each of which requires `sSize` bytes of storage. The memory is initialized to `0`. `calloc()` returns a pointer to the newly allocated memory or the null pointer `0`.

`void free( void* vpMem );`

Deallocates the memory at `vpMem` and returns it to the heap. If `vpMem` is `0` then nothing occurs. If `vpMem` was not obtained from `malloc`, `calloc`, o `realloc`, then the behavior is undefined (usually a system crash).

`void * malloc( size_t sSize );`

Allocates memory for an object occupying `sSize` bytes and returns a pointe to it. If the memory cannot be allocated, then the null pointer `0` is returned.

`void * realloc( void* vpPrev, size_t sSize );`

Tries to reallocate the memory at `vpPrev` to a new size `sSize` in bytes. `vpPre` must be previously allocated using `malloc`, `calloc`, or `realloc` (or the men ory allocator will be broken), or `vpPrev` can be the null pointer `(0)`, in whic case `realloc` acts just like `malloc`. `realloc` returns a pointer to the new allocated space or the null pointer `(0)` if it cannot allocate it.

`void abort( void);`

Causes an abnormal program termination, unless `SIGABORT` is being caug and the signal handler does not return

`int atexit( void (*pFunc)(void) );`

Registers the function referred to via `pFunc` to be called when the progra terminates. `pFunc` cannot accept or return values. Up to 32 functions can registered this way.

`void exit( int iStatus );`

Causes normal program termination. All functions registered with `atexit` will be called, the streams flushed, and temporary files removed. `iStatus` returned to the environment.

`char * getenv( const char * kcpName );`

Searches for an environment variable that matches `kcpName` in the environm list and returns a pointer to the entry. This function is implementation defir but supported by most systems. Refer to your operating manuals for detai

```
int system( const char* kcpCommand );
```

Invokes a copy of an implementation-defined command processor if possible and passes the string `kcpCommand` to it. Whether this is supported can be tested by passing a null pointer `(0)` as the argument: a nonzero value is returned if the system supports a command processor, and zero is returned if it does not support it.

```
void* bsearch( const void* kvpKey, const void* kvpBase, size_t
sNumber, size_t sSize, int (*pCompare)( const void* kvpKey,
const void* kvpArrElem) );
```

Searches the array starting at `kvpBase` with `sNumber` objects of size `sSize` for an element that matches the value referred to by `kvpKey`. To do this, `bsearch` needs to call the compare function referred to by `pCompare`, where `kvpKey` is the object to be found and `kvpArrElem` is the element to be compared with. `pCompare` should return a value less than, equal to, or greater than `0`, depending on whether `kvpKey` is less than, equal to, or greater than `kvpArrElem`, respectively. `bsearch` returns either a pointer to the element found or the null pointer `(0)` if it was not found.

```
void qsort( void* vpBase, size_t sNumber, size_t sSizeOfElem,
int (*pCompare)( const void* kvpElOne, const void* kvpElTwo ) ) ;
```

Sorts `sNumber` elements starting at `vpBase`, each of size `sSizeOfElem` bytes, using the compare function `pCompare` to order the elements. `pCompare` works the same as in `bsearch` above.

```
int abs( int iVal );
```

Returns the absolute value of the integer argument `iVal`

```
div_t div( int iNumer, int iDenom );
```

Computes the quotient and remainder of the division of `iNumer` by `iDenom`. The values are returned in the `struct div_t`, consisting of two components—`int quot` and `int rem`—representing the quotient and remainder, respectively.

```
ldiv_t ldiv( long int iNumer, long int iDenom );
```

Performs a similar computation to `div` above, except it uses `long` arguments and return values

ring Handling—`<string.h>`

```
void* memcpy( void* vpDest, const void* kvpSrc, size_t sNum);
```

Copies `sNum` characters from memory at `kvpSrc` to memory at `kvpDest`. The objects should not overlap. `memcpy` returns the value of `kvpDest`.

`void* memmove( void* vpDest, const void* kvpSrc, size_t sNum );`

Copies `sNum` characters from memory at `kvpSrc` to memory at `vpDest`. The two objects' memory may overlap. `memmove` returns the value of `vpDest`.

`char* strcpy( char* cpDest, const char* kcpSrc );`

Copies the string referred to by `kcpSrc` to memory referred to by `cpDest` (including the string-terminating null character). The memory should not overlap.

`char* strncpy( char* cpDest, const char* kcpSrc, size_t sNum );`

Copies no more than `sNum` character from the string at `kcpSrc` to the string at `cpDest`. Characters after the string-terminating null character are not copied. `strncpy` returns the value of `cpDest`.

`char* strcat( char* cpDest, const char* kcpSrc );`

Appends the source string at `kcpSrc` to the destination string at `cpDest`. `strcat` returns the value of `cpDest`.

`char* strncat( char* cpDest, const char* kcpSrc, size_t sNum );`

Appends no more than `sNum` characters from the source string `kcpSrc` to the end of the destination string `cpDest`. `strncat` returns the value of `cpDest`.

`int memcmp( const void* kvpOne, const void* kvpTwo, size_t sNum );`

Compares the first `sNum` characters from memory referred to by `kvpOne` to memory referred to by `kvpTwo` and returns a value less than, equal to, or greater than zero, depending on whether `kvpOne` is less than, equal to, or greater than `kvpTwo`, respectively.

`int strcmp( const char* kcpOne, const char* kcpTwo );`

Compares the character string referred to by `kcpOne` to the character string referred to by `kcpTwo` and returns a value less than, equal to, or greater than zero, depending on whether `kcpOne` is less than, equal to, or greater than `kcpTwo`, respectively.

`int strcoll( const char* kcpOne, const char* kcpTwo );`

Compares two strings referred to by `kcpOne` and `kcpTwo` like `strcmp`, but takes into consideration local differences in collating sequences and character s

`int strncmp( const char* kcpOne, const char* kcpTwo, size_t sNum );`

Compares two strings up to no more than `sNum` characters and returns a value like the `strcmp` function

size_t strxfrm(char* cpOne, const char* kcpTwo, size_t sNum);

Transforms the string referred to with kcpTwo and places it at memory referred to by cpOne. kcpTwo is transformed and placed in cpOne such that the results of strcmp would be the same as for the original strings using strcoll. Up to sNum characters are copied to cpOne, and strxfrm returns the length of the transformed string.

void* memchr(const char* kcpString, int iChar, size_t sNum);

Locates the first occurrence of iChar in the first sNum characters of memory referred to with kcpString, and returns a pointer to the located character or the null pointer if it was not found

char* strchr(const char* kcpString, int iChar);

Locates the first occurrence of the iChar in the string referred to by kcpString, and returns a pointer to it or the null pointer if it was not found

size_t strcspn(const char* kcpOne, const char* kcpTwo);

Computes the length of the maximum initial segment of the string referred to by kcpOne, which consists entirely of characters not from the string referred to by kcpTwo and returns the length of the segment

char* strpbrk(const char* kcpOne, const char* kcpTwo);

Locates the first occurrence in the string referred to by kcpOne of any character from the string referred to by kcpTwo, and returns a pointer to that character or a null pointer if none are found

char* strrchr(const char* kcpString, int iChar);

Locates the last occurrence of iChar in the string referred to by kcpString, and returns a pointer to it or a null pointer if it is not found

size_t strcpn(const char* kcpOne, const char* kcpTwo);

Computes the length of the maximum initial segment of the string referred to by kcpOne in the string referred to by kcpTwo, and returns that length

char* strtok(char* cpString, const char* kcpDelim);

Breaks the line referred to by cpString into a sequence of tokens where each token is delimited by a character from the string referred to by kcpDelim. The first call to strtok has the string to be tokenized as its first argument. On subsequent calls, the first argument should be the null pointer (0). kcpDelim may be changed from call to call. On the first call, strtok searches for the first character that is not in the delimiter string. This character is the start of the first token. Next, strtok searches for a character that *is* in the delimiter string, replaces the delimiter with a null character, and returns a pointer to the beginning of the token. strtok keeps a pointer to the next character so that it can start searching for tokens that may remain in the string. Each call returns a pointer to the next token in the string or to a null pointer if no tokens exist.

```
char* strerror( int iErrorNumber );
```

Maps the error number `iErrorNumber` to an error message string and returns a pointer to it

```
size_t strlen(const char* kcpString );
```

Returns the length of the string referred to by `kcpString`

Date and Time—`<time.h>`

The header file contains macros and declarations for dealing with time, such as the types `clock_t`, `time_t` for representing times, and an important structure, `struct tm`, that must at least contain the fields

```
int tm_sec;
int tm_min;
int tm_hour;
int tm_mday;
int tm_mon;
int tm_year;
int tm_wday;
int tm_yday;
int tm_isdst;
```

representing seconds, minutes, hours, the day of the month, the months sinc January, the year since 1900, the days since Sunday, the days since January 1, an daylight savings time (greater than zero if in effect, zero if not), respectively. Th functions declared in `<time.h>` are

```
clock_t clock( void );
```

Returns the processor time used by the program since the beginning of the e (implementation defined)

```
double difftime( time_t time2, time_t time1 );
```

Computes and returns the difference between the two calendar times: `time` `time1` expressed in seconds

```
time_t mktime( struct tm* stTime );
```

Converts the time broken down in the structure referred to by `stTime` ir calendar time, and returns the `time_t` value

```
time_t time( time_t* tpTimer );
```

Determines and returns the current calendar time (and, if `tpTimer` is not n also sets the time indirectly)

`char* asctime( const struct tm* ktpTime );`

Converts the broken-down time in the structure referred to via `ktpTime` into string form and returns it

`char* ctime( const time_t* ktpTimer );`

Converts the calendar time referred to via `ktpTimer` to a local time string and returns it

`struct tm* gmtime( const time_t* ktpTimer );`

Converts the calendar time referred to via `ktpTimer` into a broken-down time and returns it

`struct tm * localtime( const time_t* ktpTimer );`

Converts the calendar time referred to via `ktpTimer` into a broken-down local time and returns a pointer to it

`size_t strftime( char* cpBuf, size_t sMaxSize, const char* kcpFormat, const struct tm* ktpTime );`

Fills the string buffer `cpBuf` with a formatted time in the format specified by `kcpFormat` up to `sMaxSize` characters long using the time referred to via `ktpTime`. `strftime` returns the number of characters placed into the buffer.

REFERENCES

1. American National Standards Institute (ANSI). *ANSI Standard X3.159-1989.* ANSI, New York, 1989.
2. Arnold, K., Gosling, J. *The Java Programming Language.* Addison-Wesley, Reading, MA, 1996.
3. Boehm, B. W. A spiral model of software development and enhancement. *IEEE Computer,* **21**(5):61–72, 1988.
4. Booch, G. *Object-Oriented Analysis and Design with Applications.* 2nd ed. Benjamin Cummings, Redwood City, CA, 1994.
5. Brooks, F. *The Mythical Man-Month.* Addison-Wesley, Reading, MA, 1975.
6. Clements, P. C., Parnas, P. L., Weiss, D. M. "The modular structure of complex systems." In: *Proc. 7th International Conf. on Software Engineering,* March: 408–417, 1984.
7. Cox, T. L. *Procedures and Procedure-Oriented Languages: Encyclopedia of Computer Science.* 3rd ed. Van Nostrand Reinhold, New York, 1993.
8. Dongarra, J. J., Bunch, J. J., Moler, C. B., Stewart, G. W. *LINPACK User's Guide.* SIAM, 1979.
9. East, S. *Systems Integration—A Management Guide for Manufacturing Engineers.* McGraw-Hill, 1994.
10. Flanagan, D. *Java in a Nutshell: A Desktop Quick Reference.* 2nd ed. O'Reilly and Associates, Sebastopol, CA, 1997.
11. Goldberg, D. What every computer scientist should know about floating-point arithmetic. *ACM Computing Surveys,* **23**(1):5–48, 1991.
12. Harbison, S. P., Steele, G. L. *A C Reference Manual.* Prentice-Hall, Englewood Cliffs, NJ, 1984.
13. Jervis, R. Numerical extensions to C. *Dr Dobbs Journal,* August: 26–39, 1992.
14. Kernighan, B. W., Ritchie, D. M. *The C Programming Language.* Prentice-Hall Software Series, Englewood Cliffs, NJ, 1978.
15. Knuth, D. E. *The Art of Computer Programming: Fundamental Algorithms, Volume 2.* Addison-Wesley, Reading, MA, 1981.
16. Kulisch, U. W., Miranker, W. L. The arithmetic of the digital computer: A new approach. *SIAM Review,* **28**:1–40, 1986.
17. Lea, R., Matsuda, K., Miyashita, K. *Java for 3D and VRML Worlds.* New Riders Publishing, Indianapolis, IN, 1996.
18. Leebaert, D., ed. "Later than we think: How the future has arrived," pp. 1–38. In: *Technology 2001: The Future of Computing and Communications.* The MIT Press, Cambridge, MA, 1992.
19. Leebaert, D., Dickinson, T., eds. A world to understand: Technology and the awakening of human possibility, pp. 293–321. In: *Technology 2001: The Future of Computing and Communications.* The MIT Press, Cambridge, MA, 1992.
20. Leemis, L. M. *Reliability: Probabilistic Models and Statistical Methods.* Prentice-Hall, Englewood Cliffs, NJ, 1995.
21. Linton, M. *dbx.* Technical report, Berkeley, CA, 1982.
22. *The Student Edition of MATLAB Version 5 User's Guide: The Language of Technical Computing.* Prentice-Hall, Upper Saddle River, NJ, 1997.
23. McClure, C. *Software Reuse Techniques: Adding Reuse to the Systems Development Process.* Prentice-Hall, Upper Saddle River, NJ, 1997.

24. Meyer, B. *Object-Oriented Software Construction.* Prentice-Hall International Series in Computer Science, Hertfordshire, UK, 1988.

25. Naughton, P. *The Java Handbook.* McGraw-Hill, 1996.

26. Nievergelt, J., Hinrichs, K. H. *Algorithms and Data Structures: With Applications to Graphics and Geometry.* Prentice-Hall, Englewood Cliffs, NJ, 1993.

27. Osterhout, J. K. *Tcl and the Tk Toolkit.* Addison-Wesley Professional Computing Series, Reading, MA, 1994.

28. Parnas, D. L. On the criteria to be used in decomposing systems into modules. *Communications of the ACM,* **15**:330–336, 1972.

29. Petzold, C. *Programming Windows 3.1.* 3rd ed. Microsoft Press, Seattle, 1992.

30. Plauger, P. J. Large character sets in C. *Dr Dobbs Journal,* August: 16, 1992.

31. Plauger, P. J. *The Standard C Library.* Prentice-Hall, Englewood Cliffs, NJ, 1992.

32. Plauger, P. J. Standard C: Large character set support. *The C Users Journal,* **11**:5–7, 199

33. Press, L. Personal computing: Technetronic education: Answers on the cultural horizo *Communications of the ACM,* **36**(5):17–22, May 1993.

34. Press, W. H., Flannery, B. P., Teukolsky, S. A., Vetterling, W. T. *Numerical Recipes i C: The Art of Scientific Computing.* 2nd ed. Cambridge University Press, Cambridg UK, 1992.

35. Ressler, S. *VRML Samples from the Open Virtual Reality Testbed,* 1995. (See http: www.itl.nist.gov/div894/ovrt/projects/vrml/vrmlfiles.html.)

36. Royce, W. W. Managing the development of large software systems. In *Proceedings the IEEE WESCON,* August 1970.

37. Schrage, L. A more portable FORTRAN number generator. *ACM Transactions Mathematical Software,* **5**:132–138, 1979.

38. Smith, B. T., Boyle, J. M., Ikebe, Y., Klema, V. C., Moler, C. *Matrix Eigensystem Routin EISPACK Guide.* 2nd ed. Springer-Verlag, 1970.

39. Stallings, W. *Data and Computer Communications.* 2nd ed. MacMillan, New York, 19

40. Stevens, W. R. *UNIX Network Programming.* Prentice-Hall Software Series, Englewo Cliffs, NJ, 1990.

41. Stevens, W. R. *Advanced Programming in the UNIX Environment.* Addison-Wes Professional Computing Series, Reading, MA, 1992.

42. Stevenson, D. A proposed standard for binary floating point arithmetic. *Comput* **14**(3):51–62, 1981.

43. Sun Microsystems. *The Java Language: An Overview,* 1995. (See http://java.sun.co docs/overviews/java/java-overview-1.html.)

44. Tesler, L. G. Networked computing in the 1990's. *Scientific American,* **265**(3):86–93, 19

45. Van Der Linden, P. *Not Just Java.* Sun Microsystems Press: A Prentice-Hall Ti Mountain View, CA, 1997.

46. Wall, L., Christiansen, T., Schwartz, R. *Programming Perl.* 2nd ed. O'Reilly and Ass ates, Sebastopol, CA, 1993.

47. Weiss, M. A. *Data Structures and Algorithm Analysis in C.* Benjamin Cummings, R wood City, CA, 1993.

INDEX

Printed in the United States
100085LV00003B

9 780471 0